The American Faculty

The American Faculty

The Restructuring
of Academic Work and Careers

JACK H. SCHUSTER
MARTIN J. FINKELSTEIN

in collaboration with
JESUS FRANCISCO GALAZ-FONTES
MANDY LIU

The Johns Hopkins University Press
Baltimore

© 2006 The Johns Hopkins University Press
All rights reserved. Published 2006
Printed in the United States of America on acid-free paper

2 4 6 8 9 7 5 3 1

The Johns Hopkins University Press
2715 North Charles Street
Baltimore, Maryland 21218-4363
www.press.jhu.edu

Library of Congress Cataloging-in-Publication Data
Schuster, Jack H.
The American faculty : restructuring academic work and careers / Jack H.
Schuster, Martin J. Finkelstein.
p.   cm.
Includes bibliographical references and index.
ISBN 0-8018-8283-4 (hardcover : alk. paper)
1. Universities and colleges—United States—Faculty. 2. College
teachers—Professional relationships—United States. 3. College teachers—
Workload—United States. I. Finkelstein, Martin J., 1949– II. Title.
LB2331.72.S36 2006
378.1′2′0973—dc22
2005014180

A catalog record for this book is available from the British Library.

Contents

Tables and Figures

TABLES

FIGURES

Preface

The Project on the Future of the American Faculty and the long-standing collaboration of the authors of this volume can trace their origins back two decades. As Howard Bowen and Jack Schuster were designing the campus-visit component of the multifaceted study that ultimately yielded *American Professors* (Oxford University Press, 1986), it became apparent that it would be beneficial—necessary, actually—to invite several experts to help them conduct site visits to some of the thirty-eight campuses they had identified for the purpose of gathering data and interviewing key faculty and administrative leaders. At that time, they learned of an impressive manuscript by Martin Finkelstein based on his dissertation at State University of New York at Buffalo; the manuscript was later published as *The American Academic Profession* (Ohio State University Press, 1984).

They met with Marty in Washington, D.C., and he agreed to conduct five of the site visits. And so, the initial collaboration between Finkelstein and Schuster began. In 1994 the two of them proposed to several foundations, and to TIAA-CREF, to undertake a substantial study of the contemporary American faculty that would, in effect, bring forward their respective research agendas. The Johns Hopkins University Press agreed to publish the manuscript. But a funny thing happened on the way to the publisher. As parts of the manuscript were being researched, Finkelstein and Schuster, now joined by Robert K. Seal, became persuaded that one aspect of the new study—the striking contrast they had discerned between newer academics and their more senior colleagues—could not be addressed adequately within the confines of a single chapter of the projected manuscript.

And so in 1997 they approached their publisher proposing that the embryonic chapter on this distinctively different faculty cohort be expanded into a book-length manuscript. Jacqueline Wehmueller, editor at the Johns Hopkins Press, saw merit in this substitute proposal, and, accordingly, the original, more comprehensive project was put on hold while the authors refocused on this aspect of academic life. Meanwhile, the three coauthors had been commissioned by the National Center for Education Statistics of the U.S. Department of Education to prepare a monograph on particular facets of this new academic generation. Both manuscripts were published in 1998, the first as *The New Academic Generation* (Johns Hopkins University Press) and the second as *New Entrants to the Full-Time Faculty of Higher Education Institutions* (NCES).

Once those volumes were completed, our attention returned to the earlier, more ambitious task. The project began to crystallize into two essentially complementary dimensions, reflected in the present volume. In the first, we undertook a retrospective reanalysis and reinterpretation of trends in academic life that span the past several decades; this entailed cutting across the most prominent major national faculty surveys, starting with the landmark 1969 Carnegie Commission survey and continuing through the most recent surveys. We characterize the developments depicted by those successive surveys as nothing less than a restructuring of faculty work and careers.

The second overarching task involved squinting into an opaque future as we set off on our more speculative excursion into where the trends that we describe are propelling higher education and, at its core, the academic profession. This exercise has led us to a tangle of prospects both exhilarating and unsettling.

We argue in these pages that revolutionary changes are occurring. We are aware that such a term might seem, to some, hyperbolic, but we think the case can readily be made that the transformations—the restructuring—now afoot amount to a many-faceted revolution in academic life. Deciding what constitutes a revolution is decidedly arbitrary, but both of us, having taught doctoral seminars on the history of higher education, have arrived at our own conclusions about precedents meriting that bold label. In the United States, one revolution surely began in the 1820s; that is when academic specialization began to take a firm grip on the academy, when the first academic departments emerged, when the tilt in the direction of professional careerists who displaced tutorial generalists became clear. The academic career was never the same thereafter. All of this evolved slowly, to be sure, and so perhaps *revolution* is a misleading label. But what emerged was indisputably a transformation: an institution and practitioners markedly different from prevailing practices that had gone before.

A second revolution, we submit, took shape in the last quarter of the nineteenth century. It was fueled by the adaptation on these shores of a research university—American version. There were some not-very-successful earlier forays (at Michigan, for instance), but the founding of the Johns Hopkins University in 1876 constituted a hugely important milestone, followed by the remaking of Harvard in the 1880s under Charles Eliot, the establishment of Clark, Stanford, and Chicago in the early 1890s, and the concomitant emergence during this era of the disciplinary associations. In addition, the acknowledgment of scholarship and publishing as centrally important academic values and the consequent reprioritizing of the academic reward system led to the creation of a new academic order. One could plausibly maintain that this transformation in values had settled into place by the early twentieth century, giving rise to a system of higher education that is still more or less intact a century later. One could also insist that the "massification" of higher education since World War II—the explosive growth of community colleges, the spread of comprehensive state institutions, and the more democratized access to faculty ranks—-has constituted another revolution (Trow, 1973).

But we argue that we are now at the leading edge of, perhaps well into, yet another revolution—whether it is the third, fifth, or nineteenth—and that the consequences will be profound. It is a transformation characterized by concurrent changes, deep and wide, affecting every aspect of the academy and the faculty members who seek to carry out the amazing variety of institutional missions. Everything is "in play"; practically every aspect of the life academic is being driven by a host of interrelated developments: dazzling technological advances; globalization that continues to permeate academic boundaries; rapidly increasing numbers of tertiary students worldwide; unprecedented expansion of proprietary higher education; a blurring of the distinction between public and private or independent higher education; and innumerable entrepreneurial, market-driven initiatives from within and without the campus. Taken together, these seismic shifts are profoundly changing how knowledge is acquired and transmitted. Furthermore, all this is unfolding at an unprecedented pace, and the academy is struggling to absorb the successive shocks, to adapt, and to advance. Central to the metamorphosis is the academic profession, ever changing in composition and in role, as the faculty seek to ride the crest of change while also clinging to traditional responsibilities. The future—for the academy and its faculty—is becoming ever more difficult to predict. It is our hope, accordingly, that the information we have organized and presented here—by way of both secondary analyses of existing data sets and (in some cases) original data collection—will be beneficial to scholars, analysts, and policymakers who are trying to understand better the conditions essential to sustaining the academic profession.

Our observations—the chapters that ensue—are grouped into four parts:

Part 1 consists of three chapters that provide an overview of, and a perspective on, the academic profession. Each reflects the dual themes of continuity and change. Following an introductory setting of the stage (chapter 1), chapter 2 conducts a historical tour d'horizon of the academic profession's evolution. Chapter 3 presents a demographic profile of the faculty with an emphasis on major changes that have occurred during the past three and a half decades.

Part 2 depicts the faculty at work and the values they hold. In chapter 4 we examine how the ingredients of academic work have shifted in recent decades, and in chapter 5 we look into academic culture and the faculty's values, including how they view their professional circumstances.

In part 3 the focus shifts to various dimensions of the academic career. We explore in chapter 6 how the academic career has changed in recent years. Chapter 7 probes one pivotal element of the career: the remarkable changes in the types of academic appointments. Chapter 8 examines faculty compensation in the course of the academic career, and in chapter 9 we extend earlier work to assess whether the academic profession as a career is able to attract persons of adequate quality.

Finally, in part 4 we assess contemporary academic life. We predict where the academic profession is heading and suggest what the implications will be for the academic profession, for the academy in general, and for the larger society. Chapter 10 examines especially the many implications of the technological revolution for academic work and careers, and chapter 11 tries to place into perspective the developments addressed earlier in the book and the prospects for maintaining a vital academic profession. In this concluding chapter, we also proffer a number of recommendations, directed to individual campuses and multicampus systems, to governments, and to foundations.

Our strategy has been to lay as solid and timely a foundation as we can, grounded in data derived from the past several decades that depict in detail the major developments that have been reshaping the academy and the American faculty. Unfortunately, we have been unable to suspend, even temporarily, the relentless progress of time—the laws of physics. Just as a chapter was being completed, a new study reporting new data emerged. We were, not surprisingly, in a state of constant "updating" of our analyses—in what became a Sisyphusean struggle. At some point, however, it becomes necessary to stop: analyses must be finalized, committed to charts and prose, and at some point, new inputs must simply be set aside. That point was reached in early 2005 when the 2003 IPEDS data was publicly reported, as had been the 2004 AAUP faculty compensation data. Data from the 2004 National Study of Postsecondary Faculty had not become available by that time. So while we have fashioned a foundation, timely in the broadest sense, it did not benefit from that last contribution—even though that data indeed became available before this volume actually appeared in print. We have chosen to frame these "hard realities" of a never-slowing flow of new data into an opportunity: a invitation to readers to bring with them to each chapter the most current data of the moment—to add to the evolving mix. While we accept the inevitability that new data in some instances may compromise our own findings, we would prefer to think that the most recent data—and data yet to come—will extend the broad trend lines that we have depicted and interpreted. It is from such a layered platform we project our best sense of what lies ahead and what the plausible futures signify for the American academic profession and for the society of which they are a part.

Following the eleven chapters is a series of ten appendixes whose value to the research community, we think, will be significant. They include detailed descriptions of the major national faculty surveys that also serve as a key to survey abbreviations (Appendix A) and a "concordance" (Appendix B) that establishes which topics and items are addressed in the various surveys, providing convenient references to the field that have not heretofore been available. Among the other appendixes are one that details the methodological challenges that investigators and interpreters of faculty data must confront and resolve (Appendix C) and another that sorts through the various (and sometimes conflicting) sources of data on faculty compensation (Appendix G). To a large extent, the information presented in the appendixes has never before been available so accessibly and in such detail. Note that the numerous tables in Appendix J are intended to supplement the relatively simple tables in the text, adding further details (e.g., controlling for institutional type, race or ethnicity, and career cohort), and are not included in the list of tables at the front of the book.

In producing this book, we have become increasingly aware of a truism too easily overlooked: Whatever the distinctive contributions that have been made to society over time by universities, those contributions are overwhelmingly the work of the faculty through their teaching and scholarship. And so it is the faculty—the condition of the academic profession past, present, and future—that this project addresses. The stakes, for the world of higher learning and for the larger society, are enormous.

Acknowledgments

A project of this duration and complexity owes much to many: funders, support staff, academic and administrative colleagues qua facilitators, graduate students (functioning, as good ones do, as teacher-scholars as well as students), family, and, not least, our ever-patient publisher who kept the faith throughout this lengthy process.

Furthermore, as with any work of scholarship, we stand on the shoulders of others, some of them mentors as well as collaborators, some more distant in time and place and personally unknown to us. If we have advanced the field, it is because we have drawn on the insights and labors of such worthies as Howard Bowen, as well as our counterparts in other countries, from the United Kingdom to Australia, from Japan to Mexico. To enumerate here the many contemporary scholars who have informed, encouraged, and corrected us runs too great a risk of omission. But to begin:

The project simply would have been unrealized without the enormous efforts and skills of Dr. Jesus Francisco Galaz-Fontes, now of the Universidad Autónoma de Baja California, and Dr. Mandy Liu, of the Institute of Engineering Education Taiwan. Both completed their Ph.D. studies at Claremont Graduate University and during and after their graduate work were indispensable in crafting tables, figures, and complex appendixes drawn from disparate and sometimes barely accessible databases. Scott Snair, now completing his Ph.D. at Seton Hall University, carried the data baton for the project's final laps.

Dr. Carol Frances of Seton Hall University has contributed uniquely to the project over several years through her expertise on the economics of faculty compensation. Chapter 8 charts and tables on trends in compensation and academic careers bear her distinctive imprint.

We have received financial support, by way of grants for portions of the project, from the Lilly Endowment, the Spencer Foundation, the Andrew W. Mellon Foundation, and the Alfred P. Sloan Foundation. The Teachers Insurance Annuity Association–College Retirement Equity Fund has been especially generous; in the most recent years that support has been funneled through the TIAA-CREF Institute. Along the way additional support was provided through a contract with the National Center for Education Statistics, Office of Educational Research and Improvement, U.S. Department of Education.

We are also grateful to our respective institutions, Claremont Graduate University and Seton Hall University, for facilitating our work on this project in many ways. Perhaps foremost in this regard is the indispensable assistance provided by office staff who endured countless iterations of text. We especially single out Gwen Hoyt at CGU, who with invariable cheerfulness tended to the production and orderly maintenance of electronic files. At Seton Hall, the College of Education and Human Services through Dean Joseph DePierro and the Department of Educational Leadership, Management, and Policy through its chair, Charles Mitchel, provided extraordinary support for travel and for manuscript preparation and assigned a graduate assistant exclusively to the completion of this manuscript. Dr John Collins provided patient and tireless technical advice on arcane matters of table and figure construction and revision—at a moment's notice.

Over the long life span of this project, many of our former and some current students have assisted in very significant ways; some of them deserve special mention. In addition, through the years each of us subjected students in our respective seminars on the American faculty to drafts of chapters, asking for their critical reaction. A subset of these students were vitally involved in helping to conduct surveys and in preparing complex tables. Jesus Galaz-Fontes and Mandy Liu have already been mentioned. Among the many other students with whom it has been our good fortune to work, we express particular thanks to Gary Berg, Guy Gerbick, Cathy Heffernan, Peggy McLaughlin, Dan Walden, and Wei-jiang (Richard) Zhang in Claremont and, at Seton Hall, Lynn Mertz, Tom Green, Scott Snair, Janet James, and all spring 2004 participants in the Faculty Personnel Policies seminar. These individuals reviewed earlier versions of the manuscript and provided advice on table and figure construction. They are all accomplished professionals in their own right.

Several persons working in various capacities at the National Center for Education Statistics have been particularly helpful in assisting us as we negotiated the data maze. Valerie Martin Conley (now at Ohio University), Linda Zimbler, and Sam Bedinger come foremost to mind.

We are especially indebted to Jacqueline Wehmueller, Executive Editor at the Johns Hopkins University Press, for her guidance and patience. And we acknowledge the suggestions from reviewers both at and beyond the Press. We are grateful, too, for the excellent copyediting of our complex manuscript by Lois R. Crum.

Finally, a word of thanks is owed to our respective families. Over a decade, both of our families—especially Diane Schuster and Rena Hottinger—have "made do" with frequent, sometimes inconvenient absences and, even more frequently, the authors' preoccupations with the project. We have appreciated their patience, their belief in our project's merit, and their steadfast encouragement!

PART ONE

Overview of the
American Faculty

CHAPTER ONE

Establishing the Framework

We take as our point of departure a bold and unqualified assertion: American higher education and the academic profession that serve it are on the edge of an unprecedented restructuring that is changing the face—indeed, even the very meaning—of higher learning. Higher education, of course, has always been in transition. At a fundamental level, the knowledge base that higher education develops, preserves, and transmits is constantly expanding; that much is axiomatic. The organizational arrangements and practices of the academy—key among them the arrangements for academic staffing—also adapt continually to ever-emerging realities and to society's priorities. And the tensions that inevitably accompany change are, naturally, always present. Thus, we do not mean that this is the first time vectors of change have pushed and pulled in opposite directions: countervailing forces pressing upon higher education have always characterized the academic enterprise. Emerging knowledge and newish modes of pedagogy perennially challenge and displace—or augment—entrenched tradition and prevailing practice. The historical verity of continuity and change is "old news"; it has characterized higher education since its inception. But in these pages we argue that the coming change is *unprecedented* insofar as two powerful conditions reinforce each other: the sheer number of institution-molding forces that are in play (some of these we describe below) and the stunning rapidity with which these forces are reshaping higher education.

This arguably unprecedented transformation in American higher education is inextricably and profoundly linked with the volatile present circumstance and uncertain outlook for the academy's core resource: the faculty. That the future condition of the faculty is central to the well-being of the academy is undeniable, for without an adequately functioning faculty in place—however *adequately* may be defined—the academy would not be the academy but something else entirely. Our extensive examination of the recent past and projections about the likely future of higher education focus in particular on the academic profession, for as the venues of postsecondary education increasingly blur into the environment of the larger, information-laden society, the future of the academic profession—who the faculty are, who they will be, the nature of academic work, and the trajectories of academic careers—is perhaps less certain, more permeated with threats (and yes, opportunities) than at any time in the past. This, we recognize, is a bold assertion, but we perceive that a flood of evidence substantiates our contention.

HISTORICAL PERSPECTIVE

Some historical perspective on the pace of evolution of higher education in the United States is in order as we begin. It provides a context for our consideration of the faculty's present condition and outlook—and, accordingly, for establishing what is at stake for the American society that creates and nurtures these institutions of higher learning.

Higher education has evolved through successive stages as society's needs have changed. Each era has featured trailblazers who risked failure and who, in fact, frequently failed. They have left behind a constantly changing landscape for higher education; previous elements survive, even flourish, but the topography has become ever more complex, more accommodating to variation. Consider, for instance, the bold efforts during the early nineteenth century as innovators who promoted alternative modes of instruction or curricular content (among them Rensselaer Polytechnic Institute, Union College, and the University of Nashville) broke free of the powerful gravitational pull of the old classical English college model. Traditionalist colleges, epitomized by Yale in the 1820s, sought to beat back the incursions of heretical innovators who were markedly less interested in the traditionalists' central mission of character building (Rudolph, 1991). Or consider the introduction a half century later of the American university model, in the face of the persistent character-molding orientation of undergraduate education and the enduring practice of curricular prescription. These innovations spanned a remarkable variety of initiatives: from Andrew White and Ezra Cornell's ambitious vision for Cornell to offer "any study," to Johns Hopkins University's focused commitment to scholarship and graduate education; from Harvard's emergence under Charles Eliot's baton in the 1880s as a broad-gauged university with greater deference to student choice (that is, electives), to William Rainey Harper's daringly different concept for the organization and calendar of the University of Chicago, among other innovations. Consider, too, the remarkable but hugely controversial democratization of access to postsecondary education following World War II; opposed were such keepers of the flame as Robert Maynard Hutchins, who was aghast at what seemed to him reckless cheapening of the academic currency.

Other tension-ridden face-offs, as megaforces collided, are easy to identify. Numerous new models continue to emerge and manage still to coexist. The field is large enough, the marketplace diverse enough, to accommodate Nova University, the University of Phoenix, Western Governors University, Argosy University, and Jones International—alongside Princeton and Ohio State, Georgetown University and Pomona College, "Cal Baptist" and "Caltech," Miami Dade Community College and Agnes Scott, Southeast Missouri and Fisk University. A hundred flowers—distinctive varietals all—in fact do bloom. A *few* once-flourishing types have withered and largely disappeared: the undergraduate college for men (only four have survived into the twenty-first century from among the hundreds that once thrived)[1] and the public normal school, scores of which trained generations of future school teachers. But dozens of newish institutional models—including exotic strains cultivated in the hothouse of breathtaking new technologies—have found conditions adequate for sustenance. And each adds to the remarkable heterogeneity of *faculty* types and experiences: who the faculty are (that is, the kinds of attributes and competencies that are sought to staff these variegated enterprises) and what these faculty members actually do. The acceptance of ever greater variety among institutional types—in the marketplace and by the quality assurance (a.k.a. accreditation) guardians—in turn fuels greater variation in the ingredients that comprise academic work and in the patterns of academic career trajectories. This multihued palette of academic professionals and their work is the very essence of contemporary American higher education. The implications of these developments for the academic profession are enormous and underlie our many-faceted inquiry.

THE NEW ORDER

Now things *are* different, even radically different, for higher education and its faculty, mainly because of the accelerating pace of market-driven and technology-enabled innovations. Such change is unprecedented in terms of the confluence of four factors or megatrends.

- The pace of change is uniquely rapid and discontinuous, that is, nonlinear, resulting in "quantum" (and unpredictable) changes over very brief time frames.
- The foundations of the economy are shifting structurally, that is, how the economy is organized, and its functional "rules" are changing radically. Moreover, at the core of this dimension of change are precisely those economic arrangements related to the collection, dissemination, and management of information and knowledge: historically higher education's core social functions.
- The economic changes, especially in relation to information and knowledge, are associated with a major ideological and philosophical shift in how society views higher education, namely, increasingly as a private rather than a public good and as an "industry" that must be ever more open to competition within and from without rather than as a protected social institution.
- The growing focus on public investment in higher education and the expanding privatization movement—a "structural" concomitant of the "massification" of higher education—is truly global. In other words, developments in the United States are isomorphic, generally congruent with those in other developed nations.

Taken together, these megatrends lie at the crux of our argument that higher education is undergoing a pervasive transformation that has the most profound implications for the academy and its academic staff. Let's look briefly at each of them.

The Pace of Change Accelerated

Substantial change ordinarily has taken decades to unfold before one might plausibly label it *transformative.* It can be argued, for example, that Yale's firm hold on the template for collegiate education, prior to the mid-nineteenth century, did not begin to relax, despite a host of challengers, until some years after enactment of the Morrill Land-Grant Act of 1862; even so, traditionalist schools—Princeton perhaps at the forefront (or rearmost guard, as the case may be)—continued to exert a powerful conservative influence long thereafter.

Similarly, the university model—or more accurately, models—took form slowly at first. It was probably not until the first decade of the twentieth century, after Hopkins, Chicago, Stanford, and Clark had taken root and after Harvard's president Charles Eliot had narrowly survived the scorn heaped upon him there and from other venues for having pioneered the elective system in the 1880s (you mean let the *students* decide?), that the university paradigm, reinforced by the jelling of learned societies in the 1880s and 1890s, clearly carried the day and displaced the long-standing dominance of the collegiate model. The emergent universities surely had not vanquished the classical English college model; Swarthmore and Williams and Gettysburg and Carleton were—and are—alive and well. But a coexistence had been achieved, and pluralism, as always, prevailed.

As to the democratization of access, one change was so abrupt that it did throw its critics into a frenzy. That, of course, was the Servicemen's Readjustment Act of 1944 (the "G.I. Bill of Rights"), alluded to earlier, which funneled huge numbers of "nontraditional" students—the returning veterans—onto hundreds of campuses starved for students but hardly prepared for these new, mostly highly purposeful learners. But after the clump of veterans had made their way through the system, enrollments slumped and then rebounded more slowly, albeit steadily, over the next several decades, boosted by a growing population base, and continued to expand incrementally, following passage of the Higher Education Act of 1965 and infusions of federal student aid. The expansion of federal student financial aid remained modest, however, until about 1980 with the enactment of the Middle Income Student Assistance Act and subsequent measures that contributed to greater access to higher education. In all, though, the changes did not occur overnight. For example, it should be noted that the sweeping prescriptions offered by President Truman's visionary Commission on Higher Education in 1947, which urged expanded access and the end of racial discrimination in colleges and universities, hardly triggered swift change. Indeed, the commission's report had no significant impact "on the ground" for years; not until two decades later, after passage of the Civil Rights Act of 1964 and the aforementioned Higher Education Act of 1965, did the commission's vision even begin to approach realization.

Thus, although the previous purported "revolutions" did, in fact, signal transformations of the academy *and,* at the same time, sowed the seeds for profound change within the academic profession, these movements, however far-reaching, were much less revolutionary than *evolutionary,* given the time that proved necessary for consolidating the changes. In that same vein, it is perhaps relevant to recall the central thesis of Christopher Jencks and David Riesman's influential *The Academic Revolution* (1968); they argued that the power of professors had expanded over the years to the point where the professoriate had finally gained control over the academic core of the university. A more accurate title for their provocative book surely would have been *The Academic*

Evolution—though the effect on sales likely would not have been positive! And even that declaration of professorial triumph must be viewed in the light of Riesman's own subsequent disavowal (1981) of his and Jencks's premature assertion.

It is our contention, therefore, that over a span of years that now approaches four centuries, significant changes in the American academy and in the instructional staff have been on the whole quite gradual. In only a few instances have big changes come about in bursts, and even on those rare occasions, the shifts did not take immediate, lasting effect. We now posit, however, that the era upon which higher education has recently embarked is different, probably very different, in terms of the foreshortened time that it will take—indeed, *is* taking—for a sweeping transformation to occur. Consider for a moment, in contrast, the trajectory of teaching and learning over the past decade (or even the most recent half decade), with the universal spread of personal computing and the omnipresence of the Internet. Within a decade instructional technology has grown from not much more than a budgetary afterthought (and mostly on the capital side) to (commonly) 10% to 12% of campus "education and general" budgets (Finkelstein et al., 2000). And institutions seem to be attending in their academic offerings and in their marketing campaigns as much to their *virtual* classrooms and programs as to their traditional curriculum. For example, the Campus Computing Project in Encino, California, reported how "wired" colleges were in 1995, based on the percentage of colleges with Web site home pages (55%) and college courses utilizing e-mail (20%). As those percentages approached 100% in 2003, the project changed the conditions it measured, considering instead such statistics as the percentage of colleges with full-campus wireless networks (14.2%) and online course registration (76.6%) (Green, 1995, 2003).

A decade ago, Peter Vaill (1996) suggested that American higher education was in effect cascading through constant white-water rapids with no opportunity to seek respite in calm water before plunging into the next set of rapids. As the twenty-first century begins to unfold, it is increasingly apparent that Vaill's metaphor is apt. Change, as Heraclitus observed long ago, is perhaps the only constant, but, to repeat our thesis, change in higher education surely has never before been so rapid or so pervasive.

The Economy Restructured

Over the past decade social scientists, philosophers, and educators have described broadscale economic changes using a variety of concepts and frameworks. Charles Handy (1994), the British social philosopher, drew the distinction between "continuous" and "discontinuous" change. By that he meant to distinguish between *gradual, linear* changes whose cumulative impacts are discernible over decades, generations, or even centuries as almost linear consequences and more *abrupt* changes that promote episodic discontinuities in a decidedly nonlinear trajectory of change. We have moved, argues Handy (1998), from a world of such gradual, continuous changes to one of "unreasonable," discontinuous change in which all the established rules are vulnerable. As American society scrambles from a goods-based to a service-and-knowledge-based economy, and as globalization expands the arena in which all enterprises must compete, a greater premium must be placed on organizational efficiency, flexibility, and nimbleness. In the larger global economy, a restructuring of work is resulting: the end of secure, long-term employment for most workers (where there exists work at all) and the shift to "nonstandard" employment, including more part-time work, leaner "core" staffing levels, and greater emphasis on self-employment and entrepreneurship. Handy describes the new "shamrock" organization of the workplace as three-pronged: a shrinking "core" of professionals whose skills reflect the organization's core competencies; a growing pool of self-employed or freelance professionals and technicians who are hired on an ad hoc project basis; and an expanding corps of "contingent" workers who work by the hour—and who lack any discernible career track. These freelancers and contingents are not limited to clerical or blue-collar workers; they increasingly include lawyers, physicians, engineers, and other professionals.

From a somewhat different perspective, Carol Twigg (2002a), as part of the Project on the Future of Higher Education (www.pfhe.org), posits that the major historic functions of the university in general and scholarly activity in particular—the creation, presentation, dissemination, and preservation of knowledge—are based on a set of familiar technologies (the book, the classroom) and economic arrangements. As the technology and economic requirements change, so does the structure of the institutions performing those functions. Information technology makes it possible to disaggregate, or "unbundle," educational activities and processes and thus to reconfigure the landscape of the industry. Accordingly, "truly" new providers emerge who target specific activities and processes of the enterprise as sources of new businesses; and the pieces are reaggregated under new arrangements that are different in kind from the old arrangements. Consider the outsourcing of various "platforms" for online campus courses and the emergence of new kinds of organizations like Blackboard and eCollege that provide the tools for enhancing the academic program (Ruch, 2001). Or the development of the new "college textbook" business by publishing conglomerates and media companies. Or the outsourcing of student remedial and supplemental education services or counseling through reconfigured organizations such as Sylvan Learning Systems or Stanley Kaplan. As organizations seek to analyze their business processes in terms of how they "add value" to their product, Twigg distinguishes between the marketplace of the organization's physical activities and processes and the *virtual* market *space* of the organization's "electronic" presence. She suggests that universities, no less than other businesses in a globally competitive environment, are now thinking in terms of how they add value *virtually,* as well as physically.

The Enterprise Reconceptualized

Handy does not apply his ideas directly to colleges and university organization, but Twigg and increasing numbers of policy analysts surveying higher education are now depicting it as an "industry" or a "business"—indeed as the "core" business of the new economy. Patricia Gumport (1997) has decried the "uncritical" application of the "higher education as business" paradigm to the formulation of public policy (p. 69). She reminds us that historically higher education has been viewed by the larger society as a "social institution," as steward for a broad set of societal responsibilities to prepare young people for a democratic citizenship and to expand knowledge at least in part for knowledge's sake. Increasingly, public policy debates view colleges and universities less as "social institutions" to be supported for the long-term good of the order, than as businesses producing a product (skilled labor, new technologies) or a consumer service—and proponents of this reconceptualization choose to apply to colleges and universities the same standards that they would apply to any other business: To what extent does this entity add value? And at what cost? And can comparable value be added more efficiently by other means?

The point here is that supporting the seismic economic realignments to which we have alluded is an *ideological* posture, a basic change in how government and the public increasingly have come to think about higher education. The greater focus on performance, accountability, value added, and cost containment (or cost reduction) reflects a conception of the enterprise qua enterprise and accepts—indeed, embraces—a fundamental trade-off: the reduction of social benefits to achieve immediate short-term satisfaction of economic needs. It reflects as well the broader view of higher education as a "private" rather than a "public" benefit and invokes the application to higher education of the sovereignty of the marketplace. These trends have given broad impetus to what Slaughter and Leslie (1997) and Rhoades (1998), among others, refer to as "corporatization" and "privatization." Not only must education in this new era be treated as a commodity in the global market (witness, for example, the inclusion of higher education certification and degrees as commodities subject to "free trade" policies as part of the General Agreement on Trade and Tariffs (GATT) (see Altbach, 2004), but, as the new conceptualization would have it, this sector of the economy should be responsible for paying increasingly larger shares of its own freight. New realities, new principles.

Postsecondary ("Tertiary") Education Globalized

Higher education has always transcended national borders, ever since a handful of scholars, unhappy with their circumstances in Paris, "defected" to found a collegium across the channel in Oxford. The centuries since have witnessed incessant transnational movements, both permanent and temporary, of scholars and students. The United States, an exporter during the last quarter of the nineteenth century of scholars eager to pursue advanced study in Europe, especially at the more evolved German universities, became a huge net importer of scholars in the twentieth century.

The well-chronicled absorption of scholars fleeing Nazi persecution prior to World War II was a prelude to much larger numbers who obtained appointments in U.S. colleges and universities in the decades following that war. The importation of academic staff continued apace as U.S. immigration laws were amended—quite extensively in 1990—to explicitly facilitate that influx (Schuster, 2001). But the physical movement of bodies across international boundaries, however substantial, has become a less prominent dimension of internationalization as modes of electronic communication have obliterated borders, a process fueled by the preeminence of English as the language of scholarship and, increasingly, of instruction. In short, the clichéd "global village" is clearly manifest throughout the world of academe. It remains to be seen whether responses to threats of terrorism and the prioritization of "homeland security" will cause the U.S. government to significantly restrict entry of students and scholars from other countries. Even if such barriers to immigration were erected, the movement toward a more globalized higher education is certainly accelerating via electronic communication.

Beyond the freer flow of scholarship and teaching across increasingly porous boundaries, another prominent feature of globalization in postsecondary education is the extent to which national systems appear to be converging ideologically and in their strategic approaches, often seeming to emulate fundamental tenets of American higher education. Particularly noteworthy is the substantial expansion of access to postsecondary education in most developed countries and many developing countries over the past several decades (OECD, 2002). Comparably significant is the loosening of central control over higher education systems in favor of greater variety in types of institutions and embracing market forces to promote competition to reshape—and reenergize—national systems (Enders, 2001). (These issues are addressed in chapter 10.)

And so, the transformations manifest in American higher education cannot be understood outside the global developments that permeate other societies and the concomitant "reengineering" of higher learning. The dramatic changes in just who the American academic professionals are and what they do both shape and are shaped by counterpart institutions in other lands, and by their patterns of academic staffing.

VECTORS OF CHANGE

We suggested at the outset that the changes acting upon higher education are different from those of times past because of the number of such powerful forces and the velocity with which, acting in concert, they are effecting far-reaching transformation. We now expand on some of the dimensions of change by highlighting several key "vectors." They do not all propel higher education in a single direction, for the strong currents are sometimes in tension with one another. But the aggregate effect is transformative. Five such vectors are demographics, technology, marketplace influences, replacement rates, and changes in quality assurance.

The Demographic Transformation

The past forty years have seen perhaps the most quantum demographic transformation of the U.S. population in our history. It includes three independent, albeit mutually reinforcing, elements: the "geriatrification" of America, the reengineering of the racial and ethnic sources of immigration to the United States, and the restructuring of the family unit (Keller, 2001).

Geriatrification

If current trends continue, the cohort of America's school-age youth will be declining while the 65-plus cohort is rapidly increasing—paralleling the situation in most Western, industrialized nations. Over the next twenty years the United States will need to find ways to increase the productivity of its nonexpanding workforce. This task will require increased attention to optimizing the contribution of heretofore marginal groups, including principally women and minorities. At the same time, the nation will need to substantially increase its investment in health care and pensions (and ipso facto decrease its proportionate contribution to higher education). Already, the federal government is spending nine times as much per person on the elderly as on children and youth, and that trend will only continue.

Reconfiguration of the Racial and Ethnic Mix

The Immigration and Nationality Act Amendments of 1965 increased immigration quotas, abolished the preferences for Europeans, and stressed family connections over occupational skills—resulting in an unprecedented infusion of some 40 million immigrants, legal and otherwise. Moreover, whereas nine-tenths of U.S. immigrants hailed from Europe and Canada before 1965, since that time the proportions have been dramatically reversed: now nine-tenths of our immigrants come from Latin America and the Caribbean (50%), Asia (33%), and Africa (5%)—in all, roughly three-quarters of a million annually plus perhaps another quarter million illegally and yet another quarter million admitted via work and tourist visas but staying. Now about one in seven children over the age of 5 come from non-English-speaking homes and two-fifths from families without a completed secondary education. Not only have these facts reconfigured the work of the public school systems, but they have begun as well to recast the landscape of higher education: courses in English as a Second Language (ESL) have become more prominent, and diversity initiatives and new academic programs have emerged to accommodate these "new entrants."

The Restructuring of the Family Unit

As late as forty years ago, 90% of schoolchildren came from two-parent homes, the majority of mothers did not work outside the home (or worked part-time), and only 6% of children had been born to unmarried women. Colleges could count on parental resources and encouragement. Since then, the transformation has constituted a sea change. The divorce rate has doubled to more than 50%, 37% of children live in single-parent households (and 60% will spend part of their youth with only one parent), 70% of married women with children work outside the home, 32% of all children are born to unmarried women (the rate in 1998 was 70% among African Americans), and a million teen pregnancies are reported annually (the highest rate in the world). Today, only one-quarter of households consist of a married couple with children.

Concurrently, the number of children living in poverty has increased dramatically (38% of people living below the poverty level are children), as has the incidence of juvenile violent crime and incarceration. The available evidence suggests, not surprisingly, that family disruption has been negatively associated with school achievement and with completion of high school and college.

Technological Shocks

A powerful force permeating postsecondary education indisputably is technology (discussed at length in part 4 of this volume). Its effects are evident everywhere, including, as noted earlier, the ways technology eradicates the significance of national boundaries, at least for some scholarly purposes. Technology profoundly alters the two domains at the core of academic work: scholarship and instruction. It also changes the service component of academic work, the third (and many-faceted) function in the traditional academic triad. But relative to scholarship and the teaching-learning process, service, with rare exceptions, is not so central to the work of academics.

First, technology's impact on research, though an integral dimension of academic work since at least the emergence of the printing press a half-millennium ago, in recent years has moved so swiftly and in so many ways as to defy precise description. Technology pervades the gathering of data, its analysis, and its dissemination. Second, in the realm of teaching and learning, too, various technologies amplify, enhance, complicate, and more and more frequently redefine the very nature of the faculty's role as instructors and guides. From facilitating student access to databases that were hardly imaginable even a few years ago to organizing electronic discussion groups, the role of the faculty member as facilitator and catalyst increasingly takes on very different dimensions. The third observation for now about technology perhaps states the obvious: the rate of change continues to accelerate. What defines academic work is likely to be very different even in the proximate future from what it is today. Some important tools now commonly used by faculty members were not on the horizon a decade, even a half-decade, ago. (See chapter 4 for several illustrative vignettes by which we attempt to capture this phenomenon.) Who can foresee just how swiftly new modalities will become widely utilized and how they will alter the essence of academic work?

Marketplace Pressure

A surge of market forces has swept through the academy in recent decades, and the effects are everywhere to be found. For faculty members one of the most obvious consequences is the "liberating" of faculty salaries to respond more directly to on-the-ground realities of demand and supply—conditions that serve academic accountants well and classicists, for example, much less well. The old-fashioned notion of "*a* faculty" of approximately equal value from one specialty to another (with exceptions always made for academic lawyers and physicians) is by now a receding memory, except in the more egalitarian community colleges. (These matters are examined in some detail in chapter 8.) Moreover, a truly revolutionary reconfiguration of academic appointments (see chapter 3 and, especially, chapter 7) allows colleges and universities to respond with expanded flexibility to shifting student interests and, in the case of nearly a half million piecework-paid, benefits-free part-time faculty, dramatic cost savings as well.

Market conditions, bolstered by public policy approbation, have also given rise to a dazzling array of for-profit "knowledge service" providers. These proprietary institutions, ranging from small, niche-seeking start-ups to the far-flung University of Phoenix, compete increasingly with more traditional postsecondary institutions.[2] More to the immediate point, they employ thousands of faculty members whose work responsibilities and career paths are generally strikingly different from—much more contained than—those of their counterparts in more traditional settings. Perhaps most noteworthy (some would say sobering) is the likelihood that more providers will emerge, some probably quite well capitalized, to compete for the students' dollars. That is to say, the probability is high that the academic landscape and the distribution of faculty jobs "appertaining thereto" will undergo dramatic shifts in the foreseeable future.

Other market-driven facets of the emerging "new" higher education range from lively contests over faculty members' intellectual property interests to institutional outsourcing for curriculum content, and from the unionization of economically squeezed part time or adjunct faculty and student teaching assistants to contracts, which may involve many millions of dollars, between research-and-development-hungry corporations (sometimes foreign) and academic units to provide leading-edge research in exchange for favored access to such research results.

Although the notion of "the entrepreneurial university" is hardly new,[3] it is quite clear that entrepreneurship's presence within academe has continually broadened and deepened and that there is no end in sight (until, that is, abuses surface that may begin to arrest the pendulum's swing).

The dynamic forces that are transforming the environment and, within it, the modalities of higher education are further accelerated by two quite different factors. One is driven by demographics, the other is systematic.

The Accelerated Rate of Faculty Replacement

Faculty retirements and replacement-driven demand is a function of many factors, but the most significant among them is a raw demographic: the faculty's age. (The "uncapping" of mandatory retirement age, which went into effect January 1, 1994, has had only a modest effect on slowing the rate of retirement.) At this time the average age of faculty members is considerably greater than it was two decades ago (see chapter 3); as a function of that "graying of the faculty," scores of thousands of faculty members are retiring or moving swiftly toward retirement. A "makeover" of the faculty, in terms of who will replace retiring individuals and what conditions will define their appointments, can thus proceed at a much swifter rate than would otherwise be the case (as demonstrated in chapter 7). (The redeployment of the instructional staff and the implications of that shift is examined further in chapters 3, 6, 7, and 11.) The opportunity obtains to replace in some fashion traditional faculty—traditional, that is, in their mix of academic responsibilities—with "new look" faculty who shoulder a quite different mix of responsibilities. And this development is proceeding apace.

Quality Assurance Reformulated

A more subtle but no less profound change is occurring that has the potential for redefining higher education—and, thereby, academic work and careers. Here we refer to the substitution of new standards for regional accreditation. As emerging forces reshape American higher education, one of the fundamental issues being played out is whether standards to assure quality are changing and, if so, whether perhaps they are being relaxed in order to accommodate new modes. For many decades the responsibility for articulating standards and assuring quality has been borne by the very distinctive, peer-driven, "voluntary" system of six regional accreditation associations, augmented by "specialized" accreditation associations that define and enforce standards for particular fields. This system has evolved into a central feature of American higher education. Although perhaps all nations have *some* scheme for trying to assure quality in postsecondary education, the vehicle of regional accreditation in the United States, by buffering governmental encroachments on academic (relative) autonomy, has become the envy of much of the academic world.

But pressures on the traditional means of providing quality assurance have been buffeting the accreditation system for reasons too numerous and complex to describe here. Consequently, the regional associations in particular have been rewriting their standards in recent years, striving both to accommodate concerns by the federal government and to be more open to new market-driven and technology-facilitated "realities."

The point for present purposes is that the new look in accreditation appears to have highly significant implications for who the faculty will be and for the nature of academic work. The thrust of these changes, it can be said, is to soften, even jettison, traditional requirements for a sizable cadre of "regular," full-time faculty members who are expected to shoulder major responsibilities for governance and for shaping the academic core of the campus (Benjamin, 2003). These potentially pivotal issues are discussed subsequently. (See, for example, chapters 10 and 11.)

OUTLINE OF THE ARGUMENT

As the twenty-first century gets under way, there can be no question that higher education in the United States (and throughout the world) is undergoing rapid, far-reaching, even revolutionary change. None of the megatrends we have identified or the vectors that accelerate the changes are new; they've all been around, in one guise or another, throughout higher education's history. Yet the confluence of these forces and, in each instance, their intensification are propelling higher education into a future riddled with more uncertainties than in any previous era.

Does this depiction of changes that are sweeping through higher education and, we contend, fundamentally reshaping the academy and its faculty exaggerate either the pace of change or its scope? And what are the longer-term implications of such tumultuous change (if we are correct) for the academic profession, for the academy itself, and, in the even more important but most elusive realm to capture, for society itself?

The pursuit of answers to those questions has guided our dual, central tasks. Our inquiry has led us to describe in detail what has transpired for academics and their careers over the past three decades. Much of our effort has gone into describing this "platform" from which we seek to peer into the future. But it has obliged us to also address what the foreseeable future may hold for the academic profession and to consider how the higher education community and the wider polity should respond now to those prospects—to those threats and opportunities.

Higher education is becoming destabilized. In this process of extraordinarily rapid change, the composition of its most valuable asset—the faculty—and the essential nature of faculty work are being transformed. It is this accelerating metamorphosis of colleges and universities and their academic workforce that impels us to explore the two overarching issues joined in our inquiry: Where have we been? And where are we going?

NOTES

1. Deep Springs College (Nevada-California line), Hampden-Sydney College (Virginia), Moorehouse College (Georgia), and Wabash College (Indiana).

2. According to its Web site, the University of Phoenix has established more than 130 campuses and learning centers and has graduated more than 171,000 students since 1976. (http://online.phoenix.edu, February 18, 2004.)

3. For example, Burton Clark (1990), long an advocate for "the entrepreneurial university," was already making his case more than fifteen years ago, in his article "The Entrepreneurial University."

CHAPTER TWO

The American Faculty in Perspective

The turbulent environmental forces challenging the higher education enterprise in the closing decade of the twentieth century include, most tangibly, changes in the composition of the faculty and the nature of their appointments, in the makeup and preparation of student bodies, and in the resources available to higher education; less tangible (but no less momentous) changes have occurred in public expectations for higher education and in the technologies that influence how we go about organizing and implementing the teaching and learning enterprise.

What might these shifts mean for the American faculty? What kind of faculty will the nation require to meet these challenges? As we address this question, it is instructive to begin with a look at the historical record. That record suggests at least one striking conclusion: when the number and intensity of external social/economic/political pressures impinging on the higher education system reach a "critical mass," the system is forced to reequilibrate itself to accommodate the pressures, not only responding quantitatively, but adapting qualitatively as well. As American higher education expanded in response to the nation's transition to a secular, industrial, urban society with an emergent middle class (Veysey, 1965), it adopted new purposes, functions, and modes of operation (Trow, 1973). Shifts occurred in faculty roles, work activities, and careers, and indeed, there was a reformulation of the very definition of a college or university faculty member and of qualifications to serve in that role.

For nearly four centuries, since the founding of Harvard College, academic staff of one sort or another have stood (or sat) in front of a group, large or small, of physically present students of one sort or another. For more than half that period, college teaching changed little and could best be described as an odd job taken on by fresh graduates of baccalaureate programs as a way station on the path to some other career, for example, the ministry, business, law, medicine, government, or farming. During the past 150 to 175 years, however, an extraordinary change has occurred in the role of academic staffs—their responsibilities, backgrounds, and career paths—both reflecting and making possible in the United States the transformation to a mass system of higher education and, beyond that, practically universal access (Trow, 1973).

These historical shifts in the roles and responsibilities of academic staffs proceeded in two basic phases: professionalization in the nineteenth century, and expansion and diversification in the twentieth century (Metzger, 1987). Professionalization began in the first quarter of the nineteenth century and gained momentum after the Civil War, roughly paralleling the emergence of the American university (Veysey, 1965; Finkelstein, 1983). Expansion and diversification marked the post–World War II period; and it remains ongoing and impressive, although the rate of growth in numbers of institutions, students, and academic staff has slowed since the 1970s (Jencks and Riesman, 1968; Metzger 1987; Kerr, 1991). Current environmental turbulence suggests that we are on the cusp, as it were, of a third tectonic shift.

Reviewing such historical transitions provides an important perspective on the historical development of faculty work and careers, allowing us to unfreeze some of our assumptions about the "essentialness" and "invariability" of who faculty are and what they do and providing us with the necessary floating frame within which to contemplate the future. It is our belief that this overview of how the academic profession evolved on these shores will both allow us to perceive more clearly the current condition of academic life—poised, we argue, at the threshold of momentous change—and enable us to discern more reliably the key issues that will shape academic work and careers in the new century.

THE COLLEGE TEACHING CAREER CIRCA 1800

During the seventeenth century and the first half of the eighteenth, the teaching staffs of American colleges were composed entirely of tutors, typically young men, often no more than twenty years of age, who had just received their baccalaureate degree and were preparing for careers in the ministry (Morison, 1936). Their responsibilities were pastoral-custodial as well as pedagogical in nature. Ideally, a single tutor was assigned to shepherd a single class through the prescribed four-year curriculum. As Morison (1936, p. 127) observed, "Tutors were with their pupils almost every hour of the day [in the classroom recitations, in study halls, and at meals], and slept in the same chamber with some of them at night. They were responsible not only for the intellectual, but also for the moral and spiritual development of their charges." In reality, however, the tutorship during this era functioned more as a "revolving door," whether at Harvard or at Yale, Brown, Dartmouth, or Bowdoin. For prior to 1685, very seldom did a tutor see a class through all four years, and only six of the forty-one tutors during this period remained at Harvard for more than three years (Finkelstein, 1984, pp. 8–9).

During the second half of the eighteenth century, these staffs of tutors began to be supplemented by a small cadre of "permanent" faculty: the first professors. Carrell (1968) could identify only ten professors in all of American higher education in 1750. By 1800, while the number of colleges had doubled, professorial ranks had multiplied tenfold to more than one hundred. All in all, by the onset of the nineteenth century, some two hundred individuals had served as professors in nineteen American colleges.

The pattern that had been in place at Harvard for more than a century and at Yale for more than a half century was adopted almost immediately by those colleges founded during the second half of the eighteenth century. At Brown, for example, within five years of its founding, a core permanent faculty had already emerged with Howell's promotion from tutor to professor to join President and Professor James Manning. By 1800 Brown's five tutors had been supplemented by three permanent professors (*Historical Catalogue,* 1905). At Princeton, by 1767, two decades after its founding, three permanent professors had joined the three tutors (Wertenbaker, 1946). At Dartmouth, during the administration of John Wheelock (1779–1817), several professors were appointed to supplement the single professor who, together with two or three tutors, had constituted the entire faculty during the preceding administration of Eleazar Wheelock (Richardson, 1932, p. 820).

Although these professors discharged responsibilities very similar to those of the tutors in terms of supervising recitations, study halls, chapel, and discipline, they were distinguishable from the tutors in at least three crucial respects. First, professors did not take general charge of a whole class of students; rather, they were appointed in a particular subject area such as natural philosophy, divinity, or ancient languages and, for the most part, provided instruction in that area of specialization. Second, they were generally older than the tutors (by at least five to ten years) and more experienced (the majority had some postbaccalaureate professional preparation in theology, law, or medicine).[1] Third, they stayed on—that is, they were relatively permanent.

Carrell's analysis (1968) of 124 biographical sketches of professors during the second half of the eighteenth century illuminates the particular meaning of a "permanent" appointment prior to 1800. First, a professorship implied a career at a single institution, most frequently one's alma mater. Nearly 40% of Carrell's sample taught at their own alma mater; proportions ranged from just over one-third at the College of Philadelphia (later the University of Pennsylvania) to five-sixths (83%) at Harvard. Indeed, seven out of eight taught at only one institution during their careers, and a practically invisible one in forty taught at three or more institutions. Second, although often enduring, a professorial position was typically a "non-exclusive" career. In analyzing the lifetime occupational commitment of his sample, Carrell reported that about 15% identified themselves exclusively as professional teachers, and roughly 20% described themselves *primarily* as professional teachers but with a secondary occupation in the ministry, medicine, or law, whereas over half ($n = 68$) identified themselves primarily as practitioners of one of the traditional professions and only secondarily as professional college teachers (often having taken up professoring after a lengthy stint as a minister or a practicing physician).

Although college teaching typically was not an exclusive career, or even the first choice, of a majority of eighteenth-century professors, it became a long-term commitment for many—once the move had been made. In analyzing indicators of the extent of professors' occupational commitment *during their teaching tenure,* Carrell found strikingly varied results: 45% identified themselves as college teachers exclusively, while about one-quarter identified themselves as college teachers only primarily or secondarily. In the latter two categories, clergy were heavily represented in the first, and physicians and lawyers made up the greater portion of the second, suggesting that clergy were more likely than the other learned professions to develop a primary commitment to the professorial role, once assumed.

An important question remains: to what extent did appointments as tutors lead to professorial appointments? Alternatively, were these types of appointments typically compartmentalized from each other? In fact, the tutorship remained a separate, temporary career track for young people moving on. It rarely led to entering the professorial ranks: no tutors at Harvard became Harvard professors; one in ten tutors at Yale during this period moved on to a professorship; and one in five at Brown. The professors were typically drawn from outside the ranks of the tutors, although at a few places, such as Yale, the majority of the professors had at one time or another served as tutors (Finkelstein, 1983).

By 1800, then, college teaching was becoming a *bifurcated* occupation. The majority of college teachers were still young, inexperienced tutors, providing general custodial supervision as well as instruction to students for what would be a brief postbaccalaureate engagement before they, the tutors, moved on with their lives and into other careers. An emerging minority were more experienced professionals drawn from other fields (the ministry, medicine, law) who moved into professorships in a teaching field following a career in their profession, often at their alma mater, and who typically continued in the faculty role as a second and/or secondary career.

NINETEENTH-CENTURY PROFESSIONALIZATION

Faculty professionalization during the nineteenth century meant at least four things. First, it marked the beginnings of *specialization* in teaching; that is, faculty usually were hired to teach in a particular field rather than to lead a cohort of freshman through the entire prescribed baccalaureate course (this had begun to occur during the second half of the eighteenth century [Carrell, 1968]). Second, associated with specialization in teaching was the notion that academic staffs should have *formal preparation,* through *graduate* education, for the specializations they taught (not merely general preparation in one of the learned professions); and until the last quarter of the nineteenth century, such training was available only in European universities (McCaughey, 1974; Tobias, 1982). Third, the time dedicated to preparation meant that college teaching no longer made sense as a transitory position but ordinarily required and sustained a *lifelong career commitment* (Carrell, 1968; McCaughey, 1974). Finally, specialization, coupled with the requisite advanced subject-matter preparation, spawned the conception of the academic as *expert.* This in turn provided the basis for subsequently advancing claims to academic freedom and faculty professional autonomy (Scott, 1966; Baldridge et al., 1978; Tobias, 1982).

The professionalization phase proceeded in two relatively distinct stages—two minirevolutions separated by a half century. The first quarter of the nineteenth century witnessed the ascent of a core of permanent, specialized professors as the centerpiece of academic staffing, quickly supplanting the tutorship as the modal appointment type at the leading institutions. This new breed of older academic staff, appointed to teach a particular subject, had some "professional training" in theology, law, or medicine (if not in their teaching field) and tended to stay on in their teaching role (whatever their original career choice might have been). They remained largely independent of the more temporary tutorship, thereby perpetuating a bifurcated staffing system. However, the professors replaced the tutors as the center of academic gravity.

How can we account for this first big step in the evolving professionalization of the academic career—the rise of the permanent faculty and their displacement, in only two decades, of the class of temporary, "revolving door" tutors as the instructional heart of the academy? Several "environmental" pressures appear to provide necessary, if not sufficient, conditions for driving the shift. The first is sheer growth in opportunity: increase in size of some of the leading institutions (Yale, for example, doubled its enrollment in twenty years) and increase in the number of institutions as a result of the "College Movement," however modest that growth may seem in light of later, accelerated expansion (Rudolph, 1962; Burke, 1982). A second set of factors can be seen in changing church-related careers—the most important occupational sector competing with colleges for would-be faculty members. Calhoun (1965), examining the New Hampshire clergy in the late eighteenth and early nineteenth centuries, reports a radical shift in clerical career patterns, which he attributes to the increasing secularization and urbanization of the populace. The average terms of service in local parishes, which throughout the eighteenth century had as often as not been measured in whole adult lifetimes, began to resemble the tenures of modern college and university presidents. This new hazard of job insecurity meant that the challenge of obtaining even so tenuous a position, coupled with the low salaries of clergy hired by rural and small-town congregations, led many ministers to seek to enhance their careers by developing options—such as launching colleges and becoming professors themselves (Tobias, 1982). The correlation of these developments in clerical careers with the ascent of the permanent professorship is lent further credence by the fact that by the beginning of the nineteenth century, clergymen were demonstrably more likely than their fellow professionals in law and medicine to identify themselves primarily as college teachers.

Although the "professor movement" had created by 1825 a relatively large cohort of career college teachers, their preparation, the nature of their work, and the structure of their careers were not yet fully "professionalized" in our contemporary sense. The postgraduate preparation of faculty in their teaching specialty (as distinguished from the ministry, law, or medicine) remained a rarity, except at Harvard. The majority of faculty members continued to be drawn to their initial appointments as professor from nonacademic jobs, primarily in school teaching or the ministry, secondarily in law or medicine. Any semblance of a career grounded in their academic discipline typically ended with their *institutional* career. That is, the modal pattern at some institutions was for the majority of faculty to move into nonacademic careers following their stints, however lengthy, as college teachers (50% of the full professors at Brown did so, and 60% at Bowdoin, although this pattern did not hold at Harvard and Yale).[2] And irrespective of their length of institutional service, most faculty in the first half of the nineteenth century still evidenced relatively low engagement with a field of study in terms of their scholarly publication patterns and associational involvements. Only a single faculty member at Brown, Bowdoin, Harvard, and Yale was involved to any significant extent in the activities of the learned societies of the day. And, excluding the medical faculty, it was only these same solo faculty members who were publishing in their areas of academic appointment.[3] While many professors in the first quarter of the nineteenth century were actively pursuing concurrent "public" careers, virtually none was rooted in their academic specialization. Beyond the budding multifaceted careers of a few men such as Benjamin Silliman at Yale and Parker Cleaveland at Bowdoin, visible on the academic public lecture circuit, the vast majority of professors expended their extra-institutional time in less scholarly pursuits, devoted to church-related or civic activities. Fully three-quarters of the professors at Dartmouth, two-thirds of those at Bowdoin, and half of those at Brown were engaged in itinerant preaching and work with missionary societies. Somewhat lower proportions were actively involved in community life, principally by holding political office at the local or even national level, assuming leadership roles in civic associations unrelated to education or intellectual culture (e.g., tree-planting societies), or, in fewer cases, holding membership in state historical societies (Packard, 1882; *Historical Catalogue,* 1905; Tobias, 1982).

By mid-nineteenth century, the confluence of a number of social and intellectual forces gained sufficient momentum to propel (catapult, really) the professionalization process to the next level, and this was a critical step in the shaping of modern academic life. The progressive secularization of American society was penetrating the classical college, subjugating the demands of piety to the secular religion of progress and materialism and reflecting the needs of a growing industrial economy (Hofstadter and Metzger, 1955; Brubacher and Rudy, 1968). At the same time, the rise of science and the tremendous growth of scientific knowledge was breaking apart the classical curriculum and giving rise to the development of the academic disciplines (distinguishing, thereby, the professional from the amateur) and spawning systematic research and graduate education (Berelson, 1960; Veysey, 1965; Wolfle, 1972; Oleson and Voss, 1979). Larger numbers of Americans were studying abroad in Germany and, on their return, importing their versions of the German university and the German idea of research into the United States (Hofstadter and Metzger, 1955). Once graduate education and disciplinary specialization took hold in earnest in the last quarter of the nineteenth century, it was but a short step to the establishment of the major (now familiar) learned societies and their sponsorship of specialized, disciplinary journals: for example, the American Chemical Society began in

1876, the Modern Language Association in 1883, the American Historical Association in 1884, the American Psychological Association in 1892, and on and on (Berelson, 1960).

These developments together provided American higher education with the capability of producing graduate-trained specialists and created clear career opportunities for the specialists thereby produced. Thus the impetus was provided for furthering—completing, in some respects—a second-order restructuring of faculty roles and careers.

This second-order shift was marked by the emergence of the faculty role as specialist in a discipline. Advanced graduate training in a discipline (in contrast to professional training in theology, law, and medicine), together with scholarly publication and participation in the activities of learned societies, was already evident well before 1850 at a few institutions, most notably Harvard. By 1845, for example, some 70% of the Bowdoin faculty were publishing in their field of specialization (about half authoring primarily textbooks); nearly one-third of them were active in professional associations (Packard, 1882). About half the Brown faculty were publishing in their field of specialization at this time, and by the Civil War, fully one-half were affiliated with the major disciplinary and scientific associations of the day. It was not until the second half of the century (the 1860s and 1870s for the most part), however, that institutions such as Dartmouth and Williams began basing appointments on discipline-related credentials and began hiring individuals directly out of the European and nascent American graduate schools (Finkelstein, 1983). And it was then, too, that one discerns the emergence of interinstitutional mobility: faculty, trained in a discipline, moving to more attractive positions at other institutions as emergent disciplinary loyalties supplanted local institutional commitments.

The professorial role as expert, as it began to take form in the immediate pre–Civil War period, gave rise to two significant, interrelated shifts in the professors' institutional careers during the last quarter of the nineteenth century. First was the emergence of new academic ranks (assistant and associate professor) and the forging of these new roles into a career sequence that at once gave shape to the career course and regulated movement through the junior ranks to a full professorship. Concomitantly, there was an expansion and professionalization of the junior faculty. Together, these developments served to integrate into a seamless structure the dual career track system (temporary tutors and a small core of permanent professors) that had characterized the early part of the nineteenth century.

The ranks of instructor and assistant professor made their appearance quite early in the annals of some institutions, but they did not become standard practice anywhere until the last quarter of the nineteenth century; nor did they serve as feeders to the senior ranks initially. These junior faculty roles, however, came to represent not merely changes in nomenclature, but rather significant departures from the tutorship, leading at some institutions to the disappearance of the tutorship and at others to its transformation into an instructorship. Most critically, by the 1870s and 1880s at most institutions the junior roles came to function as feeders to the full professorial ranks. By 1880 the junior faculty grew to equal or surpass in size the senior faculty at many institutions; and they were increasingly entering their academic careers directly from graduate training in their specialties or from junior appointments at other institutions. The essential features of the twentieth-century faculty role were becoming the norm—a far cry from the composition of faculties in the first quarter of the nineteenth century.

All of these structural changes in the academic career follow from the emergence of the discipline as the central organizing principle of academic life and the university as the dominant organizational form. Beginning in the 1850s, the bare outline of a concurrent "public" career rooted in a faculty member's disciplinary expertise, as an educator and/or as a proponent of culture (rather than of religion), was becoming discernible at many institutions. At Brown, for example, the immediate pre–Civil War period saw the first instance of a faculty member using his expertise in the service of state government: the appointment of a chemistry professor to head the Rhode Island board of weights and measures. By the end of the Civil War, the proportion of the Brown faculty involved in itinerant preaching and other clerical activities had dropped from more than one-third at midcentury to one-eighth. Although a large majority of the faculty remained involved in civic and community affairs (about 75%), a change in the nature of that involvement had taken place: only a single faculty member was directly involved in elective politics, while the majority were involved in distinctively cultural, academic, or education-related activities such as membership on boards of education; holding office in national honor, art, or historical societies; and service on state and federal government commissions (*Historical Catalogue*, 1905). At Bowdoin, by the eve of the Civil War, four of seven faculty members were engaged in extra-institutional roles as specialists, educators, and public men of letters. Parker Cleaveland was holding public lectures on mineralogy, and Alpheus Packard on education; President James Woods and Professor Packard were engaging in commissioned writing for the Maine Historical Society; and Thomas Upham was producing pamphlets for the American Peace Association (Packard, 1882).[4]

The growing centrality of the discipline was intruding into new professional claims for a role in areas of college governance, especially faculty appointments and curricular decisions, that had been the province of college presidents; these areas had traditionally been driven by religious as distinguished from scholarly considerations. Such claims on the part of professors were evident during the pre–Civil War period in the struggles, albeit amicable ones, between the old- and new-guard faculty concerning the relative emphasis on moral development and student discipline versus purely academic concerns (Dwight, 1903). The assertions of faculty prerogatives were reflected both more dramatically and less amicably in the post–Civil War period; they took the form of veritable faculty revolts at some of the more traditional institutions. At Williams, for example, the faculty, concerned about student performance and academic standards, confronted Mark Hopkins, the prototypical old-time college president, over their determination to enforce regular class attendance via a marking system. Two years earlier the faculty had succeeded in instituting annual written examinations; and in 1869, at the faculty's insistence, admissions standards were tightened and the practice of sending lists of class standings (the equivalent of the modern registrar's grade report) to all parents was initiated, despite enrollment shortfalls. By 1872 these conflicts had precipitated Hopkins's resignation and the inauguration of Paul Ansel Chadbourne, who had come to Williams eight years earlier as only the second European-trained specialist on the faculty (Rudolph, 1956, pp. 223–24).

At Dartmouth a decade later, fifteen of the twenty-two resident faculty petitioned the Board of Trustees for the dismissal of President Samuel Colcord Bartlett. At issue was the president's attempt to secure the appointment of a new professor of Greek whose religious qualifications appeared to the faculty to exceed the candidate's scholarly qualifications. Although Bartlett survived the challenge and lingered on for another decade, his successor, William Jewett Tucker, recognized in his 1893 inaugural address the emergence of a "New Dartmouth," a new kind of college staffed by a new kind of faculty (Tobias, 1982).

The faculty, it could be said, by century's end had scaled one plateau. Consolidation and deeper professionalization lay ahead.

CONSOLIDATION AND ELABORATION IN THE EARLY TWENTIETH CENTURY

By 1915 one indicator that the "new" academic profession had turned a collective corner was the founding of the American Association of University Professors (AAUP). The coming together of eighteen academic luminaries from seven of the leading universities to charter the first national organization of professors suggests a newfound sense of collective professorial self-consciousness and a sense of colleagueship or fraternity in the service of scientific progress. As Edwin R. A. Seligman of Columbia, one of the founders, proclaimed: "Loyalty to our institution is admirable, but if our institution for some unfortunate reason stands athwart the progress of science, or even haltingly follows that path, we must use our best efforts to convince our colleagues and the authorities of the error of their ways. . . . In prosecuting this end, we need both individual and collective efforts. The leisure of the laboratory and of the study accounts for much; but almost equally important is the stimulus derived from contact with our colleagues" (cited by Hofstadter and Metzger, 1955, p. 471). Yet this sense of collective consciousness was, in one important sense, highly restricted: in terms of who was to be included in the collectivity. In the AAUP's initial constitution, membership was limited to "recognized" scholars with at least ten years' experience in the professoriate. Although the base was broadened in 1920 to include professors with three or more years of experience, nonetheless the cadre that was conscious of itself collectively constituted a small, exclusive contingent of professionalized scholars within the professoriate.

Initial membership included 867 research-oriented full professors; seven years later, about four thousand faculty members, constituting some 6% of the professoriate, could be counted among the AAUP's members. But among even this select group, strictly professional concerns were secondary to institutional ones. John Dewey had sought to direct the energies of the new organization toward developing professional standards for the university-based scholar and away from intervention into faculty-administrative disputes at the institutional level. But the membership clearly saw the association's primary function as that of a grievance committee assisting individual faculty in internal campus disputes, and during the early years, the organization was overwhelmed by the grievances brought to its attention (Hofstadter and Metzger, 1955).

The focus on such faculty-administrative concerns heralded the persistent, if imperfect, arrival of the modern university scholar. Indeed, the two-decade period between the world wars was largely one of consolidating the gains of the preceding quarter century. Discipline-based graduate study and research grew at an unprecedented rate. The annual production of doctorates increased fivefold: from 620 in 1920 to nearly 3,300 in 1940. More discourses and pronouncements on graduate education were published than in any previous or subsequent twenty-year period, excepting the present era. A cycle of intense, second-order specialization was evident in the differentiation of yet more specialized subareas within the disciplines. To illustrate, the social sciences spawned in quick succession the Econometric Society (1930), the American Association of Physical Anthropologists (1930), the Society for the Psychological Study of Social Issues (1936), the American Society of Criminology (1936), the Rural Sociological Society (1937), the Society for Applied Anthropology (1941), and the Economic History Association (1941), among others. And these societies, in turn, sponsored more specialized scholarly journals, for example, the *Journal of Personality* (1932), *Econometrica* (1933), *Sociometry* (1937), and the *Public Administration Review* (1940). By the mid-1940s, the dominance of the graduate research model as we know it was clearly established, as was the professoriate's claim to that crucial desideratum of professionalization, namely, specialized expertise (Berelson, 1960).

On campus, the recognition of disciplinary expertise as the sine qua non of faculty work translated into gradually relieving the faculty of responsibilities for overseeing student discipline; this had been, after all, the major noninstructional function of the faculty during the eighteenth and nineteenth centuries. Although the first deans of students emerged with the advent of the university in the last quarter of the nineteenth century (Brubacher and Rudy, 1968, p. 322), what became known as the student personnel movement began in the 1920s and gained momentum throughout the 1930s and 1940s. The movement established on campuses across the nation an infrastructure designed to address the nonintellectual, nonacademic needs of college students. This infrastructure, featuring deans of students, counseling, student health services, career development, and so on, was, to be sure, a response to a broad array of convergent forces, including the tremendous growth and diversification of student bodies; a reaction against the more narrow German influence on higher education; and an expression of John Dewey's educational philosophy. Nonetheless, these various forces also served to provide the occasion (and organizational means) for the faculty collectively to shed nonacademic responsibilities that had grown anachronistic by the interwar period.

The faculty's disciplinary expertise expressed itself on campus not only in casting off old responsibilities, but also in adding new ones. Organizationally, the increasing recognition of the faculty's claim to professional expertise brought an enhanced role in campus decision making. Faculty governance structures had existed statutorily at several leading institutions, including Harvard, Princeton, and Pennsylvania, as early as the mid-eighteenth century, closely paralleling the emergence of the professorship. And by the second half of the nineteenth century, faculty bodies had developed considerable authority at Yale, Cornell, and Wisconsin. However, although precedent may have placed student discipline and admission and graduation requirements within their purview, faculty prerogatives in key areas, such as curriculum, educational policy, and especially faculty personnel decisions (appointments and promotions) and the selection of academic administrators, were not clearly established at most institutions; not infrequently, faculty input in these areas was ignored (Cowley, 1980).

But the 1930s saw the blossoming of faculty committee structures on most leading campuses. By 1939 Haggerty and Works found that two-fifths of the faculty employed by institutions served by the North Central Association were on average sitting on two committees each. Although two-thirds of such committees concentrated on administrative functions, a significant minority focused on issues of educational policy. These developments culminated in the report of the AAUP Committee on College and University Government (Committee T) that set forth five overarching principles for faculty participation in institutional governance.[5] Taken together, these principles mandated a role for faculty in the selection of administrators, in the formulation and control of educational policy, and in the appointment and promotion process. The role promulgated was largely *consultative,* but the AAUP document has at its foundation the premise that "faculty were not hired employees to be manipulated by president and trustees, but were academic professionals whose role involved teaching and contributing to the direction and major decisions of an institution" (Orr, 1978, pp. 347–48).

Perhaps fundamentally, the expertise of professors translated on their own campuses into leverage that enabled them to win tenure rights. Throughout the nineteenth century, the professoriate had labored without provisions for job security, as mere employees of their campuses who were subject to the will of presidents and trustees. Although many full professors were on *indefinite* appointments, that simply meant that no length of term had been specified in their contract. Indefinite appointments were never the equivalent of *permanent* appointments, either in intent or in law; and individuals on such appointments could be dismissed at any time (Metzger, 1973). Moreover, for junior faculty neither a recognized set of procedures nor a timetable was yet established for attaining even these indefinite appointments that were the reward of a full professorship. An individual faculty member might serve his institution for fifteen or twenty years and be dismissed at any time—without reason and without a hearing. Such dismissals occurred again and again, even at institutions with a tradition of faculty power, such as Yale and Wisconsin. In its historic 1940 Statement of Principles on Academic Freedom and Tenure, culminating fourteen years of negotiation, the AAUP articulated the concept of *permanent* faculty tenure, designed a means for regularizing the flow of tenure decision making (that is, by stipulating a six-year probationary period), and endorsed procedures to ensure due process on nonreappointment. By that time, the AAUP had sufficient stature to gain widespread institutional acceptance of its pronouncement. And by that time, too, most institutions had already formalized the system of academic ranks to provide the infrastructure of career progression (Orr, 1978).

Off-campus, that recognition of the faculty's specialized expertise brought them into public service on a scale heretofore unknown. Although the discipline-based "public service" role of the professional scholar had germinated during the Progressive era and World War I, the number of faculty involved had been relatively small and their national exposure highly circumscribed. Thus, during the heyday of the Wisconsin Idea (1910–11), some thirty-three faculty members held official positions both with the state and within the university, mostly as agricultural experts or with the state railroad or tax commissions; thirteen others, including economists, lawyers, and political scientists, were "on call" at the capital as needed. Even so, less than 10% of the university faculty participated directly, and this group was drawn from only a handful of disciplines (Veysey, 1965).

During World War I, the faculty's public service to the nation was offered primarily through two vehicles: the National Board for Historical Service and the Committee on Public Information. The former, linked to the leadership of the American Historical Association, directed the efforts of several dozen historians for the revision of secondary-school social studies curricula. Under the Committee on Public Information, about one hundred social scientists were commissioned to prepare wartime propaganda pamphlets, while others were employed to monitor foreign-language newspaper editorials to detect disloyalty (Gruber, 1976).

The national "Brain Trust" assembled by President Franklin D. Roosevelt to address the social and economic dislocation wrought by the depression provided on an unprecedented scale a highly visible public showcase for faculty talent. Between 1930 and 1935, forty-one independent and state-supported universities granted nearly three hundred leaves to full-time faculty for the express purpose of serving the federal government (Orr, 1978). A much larger number of faculty served state and local governments "on overload." In the early 1940s, it was to academics that the federal government turned once again in support of the national defense effort associated with World War II. The Manhattan Project, which gave birth to the atomic bomb, is only the most dramatic and famous of innumerable faculty-assisted wartime projects. After the war this newfound visibility contributed to the legitimation of the professional role of the college teacher. The esteem in which members of the academic profession were held by the public increased, as did the prestige attached to an academic career.[6]

The growing recognition of faculty as professionals served not only to elevate the profession but also to broaden entry into it. Professionalization permitted (although it by no means assured) the introduction of achievement-related criteria of success and a concomitant reduction in the salience of the ascriptive characteristics of social class and religious preference. Thus, by 1940, Catholics and Jews surged to constitute nearly one-quarter of what had been an exclusively Protestant profession; the sons of farmers and manual laborers were increasingly joining the sons of businessmen and professionals; and *daughters* were now joining the sons, making up fully 13% of a sample of faculty affiliated with institutions accredited by the North Central Association (Kunkel, 1938; Lipset and Ladd, 1979).

By World War II, the various components of the contemporary academic role had thus crystallized into the highly differentiated model of today—teaching, research, and institutional and public service, all rooted in the faculty member's disciplinary expertise. The "modern era" of faculty roles and academic work had begun.

GROWTH AND DIVERSIFICATION, 1940–1969

The twenty-five-year period between the end of World War II and the close of the 1960s (when the analyses in this volume begin) was one characterized by unprecedented growth for American higher education and its academic staffs. The rate of expansion, peaking in the late 1960s with the establishment by most states of large and diverse public systems of higher education designed to achieve goals of very broad—even universal—access, nearly doubled the ranks of college faculty between 1940 and 1960, from about 120,000 to 236,000 (Harris, 1972, p. 484) and almost doubled again in a single decade, 1960–70, from 236,00 to 450,000 (NCES, 1980).[7] The number of new positions created between 1965 and 1970 alone exceeded the total number of positions extant in 1940 (Lipset and Ladd, 1979).

This explosive growth was closely associated with diversification. Most critically, faculty were pursuing careers in institutions with a much wider range of missions. By 1969 seven of ten faculty members were employed in the public sector (home to less than half of them in 1940), and fully one in six faculty were employed at two-year institutions (Harris, 1972). Although the majority of faculty were teaching in the liberal arts fields throughout this period, by 1960 the professions were beginning to rival the liberal arts in doctoral degree production (Berelson, 1960)—a harbinger of developments to come. Demographically, the gradual opening up of faculty ranks to women and to individuals from more diverse religious (non-Protestant) and racial or ethnic (nonwhite, non-European) backgrounds continued to proceed—if, initially, at glacial speed (Steinberg, 1974).

In the midst of such modest, though expanding diversification of faculty characteristics, we nevertheless find a growing normative homogenization of the profession in at least one crucial aspect: the hold of the academic disciplines on faculty loyalties and commitments. Thus while student enrollments were burgeoning and diversifying, a critical component of what Jencks and Riesman (1968) referred to as the "academic revolution," the influence of one's field, exercised primarily through the socialization experience of graduate school and later through the disciplinary associations, had been *narrowing* the definition of the proper scope and standards of academic work. This model of the university scholar and her or his scholarship suffused the early professional socialization experience of that large, dominant cohort of faculty hired to staff the great expansion of higher education during the 1960s; and the broad acceptance of this outlook and orientation, through the influence of this robust, energetic generation of faculty, had largely penetrated the whole American system by the late 1960s.

THE LAST QUARTER CENTURY: THE SEEDS
OF A THIRD REVOLUTION?

Since the consummation of the "academic revolution" described by Jencks and Riesman and the concomitant crystallization of the model of modern academic man (only more recently "woman" in any significant numbers), American higher education has been pushed, forcefully, in new directions by the economic, demographic, and technological changes to which we alluded earlier. Many believe that the face of American higher education will have changed, perhaps much of it beyond recognition, over the next generation (indeed, perhaps over the next decade). How are these competing forces of change and stasis being resolved? How are the changes that are already manifest reshaping the nature of faculty work and careers? And how will they do so in the future?

Emerging evidence, reported in subsequent chapters, suggests that the "academic revolution" of the 1960s is fraying at the edges, that changes are well under way in the nature of faculty life and work. Faculty careers, for example, appear to be becoming (1) less *exclusive,* that is, there is increasing traffic between college teaching and other employment, especially in the career and professional fields; and (2) less *preemptive,* that is, less of a career preoccupation that demands and consumes all available time. For part-time faculty, this is true by definition (except for the many part-timers holding down two or more such jobs). But increasingly, for regular, full-time faculty, there are competing claims: economic pressures have led some to redirect some of their energies to extra-mural pecuniary pursuits (other concurrent employment); a lack of congruence between individual faculty orientations and changing institutional missions has led others to disengage from institutional life and to pursue other life interests. Many observers have for some time decried the decline of "academic citizen-ship" (Cross, 1994). We note that this putative retreat comes anomalously at a time when commitments to enhancing the quality of campus life *should* be in-creasing (given the burgeoning contingent of senior faculty, who by virtue of their loyalty and know-how have traditionally been the most valuable aca-demic citizens) and when that interest needs to be intensified (as proportion-ately fewer full-time faculty positions exist, a fact that devolves more institu-tional responsibility on the shrinking proportion of regular, full-time faculty). Increasing attention has been paid in recent years to the teaching role; and in-deed a significant and rapidly growing segment of the faculty—part-timers and others not eligible for tenure—have their responsibilities *by definition* limited to teaching.

Questions such as these are relevant not only to the American faculty as an aggregate body, but especially to the cohorts of new entrants that colleges and universities have begun hiring in recent years (Finkelstein, Seal, and Schuster, 1998a, 1998b). How will the more general shifts play out with respect to this critical group who will, after all, serve as the American faculty of the first quar-ter of the twenty-first century? And to the new demographic mix of students they will encounter? Will these changes inevitably constitute a new "revolu-tion" in American academic life? Or will they merely amount to a minor turbu-lence on the order of the one the system fostered after World War II, something that can readily be accommodated? And whatever the disruption, will we have the faculty that the nation requires to staff its colleges of the new century?

It is to these and similar questions that the current volume is addressed.

NOTES

1. Seven of the eight professors at Brown during the eighteenth century had such train-ing (*Historical Catalogue,* 1905), as did all ten professors at Harvard (Eliot, 1848).

2. It should be noted, however, that those full professors who left teaching averaged nearly two decades in their institutional positions (21.2 years at Brown; 18.5 years at Bow-doin), so that college teaching still constituted a significant span in their careers.

3. The four "active" faculty were Caswell at Brown, Cleaveland at Bowdoin, Peck at Harvard, and at Yale, Silliman, who had in 1824 founded the *American Journal of Sci-*

ence. Although many of their colleagues were publishing *something,* their work consisted chiefly of collections of sermons and addresses made at commencements and other public occasions (Finkelstein, 1984, p. 16).

4. Other institutions lagged a decade or more behind these developments. At Dartmouth, as late as 1851, three-quarters of the faculty continued to participate actively in the community as preachers, licentiates, or ordained ministers, and as civic boosters. By the late 1870s, however, the proportion of faculty engaged in clerical activities had plummeted to 15%, while over half of the faculty were then significantly engaged in scientific associations in their fields of specialization (Tobias, 1982). At Wisconsin, by the early 1870s university professors were called upon to head the state geological survey (Curti and Carstensen, 1949).

5. That Committee T was the second committee organized by the AAUP (in 1916, one year after the association's founding) indicates the importance the professoriate attached to what came to be called "shared governance." The committee's name, *College and University Government,* reflects that the more contemporary *governance* is latter-day terminology; it was not customarily employed for these purposes until after World War II.

6. Bowen (1978) has documented the close association of public attitudes toward academe and levels of faculty salaries. He pinpointed World War II as marking a major upturn in both the level and the rate of real growth in faculty salaries.

7. The numbers are for faculty at the rank of instructor or above offering resident, degree-credit instruction. Both full-time and part-time faculty are included, but not those offering nondegree instruction or instruction off-campus. The figure for 1940 is estimated from the total instructional staff figure.

CHAPTER THREE

The Professoriate in Profile

The face of America's corps of college and university teachers has changed continually and dynamically over the centuries, reflecting the ever-evolving and expanding purposes of the nation's higher education system. During the past three decades, this expansion in terms of size and complexity has occurred at a decidedly accelerated rate. Toward the outset of our time frame, the American higher education system had already grown so robustly and along so many dimensions that, as Martin Trow (1973) famously suggested, the changes in *quantity* really amounted to changes in *kind*. Trow observed that this enormous expansion was tantamount to moving from mass access to the higher education system, already extraordinary by world standards, to essentially universal access. And in the three decades since Trow initially described the explosive movement toward universal access, American higher education has continued to expand and has diversified even more dramatically. Expansion and diversification, then, are the central motifs of this evolving profile of the American faculty during the last three decades of the twentieth century. Familiar themes, to be sure. But the details are often illuminating and sometimes surprising. And the implications for a strikingly different American academy in the proximate future are inescapable.

ACCELERATING GROWTH AND DIFFUSION

The systemic growth of higher education in the United States has been a function of numerous interconnected factors. Among them are the lifting of immigration restrictions since 1965, which provided an infusion of some 40 million immigrants during the last third of the twentieth century; the rebound in secondary school graduates after a prolonged dip in their numbers between 1970 and 2000 (reaching some 2.8 million in 2000); the sharply rising proportion of these graduates continuing into postsecondary education, from 53.3% in 1969 to 63.3% in 2000 (especially the much larger numbers of college-bound women and nonwhites); the greater numbers of "nontraditional-age" students, that is, adults entering initially or returning to postsecondary institutions (again, especially women); and the substantially larger numbers attending colleges and universities on a part-time, nonresidential basis. Responding to the relentlessly escalating demand for education beyond the secondary level, the existing institutions of higher education have on average grown larger—sometimes much larger—and often much more complex. In addition the number of such institutions increased to 4,168 in 2003 from 2,525 in 1969, a 65.1% increase compared to a 47.8% increase over the previous thirty-year period (NCES, 2002). Concomitantly, a sizzling variety of new kinds of institutions have sprung forth to claim "market share," some designed expressly to meet the needs of the new student demographics: to educate women, nonnative speakers, and racial and ethnic minorities. These basic measures of expansion and variety, of institutions and students, tell much of the story—more fundamentally than any other data—of higher education's transformation and, for our purposes, of the environment in which the American faculty practice their profession (table 3.1).

Although it is commonplace to think of the 1950s and 1960s as *the* era of spectacular growth in higher education—and indeed that growth was stunning—the post-1960s decades have witnessed substantial if somewhat less dramatic expansion. Observers were quick to herald, and lament, a reversal of fortune in the early 1970s as public financing of higher education abruptly slowed (see, for example, Cheit's 1971 *The New Depression in Higher Education*). Clark Kerr observed, however, that, depression or no, the 1970s came to be the decade that ranked *second* in terms of overall growth in higher education (Kerr, 1991). Indeed, the vast expansion of higher education constitutes the basic framework within which the metamorphosis of the American academic profession has taken place, as academic staffing patterns have responded to the demands upon, and opportunities opened to, the academy.

Meanwhile, a still greater force affecting the deployment of faculty has risen: the mushrooming use of information technology that is fueling a *delocalization* of instruction and scholarship (see part 4), that is, a far-reaching rearrangement of the faculty's core activities. By this we mean that (among other developments) the ready availability of a host of technologies has speedily decoupled the age-

TABLE 3.1
American Higher Education Institutions, Enrollment, and Faculty, 1939–2003

	Institutions	% Change	Total Enrollment	% Change	Faculty	% Change
1939	1,708		1,494,203		146,929	
1949	1,851	8.4	2,659,021	78.0	246,722	67.9
1959	2,004	8.3	3,639,847	36.9	380,554	54.2
1969	2,525	26.0	8,004,660	119.9	450,000	18.2
1979	3,152	24.8	11,569,899	44.5	675,000	50.0
1989	3,535	12.2	13,538,560	17.0	824,220	22.1
1995	3,706	0.5	14,261,781	−0.1	931,706	0.9
1996	4,009	8.2	14,367,520	0.7	—	—
1997	4,064	1.4	14,502,334	0.9	989,813	6.2
1998	4,070	0.1	14,506,297	0.0	—	—
1999	4,084	0.9	14,791,224	2.0	1,027,830	3.8
2001	4,179	2.4	15,927,987	3.5	1,113,183	8.3
2003	4,168	−0.3	—		1,173,000	5.4
Some summary % changes						
1939–1969		47.8		435.7		206.3
1939–2003		144.0		966.0*		698.3
1969–2003		65.1		98.9*		160.7

Sources: NCES, 2004, tables 172, 230, pp. 220, 291; UDSE, 2005, table 2, p. 6.

Notes: Faculty members include professors, associate professors, assistant professors, instructors, lecturers, assisting professors, adjunct professors, and interim professors, but not graduate assistants.

For definitions of row and column label terms, see Appendix E.

Occasionally the numbers and/or percentages in text tables differ from corresponding data in appendix tables. As noted at length in Appendix E, these differences are most often attributable to the use of different sources for the same year (e.g., difference between the National Center for Education Statistics' Integrated Postsecondary Education Data System and NCES's periodic National Study of Postsecondary Faculty. Sometimes differences may appear even from the same source (e.g., NSOPF-99) because NCES generated more than one file or data set for the same survey.

*These percentages are for 1939–2001 and 1969–2001, respectively.

old connection between physical venue (a faculty member's campus-based work site) and academic work itself.

Accordingly, the many faceted expansion of higher education and the rapidly emerging use of technologies for conducting both teaching and scholarship, along with the pressures on institutions to avoid making tenurable faculty appointments, have translated into an era of change for the American faculty that is arguably unprecedented at least since the last quarter of the nineteenth century, and in some respects ever since the origins of higher education as we know it.

This chapter traces the contours of that growth and the changing face of the American professoriate, literally as well as metaphorically, during the past three decades. The contemporary faculty is emphatically *not* the faculty of 1969, in a number of crucial respects. The point of this exercise is to demonstrate the extent and complexities of change in academic life during the proximate past, and we begin here with the challenge of describing basic demographic shifts. First comes the not-so-simple task of tabulating the faculty. From there we move on to measuring several key characteristics and how they have changed: institutional and disciplinary venue; trends in gender, race and ethnicity, age, and nativity or citizenship; the "softer" attributes of social and religious background; and several family-linked variables, namely, marital status, the education or occupation of the faculty member's spouse (including the ongoing phenomenon of dual-career couples), and number of dependents. How this array of faculty characteristics has evolved over these three decades has relevance not just for who the faculty are and who they will come to be, but also for the transformation of academic work and academic careers, issues that are explored in detail in subsequent chapters.

The Expansion of the Faculty

In 1970 the National Center for Education Statistics counted about 474,000 faculty members (the great majority, 369,000, full-time). By 2001 that base number had more than doubled to 1.11 million. This growth, though certainly impressive, was hardly on the scale, percentage-wise, realized during the previous three decades when the faculty's size more than trebled (from about 147,000 in 1939–40 to 474,000 in 1969–70). However, the expansion of the past several decades is *qualitatively* very different in terms of who the faculty are. Whereas the trebling of the faculty amounted more or less to an exercise in cloning—that is, pouring more white males into the liberal arts—the faculty growth post-1969 has been, as the following probes demonstrate, much more of an exercise in academic biodiversity.

Most noteworthy is the proliferation of part-time faculty members during this era. Between 1969–70 and 2001, the number of part-timers increased by 376%, or roughly at a rate *more than five times as fast* as the full-time faculty increase (see table 3.2). By 2001 the number of part-timers exceeded the entire number of full-time faculty in 1969–70 and was closing relentlessly on the total count of full-timers. Figure 3.1 graphically displays this remarkable growth trajectory. The proliferation of part-time (adjunct) faculty is examined in considerable detail elsewhere (see, for example, Gappa and Leslie, 1993; Conley and Leslie, 2002), and we do not address it at length. For our discussion of the crucial phenomenon of rapid changes in the distribution of types of academic appointments, see chapter 7; for career patterns and the *composition* of the part-time faculty, see Appendix D.

What is critical for our purposes is that even among the "core" full-time faculty, the primary subject of this volume, a series of striking changes is manifest.

TABLE 3.2
American Faculty, by Employment Status, 1970–2003
(in thousands)

	All	% Change	Full-Time	% Change	Part-Time	% Change
				Employment Status		
1970	474	—	369	—	104	—
1975	628	32.5	440	19.2	188	80.8
1980	686	9.2	450	2.2	236	25.5
1985	715	4.2	459	0.2	256	8.5
1991	826	15.5	536	16.8	291	13.7
1993	915	10.8	546	1.9	370	27.2
1995	932	1.9	551	0.9	381	3.0
1997	990	6.2	569	3.3	421	10.5
1999	1,028	3.8	591	3.9	437	3.8
2001	1,113	8.3	618	4.6	495	13.3
2003	1,173	5.4	630	1.9	543	9.7
Some summary % changes						
1970–2003		147.5		70.7		422.1
1980–2003		71.0		40.0		130.1
1991–2003		42.0		17.5		86.6

Sources: NCES, 2004, table 230, p. 291; USDE, 2005, table 2, p. 6.
Note: Faculty members include professors, associate professors, assistant professors, instructors, lecturers, assisting professors, adjunct professors, and interim professors, but not graduate assistants.

Included are shifting institutional and disciplinary venues, reflecting the changing configuration of the American system; basic changes in faculty demographics (gender, race and ethnicity, nativity, and age); and transitions in social background (family of origin, socioeconomic status, and religion) and family structure (marital status and dependents). As noted, there is a rich diversity of individuals among those entering the academic workforce. And those who differ from the previous faculty stereotype are beginning to attain a critical mass. Over the next decade or so, we believe, these more recent entrants to the profession will further alter the values, aspirations, and ultimately the work and career trajectories of the American faculty as they interact with the swiftly evolving environment for higher education (Finkelstein, Seal, and Schuster, 1998a, 1998b).

Shifting Institutional and Disciplinary Venues

Substantial shifts have occurred in the distribution of faculty both in the types of institutions where they practice their profession and in the academic fields in which they teach and conduct their research. This giant and ever-more-complex matrix of academic "homes" defines profoundly the variegated cultures and work of the faculty (Clark, 1987, 1997).

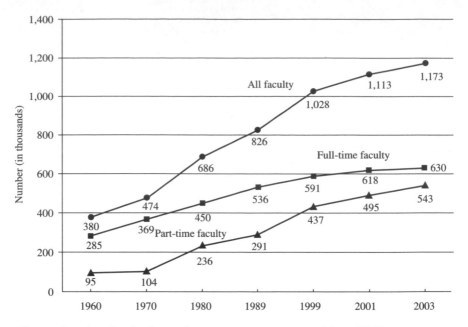

Fig. 3.1. American faculty, by employment status, 1960–2003. From NCES, 2001, 2002.
Data on 2001 were provided directly by NCES Integrated Postsecondary Education Data
System staff.

Institutional Venues

The central story line of American higher education in the twentieth century
until the late 1960s largely featured the rise of the research university, both public and independent, as the dominating organizational form (Veysey, 1965;
Geiger, 1986). Although the great expansion of the 1950s and 1960s certainly
applied to the university sector, it was the local two-year community colleges
and the emerging systems of public colleges (many of them having been con-
verted from normal schools) that marked the epicenter of enrollment growth
and, correspondingly, drove much of the accelerated demand for new faculty.
The last quarter century or so has thus seen the center of gravity shift, at least
in numerical terms, from the university sector to the two-year institutions and
to public comprehensive institutions.

In recent years, alternative types of higher education providers are becoming
more prominent. They will in time influence, perhaps heavily, the distribution
of faculty. Four such providers are scrambling for market share:

- Proprietary institutions such as Argosy University (Argosy Education
  Group), DeVry Institutes of Technology (DeVry Inc.) and, most visibly, the

University of Phoenix (Apollo Group), with more than one hundred campuses and some 186,000 students in thirty-one states (Ruch, 2001; Sperling, 2000).

- Institutions that rely exclusively on distance-learning modalities (such as Western Governors University and Jones International University), employing faculty in ways radically different from the pattern in traditional institutions.
- Emergent commercial courseware providers, that is, entities that do not themselves enroll students but are organized to produce and market specialized course materials, perhaps aggregated into degree programs, drawing in some instances on the resources and creativity of the "infotainment" industry.
- "Corporate universities," a label encompassing an amazing array of entities, perhaps numbering two thousand, some of which provide more than in-house corporate training and sometimes, in partnership with traditional universities, offer accredited courses (Luskin, 2002).

In addition, distance-learning (DL) programs operated by existing, more traditional institutions are omnipresent. The National Center for Education Statistics (NCES, 2001b) reported that a majority (56%) of all two-year and four-year degree-granting institutions in 2001 already offered such programs (and an additional 12% were planning to add DL courses by 2004) (Berg, 2002).

Concomitant with the shift in student enrollments to the two-year and public comprehensive sectors has been the steady rerouting of faculty from the research and doctoral universities to other institutional types. In 1969 nearly half (48.3%) of all full-time American professors were employed by research and doctoral universities, but by 1998 that share had slipped to 42.2% (slightly less than 30% if we limit our consideration to the 150 or so research universities) (fig. 3.2 and table 3.3). At the same time, the two-year colleges, home in 1969 to about one in eight of all full-time faculty (12.9%), accommodated nearly one-fifth of them (19.6%) by 1998. Similarly, part-time faculty, found predominantly at four-year colleges and universities in 1969, by 1998 were about twice as likely to be situated in the public two-year-college sector (almost 41% of them) as at the universities (20.7%). The part-timers now constitute a clear majority among faculty at the two-year colleges (fig. 3.3 and table 3.4). Over the three-decade span, the absolute number of full-time faculty members grew substantially (by some 181,000, or 60%), but the four-year colleges (which experienced growth of 36,000, or 31%) and the universities (59,000, or 40%), experienced much more modest gains than did the burgeoning two-year sector (55,000, or 141%). (Table A-3.1, in Appendix J, provides additional detail.)

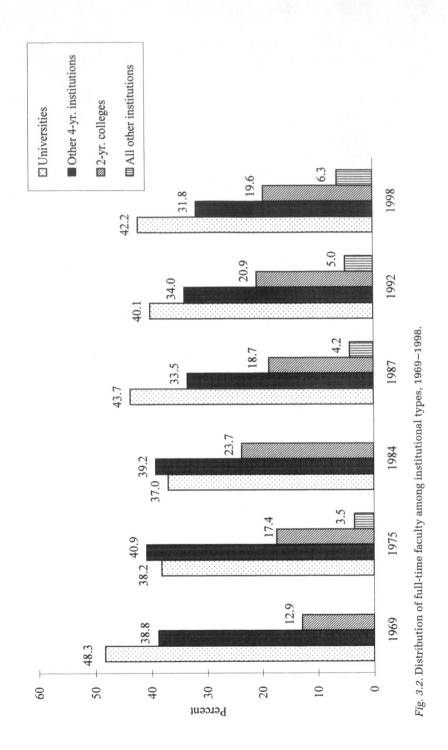

Fig. 3.2. Distribution of full-time faculty among institutional types, 1969–1998.

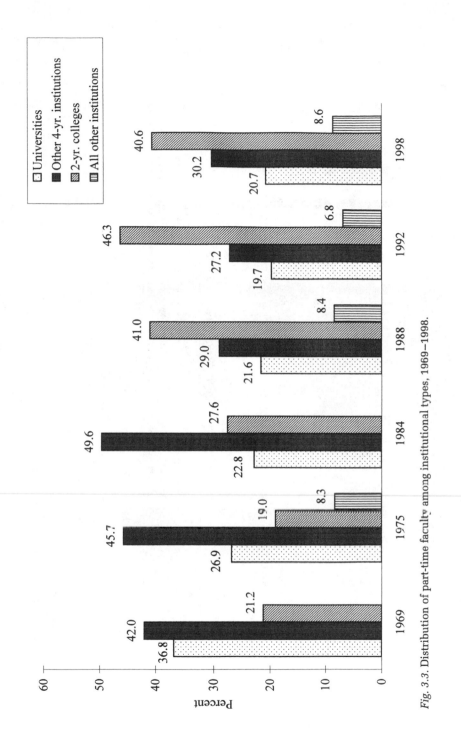

Fig. 3.3. Distribution of part-time faculty among institutional types, 1969–1998.

TABLE 3.3

Full-Time Faculty, by Institutional Type, 1969, 1987, and 1998

	1969			1987			1998			Change 1969–98		
	Number*	% All FT Faculty	% FT in Sector	Number*	% All FT Faculty	% FT in Sector	Number*	% All FT Faculty	% FT in Sector	Number*	%	Share %
All full-time faculty	303	100		516	100		484	100		181	60	
Institutional type												
Universities	146	48	85	225	44	80	205	42	76	59	40	−6
Other 4-yr. institutions	117	39	80	173	34	70	153	32	61	36	31	−7
2-yr. colleges	39	13	73	96	19	48	95	20	42	55	141	7
All other institutions	—	—	—	22	4	50	31	6	53	31	—	6

Sources: Carn-69, NSOPF-88, NSOPF-99 (see Appendix A for key).
*In thousands.

TABLE 3.4

Part-Time Faculty, by Institutional Type, 1969, 1987, and 1998

	1969			1987			1998			Change 1969–98		
	Number*	% All FT Faculty	% FT in Sector	Number*	% All FT Faculty	% FT in Sector	Number*	% All FT Faculty	% FT in Sector	Number*	%	Share %
All part-time faculty	69	100		255	100		321	100		253	369	
Institutional type												
Universities	25	37	32	55	22	20	67	21	24	41	164	−16
Other 4-yr. institutions	29	42	20	74	29	30	97	30	39	68	236	−12
2-yr. colleges	15	21	27	104	41	52	131	41	58	116	801	20
All other institutions	—	—	—	21	8	50	27	9	47	27	—	9

Sources: Carn-69, NSOPF-88, NSOPF-99 (see Appendix A for key).
*In thousands.

The typical American faculty member is no longer the research-oriented scholar whose habitat is the research university, but rather resides in the public four-year or community college, and increasingly he or she is a part-timer at that. The expansion of the part-time faculty has been huge, jumping nearly five-fold (up 253,000, or 369%). And the expansion has been pervasive: by 41,000 (164%) at the universities, by 68,000 (236%) at the four-year institutions, and by a stunning 116,000 (801%) at the two-year colleges (table 3.4). (Further details on part-time faculty are provided in tables A-3.2a and A-3.2b).

Academic Field Venues

Concurrently, the past several decades have seen major changes in how faculty are allocated among academic fields. Just as student enrollments have flowed "outward" from the historical university core to the vastly expanding "periphery" (the new core), so too have students gravitated in large numbers away from the liberal arts to the professions. Stadtman (1980) documented this gradual migration of undergraduate students to majors in the professional and vocational fields and the associated shift of enrollment-driven demand for faculty. That redistribution of demand by students and, accordingly, for the hiring of faculty has continued apace during the 1980s and 1990s. In 1969 two-thirds (67.8%) of the full-time professoriate identified the traditional arts and sciences as their disciplinary home, with less than one-third (31.3%) being situated in the professions or other fields (see table A-3.3a). By 1998, however, faculty in the liberal arts fields had shrunk to 56.4% while faculty in the professions (29.1%) and other fields (14.5%) had increased to 43.6%.

Within the liberal arts, the expansion of higher education has resulted in a larger *number* of full-time faculty in each of the four major areas but, given the deflection of faculty to program areas outside the traditional liberal arts, a smaller share for each of the areas among *all* faculty (table 3.5). Thus, as the number of humanists increased by nearly 11,000 from 66,423 in 1969 to 77,341 in 1998, the *proportion* of humanists among all full-time faculty members imploded from 22.0% to 16.1%. The natural scientists prospered most among the liberal arts and sciences, growing by some 34,500 (a solid increase of more than 47%) and accounting, by 1998, for nearly two of every five faculty members in the liberal arts and sciences; yet they still lost ground in the *proportion* of all full-time faculty, decreasing to 22.3% (a decrease in share of 1.6%). And new entrants in the liberal arts and sciences are scarce indeed among full-time faculty; they constituted only 17.1% in 1998, a mere trickle compared to 1992 (27.4%) and, especially, 1969 (45.7%) (table A-3.3b).

Among the professions, the gains were proportionately highest for the health-

TABLE 3.5

Liberal Arts Faculty, by Program Area, 1969 and 1998

	1969			1998			Change 1969–98			
	Number*	% Liberal Arts Faculty	% All Faculty	Number*	% Liberal Arts Faculty	% All Faculty	Number*	%	% Liberal Arts Faculty	% All Faculty
All liberal arts faculty	205.2	100		270.5	100		65.3	131.8		
Program area										
Fine arts	23.8	11.6	7.9	31.7	11.7	6.6	7.9	33.3	0.1	−1.3
Humanities	66.4	32.4	22.0	77.3	28.6	16.1	10.9	16.4	−3.8	−5.9
Natural sciences	72.5	35.3	23.9	106.8	39.5	22.3	34.5	47.6	4.2	−1.6
Social sciences	42.5	20.7	14.0	54.7	20.2	11.4	12.3	29.0	−0.5	−2.6

Sources: Carn-69, NSOPF-99 (see Appendix A for key).
*In thousands.

related fields, expanding more than fivefold (from 8,030 to 44,370) and from 2.7% to 9.2% of the total full-time faculty. Business faculty more than doubled during the three decades (from 17,061 to 37,338) and increased from 5.6% to 7.8% of all full-time faculty. Both education (from 9.3% to 7.2%) and engineering (from 6.8% to 4.9%) showed marked decline in market share. And if we focus on the *newest entrants* to the professoriate, the shifts among program areas are accentuated even more dramatically (Finkelstein, Seal, and Schuster, 1998a, 1998b).

But losses in share among *full*-time faculty in the arts and sciences are not matched among *part*-time faculty. The proportion of part-timers actually increased in the liberal arts and sciences (exploding almost fivefold in numbers, from 37,577 to 181,222, and edging up from 54.9% of all part-time faculty to 57.1%) (see table A-3.3c). In the professions, meanwhile, there was a marked decline in share of part-timers, from 43.4% to 29.6%, although these faculty nearly tripled in absolute numbers. (The sharp rise in the number of part-timers in fields *other than* arts and sciences and professions accounts for some of the decrease, in share, within the professions.) Thus, on balance the shifts among part-timers present an opposite image from that seen among full-time faculty.

In sum, the majority of American faculty no longer carry out their careers ensconced in the traditional arts and sciences and housed in universities. For one thing, the faculty are increasingly part-time, but even among the full-timers, the typical faculty member is now teaching in a professional or vocational field at a public comprehensive or two-year college. These shifts constitute a historic and powerful adjustment.

SHIFTING DEMOGRAPHICS

College and university faculty, like other occupation groups, can be measured in many ways. The center of gravity for college faculties has shifted not only in their institutional and disciplinary venues. Even more profound in some respects are the very substantial demographic alterations in the faculty as a group in the categories of gender, race and ethnicity, age, and nativity or citizenship. (These are, in no small measure, the legacy of larger social movements, including principally the women's movement and the civil rights movement, and the new immigration policies described in chapter 1.)

Gender

Perhaps the most striking demographic development over the past several decades is the extent to which the faculty have become increasingly *female*. The

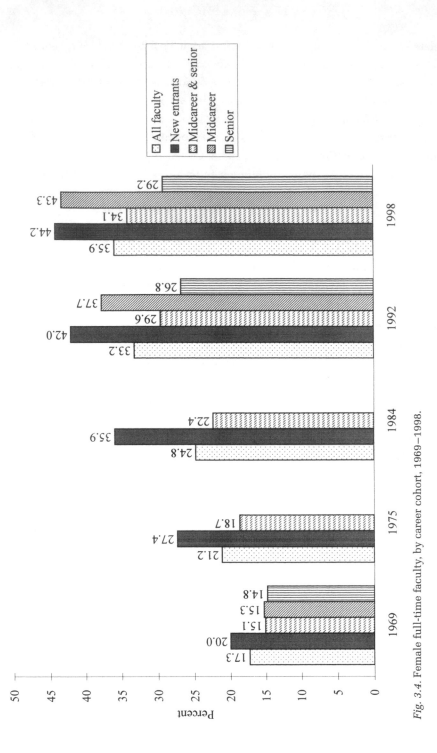

Fig. 3.4. Female full-time faculty, by career cohort, 1969–1998.

proportion of women among full-time faculty has doubled from approximately one in six (17.3%) in 1969 to more than one-third (35.9%) in 1998 (fig. 3.4). Further, if we focus on the newest cohort of full-time faculty, we find, by 1998, an even more accelerated rate of entry by women: fully 44.2% of faculty in the first seven years of an academic career were women. Moreover, that proportion increases to about half among those in the first or second year of their academic career (Finkelstein, Seal, and Schuster, 1998a). Moreover, we can see in figure 3.4 the steady growth among women within successive new-entry cohorts during our focal period: they accounted for one-fifth (20.0%) of new entrants in 1969 but, by 1998, edged toward one-half (44.2%), as noted. And as these women progress beyond entry level, their numbers swell among faculty at midcareer such that, by 1998, the proportion of women among them (43.3%) is very nearly at a parity with women among the new-entrant cohort.

However, our analysis by career cohort is consistent with evidence from other sources that the *rate* of infusion of women into the full-time faculty, having mushroomed earlier in this period, has begun to slow.

The extent of incipient faculty "feminization" varies across institutional sectors (fig. 3.5), disciplinary fields, and employment status. Women continue to be disproportionately situated in the two-year colleges. Notably, the proportion of women at research universities is rising smartly, amounting to two of every five new hires—a prospect that once seemed remote. The ascent of academic women began relatively early at the liberal arts colleges and the two-year colleges (see table A-3.4a); there already was a significantly higher representation of women in the midcareer and senior cohorts at these colleges by the 1970s and 1980s. Women now constitute the majority among new faculty at the community colleges (53.6% within the now entry cohort in 1998).

Although women's ranks are swelling across *all* fields (table A-3.4b), the feminization process has been uneven, showing the following variations, for instance, within the arts and sciences:

— in the *fine arts,* a sharp jump in the proportion of women by the mid-1980s, followed by stabilization;
— in the *humanities,* huge increases among women humanists entering in the 1990s, constituting majorities of both new-entrant and midcareer cohorts in 1992 and 1998;
— in the *natural sciences,* a substantial increase in women since the mid-1980s (primarily in the life rather than the physical sciences); and
— steady growth for women social scientists across the career cohorts, reaching nearly half (47.7%) among new entrants by 1998.

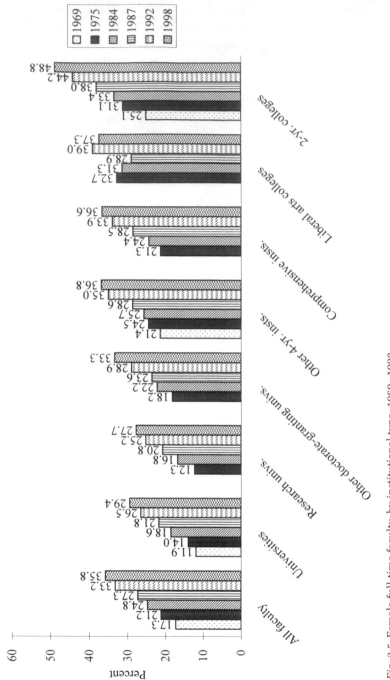

Fig. 3.5. Female full-time faculty, by institutional type, 1969–1998.

To speak of "the professions" in the academy is always hazardous because this supercategory encompasses so many disparate cultures and experiences. For example, faculty in, say, business and engineering, and their counterparts in education, social work, and nursing, may share some attributes but are likely to differ from one another in many important respects. The aggregate of faculty in the professions, that is to say, obscures very different group experiences. Nevertheless, the aggregate numbers show impressive, if mixed, advances for women. They reveal, on the whole, greater proportions of women in each year for which our data are available and, within each year, for each of the three career cohorts. The rather artificial conglomerate of the "professional fields" has done well by women, relatively speaking.

The disaggregated data, however, disclose big differences. In business, for example, women faculty have steadily progressed, constituting more than 40% of faculty in midcareer in the 1990s. In engineering, the representation of women was minuscule (less than 3% of the appointments in both the senior and the intermediate [midcareer] cohorts) but "surged" in the 1990s to exceed 12% among the new entrants. In health science—itself a label of convenience masking marked variation among components—women have accounted consistently for about half or more of the full-time appointments, holding about two of every three appointments across the cohorts of health scientists. And in education, women majorities have been a reality among full-time faculty since the early 1990s, catapulting from about one in three two decades ago.

In sum, faculty women have come to dominate numerically some professional fields that have been historically more open to women. And among the new-entrant cohort, women now account for two of three appointments in education and in the health sciences.

Race and Ethnicity

The infusion of nonwhite faculty members has been at a much more measured pace than the burgeoning influx of women, but there has nonetheless been clear movement toward diversification among faculty by race and ethnicity (fig. 3.6). In 1969 racial and ethnic minorities were scant indeed among faculty ranks: fewer than one in twenty-six (3.8%) full-time faculty were members of racial or ethnic minorities. By 1998 that proportion had grown to about one-seventh (14.5%) overall. This sharp increase in proportion (nearly quadrupling) is more emphatic when we focus on just the new entrants. In 1969 the ratio of these minorities among new entrants was pretty paltry at 3.7%; this was even slightly less than their presence in older cohorts (3.8%). But the 1990s saw a

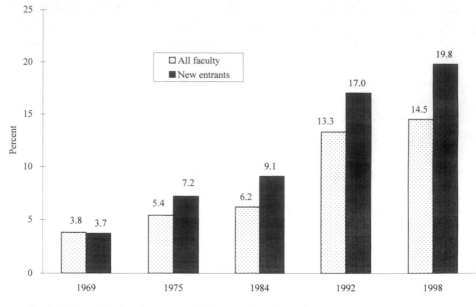

Fig. 3.6. Nonwhite faculty among all full-time faculty and new entrants, 1969–1998. (Asian Americans and Pacific Islanders are included.)

more pronounced escalation: 17.0% of all new entrants in 1992, rising to 19.8% among the new-entrant cohort of faculty in 1998 (table A-3.5a).

The various racial and ethnic groups, however, have not fared equally well. Asians and Asian Americans have proved to be the biggest "winners," nearly quadrupling their overall presence since 1969 (from 1.3% to 5.5% of all full-time faculty). They accounted for roughly one-twelfth (8.0%) of the entire new-entry cohort by 1998 and for nearly two out of five (38.1%) among *all* nonwhite faculty) (table A-3.5b). Native Americans meanwhile have benefited only somewhat; they are now represented in the full-time professoriate at about 0.7% (which is approximately their proportion in the population of doctoral recipients: 0.6% of doctorates awarded in 1998). African Americans and Hispanics occupy a middle ground. African Americans have more than doubled their representation over the past quarter century, from 2.2% in 1969 to 5.0% in 1998; among the new entrants, as of 1998, the proportion rises to 6.6%. The experience among Hispanics is more dramatic, because they more than tripled their representation from a barely visible 1% in 1984 to 3.2% in 1998 (including 4.1% of all new-entrant faculty). (It is worth noting here, as explained in more detail in Appendix I, on racial and ethnic categories, that this category did not exist in 1969 for purposes of counting faculty.) By 1998 every minority group was

proportionately better represented among new-entrant faculty than among doctorate recipients.

Rates of growth aside, as of 1999 the actual number of full-time faculty
(590,937) included 489,206 whites, non-Hispanic; 29,222 African Americans;
34,112 Asians; 16,498 Hispanics; and 2,561 Native Americans (NCES, 2002).
Thus, by 1999 the total number of nonwhite faculty (including Hispanics) exceeded 82,000.

The evidence suggests that racial and ethnic diversification has accelerated
in recent years, although clearly not on a par with the massive reconfiguration
of the general population via immigration. Thus, according to table A-3.5b, between 1969 and 1984 whites declined only moderately as a percentage of new
entrants (from 96.3% to 90.8%), but in the ensuing decade and a half their proportion among new faculty decreased more, falling to 80.2% in 1998. The corresponding growth among blacks and Hispanics was barely discernible between
1969 and 1984; yet between 1987 and 1998, their representation among new
entrants doubled. The trajectory among Asians and Pacific Islanders has been
equally dramatic, and the absolute level of representation has been higher. The
entry of all of these groups (except Asians) into faculty positions has come to
substantially outpace the growth in their representation among new doctorates.

There is another way to think about the diversification process. For the principal minority groups, the majority of faculty are relative newcomers; that is,
their presence is concentrated among the new-entry cohort. Thus, new entrants
(those in the first seven years of an academic career) constitute about one-
quarter of all Asian and Pacific Islander, black, and Hispanic faculty. Among *all*
white faculty, new entrants constitute only about one-sixth.

Diversification along racial and ethnic lines has progressed steadily across
all institutional types but is particularly notable at the universities, where minorities had been especially scarce (table 3.6). Indeed, as of 1998, the proportion of minority (nonwhite) faculty was almost identical from one institutional
type to another. African Americans show the smallest increase at research universities and Asians the largest. The pattern of growth by race and ethnicity,
however, continues to be highly circumscribed by program area (table A-3.5a).
In the liberal arts and sciences, for instance, at the universities, minorities account for 32.6% of the new-entrant cohort in the humanities but 19.4% in the
social sciences and 13.7% in the fine arts. In the professions at the universities,
in 1998 the proportion among new entrants ranged from 14.4% in the health
sciences to 33.3% in engineering (reflecting quite a few foreign-born faculty).
The Asian presence has grown principally in engineering and the natural sciences; African Americans have increased primarily in education, the social sci-

TABLE 3.6
Minority (Nonwhite) Full-Time Faculty, by Career Cohort and Institutional Type, 1969 and 1998
(percent)

	1969		1998	
	% All Faculty	% All New Entrants	% All Faculty	% All New Entrants
All minority faculty	3.8	3.7	14.5	19.8
Institutional type				
Universities	2.8	3.3	14.7	22.6
Other 4-yr. institutions	5.9	4.9	14.2	18.5
2-yr. colleges	1.4	1.8	14.3	17.4

Sources: Carn-69, NSOPF-99 (see Appendix A for key).
  Note: Asian Americans and Pacific Islanders are included in minority faculty.

ences, and the fine arts; and Hispanic growth has been limited largely to the humanities.

Moreover, as table A-3.5c indicates, men and women have been unequal beneficiaries of this racial and ethnic diversification: among Asians, it has been primarily the males whose presence has increased; women accounted for only 29.4% of full-time Asian faculty members in 1998; although a larger proportion among the new-entrant Asian faculty, women still account for a distinct minority of those appointments (37.9%). Among African Americans, by contrast, the growth has been primarily attributable to females, who comprised nearly half (46.5%) of African American faculty in 1998 and three of five (60.1%) among the new entrants. These patterns were already pronounced among new hires by 1992 (Finkelstein, Seal, and Schuster, 1998a, 1998b).

But advocates of diversity should not find solace in the gains described above. Not only is there much more to be done before parity is approached, but caution is required in interpreting the new-entrant data: such increases may not persist beyond *probationary* appointments and, accordingly, may not eventually "mature" so that they affect more permanent appointments. That is, an initial appointment may not be renewed or, in time, lead to promotion and tenure. Constant monitoring of "progress" is therefore in order.

Nativity and Citizenship

Like the increased representation of racial and ethnic minorities, the surge in the presence of foreign-born faculty has been more recent. They numbered some 28,200 full-time faculty in 1969 but had swelled to 68,600 in 1992 and 74,200 in 1998. Shown as a proportion of all full-time faculty (fig. 3.7), 10.0%

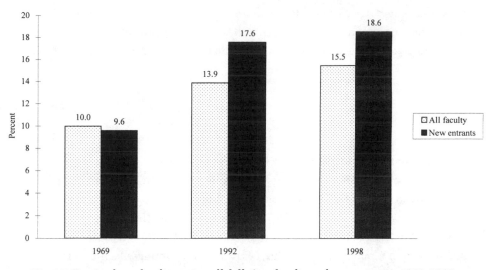

Fig. 3.7. Foreign-born faculty among all full-time faculty and new entrants, 1969, 1992, and 1998.

of full-time faculty were foreign-born in 1969, a proportion that increased by half to 15.5% in 1998. Among the new hires, in particular, the proportion of foreign-born doubled between 1969 and 1998 (from 9.6% to 18.6%). But, perhaps as a portent of what lay ahead, given the attention being paid to issues of U.S. national security, the proportion of those new entrants among all foreign-born faculty had already begun to shrink: fully 43.5% of foreign-born faculty were new in 1969, but 37.4% were new in 1992 and only 22.7% in 1998 (table A-3.6).

Historically, foreign-born faculty have been concentrated disproportionately at research universities and in several arts and science fields, but especially in engineering (table A-3.6). By 1998 their numbers remained concentrated in the natural science and engineering fields (39.9% of all foreign-born faculty in 1969; 43.5% in 1998) and even more so among foreign-born new entrants in the 1990s: 46.7% in 1992 and 46.5% in 1998.

Foreign-born faculty are increasingly female (13.5% in 1969; 29.7% in 1998). And they are increasingly Asian in origin (from 11.2% of all foreign-born faculty in 1969 to 29.6% in 1998; 36.4% among foreign-born new entrants are Asian). These numbers reflect a significant shift in the source of foreign-born faculty: from Europe in the immediate post–World War II period to Asia (as discussed in Finkelstein, Seal, and Schuster, 1998a, 1998b), giving rise to stereotypical depictions of Asian-born males teaching in science and engineering fields. In all, the number and proportion of foreign-born faculty has grown dynamically, dispersing somewhat to sectors other than universities while becoming somewhat more concentrated in natural science and engineering programs. The proportion of foreign-born faculty who are women has more than doubled during three decades, and the proportion of Asians among all foreign-born faculty has nearly trebled.

Age

While continuing to grow more diverse in terms of gender and race and ethnicity (and, at least for now, nativity), the American faculty is becoming more concentrated (and in that sense, less diverse) in terms of age. That is, the professoriate is growing considerably older, on average, as the swarm of faculty hired to staff the great expansion in the 1960s nears traditional retirement age, unbalanced in number by the smaller cohorts of new, younger faculty hired between the late 1970s and late 1990s.

The change is little short of astounding: these faculty have matured from a youthful, vital bunch of arguably inexperienced hopefuls to a corps of seasoned if sometimes weary veterans. Figure 3.8 demonstrates that the "graying" professoriate is not a mere figure of speech (see also table A-3.7). In 1969 fewer than one-quarter (22.5%) were 50 and over, but now most faculty (51.7%) are. In 1969 faculty members 60 and over were scarce (6.9%), but they have more than doubled to one in every six (16.1%). Conversely, in 1969 one-third (33.1%) of the faculty, across all institutional sectors, were 35 years of age or under, as were nearly two-thirds (64.4%) of the new hires. Images of an eager, youthful faculty were thus grounded in an age distribution skewed heavily to the under-40s. But by 1998 the faculty had aged appreciably: only about one in twelve was 35 years of age or under (roughly one-fourth the proportion of a quarter century earlier). By 1998 the mean age of full-time faculty exceeded 50: 51.7% of them were eligible to join AARP! This dramatic growth at the high end of the age continuum is illustrated in figure 3.8, where faculty over 50 emerge as the fastest-growing group.

The graying of the faculty has occurred across all institutional sectors, although it is actually now more noticeable among the public comprehensive institutions and the two-year community colleges. Although nearly one-sixth (16.3%) of university faculty are now 60 or over, the proportion in this age group at the four-year institutions and community colleges has grown to 18.0% and 12.2%, respectively (fig. 3.9). Conversely, full-timers 35 and under are becoming exceedingly rare at about 8% (fig. 3.10).

The progressive aging of faculty permeates all fields, although, of course, the

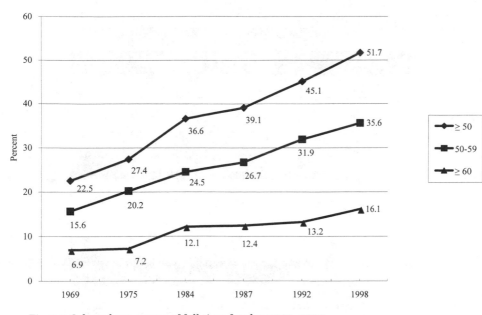

Fig. 3.8. Selected age groups of full-time faculty, 1969–1998.

incidence varies from field to field (figs. 3.11, 3.12). By 1998, among faculty in the liberal arts and sciences, those in the humanities were older on average (18.9% at least 60), and among the professions, the faculty in education were the oldest we examined (18.3% at least 60).

The aging phenomenon is more noticeable, however, when gender and race are taken into account. In 1969 academic women were slightly less likely than academic men to be 35 or under; but by 1998 women were somewhat more likely than men to fall within the under-35 age group. And men were about twice as likely as women to be at least 60 years old (19.4% versus 10.1%) (table A-3.7). Similarly, in 1969 the proportion of nonwhite faculty who were 35 and under was smaller than that for whites; by 1998 those proportions had reversed themselves, reflecting the differentiated pattern of an aging white male subgroup contrasted with a younger subgroup that is disproportionately female and more diverse racially and ethnically. Thus, racial and gender differences within the faculty vary significantly within the age distribution of the faculty as a whole.

Three further age-related phenomena merit attention. The progressive graying of the faculty has occurred despite the steady infusion of new hires amounting to roughly 3% to 4% of the total faculty annually (Finkelstein, Seal, and Schuster, 1998a, 1998b). This fact reflects in part the prevailing tight academic labor market, which enables institutions to hire new faculty who are more ex-

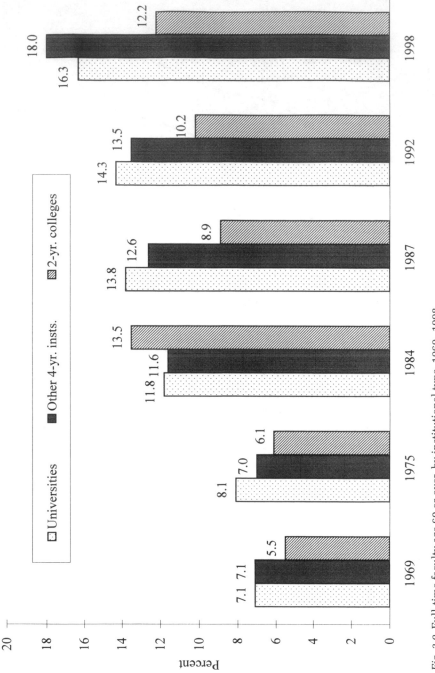

Fig. 3.9. Full-time faculty age 60 or over, by institutional type, 1969–1998.

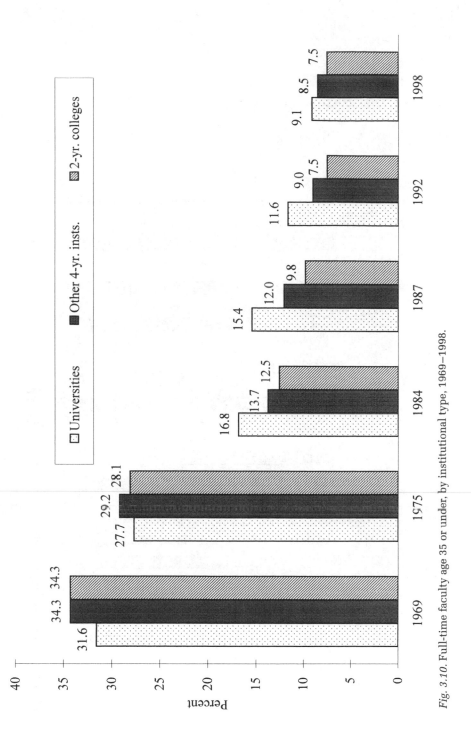

Fig. 3.10. Full-time faculty age 35 or under, by institutional type, 1969–1998.

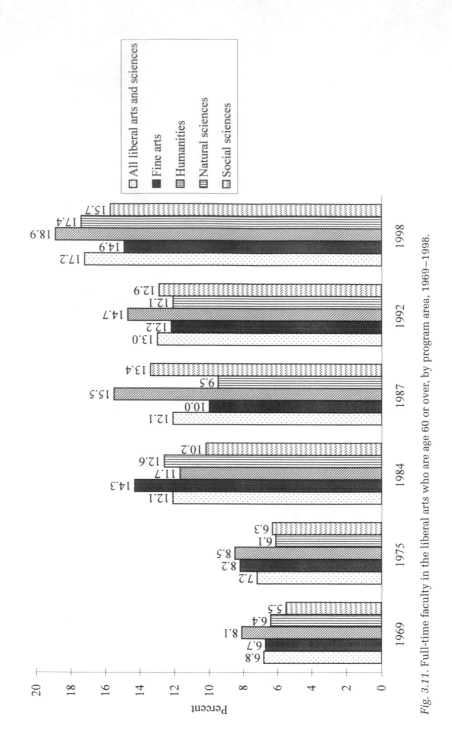

Fig. 3.11. Full-time faculty in the liberal arts who are age 60 or over, by program area, 1969–1998.

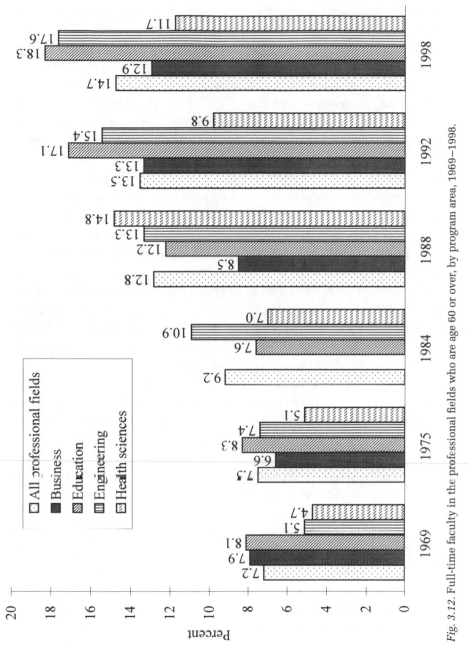

Fig. 3.12. Full-time faculty in the professional fields who are age 60 or over, by program area, 1969–1998.

perienced—and, accordingly, tend to be older—than the new hires of several decades ago. Often, faculty members in the natural sciences, especially the life sciences, will have had two or even more postdoctoral tours prior to an appointment as a full-time faculty member.

A second development that is affecting the age distribution of faculty is the "uncapping" of mandatory retirement age. Explained at greater length elsewhere (see, for example, Clark and Hammond, 2001), the change flows from a 1986 amendment to the federal Age Discrimination in Employment Act of 1967 that took effect for faculty members January 1, 1994. This legislation prohibited employers from continuing to apply a mandatory retirement age to faculty. Now free, thereby, to stay on beyond customary retirement age, except for dismissal for cause, increasing numbers of faculty have opted to remain on the job. Although it is too soon to gauge the long-term effects of uncapping, recent analyses suggest that relatively few faculty are choosing to continue full-time beyond their late 60s, contrary to the apprehensions about a senile teaching corps widely expressed when the wisdom of eliminating mandatory retirement was being hotly debated (Ashenfelter and Card, 2001; Clark and Hammond, 2001). In all, it appears that the average age at which faculty retire has remained relatively stable, although the retirement rate for faculty at the higher ages (70 and above) has declined (Clark and Hammond, 2001).

A third development, one that has had a countervailing effect on the age distribution of faculty, has been the quite widespread use by colleges and universities of retirement incentive programs to encourage older faculty to retire or phase out (Chronister and Kepple, 1987). These developments are discussed in chapter 6.

SUPPLEMENTAL DEMOGRAPHICS

Diversification of the faculty can also be plotted according to four aspects of faculty members' social and familial attributes: educational background, religious orientation, marital status, and dependents. The first two, family educational and religious background, constitute a less fundamental diversification, although chronologically these manifestations of diversity preceded the more visible infusion of women, racial and ethnic minorities, and foreign-born faculty.

Social Status

Historically, the American faculty, like that of other countries, has been drawn from the upper social strata of society. As Laurence Veysey put it, the professoriate traditionally has been recruited from among those of independent means who could afford to subsist on the compensation available for college teaching (Veysey, 1965, p. 352). As the demand for college teachers and the compensation associated with faculty appointments rose sharply in the 1960s (see chapter 8), academic careers began to offer an ever more attractive alternative path for social mobility, not unlike that provided by public school teaching a generation or so earlier, for the sons (and now the daughters as well) of the working and middle classes (Lipset and Ladd, 1979). And thus a more class-diverse set of individuals has been infused increasingly into the formerly more homogeneous upper-class and upper-middle-class mix.

One common measure of social origins and status is the formal educational attainment of one's parents. Although hardly a sufficient surrogate for class origins, the parental education record is nonetheless relevant. In 1969, according to one study, just over one-fifth of the faculty (22%) were drawn from families headed by a father who was a college graduate (at a time when only 12% of American adult men were college graduates). Even more strikingly, about one-seventh of the 1969 faculty had fathers with a graduate or professional degree, compared to about 2% (one-fiftieth) of the American adult male population (Lipset and Ladd, 1979, p. 321). By 1998 those figures had increased substantially, but the increase reflected in part the American population's overall advance in educational attainment (see table A-3.8).

This relatively high social class origin, however, masks a number of differential subgroup patterns. Faculty at the universities have always been drawn from more privileged backgrounds than their colleagues in other sectors, and that continues to be the case. Indeed, one's position in the institutional prestige hierarchy has tended to mirror quite faithfully the socioeconomic background of one's family of origin, as is clear in table A-3.8. Similarly, faculty in the liberal arts fields have historically been drawn from higher socioeconomic strata than their colleagues in professional and vocational fields. For instance, in 1998 about one-quarter (26.1%) of arts and sciences faculty reported fathers who had completed graduate or professional degrees, as compared to less than one-fifth (19.1%) of faculty in the professions. And within the professions, education and business have been, and continue to be, among the most "proletarian" in the social class origin of their faculty members (Lipset and Ladd, 1979).

At both the start and the finish of the past three-decade period, new hires boasted a better-educated parentage than their more senior colleagues, reflecting ever-increasing levels of educational attainment by the nation as a whole (Finkelstein, Seal, and Schuster, 1998a, 1998b). And academic women consistently have been drawn from higher socioeconomic backgrounds than academic men, suggesting a level of comfort with where well-bred, well-educated daughters might find suitable employment.

Inferences about faculty social origins based on the level of their fathers' education are basically corroborated by the sparse available data for fathers' occupations. A relatively stable one-quarter of the faculty in both 1969 and 1984 describe their socioeconomic background as "working class." And, as expected, more males than females and more faculty in the professions so characterize themselves (Finkelstein, 1984).

The 1990s, in sum, appear to reflect the result of these social class crosscurrents: on the one hand, a new and sizable cohort of academic women are bringing relatively high social class origins to the mix while the expanding cohort of faculty in the professions and the still sizable cohort of men supply a more proletarian leavening to the faculty demographic composition. In all, the lines of social class divisions have grown blurrier among contemporary faculty members. The current instructional corps is being drawn less along traditional social class lines; instead, they come from a richer mix of gender, racial, religious, and occupational backgrounds than their predecessors.

Religious Orientation

Whereas the academic profession has been moving over the past generation inexorably away from the modal white male stereotype, its retreat from near-exclusive Protestant family origins began a generation earlier. Steinberg (1974) has documented the infusion of Catholics and Jews into the profession in the decades following World War II. By the time our story takes up in 1969, one-third (32.3%) of the faculty could be counted as having non-Protestant origins. About one-sixth of them identified their family religious backgrounds as Catholic, and one-twelfth, Jewish. Furthermore, about one-half reported their *own* religious identity to be something other than Protestant (including almost one in five, 19.0%, who declared that they had no current religious identity [see table A-3.9]).

Religious diversification has touched all sectors and all disciplinary fields, but it has assumed some discernible patterns over the past several decades. First has been the historical overrepresentation of Jews in the research universities (25% of research university faculty are Jewish, compared to 10% of all faculty) and in the social sciences and the professions, including law and medicine. Catholics, though, have been overrepresented in the four-year collegiate sector and in the traditional humanities fields of classics, philosophy, languages, and literature (Steinberg, 1974). Together, these groups tend to be the children of early-twentieth-century immigration waves, especially the eastern European Jews and the Irish and Italian Catholics, typically the offspring of the immigrant working class. Much of the data on religious origins and current religious identity are not recent, since most substantial faculty surveys in recent years, for various reasons, fail to inquire about religious identity and background.

We can think of multiple, yet distinctive, waves of diversification of the American faculty in the post–World War II period. An initial phase of religious and social class diversification, beginning seriously in the 1940s, continued, if at a slower pace, in the 1950s and 1960s. This development was followed by a still-ongoing phase of second-order diversification: by gender and, to a lesser extent, by race and ethnicity, and by the often related characteristic of foreign nativity.

Family Structure

The demographic transformation of the nation's core faculty over the past quarter century has extended as well to the structure of faculty members' personal lives, especially the family unit (because broader national trends are reflected here, see, for example, Jacobs and Gerson, 2004). This everyday, personal context shapes both the work experience and the path within which careers are pursued. And the complexities of family life are amplified by the challenges confronting dual-career academic couples.

Marital Status

American academics are about as likely as ever to be married. In 1969 one in seven full-time faculty members (15.5%) was single and never married (Dunham, Wright, and Chandler, 1963; see also table A-3.10); in 1998 the proportion remained roughly the same (11.9%). There were two slight changes: about 3.0% of contemporary faculty members were living with someone in a "marriage-like relationship" (a response option not available in the 1969 survey), and the proportion reporting that they were divorced or widowed had more than doubled from 4.9% to 11.2%. There was one larger change: whereas the incidence of marriage declined among the men (from 87% to 80%), it has been increasing, by a more pronounced rate, among the women (44.7% to 63.2%). It now approaches parity within the new-entrant cohort (70.8% of men versus 60.7% of women are married). In the 1960s the contrast was emphatic: the majority of academic women (some 57% according to Dunham, Wright, and Chandler, 1963) were single and never married, compared to only one-eighth of the men, reinforcing the stereotype of career women who chose the role of college teacher as an *alternative* to that of parent and homemaker. By 1998, as seen in table A-3.10, the modal experience had clearly shifted; the 63% of academic women who reported their status as married was augmented by an additional 15.6% who reported that they were widowed, divorced, or separated. Only 16.9% in 1998 were "single, never married," well less than half of their counterparts a quarter century earlier.

Studies of faculty a generation ago, when the initial rise of marriage rates among academic women emerged, reported greater conflict between work and family roles for academic women than for men (Finkelstein, 1984, p. 211). These conflicting pressures, as well as the increasing social acceptance of divorce, may help explain the fact that academic women are now twice as likely as academic men to report one or more divorces (Finkelstein, Seal, and Schuster, 1998a, 1998b; Wolf-Wendel, Twombly, and Rice, 2003).

Spouses' Education and Occupations

Who were the spouses of academic men and women, and how, if at all, have they changed? Although data on spouses' education and occupations have been only sporadically available during this period, a few things are clear. First, college faculty have historically taken "highly educated" spouses when compared to the general population. Dunham, Wright, and Chandler (1963) reported that fully seven-eighths of faculty spouses had at least some college (whereas less than one-third of the general population at the time boasted some college attendance); only one-ninth had spouses whose education had proceeded no further than high school. There were no significant differences by age or gender in either the incidence of spousal college attendance or college completion, but academic women were twice as likely as academic men to report spouses with post-baccalaureate education (62% of women's spouses versus 30% of men's).

A decade later, these findings were largely corroborated by data on the *occupations* of faculty spouses. By 1975 two-fifths of the faculty reported spouses with careers in academe (12%) or in the other professions (27%), compared to only about one-fifth who reported a "homemaker" spouse (many of whom may have attended college). Two decades later, the pattern is etched ever more distinctly, reflecting the general societal trend toward *dual career couples.* According to more recent estimates (Astin and Milem, 1997), more than one-third of college and university faculty who are married or in a marriage-like relationship have spouses or partners who are also academics, and that proportion increases to nearly two in five among married academic women (Wolf-Wendel, Twombly, and Rice, 2003).

Dependents

Changing patterns of family structure are seen as well in parenting patterns, that is, the number of dependent children in faculty-led households. (Since the surveys do not distinguish between dependent *children* and general dependents in this case, it is not clear to what extent this increase in dependents may refer to elderly parents as well as children.) In 1963 one-quarter of married faculty had no children (since more than 80% of the faculty were married, that translates into roughly 20%, or one-fifth, of *all* faculty being both married and without children). As noted, some four decades ago academic women were 4.5 times as likely as academic men to be unmarried and 2.5 times as likely as men to have no children (just over half of the women versus not quite one-quarter of the men) (Dunham, Wright, and Chandler, 1963). That pattern of "lesser likelihood of marriage" among academic women has continued into the 1990s, although, as observed earlier, gender differences are clearly narrowing. So, too, is the pattern of parenthood converging. In 1969 only one-third (33.8%) of full-time academic women had one or more children, but by 1998 that number slightly exceeded one-half (50.4%). For men the pattern was reversed, if only marginally: 71.3% in 1969 had children, but the proportion of the men who were fathers had eased slightly to 68.9% by 1998 (table A-3.11).

New-entry women in 1998 are somewhat more likely to have children than their counterparts three decades before (39% in 1969, 47% in 1998). Meanwhile, the cohort of new-entry men are somewhat less likely to have children now (62% in 1998) than new-entry men in 1969 (68%). Most of that difference for new-entry women is made up for by those reporting one or two, rather than three or more, dependents.

As for larger families, the proportion of women with three or more children has edged upward (from 8% to 10%) while men reporting three or more children declined (from 28% to 23%). In all, the family patterns of men and women academics have grown more similar, in terms of marital status and parenthood, during the focal period of our study.

SUMMARIZING THE DEMOGRAPHIC TRANSFORMATION

Demographically, as summarized in table A-3.12, the American faculty over the past three decades have experienced a many-faceted transformation in age, gender, national origin, and race and ethnicity. These changes have largely reflected broader demographic restructuring in the United States (increased per-

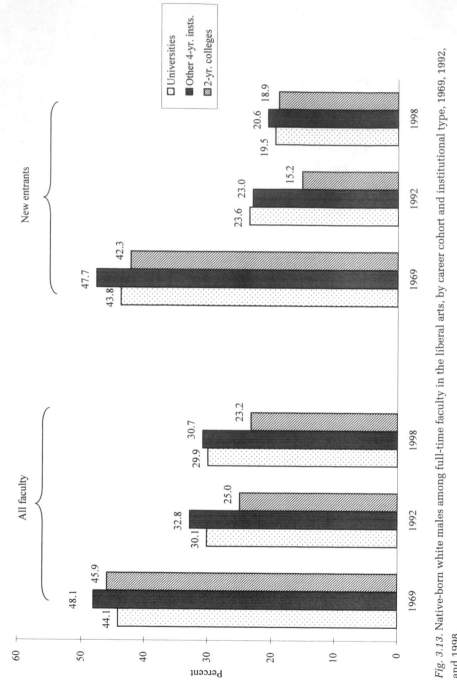

Fig. 3.13. Native-born white males among full-time faculty in the liberal arts, by career cohort and institutional type, 1969, 1992, and 1998.

centage of the elderly, immigration, and women's wholesale movement into the workforce). The faculty have been altered from a relatively young cohort of faculty members dominated by white males to a much more heterogeneous academic staff on the verge of being significantly shaped, as the trend lines suggest, by a blossoming cohort of academic women and faculty of diverse ethnicity and nativity. Roughly speaking, among the full-time faculty,

- the percentage of women has doubled,
- the percentage of nonwhites has nearly quadrupled, and
- the percentage of foreign-born persons has increased by half.

The extraordinary scope of that transformation is neatly illustrated in figure 3.13, which indicates the proportion of faculty in 1969, 1992, and 1998 that were traditional, where *traditional* is defined, albeit arbitrarily, as native-born white males in the arts and sciences. Among all full-time faculty, these modal faculty stood at about 46% in 1969 but shrank to 28.6% in 1998. Among the new-entrant cohort, the change is more pronounced. In 1969 the new entrants looked very much like their more senior colleagues: the modal native-born white males still accounted for just over 45%. By 1998 the proportion of these new-entrant traditionals, barely one in five, was a precursor of continuing change. If the whole faculty is taken into account, that is, both full- and part-time faculty, the proportion of faculty who are traditionals practically fades from view (fig. 3.13). The old modal demographic profile is virtually disappearing.

The evidence we have assembled provides, we believe, a portrait of far-reaching demographic transformation of the faculty. The American faculty have diversified substantially over the past three decades in terms of gender, race and ethnicity, nativity, and social and religious background. In 1969 the full-time professoriate was predominately male (83%) and overwhelmingly white (96%), in all, perhaps 80% white males. But the white male domination has steadily eroded to 64% male and 85% white or, in all, not much more than one-half (about 54%) white males. Although in the aggregate the faculty still constitute a *majority* (if barely) white male profession, the seeds of a sweeping demographic transformation not only have been planted, but also are clearly sprouting into, we believe, a decisive shift. While remaining distinctive in several important respects, the academic profession, not surprisingly, is repeating general trends in the larger society in terms of age, nativity, family structure, and racial and ethnic diversity. The succeeding chapters examine how these changes in who the faculty have become are affecting all aspects of the life academic: in how faculty members go about their work (chapter 4), their culture and values (chapter 5), and the career trajectories they pursue (chapter 6).

PART TWO

The Faculty at Work

CHAPTER FOUR

The Changing Complexion of Faculty Work

The general pressures on American higher education over the past decade to reduce costs and expand faculty productivity have translated into imperatives for faculty to do "more"—especially to ratchet up efforts that contribute directly to the improvement of undergraduate education. In other words, the heat has been turned up to refocus faculty attention on student learning and thereby reverse what is commonly perceived to be the inexorably expanding claim of research, at the expense of teaching, virtually throughout the academy. There are numerous signs that these vectors are significantly altering the trajectory of academic careers; among the indicators are changes in the topography of growth away from the elite research sectors, gravitating toward the teaching-oriented institutions; movement away from the traditional liberal arts fields to applied, career-oriented venues; the increasing feminization of the academic profession; and the associated infusion of more feminized academic values (particularly, a greater accent on teaching and on students). Another powerful trend (more closely examined in chapter 7) is the dramatic movement away from traditional tenure-track appointments and toward more circumscribed, specialized appointments, especially teaching-only appointments.

A host of interconnected issues bear directly on the changing nature of faculty work. For instance, Has faculty work—what faculty members actually do on the job—changed substantially, or perhaps just at the edges, during the past three decades? More broadly, in what ways and to what extent has the "academic revolution," as chronicled and celebrated by Jencks and Riesman (1968), been maintained, or even advanced, at the onset of the twenty-first century? A related question is, Has the workaday life of the faculty resisted the pressures to upgrade teaching and, instead, continued to pay homage to the research ethos? In other words, are there signs that the academic revolution has peaked and that a reversion is evident in some critical dimensions of academic life? Or is there evidence to suggest that the "revolution" is now being undermined by "counterrevolutionary" developments, that is, a return of the pendulum away from scholarly pursuits and away from faculty control over the university's academic core? We ask also whether the model of academic work that crystallized in the second half of the twentieth century—featuring the prototypical "regular" faculty member who is concomitantly engaged in teaching, research, and service—is perhaps yielding to a kind of respecialization of academic work, this time not so much by academic subfield as by academic function.

Before addressing these more sophisticated issues of change and continuity in the faculty work role, let us make sure that we have a common understanding of the baseline, the basic constellation of activities that have since World War II been subsumed as part of the faculty work role. The components of academic work have, of course, multiplied and differentiated themselves historically. There have always been internal (to the campus organization) and external (off-campus) components of faculty work. In the eighteenth and early nineteenth centuries, the major internal components included the conduct of recitations for a class of students during the day and their supervision and discipline in the dormitories (see chapter 2). The external component included ministerial work in the community (of which the campus was an important part) and sometimes various sorts of scientific or naturalistic work, usually pursued as a hobby. With the rise of the American university and, in particular, the emergence of the student personnel movement, faculty had begun by the early twentieth century "offloading" much of their responsibility for student discipline and dormitory supervision and taking on new responsibilities for research and institutional governance (Haggerty and Works, 1939). They kept their service role in their local host communities; its primary focus shifted, however, from organized religion to civic participation and cultural leadership, and faculty took on new and highly differentiated external service to their discipline and the cause of higher education.

Early on, there was fairly wide variation in these components by type of institution and academic field. The university faculty did more research and publishing; the college and community college faculty, more institutional governance and local community service, respectively. The natural scientists did more research; social scientists worked in government and industry; and the educators, nurses, and physicians worked in clinical settings. By the beginning of the period of our focus, 1969, academic work, especially at the more complex institutions (the research universities with large research enterprises and a highly differentiated constellation of colleges, research centers, departments, and other academic units) was becoming more and more complex to "match" the increasing complexity of institutional missions. Although there is a multitude of individual variations, it is important to be clear about the full range of work activities that most faculties engage in. Most of us are familiar with the basic trinity of teaching, research, and service. Teaching, that is, the staffing of for-credit course sections in the neighborhood of six to fifteen hours weekly, is the most concrete such component. Research is much less so, subject as it is to very different meanings in different institutional settings and in different academic fields. For most natural scientists, research means running their own laboratories, managing grants and armies of graduate assistants. Their laboratory may be on their campus, at the local medical center, or at a federal lab (Los Alamos, Livermore, Fermi, etc). Their research almost always requires evening and weekend work. In the humanities, research might involve archival work, the perusal of original documents and collections of unpublished letters or long-forgotten newspaper records. For the fine artist, it might consist of studio work daily or the management tasks of setting up and publicizing an exhibition or a performance. For faculty in the professional fields, it might mean direct involvement in clinical practice (e.g., clinical psychology; a physician seeing patients at the medical center or administering a double-blind drug study) or setting up and monitoring internship clinical sites for one's students. For faculty at institutions where research is not the primary mission, it might mean keeping current in one's field via library research (including the Internet) and making sure one's courses reflect the latest thinking in the field. It might involve preparing articles for local newspapers or organizations.

The service role is diverse and not always well understood (Lynton, 1995; Lynton and Elman, 1987). It includes institutional components like formal participation in department or campuswide governance committees or task forces or serving as faculty adviser to a student organization or club; off-campus activities designed to develop new on-campus academic programs; local community service and boosterism (representing the college within the geographic community), perhaps service as an unpaid consultant to a community organization; direct service to the state, regional, or national professional associations in one's discipline; and service on an accrediting team of a regional or a specialized accrediting association. Much depends on the type of institution, the academic field, and the career stage of the individual faculty member (Clark, 1997; Baldwin and Blackburn, 1981). The external, discipline-based role may also involve what is usually called consulting on specific projects with outside organizations as well as running a limited private practice (Marver and Patton, 1976; Boyer and Lewis, 1985a, 1985b; Fairweather, 1996).

The point here is that faculty work consists of a great variety of activities that are critical to the educational missions of their institutions and which go quite beyond actual hours in the class, preparation for classes, or interaction with students face-to-face or via e-mail. How do the national faculty surveys allow us to get a fix on the full range of these activities and identify changes in the nature and frequency of such activities over time? Most broadly, the national faculty surveys provide a window on the amount of time faculty spend on their work. That usually includes a global number of weekly hours or a basic distribution of those hours over the holy trinity of teaching, research, and service. For teaching, it usually includes the number and kinds of courses or student credit hours and may include the number of students. The surveys may ask for weekly office hours, time spent consulting outside, and hours spent on committee work. Also, they may inquire whether the individual holds any administrative responsibilities. When all is said and done, we are left with (1) crude self-reported estimates of weekly work hours at the institution (differentiated sometimes between paid and unpaid work) and (2) the actual (and sometimes preferred) distribution of effort across the basic tasks and some crude indicators of performance, including interaction with students, engagement in research and publishing, and sometimes even concurrent employment outside the institution.

These are the things we can count. No one of these indicators, or even their sum total, can illuminate some of the important nuances. Academic work is different from many other kinds of work. It defies the establishment of clear boundaries. The job of a good scholar and teacher is to continuously learn; and that is a tall, continuing order. So although we can look at some of the quantitative indicators and how they have changed, we need to be very careful that we not let them obscure the more nuanced gestalt and some of the tumultuous changes that information technology is bringing to the structure of academic work.

And so we probe the evidence to ascertain the extent to which what faculty actually do in their daily work has changed in recent decades. Specifically, we examine trends in the characteristics of faculty work: in the sheer amount of work effort, in faculty orientation between teaching and research, and in the distribution of faculty efforts among their various responsibilities (teaching, research, administration, departmental and institutional governance, and consulting); in the magnitude and nature of their teaching loads (the number of credit hours generated and students taught, as well as the balance between undergraduate and graduate instruction); in the amount of faculty-student interaction; in the scope of the faculty's research and scholarly activity; and in their involvement in departmental and campus governance. In chapters 10 and 11 we use the trends described in this chapter—the aspects of change and constancy in the work of American academics over the final three decades of the twentieth century—as a point of departure to speculate about the future of academic work and the outlook for the academy.

THE REDISTRIBUTION OF FACULTY EFFORT
Magnitude of Effort

Whatever concerns have been expressed by critics that the faculty has been paying attention to the wrong things, the surveys provide no basis for suggesting that they are working less. Table 4.1 illustrates how since 1984 the weekly work effort of the faculty has increased in almost liner fashion from about 40 hours per week to nearly 49 (48.6)—about 20%. Moreover, during the same period, outside work commitments (consulting, public service, etc.) have remained stable or decreased slightly following a spike in the late 1980s (see fig. 4.1). What this means is that, taken together, outside commitments by faculty have stabilized (or declined slightly) as the time allocated to their professional tasks inside the institution has increased markedly over the past two decades, a period when the average work week of the American worker was holding steady (Jacobs, 2004). The faculty are, it appears, putting in more time, and becoming, together with other professional and managerial workers, the exception to the rule (Jacobs and Gerson, 2004).[1]

When we focus explicitly on work effort patterns across institutional types (table 4.1, fig. 4.1), we find that work effort has increased in all types of institutions, although it has increased most dramatically at the research universities, where faculty have been subjected to increasing instructional demands *and* increasing research demands. Similarly, faculty in other four-year institutions

TABLE 4.1
Weekly Hours Worked Inside Home Institution by Full-Time Faculty, 1972–1998

	1972	1984	1987	1992	1997	1998
Mean total hours worked in institution (all faculty)	42.9	40.2	46.4	47.1	41.8	48.6
Institutional type						
Universities	43.7	40.3	50.2	50.6	43.9	50.6
Other 4-yr. institutions	41.2	40.0	45.6	46.8	41.2	48.3
2-yr. colleges	40.4	40.3	40.0	41.8	39.9	45.1

Sources: ACE-72, CFAT-84, NSOPF-88, NSOPF-93, CFAT-97, NSOPF99 (see Appendix A for key).
  Note: For definitions of row and column label terms, see Appendix E.

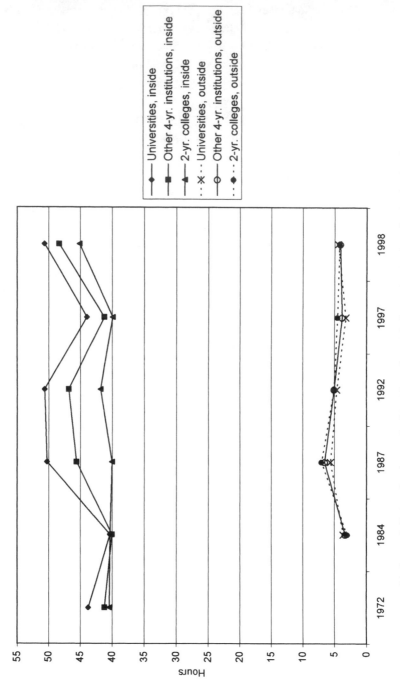

Universities, inside
Other 4-yr. institutions, inside
2-yr. colleges, inside
Universities, outside
Other 4-yr. institutions, outside
2-yr. colleges, outside

Fig. 4.1. Mean weekly hours full-time faculty worked inside and outside home institutions, by institutional type, 1972–1998.

have been subject to increasing instructional, research, and community building or maintenance demands. These confirmatory trends across institutional
types are significant for two reasons. First, they demonstrate that the overall
finding of increased work effort is not an artifact of differences in survey sampling frames. Second, they provide a quantitative context within which to interpret the data on changes in the faculty's efforts in both the teaching and the
research areas.

Taking the analysis one step further, we examined trends across surveys in
the proportion of faculty who reported working more than 50 and more than 55
hours weekly at their employing institutions. These faculty may be considered
the "driven" or "committed" faculty about whom one rarely hears in the popular press but who are frequently encountered by those who spend time on any
campus in America. Those data, reported in figures 4.2a, 4.2b, and 4.2c., reveal
a striking pattern: the proportion of faculty working more than 50 hours a week
has *doubled* since 1972, rising from a significant minority (23.2% in 1972) to
nearly two-fifths by 1998. That means that a plurality (and near majority) of the
American faculty can be labeled "driven" or "highly committed" to their jobs.
Furthermore, the data indicate that the proportion of faculty spending more
than 55 hours a week on their institutional responsibilities has climbed from
about one in eight to one in four (13.1% to 25.6%), now constituting one-
quarter of the working faculty. Although this number rose less dramatically than
the proportion working more than 50 hours weekly, the graph makes it clear that
more than half of the "driven" or "committed" faculty, defined as those who
work 50 hours plus weekly, actually fit into the category of those working 55
hours plus weekly. Once again, when we examine patterns by institutional type
(figs. 4.2b, 4.2c), we find a consistent pattern, but one that suggests that faculty
work intensity has affected the four-year, and particularly the university, sector
more than the two-year sector. But there too, following a brief dip in the 1980s,
work effort has increased inexorably, reflecting, in part, the increasing economic
pressures on American workers generally.

Finally, it is useful to control some basic demographics—gender, race, age,
academic field, and career cohort—and examine the demographic topography
of work commitment in academe. The data in table A-4.1a demonstrate that
mean weekly work hours are, as we have seen, highest at research universities
and lowest at two-year colleges. They are higher as well for faculty in the natural sciences and engineering (maintaining a research laboratory is a 24/7 responsibility). The overall mean differences between the genders, the races, and
the career cohorts are minimal. When, however, we focus on work commitment
surpassing 50 or 55 weekly hours, we find a clearer pattern. The data in table

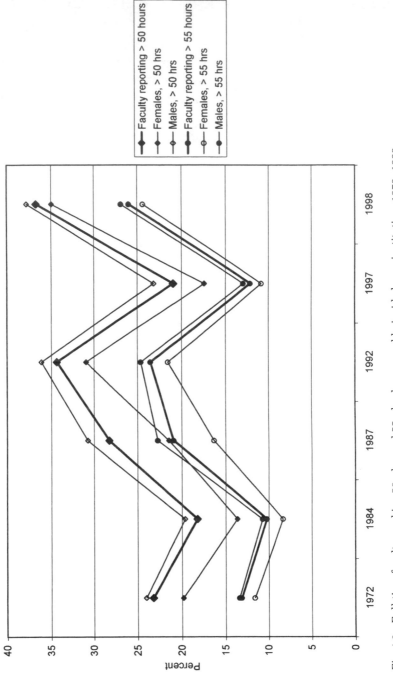

Fig. 4.2a. Full-time faculty working 50-plus and 55-plus hours weekly inside home institution, 1972–1998.

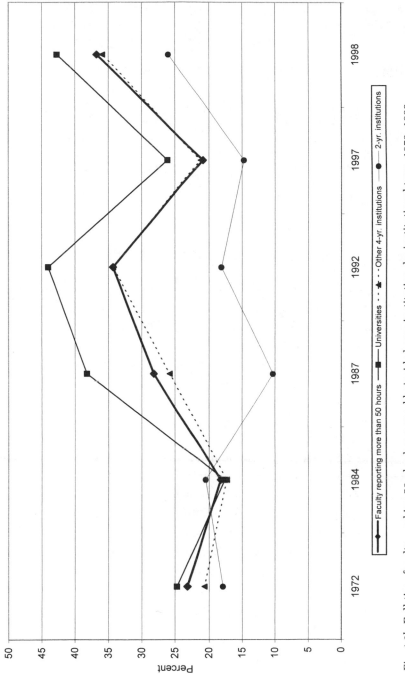

Fig. 4.2b. Full-time faculty working 50-plus hours weekly inside home institution, by institutional type, 1972–1998.

Legend:
- Faculty reporting more than 50 hours ◆
- Universities ■
- Other 4-yr. institutions ▲
- 2-yr. institutions ●

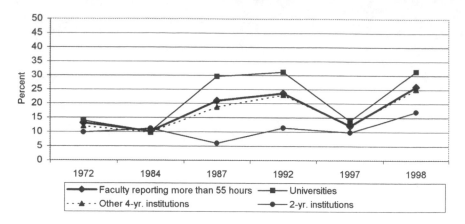

Fig. 4.2c. Full-time faculty working 55-plus hours weekly inside home institution, by institutional type, 1972–1998.

A-4.1a reveal that at the high end of the working-hours continuum, demographics are distinguishing features. Specifically, at the 50 or near-50 level, the majority of research university faculty, the majority of natural scientists and engineers, and near-majorities of males and Caucasian and Asian faculty are represented. The differences at the 55+ level (fig. 4.2c) are much less pronounced among faculty subgroups—except for those defined by institutional type, where more than one-third of research university faculty reported 55+ hours weekly, as compared to nearly one-quarter of the four-year faculty and one-sixth of the community college faculty.

When we turn to weekly work hours outside the employing institution, we find quite a different pattern. First, as figure 4.1 and table A-4.1b indicate, although the mean number of hours of outside work has remained fairly stable (or declined slightly), and faculty subgroup differences are minimal, that the proportion of faculty reporting work outside their employing institution appears to have peaked in the late 1980s and early 1990s and then to have declined to earlier levels. Moreover, as compared to patterns for hours worked inside the institution, discernible subgroup differences emerge. Thus, two-year community college faculty are significantly more likely than four-year faculty to spend 10% or more of their work time (i.e., 10+ hours) outside the institution (see table 4.2); the same relationship holds for faculty in the professions versus liberal arts faculty, male faculty versus female faculty, and non-Asian faculty as compared to Asian faculty. These findings make some basic sense: faculty in the four-year sector are spending more time with a more complex set of institutional responsibilities, as are faculty in the natural sciences (who are disproportionately

TABLE 4.2
Full-Time Faculty Allocating More than 10 Percent of Total Work Time to Consulting, 1969–1998
(percent)

	1969	1975	1984	1987	1992	1997	1998
All faculty with							
>10% in consulting	17.5	17.4	12.2	6.6	6.2	7.9	5.9
Institutional type							
Universities	16.7	15.5	16.0	5.9	6.1	9.3	5.0
Research	—	15.1	17.2	5.9	6.3	9.3	4.6
Other doctorate-granting	—	16.6	13.7	5.9	5.8	9.6	6.0
Other 4-yr. institutions	18.6	17.5	11.7	7.1	6.2	8.6	5.7
Comprehensive	—	17.6	12.3	7.5	6.6	9.8	6.5
Liberal arts colleges	—	17.1	9.0	5.9	4.9	5.7	3.7
2-yr. colleges	16.9	20.3	7.1	6.7	6.6	5.6	6.5

Sources: Carn-69, CFAT-75, CFAT-84, NSOPF-88, NSOPF-93, CFAT-97, and NSOPF-99 (see Appendix A for key).
   Notes: The 1984 figures are based on item 6e: "How many hours per week on the average are you spending in each of the following activities: . . . consulting (with or without pay)?"
   The 1987 figures are based on item 37k: "Percentage of total work time spent in outside consulting or freelance work, working at self-owned business."
   The 1992 figures are based on item 37e: "Percentage of total work time spent in outside consulting or freelance work."
   The 1998 figures are based on item 31g: "Percentage of total work time spent in outside consulting, freelance work, other outside work, other non-teaching professional activities."

Asian); faculty in the professions would be expected to show more outside commitments because of the nature of their fields. Male-female differences presumably reflect the greater set of nonwork family responsibilities assumed by academic women that preclude non-institution-related outside work.

The surveys also allow us to focus explicitly on the proportion of time faculty spend on consulting. Table 4.2 confirms the same picture for faculty consulting activity that we saw for the overall proportion of time faculty spend in work outside their institution. The percentage of faculty spending more than 10% of their work time in consulting dropped overall from about one-sixth (17.5%) in 1969 to only about 6% in 1998; and the decline holds across all institutional types, program areas, and faculty demographic groups (table A-4.2).

Faculty Role Orientation

Beyond the total work effort that faculty actually devote to teaching, research, and other institutional responsibilities, is the matter of how they apportion their time among these competing responsibilities. The faculty surveys offer two lenses through which to view faculty division of labor. Although they provide self-reports of actual division of labor, they also give insights into the *preferred*

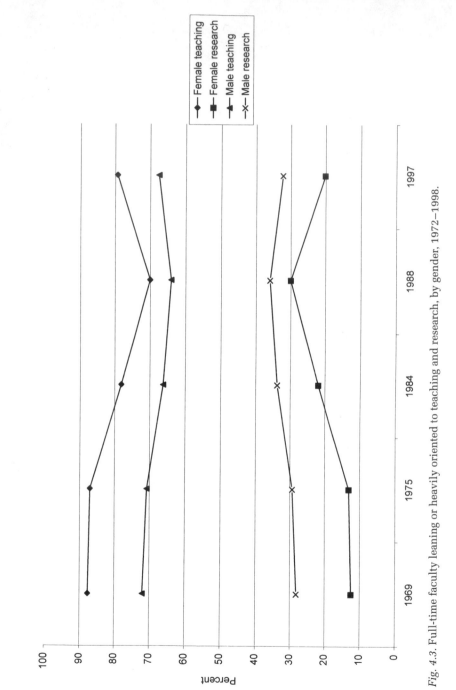

Fig. 4.3. Full-time faculty leaning or heavily oriented to teaching and research, by gender, 1972–1998.

division of labor, that is, the value that faculty place on these activities both personally and professionally. For American academics, questions of work-related values are particularly significant, and revealing, since the available evidence suggests that, compared to persons in other professions, academics are more strongly shaped by professional values and are among the most likely—given the relative autonomy they enjoy—to "act out" their values in fulfilling their professional responsibilities. That means that though faculty members must respond in their work behavior to organizational workload expectations, when those immediate imperatives or constraints are relaxed, they are likely to gravitate to their "most valued" activities (Finkelstein, 1984). Moreover, when organizational expectations diverge from those activities that individual faculty members value most, they are likely to experience considerable strain that may negatively affect their work—or, more problematically, they may find ways to passively circumvent organizational expectations.

Since 1969 five Carnegie surveys have asked faculty members to describe their orientation to research and teaching on a continuum from "primarily teaching" to "primarily research." The surveys allow us to track shifts, using the same item, over this time period. As displayed in figure 4.3, the data indicate a very modest increase between 1969 and 1998 in the proportion of faculty who report themselves "leaning or heavily oriented to research"; it rises from about one-fourth to one-third of the faculty in the 1980s and recedes again to one-fourth in the 1990s. At the same time, the proportion of faculty who describe themselves as "leaning or heavily oriented to teaching" drops from about three-fourths to two-thirds and then rises again.

Another way to view the tension between teaching and research is to compare faculty *preferences* for allocating their time to how they actually spend their time. Both the 1993 and the 1999 National Study of Postsecondary Faculty asked faculty to estimate the actual distribution of their effort across work roles and then asked them to indicate the "preferred" distribution of their time. One analysis of faculty responses discovered that faculty members almost universally expressed a desire to shift some portion of their time from teaching to research (Finkelstein, Seal, and Schuster, 1998a). This result—which surely must be disappointing to individuals and groups, both inside and outside of the academy, who have urged a rehabilitation of teaching and undergraduate education—suggests that faculty members remain generally more oriented to research than their job allows them to be despite the blandishments visited upon them to pay more attention to teaching. That is, their orientation toward research outruns the opportunity afforded by their jobs to engage in research. This, together with the data in table A-4.3, suggests that there remains a residual interest in re-

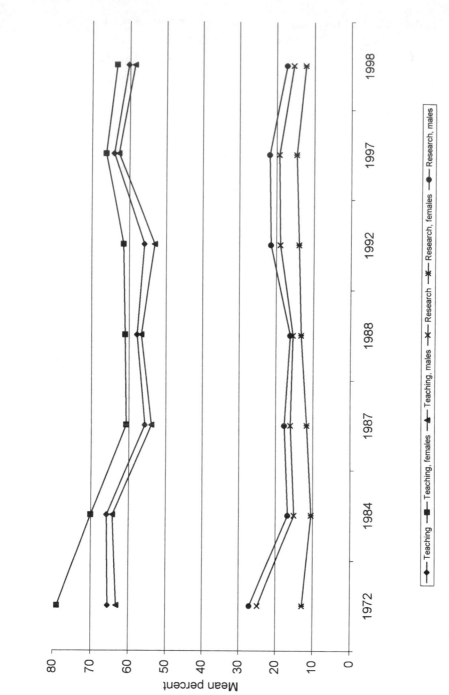

Fig. 4.4. Full-time faculty effort allocated to teaching and research, by gender, 1972–1998.

search across all institutional types, academic fields, and demographic subgroups of faculty that is not now finding expression in faculty members' day-to-
day work.

The differences among institutional types are striking. As would be expected,
faculty at research universities and other doctorate-granting universities report
a significantly greater orientation to research than those at other types of institutions (table A-4.3). The magnitude of research orientation also varies by field
in predictable ways, with natural scientists and engineers at the high end. Men
show a consistently higher research orientation than academic women: about
one in three men say that they are either heavily oriented or leaning toward research compared to only one in five or one in six women. And that male-female
difference holds across most academic fields.

Another means for assessing the focus on teaching versus research is to examine, as in table A-4.4, changes in the ratio (proportion) of faculty championing teaching to those championing research. The data here indicate quite conclusively an overall, albeit modest, decline in that ratio. In 1969 the number of
faculty leaning or heavily oriented to teaching was three times greater than the
number oriented to research; by 1997 the ratio had declined slightly from 3 to
2½. Some interesting departures from these aggregated averages are, however,
evident. Among institutional types, it is in the four-year nonuniversity sector
that the shrinkage in teaching supremacy is greatest (the ratio actually increases
in the two-year sector). Among academic fields, both education and business
show the greatest decline in the teaching orientation, while the health sciences
show an increase. And among faculty demographic groups, it is among women
and blacks that we see the largest aggregate proportionate shifts from teaching
to research (presumably reflecting the pressure among newer entrants to meet
the widely perceived "publish or perish" standard).

Allocation of Effort: Teaching versus Research

To what extent is the clear, if modest, shift in aggregate faculty preferences
reflected in their actual division of labor? During the first several decades following World War II, faculty members spent a majority of their work time, as
much as two-thirds, directly engaged in instructional duties (Dunham, Wright,
and Chandler, 1963, p. 36). Between 1984 and 1997, however, the portion of
their effort devoted to teaching declined—to about half of their overall effort by
1987—but then rose again in the mid-1990s to approach former levels (fig. 4.4).
During that same period the effort devoted to research increased overall—but
only moderately—from roughly one-seventh to about one-fifth of the faculty's

overall commitment. The picture that emerges is one that validates the common perception during the 1980s, reflected in such critiques as Boyer's *Scholarship Reconsidered* (1990), that among the faculty's priorities teaching was losing ground to research, as well as the observation that a significant teaching-friendly "correction" ensued in the 1990s. This picture also suggests that the expansion of effort directed to research in the 1980s may not, in itself, explain the dip in the effort going into teaching. As other studies have suggested, it appears that the expanded research effort evident by the late 1980s may prove to be a short-lived aberration: not so much accomplished at the direct expense of teaching activities as reflecting "additional" faculty work prompted by heightened expectations, especially for junior faculty (Rice and Sorcinelli, 2002).

This "U-shaped" pattern—of decline followed by increase in teaching effort, accompanied by a consistent modest increase in research effort—spread throughout higher education's landscape. As can be seen in table A-4.5, the pattern holds across all types of institutions, spanning research universities and liberal arts colleges; but as should be expected, the absolute magnitude of teaching and research efforts (and the ratio between them) varies substantially by type of institution. At research universities, the teaching effort constituted roughly 50% of faculty members' time in the mid-1980s but then declined sharply to just over one-third in the early 1990s, while the effort these faculty members invested in research fluctuated between approximately one-fourth and one-third of their time. Similarly, at the liberal arts colleges, teaching effort, which had commanded about 75% of faculty members' time in the 1980s, dipped to the mid-60% range in the 1990s.

Generally speaking, we found in *The New Academic Generation* (Finkelstein, Seal, and Schuster, 1998a) less intercohort differentiation in work activities than in either the faculty's demographic or career trajectory characteristics. So it is not surprising that no large differences were detected among the three career cohorts in the overall allocation of their time between teaching and research (table A-4.5). Indeed, what is detectable is a small but perceptible increase in time allocated to teaching, especially among new entrants, and a stabilization in time allocated to research among all career cohorts—following a small but discernible increase.

Gender, too, proves to be an influential variable. According to table A-4.5, academic women devote more of their time to teaching than do their male counterparts and, correspondingly, considerably less time to research. Indeed, the distribution of work activity varies consistently by gender *across* the institutional sectors. That is, no matter the type of institution, even at research universities, female faculty members are more likely than their male colleagues to be somewhat more engaged in teaching activity and less involved in research (table A-4.10). By the late 1990s, these gender disparities largely maintained themselves, although the disparity in research activity seemed to be narrowing somewhat (see the discussion of publication prolificity below).

When we examine differences by academic field (table A-4.5), we observe the same overall U-shaped trend in teaching effort over time as well as the same pattern of gender differences. As for research, the basic pattern of modest increases in overall research effort, from 1984 to 1997, is accounted for largely by the persistent and growing research efforts of the natural and social sciences and engineering, while other fields show modest declines. Indeed, it is these fields that show the highest proportionate research effort.

Finally, when we control for race and ethnicity, we find that the race variable only moderately influences the distribution of faculty effort between teaching and research. Even so, some differences are evident. Table A-4.5 indicates, for example, that Asian faculty members as a group devote less time to teaching and significantly more time to research than any of the other race or ethnicity groups. The proportion of Asian faculty members' efforts committed to research is typically two to three times greater than those of the comparison groups. With regard to time devoted to teaching, Caucasians and Asians consistently rank fourth and fifth, respectively, among the five groups. In large measure, however, these racial differences appear to be attributable to differences in the distribution of the racial and ethnic groups according to academic field—reflecting, for instance, the high concentration of Asians in the research-intensive engineering and natural science fields as well as the high proportion of blacks in the less-research-oriented humanities and education.

Another angle on stability and change in the faculty's division of labor is provided when we look (as we did for faculty work orientation and preferences in the previous section) at the ratio of teaching to research effort for full-time faculty. That is, beyond the self-contained trends in teaching activity, on the one hand, and research activity, on the other, what can we say about trends in the *balance* between teaching and research effort for individual full-time faculty over our time period. Figure 4.5a graphs the median of the ratio between individual teaching and research effort for full-time faculty by gender over time. In 1972 full-time faculty *on average* (at the middle of the distribution of all faculty, i.e., the typical faculty member) spent 3.6 times more effort in teaching than research; by 1998 that ratio had doubled to 7.0 times. Most of the increased effort is represented by increased emphasis on teaching (a teaching "correction") among male faculty; the prominence of teaching for female faculty has actually plummeted, bringing them more closely in line with males. This means that at the 50th percentile (the median), the teaching multiple over research actually doubled since 1972—presenting a picture of much more dramatic shifts toward a greater emphasis on teaching. Among institutional types, the median ratio of teaching to research effort at the universities was relatively stable over the twenty-six-year period, accounted for largely by stability among men and a dramatic decline in the predominance of teaching over research for women (fig. 4.5b). Among other (i.e., nonuniversity) four-year institutions, the ratio declined as well (reflecting the infusion of the research culture into the four-year sector that we discuss in greater length in chapter 5). A decline is notable even in the two-year sector, though with absolute ratio values of an entirely different order from that for the four-year sector. Among program areas (table A-4.6), we find consistent increases in the predominance of teaching across the board; they are especially dramatic in the natural sciences (tripling from a bare two times to nearly six times). Finally, among career cohorts, we find a modest decline in the ratio for midcareer and senior faculty (actually a U-shaped pattern consistent with the shape of the distribution of teaching effort) and a noticeable rise in teaching emphasis for new entrants—illustrating dramatically the increasing teaching and research pressures on junior faculty.

Administration

Beyond the faculty's shifting involvement in teaching and research, an overall decline in the time that faculty members devote to administrative activities has been evident since the beginning of the era we are examining (table 4.3, fig. 4.6, and table A-4.7). In 1969 about one-half of the faculty reported spending 10% or less of their time in administration; by 1998 that proportion had swelled to more than two-thirds (68.9%). This pattern of diminishing faculty administrative involvement is widespread, holding across types of institutions, academic fields, and career cohorts (table A-4.7), although it appears to increase slightly with career age. That is, it is the senior faculty who are redirecting their energies to a large extent away from administration, followed by midcareer and junior faculty, and they are doing so across all types of institutions and academic fields. This apparent shrinkage of administrative effort may reflect the extent to which faculty members have succeeded in offloading such tasks (often deemed to be undesirable), as evinced in the oft-reported expansion of administrative staff (Frances, 1998; Leslie and Rhoades, 1995). Among academic fields, the magnitude of administrative effort appears to be higher in both education and the health sciences and lowest in the natural sciences and engineering.

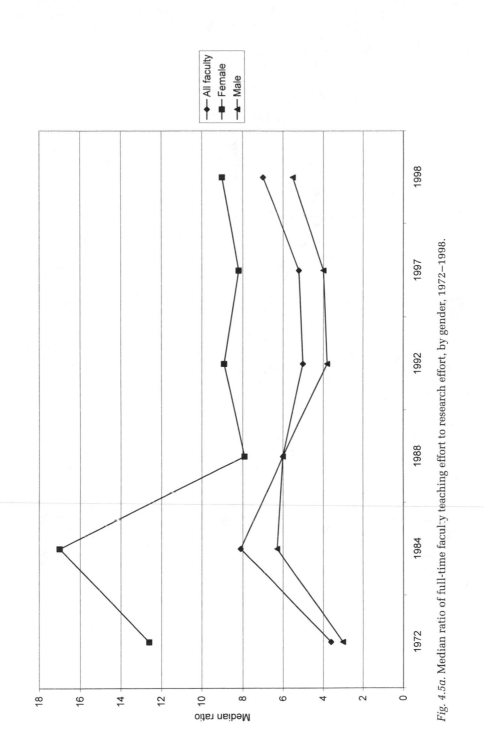

Fig. 4.5a. Median ratio of full-time faculty teaching effort to research effort, by gender, 1972–1998.

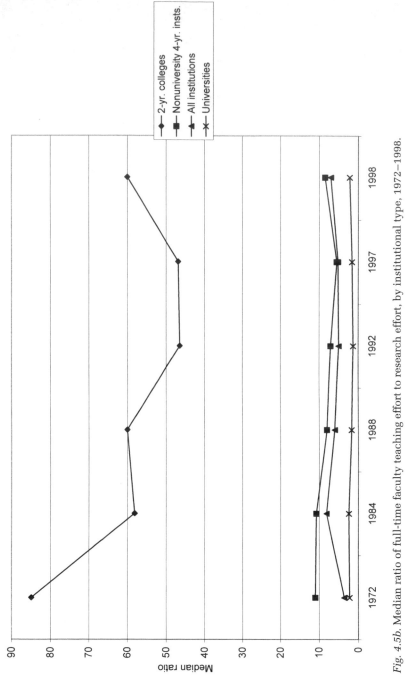

Fig. 4.5b. Median ratio of full-time faculty teaching effort to research effort, by institutional type, 1972–1998.

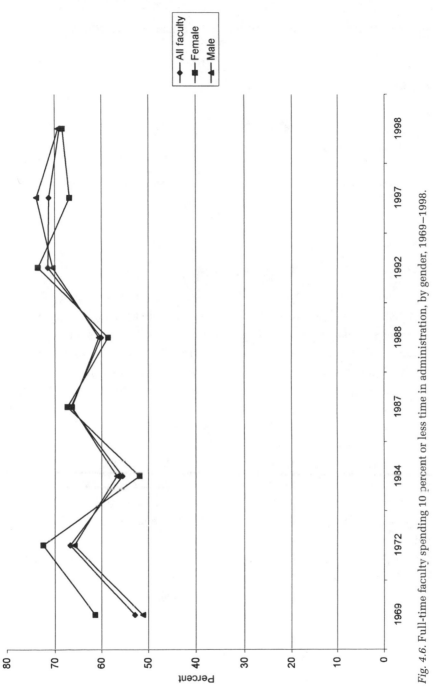

Fig. 4.6. Full-time faculty spending 10 percent or less time in administration, by gender, 1969–1998.

TABLE 4.3

Full-Time Faculty Allocating 10 Percent or Less Time to Administration, 1969–1998

(percent)

	1969	1972	1984	1987	1988	1992	1997	1998
All faculty	52.8	66.7	55.5	66.6	60.0	71.4	71.2	68.9
Institutional type								
Universities	51.5	65.7	52.6	63.4	58.1	70.1	67.4	67.6
Research	—	64.8	51.9	63.4	57.1	69.7	68.1	68.1
Other doctorate-granting	—	68.0	53.8	63.3	59.4	70.8	65.0	66.6
Other 4-yr. institutions	53.0	67.6	53.0	66.2	56.2	71.4	69.2	68.8
Comprehensive	—	70.0	53.6	67.4	56.5	72.4	70.0	70.1
Liberal arts colleges	—	64.5	50.9	61.7	55.5	67.8	67.2	65.6
2-yr. colleges	57.0	80.4	63.9	75.6	69.2	74.9	77.7	73.8

Sources: Carn-69, ACE-72, CFAT-84, NSOPF-88, NCRIPTAL-88, NSOPF-93, CFAT-97, NSOPF-99 (see Appendix A for key).

TEACHING LOADS

Whatever the allocation of faculty work effort and the congruence (or incongruence) of actual and preferred distributions of effort, some concrete measures are available to illuminate academic practice. These include the actual (self-reported) number of hours engaged in classroom teaching and the type of students taught (particularly undergraduate versus graduate). What do the trends show? Insofar as the distribution of teaching hours is quite skewed, table 4.4 shows the ratio of those faculty teaching high loads (defined as nine or more weekly hours) to those faculty teaching low loads (defined as six hours or less) as a good indicator of the proportion of faculty teaching more than the median compared to those teaching less. According to the data, whereas one and a half times more faculty taught high as compared to low loads in 1969, that ratio had increased modestly to twice as many teaching high loads by 1998. With the exception of the research universities, where the ratio remained both stable and low (about three-fifths as many faculty taught high as low loads), the ratio of high to low teaching load increased for all faculty demographic groups with the sole exception of women and new entrants (table A-4.8), where the ratio was about the same in 1998 as in 1969 after having dipped slightly in the 1980s. That means that irrespective of periodic swings in numbers of hours of teaching, the basic ratio of those teaching more to those teaching less has either remained stable or increased.

Taken together with our earlier findings of demonstrably increased research involvement and overall work effort on the part of the faculty over the past generation, these data suggest that increased research involvement has *not* been

TABLE 4.4

Ratio of High to Low Teaching Loads among Full-Time Faculty, 1969–1998

	1969	1975	1984	1987	1992	1997	1998	Difference in ratios 1969–98
All faculty	1.5	2.2	2.0	1.7	1.8	2.0	2.0	0.5
Gender								
Female	2.5	2.4	2.2	2.2	2.2	2.1	2.5	0.0
Male	1.3	2.2	2.0	1.5	1.6	1.9	1.8	0.5
Institutional type								
Universities	0.6	0.8	0.7	0.6	0.5	0.6	0.7	0.1
Other 4-year institutions	3.2	4.0	3.0	3.6	3.6	3.2	3.9	0.7
2-year colleges	6.9	6.0	6.9	8.1	7.6	7.3	11.9	5.0
Institutional type								
Universities	0.6	0.8	0.7	0.6	0.5	0.6	0.7	0.1
Female	1.1	1.1	0.8	0.9	0.7	0.6	0.8	
Male	0.5	0.8	0.6	0.5	0.4	0.5	0.6	
Other 4-year institutions	3.2	4.0	3.0	3.6	3.6	3.2	3.9	0.7
Female	3.5	3.0	2.6	3.1	3.1	2.6	3.8	
Male	3.2	4.5	3.2	3.7	3.9	3.8	4.0	
2-year colleges	6.9	6.0	6.9	8.1	7.6	7.3	11.9	5.0
Female	5.8	3.7	4.5	6.0	5.8	4.8	7.8	
Male	7.4	8.0	9.41	0.1	9.7	11.6	21.7	

Sources: Carn-69, CFAT-75, CFAT-84, NSOPF-88, NSOPF-93, CFAT-97, NSOPF-99 (see Appendix A for key).
Note: High teaching load ≥ 9 hours/week; low teaching load ≤ 6 hours/week.

achieved at the overall expense of teaching. Thus it would appear, first, that teaching has *not* for the most part lost out to the increasing emphasis on research, although there has been an effort to "balance" the workload of junior faculty in particular, who experience the greatest research pressures—a balance that the data suggest has been achieved largely at the expense of the senior faculty's workload, to be sure. Second, academic women may have received over the past generation something of an equity adjustment in teaching load: their historically higher teaching load vis-à-vis men may be disappearing, or at least declining. To the extent that both teaching and research pressures have increased, the resolution of those forces has apparently been achieved via a combination of decreased time allocated to administration and a greater aggregated volume of work effort.

The data in figure 4.7, moreover, suggest that the consistent movement toward higher teaching loads has coincided with a greater focus on undergradu-

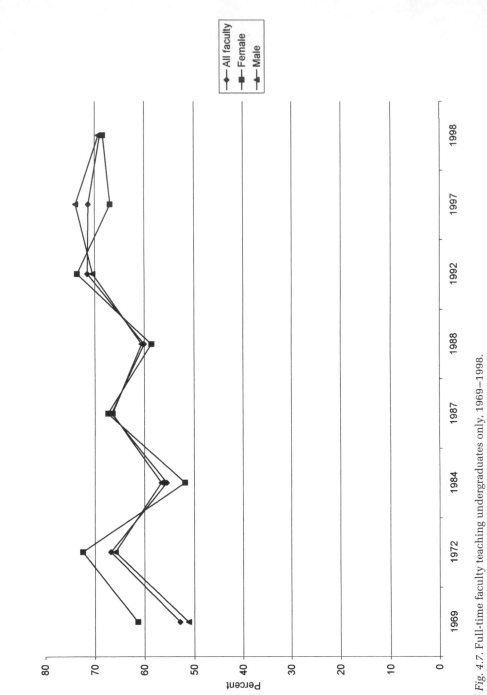

Fig. 4.7. Full-time faculty teaching undergraduates only, 1969–1998.

ates (versus graduate students). In 1969 about half of all college faculty taught undergraduates only; by 1998 that proportion had increased in linear fashion to about two in three. In large part the overall increase was attributable to the rising proportion of faculty at the research and other doctorate-granting universities who are teaching only undergraduates. This has been achieved largely by the resort to "teaching only" term appointments at the research universities (see chapter 7). Tenured and tenure-track faculty are much less likely to be teaching undergraduates only, although the proportions have certainly risen substantially since 1975.

RESEARCH AND SCHOLARLY ACTIVITY

To what extent has the increased orientation to research and the modest increase in the allocation of faculty members' effort to their scholarship been reflected in the level of faculty publication and sponsored research? Have changes in publication rates—however crude such a measurement must be—been commensurate with the reallocation of the faculty's efforts? The overall trend is clear; the numbers show that ever-larger proportions of the faculty have engaged in scholarly publication. Their effort can be measured in two ways based on faculty survey items: publication activity during the two previous years and publications spanning one's entire academic career.

Three decades ago the American professoriate was not notably immersed in writing for publication (table 4.5, fig. 4.8). In 1969 fully half of the faculty reported no publishing—either articles or books—during the previous two years. Since then, however, the act of publication has become much more the norm. Thus by 1998 the proportion of faculty who published had risen sharply from one-half to two in three. And the publication contagion was widespread, plainly affecting faculty at all types of institutions and in most fields of the arts and sciences (table A-4.9). Of course, absolute levels of faculty members' publishing continue to be shaped heavily by their institutional environment and disciplinary affiliation: publication activity was highest, naturally, at research universities and, among fields, in the social and natural sciences. The principle of "small worlds, different worlds" endures. True to their self-reported orientation and actual time commitments, academic women at all types of institutions consistently published less than men, although the vast majority of both men and women at research universities do publish; indeed, by 1998 only one-quarter of the women (and only one-sixth of the men) had not published over their career (roughly half the proportion of nonpublishers reported in 1969).

Viewed through a different lens—publication rates over the course of an en-

TABLE 4.5

Research and Publication Activity of Full-Time Faculty, 1969–1998
(percent)

	1969	1972	1975	1984	1987	1988	1992	1997*	1998
All faculty									
No publications in past 2 yrs.	49.5	35.6	47.7	44.6	54.7	38.2	40.4	41.5	33.4
5 or more publications in past 2 yrs.	11.1	18.0	11.3	14.8	14.2	19.5	12.7	9.2	22.5
Engaged in funded research in past 2 yrs.	37.1	48.9	38.9	40.6	21.9	63.7	27.4	47.6	33.9
No publications in past 2 yrs.									
Universities	28.8	23.1	23.0	20.0	29.1	12.0	21.0	13.8	14.0
Other 4-yr. institutions	62.5	59.2	55.7	45.6	64.4	42.9	40.1	37.5	35.1
2-yr. colleges	85.9	87.8	81.8	81.3	91.8	72.8	73.4	80.1	69.1
5 or more publications in past 2 yrs.									
Universities	19.4	24.2	23.1	29.6	28.6	40.6	26.4	21.5	40.9
Other 4-yr. institutions	4.3	4.7	4.8	8.8	4.5	10.7	5.5	3.8	3.5
2-yr. colleges	1.5	0.8	1.3	1.8	0.9	3.3	1.2	0.0	3.3
Engaged in funded research in past 2 yrs.									
Universities	57.7	59.0	63.4	65.5	37.9	80.3	49.3	68.4	52.4
Other 4-yr. institutions	23.0	29.1	29.4	36.5	12.4	61.9	18.2	48.4	26.3
2-yr. colleges	4.9	10.3	9.5	8.7	6.1	39.2	5.7	22.5	13.6

Sources: Carn-69, ACE-72, CFAT-75, CFAT-84, NSOPF-88, NCRIPTAL-88, NSOPF-93, CFAT-97, NSOPF-99 (see Appendix A for key).

*For CFAT-97 the corresponding items asked for a three-year period. In the case of no publications, the "0" figure was simply maintained. In the case of 5 or more publications, the answer provided by each respondant was multiplied by 2/3 in order to obtain a figure comparable with those of the other surveys. The reported answer was kept for the item relative to funded research.

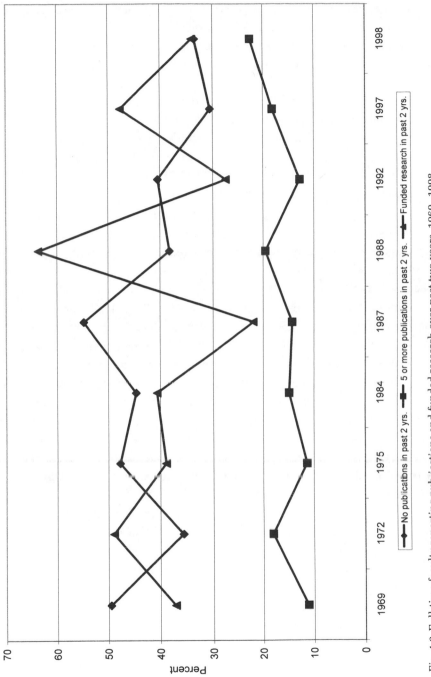

Fig. 4.8. Full-time faculty reporting publications and funded research over past two years, 1969–1998.

tire career rather than during just the preceding two-year period—we find a similar pattern over time: in 1969 about one-third of the professoriate reported no publications over their careers, but by 1998 that proportion had dropped to one-fifth. Conversely, from two-thirds in 1969, fully four-fifths now report publication during their careers.

Differences in career publication according to institutional type and disciplinary field are obvious (table A-4.9). Gender disparities are evident as well, across both institutional types and disciplines. There is, however, some evidence that these male-female disparities in the proportion who publish are narrowing—just as the gender gap is narrowing for those who report publishing in the past two years (see table A-4.10).

The data in table A-4.9 reveal that the senior cohort, congruent with their time-allocation patterns, are slightly less active in publication than their junior and midcareer colleagues, at least as measured (however crudely) by the proportion in each career cohort who did not publish in a refereed journal during the past two years. The data also confirm the change in generational patterns of publication activity. In 1969 new faculty were 12% *more* likely than midcareer or senior faculty to be counted among the nonpublishers; by 1998 the disparity was cut in half: new entrants showed an 18% decline in nonpublishers, whereas older cohorts showed a barely perceptible decline in nonpublishers (3–4%). This pattern of increasing publication activity for *new* faculty holds across institutional types (excluding two-year colleges), although the absolute proportion of nonpublishers at the research universities is about half that at other four-year institutions. What is striking, however, is that in 1998 nonpublication declines among both the midcareer and senior cohorts (as well as the new cohort) for faculty at *other four-year* institutions (as distinguished from research university midcareer and senior faculty, who show no such change). This suggests two trends: first, the increasing pressure over the past generation on junior faculty to publish and achieve distinction in their discipline; second, the extension of that pressure out of research universities to other four-year institutions, where midcareer and senior as well as junior faculty are now subject to increasing publication pressure (although, again, not as severe as at the research universities).

Having documented the shrinking proportion of the faculty at the bottom of the publication curve, what can we say about the top of the distribution? That is, if fewer faculty are not publishing, are more faculty publishing prolifically? Based on an operational definition of "prolific" publication as five or more publications in the past two years, the data in figure 4.8 (table A-4.9) indicate that as nonpublishers have shrunk from one-half to one-third of the faculty, the prolific publishers have grown from one-ninth to nearly one-fourth of the faculty. Not only are more faculty publishing, but more faculty are publishing *more*. Prolificity, moreover, no less than the fact of publication, appears to be growing quite uniformly across the four-year college and university sector. Prolificity has increased impressively at the universities (where the proportion of faculty with five or more publications exploded from about one-quarter in 1987 to nearly two-thirds by 1998); but, though at lower absolute levels, it has grown even more dramatically in the nonuniversity four-year sector (from one-twentieth in 1987 to about one-third by 1998) (table 4.5). Similarly, it has grown across all program areas—although still highest in the natural and social sciences—and across all career cohorts (senior as well as new entrant faculty) (table A-4.9). The case of gender is particularly interesting. The proportion of prolific publishers among men remains almost twice as great as among women (26.6% versus 15.1% in 1998 as compared to 16.8% versus 7.2% in 1987), although it appears to be shrinking—most dramatically at the research universities and in the social sciences (table A-4.10).

The overall pattern, then, is one of increasingly widespread publication extending well beyond the research university sector. Although one-third of all faculty have always published something over the course of their careers, the proportions who are publishing and who are publishing prolifically have increased across all sectors and all fields, and among women as well as men. Taken together with the evidence of research orientation and increased allocation of effort to research, the data clearly suggest a system that expects research and publication almost across the board—even as it is imposing a return to heavier teaching loads.

Still another relevant vantage point is faculty participation in externally funded research, a vital factor because extramural support is not only increasingly a precondition for conducting research that can lead to publication in many (perhaps most) fields, but also, by faculty accounts, an increasingly competitive arena. The data in figure 4.8 reveal a doubling between 1969 and 1988 in the proportion of faculty involved in funded research, building from just over one-third in 1969 to two-thirds by 1988, and then a sharp falloff by half in the 1990s, reflecting the decline in federal research funding. The initially rising tide of faculty members who report obtaining funded research is discernible across all institutional types, but it was primarily at the research and other doctorate-granting universities where the involvement was (and is) greatest (table A-4.11). Indeed, a majority of faculty at these institutions are so engaged: about three-fourths at the former and approximately one-half at the latter. Only a minority of faculty everywhere else—although significant minorities at the comprehensive universities and the liberal arts colleges—succeed in obtaining extramural support.[2]

Although large male-female disparities in obtaining outside funding were reported in 1969 and again in 1975, the gender difference had mostly disappeared by the mid-1990s—with institutional type clearly asserting its primary influence. However, differences by field (table A-4.11) and gender-field interactions persist: the proportion of faculty obtaining extramural support has declined in the social and natural sciences (no doubt in direct proportion to falloffs in federal funding) while increasing in the humanities and the fine arts. The gender gap persists in several of the professions (most notably the health sciences and engineering), but women have achieved proportionate presence with men in the natural sciences and business and have actually come to surpass their male colleagues in obtaining funded research in the social sciences and, to a lesser extent, in the humanities. Again, the basic pattern of increasing gender convergence in research and scholarly activity is evident.

Most of the publication activity in American higher education is accounted for by a minority, albeit a growing minority, of faculty at research universities. According to the data in tables A-4.9 and A-4.10, university faculty continue to account for four-fifths of the research output. What is interesting here is that the proportionate representation of women in these ranks has tripled from about one-twenty-fifth to one-sixth, suggesting that male-female disparities are narrowing not only on average but also at the highest levels of research productivity; and it is women in the health and social sciences and the fine arts who are contributing most to the narrowing of that gap.

FACULTY PARTICIPATION IN DEPARTMENT AND CAMPUS GOVERNANCE

A significant if less time-consuming component of faculty work is participation in the governance of academic departments and the wider campus. Current debates in higher education suggest that academic citizenship may be withering—a victim at once of declining loyalty of faculty members to their home institutions (a function in part of the rise of temporary and part-time appointments) and the increasingly managerial orientation of administrative leadership (Slaughter and Leslie, 1997; Baldwin and Chronister, 2001). What do the national faculty surveys tell us about changes, if any, in faculty members' perceptions of their role in departmental and campus affairs over the past quarter century?

Perhaps surprisingly, an increasing proportion of faculty members report "more than average" involvement in departmental affairs (escalating from about three-fifths to nine-tenths) and, to a lesser extent, in campuswide affairs as well (rising from about 30% to roughly 40%) (fig. 4.9). (One may ponder how such large proportions of faculty can be "above average" in their rates of participation, but that is another matter.) Thus self-reported involvement in governance (as seen relative to that of colleagues) has become more rather than less pervasive, contrary to general opinion. Not surprisingly, twice as many faculty members report high levels of involvement in departmental decision making as those who report significant participation in campuswide affairs. Involvement in the former is modal; involvement in the latter is not. Controlling for faculty career age, we find—again, as would be expected—that new faculty (those in the first six or seven years of an academic career) are significantly less likely than their more senior colleagues to report involvement in campus affairs, both a quarter century ago and now (table A-4.12b). However, these new entrants are involved in department affairs almost as much as their more senior colleagues (table A-4.12a). The senior faculty cohort, meanwhile, show a rising trajectory of departmental involvement along with a lower, albeit consistent, involvement over time in institutional affairs (tables A-4.12a and A-4.12b).

How should this pattern of rising faculty involvement in governance be interpreted? In part, it may be a consequence of trends in the increased use of part-time and temporary full-time appointments. That is, perhaps fewer faculty, by virtue of the kind of "regular" appointment they hold, are now expected to participate in governance, with the result that these core faculty who are "eligible" for governance must shoulder greater responsibility and involvement in it. Or, the self-reported statistics may mean that most faculty simply rate themselves as "more than average" on any measure you care to take. Then again, it may simply be that the (self-reported) greater involvement, perhaps occasioned by the advent of new committees and task forces, is at least as demanding as ever, leaving aside whether the results of faculty involvement—that is, actual faculty influence—may have dwindled at the same time.

The data on that score shown in figure 4.9 (faculty influence as distinguished from mere involvement) suggest, first, a strong and consistent pattern of about two of every three faculty members perceiving a high level of influence on their department. At the same time, many fewer faculty (15% to 20%) report wielding high levels of influence over campuswide affairs. Moreover, there appears to be a subtle pattern of declining influence over time: the one-sixth of faculty members who reported "high" campus influence in 1969 had declined to about one-seventh by 1997. But the proportion reporting no campus influence rose from one-third to about 40%. When we control for career age (tables A-4.13a

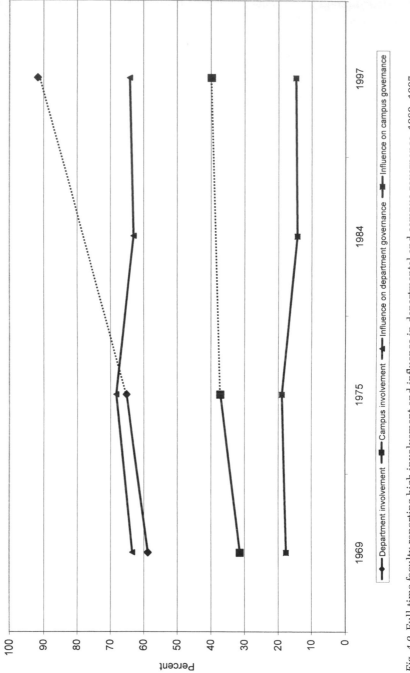

Fig. 4.9. Full-time faculty reporting high involvement and influence in departmental and campus governance, 1969–1997.

and A-4.13b), we find, as would be expected, that senior faculty members are much more likely than their junior colleagues to report higher influence on both department and campus affairs. For both groups, however, substantial proportions report considerable intradepartment influence over time, whereas only a small and declining minority report high campuswide influence. For the senior faculty cohort, the 25.8% reporting high campus influence in 1969 had shrunk to 17.1% by 1997.

The picture that emerges is one of a profession consistently involved, especially at the senior ranks, in processes to shape their academic units and, to a considerably lesser degree, their campuses. Thus many faculty members experience an increasing disjunction between their departmental and their institutional spheres of influence; in their perception they are losing their grip on institutional affairs while they continue, and even reinforce, their focus on their own departments.

THE INFORMATION TECHNOLOGY WILD CARD

Some basic changes have been afoot in the definition of faculty work (largely, it would seem, toward a narrowing of work responsibilities), but two key external developments since 1994 promise to reshape the faculty role to an extent not seen since the emergence of graduate education in the nineteenth century or the birth of Big Science during and after World War II:

- ubiquitous computing capability (24/7 availability via PC or laptop) for communication and access to information, and
- the Internet as a source of global content accessible to anyone.

These developments together change the relationship between faculty and learners and promise to recast the role of college faculty as experts and gatekeepers—the great addition to academic work in the twentieth century.

Although the full impact of information technology on faculty roles and work may not be discernible for another generation, incipient realignments are already demonstrable. Most obviously, there is the impact on *faculty workload*. Faculty have had to learn new technologies and instrumentalities (the use of presentation software, courseware management policies, course Web page design) and revise course content more often (e.g., maintain a good course Web site), since students are no longer dependent on them exclusively for access to the latest information on the course topics; and their courses have become in some sense much more "public" (a not-unwelcome change; see Shulman, 2004). They must contend with e-mail and the consequent 24/7 accessibility to students, deal with the ubiquitous technical snafus, and even assume new kinds of secretarial duties as the departmental typist and filer fast disappears and professors are expected to word process their own syllabi and writing and maintain their own electronic files. Recognition of the resulting workload increase has already begun to find its way into faculty collective-bargaining contracts. Rhoades and Maitland (2000) reported, based on a content analysis of new National Education Association contracts, the introduction of specialized clauses related to information technology (IT) as a new trend in renegotiation of the particulars of faculty workload, compensation, and evaluation.

IT is also changing the kind of work and work roles that faculty take on. Perhaps most momentous is what analysts have referred to as the "unbundling" of faculty work roles. By that we mean the separation of teaching from research and service in ways that permit and accommodate the emergence of part-time and even full-time teaching-only (or research-only) appointments (see chapter 7). In particular, IT makes possible a second-order "unbundling" of the teaching role itself. Jewett (2000) describes how IT provides a practical means for dividing the teaching function into its constituent parts and reorganizing it into more cost-effective structures. Thus, teaching is defined as including, at minimum, four analytically distinct activities: material preparation, presentation or delivery of the material, assessment of student learning, and interaction with students about course content. IT allows us to now ask the question, Can teaching labor be divided in a given course so as to reduce the amount of faculty time spent (the very expensive labor-intensive model of having one person, the professor, take responsibility for all four activities) and increase the proportion of investment in capital, the computer, whose costs rise more slowly and are more controllable? In an important sense, of course, research universities have for two generations been working with the "TA" model, which, in effect, increases class size by dissociating the professor from assessment and interaction with students and limiting her or his expensive labor to preparation and delivery. IT provides an opportunity for nonresearch universities to experiment with different divisions of teaching activities and thereby change the nature of faculty teaching on a much grander scale.

Second-order revisions are now feasible for the course-preparation and delivery functions. For example, in large, multisection introductory courses, the possibility now arises of having a single international expert or team of experts take responsibility for the preparation of course materials for *all* sections, thus saving the not-inconsiderable costs of having perhaps eighty individuals prepare largely similar materials for English 101. Delivery of materials then can occur through the Internet and the campus network, with the faculty member (or an appropriate substitute) serving in a "facilitative" capacity (see, for example, Twigg, 2002b).

New questions are emerging about the ownership of the intellectual property that course syllabi and materials constitute. Institutions that are providing the infrastructure and technical support for faculty course development are now establishing claims to ownership in the course material as "works for hire." And new kinds of arrangements are being made for institutional "buyouts" of faculty courses and/or payments to faculty for residual rights—not unlike a dose of Hollywood in academe. These developments raise fundamental questions about the relationship between faculty and their institutions and may yet provide the third phase in the transition of faculty from fellows and owners of the college property (the English model) to civil servants (western Europe) and employees (the American model) and ultimately to freelancers or, at least, consultants with a primary client (the employing institution) (see Metzger, 1969).[3]

Quite aside from these impressions and speculation, to what extent is there evidence that allows us to begin assessing these new developments? Although the available data are scattered and sporadic, there are nonetheless at least two kinds of sources (evidence) that enable us to begin evaluating empirically the impact of IT on faculty work. They include

- self-reported data on faculty activities in the national surveys, and
- scenarios that can be developed of a typical work day (a day in 1972, 1986, 1998, 2012).

Indicators of Realignment

Several independent sources of empirical evidence exist about how technology is intruding into and transforming faculty work:

- The Rhoades/Maitland analysis of NEA contracts (evidence regarding workload)
- Kenneth Green's *Campus Computing Survey*[4] (trends over the 1990s in e-mail use, use of the Web in instruction, etc.)
- The Carnegie 1997 Faculty Survey (a section on technology use)
- National Study of Postsecondary Faculty for 1993 (NSOPF-93) and the NSOPF-99 (items on the use of IT in courses; types of IT used; distance education)
- NCES survey of distance education (USDE, 1997)

Kenneth Green's Campus Computing Survey provides a trend line on the spectacular rise of IT applications in faculty teaching as reported by campus chief information officers. Figure 4.10 details the rising use of e-mail, Internet resources, course Web pages, and presentation handouts in the new age classroom (Green, 2002). Two observations are in order here: first, in a matter of six years, e-mail and Internet resources catapulted from a curiosity in one of ten courses in 1994 to a dominant instrument in the majority of courses by 2000—*an utterly unprecedented rate of change.* This rise does suggest increased faculty workload in terms of availability to students and increased time in professional development related to the new technologies, but it is difficult to assess empirically either the extent to which instruction has been "unbundled" or any attendant reorientation in faculty roles. Some documented developments are suggestive. The vast majority of campuses are moving quickly to adopt standard course-management tools (software), which shape how faculty structure their courses, although only about one-quarter of all courses used such tools in 2000 (fig. 4.10). Moreover, the data on distance education suggest a clear reorientation in delivery—at least through administrative eyes. According to the U.S. Department of Education, nearly 2.9 million students enrolled in college level courses hosted online in the academic year 2000–2001, and fully nine-tenths of public colleges, universities, and technical training schools ran online courses (CNN, 2003).

This administratively drawn picture is confirmed in its broadest strokes through the results of the national faculty surveys. More specifically, the national faculty surveys confirm the timing of some of the changes in faculty use of IT and the pervasiveness of IT's penetration into teaching and research (although not its *depth* of penetration). Thus, in 1987 the National Study of Postsecondary Faculty included only a single item on IT (a question asking whether faculty had developed computer software), and nearly 99% of responses indicated a lack of involvement in software development. By fall 1992, the survey had added several questionnaire items that together yielded a different picture of IT, but still the responses confirmed an emerging theme rather than a sweeping tide. Forty-four and one-half percent of faculty had in 1992 used computational software, especially in business, engineering, and the professions (obviously a limited and non-role-transforming use of IT), and about one-third had used computer-aided instruction, with proportions significantly higher in the natural sciences and engineering. This, of course, means that the majority of faculty (55.4%) had *not* used computational software and that fully two-thirds had made no use of computer-aided instruction (figures that rise by at least 10–15% when we exclude engineering, business, and the natural sciences). Nearly two

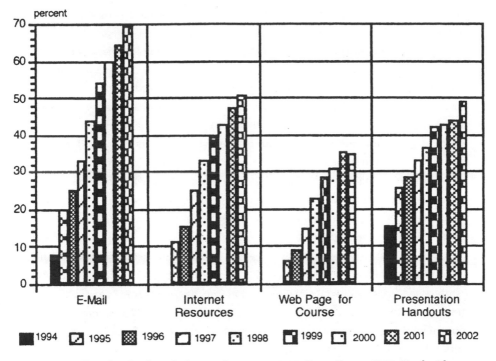

Fig. 4.10. Use of technology in instruction, 1994–2002. From Green, 2002. Used with permission of Kenneth C. Green.

out of three faculty (63%) reported using the lecture as their primary method of instruction—a figure that jumps to 87% when seminar and discussion are added in to lecture. Five years later, still only about 6% (compared with less than 1% in 1987) had developed computer software (USDE, 1998b).

By 1998 a clear, if not quite seismic, shift was discernible. The vast majority of faculty still had not developed computer software, and 90% reported face-to-face as the primary medium of instruction (only 10% reported that their primary method of instruction was not face-to-face, and only 6% said the computer served as the primary medium of instruction in any class). But the use of the Web and electronic mail as instructional tools had emerged from nowhere to become virtually standard practice. Seven of ten faculty in 1998 reported using e-mail to communicate with students (from a high of five-sixths at research universities to fully one-half at two-year community colleges), men and women alike across all fields—reaching more than one-third of their students this way. Moreover, four in ten reported the use of Web sites for their courses to post general course information, links to outside resources, and information on home-

work and, in less than half the cases, to provide for student-to-student chat fo-
rums (USDE, 2001a).

It is clear that between 1992 and 1998, the Web and e-mail emerged on campus, much as they did off campus, as important vehicles to convey information
and facilitate communication. What is less clear is the extent to which such
technologies have actually increased faculty workload and substantively transformed the nature of the work. In 1998 faculty reported that they spent an average of 2.75 hours per week communicating with students via e-mail; the figure is slightly higher for women and minority faculty. Among the decile (10%)
of faculty reporting the highest average time spent on e-mail with students, the
average number of hours rises to as many as 6 or 8. But how much were these
increases in electronic communication offset by decreases in face-to-face communication? How much was the time involved in preparing and updating course
Web sites offset by a decline in face-to-face course-administration-related rou-
tines? ("Can I get last week's handouts?" "I missed the homework assignment?")
And to what extent do Web sites function merely as "electronic" versions of the
traditional library reserve desk and the traditional handout? Have they actually
contributed to a change in the instructional process or the unbundling of faculty roles? Indeed, the data on instructional methods mentioned above suggest
that the lecture and the lecture-discussion tradition remain powerful shapers
of faculty behavior. What remains to be determined is the depth of the penetration of IT into faculty behavior and work roles and the meaning, or changes
in meaning, to which it may lead. For answers to such uncertainties, we will
need to continue to monitor faculty activity patterns over time. We will also
need to disentangle the effects of increasing managerialism on campus (and
attendant declines in faculty participation in governance) from the IT-related
rise in faculty entrepreneurialism and the questions of intellectual-property
ownership that threaten to reconfigure the faculty-campus employment relationship.

In sum, just as a first-order narrowing, or functional respecialization, of faculty work roles was coming to the fore in American higher education, supported
in no small measure by the structuring of new kinds of faculty appointments,
including specialized full-time as well as part-time appointments, the advent of
new information technologies seems to be both reinforcing that trend and spawning a second-order respecialization of its own. We await the empirical data that
will demonstrate the specifics of the second-order change, but in the meantime
we have identified a series of faculty work scenarios that, in the absence of data,
provide a sense of the magnitude and depth of the changes we are discussing.

The Scenarios

Static snapshots of discrete and isolated behaviors at one point in time provide one sort of evidence of emerging trends. A very different, and perhaps more revealing, perspective is gained when we look at the typical workday of a faculty member as it has evolved over a generation or two. The following four scenarios attempt to capture the daily work life of a typical faculty member at four points in time: in 1972, at the height of higher education's boom and the ascent of the "one professional does all" model; in 1986, when the first intimations of the potential of IT poked their head into the classrooms of a few vanguard faculty; in 1998, when the advent of the Internet and the personal computer were already shaking up the academic mix; and as we project in 2012, when the mix begins to settle at a new equilibrium or set of equilibriums.

A day in the life of . . .
John Scherff, physics professor, University of the Midwest, September 15, 1972

What a difference a weekend made, John thought as he rolled up the window of his VW Super Beetle, pulled out the 8-track tape, and stashed it in the glove compartment. Last week he was just a former liberal arts college professor in his first week at the premier research university in the Midwest. This week he was a former liberal arts college professor in his first week at the premier research university in the Midwest *with a grant.*

He smiled to himself as he locked the car. They ought to get his acceptance letter by the end of the week. Then, within a month, his first check would arrive. He looked up at the weathered brick buildings of the science quad and thought about the lab with all the latest equipment that would now be available for him inside one of them. He'd check into it today. Life was definitely good.

The letter from the foundation had arrived on Saturday, with a cover memo apologizing for the delay due to late mailing. Its arrival had brought to a halt the in-depth preparations for two of his assigned classes. Those he could hand over to grad students now. On the advice of his friend Charlie Furtch, a chemistry professor at VPI and, without a doubt, the most brilliant of his close colleagues, he would keep the intro class for himself. If things worked out for him as they had for Charlie, he'd get a kick out of introducing freshman to the wonders of physics.

On his way to the office, he stopped by the library to check the availability of the journals and other resources he needed for his background research. He was in luck; the card catalog showed more than a dozen texts he could use, and the periodicals list indicated that almost every journal was available, either bound or on microfiche. These resources bordered on luxurious compared to the slim collection on the sciences at his former college.

Lucille was already hard at work. No surprise there. If he believed in omens, he'd take having Lucille as the department secretary as yet another very good sign. He greeted her cheerfully as he pulled what looked like a hundred phone messages and interoffice memos from his mailbox. Most seemed to be the usual first-of-the-year notices and pleas to serve on this or that committee. Unlike the stereotypical scientist, John liked committee work. But he'd have to choose carefully this year; he didn't want all the meetings to cut into his research time. He carried the mail and his briefcase into his newly established tiny office.

Lucille knocked lightly at the door, then carried in a steaming cup of Sanka. Thanking her kindly, he gave her the rough of the syllabus for the intro class, greatly relieved at knowing that she was more than up to the task of deciphering his hit-or-miss spelling. He asked her to run off one hundred copies, adding that he hoped the department ditto machine could produce that many clear copies from one master. At his old school, she would have had to type two.

John humbly broke the news about winning the grant and was gratified at her enthusiastic reaction, especially since it would likely mean several weeks of overwhelming work for her more than a few times over the year. Together, they figured out the wording of the ads for lab aides that he need to post on bulletin boards around the campus.

After Lucille left, John decided to phone Charlie in Virginia. He called the campus operator for an outside line and waited while the connection was made. Unfortunately, it wasn't Charlie, but his secretary, who answered. Charlie wasn't back from his speaking date at a conference, so John left the good news about the grant with his secretary. He returned several of the calls he had message slips for, but was frustrated when he only got through to a few of the callers. Maybe Monday morning was not the time to catch his colleagues in their offices.

John spent the next few hours reworking some old lab assignments to fit his introductory course. His fancy new ten-function calculator expedited his calculations. Although it had cost him one hundred dollars, John considered it a bargain. Always a sucker for gadgets, he was one of the first of his colleagues to abandon his slide rule.

He didn't get away for lunch until 2:00 p.m. On his way out, he gave Lucille the instructions for three labs along with a description of the format he liked to use. She, in turn, handed him ten neatly typed 3x5 cards to post. He made a mental note to get them up before he left for the day. He needed four able lab assistants, and soon, if he wanted any results by the end of the semester. Hopefully at least one would be able to back him up preparing the data for the mainframe. Although more than worth the trouble, keypunching the hundreds of cards required was not a job he anticipated with any relish. Perhaps the cost of an ad in the weekly student newspaper would be justified if he ended up with the right group.

After lunch he checked in with the department chairman about his new lab. The result was a guided tour of the huge basement that held most of the labs. In general the labs were well equipped for physics experiments. But one was perfect for his work with fiber optics. Nevertheless, the chairman asked him for his top three choices—rookies rarely got their heart's desire. John was happy to report that his grant would cover the purchase of a reasonable amount of equipment. The chairman was pleased to hear it.

The day was winding down, so John made the rounds with his 3x5 cards, then headed out to the parking lot and home. Despite all the decisions yet to be made, he felt this was a great way to start a year.

* * *

A day in the life of . . .

Máximo Ruiz, associate professor of mathematics, Eastern Land Grant University, October 10, 1986

Max hurried over to the graphic arts building. He had barely an hour before class, and he was determined to review the Mathematica software demo his friend at MIT had sent. Vigi said it was an exciting breakthrough in teaching math. Unfortunately, it didn't run on either Max's Leading Edge Model D IBM clone or his Apple II. The graphic arts group used Macintosh computers exclusively, and a Mac was what he required.

Grace Boerner was available to get him started. He was surprised at how different the Mac was from his other machines. Instead of typing in commands, he used a mouse to click (sometimes twice) on pictures of files and folders and pull down menus of options. The concept was interesting, but Max was sure he'd never get used to the mouse.

The software turned out to be amazing. Visual representations of equations and functions displayed clearly and smoothly—like real drawings. The speed at which they were executed made it simple to show how changes in variables affected the graphs. Max could see what all the excitement was about: relationships between and among variables would be more comprehensible to his more concrete thinkers. He made a mental note to discuss with his department chair a pilot program using Mathematica.

He made it to class on time. He was teaching recursion in his BASIC programming class. It reminded him of his discussion with his son Julio the night before. The high school had just begun a computer literacy class. They were using LOGO to program the Apple II's in their lab of fifteen computers. Julio was explaining how he used the Repeat command to get the LOGO turtle to draw recursive patterns. Max was so pleased to see his son's excitement for learning. If high school kids were learning to program, there would be no stopping them in college. That got him to thinking that LOGO might be a good addition to his "Math as a Liberal Art" course geared toward teachers. He was already having them explore using Math Blaster and Number Munchers as alternatives to practice worksheets.

On the way back to his office, he ran into Gail, the student intern who had been assigned to work with him in his role as faculty moderator. He was able to give her the agenda for the next faculty meeting to take to the university print shop to be Xeroxed. He took a minute to admire his handiwork before he passed it on. He was amused at how much he enjoyed inserting clip art and using different fonts in his publications. He double-checked the spreadsheets on comparing faculty salaries he had included in the packet. Thanks to a new ribbon in his Epson printer, they had printed out just fine and should reproduce well. Gail showed him the labels with the senators' names and departments that she had made from his database. They both agreed that Appleworks made this part of their jobs much easier.

After 90 minutes of office hours, he closed up his office for the day and ambled over to the computer lab. He was working on his dissertation and had some more data to enter into his SPSS file on the mainframe. He found an empty terminal and logged on. It was a tedious process. He had to call up the line editor several times to fix his typing errors. He ran some frequencies to see how it was going and sent the results to the printer. The lab was swamped, so it took half an hour for his run number to be called by the lab assistants. The results showed that multivariate analysis was definitely in order, but Max couldn't remember the exact commands and syntax required. He decided to work on it the next day.

It was a warm afternoon, so Max rode home with the top down on his '78 MGB. The department secretary had passed on a message from his wife that she was running late and would bring home some burgers. He might have an hour to chase down the short in his trunk light before dinner. Better yet, he should put it off. None of his other forays into the electrical system had taken as little as an hour—one definitely had to like fooling with wiring to own an MGB. He would use the time to check out the batteries and AC connection for the Beta video recorder. Julio would turn 18 this weekend, and though he would gripe about it, they were going to tape the family party.

It would be huge. Three generations of relatives were converging on the town, some coming all the way from Guadalajara to help usher his son into adulthood. Max considered all of the changes he had seen in his life since he had turned 18. How different the future promised to be for Julio!

A day in the life of . . .
Charlotte Durfield, English professor, Suburbia College, January 5, 1998

It was surprisingly good to be starting the second semester. Charlotte might have attributed her renewed zest to the exhilarating mountain biking trip she'd taken over the break, but she knew it was more. After twenty years of teaching graduate and undergraduate English courses, she was headed down a new professional path: she was taking on the challenge of technology.

She reflected on the events that had led her to her new goal. There were two that came to mind.

The first occurred during a visit to her former student's sixth-grade class. As a student, Chuck Brightup had been loaded with enthusiasm for new ideas. It didn't surprise Charlotte that, after becoming a teacher, he had jumped onto the technology bandwagon. She had the good fortune to be in his classroom the first day that he and the other sixth-grade teachers were trying out their network's new synchronous chat capability.

Three groups of four students each were to plan the school dance while in chat mode. As each group's posting appeared on the screen, the "conversation" quickly deteriorated:

From Group A: "Let's have T-shirts."
From Group B: "We should decorate the gym."
From Group C: "I like black."
From Group A: "We should have a band."
From Group C: "Black Lights would be cool."
From Group B: "That would be expensive."
From Group A: "I agree."

And then came the posting that warmed Charlotte's English-professor heart:

From Group C: "This is getting confusing. I think we should answer *in complete sentences.*"

Chuck called all the groups together to help them work on protocols for their sessions, but Charlotte was too busy considering the ramifications of online exchange for her own students to pay much attention. Clearly, communicating via Internet technologies was a challenge to students. There were technology-specific writing issues to be explored. More than ever, she was anticipating "observing" their subsequent chat sessions with other schools, and she looked forward to helping them study the pedagogical ramifications of using this technology.

The other incident that got her excited about technology was her first stab at online research. The librarian, Steve Quast, assigned a student aide to introduce her to online reference. She and the student spent two hours online, searching for articles that offered solutions to writing challenges of nonnative speakers. She found more than enough, and thanks to First Search, she was able to save the full text of several to her disk. Those not available in the Suburbia collection or from First Search could be ordered via Interlibrary Loan directly from her computer. It was amazingly convenient.

When Steve stopped by to check on her progress, he introduced her to the Gutenberg Project, a World Wide Web site containing the full text of a number of out-of-copyright classics and government texts. He explained how she could copy the text into a word processor, then use her word processor's search feature to explore characters, follow themes, and trace patterns. More ideas for challenging her students with technology activities blossomed.

She had spent valuable time and money over the summer learning the technology she needed to carry out her ideas, but it was already paying off professionally. The Teaching Learning Technology Roundtable, a group of campus technology leaders led by the provost, had voted to pilot distance education courses. The college would offer twenty online courses beginning this fall. The target group for the pilot program included Suburbia's adult students: the graduate students, most of whom studied off-campus in the college's outlying centers, and the adult degree completion students, who also had time and travel issues. The provost offered an incentive—a laptop computer—for each faculty member whose course proposal was accepted.

Charlotte had designed a Web-based creative writing course that, with an adjustment or two in assignments, could apply to both English master's degree students and fifth-year Education students. She had done her best to include a variety of activities that took advantage of the system's capabilities: asynchronous chat for idea exchanges and feedback among students, an FAQ area where she could post suggestions and address challenges, and connections to several creative-writing-oriented Web sites for reference and inspiration. She was particularly happy that she had been able to arrange for e-mail partnerships for each student with a member of the Senior Citizens Center Creative Writing Club. The TLTR had accepted the idea. Now she was looking forward to the first meeting with the company that would provide technical and curricular service and support for the courses. She was also excited about the idea of having her own laptop.

That thought reminded Charlotte of her current errand. She was determined to be assigned one of the Smart (multimedia) classrooms for her spring poetry class. Her plans for the course included having students listen to recordings of poets reading their works, studying music lyrics as poetry, and using filmed images and scenes to inspire her budding poets. Large pieces of the plan just would not be feasible without the proper equipment for sound and display. She had sent both voicemail and e-mail messages to the registrar's office stating her need. But the Smart classrooms were in short supply, and Charlotte knew her chances of getting one would be better if she rubbed elbows a bit with the folks doing the scheduling. Although sold on technology's promise for teaching and learning, Charlotte still felt that negotiating a favor was best done face-to-face.

A day in the life of . . .
Reiko Obuchi, political science professor, Big State University,
Tokyo Campus, October 5, 2014

Reiko said goodbye to the members of Study Group 3 of her Politics of Elections course and spoke the command that returned her computer to environmental display. She had enjoyed the twenty minutes or so of their meeting that she had viewed. Her students were coming along nicely with their comparison study of unsuccessful presidential/ministerial elections of twentieth-century America and Japan. This session they were finding interesting parallels between the campaigns of Ross Perot in the '90s and Bill Gates's current bid. It would be interesting to see if his choice of VP would do more to advance his cause. Al Gore was a surprisingly good match. Although neither candidate would win many points in the charisma department, they were making expert use of the multimedia features of the National Interactive Election Forum carried on Internet 37. She herself had received a detailed video-mail response from the Gore camp to her question about equitable access to vote via the Internet. And it had come within three hours. There was no denying it: both their response and its timeliness impressed her more than the voice-only messaging used by Amanda Gingrich's campaign. Only time would tell if the general populace would warm to such attention.

Reiko requested access to voice messages from individual students in her Intro course. Instead, she got the chat room. Apparently the support staff was still working on the new classroom-management software. She was about to try again when she noticed the name Perot among the descriptors the computer had generated for each student's contribution to the chat. There was a discussion in progress about the influence of business on government policy, and he was a topic under consideration. Interesting. She had several online consulting vouchers accrued. She asked her online assistant to find out if Ross Perot was making himself available to consult with colleges and universities to fulfill his Thousand Points National Service requirement. If so, the assistant was to check for dates when Perot was available and both classes would be meeting. She commanded the computer to change to Quick-Listen mode and aurally scanned several more lines of the chat. Then she tried to access individual messages again, this time from the keypad.

Successful this time, she spent an hour listening and responding to students' video messages from her international feed. Two of her students in Britain reported disappointment with their service learning project. Instead of participating in analyzing the transcription of the recorded interviews from citizens involved in the turnover of Hong Kong, they were being used to make backup CD-ROMS of old documents from the library at Brasnose College. It was time to meet with the director face-to-face. She would have to set her alarm tonight so she could call at the appropriate time. She asked her online assistant to establish the connection ten minutes after the system activated to awaken her.

As she switched back to environmental mode, she couldn't help but recall the days of manual input of messages. What a pain, and how time-consuming! Now interaction with students seemed more like an ongoing dialogue than a writing exercise. Still, Reiko hadn't broken herself of the habit of hooking up the old keyboard and drafting her own publications manually. She could still think better that way.

It was time to prep for her Sociopolitics of Colonization and Domination class. She asked the assistant to display the resources, about fifty chapters and articles she'd collected from the online research center. It hadn't been easy to glean exactly what she needed, but with the help of her smart search engine, she had a good representation from all major cultures from the fifteenth century forward. She was Quick-Listening to "The Other Civil War" from Howard Zinn's 1997 work on American history when the edge of the screen flashed an urgent message.

CCR (Central Course Resources) was notifying her that the copyright had expired on the virtual simulation of the antiwar demonstrations of the '60s and '70s. Reiko's younger students really responded to the activity. (Her adult students got more out of participating in the Social Security sit-ins of 2009.) She requested renewal for two thousand additional uses and provided her vocal thumbprint for budgeting.

It was time to attend a colleague's on-site course in the School of Business and Civilian Service building. She was looking forward to the panel discussion about the politics of the graduated income tax. It was one of her favorite topics. Reiko hung her professional-look screen clothes on the valet rod of her computer center next to her wig and casual-look attire and went to get ready. Before leaving, she requested the supermarket, swiped her debit card, and entered her request for 4:30 pickup. That should put her back home by the time the kids were home from their twice-weekly life-skills encounter at 5:00.

The panel discussion had gone well. She was glad she had decided to set her Translation Broadcaster to "From Japanese" and had spoken Japanese during the presentation. Although there were more English-speaking attendees than Japanese, she was representing the Asian view of the tax system. Not speaking English accomplished the desired effect of adding to her credibility with the audience. After the panel discussion, she had facilitated a breakout session in which she discussed related issues with a small group of students and faculty. The session went overtime by a half hour, and although she was invigorated by the sometimes heated exchange of ideas, she was running behind. She scurried to the car.

After punching in the coordinates for the market, she settled back for the ride. En route, she commanded the onboard computer to activate. Calling up the supermarket, she amended her previous order to include a ready-made meal. As far as she was concerned, she had cooked up enough for one day.

SUMMARY: ACADEMIC WORK RECONFIGURED

A variety of indicators clearly suggests an evolution in the nature and scope of the faculty's work over the past quarter century. An increased allocation of effort to teaching (following a slide in the 1980s) is evident, including a greater focus on undergraduates (typically in larger classes). Simultaneously, a greater focus on research is reflected in the growing pervasiveness of faculty publication, which reaches well beyond the research university. These activities appear to be partially offset by a progressive diminution in administrative responsibilities (presumably a function of the increasing professionalization of academic management) and a contraction in the arena within which faculty operate as academic citizens, that is, a retreat to the department at the expense of the wider campus. Most recently, it seems that new developments in IT are accelerating the pace of functional respecialization among faculty roles and even contributing to a second-order respecialization centered around the teaching role.

Taken together, these trends suggest what amounts to a sharpening of focus— a narrowing of the scope—of faculty activities: teaching and, increasingly, research form the dyadic core, while other activities, such as administration and academic citizenship, are being relegated more and more to the periphery. Such a sharpened focus presumably is appealing to those policymakers and public officials concerned with the costs of higher education and, most particularly, the adequacy of faculty productivity. Although these developments may be viewed at first glance as "productivity enhancing," arguably boding well for American higher education, they hide beneath the surface a more momentous, less clearly defined, and surely more controversial issue. This can be described as a redefinition—albeit largely silent—of faculty work roles and the associated "stratification" of the faculty into more and more specialized groups based on the increasing popularity of nontraditional academic appointments, as examined in more detail in chapter 7.

NOTES

1. The NSOPF-88, -93, and -99 surveys distinguish explicitly in their questions between paid and unpaid work within the institution—unpaid work including such "fuzzy" items as attending student performances or exhibitions, advising a student club, and so forth. When the distinction between paid and unpaid is not made, (e.g., in Carnegie surveys), the survey tends to underestimate total weekly work hours.

2. It is not clear that faculty at different types of institutions and in different academic fields mean the same thing when they speak of research. Some in the two-year colleges and the nonuniversity four-year institutions, for example, may not distinguish funding of teaching innovations, program evaluations, and textual analyses and commentary from theoretically based empirical or experimental inquiry. In the fine arts or the clinical health sciences, research may include aspects of performance, whereas in the humanities it may include textual explication, as distinguished from the conduct of experimental work in the physical and life sciences. We should keep in mind such differences in meaning attributed to *research* as we interpret these results.

3. The phrase *delocalization* of academic work was coined by Walter Metzger in his essay "Academic Freedom in Delocalized Institutions" (1969).

4. The most recent information is available from "The 2004 National Survey of Information Technology in U.S. Higher Education," by Kenneth C. Green. The report, which provides several excellent charts, can be accessed at www.campuscomputing.net/.

CHAPTER FIVE

Academic Culture and Values and the Quality of Work Life

For three decades now, much has been made of the growing diversification of the faculty—a development universally acknowledged and widely applauded. The evidence of this substantial change is spread across chapter 3. Arguably, that demographic transformation, in both magnitude and pace, has no equivalent in the near-millennium span of higher education history. Historically, academics have shown themselves to be notoriously "normative" creatures. Their work and their careers are at once governed and enabled by a set of values and customs that hark back to the medieval guilds of Europe, emphasizing core academic values. Key among these are professional autonomy, freedom of inquiry, and verifiable testing of scientific truth. To be sure, those venerable values have been universally practiced neither in time nor in place; exceptions were not exactly rare. But "the idea of the university," as Cardinal John Newman so simply put it (Newman, 1907), and the guiding values of the academics who do the work of universities, have persisted, in the main, over time—with whatever accommodations and compromises were deemed necessary or perhaps merely expedient. The very history of higher education can be recounted as a struggle between adherence to traditional academic values and the need to operationalize them in ways responsive to a societal environment ever in flux and always dubious, in one degree or another, about the unique status of the university and its claim to special treatment. Thus the conventional wisdom that universities are doggedly slow to change is belied by their amazing adaptability and their extraordinary persistence. These qualities are perhaps best symbolized by the scores of medieval universities that endured all manner of societal upheavals—wars, plagues, church-state face-offs, depressions—to survive to this day (not always, it might be added, by having adapted with honor). But the point, for our purposes, is plain: the idea of the university has endured, and the institutional culture and the values of its practitioners, albeit with many, many variations, have persisted across the centuries.

Now we turn to a more focused examination of a tiny slice of that saga—the past three decades. When higher education is viewed from a great distance, the theme that shines through is continuity. But probed and fine-tuned, interesting subplots emerge; the persistence of institutional core values may well be undergoing testing by the unprecedented demographic diversification of the faculty, as well as the restructuring of global economic life and the effects of market pressures on the academy.

As noted earlier, academics *historically* have been a demographically homogeneous lot: white, male, and middle- or upper-class. The past thirty years have been a time not only of accelerating diversification, especially with the emergence of women and foreign nationals in the American faculty ranks, but also of fiscal pressure and, in some respects, declining opportunity. We now ask: What has diversification amid financial constraints meant for academic culture generally, and for the quality of work life in particular? To what extent has the accelerating demographic diversification of the professoriate intruded on or compromised that cultural hegemony? Has demographic diversification, as well as divergent statuses by type of academic appointment, fragmented professional culture at the very time that navigating the extraordinary turbulence of higher education's environment would seem to require a stable rudder? Has diversification brought integration—or stratification—of the work experience for different demographic subgroups of faculty?

Then, there is the matter of economic restructuring. To what extent do the trends we uncover reflect broader developments in the restructuring of work in a global, knowledge-based economy, affecting faculty no less than physicians, attorneys, or engineers? Or to what extent is there something distinctive in the case of the faculty vis-à-vis developments in the other learned professions. Moreover, it is important as well to distinguish what may be distinctive trends in America as compared with the academic profession in other nations across the globe.

In this chapter we examine the constancies and changes in the faculty's own views of the higher education enterprise, its goals, roles, and condition. Under ideal conditions, we would be able to address faculty attitudes and perceptions of their work systematically, or at least coherently, from a conceptual perspective—moving from an examination of attitudes about the content and substance of their work to perceptions of the "changing" environment (internal and external to the campus) within which that work is practiced, and then to more global assessments of their overall satisfaction with their work and careers. Although the national surveys do not proceed from a systematic conceptualization, they do nonetheless allow us to probe at once faculty perceptions of the substance of the higher education enterprise, of the quality of their work lives, especially of the state of academic freedom and tenure—traditional bellwethers of professional status—and of the overall balance between costs and benefits in their work role. Specifically, we treat in turn the importance the faculty attach to undergraduate education and their identification with its various goals; their assessments of the status of the American academic profession generally; their evaluation of their campus as a workplace, including student quality, faculty-student and collegial relationships, department operations, and administrative leadership; their understanding of their own autonomy and academic freedom and the reward system; and their political self-identification. Finally, we note how the faculty's overall assessment of their work—the quality of their work life as reflected in their self-reported job satisfaction—has shifted over these several decades. Taken together, this montage depicts a profession both clinging to some core values and adapting to emerging societal realities and their own changing composition.

INTEREST IN UNDERGRADUATE EDUCATION

Are faculty attitudes toward undergraduates and their education changing? The American faculty reports its own interest in undergraduate education (in contradistinction to research and graduate education) to be on the rise. In 1997 fully four out of five faculty members agreed "very much" or "somewhat" that faculty interest in the academic progress of undergraduate students was gaining strength, in contrast to about three out of five (61.6%) who said so in 1969 (fig. 5.1). Moreover, the proportion of faculty agreeing "strongly" more than doubled over the past three decades (from 18.9% to 40.4%). And agreement has risen consistently throughout the higher education enterprise: across all institutional types (including university faculty, although by lesser margins than faculty at other four-year and two-year institutions) and program areas, and among both men and women (although, absolutely speaking, women consistently express support for undergraduate education by some 10% more than do men).

This ascent of interest in undergraduate education, though widespread, varies across the higher education spectrum. Demography shapes faculty perceptions here. Women academics, traditionally more student- and teaching-oriented than men, report greater interest in undergraduate education (by some

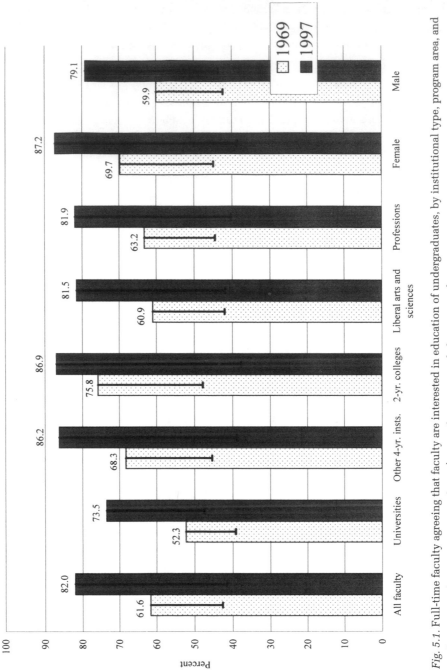

Fig. 5.1. Full-time faculty agreeing that faculty are interested in education of undergraduates, by institutional type, program area, and gender, 1969 and 1997. Note: area above]: strongly agree; area below: somewhat agree.

10%) than men do. Among racial subgroups, Asian faculty are about 10% less likely than white and 5% less likely than other nonwhite faculty members to report an increased focus on undergraduate education, although their interest has strengthened over the past generation (table A-5.1). Differences are also visible generationally. Senior faculty are more likely, albeit slightly, to express interest in undergraduate education than are newer faculty.

The claim of increased interest in undergraduates based on attitudinal shifts appears to be translating into *behavioral* support for the assessment and improvement of undergraduate teaching. In 1997 nearly two-fifths (38%) of the faculty reported the introduction of new methods in their departments for evaluating teaching; this is roughly three times the number of faculty who perceived new developments for evaluating faculty in areas other than teaching (table A-5.2). And those reports were consistent across institutional types, academic fields, and faculty career cohorts.

VIEWS OF THE PRIMACY OF RESEARCH

Concurrent with this apparent rise in faculty interest in undergraduates, a powerful countervailing trend is unmistakable: a clear faculty perception of the increasing importance of research and publication for purposes of promotion and tenure. The proportion of faculty agreeing that it is difficult to attain tenure without research or publications rose steadily from about two in five (39.9%) in 1969 to nearly two-thirds (65.0%) by 1997 (fig. 5.2). (The proportion "strongly" agreeing more than doubled during the same period). Moreover, that increase has coexisted with a persistently high endorsement of teaching effectiveness as the primary criterion for promotion. Table A-5.3 demonstrates that the increased focus on research was most striking at four-year colleges *outside* the university sector: nearly two-thirds (63.8%) now agree, versus just one-fifth (19.8%) three decades earlier. Thus, a pivotal sector of higher education that several decades ago had only marginally bought into the expectation of research and publication as a crucial gatekeeping function for admission into the "guild" has tilted heavily in that direction.

The professed interest in undergraduates, bolstered by some behavioral evidence, is rising—even as research and publication pressures have been steadily mounting. One reasonable interpretation is the conventional perception that in the current environment of higher education, faculty are expected to do more—of everything.

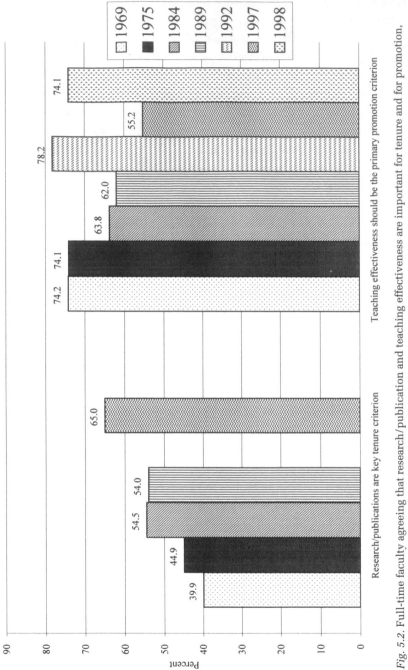

Fig. 5.2. Full-time faculty agreeing that research/publication and teaching effectiveness are important for tenure and for promotion, 1969–1998.

VIEWS OF THE GOALS OF UNDERGRADUATE EDUCATION

Although interest in undergraduate education seems to be rising, genuinely, in importance (long overdue, some would say), even amid the pressures promoting research and publication, the question remains whether faculty views of the thrust and substance of undergraduate education are in flux. Here we ask, How have faculty views of the goals of undergraduate education changed? In fact, a remarkably consistent agreement on four key goals is evident (table 5.1). More than 90% of all faculty endorse the dual objectives of "a broad liberal arts education" and "increasing tolerance for diversity." More than 80% consistently endorse the goals of "career preparation," "developing moral values," and "in-depth knowledge of one subject" (fig. 5.3). Meanwhile, faculty seem to have lost some interest in two goals that traditionally have been highly valued among academic imperatives: the preparation for graduate and professional school (importance rating down from three-fourths to one-half) and the in-depth knowledge of one subject and tolerance for diversity (both down by 5%). Although the decline of graduate school as a guiding force to undergraduate education is certainly understandable in light of the widely perceived decline in the opportunity structure of academic careers (that is, an awful academic marketplace in most fields), the slight drop in the goals of in-depth knowledge of a single subject and diversity tolerance is less understandable. Has the diversity imperative lost support because of its striking success? Or has the anti–affirmative action backlash that has surfaced in recent years taken a toll?

Devotion among academic subgroups to the importance of a broad liberal arts education, always uneven, and historically the province of the freestanding liberal arts college, appears to be rising across all institutional types (table A-5.4). The two-year public community colleges, once bastions of career preparation, appear to be strengthening their commitment to a broad liberal arts education as they enhance their transfer function. Much of the rest of higher education seems to be divided by program area, race, and gender. Thus, unsurprisingly, broad exposure to the liberal arts is a more common objective among the arts and sciences fields than in the professions. Concomitantly, faculty in the professions are more likely than their liberal arts colleagues to endorse "career preparation" and "developing moral values" as critical—again hardly surprising. The one striking exception is provided by faculty in the health sciences who are significantly *more likely* than even their humanities colleagues to emphasize the "development of moral values" as a central goal of undergraduate education (table A-5.8).

Full-Time Faculty Rating Various Goals of Undergraduate Education as Important, 1969–1997
(percent)

	1969	1975	1984	1989	1997	Change in % 1975–97
Broad liberal arts education[a,b]	—	86.7	89.8	91.0	90.9	4.2
Fairly important		49.7	42.7	41.0	42.2	−7.5
Very important		37.0	47.1	50.0	48.7	11.7
Career preparation[a,c]	—	84.5	77.9	75.0	88.1	3.6
Fairly important		46.7	43.4	44.0	43.1	−3.6
Very important		37.8	34.5	31.0	45.0	7.2
In-depth knowledge of one subject[a,d]	—	85.9	81.3	77.8	80.6	−5.3
Fairly important		50.8	47.9	46.0	48.0	−2.8
Very important		35.1	33.4	32.0	32.5	−2.6
Developing moral values[a,e]	—	82.3	79.4	85.0	83.8	1.5
Fairly important		36.3	38.3	44.0	36.3	0.0
Very important		46.0	41.0	41.0	47.5	1.5
Increasing tolerance for diversity[a,f]	—	95.7	93.6	—	91.3	−4.4
Fairly important		31.4	31.7	—	31.1	−0.3
Very important		64.3	61.9	—	60.2	−4.1
Preparation for graduate school						
Important (only one degree of response)	79.4	—	—	50.7	—	—

Sources: Carn-69, CFAT-75, CFAT-84, CFAT-89, CFAT-97 (see Appendix A for key).
Notes: For definitions of row and column label terms, see Appendix E.
1969: N = 302, 585; 1975: N = 20,788; 1984: N = 4,479; 1989: N = 9,666; 1997: N = 4,430.
[a]The item reads, "Many goals have been proposed for undergraduate education. On the following list, please indicate how important you consider each of the following possible outcomes for the undergraduate." The results combine responses of "very important" and "fairly important" on a 4-point scale (very important, fairly important, fairly unimportant, very unimportant).
[b]The item numbers for the surveys are CFAT-75, item 48a; CFAT-84, item 34-1; CFAT-89, item 32a; and CFAT-97, item 55a; and the goal is "Appreciation of literature and the arts."
[c]The item numbers for the surveys are CFAT-75, item 48e; CFAT-84, item 34-5; CFAT-89, item 32e; and CFAT-97, item 55d; and the goal is "Preparation for a career."
[d]The item numbers for the surveys are CFAT-75, item 48h; CFAT-84, item 34-8; and CFAT-97, item 55g; and the goal is "Knowledge of a subject in depth."
[e]The item numbers for the surveys are CFAT-75, item 48b; CFAT-84, item 34-2; CFAT-89, item 32b; and CFAT-97, item 55b; and the goal is "Firm moral values."
[f]The item numbers for the surveys are CFAT-75, item 48f; CFAT-84, item 34-6; and CFAT-97, item 55e; and the goal is "Tolerance of diversity."

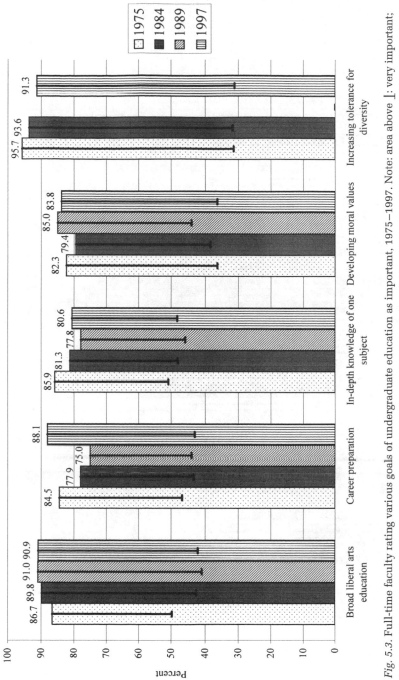

Fig. 5.3. Full-time faculty rating various goals of undergraduate education as important, 1975–1997. Note: area above ⌊: very important; below: fairly important.

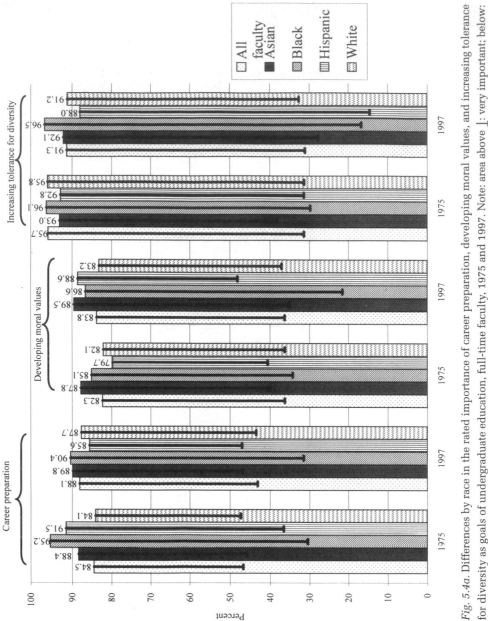

Fig. 5.4a. Differences by race in the rated importance of career preparation, developing moral values, and increasing tolerance for diversity as goals of undergraduate education, full-time faculty, 1975 and 1997. Note: area above ⌉: very important; below: fairly important.

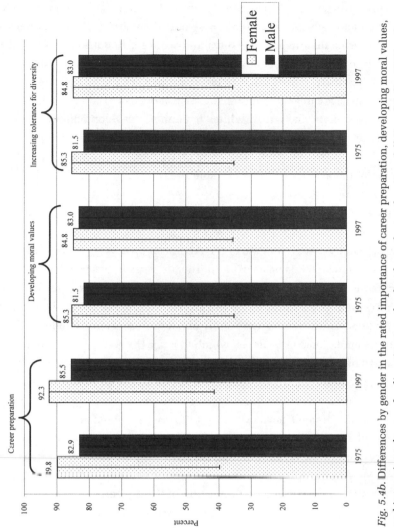

Fig. 5.4b. Differences by gender in the rated importance of career preparation, developing moral values, and increasing tolerance for diversity as goals of undergraduate education, full-time faculty, 1975 and 1997. Note: area above ⌐: very important; below: fairly important.

Academic women and blacks are significantly more likely to endorse the "broad liberal arts education" (table A-5.4) and "diversity" (figs. 5.4a and 5.4b, table A-5.5) goals than men and Asians and whites are. Both groups are also more likely to endorse career-development-related goals (table A-5.6). Thus, perhaps surprisingly, it is women rather than men who are about 10% more likely to emphasize career preparation (fig. 5.4b, table A-5.6) and minorities who are nearly 10% more likely than whites to support "development of in-depth knowledge of a single subject" (table A-5.7). Moreover, minority faculty diverge slightly (about 5%) from majority faculty in placing greater emphasis on the "development of moral values" (fig. 5.4a, table A-5.8).

VIEWS OF THE CURRENT STATE OF THE PROFESSORIATE

How do faculty assess the state of the American professoriate generally and the direction in which it is headed? Most directly, the surveys have persistently elicited the extent of faculty agreement with the item "Respect for the academic profession is declining"; less directly, but no less importantly, the surveys have persistently queried the faculty about their academic freedom. There is no more foundational criterion by which to judge the quality of academic life than faculty members' sense of academic freedom, and so the extent to which pessimism about the American academic profession may be linked to concerns about this most basic building block of the profession is revealing. The national surveys over the decades have asked faculty members about two vital dimensions of academic freedom: their sense of freedom to express ideas in class and their perception of the extent of administrative support of academic freedom (see fig. 5.5).

Concerns are widespread. The proportion of faculty perceiving that the status of the academic profession has declined rose substantially from just over one-half in 1969 to nearly three-quarters in 1997. Moreover, and perhaps more unexpectedly, there is a large, commensurate decline in faculty reporting that they are free to express their ideas in class (from 83.9% to 62.9%) and that the administration is supportive of academic freedom (76.1% to 55.3%). This troubling perception of a weakened environment for academic work is evident across all institutional types (table A-5.9), but the decline is steepest at research universities, which historically have been more sanguine about the status of the profession. Perceptions of decline have risen more among the traditional arts and sciences faculty than in the professions (the undisputed growth sector in American higher education) and, tellingly, more among new entrants than senior faculty (although the new entrants lack the longer-view perspective that

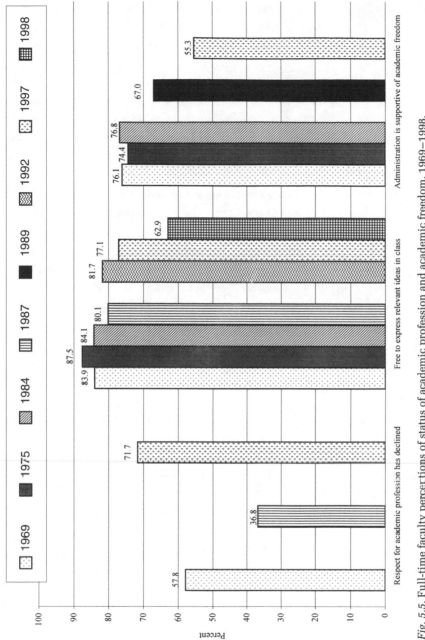

Fig. 5.5. Full-time faculty perceptions of status of academic profession and academic freedom, 1969–1998.

their more experienced colleagues have, their briefer experience has been marked by a less sanguine outlook).

As to perceptions of academic freedom, whereas a solid majority (two-thirds) of faculty report general satisfaction with their freedom of expression in class, that nonetheless constitutes a sharp decline, in the neighborhood of 20%, over the past quarter century. And the extent to which faculty have been losing confidence in administrative support for academic freedom can be clearly seen: the proportion of faculty who perceive administrative support for academic freedom has eroded, over several decades, from nearly four in five to less than two-thirds (fig. 5.5).

How widespread are these perceptions across various faculty subgroups? The answer: widespread. A loss of confidence is pervasively evident across institutional types and fields and across faculty demographic groups (tables A-5.9, A-5.10, A-5.11). As might be expected, given the relatively greater security of their positions, senior faculty are slightly more likely to have confidence in administrative support for academic freedom on their campus than are junior (read, more vulnerable) faculty. However, faculty at the research universities and liberal arts colleges are no more likely than their colleagues at the two-year colleges to express a relatively greater sense of control and freedom.

What is the source of that loss of confidence? Although the data are not clear, and although this is not the place to speculate more broadly on the sources of the perceived decline of the American academic profession, it does appear that faculty are responding to the increasing commodification and commercialization of higher education and the perceived decline of purely academic values (see chapter 10 for fuller discussion).

APPRAISALS OF WORK LIFE: STUDENTS, COLLEAGUES, THE ACADEMIC DEPARTMENT, AND ADMINISTRATORS

If faculty continue to feel, at the least, ambivalent about the prospects for the academic profession writ large, what do they say about the work life they experience? Are the complaints and the laments for some long-ago "golden era" nothing more than nostalgia? Or maybe an illusion altogether? Or do these longings reflect a genuine decline in the quality of academic work life? And are these perceptions, whatever their basis in fact, largely shared across the profession? Or has increasing stratification within the profession brought with it a divergence of work-life quality as experienced by different classes of faculty? The national faculty surveys provide a wide variety of items that bear on this "quality of work life" question, including faculty perceptions of student quality, both undergraduate and graduate; of personal relations among faculty and between faculty and students; of "equity" for underrepresented groups in the workplace; of their own academic home, that is, their department unit; and more broadly, of the administration and management of their own institution. Taken together, this array of work-life dimensions constitutes the character of the workplace, including its functioning as a community and the faculty's role within it.

We examine first the faculty's perceptions of student relationships and colleague congeniality, and then their views of equity, department operations, and institutional leadership. Table 5.2 reveals a pattern of relative stability in collegial relationships and in faculty-student relations: the Carnegie data suggest a modest decline in the 1970s and 1980s in the quality of interpersonal relations among faculty, followed by an upswing in the 1990s. The vast majority of faculty—about four of five—continue to rate their relations with students as good (although the proportion rating their relationships as "excellent" has declined perceptibly). Moreover, over the last generation, faculty are reporting a dramatic change for the better as far as equity in the workplace is concerned: thus, four-fifths of all faculty (but not four-fifths of women or four-fifths of nonwhites) now agree that equity exists for women faculty and for minority faculty. Academic women are less sanguine in their assessments than their male colleagues: they continue to be 20% less likely than men to perceive equitable treatment. Moreover, the percentage of women *strongly* agreeing that gender equity has been achieved is only half that of men (fig. 5.6a). In the case of minority faculty, the proportion reporting equitable treatment has remained constant—although, as in the cases of women, the proportion who "strongly" agree about equitable treatment of minority faculty has declined over the past decade (fig. 5.6b). The single area in which faculty provide a clear negative report is in administration and institutional management: the bare majority reporting satisfaction with administration in 1975 has been lost; some 55% are now *not* satisfied.

Indeed, the American faculty has become much more diverse in terms of race or ethnicity and gender during the past three decades. Not surprisingly, the faculty's perceptions of equitable treatment of women and minorities have changed significantly during the same period. As late as 1975, fewer than one faculty member in four reported that either women or minority colleagues were treated fairly. By the 1990s, however, that proportion had flip-flopped: three of four faculty members perceived that their female colleagues and their minority colleagues were being treated equitably. These perceptions hold, with minor variations, across all institutional types and all academic fields (table A-5.12). Differences do emerge, however, across racial lines: minority faculty consistently perceive less equity than white faculty (fig. 5.6b). Moreover, while male-

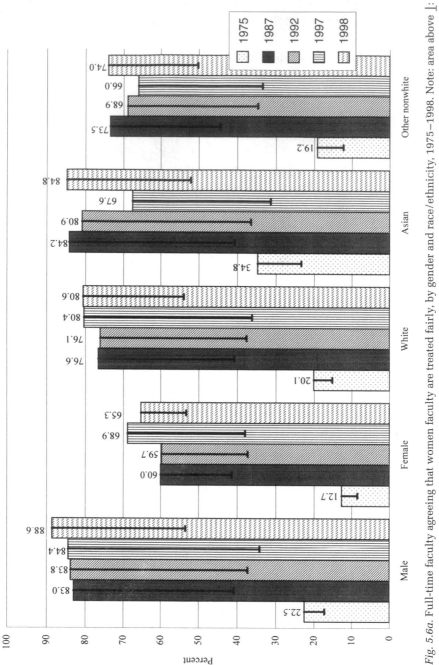

Fig. 5.6a. Full-time faculty agreeing that women faculty are treated fairly, by gender and race/ethnicity, 1975–1998. Note: area above ⌐: strongly agree; below: somewhat agree.

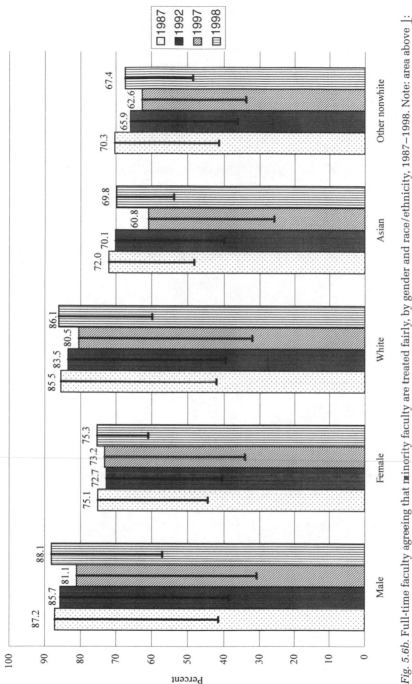

Fig. 5.6b. Full-time faculty agreeing that minority faculty are treated fairly, by gender and race/ethnicity, 1987–1998. Note: area above]: strongly agree; below: somewhat agree.

TABLE 5.2
Full-Time Faculty Perceptions of Intracampus Relations, 1969–1998
(percent)

	1969	1975	1984	1987	1989	1992	1997	1998	Change in %[a]
Department Level									
Faculty/student relations are good/excellent[b]	80.7	82.2	—	—	—	—	78.1	—	-2.4
Good	(56.0)	(55.4)					(59.9)		3.9
Excellent	(24.7)	(26.8)					(18.2)		-6.5
Personal relations among faculty are good/excellent[c]	73.9	69.8	65.5	—	—	—	81.1	—	7.2
Good	(43.8)	(42.1)	(43.1)				(41.4)		-2.4
Excellent	(30.1)	(27.7)	(22.4)				(39.7)		9.6
Campus Level									
The administration is good/excellent[d]	52.2	36.5	33.7	57.0	36.0	—	46.5	—	-5.7
Good	(42.0)	(31.5)	(29.3)	(39.8)			(34.5)		-7.5
Excellent	(10.2)	(5.0)	(4.4)	(17.2)			(12.0)		1.8
The sense of community on campus is good/excellent[e]	—	—	—	—	37.0	—	26.9	—	—
Somewhat agree							(22.0)		
Strongly agree							(4.9)		
Women faculty are treated fairly[f]	—	20.3	—	76.7	—	75.8	78.5	80.2	59.9
Somewhat agree		(15.2)		(41.0)		(37.3)	(35.6)	(53.4)	38.2
Strongly agree		(5.1)		(35.7)		(38.5)	(43.0)	(26.8)	21.7
Minority faculty are treated fairly[g]	—	—	—	84.0	—	81.4	78.1	83.5	-0.4
Somewhat agree				(42.4)		(39.3)	(32.0)	(58.4)	16.0
Strongly agree				(41.6)		(42.1)	(46.1)	(25.1)	-16.5

Sources: Carn-69, CFAT-75, CFAT-84, NSOPF-88, CFAT-89, NSOPF-93, CFAT-97, NSOPF-99 (see Appendix A for key).

Notes: 1969: N = 302,585; 1975: N = 20,788; 1984: N = 4,479; 1987: N = 491,500; 1989: N = 9,666; 1992: N = 495,061; 1997: N = 4,430; 1998: N = 483,690. Parentheses denote subsets of larger percentages.

[a] The time period covered by the % change varies by row, depending on the initial availability of data from the various surveys for the item in question.

[b] Carn-69 (item 75o), CFAT-75 (item 45n), and CFAT-97 (item 58i) read, "How would you rate the following: Faculty/student relations in your department." Reported results combine responses of "excellent" and "good" on a 4-point scale (excellent, good, fair, poor).

[c] Carn-69 (item 75n), CFAT-75 (item 45m), and CFAT-84 (item 47–10) read, "How would you rate the following: Personal relations among faculty in your department." Reported results combine responses of "excellent" and "good" on a 4-point scale (excellent, good, fair, poor). CFAT-97 (item 21d) reads, "To what extent are you satisfied with the following aspect of your job: Relationships with colleagues." Reported result combines responses of "very satisfied" and "somewhat satisfied" on a 5-point scale (very satisfied, somewhat satisfied, neutral, somewhat dissatisfied, very dissatisfied).

[d] Carn-69 (item 75h), CFAT-75 (item 45h), and CFAT-84 (item 47–8), and CFAT-89 (item 40g) read, "How would you rate the following: The administration at your institution." For Carn-69, CFAT-75, and CFAT-84, reported results combine responses of "excellent" and "good" on a 4-point scale. For CFAT-89, reported result combines responses of "excellent" and "good" on a 5-point scale (excellent, good, fair, poor, not applicable). NSOPF-88 (item 19p) reads, "How satisfied or dissatisfied do you personally feel about each of the following aspects of your job at this institution? Quality of chief administrative officers at this campus." Reported result combines responses of "somewhat satisfied" and "very satisfied" on a 4-point scale (very dissatisfied, somewhat dissatisfied, somewhat satisfied, very satisfied, and a category for "does not apply"). CFAT-97 (item 52a) reads, "Please indicate how you feel about the following statement which relates to management and the decision-making process: Top-level administrators are providing competent leadership." Reported result combines responses of "strongly agree" and "somewhat agree" on a 5-point scale (strongly agree, somewhat agree, neutral, somewhat disagree, strongly disagree).

[e] CFAT-89 (item 40i) and CFAT-97 (item 58e) read, "How would you rate each of the following at your institution: The sense of campus community." Reported results combine responses of "excellent" and "good" on a 4-point scale (excellent, good, fair, poor).

[f] CFAT-75 (item 9ii) reads, "Please indicate your agreement or disagreement with the following statement: On the whole, women have not been discriminated against in academic life." Reported results combine responses of "strongly agree" and "agree with reservations" on a 4-point scale (strongly agree, agree with reservations, disagree with reservations, strongly disagree). NSOPF-88 (item 48l), NSOPF-93 (item F59e), CFAT-97 (item 59b), and NSOPF-99 (item 92f) read, "Please indicate your agreement or disagreement with the following statement: Female faculty are treated fairly at this institution." For NSOPF-88, reported result combines responses of "strongly agree" and "somewhat agree" on a 4-point scale (strongly agree, somewhat agree, somewhat disagree, strongly disagree.) For NSOPF-93, reported result combines responses of "agree somewhat" and "agree strongly" on a 4-point scale (disagree strongly, disagree somewhat, agree somewhat, agree strongly). For CFAT-97, reported result combines responses of "strongly agree" and "somewhat agree" on a 5-point scale (strongly disagree, disagree, agree, strongly agree). For NSOPF-99, reported result combines responses of "strongly agree" and "somewhat agree" on a 4-point scale (strongly disagree, disagree, agree, strongly agree).

[g] NSOPF-88 (48m), NSOPF-93 (F59f), CFAT-97 (item 59a), and NSOPF-99 (item 92g) read, "Please indicate your agreement or disagreement with the following statement: Faculty who are members of racial or ethnic minorities are treated fairly at this institution." Reported results combine responses of "agree somewhat" and "agree strongly" on a 4-point scale (disagree strongly, disagree somewhat, agree somewhat, agree strongly)." For CFAT-97, reported result combines responses of "strongly agree" and "somewhat agree" on a 5-point scale (strongly agree, somewhat agree, neutral, somewhat disagree, strongly disagree). For NSOPF-99, reported result combines responses of "agree" and "strongly agree" on a 4-point scale (strongly disagree, disagree, agree, strongly agree).

female differences in the perception of gender and racial equity were modest in 1975, by the 1990s the disparity had widened (although both groups acknowledged significantly greater equity than had their earlier counterparts) (figs. 5.6a and 5.6b). These more positive perceptions of the equity accorded women and minority scholars are reflected, at least in the case of women, by the increased proportion agreeing that faculty relations on campus are good. By 1998 academic women were 5% *more* likely than men to report good relations on campus (women were about 5% *less* likely than men to do so in 1969) (table A-5.13).

The overall portrait of positive relationships and congenial department life, however, masks some clear lines of cleavage. Most prominent are the differences evident among institutional types. The freestanding liberal arts college emerges alone, although occasionally in tandem with the community college, as a bastion of "community" in academic life. Faculty at liberal arts colleges, compared to their counterparts at other types of institutions, consistently report better relations with students and with colleagues (table A-5.13) and a higher institutional priority on developing a sense of campus community (table A-5.14). Differences among academic fields, although discernible, are uniformly smaller than among institutional types.

Within the campus, differences along both racial and gender lines appear to be shrinking. By 1997 women were more likely than men to report developing a "sense of campus community" as an institutional priority (table A-5.14) and also to report that good relations obtained with faculty colleagues (table A-5.13) and with students (table A-5.15). Minority faculty, who were much less likely (by some 10% to 20%) to report good relations with colleagues in the 1970s and 1980s, by 1997 were reporting perceptions of colleague relations on a par with white faculty (table A-5.13).

Administration and institutional management remains the single very widespread area of concern for most faculty—although even here there are minor cleavages (table A-5.16). Among institutional types, liberal arts colleges are the exception: their faculties actually report *increased* satisfaction with administrative leadership and thereby stand out from the pack. University faculty have lost confidence to the greatest degree. Women and non-Asian minorities are significantly more satisfied with administrative leadership than males and white faculty, respectively, a reversal of earlier patterns and a function perhaps of their view of administrators as a "defense" or bulwark for enforcement of equity values and regulations. Similarly, junior faculty are more satisfied than senior faculty, a reversal of historic patterns.

POLITICAL VIEWS

In their landmark 1975 volume *The Divided Academy,* Ladd and Lipset presented a portrait of a disproportionately politically liberal profession that defied the iron rule of political science that political orientation was shaped heavily by "class interest." The rule says that those toward the bottom rungs of the socioeconomic status ladder are likely to be more liberal, whereas those toward the top tilt toward conservativism. Among American academics, those in the top stratum of the conventional hierarchy of institutions (professors at the research universities) have tended to be the most liberal, while those at the bottom (the "lesser" four-year institutions and the community colleges) have been more conservative. Moreover, Ladd and Lipset found that one's academic field was a powerful determinant of political orientation: faculty in the professions leaned toward conservative views, and those in the arts and sciences (except for the natural sciences) were more liberal.

The ability to track the professoriate's political predilections is limited by the unwillingness of some surveyors to raise questions about faculty members' political (or religious) leanings. Thus the U.S. Department of Education's faculty surveys (those of 1988, 1993, and 1999) have assiduously steered clear of such potentially sensitive items. Inquiring minds will need to look elsewhere. However, surveys by the Carnegie Foundation for the Advancement of Teaching are helpful here. Together, as seen in figure 5.7, they suggest that the basic pattern discernible in the past quarter century since the immediate post–Vietnam war era has become more accentuated. Now nearly three-fifths of faculty describe themselves as "liberal," basically another one-quarter as conservative, and the rest (barely one-fifth) as "middle of the road." There has been a slight shrinkage both at the conservative ideological extreme and in the middle and a discernible drift to the left (just as the general public was moving to the center of American politics in the 1990s).

Figure 5.8 suggests that the leftward shift is largely accounted for by the infusion of academic women. Liberal political views have been on the decline among new-entry males, but they have sharply increased for new-entry females (yielding a "gender gap" of about 20% in the percentage characterizing themselves as liberal). Similarly, among midcareer and senior faculty who came of age during the Vietnam war, it is the females who are more liberal, though by a smaller margin (two-thirds of the women, about one-half of the men). Moreover, although some portion of this gender gap may be attributable to differences in the gender makeup of academic fields, we can see from the data in table A-5.17

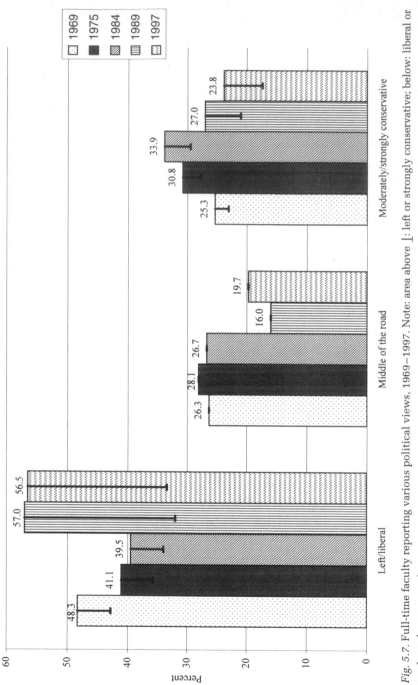

Fig. 5.7. Full-time faculty reporting various political views, 1969–1997. Note: area above ⌐: left or strongly conservative; below: liberal or moderately conservative.

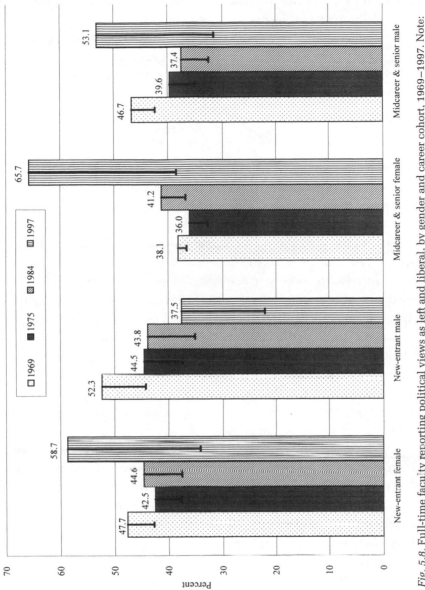

Fig. 5.8. Full-time faculty reporting political views as left and liberal, by gender and career cohort, 1969–1997. Note: area above ⌐: left; below: liberal.

that women's distinctively stronger liberalism persists across all academic fields, with the exception of education.

Political orientation also boasts a race and minority gap. Among racial and ethnic groups, blacks and Hispanics tend to be the most liberal, while Asians are the most conservative compared with whites (table A-5.17). Here, academic field appears to account for more of the variance.

JOB SATISFACTION

Over the years faculty members have been queried, on many national surveys, about their level of satisfaction with many aspects of their work, from their compensation to their role in governance, from the manageability of their workload to the clarity of what is expected of them for tenure and promotion, and so on. Often the surveys contain one or two summative items that attempt to gauge how satisfying faculty members find their work (their jobs) and, similarly but more expansively, their career in academe. Plotting these levels of satisfaction or frustration over time provides a succinct if crude measure of the quality of the life academic and, in that sense, the health of the academic profession.

The starting point for this trend-line analysis is not a happy one: faculty job satisfaction has eroded significantly over the past generation (fig. 5.9). Whereas about half the faculty characterized themselves as "very satisfied" both in 1969 (48.1%) and 1975 (50.3%), that figure skidded over the subsequent decades to about one-third: 35.5% in 1987, 36.7% in 1992, 33.8% in 1997, and 38% in 1998.[1] Moreover, the proportion of faculty who reported that they were dissatisfied (either "somewhat" or "very") essentially doubled from one in roughly fourteen a generation ago (8.9% in 1969, 7.2% in 1975) to one in seven more recently (14.7% in 1988, 15.8% in 1993, 15.1% in 1997, and 15.3% in 1998).

The decline in job satisfaction appears to have permeated the faculty. Figure 5.10 indicates that even for tenured faculty, the proportions reporting high levels of satisfaction declined sharply from the era of the earlier surveys to the more recent ones *in all institution types.* At the other extreme of the scale, however, the proportion of tenured faculty members reporting that they were "very dissatisfied" remained at very low levels across all of the surveys for all institution types. Among faculty members with tenure, those at two-year colleges tended to express the highest levels of satisfaction. In fact, the most recent surveys— the 1993 and 1999 NSOPF and 1997 Carnegie—show the community college faculty reporting very high levels of satisfaction. More than half of tenured community college faculty (51.1%) reported in 1997–98 that they were "very satisfied" with their "job situation as a whole," far outstripping the proportion of

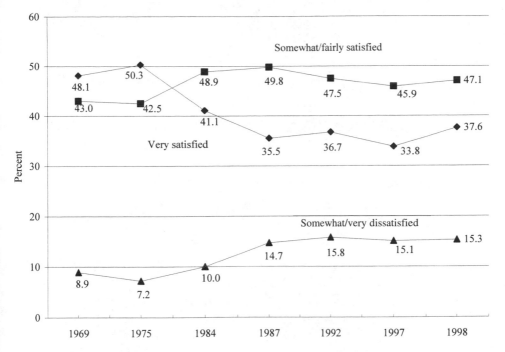

Fig. 5.9. Full-time faculty satisfied with their job, 1969–1998. Data from Carn-69, CFAT-75, CFAT- 84, NSOPF-88, NSOPF-93, CFAT-97, and NSOPF-99.

such contented faculty at the four-year institutions: about one-third at the research universities (33.5%) and liberal arts colleges (34.2%), roughly one-fourth at the comprehensives (26.9%), and an even smaller proportion at the other doctorate granting universities (22.8%).

Women faculty have tended to report marginally greater satisfaction levels than have their male colleagues—although two NSOPF surveys (1988, 1993) showed the opposite. For both genders, however, the proportion of highly satisfied faculty has receded significantly since the 1969 and 1975 markers (table A-5.19a), and, correspondingly, the proportion who reported that they were somewhat or very dissatisfied nearly doubled over the same span of years (table A-5.19b).

Turning to breakouts by race and ethnicity, a comparison of Caucasian to all non-Caucasian faculty (table A-5.19c) shows that the latter have tended to be significantly less satisfied than the former—a gap that is apparent for both genders, that is, in comparing minority to majority males and minority to majority females. The differentials for the most recent surveys, however, suggest a considerable attenuation of the white-nonwhite gap. Thus, by 1997 and 1998, the

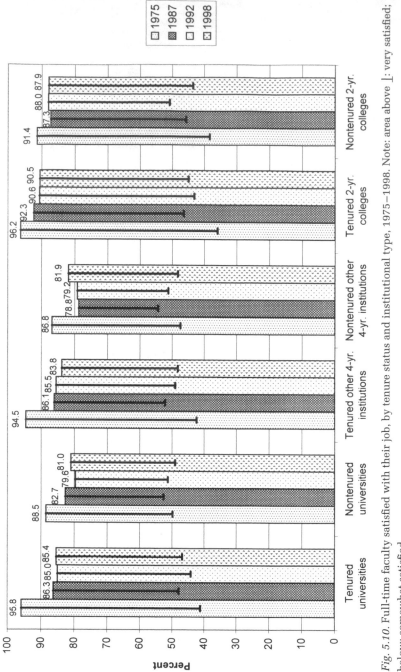

Fig. 5.10. Full-time faculty satisfied with their job, by tenure status and institutional type, 1975–1998. Note: area above |: very satisfied; below: somewhat satisfied.

gap in satisfaction between majority and minority faculty reported a generation earlier had largely been bridged—unfortunately via the route of everyone reporting lower satisfaction!

The general decline in satisfaction appears to be a function in part of increasing workload, in particular, research and publication pressures (tables 5.3a, 5.3b). The data suggest that it may also be attributable to salary. Although junior faculty report slightly higher satisfaction with salary since 1969, senior faculty report a significant decline since 1969—a decline nearly perfectly commensurate in magnitude with their decline in overall job satisfaction (some 10% to 12%). These generational differences appear to reflect the empirical trends in faculty compensation documented in greater detail in chapter 8. Academic compensation has declined relative to salaries in other professions, especially at the later career end rather than at the entry level; and this relative decline has occurred just as research pressures have increased and the organizational influence of the faculty has decreased—certainly a recipe for declining job satisfaction levels.

This finding parallels faculty perceptions at all but the elite research universities of a decline in institutional academic support, in overall resources, and in real compensation, and a less significant role for faculty in the governance of increasingly "managed" campuses (Rhoades, 1998). Decline aside, tenured faculty are still slightly more satisfied in absolute terms than their nontenured colleagues. As tenured faculty members become less satisfied, though, their degree of unhappiness appears to be converging with that of their probationary and non-tenure-track colleagues. Indeed, the "satisfaction gap" appears to be narrowing in most sectors: the divide between tenured and untenured faculty closed almost entirely at the nonresearch doctorate-granting and, to a lesser extent, at the research and comprehensive campuses. At the community colleges the gap, while remaining quite wide, narrowed the most. The picture at the liberal arts colleges is different; in that sector the gap continues essentially unchanged. But in all instances—and this is the important point—the narrowing phenomenon is attributable to the considerably smaller numbers of tenured faculty who express high satisfaction with their jobs. That is, the diminished morale among tenured faculty propels them lower on the satisfaction scale, toward the levels of their less established colleagues. As for the liberal arts colleges, there, too, despite little change in the gap, all types of faculty—tenured, probationary, and tenure-ineligible—report sharp drop-offs in satisfaction.

In sum, variations in the amount and rate of decline in satisfaction are evident. But the overall finding is unsettling: in all facets of academic life—by institutional type, by field, by gender, by race, and by tenure status—job satisfac-

TABLE 5.3A

Full-Time Faculty Satisfied with Various Job Aspects, by Tenure Status, 1969–1998

(percent)

Job Aspect	1969	1975	1984	1987	1992	1997	1998	Change in % 1975–97 (CFAT)	Change in % 1987–98 (NSOPF)
Job overall[a]	91.0	92.7	90.0	85.2	84.3	91.9	84.7	-0.8	-0.5
Tenured	—	95.4	91.3	87.3	86.4	93.5	86.0	-1.9	-1.3
Nontenured	—	88.4	86.6	82.1	81.3	88.4	83.0	0.0	0.9
Workload	—	—	—	72.8	68.7	—	67.2	—	-5.6
Tenured	—	—	—	73.5	70.6		68.0		-5.5
Nontenured	—	—	—	71.8	66.1		66.0		-5.8
Job security	—	—	—	84.0	81.5	81.1	83.6	—	-0.4
Tenured	—	—	—	96.5	93.9	90.5	94.7		-1.8
Nontenured	—	—	—	65.1	64.4	60.1	68.7		3.6
Advancement opportunities	—	—	—	69.1	69.6	56.2	72.0	—	2.9
Tenured	—	—	—	74.3	76.2	58.0	78.5		4.2
Nontenured	—	—	—	62.3	60.5	53.4	63.5		1.3
Time for keeping current in field	—	—	—	—	47.8	—	50.9	—	
Tenured	—	—	—	—	51.3		51.9		
Nontenured	—	—	—	—	43.1		49.7		
Freedom for consulting	—	—	—	89.3	79.6	—	84.6	—	-4.7
Tenured	—	—	—	91.6	82.8		86.3		-5.3
Nontenured	—	—	—	85.8	75.1		82.4		-3.4

Salary[b]	56.0	44.1	40.2	58.3	54.2	49.1	57.3	5.0	−1.0
Tenured	—	49.8	43.0	59.4	57.3	53.1	60.6	3.3	1.2
Nontenured	—	35.2	32.2	56.6	50.0	39.6	52.8	4.4	−3.8
Benefits	—	—	—	76.5	74.5	—	77.9	—	1.4
Tenured				76.5	75.2		78.9		2.4
Nontenured				76.4	73.6		76.4		0.0
Spouse employment opportunities	—	—	—	73.2	73.3	—	76.6	—	3.4
Tenured				74.0	76.2		77.5		3.5
Nontenured				71.9	69.2		75.3		3.4

Sources: Carn-69, CFAT-75, CFAT-84, NSOPF-88, NSOPF-93, CFAT-97, NSOPF-99 (see Appendix A for key).

Notes: Respondents were considered "satisfied" if they marked one of the two highest categories in the scale used to evaluate each particular item.

Item wording: For the NSOPF questionnaires, data reported combine "somewhat satisfied" and "very satisfied" on a 4-point scale (very dissatisfied, somewhat dissatisfied, somewhat satisfied, very satisfied). For the CFAT questionnaires, data reported combine the two highest categories out of three and four, respectively, for overall job satisfaction and satisfaction with salary, and the two highest categories out of five for satisfaction with job security and advancement opportunities.

1969: *N* = 337,250; 1975: *N* = 20,739; 1984: *N* = 4,313; 1987: *N* = 489,260; 1992: *N* = 476,328; 1997: *N* = 4,444; 1998: *N* = 483,690.

[a]The CFAT questionnaire asked respondents, "In general, how do you feel about this institution?" Valid response alternatives were "It is a very good place for me," "It is a fairly good place for me," and "It is not the place for me." The NSOPF questionnaire asked, "How satisfied or dissatisfied do you personally feel about each of the following aspects of your job at this institution? My job here, overall." Valid response alternatives were "very dissatisfied," "somewhat dissatisfied," "somewhat satisfied," and "very satisfied."

[b]The CFAT quesionnaire asked respondents, "How would you rate your own salary?" Valid responses were "excellent," "good," "fair," and "poor." The NSOPF questionnaire asked, "How satisfied or dissatisfied do you personally feel about each of the following aspects of your job at this institution? My salary." Valid response alternatives were "very dissatisfied," "somewhat dissatisfied," "somewhat satisfied," and "very satisfied."

TABLE 5.3B

Full-Time Faculty Satisfied with Various Job Aspects, by Career Cohort, 1969–1998
(percent)

Job Aspect	1969	1975	1984	1987	1992	1997	1998	Change in % 1975–97 (CFAT)	Change in % 1987–98 (NSOPF)
Job overall[a]	91.0	92.7	90.0	85.2	84.3	91.9	84.7	−0.8	−0.5
New entrants	86.3	89.3	87.1	—	82.1	88.4	82.6	−0.9	—
Midcareer & senior faculty	94.8	94.7	90.8	—	85.2	92.4	85.2	−2.3	—
Workload	—	—	—	72.8	68.7	—	67.2	—	−5.6
New entrants				—	66.6		68.9		2.3
Midcareer & senior faculty				—	69.5		66.8		−2.7
Job security	—	—	—	84.0	81.5	81.1	83.6	—	−0.4
New entrants				—	70.0	65.0	70.9		0.9
Midcareer & senior faculty				—	86.2	83.3	86.4		0.2
Advancement opportunities	—	—	—	69.1	69.6	56.2	72.0	—	2.9
New entrants				—	66.2	62.7	69.0		2.8
Midcareer & senior faculty				—	71.0	54.6	72.7		1.7
Time for keeping current in field	—	—	47.8	—	50.9	—			
New entrants					43.6		51.4		
Midcareer & senior faculty					49.6		50.8		
Freedom for consulting	—	—	—	89.3	79.6	—	84.6	—	−4.7
New entrants				—	76.5		83.0		6.5
Midcareer & senior faculty				—	80.9		84.9		4.0

Salary[b]	56.0	44.1	40.2	58.3	54.2	49.1	57.3	5.0	−1.0
New entrants	49.9	37.3	34.4	—	52.3	41.7	53.7	4.4	1.4
Midcareer & senior faculty	61.0	48.7	41.7	—	55.0	50.1	58.1	1.4	3.1
Benefits	—	—	—	76.5	74.5	—	77.9	—	1.4
New entrants	—	—	—	—	74.6	—	77.5	—	2.9
Midcareer & senior faculty	—	—	—	—	74.5	—	78.0	—	3.5
Spouse employment opportunities	—	—	73.2	73.3	—	76.6	—	3.4	
New entrants	—	—	—	—	67.8	—	72.1	—	4.3
Midcareer & senior faculty	—	—	—	—	75.5	—	77.6	—	2.1

Sources: Carn-69, CFAT-75, CFAT-84, NSCPF-88, NSOPF-93, CFAT-97, NSOPF-99 (see Appendix A for key).

Notes: Respondents were considered "satisfied" if they marked one of the two highest categories in the scale used to evaluate each particular item.

Item wording: For the NSOPF questionnaires, data reported combine "somewhat satisfied" and "very satisfied" on a 4-point scale (very dissatisfied, somewhat dissatisfied, somewhat satisfied, very satisfied). For the CFAT questionnaires, data reported combine the two highest categories out of three and four, respectively, for overall job satisfaction and satisfaction with salary, and the two highest categories out of five for satisfaction with job security and advancement opportunities.

1969: N = 337,250; 1975: N = 20,789; 1984: N = 4,313; 1987: N = 489,260; 1992: N = 476,328; 1997: N = 4,444; 1998: N = 483,690.

[a]The CFAT questionnaire asked respondents, "In general, how do you feel about this institution?" Valid response alternatives were "It is a very good place for me," "It is a fairly good place for me," and "It is not the place for me." The NSOPF questionnaire asked, "How satisfied or dissatisfied do you personally feel about each of the following aspects of your job at this institution? My job here, overall." Valid response alternatives were "very dissatisfied," "somewhat dissatisfied," "somewhat satisfied," and "very satisfied."

[b]The CFAT questionnaire asked respondents, "How would you rate your own salary?" Valid responses were "excellent," "good," "fair," and "poor." The NSOPF questionnaire asked, "How satisfied or dissatisfied do you personally feel about each of the following aspects of your job at this institution? My salary." Valid response alternatives were "very dissatisfied," "somewhat dissatisfied," "somewhat satisfied," and "very satisfied."

tion has been waning, often amounting to a substantial decline. Yes, the ratio of very satisfied to very unsatisfied faculty remains high, more than two-to-one across all categories. But that ratio has shrunk substantially from two and three decades ago. Back then, with about half of the faculty—compared to one-third more recently—reporting high levels of satisfaction, the ratio of very satisfied to very dissatisfied full-time faculty members was much greater: more than 5:1 in 1969, nearly 7:1 in 1975, and more than 4:1 as late as 1984. To be sure, these declines reflect in part a more general decline in job satisfaction reported among workers in the United States in the 1990s—although it appears that the faculty's decline began earlier, in the 1980s—and the declines certainly appear congruent with reported declines in the job satisfaction of physicians and attorneys in response to a changing professional environment (Conference Board, 2003). Furthermore, they perfectly parallel the situation of faculties in Europe (Enders, 2001) and elsewhere across the globe (Altbach, 2004). So the declines in faculty job satisfaction are clearly part of a global "academic" decline and a decline in the learned professions.

SUMMARY: CONTINUITY AND RECALIBRATION

Figure 5.11 provides a thumbnail summary of trends in academic values and culture and subgroup variations as revealed by the national faculty surveys. The picture is one of diversification amid basic stability. Three decades of national surveys capturing the pulse of American academics suggest that in the face of declining job opportunities, fiscal constraint, and challenges to academic standards, the quality of academic work life has remained surprisingly stable in many respects (including, for example, relations with colleagues and with students). Faculty increasingly are expressing interest in undergraduate education. They express concern more generally, however, about the declining status of the academic profession itself and about the imbalance between teaching and research.

There is, however, evidence of continuing fragmentation of the profession over the past quarter century. First, the observation of Burton Clark (1987) that the American academic profession is divided along the lines of institutional type and discipline—"small worlds, different worlds"—continues to hold, although those differences may be at once attenuating and recalibrating themselves. While the type of institution in which a faculty member is employed continues to shape his or her work experience and norms, fewer gradations are apparent, and differences seem, in large measure, attenuated. Similarly, academic discipline maintains its shaping influence, but, once again, with the sig-

Variable	Trend 1969–1998
Importance of undergrad education	↑
Goals of undergrad education	
Liberal ed	↑
Moral development	↓
Diversity	↓
Status of academic professoriate	↓
Student relations	↑
Colleague relations	↔
Equity perceived	↑
Quality of community	↔
Autonomy and academic freedom	↓
Perception of rewards: Research	↑
Political liberalism	↑
Job satisfaction	↓

Key:
↑ = Trend is upward
↓ = Trend is downward
↔ = Recent trend is no change

Fig. 5.11. Trends in academic values, 1969–1998.

nificant differences largely reduced to those between the traditional arts and sciences, on the one hand, and the professions, on the other (although the natural scientists may look more like faculty in the professions than their liberal arts peers).

Within the context of this "blurring" and reduction of institutional type and disciplinary demarcations (that is, distinctions), the data suggest, perhaps surprisingly, that internal demographic diversification is *no longer* expressing itself in terms of increased *cultural* diversity, nor in the accentuation of distinctive faculty subcultures or communities based on gender and race. Women academics are more attuned to undergraduate education, more attuned to student career aspirations and to diversity issues, and more politically liberal than academic men. Black and Hispanic faculty, too, are more liberal and are more concerned about diversity and developing student character. They are not, how-ever, any less sanguine than white males about the quality of community life on campus (whatever differences may have existed now appear to be attenuating). There remains much in common that is discernible, but academic life appears, from the numbers, to be at once regressing toward a mean—one might argue a more tepid mean—and blurring fissures along racial and ethnic lines. If this in-terpretation indeed emerges from the sea of data, it is remarkable—and proba-bly counterintuitive to what many observers of higher education's varied topog-raphy likely assume. For herein we find areas of convergence in the values held by academics who inhabit the myriad of cells that comprise the huge matrix of higher education formed by multitudinous institutional types and academic fields. This may be all the more surprising given the changes washing over higher education and transforming just who the faculty are and what they do (see especially chapters 7 and 11). But it is at least arguable that at the begin-ning of this century, despite the formidable forces pulling and pushing at the higher education enterprise, certain core academic values endure and permit us to speak, at least in guarded tones, of *an* American faculty.

NOTE

1. If the Carnegie 1997 survey oversampled *established* faculty members, the slump recorded there—a highly satisfied cohort of only 33.8%—arguably is all the more reveal-ing of discontent in the professoriate.

PART THREE

The Academic Career

CHAPTER SIX

The Changing Academic Career

We have argued that the modern academic career, characterized by its exclusivity, its specialization, and its professionalization, became increasingly routinized following World War II after nearly a century of evolutionary transition. An ever more formalized "lockstep" from graduate study (meaning, more and more, the doctorate) into a first full-time position was followed by progression through the academic ranks to tenure, culminating in a full professorship. The typical professor served many years at the top rank and retired at or around age 65. Thus crystallized the twentieth-century career for American academics. To be sure, there were innumerable variations on that central—almost surely modal—theme. Individuals may have made forays into departmental or campus administrative roles or into discipline-based roles in government or industry, but the faculty career remained the undisputed anchor, pulling the individual back to the basic tasks of teaching, research, and service with reasonable prospects for security, even if the price for stability was compensation incommensurate with the rigor and duration of the necessary preparation.

How is that pattern faring in light of the far-reaching changes sweeping through the higher education system? Does the changing demographic profile of those who are being drawn into academic careers affect the contemporary progression of academic careers? And perhaps most consequential, to what extent are the multiple pressures on higher education—and, thereby, on academic personnel policies and practices—reshaping, even redefining, the substance and trajectory of academic careers as we have come to know them? So striking is the redistribution of the types of academic appointments as a new century begins (see chapter 3), that we must ask whether the traditional academic career, which solidified during the quarter century following World War II, is rapidly becoming an anachronism, possibly to be reserved in the future for a relatively few men and women who will perform a traditional mix of academic tasks at a diminishing number of traditional institutions. These are matters that we delve into more systematically in chapter 7; in this chapter we examine the indicators drawn from the most recent three decades of national faculty surveys in order to illuminate the changing facets of academic careers. We attempt to answer a key question: Have we entered into a "postconsolidation" period wherein the givens of the 1970s and 1980s appear to be yielding to destabilizing new realities? Or, in still blunter terms, are the prospects for realizing a traditional academic career—by which we mean something considerably more than a series of academic "jobs"—growing perceptibly slimmer? Even before the full onslaught of distance learning and new providers is felt? Or, to put it another way, are the hard-won gains of the academic profession, achieved over the decades of the twentieth century—and celebrated by Christopher Jencks and David Riesman (1968) and many others—now so threatened by the new realities pervading postsecondary education that the "traditional" career is already giving way? Such speculation aside, what does the evidence based on recent decades reveal?

We begin with an overview of the growth of graduate education (the supply line, so to speak) and the nature of demand for faculty. An examination of these dimensions of the early career is intended to establish the changing contexts within which academic careers are being launched. We undertake next to compare characteristics of careers evident in the national faculty surveys of 1969 and 1975 to the patterns visible in the more recent surveys of 1988, 1993, 1997, and 1999. Specifically, first we examine changes in the educational background of new faculty (highest degree attainment and graduate school support); the nature of the previous employment experience that they bring to their current job (experience in educational versus noneducational settings; responsibilities for teaching, research, administration, or other tasks); the age at which they reach important career milestones (e.g., age at receipt of their highest degree, at appointment to their first full-time job, and at attainment of tenure), and the rising incidence of off-track, that is, fixed term, appointments, as opposed to tenure-eligible and continuous, presumably permanent appointments. Finally, we look at changing patterns in the exit from academic careers: the timing and outcomes of retirement.

THE CONTEXT FOR ACADEMIC CAREER

The authors' recent examination of entrants to faculty careers in the 1990s (Finkelstein, Seal, and Schuster, 1998a, 1998b) revealed that fully one-third of the body academic was, in fact, composed of new entrants: 33% of all full-time faculty were in the first seven years of their academic careers. This represents a "turnover" rate of roughly 4.5% annually, a figure that precisely mirrors the average annual infusion rate that Bowen and Schuster (1986) found to characterize the American faculty in the earlier post–World War II period (except for the brief aberration of explosive hiring that took place during the six-year period of 1967–73). Contrary to the prevailing view, then, there has been a steady, roughly consistent demand for full-time academic workers over the past thirty years. Moreover, the portion of the demand that is driven by replenishment needs (to replace retiring faculty or those who leave the academy for other reasons) may be about to peak. The faculty hired to staff the massive expansion of higher education in the late 1960s and early 1970s are now entering their sixties after nearly three decades of service. The available data suggest that irrespective of the uncapping of mandatory retirement in 1994, the vast majority of academics (with the possible exception of those at the top-tier research universities, especially private universities) are continuing to retire at or around the age of 65 (Chronister, Baldwin, and Conley, 1997; Leslie and Janson, 2005; Clark and Hammond, 2001). This means that, subject to the vagaries of the economy, higher education is likely to experience a significant increase in vacated positions in the early twenty-first century. And those vacancies seem scheduled to coincide almost "on cue" with the surge in the number of 18-to-22-year-olds, the sons and daughters of the baby boomers, that is destined to drive up the "expansion-related" demand for traditional higher education—presumably creating even more opportunities for full-time faculty (Frances, 1998). (We leave aside, for now, the question of how much of the replacement- and enrollment-driven demand is likely to be filled by full-time recruits rather than by part-time appointees.)

The magnitude and consistency of demand, however, has been exceeded—substantially exceeded—by the supply of persons who trained for, and who possess the customary qualifications for, academic positions. One crucial measure is that annual PhD production at the close of the twentieth century had reached an all-time high. As Figure 6.1 indicates, annual PhD production, after a brief interlude of nongrowth in the 1970s, has continued its inexorable ascent, at least until 1997, when it appeared to stabilize. In fact, more doctorates than ever before are now being awarded in such low-demand fields as physics and English (AAUP, 2004). And there remains in many, if not most fields (the few exceptions include some types of engineering) a residual oversupply of academically "underemployed" PhDs, some portion of whom continue to seek academic positions. Moreover, the latest data imply that if doctoral degree production has

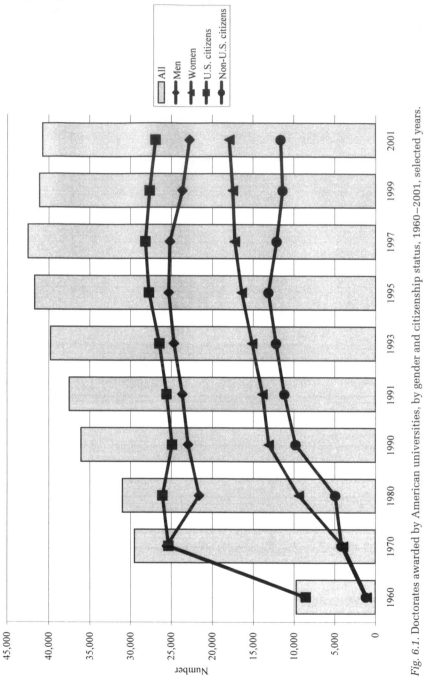

Fig. 6.1. Doctorates awarded by American universities, by gender and citizenship status, 1960–2001, selected years.

stabilized or slightly declined, enrollment in doctoral programs is once again on the rise, suggesting that any modest decline may be short-lived (Syverson, 2003).

What has changed is the demography of the new doctoral cohort, their gender and citizenship status. Figure 6.1 reveals that although overall levels are remaining largely constant, the share of women has increased substantially over the past decade, while the numbers of men have held relatively steady or even declined slightly. According to data from the National Research Council's annual Survey of Doctoral Recipients, in 2002 for the first time among U.S. citizens the number of women doctoral recipients surpassed the number of men (Smallwood, 2003). The proportionate increase of noncitizen, foreign-born members of the doctoral cohort has also moderated vis-à-vis native-born U.S. citizens.

This is the context within which academic careers are being chosen and entered upon at the threshold of the new century. Now to the surveys.

EDUCATIONAL BACKGROUND

The data confirm what many observers have been noting about the academic marketplace for nearly a generation: it is increasingly competitive. That is to say, the prevailing strong buyer's market in most fields has prompted a ratcheting up of educational qualifications for most faculty positions. The proportion of full-time faculty holding the doctorate has increased steadily over the past quarter century from 57.3% in 1969 to around 62.8% in 1998 (fig. 6.2a), while the proportion holding a master's as a highest degree has remained largely unchanged.

As figure 6.2b indicates, all institutional sectors have recorded a sharp rise in the faculty's educational qualifications, although it has not been occurring at the same pace throughout higher education. For the research universities—whose faculty members were far better credentialed in 1969 than other faculties, with three in four holding a doctorate—the doctorate is now nearly universal (taking into account the fields for which a master's degree is the conventional terminal degree). Even at the two-year institutions, never a site for many doctorate holders, the proportion has more than doubled in recent years to nearly one in five by 1998. The comprehensive and liberal arts institutions may have experienced the most emphatic rise during this era, climbing from about one-half (52.2% in 1969) to 69.2% in 1998. The most recent data suggest that for the nonresearch doctorate-granting universities, the rise has crested at over 80%, thus minimizing any differences between those institutions and the research universities in terms of proportions of doctorate holders. This is a crude measure, some would say, because it neglects to take into account just which

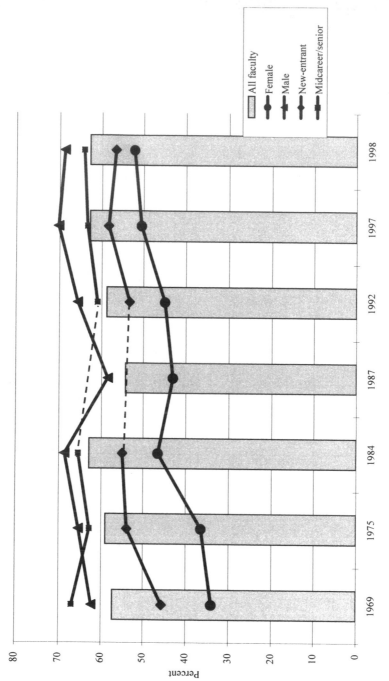

Fig. 6.2a. Full-time faculty holding doctorate, by gender and career cohort, 1969–1998. Note: Data for career cohorts in 1987 are not available.

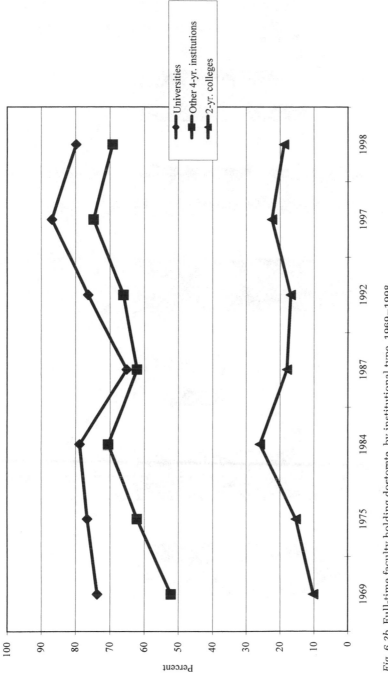

Fig. 6.2b. Full-time faculty holding doctorate, by institutional type, 1969–1998.

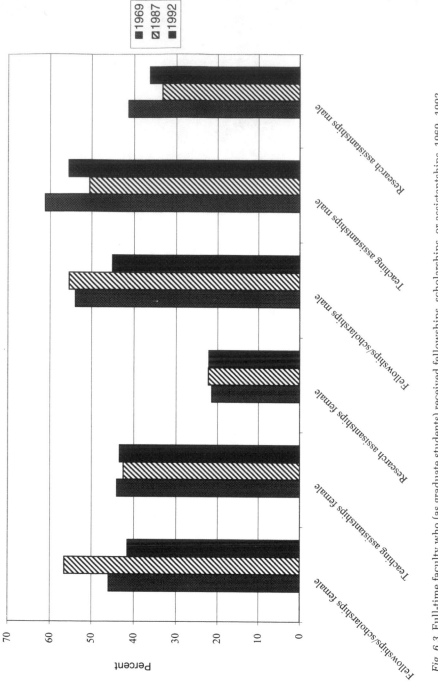

Fig. 6.3. Full-time faculty who (as graduate students) received fellowships, scholarships, or assistantships, 1969–1992.

universities granted the degrees; in some circles it would matter greatly whether the doctorate's source was a top-ranked program or a "lesser" one. Nonetheless, the overriding message is that the doctorate has become essentially the entry-level qualification, save for the two-year sector.

The credentials for *new entrants* in particular have increased substantially over the past generation (fig. 6.2a). In 1969 junior faculty were 20% less likely than their senior or midcareer colleagues to hold the terminal degree; by 1998 that difference had been cut in half. When combined with the evidence of the dramatic decline in the under-35 age cohort among the junior faculty, what emerges is clearly a picture of a profession that is drawing an *older* group of entrants, persons who are more highly credentialed and more likely to be coming from other work experience.

Upon closer examination, it is evident that much of this rise in faculty qualifications has been achieved by the increase in the proportion of women faculty holding the doctorate—from one-third in 1969 to fully one-half (52.2%) by 1998 (fig. 6.2a). Thus, not only have women joined the faculty in increasing numbers and proportions, but in addition a growing proportion of them possess doctoral degrees.

As the faculty's educational qualifications have expanded, however, the faculty-members-to-be have been asked to shoulder a greater proportion of the costs incurred in their graduate training. The rise in qualifications, at least insofar as it is measured by degrees held, has occurred while financial support for graduate study has ebbed (fig. 6.3). In 1969 over half the faculty reported that they had received scholarship support (52.5%) and/or a teaching assistantship (58.2%) during graduate study, and more than one-third (37.9%) had held some kind of research assistantship. By 1992 those percentages had slipped markedly to 43.9% for scholarships, 51.5% for teaching assistantships, and 31.5% for research assistantships (data on this item are not included in NSOPF-99). Loans have figured more prominently in recent years. Although no directly comparative data are available for 1969, the fact that nearly one-quarter (22.6%) of faculty in 1992 reported borrowing as a source of graduate school support suggests that loans increasingly have taken up some of the slack (this was not even a response alternative in the 1969 survey). We do not have any estimates of the magnitude of indebtedness for graduate school loans that faculty are carrying, although we can expect that those faculty members who report loan indebtedness are more likely to be found among the more recent faculty hires. These survey data also do not establish the numbers of faculty members who financed their undergraduate educations in part via loans or the magnitude of such indebtedness that they carried forward into their postbaccalaureate education.

The data indicate that the pressures resulting from decreasing graduate study support have affected faculty unevenly. Contrary to conventional expectations, it appears that faculty members in the natural sciences, and to a lesser extent in the social sciences, have been harder hit than their colleagues in the humanities and fine arts (table A-6.2). Similarly, among faculty in professional schools, those in engineering and the health sciences have been most burdened as students by a decline in the availability of extramural (usually federal) funds. Despite declines across all academic fields (except for the fine arts) in the proportion of faculty members who had received scholarship or fellowship support as graduate students, the rank order among the fields has remained roughly the same over the years—indeed, the order was exactly the same for the 1987 and 1992 measures. Perhaps surprising to some, the social scientists surveyed in 1969, 1987, and 1992 fared best in terms of the proportion of them who received scholarship or fellowship support, with humanists and natural scientists in a second tier. Faculty members in business and, especially, education lagged behind the other fields.

Again defying the conventional wisdom, figure 6.3 indicates that most of the decline in support has been absorbed by men rather than women. The proportion of women receiving all categories of financial support for graduate study has remained virtually unchanged since 1969: just over 40% had received teaching assistantships and scholarships or fellowships and about 20% had received research assistantships over these decades, while during the same quarter century the proportion of men who had received teaching or research assistantships or scholarship or fellowship aid declined by roughly 7% in each category. Academic women are still, however, considerably less likely to have received teaching (43.4% versus 55.5%) or research assistantships (22.1% versus 36.2%) than academic men. Moreover, among racial and ethnic groups, it has been Asians who have been hardest hit—reflecting undoubtedly their overrepresentation in the natural sciences and engineering, where support has become less plentiful (table A-6.2).

PREVIOUS EMPLOYMENT EXPERIENCES

The national faculty surveys allow us to compare the previous employment experiences of faculty in the 1990s with those of their predecessors in 1969 and 1975. These aspects of their early careers include both the employment sector (in higher education, K-12 education, or a variety of settings outside education) and the major type of responsibility held (teaching, research, administration, clinical, or other). Unfortunately, the response categories changed in NSOPF-

99: teaching was combined with research and service into a single "instruction/research/service" response category in contradistinction to "administration and technical services," effectively obliterating the clean distinctions among teaching and research and clinical activities that were drawn in both NSOPF-88 and NSOPF-93 *within* the college and university employment sector. To compensate for this interpretive wrinkle, we have focused initially on NSOPF-93 as the outside bookend in our analyses and then have brought NSOPF-99 into the picture only insofar as it can provide a clear elaboration of the trends discerned by 1992.

When we compare the early job market experiences of the faculty of the 1990s with those of the faculty of the late 1960s and mid-1970s, we find some clear and stark differences between 1969–75, on the one hand, and 1992, on the other. In the first place, according to figure 6.4, 1992 faculty were significantly less likely to report previous college teaching experience, though considerably more likely to report previous nonteaching employment in higher education, presumably in administration, research, or technical services. Practically speaking, this means that the faculty of the early 1990s were experiencing significantly less choice and mobility among academic options relatively early in their careers, although they had managed to latch onto some kind of job within the university. Whereas faculty members three-plus decades ago characteristically were able to "trade up," moving from one faculty position to another in a robust buyer's market, the more recent data depict much less fluidity. This new pattern of remaining at the institution where one is first appointed holds for all types of institutions. The experience among institutional types does not vary greatly, but the "velcro phenomenon" is more pronounced at the research universities and the community colleges and less so at the comprehensives and the liberal arts colleges. The case of the community colleges may reflect higher levels of tenure, as well as faculty receiving tenure earlier in their careers compared to faculty members at four-year institutions (see Finkelstein, Seal, and Schuster, 1998a).

Not only do the faculty of the 1990s report having held fewer previous full-time academic jobs; they also report a greater variety of jobs prior to their full-time academic appointment. Table A-6.3 establishes three relevant developments. Perhaps most interestingly, the proportion of faculty who report having previously worked at a job *outside* education declined slightly (49.9% in 1969; 49.7% in 1992). Second, within the university sector, a significant increase can be seen among faculty reporting previous *nonteaching* employment at a college or university, rising from 6.2% in 1969 to 38.1% in 1992 and in part reflecting a growth in postdoctoral research appointments. Third, a significant decline is evident in the overall proportion of faculty reporting prior employment in the K-12 sector (falling from 25.8% in 1969 to 13.9% in 1993).

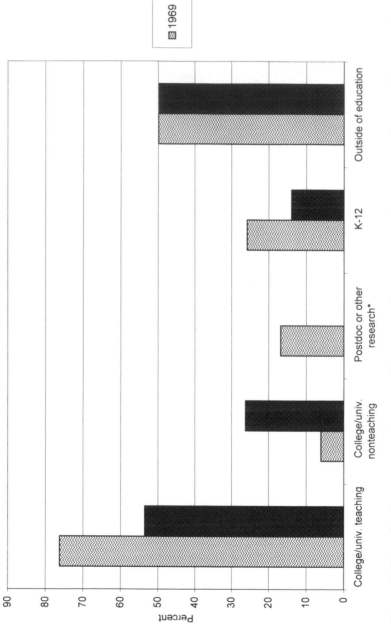

Fig. 6.4. Full-time faculty reporting various types of previous employment, 1969 and 1992. * 1992 data unavailable.

The decline in faculty members' previous public school employment experiences is extensive and is particularly notable at the two-year community colleges (from nearly one-half [47.8%] in 1969 to one-quarter [24.8%] in 1992) (table A-6.3). That decline may be attributable, in part, to an increasing tendency for community college faculty to be drawn from positions outside education (47.9% in 1969 versus 59.0% in 1992), reflecting increased staffing needs in the vocational fields, as well as to the general decoupling of the two-year sector from its K-12 origins.

When we look at patterns by academic field (table A-6.3), some striking contrasts are evident. First, the proportion of natural science faculty reporting previous nonteaching college and university employment has almost doubled (21.9% in 1975; 41.0% in 1992), undoubtedly a function of widespread postdoctoral experiences prior to landing a teaching position. Less expectedly, a widening experience gap is discernible between the professions and the liberal arts and sciences. The vast majority of faculty in business (61.2% in 1992), engineering (64.8% in 1992), and especially the health professions (73.3% in 1992) continued to report previous work experience outside education, while the proportion of liberal arts and sciences faculty reporting such outside experience continued to shrink from 44.9% in 1969 to 38.6% in 1992. These data are not unexpected, but they make it abundantly clear that the fastest-growing segments of the faculty are precisely those bringing work experiences from outside academe to their academic positions; and the background gap between liberal arts and professional faculty is widening. For education, there is a striking decline in the proportion of faculty members reporting work experience in the public schools (from nearly three-fourths in 1969 to less than one-half in 1992). This increasing distance between school sites and schools of education no doubt documents the extent to which the "ed schools" have looked less and less to public school administrators to stock their faculties; they have turned more and more to university-trained researchers to meet their needs.

The rise in previous nonteaching collegiate employment together with the decline in public school teaching as a significant job background is perceptible for both men and women, but it is especially striking for academic women (table A-6.3). In 1969 43.1% of the female faculty reported a background in public school teaching (twice the proportion of men), but by 1992 that proportion had been pared in half to 20.9% (and only 10.0% for the men).

If we can discern clear and compelling trends between 1969–75 and 1992, the data for 1998 introduce some new uncertainties into the equation. While the declines since 1969–75 in previous K-12 experience continue and redistribution of previous experience from outside the education sector continues to in-

TABLE 6.1
Non-Tenure-Eligible Full-Time Faculty, 1969–1998
(percent)

	1969	1975	1984	1987	1992	1997	1998	Change in % 1969–98
All faculty	3.2	13.2	9.0	9.1	10.3	14.2	14.5	11.3
Not on tenure track although institution has a tenure system, among all institutions	—	—	—	7.9	9.0	—	13.1	—
Not on tenure track although institution has a tenure system, among institutions with tenure system	—	—	—	9.1	10.3	—	14.5	—
Not on tenure track because institution has no tenure system, among all institutions	—	—	—	12.7	12.4	—	10.0	—

Sources: Carn-69, CFAT-75, CFAT-84, NSOPF-88, NSOPF-93, CFAT-97, NSOPF-99 (see Appendix A for key).
Note: For definitions of row label terms, see Appendix E.

crease for professional and decline for liberal arts faculty, there appears to be a stark "reversal" between 1992 and 1998: a marked increase of nearly 10% in the proportion reporting previous college teaching experience and a concomitant decline in the proportion reporting non-teaching-related college and university employment. To what extent this represents a "real" change in the early career experiences of American faculty—an opening up of the market perhaps attributable precisely to the plethora of nontraditional appointments—or an artifact of changes in survey response categories is not yet clear. One way to weigh these alternative explanations would be to differentiate analytically between the career experience of new entrants and that of midcareer and senior faculty in 1998—assuming that any new trends would be visible for the new entrants. With the lack of comparability between item response categories, however, precise comparison remain elusive.

THE GROWTH OF THE NEW APPOINTMENTS

Although American faculty are coming to their first academic jobs at a somewhat later age, more highly credentialed than their predecessors, and with less previous full-time faculty experience, the "drag" on their careers does not stop there. They are—and this is perhaps the most critical change—beginning their first full-time appointments under conditions that are significantly different in at least one crucial respect from their predecessors': sharply reduced tenure eligibility. Table 6.1 indicates the striking increase in the proportion of full-time faculty reporting that they are not eligible for tenure consideration. Moreover, it shows that most of that increase has come not from a rise in institutions that are abandoning tenure systems wholesale (the number of which has actually declined), but rather from institutions that are quickly developing off-track systems to parallel their existing shrinking tenure systems. Ironically, then, although the "aging" faculty of the 1990s are only slightly more likely than the faculty of a generation earlier to have achieved tenure (53.1% in 1998 versus 52.1% in 1969), they are significantly less likely overall—by a ratio of three to one—to occupy positions that are tenure-eligible (See Parsad, Glover, and Zimbler, 2002). The message that inheres in these data is that the proportion of full-time faculty who are *either* tenured *or* tenure-eligible (that is, on the tenure track) has diminished: 96.8% in 1969 (only about one in thirty were off the tenure track) compared to 85.4% in 1998 (about one in six off the tenure track). The transformation is remarkable: from 1969 to 1998, a decline by one-half in faculty members occupying tenure-eligible positions and a sevenfold increase in faculty reporting non-tenure-eligible appointments (USDE, 1996a, 1998a, 2000). (For greater detail, see chapter 7.)

When the transformation is viewed by institutional type and academic field (fig. 6.5a), we begin to see how pervasive it is. The shift toward these full-time term appointments is manifest everywhere, visible across all types of institutions and all academic fields. It is less notable, however, in the two-year community colleges, which have moved to part-time appointments, rather than full-time term appointments, as their primary vehicle for ensuring flexibility in staffing (more than half of all head-count faculty in community colleges are part-time (see table 3.4). Thus, counting only the "not on tenure track" category (and disregarding, for now, both the "no tenure for faculty status" and "no tenure system at institution" categories in those surveys), the proportion of off-track appointments among the new-entrant faculty cohort is consistently double or nearly double that of the intermediate faculty cohort. The change is particularly accentuated at the universities. Among full-time faculty in the universities, a barely visible fraction of 3.4% who were tenure-ineligible in 1969 had mushroomed to 16.4% by 1998. Although the flight from tenure-eligible appointments is manifest across all academic fields, as noted, it is especially acute in the professions, and within the professions in the health-related fields, soaring from 1.9% tenure-ineligible in 1969 to 22.4% in 1998.

When we control for race or ethnicity and gender (fig. 6.5b), we find several noteworthy developments. Whereas the proportion of non-tenure-eligible white faculty has increased from 8.8% to 14.7% since the mid-1980s, the proportion of Asian, Hispanic, and black faculty who are non-tenure-eligible actually declined until 1998, effectively resisting the otherwise widespread circumvention of tenure or tenure-track appointments.[1] Thus the proportion of Hispanic faculty holding tenured or tenure-eligible appointments declined minimally (from 83.7% to 82.4%), while the corresponding proportion of black faculty members actually rose somewhat (from 72.7% to 77.2%). Note, however, that the proportion of black faculty holding tenured appointments shrank perceptibly (from 55.1% in 1969 to 47.2% in 1992)—in contrast to the experience of Asian and Caucasian faculty members.

Academic women, despite their infusion into the academy in large numbers, suffer in comparison to men in the types of academic appointments they hold. Reflecting with a vengeance the overall trend toward off-track appointments, the women are twice as likely as the men to be found in non-tenure-eligible positions (21.2% versus 11.0%). This roughly two-to-one ratio has persisted. The proportion of women who are tenured has also continued at much lower rates

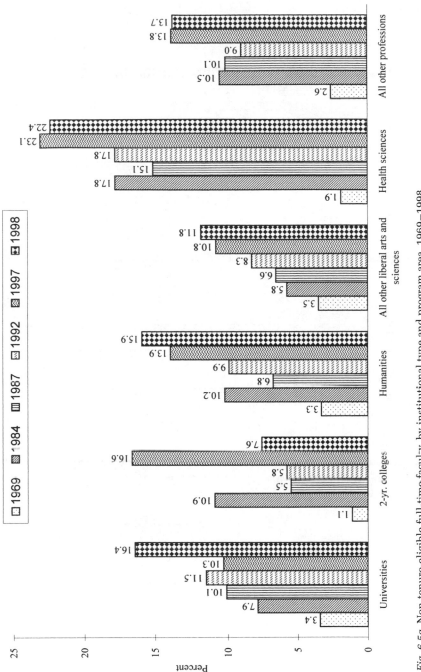

Legend: □ 1969 ▨ 1984 ▥ 1987 ▦ 1992 ▩ 1997 ▦ 1998

Universities
3.4
7.9
10.1
11.5
10.3
16.4

2-yr. colleges
1.1
10.9
5.5
5.8
16.6
7.6

Humanities
3.3
10.2
6.8
9.9
13.9
15.9

All other liberal arts and sciences
3.5
5.8
9.9
8.3
10.8
11.8

Health sciences
1.9
17.8
15.1
17.8
23.1
22.4

All other professions
2.6
10.5
10.1
9.0
13.8
13.7

Percent (0, 5, 10, 15, 20, 25)

Fig. 6.5a. Non-tenure-eligible full-time faculty, by institutional type and program area, 1969–1998.

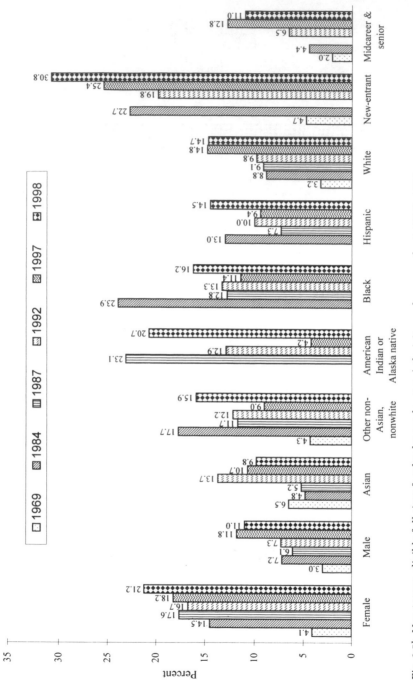

Fig. 6.5b. Non-tenure-eligible full-time faculty, by gender, race/ethnicity, and career cohort, 1969–1998.

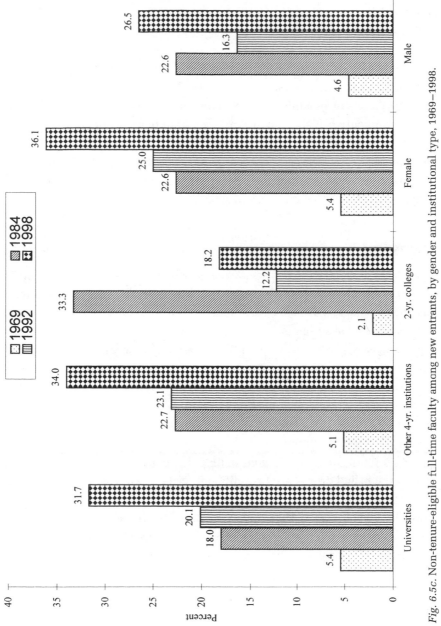

Fig. 6.5c. Non-tenure-eligible full-time faculty among new entrants, by gender and institutional type, 1969–1998.

than for men (41.6% of women versus 59.7% of men in 1998 [Parsad, Glover, and Zimbler, 2002]).

Once again, these aggregated comparisons appear to underestimate the magnitude of change. Comparing new and senior faculty according to the types of appointments they held, Finkelstein, Seal, and Schuster (1998a, p. 56) found much larger differences in the 1990s. Among the full-time new entrants in the early 1990s, about one-third (33.2%) were in non-tenure-eligible positions, compared to only half that proportion (16.5%) of their senior colleagues. The more recent the entry into a full-time appointment, the more likely, by far, that the appointment will be term-limited. Figure 6.5c dramatically illustrates the growth of these new appointments among new entrants to the profession, across all types of four-year institutions and among academic women.

Career Progress

We have established that academic careers are more likely than previously to begin under less-than-propitious conditions insofar as careers are increasingly being launched at a later age and "off-track." Moreover, academic careers in recent years have begun under unfavorable marketplace conditions (as the large number of persons seeking traditional academic careers affords opportunities for the employing institutions to replace less-than-excellent probationary faculty members ordinarily without great difficulty). But can we discern whether the individual career situation tends to improve down the stretch? Are traditional career milestones (receipt of doctorate, appointment to first position, achieving tenure, and an associate or full professorship) continuing to arrive "on time"? Do those who begin in nontraditional appointments (part-time or full-time off-track) find their way into traditional academic careers? Or does launching a career with a nontraditional appointment foreclose the possibility of a traditional academic career? For everyone? For identifiable subgroups? And what of the experiences of those faculty members who were able to launch their careers in the traditional way, that is, on-track? Has their career trajectory changed over time?

As we suggested earlier, the evidence on academic career trajectories is slender; until recently, it did not discriminate between fixed-term (off-track) and tenure-eligible (on-track) faculty. Therefore we could examine only aggregated differences over time in the distribution of academic ranks (presumably reflecting macro patterns in movement throughout the professorial ranks) and the timing of career milestones. Nonetheless, several windows exist through which career progress can be viewed. First are aggregate changes, from 1969 to 1998, along several dimensions: in the distribution of faculty across the academic ranks, in their age at first appointment, and in their age at receipt of tenure. A second set of data probes the widening differences in 1998 between the new career entrants and their senior colleagues over time (defined as those with seven or more years of full-time college teaching experience). Moreover, there is newly available data since 1999 from NSOPF that includes information on tenure status (tenured, tenure-eligible, no tenure system at institution, no tenure for this faculty status) as well as employment status (full-time versus part-time) at the time of appointment to first position, for the immediately previous position, and for the current position (see chapter 7). This allows us *at least for current faculty in 1989* to trace *retrospectively* mobility across tenure and employment statuses to date. We turn now to the aggregate evidence on career markers.

Rank and Time to Tenure as Indicators of Career Progress

Table A-6.4 examines changes in the distribution of academic ranks over a three-decade period. Not surprisingly, we find a steadily increasing top-heaviness in academic ranks as the large cohort of faculty recruited to guide higher education's powerful expansion in the 1960s "moved up." They began their careers, for the most part, "on-track."[2] By 1998 about one-third (33.4%) of all full-time faculty were at the rank of professor as compared with about one-quarter (27.1%) a generation earlier. Correspondingly, the proportion of faculty at the rank of assistant professor has steadily declined (from 29.6% in 1969 and 30.4% in 1975 to 23.5% in 1992 and 22.5% in 1998) as the combined proportions of faculty in the ranks of professor and associate professor have expanded inexorably from about half (50.5% in 1969 and 55.6% in 1975) to 57.9% in 1992 and 58.5% in 1998.

In other respects, especially in terms of type of appointment (term versus tenurable), the 1969 versus 1998 comparisons are less clearly confirmatory. According to the data in table A-6.4, the proportion of *new-entrant* faculty in the ladder rank of assistant professor is larger in 1998 than it was in 1969—although the percentage of the associate professor and instructor ranks actually declined. The proportion of midcareer and senior faculty holding ladder ranks shows a consistent decline from 1969. Moreover, the data indicate no change in percentage of junior faculty holding tenure in 1998 compared with 1969 (about one-fifth), albeit a decline in the percentage of *senior* faculty holding tenure in 1998 compared to 1969 (about three-fourths versus seven-eighths a generation earlier). These data might be interpreted in a number of ways. First, it may be that the use of *ladder rank* to mean a tenure-eligible appointment actually underes-

TABLE 6.2
Mean Age of Full-Time Faculty at Highest Degree, at First Full-Time Academic Job, and at Tenure, 1969–1998

	1975	1984	1992	1998	Change 1969–98
All faculty					
At highest degree					
Doctorate	32.5	32.4	32.5	33.0	0.5
Master's or less	30.5	30.4	30.9	31.7	1.2
At 1st full-time academic job	—	—	34.8	—	—
At tenure	38.2	37.9	39.4	—	—
Female					
At highest degree					
Doctorate	34.9	34.9	35.0	35.3	0.4
Master's or less	31.4	31.0	31.7	32.3	0.9
At 1st full-time academic job	—	—	35.5	—	—
At tenure	40.7	39.8	40.4	—	—
Male					
At highest degree					
Doctorate	32.1	31.8	31.6	32.0	−0.1
Master's or less	30.1	30.1	30.1	31.2	1.1
At 1st full-time academic job	—	—	34.5	—	—
At tenure	37.7	37.5	39.1	—	—
New entrants					
At highest degree					
Doctorate	31.6	31.3	32.4	33.2	1.6
Master's or less	29.5	28.2	30.9	32.0	2.5
At 1st full-time academic job	—	—	38.4	—	—
At tenure	36.9	37.0	40.4	—	—
Female					
At highest degree					
Doctorate	33.0	33.7	34.4	34.1	1.1
Master's or less	30.0	29.0	31.6	32.2	2.2
At 1st full-time academic job	—	—	38.2	—	—
At tenure	38.4	37.1	40.2	—	—
Male					
At highest degree					
Doctorate	31.2	30.2	31.5	32.6	1.4
Master's or less	29.3	27.6	30.1	31.8	2.5
At 1st full-time academic job	—	—	38.6	—	—
At tenure	36.5	36.9	40.5	—	—
Midcareer & senior					
At highest degree					
Doctorate	32.8	32.6	32.5	33.0	0.2
Master's or less	31.0	31.0	30.8	31.6	0.6
At 1st full-time academic job	—	—	33.3	—	—
At tenure	38.3	38.0	39.2	—	—
Female					
At highest degree					
Doctorate	36.0	35.4	35.4	35.6	−0.4
Master's or less	32.5	31.6	31.7	32.3	−0.2
At 1st full-time academic job	—	—	33.8	—	—
At tenure	41.0	40.1	40.4	—	—
Male					
At highest degree					
Doctorate	32.3	32.1	31.7	32.0	−0.3
Master's or less	30.4	30.7	30.1	31.0	0.6
At 1st full-time academic job	—	—	33.1	—	—
At tenure	37.8	37.5	38.9	—	—

Sources: CFAT-75, CFAT-84, NSOPF-93, NSOPF-99 (see Appendix A for key).

  Note: "Doctorate" refers to doctoral (PhD, EdD, etc.) and first professional (MD, DDS, LLB, etc.) degrees.

timates the proportion of regular, tenure-eligible, full-time appointments among junior faculty in 1969. Certainly in 1998, in the four-year institutions, ladder rank provides a good indicator of "regularity" of appointment. In 1969, however, it may not, since "instructor" was still at many institutions the entry-level rank for full-time faculty, especially those who had not yet completed their doctorate. About half of those new-entrant faculty holding the rank of instructor in 1969 reported that they were on "regular" appointments; by 1998 only about one-fifth of instructors said they held "regular" appointments; so the exclusion of one-half of the instructors in 1969 from classification as holding ladder rank may simply give the appearance of an increasingly "regularly appointed" junior faculty. Second, if this is true, then the decline in ladder-rank occupancy among midcareer and, to a lesser extent, senior faculty may confirm that the effect of nontraditional appointments was actually operating much earlier, even in the early 1980s, when many of the midcareer and even a few of the senior faculty in 1998 were entering the professions.

Among academic women, the progress has been slow, if steady. Their rate of movement into the top rank has picked up—but only modestly. A generation ago the gender gap was very big. Nearly one-third of men had attained the rank of full professor (30.1% in 1969; 33.1% in 1975), whereas barely more than one of eight women academics were full professors at that time (12.5% in 1969; 13.7% in 1975). For men, full professor had already become the modal rank by 1969 and has remained so at each of the ensuing data points, more recently climbing to 41.1% in 1993 and 40.9% in 1998. Meanwhile, for the women, the ascent had reached only 19.9% in 1998 (lagging behind associate and assistant professors and instructors), although the 1997 Carnegie survey puts the percentage of women in the full professor rank at 27.4. In any event, the rank deficit for women persists, though the gap—formerly a chasm—may well be narrowing. Such a convergence would certainly be expected, given the women's relatively later entry to academe in large numbers, but the sizable gap that persists demonstrates how slow progress has been.

The Chronology of Career Milestones: Doctorate, First Appointment, and Tenure

Given that the substance of faculty members' early career experiences has changed over the span of these past several decades, we turn now to issues of timing—the chronology of academic career milestones. Has career timing changed substantially during this era? In fact, there has been remarkable constancy in the timing of the first academic career milestone. Faculty holding the doctorate report in 1998 a mean age of 33.0 at receipt of that degree—only about one-half year later than reported by faculty members a generation earlier (32.5 in 1975) (table 6.2). Faculty who hold a master's as their highest degree report in 1998 a mean age at receipt of that degree as 31.7 compared to 30.5 in 1975—a delay of just over one year, but one that is discernible only in the late 1990s.

But what about actually embarking on one's career, that is, obtaining a full-time academic appointment? Reaching this second milestone is a different story. Although we have no comparable data for the early period (the item was not included in NSOPF-99), faculty in 1992 were reporting a mean age at appointment to their first faculty position of 34.8 years—approximately two years on average following degree receipt for those holding the doctorate. Or viewed through another lens, this more recent cohort of faculty members have waited (that is, studied and worked) on average a dozen or so years, since most of them would have completed their baccalaureate degrees before attaining a full-time academic appointment. This undoubtedly constitutes a protracted deferral compared to the commonplace experience during the very brisk academic marketplace of the late 1960s and early 1970s when prospective faculty members often were being plucked from their graduate school program prior to completion of their dissertations (that is, their appointments commonly preceded the awarding of their terminal degree, as noted earlier).

An earlier examination of faculty career age suggests that the aggregated data likely underestimate the extent of change. When we compared faculty in the first seven years of a full-time academic career with their more senior colleagues (that is, those with eight or more years of full-time faculty experience), we found that the gap between receipt of doctorate and first faculty appointment had grown from barely two years among the more senior cohort to almost five years for the more recent entrants (Finkelstein, Seal, and Schuster, 1998a, p. 50). This suggests that the "early career" years have stretched out for contemporary faculty, entailing fewer opportunities than their more senior colleagues experienced in launching their careers.

Over the past generation, the age at which faculty have achieved tenure has increased for males (from 37.7 in 1975 to 39.1 in 1992), but not for females (40.7 in 1975 versus 40.4 in 1992) (table 6.2), shrinking the gender gap from three years to one (although these timing differences say nothing about gender differences in pretenure attrition, which we know to be higher for women than men (Mason and Goulden, 2002). This finding should be viewed in the context of our earlier cross-sectional findings (based on 1992 data) that although new entrants had received their highest degree at about the same age as their senior colleagues, these new entrants reported that they took up their first full-time appointment, on average, four years later than their senior colleagues had (age 36 versus age 32) (Finkelstein, Seal, and Schuster, 1998a). It is apparent that academic careers today are beginning later than a generation ago. With careers ordinarily beginning in earnest after age 35, rather than in the early 30s, achieving tenure naturally comes at a still later age. Thus, in 1975, 64.9% of men and 74.3% of women had not become tenured until they were at least 35 years old. By 1992 a further delay is evident: 74.0% of the men and 78.6% of the women were not tenured prior to age 35. The phenomenon of delayed career markers is a hard reality for men and women alike.

Academic women hit these career markers at a later age than their male counterparts: when they earn their highest degree, when they obtain their first full-time faculty appointment, and when they are granted tenure. With regard to age at highest degree, the pattern is unchanged across recent decades. Thus, women are consistently two–three years older than men at receipt of the doctorate. The differential attenuates slightly for age at receipt of master's degrees. Further, women are perceptibly older than men when they begin their academic careers; for instance, in 1992 they had received their first full-time academic appointments on average one year later than men. Still further, the same pattern holds for age at receipt of tenure—although, again, the differential appears to be shrinking from 3.0 to 2.3 to 1.3 years in 1992. At least some portion of these differences undoubtedly can be explained by women's time out for childrearing and by women's disproportionate presence in fields—the humanities and education, for instance—in which time-to-degree historically has been longer (see chapter 3). Also, women clearly are more likely than men to bring part-time college teaching experience with them to their first full-time appointment, contributing still further to time lags in hitting the key academic milestones. Whatever the reasons, the track continues to be slower for academic women.

RETIREMENT OR NEW PATTERNS IN EXITING
FROM ACADEMIC CAREERS

Federal age-discrimination legislation in the late 1970s and early 1980s ushered in a new era of concern about, and study of, faculty retirement. The legislation, of course, intruded into a rather stagnant academic marketplace where major concerns arose about the increased costs associated with senior faculty staying on "indefinitely" as well as the resulting diminished opportunities for young scholars. Thus, the timing of faculty retirement decisions has become the focus of empirical attention in an era when those decisions have been transferred from the institution's discretion to that of the individual faculty member.

Hansen and Holden (1981) were commissioned by the U.S. Congress to study the possible repercussions for colleges and universities of raising the mandatory retirement age from 65 to 70. Systematic studies of retirement in the 1990s were also commissioned as a result of temporary faculty exemptions from the new federal legislation and the attempt to determine whether the temporary exemption needed to be made permanent or might be relinquished. Among the studies were those undertaken under the aegis of the National Academy of Sciences (Hammond and Morgan, 1991), including the North Carolina Studies (Clark and Hammond, 2001) and the Faculty Retirement Survey of research universities and elite liberal arts colleges, carried out initially by Albert Rees and Sharon Smith (1991) and later by Orley Ashenfelter and David Card for the Andrew Mellon Foundation (Ashenfelter and Card, 1998, 2001). Both of these, like the Hansen and Holden study before them, were focused specifically on the timing of the retirement decision and the impact of legislative changes relative to other institutional policies and individual variables in shaping that timing.

The concern, of course, was that the transfer of what had been an institutional decision into the hands of individual faculty would effectively extend faculty tenure benefits indefinitely, thus placing heavy financial burdens on institutions and preventing them from infusing new blood into their faculties. All of these studies together provide remarkably consistent conclusions: that faculty generally retire around 65 *irrespective* of the existence of any mandatory retirement policy; that uncappping affects primarily the retirement decisions of that small contingent of faculty who continue their employment to age 70 (clearly encouraging much lower retirement rates at age 70 and beyond but having little impact on the large contingent who retire earlier); that those faculty most likely to continue their employment are located at private research universities and elite liberal arts colleges with relatively light teaching obligations and relatively rich research opportunities and are those who are most professionally active and productive; and finally, that "incentive programs" could be designed by institutions, either stand-alone or as one piece in a larger posttenure review initiative, that would encourage the departure of less productive faculty at or before the normal retirement age. For the most part, experience to date suggests that these conclusions hold up well (Holden and Hansen, 2001). Moreover, the retirement decision has been shown to be quite a complex one involving the assessment of many potential trade-offs of the benefits and costs of remaining employed versus retiring (for a model, see Keefe, 2001), as these may change for any given individual over time.

In addition to what we are learning about the determinants of the timing of faculty retirement decisions, two other sorts of evidence are available to inform our understanding of retirement. First, there are the national faculty surveys (especially NSOPF-93 and -99) that provide two sorts of windows on retirement: from the survey of individual faculty, indications of individual retirement plans, based on questions such as, "Within the next three years, how likely are you to (a) retire from employment at this institution and (b) retire from all paid employment?" and from the institutional survey, actual data on retirement rates of faculty, as well as data on the existence and popularity of "early retirement" incentive programs. These data demonstrate that a consistent 2–3% of faculty have retired (from their current employer) annually, both before (NSOPF-93) and after (NSOPF-99) uncapping, and that those rates are demonstrably lower for faculty at research universities, especially private research universities. Retirements constitute a consistent 30% or so of all faculty separations reported— closer, however to 12% at private research universities (21% at public research universities), while accounting for about half of all separations at the two-year community colleges. Many faculty also report simply not knowing when they are going to retire—either from their current institution or from all paid employment; and significantly greater proportions of faculty anticipate retiring (7–8%, in NSOPF-93 and -99) than actually retire (2–3%)—suggesting that faculty intentions are a notoriously unreliable indicator of their behavior here. Between 1987 and 1992, about 40% of all institutions offered some kind of early retirement incentive program (about three-fourths of the research universities, both public and private, about half of the other public institutions, and only about one-third of the private, nonresearch institutions). The faculty who accept these incentive offers, however, amount to only a small percentage, ranging from nearly one-third at the two-year community colleges to about 3% at the private research universities. Keefe (2001) has provided an analytical model of the costs and benefits of an early retirement incentive, showing the quite complex interaction between financial and nonfinancial issues.

The second source of evidence comes from studies of faculty who are already retired or in the process of a "phased" retirement. Leslie and Janson (2005) began a study of faculty in phased retirement arrangements in order to understand the process of adjustment to retirement. Those findings suggest, first, that retirement decisions are quite individualized—subject to an idiosyncratic combination of factors, including health, spouse's situation, and so forth. Second, many fewer faculty than expected have taken advantage of such arrangements when available—although the evidence suggests that, with appropriate flexibility, phased retirement works well for both the individual and the institution. The NSOPF-99 (and -93) provides a second, more direct though less obvious, source of information on retired faculty. One of the NSOPF questions asks fac-

ulty respondents whether they have retired from another position. The data
show that nearly one-tenth of the faculty had retired from another position and
were working in their second career. Moreover, most of those retirees were from
other faculty positions at institutions of higher education. Once having identified such a subgroup, we can use the considerable available information on
NSOPF to paint a portrait, at least in gross strokes, of the "retired" faculty who
have chosen to continue their careers in another institution of higher education.
What do the data tell us about this subgroup of faculty retirees? Most of these
retirees (n = about 7,800) are now part-timers who have retired from a previous
full-time job, whether that job was academic or nonacademic (e.g., military, law
enforcement, or business) (see chapter 7, the section titled "Mobility between
Part-Time and Full-Time Appointments"). For these "retired" individuals, part-
time work appears to constitute a kind of phased retirement from full-time faculty or nonacademic work. (As our analysis elsewhere has shown, this subgroup
of retirees, together with aspiring full-timers who are holding down multiple
part-time academic jobs, is the fastest-growing segment of the part-time professoriate (see Appendix D).

SUMMARY

What have we learned about the evolving shape of academic careers? The
data suggest a range of important changes. The pace and magnitude of these
changes naturally have varied depending on the particular career dimension being examined. What is clear, however, is that key aspects of academic careers,
from inception to conclusion, have undergone consequential transformations.
The expectations about one's career prospects that an entering academic could
have reasonably entertained a generation ago differ strikingly from current realistic expectations. The passageways have become bumpier. Consider the following.

First, career entry has become substantially more competitive in purely numerical terms. While overall demand for faculty has remained relatively stable,
the supply, in terms of PhD production, continued to mount in most fields
throughout the 1990s, translating into substantially greater difficulty for the person who wished to break into the traditional faculty ranks. Tighter ingress is reflected in the progressively lengthening period between receipt of one's terminal degree and appointment to an initial full-time academic position. During
this time of treading water academically, prospective faculty are more and more
likely to be employed outside the "traditional faculty track," whether in nonteaching roles in colleges and universities or outside academe. The greater bar-

riers to latching on are reflected also in the growth of off-track, full-time appointments. These non-tenure-eligible term appointments differ not only in their limited time horizon and murky career prospects, but also in the nature of the substantive work that such positions typically entail (see chapter 7). Baldwin and Chronister (2001) found in their national study that for a majority of term-limited, non-tenure-track full-time positions, the appointees performed more limited roles than tenure-track faculty did, specializing in either teaching or research.

A second key change derives from the institutional and disciplinary matrix within which academic careers are pursued. Since most faculty, especially new entrants, are increasingly employed in institutional sectors other than the research university (see chapter 3), the nature of their academic work is likely to differ from that of the typical research university scholar. In other words, increasing proportions of new-entry faculty will not be pursuing institutionally sanctioned careers that emphasize scholarship in their discipline; instead, for more and more faculty members, their academic responsibilities focus on the teaching role. This tendency is reinforced by a concomitant development in academic fields, namely, the redistribution of faculty appointments away from the traditional liberal arts and into professional and career-oriented programs.

Third is the progressive feminization of the academic career. The ascent of women in the academy (chapter 3) is especially evident among new career entrants and even more among appointees to full-time non-tenure-track positions. Given the tendency of this new cohort of women academics to be married, increasingly to other academics concurrently juggling similar career pressures (Wolf-Wendel and Ward, 2003), new projects are emerging, such as the American Association of University Professors' Balancing Academic Career and Family Work initiative (see AAUP, 2004), supported by the Sloan Foundation's emerging Workplace, Workforce, and Working Families program, that squarely place on the national policy agenda issues related to the restructuring of the workplace to meet the needs of an increasingly diverse workforce. Many academic women appear to be increasingly willing to forgo the rewards (and commitment pressures) of traditional probationary positions, so that—it would appear—they can pursue a more balanced family and work life.

Finally, there is the matter of career exit. Although there appears to be limited evidence of any great change in the timing of retirement—except at the research universities—it is quite clear that we will be dealing for some time to come with an aging faculty, but one that is healthier and more energetic than ever before. Retirees from full-time faculty positions (along with retirees from outside academe) are the fastest-growing segment of the part-time faculty (see chapter 3); and the academic profession is serving a growing cohort of faculty in their second career.

NOTES

1. The N's for Native Americans are too low to permit confident comparison.

2. Analyses of faculty rank are complicated because the instructor rank is commonly used in two quite different ways: (1) for entry-level tenure-track appointments of new faculty in four-year institutions who have not yet completed their doctorates, and (2) for faculty at numerous "rankless" two-year institutions that have disavowed a traditional rank hierarchy, where all full-time faculty, from most junior to most senior, hold the rank of instructor.

CHAPTER SEVEN

The Revolution in Academic Appointments

A Closer Look

Of the two most significant developments in recent years that have been re-shaping academic work and careers, one is obvious and ubiquitous: the technological revolution that permeates the academy. Its effects already are profound. Furthermore, instructional technology indisputably will continue to transform how academic work is done and, though less obviously, will affect significantly how academic careers are constructed. Some of those issues are considered in chapter 4 and in our earlier volume (Finkelstein et al., 2000). Here we address the second momentous change, which emerged full-blown in chapter 6: the sweeping reconfiguration of academic appointments. In contrast to the palpable technological revolution, the restructuring of academic appointments is at once more amenable to measurement—after all, noses can be counted—and somehow less visible even to close observers of academic life. The likely effects of this redeployment of appointments on academic work and careers, we contend, have been seriously underestimated. But unlike technology's irreversible advance, the sweeping changes in the types of academic appointments being made could be checked, even reversed, if institutional will so dictated.

The most visible manifestation of the reconfiguration and redeployment of instructional staff over the past three decades has been, of course, the remarkable expansion in the use of part-time appointments (see chapter 3). Although it has not always been clear to what extent the part-time role has constituted a distinctive and separate career track (i.e., an alternative to full-time employment that better fits the needs of a demographically more diverse population) or merely served as a temporary way station on the increasingly overcrowded pathway to a traditional academic career (a career beset by a long-prevailing buyer's market), the work of Tuckman (1978) and Gappa and Leslie (1993), among others, has established that a "contingent"—or, as the Australians call it, a "casual"—academic workforce has exploded from the periphery of our awareness to the dead center of academic life. The remarkable growth of this sector is described in chapter 3 (see table 3.2). The presence of part-time instructional staff has always been distributed unevenly by institutional type (especially prominent in two-year community colleges) and has been more pronounced in such academic fields as English composition, foreign languages, mathematics, and business (see tables A-3.2a and A-3.2b). Nonetheless, most observers have agreed that an unambiguous signal of a revolution in academic appointments was emerging, although opinions have varied greatly about the likely longer-term consequences of this development. In any event, it is old news.

We argue that a comparably powerful indicator of the faculty's structural evolution over the past two decades has been less visible, indeed, has largely escaped major attention: the advent and expansion of full-time faculty appointments *off* the tenure track. We refer here to the rapid emergence of fixed-term, that is, non-tenure-eligible full-time appointments, which have become widespread—even modal—among new entrants to the profession (Finkelstein, Seal, and Schuster, 1998a; Baldwin and Chronister, 2000; see chapter 6).

The purpose of this chapter is to estimate empirically the scope of the appointments revolution and to assess the empirical evidence about its implications for academic work and careers. We address five clusters of questions: (1) What is the latest available evidence on the magnitude (scope) and venues of these nontraditional, full-time appointments. Where are they located? (2) Who occupies these new appointments? That is, what are the appointees' demographic characteristics? And how do these faculty members differ from those holding traditional full-time appointments? (3) What do the new appointees do? How does the work they perform compare to that of their colleagues in traditional appointments? Are these appointments merely contractual artifacts—essentially a technicality—superimposed on what is substantively the same kind of work and configuration of responsibilities, or do they constitute an essential redesign of academic work as we have come to know it? Put another way, does this rapidly emerging category of new appointments materially affect the nature of the job itself—either the work or its content organization? Are they new names for essentially the same job description? Are the tangible rewards (organizational perquisites and compensation) the same? (4) How permeable are these new appointments? Are they newly identified tributaries to an otherwise prototypical full-time academic career? To what extent do they represent new and independent career tracks that, in effect, compete with the traditional academic career? (5) Given the similarities and dissimilarities between the different types of appointees (who they are and the work they do), what can be said about how satisfying faculty in each subset of appointees find their jobs and their careers? And, finally, does the answer differ by institutional type and field (and perhaps even by gender)? How did the movement between full-time and part-time change in the anemic academic job market of the 1980s and 1990s?

To answer these questions, we have relied primarily on two sources of data from the U.S. Department of Education: (1) the "New Hires" section of the biennial Fall Staff Survey conducted as part of the IPEDS (Integrated Postsecondary Education Data System), the successor to the HEGIS (Higher Education Government Information Survey)—a survey taken over by the National Center for Education Statistics (NCES) in 1991 from the department's Office of Civil Rights; and (2) three national faculty surveys—the 1988, 1993, and 1999 National Studies of Postsecondary Faculty (NSOPF). The former source provides an institution-based "census" of the faculty population, and the latter surveys provide population estimates of the nontraditional appointments and their institutional and disciplinary venues. These surveys allow us to trace the emergence of such appointments, to identify the demographic characteristics of their incumbents, and to provide detailed workload data that can help us understand how these faculty members' roles and work activities compare with those of their traditionally appointed colleagues. Moreover, the 1999 NSOPF includes for the first time a series of detailed questions about respondents' initial, current, and immediate past positions, thereby enabling us to examine mobility across these various types of full- and part-time appointments. Although these data are cross-sectional rather than longitudinal in nature, they nonetheless enable us to reconstruct career trajectories (mobility among types of full-time appointments as well as between part-time and full-time) for *current faculty*.[1] In addition, we provide further perspective through our analysis of appointment trends by faculty career cohorts, that is, broken out by new-entry, midcareer, and senior faculty "generations."

THE FULL-TIME OFF-TRACK PHENOMENON: THE LATEST EVIDENCE

Our analyses of career cohort differences in chapter 6 demonstrates at once that fixed-term, off-track appointments have grown substantially among new entrants to the profession, especially newly entering women and Caucasian as opposed to minority scholars, and that such appointments occur among the full spectrum of institutional types and academic fields. In the span of relatively few

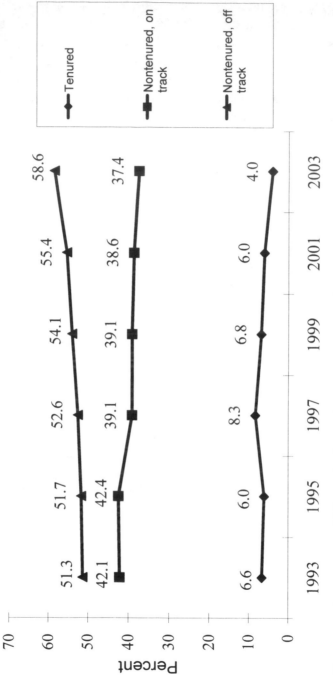

Fig. 7.1. Appointment status of full-time faculty new hires, 1993–2003. Data from USDE, 1998a, 1998b, 2000, 2001a, 2003.

years, among newly entering faculty the proportion occupying tenure-eligible positions has declined by one-third while the proportion reporting non-tenure-eligible appointments has shot up nearly sevenfold. And these analyses may actually underestimate—by a considerable margin—the scale and inexorability of the change.

Figure 7.1 charts the distribution of types of appointments for new full-time hires during the 1990s, based on NCES census data.[2] The pattern is striking and unequivocal: among new full-time hires reported by institutions of higher education to the National Center for Education Statistics, the *majority* were being appointed to non-tenure-eligible positions as early as 1993. This pattern was replicated in 1995 and again in 1997, 1999, 2001, and 2003 (USDE, 1998a, 1998b, 2000, 2001a, 2003b, 2005), with slight, though discernible, *increases* each biennium. That is to say, *term-limited full-time positions have become the modal type of full-time appointment for new entrants to academic careers.* The implications of this remarkable—we would say astonishing—development are examined later in this chapter; it will suffice for now to say that the change marks a seismic shift in the types of faculty appointments that are being made— from essentially an unknown phenomenon in 1969 to an absolute majority of full-time appointments at the onset of the twenty-first century.

DEMOGRAPHICS OF THE NEW APPOINTEES

For the demographics of the part-time faculty and the nature of their work, see chapter 3 and Appendix D. Here we employ the National Study of Postsecondary Faculty to document in precise ways the dimensions of diversity among the full-time term appointees. One major role-related variable that shows suggestive differences between tenurable and term appointees is the *type of principal activity.* Term appointees were 5% more likely than their tenure-track colleagues in 1992 to report research and administration as their principal activities and conversely 5% less likely to report teaching as their principal activity (table 7.1). And although many of these differences hold across institutional types, academic fields, race or ethnicity, gender, and career cohorts, there are a number of noteworthy exceptions (table A-7.1). In 1992, term faculty at *universities* were 5% less likely to report teaching as their principal activity (table 7.1) and 8% more likely to report research as their principal activity; that is, off-track appointees were disproportionately focused on research. By 1998, the proportions of these differences had reversed themselves—with term faculty more likely than tenurable faculty to report teaching as their principal activity and less likely to report research as their principal activity. The teaching-

TABLE 7.1

Principal Activities of Full-Time Faculty, by Appointment Status, 1992 and 1998
(percent)

	1992					1998				
	All	Teaching	Research	Admin.	Sabbatical	All	Teaching	Research	Admin.	Sabbatical
All faculty	100.0	76.9	11.7	8.5	2.9	100.0	78.5	11.4	9.1	1.0
Type of appointment										
Tenured/tenure track	89.8	77.4	11.2	8.4	3.1	85.5	78.6	11.5	8.7	1.2
Tenured	65.5	75.7	10.3	10.3	3.7	63.7	77.2	11.0	10.4	1.5
Tenure track	24.3	81.8	13.4	3.4	1.3	21.8	82.9	13.0	3.9	0.2
Non-tenure-track	10.3	73.0	16.3	9.8	0.9	14.5	78.0	10.6	11.4	0.0

Sources: NSOPF-93, NSOPF-99 (see Appendix A for key).
Note: "Non-tenure-track" does not include faculty in institutions with no tenure system.
For definitions of row and column label terms, see Appendix E.

only appointments had come of age. Even within the university sector, however, we find that natural science faculty on term appointments are 7–10% more likely to report research as their principal activity (15–30% more likely than term faculty in other liberal arts fields) and 5–7% less likely than their tenurable colleagues to report teaching as their principal activity. These differences tend to be larger among new entrants than among midcareer and senior faculty. In short, term faculty are significantly more likely to report research or administration as their principal activity at nonuniversity four-year institutions and two-year colleges and to report teaching as their principal activity at universities. Moreover, beyond institutional type, term faculty in certain fields (e.g., humanities versus natural sciences) are either more or less likely than their tenured or tenurable colleagues to report teaching as their principal activity. What these data suggest is that term appointments have taken somewhat different shapes in universities than in liberal arts colleges, comprehensive universities, and community colleges; and in the natural sciences than in other fields. Moreover, these differences are accentuated among new entrants to the profession, implying that the new roles have developed primarily in the last decade.

Comparisons among Teaching-Intensive Faculty

Who are the new appointees, and what is their role? Table 7.2 compares the regular and term faculty by highest degree, gender, racial or ethnic characteristics, age, and academic field, controlling for principal activity. Beginning with those faculty members who reported in 1992 that their principal activity was teaching, we find that term faculty were about half as likely as their regularly appointed colleagues to hold the doctorate (31.2% versus 61.4%), nearly twice as likely to be under age 45 (57.8% versus 32.3%), and more than twice as likely to be at the earliest (i.e., new-entrant) stage of their academic career (52.2% new entrants versus 22.9% in other career stages). Moreover, women were nearly twice as likely as men (54.6% versus 30.5%) to be represented among these term full-time teaching faculty, and that is especially evident in the liberal arts fields (particularly in English and modern languages). Indeed, academic women constituted the *clear majority* (50.8%) of all term faculty. This is doubtless attributable in part to the increasing prevalence of off-track appointments made recently—during the last decade or so—when most younger and women faculty would have begun their initial appointments. (It is instructive, however, to note that there were not equally substantial differences between term faculty and regular appointees in race and ethnicity, even though faculty of color, like women, have been increasingly hired over the past decade.) Furthermore, the data in

TABLE 7.2

Selected Characteristics of Tenured or Tenure-Track vs. Non-Tenure-Track Full-Time Faculty, by Principal Activity, 1992 and 1998
(percent)

	1992								1998							
	All		Principal Activity						All		Principal Activity					
			Teaching		Research		Admin.				Teaching		Research		Admin.	
Characteristics	TT	NTT	TT	NTT	TT	NTT	TT	NTT	TT	NTT	TT	NTT	TT	NTT	TT	NTT
Degree																
PhD	66.2	37.3	61.4	31.2	89.2	70.2	75.6	29.5	71.5	38.5	67.3	32.8	94.4	83.1	76.9	35.7
Gender																
Women	29.0	50.8	30.5	54.6	18.3	31.7	28.1	53.4	31.9	50.5	33.5	52.3	22.0	32.8	30.2	54.8
Marital status																
Married*	78.4	70.4	76.9	70.0	84.3	72.8	83.5	68.2	77.3	72.9	76.5	72.0	79.8	77.3	79.8	75.5
Race/ethnicity																
Asian	5.2	7.3	5.2	5.5	7.5	18.5	2.4	2.4	6.2	4.0	5.7	3.6	12.6	10.6	3.1	0.5
Other nonwhite	8.1	9.8	8.6	10.8	4.2	5.1	9.3	8.7	8.4	9.9	8.9	10.5	9.4	5.8	6.0	9.8
White	86.7	82.9	86.2	83.6	88.3	76.5	88.3	88.8	84.9	86.1	84.9	85.9	81.4	83.6	89.0	89.7
Age																
<45 years	34.9	58.9	32.3	57.8	52.0	75.6	14.7	40.7	28.4	44.4	28.0	44.2	44.7	57.5	11.0	33.8
Rank																
Professor	38.3	4.5	35.4	4.4	40.4	3.5	58.2	7.9	39.5	6.4	37.1	5.3	41.3	14.9	57.0	5.6
Associate professor	27.6	8.1	27.3	6.8	29.6	12.3	24.5	10.1	29.1	5.9	28.7	5.0	31.4	7.4	27.4	10.9
Assistant professor	23.0	30.9	24.3	31.9	28.1	31.1	8.4	23.1	22.0	24.9	23.4	24.4	25.7	38.0	6.6	16.2

Sources: NSOPF-93, NSOPF-99 (see Appendix A for key).

Notes: "TT" means "Tenured or tenure-track"; "NTT" means "Non-tenure-track."
"Non-tenure-track" does not include faculty in institutions with no tenure system.
*Married includes living with someone in a marriage-like relationship.

table A-7.2 suggest that these differences between term and regular appointees are largely confined to faculty in the four-year institutional sector; differentials in the two-year sector are minimal. Between 1992 and 1998, these differences between term and regularly appointed faculty in age and career cohort in the four-year sector become perceptibly smaller, suggesting that the new appointments and their incumbents are "working their way" out of the young and the new into the midcareer cohort of faculty.

Comparisons among Research-Intensive and Administration-Intensive Faculty

Next we make the same comparisons between those regular and term full-time faculty for whom *research* is the principal activity. Although research-intensive term faculty, like teaching term faculty, tend to be younger than their tenure-track or tenured counterparts, women are much more scarce among the ranks of the research-intensive term faculty. Among racial and ethnic groups, Asians are disproportionately represented among the research-intensive term faculty, as are, more generally, faculty in the natural sciences and engineering, especially in the four-year sector. Finally, among research-intensive faculty, the huge differences between term and regular appointees in percentage holding the doctorate as the highest degree largely disappears by 1998. Clearly, for these research-intensive term faculty, such appointments are more clearly postdoctoral in nature.

Finally, the data in table 7.2 reveal that those term appointees whose principal activity is administration tend to resemble more their teaching than their research-intensive colleagues insofar as they tend to be disproportionately lacking the PhD degree and to be women—although they differ much less from their regularly appointed colleagues in age. Such term appointments are disproportionately found in education and the professions.

WORK ACTIVITIES OF THE NEW APPOINTEES

We turn now to the question of whether—within principal activity categories—the work of full-time term appointees differs significantly from that of their tenure-track or tenured colleagues. We confine our attention to term faculty in the four-year college and university sector, since our preliminary analyses suggest that that is where the significant differences reside.

We have established that, demographically, term teaching faculty and, to a lesser extent, term research and administration faculty differ from their regular counterparts in age, gender, and highest degree and that those differences are accentuated in the four-year college and university sector and minimized in the two-year college sector. Now we ask, To what extent are the off-track appointees nevertheless engaged in the same type of work, in the same distribution of activities, as their "core" counterparts? Are both the teaching-intensive and research-intensive term faculty contributing equally to the trend toward the increased *functional specialization* (that is, refocusing) of academic work? Or are we witnessing a differentiation among full-time academics, between the traditional *functional generalists* (that is, "all-purpose" faculty members who are expected to do everything—teaching, research, and service) and the newly emergent *functional specialists?*

Comparisons among Teaching-Intensive Faculty

Among the *teaching-intensive* faculty, the term appointees show a rather different activity pattern than the regular appointees (tables 7.3, 7.4, and 7.5). In the first place, these term teaching faculty spend overall about three to five hours less weekly on the job (perhaps as much as ten hours less weekly at research universities, where differences are largest; such differences disappear in the two-year sector) (table 7.3). They allocate a greater percentage of their time to teaching (by about 5%) but allocate proportionately less of their time to research

TABLE 7.3

Mean Weekly Hours Worked by Full-Time Faculty, by Appointment Status, 1992 and 1998

| | 1992 | | | 1998 | | |
| | Principal Activity | | | Principal Activity | | |
	Teaching	Research	Admin.	Teaching	Research	Admin.
Female						
Tenured/tenure track	40.6	49.5	46.2	45.0	50.2	48.6
Tenured	39.9	48.6	45.6	44.2	49.9	48.7
Tenure track	41.8	50.5	48.4	46.4	50.6	48.3
Non-tenure-track	37.5	48.6	43.2	41.3	47.2	47.0
Male						
Tenured/tenure track	42.3	50.9	48.0	45.5	52.0	50.6
Tenured	41.9	49.7	48.2	45.2	51.3	50.3
Tenure track	43.5	53.7	46.7	46.4	53.9	54.3
Non-tenure-track	38.7	48.0	42.7	41.1	48.1	48.7

Sources: NSOPF-93, NSOPF-99 (see Appendix A for key).

Notes: The hours worked include all paid activities at this institution in teaching, research, and administration. "Non-tenure-track" does not include faculty in institutions with no tenure system.

TABLE 7.4

Allocation of Effort by Full-Time Faculty, by Appointment Status, 1992 and 1998
(percent)

	1992						1998					
	Principal Activity						Principal Activity					
	Teaching		Research		Admin.		Teaching		Research		Admin.	
	TT	NTT	TT	NTT	TT	NTT	TT	NTT	TT	NTT	TT	NTT
Female												
Teaching	67.5	71.6	27.0	8.8	23.3	13.7	68.5	74.3	34.9	24.8	31.2	33.7
Research	11.6	8.6	55.1	71.4	9.1	10.2	10.2	5.9	47.0	64.5	9.7	6.8
Administration	7.7	6.3	7.6	3.3	55.7	65.8	10.3	6.4	8.8	5.4	47.2	42.0
Professional growth	5.4	5.4	2.6	11.0	3.3	3.7	4.8	5.2	2.9	2.7	3.9	7.8
Consulting	1.8	2.3	1.2	0.6	1.3	0.7	2.3	3.7	2.2	0.7	3.1	3.9
Service	5.9	5.7	4.9	5.0	7.3	5.9	4.0	4.4	4.2	1.9	5.0	5.8
Male												
Teaching	61.5	65.1	24.1	7.4	20.5	20.0	65.6	71.0	32.8	20.4	28.8	26.8
Research	17.0	11.3	56.6	81.1	11.4	4.4	14.1	7.4	47.1	60.9	11.6	7.0
Administration	8.5	8.6	9.5	3.1	58.6	66.5	8.9	9.1	9.6	8.4	48.5	56.4
Professional growth	4.6	6.0	2.7	3.2	2.7	3.0	4.2	4.3	2.6	3.4	3.2	4.0
Consulting	3.2	3.9	2.5	1.6	2.4	1.5	3.0	4.7	3.0	2.2	3.1	2.7
Service	5.1	5.2	4.3	3.6	4.5	4.6	4.2	3.4	5.0	4.7	4.8	3.2

Sources: NSOPF-93, NSOPF-99 (see Appendix A for key).

Notes: "TT" means "Tenurable or tenured"; "NTT" means "Non-tenure-track."
"Non-tenure-track" does not include faculty in institutions with no tenure system.
Effort refers to all paid activities at this institution (teaching, research, administration, etc.)

TABLE 7.5

Selected Work Activities of Full-Time Faculty, by Appointment Status, 1992 and 1998
(percent)

Work Activities	1992						1998					
	Principal Activity						Principal Activity					
	Teaching		Research		Admin.		Teaching		Research		Admin.	
	TT	NTT	TT	NTT	TT	NTT	TT	NTT	TT	NTT	TT	NTT
Female												
Teaching undergraduates only	44.6	45.8	10.6	8.8	30.4	29.5	59.8	62.4	7.3	22.0	38.6	54.9
No publications during career	31.5	45.1	8.5	28.5	20.5	29.8	23.4	40.4	1.2	8.0	17.2	35.0
No publications during past 2 years	46.9	59.3	13.1	34.0	35.1	56.8	35.8	53.3	2.3	15.4	26.4	49.6
Have funded research	29.0	23.8	78.6	87.4	39.0	27.5	18.3	29.1	84.2	74.6	28.5	42.7
No informal contact hours with students	10.9	13.5	20.2	44.6	14.3	30.1	29.4	47.5	31.7	49.0	28.1	37.8
Male												
Teaching undergraduates only	36.5	41.5	10.3	9.2	21.8	32.3	49.5	64.1	4.2	15.4	25.8	58.5
No publications during career	21.7	37.5	3.9	3.0	12.0	39.0	15.2	37.3	0.2	3.5	5.6	29.5
No publications during past 2 years	37.0	52.6	5.6	7.2	29.8	46.3	29.8	48.5	1.4	3.5	17.9	49.1
Have funded research	34.4	22.0	82.1	86.4	44.8	30.4	31.6	15.6	86.3	88.1	43.3	21.8
No informal contact hours with students	11.6	18.1	14.6	53.5	14.5	18.4	29.3 4	1.8	33.0	47.1	27.3	38.7

Sources: NSOPF-93, NSOPF-99 (see Appendix A for key).
Notes: "TT" means "Tenurable or tenured"; "NTT" means "Non-tenure-track."
"Non-tenure-track" does not include faculty in institutions with no tenure system.

(about 5% less, although differences are greater for men than for women) (table 7.4). They are more likely to be teaching only undergraduates (table 7.5). However, they are less likely to report that they interact informally with students. Indeed, the data on this latter point suggest that disparities between term and tenurable faculty grew considerably between 1992 and 1998. Term teaching faculty are also less likely than regular appointees to have published anything during the previous two years or to have been engaged in funded research.

Comparisons among Research-Intensive and Administration-Intensive Faculty

When we turn to a comparison of activity patterns among those faculty members for whom *research* or *administration* is their principal activity, we find corroboration of a portrait of increased functional specialization. Teaching constitutes a quite small part of their work activity—although typically it is larger for those whose principal activity is administration (table 7.4). The teaching component ranges from a low of about 7% of time for male university research-intensive faculty to a high of only about 20% for research-intensive faculty at any four-year institution and 33% for administration-intensive faculty (table A-7.4). Among the research-intensive term faculty, the vast majority spend 60–80% of their time in research. And with the exceptions of faculty in business, education, and the social sciences, the term-appointed research faculty spend considerably more time engaged in research than do even their regularly appointed colleagues for whom research is their principal activity. Moreover, the data suggest that term research faculty interact informally with students much less frequently; in fact, zero is the modal response. And they are about equally as likely as regularly appointed research-intensive faculty to be engaged in conducting grant-funded research (table 7.5). They do *not* differ from their regularly appointed colleagues in self-reported weekly work hours as much as the teaching-intensive faculty do (table 7.4).

As for administration-intensive faculty, they, not unexpectedly, allocate most of their effort to administration—roughly one-half to two-thirds. Their modest involvement with teaching is, according to table 7.5, more likely to be limited to undergraduates than are the teaching duties of their regularly appointed colleagues. Unlike the research-intensive faculty, they are as likely to be found in the two-year as the four-year sector.

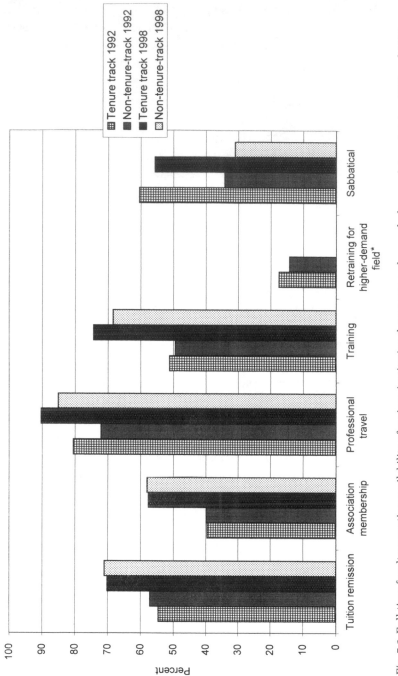

Fig. 7.2. Full-time faculty reporting availability of various institutional supports and rewards, by appointment status, 1992 and 1998.
*Data available only for 1992.

INSTITUTIONAL SUPPORT AND BENEFITS

Term faculty differ from their regularly appointed colleagues not only in their work activities, but also in the kinds of support they receive from their institutions—although, in this regard the difference is not as great as might be expected. Thus, term faculty whose principal activity is teaching compare unfavorably to their regular colleagues only in regard to the more limited availability of sabbatical leaves and professional travel support (fig. 7.2). But in other respects, the teaching-oriented term faculty appear to receive roughly equal treatment in such areas as training benefits, tuition remission, and professional association dues. Among faculty members whose principal activity is research, only the lesser availability of sabbatical leaves appears to distinguish between term faculty and their regular counterparts. Otherwise, the research-intensive faculty (regular and term appointees) receive comparable institutional support. Among faculty whose principal activity is administration, off-track faculty are actually more likely than on-track faculty to have tuition remission and professional association membership benefits. Only sabbaticals and released time are less likely to be available to them (table A-7.6).

THE CHANGING TRAJECTORY OF ACADEMIC CAREERS

If term faculty differ from their regular colleagues in who they are (younger, more women, more in the professions) and what they do (type of principal activity, time commitment, and allocation of effort), what can we say about their career trajectories? Although there has been growing recognition of the emergence of more variegated academic appointments and career paths (and not a little anecdotal material), little systematic empirical evidence has surfaced to describe actual career trajectories of the "new" American faculty.

The 1999 National Study of Postsecondary Faculty (NCES, 2001b) makes possible for the first time some systematic, albeit preliminary, answers to this question. Faculty members in a nationally representative sample were asked to describe their current job as well as both their first academic job (beyond graduate assistant) and the academic job immediately preceding their current one. The description included their *employment status* (part-time or full-time) and, if full-time, their *appointment status* (on-track or off-track) both at *hire* and at *exit*. We can thus trace, retrospectively, the career paths of current part-time and full-time faculty across both their employment and appointment statuses, although our conclusions are constrained by the fact that respondents provided data on no more than three academic jobs. As drawn from the NSOPF-99 data file, both part-time faculty (projecting to a national total of 317,210) and full-time faculty (projecting to 479,610) answered questions about their previous employment, thereby constituting our sizable "usable" population.

We conducted separate analyses for current part-time and current full-time faculty subgroups. In each case, we identified three subsets of faculty: those who reported having held (1) only one academic job during their career, that is, the current job; (2) two jobs, that is, one previous academic job (their initial one in addition to their current job); and (3) three (or more) jobs during their careers (i.e., a first academic job *and* another academic job, the one immediately prior to the current job). For each of these subgroups, we examined the distribution of employment and appointment statuses at those three career stages: at initial career entry (first job), at immediately prior job, and at current job.

In tracking academic careers, then, we have had to begin with currently appointed faculty and, by working backward, seek to recreate their career trajectories. This approach (the only one available) has at least two serious limitations. First, excluded from the analysis are a large but unknown number of individuals who for personal or professional reasons have "dropped out" or have been obliged to depart from academic jobs and who obviously were not available to participate in the survey. Regarding these missing former faculty, current estimates, based on responses to the NSOPF-99 Institutional Questionnaire (as distinguished from the questionnaire answered by individual faculty members), are that annually about 2% of the aggregate faculty separate from their institutions for reasons other than retirement (NCES, 2001b)—although it is not clear what percentage of institutional separations constitute movement to another academic institution rather than leaving academe entirely. Moreover, these dropouts are likely to be disproportionately women and members of racial and ethnic minorities. Accordingly, because we are reconstructing the careers only of the "survivors," our perspective may be distorted. A further limitation is that the NSOPF-99 provides data on a maximum of three jobs: first job, current job, and job immediately preceding current one. Obviously, a larger number of data points, had they been available, would have allowed us to trace more accurately the peregrinations across employment and appointment statuses in current faculty members' careers. Nonetheless, such is the available data. And whatever limitations need to be acknowledged, it seems fair to suggest that we do have a large and very representative segment of the faculty who have persisted at least to this point in academic careers. More importantly, these data allow us, for the first time to our knowledge, to estimate mobility *across* employment and appointment statuses—at least at three key career stages for this representative group of faculty.

What can we say about the careers of these academic persisters? Undergirding our analysis is the overarching question, To what extent does the academic career remain a unitary one? That is, to what extent has the single prototypical career that crystallized in the post–World War II era endured relatively intact for full-time academics—despite the proliferation in more recent years of new types of appointments? We now ask, Have these new types of appointments simply been absorbed into the prototypical career track (terminal degree leading to probationary, junior appointment, then on to tenure, and eventually promotion to full professor)? Or have the new appointments created alternative, separate career tracks, which would presumably mean that the profession is giving rise to a further and significant differentiation and diversification of academic careers?

MOBILITY BETWEEN PART-TIME AND
FULL-TIME APPOINTMENTS

We begin by focusing on the careers of current part-time faculty and then turn to those of current full-time faculty. To what extent is there considerable porosity between part-time and full-time faculty status during the course of an academic career? Embedded in this part of our inquiry is how often a part-time appointment actually leads to securing a full-time faculty appointment. A preliminary word needs to be said about overall mobility rates. Table 7.6 indicates the proportion of faculty reporting one, two, or three previous jobs. What do we learn? In the first place, the data tell us that about two-fifths (40.4%) of current part-timers (n = 128,153) report *no previous* job, meaning that their current part-time position is their first and (thus far) only academic work experience. The majority, however—three of five (59.6%)—report having held one or more previous academic positions, and it is to these roughly 189,100 faculty that we now turn our attention. (Among full-time faculty, there is slightly more previous experience: about one-third have had only one job, another one-third have had two, and another one-third have had three.)

Tables 7.7a and 7.7b report the extent of previous work experience for currently employed part- and full-time faculty. Figure 7.3 illustrates graphically the distribution of that previous academic work experience (whether part- or full-time) among part- and full-time roles, controlling for highest degree. The big story beyond mobility rates, here, is clearly in the distribution of previous em-

TABLE 7.6

Basic Mobility Rate of Faculty, by Employment Status and Highest Degree, 1998
(percent)

Number of Jobs	All Faculty		Doctorate or 1st Professional Degree		Master's or Less	
	Part-Time	Full-Time	Part-Time	Full-Time	Part-Time	Full-Time
	$N = 317,210$	$N = 479,610$	$N = 82,780$	$N = 321,540$	$N = 234,430$	$N = 158,070$
One (current job is 1st)	40.4	33.7	26.0	29.8	45.5	41.6
Two (current job + 1st)	27.1	29.9	25.5	31.3	27.6	27.0
Three (current job + 2)	32.5	36.4	48.6	38.8	26.9	31.4

Source: NSOPF-99 (see Appendix A for key).

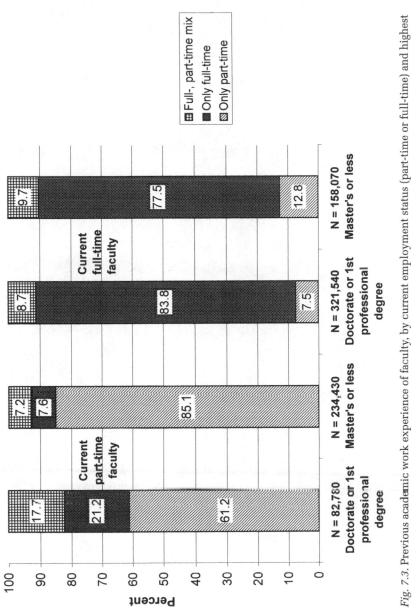

Fig. 7.3. Previous academic work experience of faculty, by current employment status (part-time or full-time) and highest degree, 1998. Data from NSOPF-99.

TABLE 7.7A

Employment Status at First and Most Recent Academic Jobs for Current Part-Time Faculty, by Highest Degree, 1998

	All Faculty		Doctorate or 1st Professional Degree		Master's or Less	
	N	%	N	%	N	%
All faculty	317,210	100.0	82,780	100.0	234,430	100.0
Part-time faculty with no previous job						
1st job part-time (i.e., current job)	128,153	40.4	21,523	26.0	106,666	45.5
Part-time faculty with 1 previous job	85,880	27.1	21,110	25.5	64,770	27.6
1st job part-time	(65,784)	(20.7)	(12,813)	(15.5)	(52,982)	(22.6)
1st job full-time	(20,096)	(6.3)	(8,296)	(10.0)	(11,788)	(5.0)
Part-time faculty with 2 or more previous jobs	103,180	32.5	40,200	48.6	62,980	26.9
both 1st and most recent jobs part-time	(56,250)	(17.7)	(16,341)	(19.7)	(39,928)	(17.0)
both 1st and most recent jobs full-time	(15,403)	(4.9)	(9,242)	(11.2)	(6,156)	(2.6)
1st job part-time, most recent job full-time	(11,440)	(3.6)	(5,189)	(6.3)	(6,232)	(2.7)
1st job full-time, most recent job part-time	(20,087)	(6.3)	(9,428)	(11.4)	(10,663)	(4.5)

Source: NSOPF-99 (see Appendix A for key).
Note: Parentheses denote subsets of larger numbers.

TABLE 7.7B

Movement between Full-Time and Part-Time by Current Full-Time Faculty with One or More Previous Jobs, 1998

	All Faculty		Doctorate or 1st Professional Degree		Master's or Less	
	N	%	N	%	N	%
All full-time faculty	479,610	100.0	321,540	100.0	158,070	100.0
Full time faculty with no previous job						
1st job full-time (i.e., current job)	161,629	33.7	95,819	29.8	65,757	41.6
Full-time faculty with 1 previous job	143,440	29.9	100,740	31.3	42,700	27.0
1st job part-time	(28,688)	(6.0)	(15,615)	(4.9)	(13,024)	(8.2)
1st job full-time	(114,752)	(23.9)	(85,125)	(26.5)	(29,677)	(18.8)
Full-time faculty with 2 or more previous jobs	174,470	36.4	124,860	38.8	49,620	31.4
Both 1st and most recent jobs part-time	(15,562)	(3.2)	(8,207)	(2.6)	(7,346)	(4.6)
Both 1st and most recent jobs full-time	(115,567)	(24.1)	(88,581)	(27.5)	(26,961)	(17.1)
1st job part-time, most recent job full-time	(28,028)	(5.8)	(17,123)	(5.3)	(10,925)	(6.9)
1st job full-time, most recent job part-time	(15,313)	(3.2)	(10,948)	(3.4)	(4,389)	(2.8)

Source: NSOPF-99 (see Appendix A for key).

Note: Parentheses denote subsets of larger numbers and percentages.

ployment statuses. Among current part-time faculty, the vast majority (more than three-fifths, or 61.2%, of the 82,780 doctorate holders and five-sixths of the 234,430 master's degree holders) report *only part-time experience* (counting their current job). This suggests that current part-time faculty predominantly live an "exclusive" pattern of part-time employment; the vast majority of current part-timers who report any previous employment moved to their current part-time job from other part-time jobs. In all, only 66,000 (34.9% of those with any previous academic employment, or 20.8% of the total group of 317,200 part-time faculty) have had any previous full-time academic employment. If it is not exactly rare to have moved from full- to part-time teaching, it is distinctly uncommon. This leaves aside, for now, how many of the track-switchers switch by choice.

As to highest degree earned, when we distinguish between holders of the doctorate and the master's degree or less, we find an even more pronounced pattern of divergent experiences: among those with a master's degree or less, only 34,800 out of 234,400 (14.9%) have had any previous full-time experience. By contrast, just over half of the doctorate holders (32,200 of 61,300, or 52.4%) with previous academic job experience indicate having had at least some full-time academic experience. Another lens: These 32,200 former full-timers constitute nearly two of every five (38.8%) current part-time faculty (82,800) who hold the doctorate.

So, just who are the 32,200 part-timers with doctorates who have made the transition from full- to part-time experience? The data suggest two dominant patterns. In the first place, a sizable one-fourth (some 7,800) of these "be-doctored" part-timers with previous full-time academic experience are "retirees" from a previous full-time job, whether that job was academic or nonacademic (e.g., military, law enforcement, business). For these "retired" individuals, part-time work appears to constitute a kind of "phased" retirement from full-time faculty or nonacademic work. (As our analysis elsewhere has shown, this subgroup of retirees, together with "aspiring" full-timers who are holding down multiple part-time academic jobs, is the fastest-growing segment of the part-time professoriate [see chapter 6, page 188].) However, the substantial majority—about three-fourths or some 24,500 of these doctorate-holding part-timers with previous full-time experience—are *not* retired. This group is approximately two-thirds male, mostly teaching in the traditional liberal arts and sciences. Between 70% and 90% of these nonretirees with *previous* full-time experience report other *concurrent* employment. In particular, the majority of them report having previous full-time employment that is also *concurrent* full-time employment (in instruction, research, and service, as opposed to administrative roles) at *four-year* colleges and universities. We expected that these individuals would primarily include full-time faculty at two-year community colleges who are teaching part-time at four-year institutions, but we found rather that they were primarily full-time faculty at *four-year* colleges and universities who were teaching also at *another* campus (two- or four-year). So a considerable amount of "moonlighting" appears to be taking place, and it accounts for a significant amount of the full-time experience of doctorate-holding faculty members who received and completed the questionnaire in their capacity as part-timers.

When we turn to current full-timers (table 7.7b), about four-fifths report a pattern of only full-time experience (counting their current job). Of the 317,900 current full-time faculty who report having had some previous academic employment beyond teaching assistant, fully 230,300 (72.4%) report *only* full-time previous experience. The remaining 87,600 full-timers are evenly divided between those reporting a "mix" of part- and full-time experience (43,300, or 13.5%) and those whose previous experience was limited to part-time appointments (44,300, or 13.9%). When we combine the 230,300 faculty whose previous experience was limited to full-time academic appointments with the 161,600 current full-timers who had no previous academic job experience, it is clear that the overwhelming majority—fully 391,900 of the 479,600 current full-timers, or 81.7%—have had *only* full-time experience.

These data suggest a corollary to our "rule" about the "part-time-exclusive" track: nearly three-fourths of the current full-time faculty who report previous academic employment indicate having moved to their current full-time position from another full-time academic position. Moreover, it should be noted that fewer than one-fifth of all current full-timers (87,600/479,610, or 18.3%) report *any* previous part-time faculty experience.

As is the case with current part-timers, the basic pattern is even more pronounced when we compare full-timers who are doctorate holders (or who have a first professional degree) with full-timers who hold a master's degree or less. Of the 225,600 full-timers holding the doctorate who report having any previous academic experience, 173,700 (77.0%) have had *only* full-time previous experience, while small fractions have had any part-time appointment: 23,800 (10.6%) report only previous part-time experience, and 28,000 (12.4%) report a mix of part- and full-time experience.

Among the 92,300 full-time faculty holding master's degrees or less who report previous academic experience, 56,600 (61.3%) report only full-time previous experience, while considerably smaller proportions have some part-time experience in their academic history: 20,400 (22.1%) report only part-time experience, and

TABLE 7.8
Characteristics of Faculty Moving from Part-Time to Full-Time vs. Those Staying Part-Time, 1998

	Movers						Stayers					
	All		Doctorate or 1st Professional Degree		Master's or Less		All		Doctorate or 1st Professional Degree		Master's or Less	
	N	%	N	%	N	%	N	%	N	%	N	%
All faculty	59,520	100	34,789	100	24,740	100	142,170	100	38,570	100	103,610	100
Institutional type												
Universities and other												
4-yr. institutions	39,536	67	27,936	80	11,650	47	70,936	50	25,960	67	45,863	44
2-yr. colleges	14,932	25	4,194	12	10,724	43	57,136	40	7,778	20	49,340	48
Other institutions	5,003	8	2,671	8	2,355	10	14,175	10	5,732	15	8,460	8
Program area												
Liberal arts and sciences	38,199	64	23,710	68	14,494	59	90,831	64	23,012	60	67,804	65
Humanities	14,414	24	9,462	27	4,927	20	33,742	24	780	20	25,897	25
Natural sciences	10,793	18	6,550	19	4,242	17	23,955	17	7,708	20	16,946	16
Professions	14,104	24	6,885	20	7,219	29	31,681	22	9,619	25	22,071	21
Gender												
Female	28,393	48	15,394	44	13,000	53	65,251	46	11,361	29	53,836	52
Male	31,155	52	19,386	56	11,740	47	76,919	54	27,209	71	49,774	48
Race/ethnicity												
Asian	2,266	4	1,466	4	805	3	4,125	3	1,604	4	2,491	2
Other nonwhite	5,231	9	3,206	9	2,032	8	13,693	10	2,790	7	10,985	11
White	52,022	87	30,127	87	21,903	89	124,352	87	34,176	89	90,187	87
No publications in past 2 yrs.	23,379	39	8,897	26	14,496	59	88,518	62	17,681	46	70,944	68
Doctorate or 1st professional degree	34,780	58	34,789	100	0	0	38,570	27	38,570	100	0	0

Source: NSOPF-99 (see Appendix A for key).
Note: "Other institutions" include private, not-for-profit associate degree institutions, public baccalaureate institutions, and other "specialized" institutions (e.g., technology institutes, service academies).

15,300 (16.6%) report a "mix" of previous experience. Presumably these include a preponderance of faculty at the two-year community colleges.

Overall, by including those current full-timers without previous academic job experience, the overwhelming proportion of current full-timers who hold the doctorate (269,500 out of 321,500, or 83.5%) report *only* full-time academic work experience, while fewer of the current full-timers who hold a master's degree or less (122,400 out of 158,000, or 77.4%) have, similarly, had only full-time experience.

On the face of it, then, part-time work would appear to play a significantly different role in the careers of faculty with doctoral degrees compared to those with master's degrees or less. For a substantial proportion of the doctorate holders, part-time employment would seem to represent either a supplemental source of income for those holding full-time appointments at another, usually four-year, institution, or perhaps a stepping-stone to retirement following a full-time career in academe or elsewhere. For the no-higher-than-master's holders, part-time work represents a more distinct career track, affording considerably less opportunity for mobility across tracks. (And the attrition problem noted earlier probably results in a serious underestimation of the durability of the part-time track for nondoctorates, since presumably many of them either abandon academe or return to school to get the doctorate.)

Accordingly, it would appear that part-time and full-time academic work tend to constitute fairly independent career tracks. Current part-timers without the doctorate largely move among part-time positions. And current part-timers with the doctorate who report previous full-time experience often are faculty members who have retired from full-time positions or faculty who hold full-time appointments at four-year colleges and universities and are moonlighting. Among full-timers with the doctorate, full-time employment constitutes a largely independent career track—and crossing from part-time to full-time is the decided exception.

What factors appear to affect the permeability of the boundaries between part-time and full-time career tracks? Table 7.8 examines the institutional and disciplinary venues, as well as the demographic and other characteristics that differentiate (1) those current full-time faculty who *moved* to their full-time positions from previous part-time academic jobs from (2) those current part-time faculty who *stayed* in part-time positions in the course of their job moves. The first observation to be made is this: whether we look at one or at multiple job changes, more than twice as many current faculty stayed part-time ($n = 142,000$) as moved from a part-time to a full-time position ($n = 59,500$). When we examine mobility by highest degree, we find that among doctorate holders (combining those with one and with two or more previous academic jobs), about as many moved to full-time status (34,800) as remained in part-time positions (38,600). In contrast, among those holding master's degrees only, the stayers outnumbered the movers by a ratio of more than four to one. Put another way, doctorate holders were overrepresented among the movers to full time (58.4% of all movers, leaving just 41.6% of all movers to those holding only master's degrees). Correspondingly, the doctorate holders were *under*represented among the stayers: 27.1% of all stayers versus 72.9% of all stayers holding master's degrees. Clearly, for those who had earned the doctoral degree, part-time academic jobs are as likely as not to lead eventually to full-time jobs, whereas for those who do not earn a degree beyond the master's level, movement from part-time to full-time is decidedly less common.

Next we ask what characteristics, beyond highest degree held, differentiate between the profile of current full-timers who began as part-timers (the movers) and those current part-timers who have remained part-time (the stayers). Among the relatively small number of full-time faculty who succeeded in making the move from a part-time appointment ($n = 59,520$), table 7.8 shows that

1. Movers disproportionately represent faculty at four-year colleges and universities, while stayers disproportionately are found among two-year college faculty.
2. Movers and stayers do not differ in their broad disciplinary area profiles.
3. Females and males and racial subgroups are approximately equally distributed in both groups (movers and stayers).
4. Faculty who do not publish are overrepresented among stayers (62%) but underrepresented among movers (39%).

If we ask how the profile of movers versus stayers differs between the two highest-degree subgroups, we find that among doctorate holders (including first professional degree),

5. Movers are more likely to be affiliated with four-year colleges and universities than master's degree holders are (hardly surprising).
6. Movers are more likely to be in the liberal arts, especially the humanities, than stayers are.
7. Stayers are much more likely to be male (71%) than movers (56%) are.

Taken together, these findings suggest that what modest movement does exist between part-and full-time employment tends to occur more frequently for holders of the doctorate than for master's degree holders and for faculty who have published than for those who have not. Furthermore, cross-boundary movement occurs more in the four-year than the two-year sector and more among faculty in the traditional arts and sciences, especially the humanities, than faculty in the professions. For doctorate holders, but much less so for master's holders, permeability or mobility between part-time and full-time appointments is affected by program area (more mobility in the liberal arts and humanities than in the professions) and by gender (to the disadvantage of males).

MOBILITY ON AND OFF THE TENURE TRACK

Full-time but off-track (that is, fixed-term) appointments numbered 111,000 out of the 479,000 full-time faculty appointments in 1998, or 23.1%. (A much larger proportion of newly hired full-time appointees are off-track, as noted previously, but that's another story.) If part-time and full-time faculty tend to occupy largely separate career channels (except for faculty holding the doctorate in the four-year sector), what about the permeability of boundaries between "regular" (tenure-bearing) and fixed-term full-time appointments? And how do these faculty subsets interact with part-time jobs? That is, to the extent that part-time jobs pave the way to full-time academic positions, do they lead to off-track full-time positions or to on-track (regular) appointments? Table 7.9 displays the

TABLE 7.9

Job Mobility Patterns of Current Full-Time Faculty, by Appointment Status, 1998

| | Current Appointment Status | | | | | |
| | All Faculty | | Tenured or Tenure Track | | Non-Tenure-Track | |
	N	%	N	%	N	%
All faculty	479,523	100.0	368,523	100.0	111,000	100.0
No previous job	101,700	33.7	118,526	32.2	43,174	38.9
One previous job	143,353	29.9	114,608	31.1	28,745	25.9
PT	(28,598)	(6.0)	(19,025)	(5.2)	(9,573)	(8.6)
FT on-track	(58,437)	(12.2)	(55,699)	(15.1)	(2,738)	(2.5)
FT off -track	(56,432)	(11.8)	(39,998)	(10.8)	(16,434)	(14.8)
Two previous jobs	174,470	36.4	135,389	36.7	39,081	35.2
Both PT	(15,575)	(3.2)	(10,923)	(3.0)	(4,652)	(4.2)
1st PT, 2nd FT (off)	(11,280)	(2.4)	(6,369)	(1.7)	(4,911)	(4.4)
1st PT, 2nd FT (on)	(13,990)	(2.9)	(13,500)	(3.7)	(490)	(0.4)
Both FT (off)	(34,791)	(7.3)	(18,521)	(5.0)	(16,270)	(14.7)
1st FT (off), 2nd FT (on)	(28,400)	(5.9)	(26,706)	(7.2)	(1,694)	(1.5)
1st FT (off), 2nd PT	(9,900)	(2.1)	(5,791)	(1.6)	(4,109)	(3.7)
Both FT (on)	(41,480)	(8.6)	(40,319)	(10.9)	(1,161)	(1.0)
1st FT (on), 2nd FT (off)	(10,904)	(2.3)	(8,641)	(2.3)	(2,263)	(2.0)
1st FT (on), 2nd PT	(5,390)	(1.1)	(4,641)	(1.3)	(749)	(0.6)

Source: NSOPF-99 (see Appendix A for key).
  Note: Parentheses denote subsets of larger numbers.

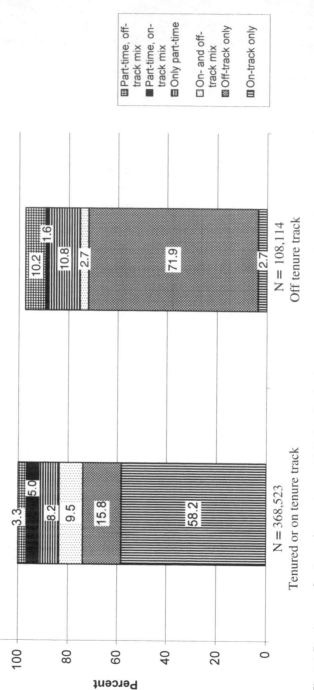

Legend:
- ⊞ Part-time, off-track mix
- ■ Part-time, on-track mix
- ☰ Only part-time
- ☐ On- and off-track mix
- ▨ Off-track only
- ▥ On-track only

Tenured or on tenure track (N = 368,523):
3.3, 5.0, 8.2, 9.5, 15.8, 58.2

Off tenure track (N = 108,114):
10.2, 1.6, 10.8, 2.7, 71.9, 2.7

Percent

Fig. 7.4. Previous academic work experience of full-time faculty, by current tenure status (on-track or off-track), 1998. Data from NSOFP-99.

distribution of *previous* employment experiences of current full-time faculty shown by *current* appointment status (on-track or off-track). The three sub-groups are quite evenly divided: as we saw previously (table 7.7b), about one-third (33.7%) of full-timers report having had no previous jobs, slightly fewer (29.9%) indicate having held a single previous academic job, and somewhat more than one-third (36.4%) report at least two previous jobs. However, full-timers who are *off*-track are more likely (38.9% of them) than their *on*-track counterparts (32.2%) to have held no previous job, since they are presumably more likely to be at the early part of their academic career. (By a similar margin, the off-track appointees are *less* likely than the on-track faculty to have had one previous position: 25.9% versus 31.1%.)

Figure 7.4 graphically contrasts the mix of work experience of current full-time faculty (counting their current job) by their current tenure appointment status. The data indicate quite clearly that the majority (58.2%) of on-track faculty report *only* full-time on-track experience, whereas an even larger majority of off-track faculty (68.4%) report *only* full-time off-track experience. However, figure 7.4 (as well as table 7.9) suggests a situation of much greater permeability *within* full-time tracks than *between* part-time and full-time statuses. Nine distinct permutations are required to encompass faculty mobility experiences across three academic jobs—although some are clearly more *modal* than others.

What distinguishes those who move onto the tenure track from those who remain off-track? As seen in table 7.10, the importance of the highest degree in facilitating a move from off-track to on-track in the four-year college and university sector is clearly reinforced: three-fourths of the "successful" movers held doctorates versus only 42% of those who stayed in off-track positions. Within the four-year college and university sector, 85.5% (72,859 of 85,222) of movers, but only 50.8% (19,860 of 39,082) of stayers, are doctorate or first professional degree holders. Faculty in this four-year sector were disproportionately represented among the movers, as were faculty in the liberal arts, especially the natural sciences (and, conversely, faculty in the professions were overrepresented among the stayers). As to gender, males were overrepresented among movers (64.5%) while females were overrepresented among the stayers (48.1%). Barely half (51.9%) of the stayers were male. Moreover, movers are much more likely than stayers to have published something (73.6% versus 52.1%).

What these data suggest (interpreted in the light of table 7.8 on mobility of another kind, i.e., from part-time to full-time) is that there is some considerable permeability between off-track and on-track full-time appointments. This is especially the case among those who have earned the doctoral degree. At the same time, three other observations can be made:

TABLE 7.10
Characteristics of Faculty Moving from Off Tenure Track to On Tenure Track vs. Those Staying Off-Track, 1998

	Movers						Stayers					
	All		Doctorate or 1st Professional Degree		Master's or Less		All		Doctorate or 1st Professional Degree		Master's or Less	
	N	%	N	%	N	%	N	%	N	%	N	%
All faculty	111,540	100.0	84,800	100.0	26,740	100.0	61,590	100.0	25,850	100.0	35,720	100.0
Institutional type												
Universities and other												
4-yr. institutions	85,222	76.4	72,859	85.9	12,347	46.2	39,082	63.5	19,860	76.8	19,195	53.7
2-yr. colleges	19,200	17.2	6,084	8.2	13,147	49.3	15,108	24.5	3,229	12.5	11,878	33.3
Other institutions	7,117	6.4	5,813	6.9	1,261	4.7	7,436	12.1	2,772	10.7	4,683	13.1
Program area												
Liberal arts and sciences	71,396	64.0	55,435	65.4	15,931	59.6	31,739	51.5	16,574	64.1	15,160	42.4
Humanities	21,314	19.1	16,690	19.7	4,628	17.3	11,736	19.1	5,091	19.7	6,635	18.6
Natural sciences	28,900	25.9	24,051	28.4	4,839	18.3	11,827	19.2	7,375	28.5	4,444	12.4
Professions	26,287	23.6	19,319	21.6	6,959	26.0	20,513	33.3	6,289	24.3	14,185	39.7
Gender												
Female	39,570	35.5	27,080	31.9	12,491	46.7	29,617	48.1	10,539	40.8	19,078	53.4
Male	71,970	64.5	57,720	68.1	14,250	53.3	31,973	51.9	15,311	59.2	16,642	46.6
Race/ethnicity												
Asian	6,666	6.0	5,452	6.4	1,205	4.5	1,789	2.9	972	3.8	810	2.3
Other nonwhite	9,863	8.8	7,248	8.5	2,647	9.9	6,041	9.8	2,357	9.1	3,715	10.4
White	95,985	86.1	72,060	85.0	22,889	85.6	53,786	87.3	22,547	87.2	31,231	87.4
No publications in past 2 yrs.	29,436	26.4	14,416	17.0	15,050	56.3	29,522	47.9	7,620	29.5	21,919	61.4
Doctorate or 1st prof. degree	84,800	76.0	84,800	100.0	0	0.0	25,850	42.0	25,850	100.0	0	0.0

Source: NSOPF-99 (see Appendix A for key).

Note: "Other institutions" include private, not-for-profit associate degree institutions, public baccalaureate institutions, and other "specialized " institutions (e.g., technology institutes, service academies).

1. Permeability clearly varies by gender, with men more likely to move onto the tenure track than women.
2. Permeability varies, too, by traditional academic productivity: a publishing record, it appears, facilitates gaining access to the tenure track. To a lesser extent, program area matters, too. (Moves onto the track are more frequent in the natural sciences, presumably based on the long tradition of the postdoctoral research appointment.)
3. The modal situation, however, is still nonpermeability; that is, most faculty who currently are in an off-track position began that way, and only about one-third of those currently in full-time tenured or tenure-track positions moved to these positions from full-time off-track jobs.

The foregoing analyses are summarized in table 7.11. They suggest that, at a minimum, we have seen over the past generation of academics a *bifurcation* of the traditional academic career into full-time and part-time *tracks*. A whole corps of master's-level instructors (predominantly at the two-year colleges) have emerged, who are pursuing a career track wholly different from that of traditional full-time faculty—and they now constitute a significant fraction of the college teaching profession in the United States. For those who hold the doctorate, especially in the natural sciences and the humanities, a significant subgroup is now pursuing, in stages, rather traditional academic careers through the stepping-stone of an initial part-time or non-tenure-track full-time academic appointment that leads to a traditional tenure-track position. Perhaps this constitutes, in effect, a new rung on the academic career ladder in these fields. More-

TABLE 7.11

Movement between Part-Time and Full-Time and between On Tenure Track and Off Track, Current Full-Time Faculty, 1998

	All Faculty		Doctorate or 1st Professional Degree		Master's or Less	
	N	%	N	%	N	%
All faculty	317,815	100.0	225,759	100.0	92,312	100.0
Moved from part-time to full-time	87,570	27.6	51,890	23.0	35,683	38.7
Moved from on to off tenure track	9,103	2.9	6,226	2.8	2,875	3.1
Moved from off to on tenure track	105,929	33.3	86,402	38.3	19,446	21.1

Source: NSOPF-99 (see Appendix A for key).

over, an expanding group of part-time faculty are emerging who have retired from full-time academic jobs and are using part-time teaching appointments as a venue for a kind of phased retirement.

The preliminary evidence suggests that *for the most part* these fixed-term, full-time appointments seem to constitute a discernibly different career track from that of traditional, tenure-eligible appointments. That is, the modal pattern discernible among current full-time faculty is one of movement *among* off-track appointments or *among* on-track appointments. Crossover from one track to another appears limited to about one-third of the current tenurable full-timers and to a significantly lower proportion of current full-time faculty on fixed-term contracts. Because we must limit our observations to the "survivors," that is, current faculty who have persevered, it seems most probable that we have *over-*estimated the extent of actual crossovers (by having excluded from the denominator the relevant fraction those who dropped out for one reason or another). In other words, the proportions of crossovers undoubtedly would shrink if we could somehow count those who were "trapped" off-track and have departed from academic careers.

Moreover, our analyses have identified a few discernible patterns in the crossover phenomenon. Most generally, attainment of the doctoral degree appears to be a major facilitator influencing whether individuals wind up pursuing traditional, full-time academic careers. Now more than ever, the doctorate, undoubtedly abetted by a strong buyer's academic labor market that enables employers to be choosy in most fields, has become the basic qualification for faculty appointments at all four-year colleges and universities. More pointedly, women are significantly *less* likely than men to cross over; though more likely to move from part-time to full-time, women are markedly less likely than men to make the move from off-track to on-track. The extent to which this relative immobility represents system choices or individual choices remains unclear. But it is surely a critical matter to address from a human-resource and equity policy perspective. Although the impact of highest degree is clearly affirmed by our analyses, what is less clear is the timing of that influence. Among those holding the doctoral degree, to what extent does the more frequent movement from a part-time to a full-time appointment, or from off-track to on-track, occur *after* or *before* receipt of the doctorate? Is movement a "rite of passage" that coincides closely with attainment of the highest degree? Or do those who already possess the doctorate, especially in the humanities and natural sciences, struggle *post-degree* to obtain full-time or tenure-track positions? Answers to such questions of timing will be required in order to determine more definitively to what extent we are witnessing a new pre-PhD rung on the career ladder or whether this phenomenon constitutes in actuality an alternative career track.

For the moment, we can observe that the American college teaching force has become increasingly stratified into relatively independent part-time and full-time career tracks. And even the full-time career may be differentiating into dual independent career tracks, maybe even quite deep "troughs," with crossovers occurring only at the margins. Changes in the nature of academic appointments are extraordinarily dynamic; indeed, these changes are taking place at a rate faster than we can measure them—much less comprehend all of the implications.

NEW APPOINTEES AND JOB SATISFACTION

When we examined general trends in the job and career satisfaction of faculty over the past generation (chapter 5), we found, despite some slight decline overall (largely accounted for by declines in high satisfaction among senior faculty and the narrowing junior-senior faculty satisfaction gap), a basically stable pattern of job and career satisfaction over time. We did not, however, focus on the new appointments as a factor affecting job and career satisfaction. So we turn here to a consideration of the impact of the new appointments on faculty job and career satisfaction.

Elsewhere we have shown that part-timers—at least those who are part-time by choice—compare favorably with full-timers generally in overall job satisfaction (See Appendix D). How do those "other" new appointees, off-track full-timers, compare with their tenurable or tenured colleagues in the degree of satisfaction they experience? We compare levels of satisfaction on three dimensions: first, and most specifically, satisfaction with various aspects of their instructional responsibilities (decision making about course content and methods; time available for working with students; and student quality); second, satisfaction with the typical general facets of any job (that is, facet-related satisfaction with, e.g., workload, salary, benefits, and discretionary time); and third, most generally, overall satisfaction with the general conditions of their employment.

When we look at faculty whose principal activity is *teaching* (table 7.12a), we find a rather consistent, albeit highly differentiated, pattern. On those aspects of their instructional responsibilities associated with autonomy to determine course content and schedules, fixed-term faculty are less satisfied by 3–5% than their regular colleagues. This applies especially to their authority to

TABLE 7.12A

Satisfaction with Instructional Responsibilities and Other Job Dimensions, Full-time Faculty with Principal Activity of Teaching, 1992 and 1998
(percent)

Job Dimensions	All Faculty								Males								Females							
	1992		1998		Change in % 1992–98		% Difference TT vs. NTT		1992		1998		Change in % 1992–98		% Difference TT vs. NTT		1992		1998		Change in % 1992–98		% Difference TT vs. NTT	
	TT	NTT	TT	NTT	TT	NTT	1992	1998	TT	NTT	TT	NTT	TT	NTT	1992	1998	TT	NTT	TT	NTT	TT	NTT	1992	1998
Instructional responsibilities																								
Authority to make decisions about content and methods in the course	94.8	92.1	95.7	93.1	0.9	1.0	−2.7	−2.6	95.2	91.2	95.7	93.0	0.5	1.8	−4.0	−2.7	93.8	92.8	95.6	93.1	1.8	0.3	−1.0	−2.5
Authority to make decisions about other aspects of the job	74.2	73.8	76.4	73.9	2.2	0.1	−0.4	−2.5	75.9	74.8	77.2	73.3	1.3	−1.5	−1.1	−3.9	70.5	73.0	74.8	74.4	4.3	1.4	2.5	−0.4
Authority to make decisions about what course to teach	86.1	74.9	89.3	82.0	3.2	7.1	−11.2	−7.3	87.2	74.5	89.8	81.4	2.6	6.9	−12.7	−8.4	83.5	75.2	88.2	82.6	4.7	7.4	−8.3	−5.6
Time available for working with students as an adviser	80.8	79.4	78.4	80.8	−2.4	1.4	−1.4	2.4	83.6	83.1	79.6	82.4	−4.0	−0.7	−0.5	2.8	74.4	76.3	76.0	79.3	1.6	3.0	1.9	3.3
Quality of undergraduate students	66.3	69.4	68.2	73.5	1.9	4.1	3.1	5.3	65.6	63.3	67.3	74.5	1.7	11.2	−2.3	7.2	67.9	74.4	70.1	72.5	2.2	−1.9	6.5	2.4
Quality of graduate students	77.2	83.5	79.3	83.6	2.1	0.1	6.3	4.3	76.3	84.3	79.4	86.3	3.1	2.0	8.0	6.9	79.5	82.8	79.1	81.2	−0.4	−1.6	3.3	2.1

Other job aspects

Workload	67.9	73.1	66.3	71.4	-1.6	-1.7	5.2	5.1	71.4	74.7	68.6	72.6	-2.8	-2.1	3.3	4.0	59.9	71.8	61.7	70.3	1.8	-1.5	11.9	8.6
Job security	86.7	47.1	90.1	53.4	3.4	6.3	-39.6	-36.7	88.2	50.4	91.5	55.7	3.3	5.3	-37.8	-35.8	83.5	44.4	87.2	51.2	3.7	6.8	-39.1	-36.0
Advancement opportunity	73.1	44.9	77.3	45.9	4.2	1.0	-28.2	-31.4	75.2	51.3	77.7	46.3	2.5	-5.0	-23.9	-31.4	68.3	39.6	76.7	45.5	8.4	5.9	-28.7	-31.2
Time available for keeping current in the field	47.4	46.6	49.0	54.3	1.6	7.7	-0.8	5.3	52.2	54.4	52.0	53.5	-0.2	-0.9	2.2	1.5	36.7	40.1	43.2	55.0	6.5	14.9	3.4	11.8
Freedom to do outside consulting	79.5	76.3	84.5	82.5	5.0	6.2	-3.2	-2.0	81.7	76.4	86.0	79.0	4.3	2.6	-5.3	-7.0	74.6	76.3	81.6	85.6	7.0	9.3	1.7	4.0
Salary	53.5	49.0	56.6	50.0	3.1	1.0	-4.5	-6.6	55.6	52.1	58.0	51.3	2.4	-0.8	-3.5	-6.7	48.6	46.3	53.8	48.8	5.2	2.5	-2.3	-5.0
Benefits	74.3	73.4	77.0	77.9	2.7	4.5	-0.9	0.9	74.3	69.4	77.3	76.8	3.0	7.4	-4.9	-0.5	74.3	76.7	76.5	78.9	2.2	2.2	2.4	2.4
Spouse or partner employment opportunities in the area	72.7	71.8	75.1	77.8	2.4	6.0	-0.3	2.7	72.9	72.2	75.4	75.8	2.5	3.6	-0.7	0.4	72.3	71.5	74.4	79.7	2.1	8.2	-0.8	5.3
Job overall	84.0	80.8	84.8	82.8	0.8	2.0	-3.2	-2.0	84.9	80.1	85.0	82.1	0.1	2.0	-4.8	-2.9	82.0	81.3	84.3	83.4	2.3	2.1	-0.7	-0.9

Sources: NSOPF-93, NSOPF-99 (see Appendix A for key).
Notes: "TT" means "Tenurable or tenured"; "NTT" means "Non-tenure-track."
"Non-tenure-track" does not include faculty in institutions with no tenure system.
Cell entries reflect percent of faculty reporting that they were "fairly" or "very" satisfied with each job aspect.

TABLE 7.12B

Satisfaction with Instructional Responsibilities and Other Job Dimensions, Full-Time Faculty with Principal Activity of Research, 1992 and 1998

(percent)

Job Dimensions	All Faculty								Males								Females							
	1992		1998		Change in % 1992–98		% Difference TT vs. NTT		1992		1998		Change in % 1992–98		% Difference TT vs. NTT		1992		1998		Change in % 1992–98		% Difference TT vs. NTT	
	TT	NTT	TT	NTT	TT	NTT	1992	1998	TT	NTT	TT	NTT	TT	NTT	1992	1998	TT	NTT	TT	NTT	TT	NTT	1992	1998
Instructional responsibilities																								
Authority to make decisions about content and methods in the course	95.5	87.7	93.4	87.1	-2.1	-0.6	-7.8	-6.3	95.8	89.3	93.2	89.8	-2.6	0.5	-6.5	-3.4	94.2	84.6	94.3	81.6	0.1	-3.0	-9.6	-12.7
Authority to make decisions about other aspects of the job	83.2	74.0	82.0	79.6	-1.2	5.6	-9.2	-2.4	84.1	76.5	82.5	83.8	-1.6	7.3	-7.6	1.3	79.0	68.2	80.0	71.2	1.0	3.0	-10.8	-8.8
Authority to make decisions about what course to teach	87.7	61.0	85.7	80.5	-2.0	19.5	-26.7	-5.2	89.4	71.3	85.0	82.1	-4.4	10.8	-18.1	-2.9	80.0	43.2	87.8	77.3	7.8	34.1	-36.8	-10.5
Time available for working with students as an adviser	82.3	50.4	79.3	82.7	-3.0	32.3	-31.9	3.4	83.4	58.4	79.7	82.8	-3.7	24.4	-25.0	3.1	77.1	32.5	77.9	82.4	0.8	49.9	-44.6	4.5
Quality of undergraduate students	64.3	71.8	59.7	73.4	-4.6	1.6	7.5	13.7	62.8	69.4	59.8	76.2	-3.0	6.8	6.6	16.4	70.7	75.5	59.4 low n	—	-11.3	—	4.8	—
Quality of graduate students	78.3	85.5	72.7	79.9	-5.6	-5.6	7.2	7.2	78.1	88.9	71.8	82.1	-6.3	-6.8	10.8	10.3	79.6	78.6	76.8	75.7	-2.8	-2.9	-1.0	-1.1

Other job aspects

Workload	73.8	77.0	70.2	77.0	-3.6	0.0	3.2	6.8	75.1	76.6	71.8	75.0	-3.3	-1.6	1.5	3.2	68.1	77.9	64.6	81.3	-3.5	3.4	9.8	16.7
Job security	84.6	43.3	87.7	55.8	3.1	12.5	-41.3	-31.9	86.3	36.9	88.4	58.8	2.1	21.9	-49.4	-29.6	76.9	57.0	85.0	49.7	8.1	-7.3	-19.9	-35.3
Advancement opportunity	81.3	38.6	79.3	50.8	-2.0	12.2	-42.7	-28.5	82.0	36.1	81.8	57.1	-0.2	21.0	-45.9	-24.7	78.2	44.0	70.7	37.9	-7.5	-6.1	-34.2	-32.8
Time available for keeping current in the field	61.3	56.7	57.4	73.9	-3.9	17.2	-4.6	16.5	63.3	62.0	61.6	75.2	-1.7	13.2	-1.3	13.6	52.2	45.4	42.4	71.4	-9.8	26.0	-6.8	29.0
Freedom to do outside consulting	88.7	78.3	86.8	87.1	-1.9	8.8	-10.4	0.3	90.0	79.0	87.1	87.1	-2.9	8.1	-11.0	0.0	83.1	76.9	85.5	87.2	2.4	10.3	-6.2	1.7
Salary	57.3	52.5	61.7	60.0	4.4	7.5	-4.8	-1.7	57.6	57.6	63.0	69.2	5.4	11.6	0.0	6.2	56.4	41.5	57.0	41.0	0.6	-0.5	-14.9	-16.0
Benefits	73.6	78.7	78.9	79.9	5.3	1.2	5.1	1.0	73.4	86.9	78.8	84.1	5.4	-2.8	13.5	5.3	74.7	61.0	79.0	71.4	4.3	10.4	-13.7	-7.6
Spouse or partner employment opportunities in the area	72.3	72.4	73.6	78.7	1.3	6.3	0.1	5.1	72.0	70.6	72.5	81.1	0.5	10.5	-1.4	8.6	73.2	76.4	77.7	73.3	4.5	-3.1	3.2	-4.4
Job overall	85.7	76.8	81.7	81.4	-4.0	4.6	-8.5	-0.3	85.9	75.7	82.2	84.5	-3.7	8.8	-10.2	2.3	84.4	79.1	80.1	75.1	-4.3	-4.0	-5.3	-5.0

Sources: NSOPF-93, NSOPF-99 (see Appendix A for key).

Notes: "TT" means "Tenurable or tenured"; "NTT" means "Non-tenure-track."

Cell entries reflect percent of faculty reporting that they were "fairly" or "very" satisfied with each job aspect.

TABLE 7.12C

Satisfaction with Instructional Responsibilities and Other Job Dimensions, Full-Time Faculty with Principal Activity of Administration, 1992 and 1998
(percent)

Job Dimensions	All Faculty 1992 TT	1992 NTT	1998 TT	1998 NTT	Change in % 1992–98 TT	1992–98 NTT	% Difference TT vs. NTT 1992	1998	Males 1992 TT	1992 NTT	1998 TT	1998 NTT	Change in % 1992–98 TT	1992–98 NTT	% Difference TT vs. NTT 1992	1998	Females 1992 TT	1992 NTT	1998 TT	1998 NTT	Change in % 1992–98 TT	1992–98 NTT	% Difference TT vs. NTT 1992	1998
Instructional responsibilities																								
Authority to make decisions about content and methods in the course	97.8	98.1	96.8	96.9	-1.0	-1.2	0.3	0.1	98.0	99.8	97.5	96.6	-0.5	-3.2	1.8	-0.9	97.1	96.3	95.1	97.1	-2.0	0.8	-0.8	2.0
Authority to make decisions about other aspects of the job	84.8	83.3	84.4	82.8	-0.4	-0.5	-1.5	-1.6	86.1	90.6	87.5	83.3	1.4	-7.3	4.5	-4.2	81.6	74.9	77.2	82.5	-4.4	7.6	-6.7	5.3
Authority to make decisions about what course to teach	93.5	88.3	96.8	88.3	3.3	0.0	-5.2	-8.5	94.0	82.9	97.5	91.2	3.5	8.3	-11.1	-6.3	92.3	94.3	95.1	86.0	2.8	-8.3	2.0	-9.1
Time available for working with students as an adviser	75.9	72.2	72.5	80.9	-3.4	8.7	-3.7	8.4	78.6	65.9	72.8	86.0	-5.8	20.1	-12.7	13.2	69.3	79.9	71.7	76.9	2.4	-3.0	10.6	5.2
Quality of undergraduate students	72.9	79.2	74.3	81.4	1.4	2.2	6.3	7.1	72.6	80.5	72.2	89.2	-0.4	8.7	7.9	17.0	73.7	77.9	79.5	74.9	5.8	-3.0	4.2	-4.6
Quality of graduate students	83.9	80.3	84.6	93.3	0.7	13.0	-3.6	8.7	83.0	87.4	86.4	95.1	3.4	7.7	4.4	8.7	86.5	72.9	80.0	91.8	-6.5	18.9	-13.6	11.8

Other job aspects

Workload	67.8	75.9	63.3	69.0	-4.5	-6.9	8.1	5.7	71.2	76.4	66.7	78.6	-4.5	2.2	5.2	11.9	59.0	75.5	55.3	61.1	-3.7	-14.4	16.5	5.8
Job security	91.5	58.2	95.2	67.7	3.7	9.5	-33.3	-27.5	92.5	58.5	97.0	77.7	4.5	19.2	-34.0	-19.3	88.9	57.9	90.9	59.5	2.0	1.6	-31.0	-31.4
Advancement opportunity	79.5	40.8	82.1	49.2	2.6	8.4	-38.7	-32.9	80.5	46.9	84.8	50.7	4.3	3.8	-33.6	-34.1	76.8	35.6	75.8	48.0	-1.0	12.4	-41.2	-27.8
Time available for keeping current in the field	45.8	47.2	45.5	52.6	-0.3	5.4	1.4	7.1	48.3	56.9	45.2	55.8	-3.1	-1.1	8.6	10.6	39.5	38.7	46.4	49.9	6.9	11.2	-0.8	3.5
Freedom to do outside consulting	80.0	77.8	88.6	87.0	3.6	9.2	-2.2	-1.6	82.1	75.2	89.7	86.0	7.6	10.8	-6.9	-3.7	74.6	80.0	86.1	87.8	11.5	7.8	5.4	1.7
Salary	63.7	63.7	71.7	60.6	3.0	-3.1	0.0	-11.1	65.4	77.1	72.4	73.2	7.0	-3.9	11.7	0.8	59.3	52.1	70.2	50.3	10.9	-1.8	-7.2	-19.9
Benefits	77.1	85.1	85.1	85.4	8.0	0.3	8.0	0.3	78.0	83.3	85.4	81.4	7.4	-1.9	5.3	-4.0	77.1	86.6	84.5	88.6	7.4	2.0	9.5	4.1
Spouse or partner employment opportunities in the area	75.6	84.5	82.0	76.8	6.4	-7.7	8.9	-5.2	77.7	87.3	83.0	80.0	5.3	-7.3	9.6	-3.0	70.2	82.2	79.3	73.9	9.1	-8.3	12.0	-5.4
Job overall	88.9	82.3	89.3	90.1	0.4	7.8	-6.5	0.8	89.8	84.6	92.3	93.2	2.5	8.6	-5.2	0.9	86.4	80.3	82.2	87.6	-4.2	7.3	-6.1	5.4

Sources: NSOPF-93, NSOPF-99 (see Appendix A for key).

Notes: "TT" means "Tenurable or tenured"; "NTT" means "Non-tenure-track."
"Non-tenure-track" does not include faculty in institutions with no tenure system.
Cell entries reflect percent of faculty reporting that they were "fairly" or "very" satisfied with each job aspect.

choose the courses they teach. The regular-versus-term disparities are greater among males than among females and generally hold across academic fields. Among those aspects of their instructional responsibilities related directly to use of time for working with students, however, fixed-term faculty actually report slightly more satisfaction than on-track faculty. That is, off-track faculty typically are *equally* or *more* satisfied with the time they have to work with students as an adviser and more satisfied with the quality of students. This pattern of lower satisfaction with organizational status and perquisites, but a greater sense of temporal freedom, is replicated when we examine how faculty assess their facet-related satisfaction. Regularly appointed faculty are 30–40% more likely to express satisfaction with job security and advancement opportunities (and slightly more likely to express satisfaction with salary and benefits) than their fixed-term colleagues, but a higher proportion of term faculty report satisfaction with items related to control of their use of time: specifically, they are more satisfied with workload and with time available for keeping current in the field—and the term-regular differences are twice as great for women (10% versus 5% term-regular differential for men). What this pattern suggests is that term faculty, especially women, are more satisfied with their capacity to manage their workload and their time—a finding perfectly consistent with the pattern of actual work activity differences between term and regular faculty that we reported earlier in this chapter.

In global or composite ratings of job satisfaction, we find further support for this interpretation: among men, regular faculty are 5% more likely to report high satisfaction, while among academic women, off-track–on-track differentials in overall satisfaction virtually disappear. That is, the calculus reflected in trading off control of workload and greater time balance appears to offset any decrements in organizational status associated with the nonregular appointments for academic women, but not for men. Nonetheless, the satisfaction differentials, even for men, appear minimal.

When we turn to faculty whose principal activity is *research* (table 7.12b), the pattern of term-regular satisfaction differentials that we found for teaching-intensive faculty is largely replicated—with some important exceptions. First, it should be noted that we are dealing here with significantly smaller *N*'s, especially for women, which makes it difficult to assert fine distinctions with confidence. Nonetheless, research-intensive term faculty are 3–5% less satisfied with their instructional autonomy in matters of course scheduling and content than their regular colleagues are (it is useful to remember, though, that they do much less teaching than their teaching-intensive colleagues) and slightly more satisfied with their time available for working with students (but again, they re-

port significantly lower levels of interaction with students). They are more satisfied than regular faculty with their workload (and that differential is greater
for women than for men) and their discretionary professional time (keeping current and consulting), at least in 1998, and less satisfied with their organizational
status and advancement opportunities and, in the case of academic women,
with salary and benefits. In terms of overall or composite satisfaction, the term-
regular differential favoring regulars persists for academic women (term faculty
are slightly lower) but disappears by 1998 for academic men.

Among faculty whose principal activity is *administration* (table 7.12c), we
find the smallest differences in job satisfaction between term and regular faculty; indeed, overall job satisfaction is slightly greater in 1998 for term faculty
than for regulars. While the overall pattern of higher satisfaction with workload
and discretionary time for term faculty and lower satisfaction vis-à-vis regular
faculty with job security and advancement obtains, there appear to be only minimal differences in satisfaction with instructional responsibilities (not surprising since administration-intensive faculty have limited teaching responsibilities). Caution should be used, however, in interpreting the differences between
term and regular faculty whose principal activity is administration because of
the relatively low N's.

In all, in comparing regular and term full-time appointees in regard to their
satisfaction with their work, the patterns are clear, and they largely hold across
principal-activity categories. Term faculty are less satisfied with their organizational status, perquisites, and prospects and more satisfied with their workload
and control over their professional time. Since the differences in overall satisfaction are relatively small, and those with respect to organizational status,
perquisites, and prospects are visibly large, it appears that control over time and
workload makes up substantially for the loss of organizational status. What
these findings suggest initially is that time on the job may be the critical variable: term faculty appear to be trading off security and advancement potential
for a more manageable workload and the time to pursue their own interests. And
that trade-off may be particularly attractive to academic women in the early
stages of their careers. Thus, these relatively insecure appointments, which one
might expect would be experienced negatively by their incumbents, in fact appear, on balance, to be experienced positively.

SUMMARY: NEW KINDS OF JOBS

Taken together, these trends suggest what amounts to a largely silent redefinition of faculty work roles and the associated stratification of the faculty into

increasingly specialized groups derived from the proliferation of nontraditional academic appointments. The phenomenon of part-time appointments (and the creation of a huge—and growing—cadre of teaching-only faculty) is old news. What is far less understood—either in terms of measuring the phenomenon itself or in beginning to comprehend the implications of it—is the restructuring of *full-time* academic work and careers. Our analysis thus far has led to the following salient findings.

1. A quite new and distinctive, nontraditional track has been opening up within the academic career: a full-time term track supplementing the traditional full-time, on-track appointment and the part-time track.

2. Movement among the several tracks is possible, from part-time to full-time (and, to a greater degree, among full-time appointees, from term to tenure-track), but movement ordinarily does not flow in the opposite direction, that is, either from a full-time to a part-time appointment (except for full-time tenured faculty who, in retirement, move into part-time roles compatible with a more leisurely lifestyle) or from a tenure-track to an off-track appointment. It is difficult to assess the magnitude of such mobility in the absence of longitudinal data on individuals.

3. Career trajectory and mobility is not serendipitous. Rather, the career trajectories of PhD holders, especially in four-year institutions, differ appreciably from the career patterns of those who hold master's degrees. Traditional PhDs are increasingly likely to start their careers in a part-time position or a full-time off-track position. They are much more likely than non-PhDs to move from part-time into full-time positions and from non-tenure-eligible term appointments to tenurable or tenured positions. Concurrently, an increasingly large secondary market for non-PhDs has grown up in the two-year community colleges and even in the four-year sector. These non-PhDs have become prime candidates for the new appointments.

4. It appears that we have only just begun to acknowledge that large, and growing, subgroup of non-doctorate-holding faculty who pursue college teaching careers outside the traditional boundaries of careers in their respective academic disciplines (i.e., without earning the PhD or without doing so at the early stages of their careers).

5. New appointment types translate into differentiated and more specialized work roles. Not only are the timetable and the exclusivity of academic careers changing, but the ideal typical role (combining teaching with equal measures of research and service) is giving way increasingly to staffing in-

stitutions of higher education by teaching, research, and service specialists. Although full-time term appointments tend, in general, to involve
more specialized work activities, the role of term faculty appears to vary
by institutional type and field. That is, there are multiple variants of the
faculty role emerging in different types of institutions and in different
fields.

6. New types of appointments and the new kinds of roles that they offer affect the levels of satisfaction experienced by faculty. Term faculty are less
satisfied with their organizational status, perquisites, and prospects and
more satisfied with their workload and control over their professional
time. To the extent that the differences in overall satisfaction are relatively
small, and those with respect to organizational status, perquisites and
prospects are visibly large, it appears that control over time and workload
makes up substantially for the loss of organizational status—especially so
for women faculty.

NOTES

1. Historical perspective requires noting that part-time appointments, although escalating rapidly these past three decades, certainly did not originate circa 1970. In fact,
though seldom recalled, the proportion of all academic appointments that were part-time
at the beginning of the era we are scrutinizing—comprising about 22% of all faculty in
1970—actually represents a sharp decline from a decade earlier. That is, in 1960, as the
rapid expansion of higher education created a demand for faculty that far outstripped the
production of persons well qualified to become faculty members, many persons, often
with marginal credentials, were hired to teach on a part-time basis. Indeed, that group by
head count had swelled by 1960 to about one-third of all faculty members who were part-
time (Bowen and Schuster, 1986, p. 61). Even taking into account the dip between 1960
and 1970, the steady increase in the use of part-timers over the past three decades, with
no apparent reversal in sight, constitutes the single most dramatic redeployment of academic staff. (As noted elsewhere, the use of part-timers may be plateauing, and if so, that
leveling may be in part a function of greater use of full-time term appointments.) But because the part-time phenomenon has been examined so extensively, our attention in this
chapter is disproportionately devoted to the relatively recent and decidedly underexam-
ined phenomenon of off-track appointments.

2. IPEDS survey instructions define *new hires* as "full-time permanent employees, in
the respective activities, who were included on the payroll for the first time between July
1 and October 31 of the survey year." They are "persons who were hired for full-time permanent employment for the first time or after a break in service," but do not include those
"who have returned from sabbatical leave or full-time faculty with less than 9-month contracts." http://nces.ed.gov/ipeds/pdf/webbase2003/S1_form.pdf.

CHAPTER EIGHT

Compensation and Academic Careers

Trends and Issues

The condition of the American professoriate and prospects for its future are a function of many elements. Among them, the changing patterns of faculty compensation constitute one of the basic—and most intriguing—factors that now shape, and will continue to mold, the academic experience. As we examine in this chapter many aspects of the academic reward structure, we highlight recent trends that describe a degree of responsiveness to market forces that likely is unprecedented in the long history of the profession.

CONCEPTS AND DEFINITIONS

Academic compensation is important for many reasons, but it is not easy to ascertain exactly how important. It is a core element of the financial incentive system that significantly defines and calibrates incentives for academics. Yet debate has long swirled about the extent to which faculty members are motivated by external, material rewards and how much they are driven by satisfactions internal to their psyche. Whatever weight is appropriately attributed to extrinsic versus intrinsic factors as motivators, compensation is unquestionably connected to the ability of academic institutions to attract able individuals and to retain them in academic careers. And, as numerous surveys of faculty have demonstrated over the years, compensation is closely interwoven with faculty morale. Another distinctive feature of academic compensation is that it is actually measurable, in contrast to more qualitative and heavily nuanced aspects of the faculty experience—although measuring compensation, not to mention interpreting its effects, is hardly as simple as might first be supposed. (Appendix

G provides a discussion of the methodological challenges in explicating faculty compensation.)

In this chapter we describe briefly patterns of academic compensation in recent decades after first sketching a historical overview. Gender and racial or ethnic salary equity, as well as issues of salary compression (by rank) and dispersion (by field), are discussed. We then attempt to relate the significance of trends identified in other chapters—such as the aging of the faculty, the changing distribution of academic appointments, and the impact of information technology—to the future of faculty compensation. En route we touch on the challenges of measurement, and we seek perspective by comparing faculty compensation with administrators' earnings and compensation in comparable, sometimes "competing" professions. We have, in these pursuits, sought to provide fresh ways of understanding the compensation factor rather than simply reporting the data available from conventional sources.

Before we proceed, it will be useful to clarify a few terms. Faculty compensation consists of several distinct components. First is the *base salary* paid by the "home" college or university for the standard nine-to-ten-month academic-year appointment, with actual payments commonly spread over a twelve-month period. (This is the base upon which annual cost-of-living increments are typically calculated.) Beyond the base salary, there is supplemental income paid by the home institution for "extra" work, including, for example, summer teaching, teaching overloads during the academic year, and special administrative assignments. Additional compensation may come from outside grants that typically are funneled through the institution, which serves as a fiscal agent. Such grants may include compensation during summer months and/or buyouts of a faculty member's time during the academic year.[1]

A very significant component of compensation is *fringe benefits*. These include, most importantly, institutional contributions to retirement or pension plans, medical and dental insurance, life insurance, and—primarily in the independent sector—tuition remission for dependents.

There also exists an assortment of other possible benefits spanning, for example, disability insurance, unemployment insurance, and worker's compensation; these become tangible benefits if the faculty ever use them, although they rarely do. As it turns out, then, these "benefits" in reality function more like taxes on faculty income than as benefits that augment compensation.

Social security is also considered by many to be closer conceptually to a tax on current employment income than to a current benefit. Unlike private pension plans, in which contributions accumulate and accrue to individuals who have legally enforceable claims on those funds, the social security contributions of current workers fund the benefits of *current retirees.* The future benefit for current employees when they become retirees in the future will depend primarily on the social security contributions, that is, taxes on the employment income, of *future* workers.

To these sources of *institutionally derived* income must be added other *earned* income that is linked to the faculty member's professional expertise. Included may be royalties and income from patents (sometimes shared with the institution) and income from part-time professional practice (for instance, from financial or legal consulting, music lessons, or math tutoring). Some work by faculty members, though similar or even indistinguishable in nature from work supported by grants that pass through their home institution, may be compensated by payments made directly to the individual faculty member by another entity in the form of a stipend or consulting fee. Additionally, faculty members, especially part-timers, commonly earn income from teaching at another traditional nonprofit college or university or, increasingly, at a for-profit teaching institution. On top of the foregoing sources, which are products of the person's academic expertise, are income sources that are unrelated, or only peripherally related, to academic expertise, for example a private non-academic-related business (say, selling real estate or Internet-facilitated services).

There is also *unearned* income, that is, income from investments; such income represents the return on non-work-related assets and typically is not included in discussions of faculty compensation. Although, strictly speaking, the exclusion of unearned income is understandable for most analytical purposes, we mention it here because it may contribute usefully to the socioeconomic profile of a profession that has historically relied to some extent on private wealth to supplement limited earnings from academic employment.

Yet another increasingly prominent element is family—typically spousal—income. The dual-income family phenomenon has mushroomed in recent decades and adds a crucial on-the-ground dimension to the faculty compensation/standard-of-living picture. These components of faculty compensation and their relationship to base salary are depicted in table 8.1 with income sources derived from the employing institutions shown first. Based on 1998 income as self-reported in the 1999 NSOPF survey, table 8.1 indicates what proportion of the faculty derives some income from each source.

As becomes readily apparent, faculty income is a many-faceted phenomenon. Accordingly, computing averages and plotting trends in faculty compensation entail choosing just which facets—all of them capturing a slice of real-

TABLE 8.1
Components of Faculty Income, 1998 Calendar Year

Sources of Compensation	Faculty Receiving This Source (%)
Academic sources	
Base salary from home institution	98.8
Other income from home institution	34.3
Nonmonetary income from home institution	1.2
Grants/fellowship	0.7
Other academic institution	17.2
Related professional sources	
Consulting	20.0
Professional performances/exhibits	4.0
Legal/medical/counseling	3.8
Royalties/commissions	8.3
Speaking fees/honoraria	14.4
Nonacademic sources	
Earned income	
Any other employment	25.6
Outside income, unspecified	0.8
Self-owned business	6.7
Investments and other income	
Dividends	
Real estate/rental income	0.7
Military/pensions	0.6
Retirement/pension income	2.2
Household income of spouse or significant other	64.1

Source: U.S. Department of Education, National Center for Education Statistics, National Survey of Postsecondary Faculty: 1999, Data Analysis System.

ity—are to be measured. There are, that is to say, many parallel or coexisting realities. Such complexity is not unique to the academic profession, but especially given the flexibility typical of academic work, the income patterns in academe are likely to be more variegated than in most, perhaps all, other professions. Having drawn these distinctions, we can now identify several further conceptual issues.

First, most discussions of compensation do not extend beyond measuring trends in *institutional base salary.* Though the value of fringe benefits is often noted, infrequent reference is made in the literature to gross institutional salaries or gross faculty earned income; we discuss faculty income beyond base pay, but only with proper specification.

Second, the literature on faculty compensation infrequently reports averages for part-time faculty. It is much easier to find useful discussions of policies (both descriptive and prescriptive) for paying part-time faculty than it is to locate reliable data. This empirical weakness creates problems for understanding "the big picture" of faculty compensation because such a large proportion of faculty members teach part-time.

Third, there is a paucity of faculty compensation data that reports individuals' income from multiple institutions. As a result, faculty income from teaching tends to be underreported since a significant number of faculty members either teach part-time at another campus in addition to teaching full-time at their home institution or teach part-time at more than one institution.

Fourth, several key economic terms require explanation. Briefly, *salary* for our purposes means base pay, ordinarily calculated for an academic year. *Compensation* is a broader term that also includes the dollar value of fringe benefits (as described previously). It is also necessary to distinguish between salary or compensation that is reported in *current* dollars (sometimes referred to as *nominal* salary or compensation) and *real* salary or compensation. Current dollars reflect actual dollar amounts at a given time. *Real* income is computed in dollars held constant over time—that is, by adjusting current dollars for inflation. This adjustment ordinarily requires *deflating* current dollar amounts to take into account the reduced purchasing power of those dollars because of the increased costs of goods and services over time. We will sometimes refer to real (adjusted) compensation in our text in order to more realistically capture changes in faculty members' purchasing power.

Note, too, that in calculating trends in faculty compensation, it is important to distinguish between averages for "all faculty" and for "continuing faculty." Each provides a different measure of year-to-year change. Averages for "all faculty" reflect how much institutions are paying to compensate faculty (ordinarily only full-time faculty). Averages for "continuing faculty" provide a different, arguably more accurate, measure of progress (or the absence thereof), since these figures are limited to faculty members who are continuing at their institution from one year to the next. The all-faculty averages naturally do not include faculty members who have left the profession (many of whom are likely to be retirees who *were* relatively highly paid faculty) but do "substitute" for them the newly hired faculty members, who are likely to be paid lower, entry-level salaries. Thus, the year-to-year percentage increase in continuing faculty salaries in current dollars in recent years is invariably greater than the increase for all faculty (including the "continuing" faculty). Almost always the difference—the higher percentage increase for continuing faculty—is about 1 percentage point (plus or minus 0.5 percentage point).[2]

Another factor in calculating trends in faculty compensation is the extent to which measurements of compensation differ depending on how *faculty* are designated. The recently developed Data Analysis System of the National Center

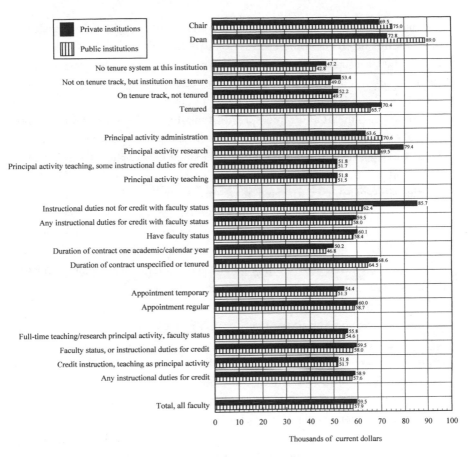

Fig. 8.1. Effect of alternative faculty designations on estimates of faculty salary, 1998–99. Data from NSOPF-99, Data Analysis System.

for Education Statistics permits almost twenty different ways to designate "faculty," grouped by such characteristics as principal activity, type of appointment, and tenure eligibility. To illustrate, figure 8.1 shows a range of salary estimates for academic year 1998–99 at both public and private institutions, depending on various delineations of faculty—quite apart from the common delineations by type of institution or academic field. We turn now to a brief historical account of faculty compensation.

HISTORICAL PERSPECTIVES

In his prefatory note to Charles Homer Haskins's *The Rise of Universities,* Theodore Mommsen notes that "after twelve years at the University of Wisconsin, Haskins was *called* to Harvard University in 1902 and taught there until 1931" (italics supplied). Mommsen's choice of the verb "to call" packs a special meaning, for throughout the centuries it has been commonplace to regard the academic profession as a calling—indeed, a calling not unlike that for the ministry, from which it evolved. As the twentieth century unfolded, perhaps especially after the advent and rapid spread of faculty unionism in the late 1960s and 1970s, it became unfashionable to describe one's commitment to an academic career as a calling. Such a notion, in some minds, depicted the faculty with a softness that suggested that they were ripe for exploitation in the rough-and-tumble, ever-more-variegated marketplace and, further, that this duty-grounded sense of calling unduly deflected attention from inadequate pay and working conditions.[3] The proportion of faculty members who today think of their own careers as bearing responsibilities one might associate with a "sanctified" vocation is unknown—although that age-old sense of a higher calling undoubtedly remains strong among many faculty members, perhaps especially at church-related colleges (to which, it might be argued, their customary very low pay attests). The point for present purposes, however, is that historically a "calling" was associated with marginal compensation; if the called were not exactly required to take vows of poverty reminiscent of religious orders, then at least the de-emphasis on material expectations—and commensurate material rewards—was implicit in the bargain. And so, over the centuries, academic compensation has been modest (or worse), although other attractive features of academic careers have served to compensate in large or small measure for the profession's financially challenged status.

The Long View

From the beginning the teaching profession, at all levels, received very low compensation in the United States. Reflecting on the financial marginality of so many colleges and universities in the nineteenth century, historian Helen Horowitz observed, "It is a truism that the greatest philanthropy of American colleges in the nineteenth century was the willingness of professors to teach for very low wages" (Horowitz, 1984, p. 185). Indeed, normal academic compensation was so pathetic that in 1902 Andrew Carnegie devised a plan to provide faculty members, at institutions deemed to be qualified, with a modest measure of financial security through creating a pension plan. It evolved, over time, into the massive Teachers Insurance and Annuity Association–College Retirement Equities Fund (TIAA-CREF).[4]

During the Great Depression of the 1930s, faculty compensation suffered

only marginally—a function in part of the lamentably low levels it already ha-
bitually occupied. In contrast to the widespread experience of other workers
throughout the nation, few faculty members were terminated or even temporarily laid off during the depression. The faculty often were obliged to agree
to salary reductions; indeed, some received as little as half-time wages for full-
time work. Between the academic years 1931–32 and 1934–35, real faculty
salaries declined by a modest 3% annually. Faculty appear to have sacrificed
significantly less financially than other professionals, for whom unemployment
was rampant. This "bargain" further illustrates the trade-off that faculty members as a whole have historically made between high levels of job security and
low remuneration. Assaying educators' salaries during the first half of the twentieth century, Beardsley Ruml and Sidney Tickton, in the most comprehensive
such study to that time, found in 1953 that there had been no progress "at the
top" for university professors and presidents. Professors' real salaries over this
fifty-year period had lost 2% (72% in then-current dollars) compared to their
economic position in 1904 (Ruml and Tickton, 1955, p. 21; Orr, 1978).[5]

Compensation in the Post–World War II Period

No significant improvement in faculty compensation materialized in the immediate post–World War II period. However, as economist Howard R. Bowen
observed, "in the early 1950s . . . a national consensus was reached to the effect
that academic compensation rates were so low that they failed to attract and
hold faculty and staff of adequate capability" (1980, p. 53). The war, he noted,
had served as a "major watershed in the evolution of faculty compensation"
(p. 54), prompting substantial salary increases after the long depression-era
drought.[6] Thus, following a moderate postwar decline in real terms, faculty
compensation developed considerable momentum through the 1950s and
1960s, posting average annual increases of about 3.6% in constant dollars. However, academic salaries fell victim to inflation-induced erosion in the 1970s, and
faculty members lost more than 15% of their purchasing power during that
decade. No other nonagricultural occupational group—professional or otherwise—appears to have fared so poorly; for example, blue-collar workers, clerical workers, and (notably) elementary and secondary classroom teachers fared
far better than postsecondary faculty members during this period. The 1980s did
bring partial recovery, but over time, these adjustments have consistently lagged
behind ever-rising living costs.

Not until the mid-1990s did faculty salaries, in constant dollars, recover from
the significant drop in purchasing power experienced in the 1970s. After some

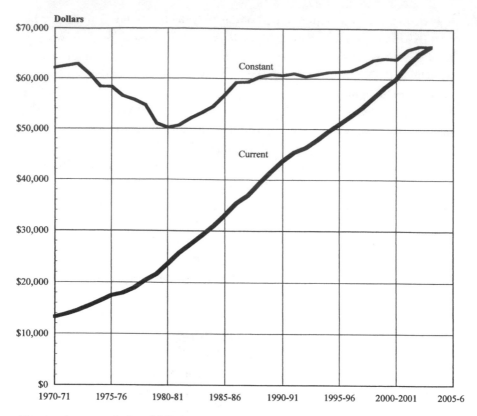

Dollars

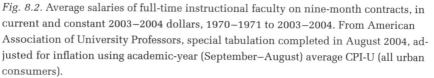

Fig. 8.2. Average salaries of full-time instructional faculty on nine-month contracts, in current and constant 2003–2004 dollars, 1970–1971 to 2003–2004. From American Association of University Professors, special tabulation completed in August 2004, adjusted for inflation using academic-year (September–August) average CPI-U (all urban consumers).

progress in the early 1980s and moving mainly sideways for a decade, faculty salaries on average finally in 1997–98 drew even with the real level that had been attained in 1970–71 (see fig. 8.2). The recovery of real income had taken more than a quarter of a century.

In sum, viewed over the three decades on which our study focuses, basically from 1970 into the early 2000s, we see that the average salaries of full-time faculty members in *current* dollars have risen more than fourfold (fig. 8.2). Adjusting for inflation, however, reveals that there has been little increase over 1970–71 levels.

But an important caveat is necessary, for the apparent recovery, which has been achieved in the average salary for all faculty ranks over the 1980s and

1990s—following that calamitous slide in real earnings in the 1970s—is actually something of an illusion. Why? Because much of the apparent rebound is attributable to an artifact, namely, the proportion of all faculty members who have become full professors—a much larger proportion in these recent years than was the case several decades ago. That is, as large numbers of faculty members advanced through the academic ranks from assistant to associate professor and then to full professor, they naturally earned higher average base salaries. (See the discussion below of academic rank as a key structural determinant of salaries.) Indeed, if we control for academic rank, we find that the average *real* salary *at both the assistant and associate professor ranks* currently barely rises above 1970–71 levels, as figure 8.3 makes painfully clear. In other words, as doc-

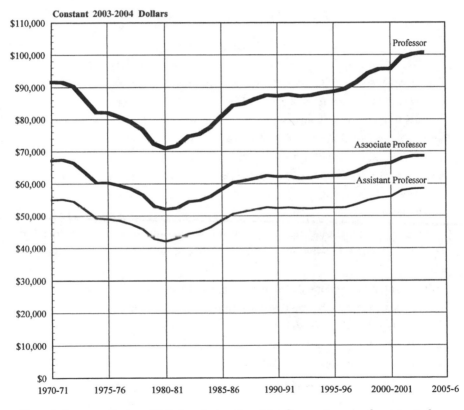

Fig. 8.3. Average salaries of full-time instructional faculty on nine-month contracts, by rank, in constant 2003–2004 dollars, 1970–1971 to 2003–2004. From American Association of University Professors, special tabulation completed in August 2004, adjusted for inflation using academic-year (September–August) average CPI-U (All Urban Consumers).

umented in figure 8.3, the *real* salaries of full-time assistant and associate professors, on average, had not risen appreciably by 2004 over their 1970–71 levels. Only at the level of full professors had *real* salaries increased—albeit modestly—by about 10%. Expressed differently, higher average salaries for faculty
overall are artificially inflated by natural maturity, that is, by the average increase in faculty members' age and experience. Or, put another way, as the
faculty have grown older and have advanced in rank, they have been able to
command higher salaries; and as senior faculty have become more numerous
relative to entry-level faculty, the average faculty salary has been boosted in part
simply because of this statistical artifact. The point: Disregarding the effects of
the changing distribution of faculty by age and rank seriously distorts the analysis of salary trends—in this case, suggesting more progress than has actually occurred.[7]

COMPARING FACULTY COMPENSATION TO
THAT OF OTHER PROFESSIONS

Two aspects of faculty compensation merit special attention: how academic
salaries compare to salaries of other professionals (providing a context in which
to assess the economic well-being of the faculty), and fringe benefits. Since the
late 1970s, college and university faculty have experienced a consistent "earnings disadvantage" relative to other "highly educated" professions: they earn
about 70% of the median salary of other such professionals (and have done so,
with only a few percentage-point variations, over the past quarter century) (see
table 8.2). Moreover, if we compare faculty to other workers who hold advanced
degrees, we find that a virtual parity was maintained from 1975 until 1990, but
thereafter a faculty disadvantage materialized and actually began to grow appreciably.

Furthermore, if we focus on new entrants to the academic profession, that is,
the prototypical assistant professor, we find that the "signal" to the prospective
academic is one of salary disadvantage, a disadvantage that appears to have
widened over the past quarter century. To illustrate: the average salary for assistant professors in relation to national median family income is an important
indicator of how well those in early academic careers are faring. In 1975 salaries
at the point of entry to the academic profession exceeded the median *family* income in the country as a whole by approximately 3%. Since then, however, a
reversal has occurred: the average salary of assistant professors as a percentage
of median family income, after fluctuating, has headed downward and by 1999–
2000 had fallen to about 92%. (To be sure, a considerable portion of that lag can

TABLE 8.2
*Salary Disadvantage of Faculty of All Ranks, Compared with Other Professionals,
1999 and 2003*

Compensation Profession	1999		2003		
	Annual Salary ($)	Faculty Salary Disadvantage (%)	Annual Salary (%)	Faculty Salary Disadvantage (%)	% Change 1999–2003
Lawyers	90,360	50.4	107,800	63.9	13.5%
Legal professions (weighted)	85,786	42.8	105,325	60.2	17.4
Medical professions (weighted)	90,718	51.0	106,525	62.0	11.0
Computer and information scientists, research	67,180	11.8	84,530	28.6	16.7
Engineering professions (weighted)	66,104	10.0	68,349	3.9	−6.1
Life and physical scientists (weighted)	51,940	−13.5*	1,276	−6.8*	6.7
Above occupations (weighted)	75,369	25.5	83,955	27.7	2.2
Totals for faculty (all ranks)	60,070		65,752		

Sources: 1999: American Association of University Professors, "The Annual Report on the Economic Status of the Profession: 2000–2001," *Academe,* March–April 2001, p. 29; 2003: U.S. Department of Commerce, Bureau of Labor Statistics, 2003 Occupational Employment Statistics Survey Web site.
    *Faculty salary advantage.

be attributed to the rise in the number of two-income families—contributing to the increase in family income—but the lens is nevertheless a revealing one through which to view the economic status of the profession.) Thus, except for a partial recovery during the 1980s and into the early 1990s, the average salary of assistant professors has continued to compare unfavorably with median family income (fig. 8.4).

As another concrete example of their weakening economic competitiveness, consider the compensation of postsecondary faculty relative to that of teachers in public elementary and secondary schools. An assistant professor in 1970, ordinarily having acquired substantial postbaccalaureate training, usually commanded a somewhat higher salary than the average elementary or secondary school teacher. But by the late 1980s, on average, public school teachers' salaries had almost drawn even, and since then, as increases in teachers' salaries have slowed in the 1990s relative to the increases in wages of all full-time workers, assistant professors have inched up a couple of percentage points. Although the classroom teachers are generally older and more experienced than the typical assistant professors, the relative advantage enjoyed by assistant professors in the 1970s vanished in the 1980s. There is some indication that the salary advantage

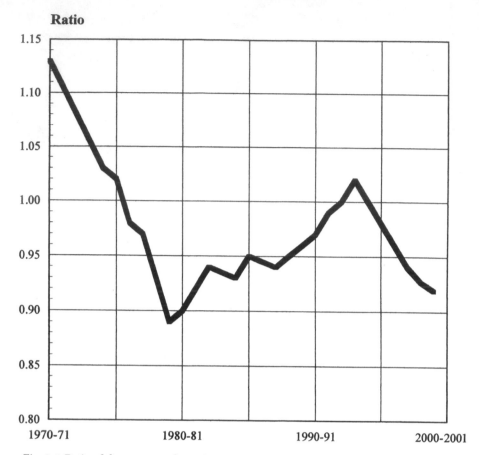

Fig. 8.4. Ratio of the average salary of assistant professors to the median family income, 1970–1971 to 1999–2000. The ratio is calculated using data from NCES, 2001a, and from the NCES and Bureau of the Census Web sites. Note: gaps in the data for the years 1972, 1978, 1988, 1990, and 1992 are spanned.

of the assistant professors may have reemerged in the late 1990s and continued into the current decade (fig. 8.5).[8] But even if that is so, the economic prospects facing would-be junior faculty members are clouded by the uncertainties of job security that accompany the rising proportion of academic appointments that are not tenurable and are term-limited (see chapter 7).

If recruitment to the academic profession is compromised by stagnant or even declining real entry-level salaries, the relative earnings potential for experienced academics paints an even grimmer picture. Over the past two decades the average faculty salary for all ranks has lagged substantially, by about 30%, behind the average salaries of a comparison group of well-educated professionals

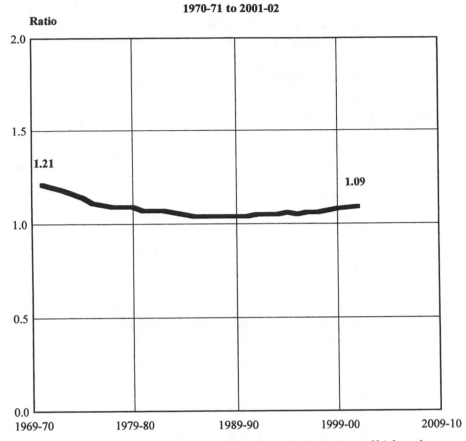

1970-71 to 2001-02

Fig. 8.5. Ratio of average salaries of assistant professors in institutions of higher education to those of elementary and secondary school teachers, 1970–1971 to 2001–2002. Calculated using data from NCES, 2004, table 239.

(holding at least a master's degree) (table 8.2). So not only have the salaries of academics not recovered fully from the substantial loss of earning power that occurred in the 1970s, but the gap between faculty salaries and those of other professionals is widening.

A WORD ABOUT FRINGE BENEFITS

Having painted a discouraging broad-brush picture of academic salary trends, we should note, by way of contrast, that fringe benefits have increased significantly until recently, both in dollar amounts and as a percentage of base salaries. They now constitute in many cases more than 20%—sometimes as much as 30%—of base salaries. Much of the increase is invisible to the individual faculty member, however, because the benefits that account for most of the reported percentage increases do not, in the main, improve the faculty member's current economic status. This is true even though the institution must pay more—even much more—than for earlier fringe benefits. The increased cost of the benefits, which boost overall *compensation* rates, derives largely from higher contributions that many institutions must make for social security coverage of their staff and for health insurance, with its exploding costs (Chronister, 2000).[9]

THE DETERMINANTS OF FACULTY SALARIES: CONTINUITIES AND CHANGES

Understanding faculty compensation and its impact on the academic profession requires not only an understanding of trends in the *level* of compensation, but trends in the *structure* of compensation as well. Some of these components have remained virtual constants throughout the second half of the twentieth century; others, to varying degrees, represent a significant restructuring of faculty compensation—with potentially powerful implications for academic work and careers. Two of the consistently most influential determinants of base salary levels are academic rank and institutional type.

Academic Rank

Since the system of academic ranks emerged clearly toward the beginning of the twentieth century, there has always been a strong positive relationship between rank and base salary: higher rank, naturally, is associated with higher base salary. Thus, in academic year 2003–4, the average salary of assistant professors (all categories of institutions) was $52,788, while that of associate professors was $63,063, and full professors were paid $88,591 (AAUP, 2004). Associate professors earned, on average, 19.5% more than assistant professors did in basic salary in 2003–4, and full professors earned 40% more than associate professors and nearly 68% more than assistant professors. So differences among ranks continue to be substantial, as they always have been. But an important question is whether those differences by rank have shrunk in recent years.

Salary Compression by Rank?

Prevailing opinion holds that differences in salary by rank have diminished in recent decades. The commonly expressed notion is that entry-level salaries have been forced upward to compete for the "best" new talent, especially in academic fields for which demand is highest. The usual assumption is that marketplace pressures, accordingly, have reduced the salary differential between these new entrants and their more senior colleagues (whose salaries, once established, presumably have tended to rise more slowly). Most academics can cite—with glee or dismay, depending upon their vantage point—examples of the new assistant professor of information science or accounting who commanded a higher salary than some greybeard philosophers or historians. Upon closer inspection, however, the data on average salary by rank suggest that, poignant anecdotes aside, salary compression has *not* been occurring across the board. That is, plotting the average salaries of associate and assistant professors as a percentage of the average salary of full professors from the 1970s to the present does *not* show, in the aggregate, any convergence or compression among the ranks (fig. 8.6). In fact, over the three-decade span, the average salaries of assistant and associate professors have declined slightly compared to the average salary of full professors. Specifically, the salaries of assistant professors have slipped a few points, from 60.0% to 58.2% of full professors' salaries. The salaries of associate professors have lost even more ground, from 73.4 to 68.2% of full professors' salaries. Thus the overall pattern of faculty salaries by rank has not been convergent, but instead slightly divergent (see table 8.3).[10] That finding, though basic, masks important specific examples of salary compression that have been occurring, as described subsequently in the discussion of salary *divergence* among academic fields. In other words, averages are just that; they obscure the convergence of faculty salaries by rank in some academic fields and the divergence in others. Nevertheless, contrary to commonly held perceptions, the national averages by rank do not reveal salary compression over the last thirty years.

Type of Institution

In general, salaries also vary systematically by institutional type, with average salaries at the doctorate-granting universities greatly exceeding those at institutions granting no degree higher than the master's or the bachelor's, and at two-year institutions (fig. 8.7). As reported by the AAUP, the average faculty salary in 2003–4 at doctoral institutions was $75,863, as compared with $59,400 at master's institutions, $55,851 at baccalaureate institutions, and $50,800 at two-year colleges. Moreover, as the data in table 8.4 suggest, institutional type differences are increasing significantly—suggesting a considerably more stratified system than previously existed. For example, full professors and assistant

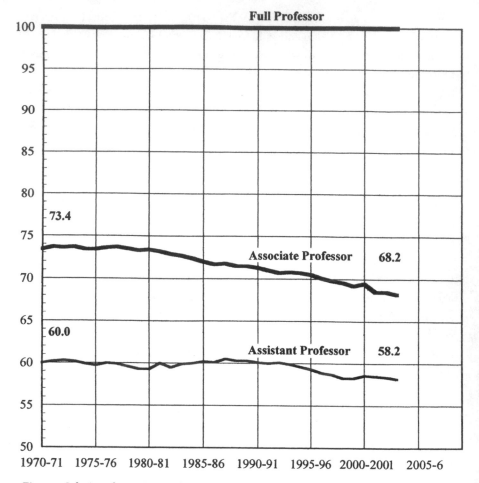

Fig. 8.6. Salaries of associate and assistant professors as a percentage of the salaries of full professors, 1970–1971 to 2003–2004. Calculated using data obtained from the American Association of University Professors, "Annual Report on the Economic Status of the Profession," *Academe* (generally found in the March–April issue for each year).

professors at doctoral-level institutions in 1984–85 earned 18.6% and 8.8% more, respectively, than their counterparts at comprehensive (master's) institutions. But not quite two decades later, by 2003–4, the advantage they enjoyed— that is, the premium for working at a doctoral-level institution—had mushroomed to 32.3% and 17.2% (fig. 8.7). The 17% advantage enjoyed by faculty at doctoral-level institutions (across all ranks) in 1984–85, compared to the comprehensive institutions, had swelled to 27.7% by 2003–4. Similar disparities are evident when doctoral institutions are compared to two-year institutions;

TABLE 8.3

Average Salaries of Full-Time Instructional Faculty on Nine-Month Contracts in Degree-Granting Doctoral Institutions, Selected Years, 1970–1971 to 2003–2004

(current dollars, in thousands)

	All Full-time Faculty	Full Professors	Associate Professors	Assistant Professors	Associate Professors as % of Full Professors	Assistant Professors as % of Full Professors
1970–71	—	19.6	14.4	11.8	73.5	60.0
1980–81	26.1	33.5	24.6	19.9	73.4	59.4
1990–91	49.3	62.9	44.9	37.8	71.4	60.1
1995–96	57.8	73.6	51.9	43.7	70.5	59.4
2000–2001	68.6	89.8	62.4	52.7	69.5	58.7
2003–4	75.9	100.7	68.6	58.6	68.1	58.2

Source: Derived from AAUP Faculty Compensation Survey, 1970–71 to 2003–4. Weighted average for Category I (Doctoral) Institutions.

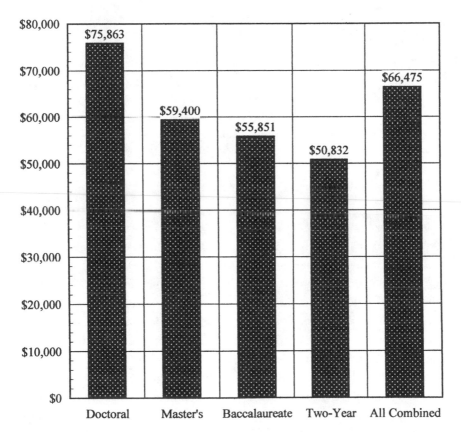

Fig. 8.7. Average faculty salary, by institutional type, 2003–2004. From AAUP, 2004, table 4.

TABLE 8.4
Salary "Premiums" to Faculty at Doctoral-Level Institutions, by Rank,
Selected Years, 1984–1985 through 2003–2004
(percent)

	1984–85	1989–90	1994–95	1999–2000	2003–4
Doctoral level (Category I) institutions compared with comprehensive (Category IIA) institutions					
Full professor	18.6	20.5	23.2	29.9	32.3
Associate professor	7.8	8.3	8.6	16.1	14.4
Assistant professor	8.8	10.6	10.3	18.0	17.2
All ranks	17.0	17.7	19.9	26.1	27.7
Doctoral level (Category I) institutions compared with general baccalaureate (Category IIB) institutions					
Full professor	34.4	42.1	37.7	50.0	40.2
Associate professor	21.7	25.9	22.2	32.2	23.8
Assistant professor	21.2	28.0	23.1	31.2	27.1
All ranks	36.1	41.0	41.0	44.4	35.8
Doctoral level (Category I) institutions compared with 2-year (Category III) institutions					
Full professor	34.1	42.1	39.6	54.1	56.7
Associate professor	14.2	20.5	20.4	33.5	32.7
Assistant professor	13.3	20.1	19.3	30.3	30.1
All ranks	33.4	38.7	37.1	49.4	49.2

Source: Calculated using data from the American Association of University Professors' annual survey of faculty salaries generally published in the March–April issue of Academe.
Note: Percentage premium equals percentage differences between average faculty salaries, by institutional category.

the advantage across all ranks climbed sharply from 33.4% in 1984–85 to 49.2% in 2003–4.

Public-Private Differences

In 1970–71 average faculty salaries in the public institutions were just over 10% higher than in the private institutions. The public salary advantage slipped to about 4% in the mid-1980s and vanished altogether by about 1990–91. Indeed, by 1999–2000, the average faculty salary in private institutions had climbed to just over 5% higher than in the public institutions—resulting in a swing in relative position of more than 15 percentage points. Differences in average faculty salaries between the public and the private sectors are explained in part by differences in the mix of institutions by type and also by differences in the mix of faculty by rank. Thus, faculty salaries are slightly higher at the preeminent private research universities than at the flagship public universities. But faculty salaries at the public comprehensive four-year and the public two-year colleges are somewhat higher than those at the corresponding independent institutions.

The public-private differences continue to increase; that is, a progressive

Constant 2001-2 Dollars

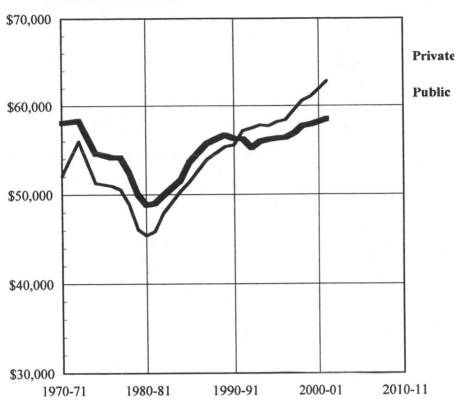

Private

Public

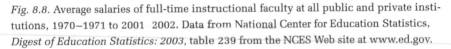

Fig. 8.8. Average salaries of full-time instructional faculty at all public and private institutions, 1970–1971 to 2001 2002. Data from National Center for Education Statistics, *Digest of Education Statistics: 2003,* table 239 from the NCES Web site at www.ed.gov.

widening of the disparity in favor of the private institutions has become evident. Figure 8.8 illustrates the differences between public and private institutions over the three decades since 1970.

This public-private disparity may reflect declining government support for public higher education (see discussion below), resulting in the relative underfunding of the public sector. At work also may be a decline in the economic impact of collective bargaining that until the 1980s may have shored up the public-sector salaries. Notwithstanding this growing difference between sectors, a consistent compensation hierarchy, defined by rank and institutional type, remains a central feature of academic compensation. The story may be quite varied, however, within particular disciplines or program areas—a matter to which we shall return.

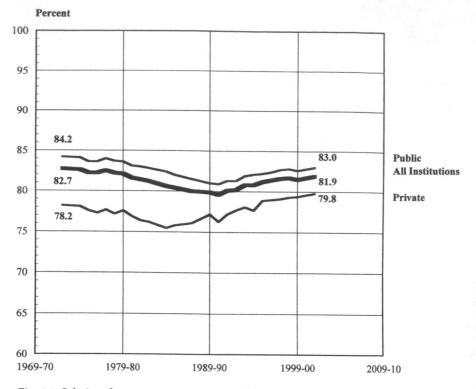

Fig. 8.9. Salaries of women as a percentage of the salaries of men, by sector, full-time instructional faculty at all institutions, 1972–1973 to 2001–2002. Data from U.S. Department of Education, National Center for Education Statistics, *Digest of Education Statistics: 2003,* table 239 from the NCES Web site at www.ed.gov.

Gender Differences

Currently, close to 40% of the faculty teaching at American colleges and universities are women, up from only about 24% in 1972. Women account for over one-third of the full-time faculty but nearly half of the part-time faculty, according to recent data (NCES, 2003).

While the percentage of the faculty who are women has increased markedly over the last several decades, the gap between the average salaries of men and women has not narrowed during the same period, as shown in figure 8.9. Overall, relatively speaking, women faculty lost some ground versus men in the 1970s and 1980s, as their average salary slipped from a high at the beginning of the 1970s, of 82.7% of the average salary of faculty men to a low of 79.6% at the beginning of the 1990s. Their situation brightened somewhat in the 1990s, but

TABLE 8.5
Comparison of Average Salaries of Men and Women Faculty, Selected Academic
Years, 1972–1973 through 1999–2000
(current dollars)

	Men	Women	Difference	Women's Salaries as % of Men's Salaries
1972–73	14,422	11,925	−2,497	82.7
1980–91	24,499	19,996	−4,503	81.6
1990–91	45,065	35,881	−9,184	79.6
1999–2000	60,084	48,997	−11,087	81.5

Source: Derived using data from the National Center for Education Statistics, *Digest of Education Statistics: 2002*, table 235 on the NCES Web site.

by 2001–2, still at only 81.9%, women had not yet regained the salary position relative to that of men they had reached in the early 1970s (fig. 8.9; see also table 8.5).

The gap between the average salaries of women and men faculty is somewhat smaller in the public sector than in the private (fig. 8.9). In both the public and the private sectors the gender gap widened slightly during the 1970s, but the differential between the sectors began to narrow in the mid-1980s and continued to shrink through the late 1990s. Although the gender gap in faculty salaries in the private institutions was somewhat narrower in the late 1990s than in the early 1970s, it still remained wider than the gap in the public institutions, and— it should be noted—the public gap was larger in the late 1990s than it had been in the early 1970s. Of course, the average salaries by gender are affected by many factors, including differences in employment patterns by institutional type, faculty rank (which, in turn, is closely associated with seniority, that is, length of service), and field of specialization, as well as the vestiges of discrimination that persist in spite of decades of affirmative action and other initiatives to promote gender equity.

Viewing the salary-compression issue through the lens of gender, the salaries of women faculty members can be seen as a percentage of the salary of men faculty within each rank (fig. 8.10). It does not appear, using this finer focus, that salary compression, discussed earlier, has occurred during the period from the early 1970s to the late 1990s for either men or women. Indeed, at all three ranks— full, associate, and assistant professor—women faculty lost some ground in salaries, relative to salaries of male full professors. It is true, however, that the salaries of women assistant and associate professors constitute a higher percentage of the salaries of *women* full professors than is the comparable case for the men. The explanation, however, is related to the fact that women full professors' salaries are further below those of the men full professors than are the

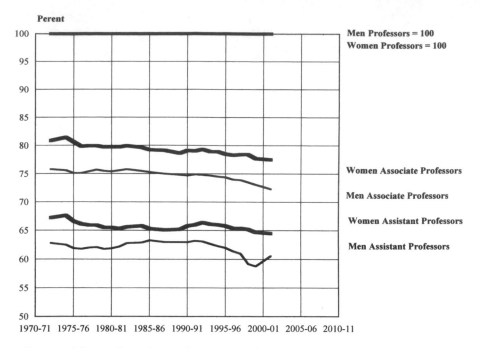

Fig. 8.10. Salaries of associate and assistant professors as a percentage of the salaries of professors, by rank and gender, 1972–1973 to 2001–2002. Data from NCES, 2004, and the NCES Web site at www.ed.gov.

salaries of women assistant and associate professors compared to their male colleagues.

Race and Ethnicity

Salaries differ by race and ethnicity as well as by gender. On average, Asians and Pacific Islanders had the highest average salary among full-time faculty whose primary responsibility was teaching, according to the National Study of Postsecondary Faculty (NSOPF-1993 and -1999). Consistent with income statistics by race and ethnicity nationwide, the next highest salaries were those of white non-Hispanics, followed by Hispanics and African Americans, as shown in figure 8.11. The average faculty salary of Asians (in the NSOPF-99 database) of $55,800 is almost $5,000 higher than the average salary of whites and close to $7,000 higher than that of Hispanics and African Americans. There is more than a $10,000 gap between the average salaries of Asian and American Indian faculty, but there are so few American Indians in the sample that conclusions based on their salary data cannot be very reliable. Of course, the average salaries are shaped by the different employment patterns with respect to institutional type, academic rank, and field of specialty. Asians tend to be more than proportionately represented in engineering and science, which are among the higher-paying academic fields.

The overall pattern of relative differences in faculty salaries by race and ethnicity in 1998 was almost the same as it was in 1992, except for a slight convergence. This convergence phenomenon in average faculty salary by race and ethnicity in the 1990s does contrast, however, with the slight *divergence* in average faculty salary by gender.

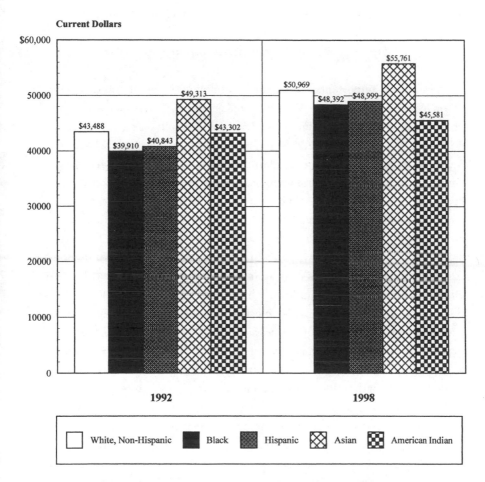

Fig. 8.11. Average base salary of faculty with primary responsibility of teaching, by race/ethnicity, fall 1992 and fall 1998. Data from NSOPF-93 and NSOPF-99. The data were generated using the NCES Data Analysis System.

THE DIMENSIONS OF RESTRUCTURING

Compensation of faculty has historically varied, as illustrated previously, depending on where faculty teach (that is, by institutional type) and on their level of experience or longevity, as largely reflected in academic rank. We have seen that institutional type (universities, other four-year institutions, two-year colleges) is more influential in determining salary than is institutional control, that is, whether faculty are teaching in a public or an independent institution. During the last quarter century those factors have begun to vary in a number of new ways with significant implications for the profession. But more influential, still, has been the increasingly salient role of academic field or discipline.

The Increasing Power of Disciplinary Markets

Of increasing importance among the determinants of faculty salaries—in addition to academic rank, type of institutional employer, and gender—is academic field, or discipline. Until the mid-1970s, disparities in the salaries of faculty in different fields were small and had remained quite stable over time (Bowen and Schuster, 1986). This pattern of modest differences in compensation among academic fields has had a long and honorable history, probably spanning centuries. In a highly meaningful sense, "the faculty were the faculty." They were all equal, or at least roughly equal, one to another; no particular field was held to be more valuable, at least as measured by the reward system. But even if all the barnyard animals *were* equal, a few—in Orwellian fashion—were demonstrably "more equal" than the others. Thus, faculty in a few areas—medicine and law, especially—stood apart; their significantly higher compensation reflected their very different positioning in the wider marketplace. The rest, whether physicists, classicists, art historians, or political scientists, looked *about* the same on the pay scales. That cohesion may have been reinforced, in part, through the upsurge of collective bargaining that exerted egalitarian—and therefore centripetal—pressures across the board, especially in the large public systems.

Beginning in the mid-1970s, however, a sharp and accelerating divergence in salaries surfaced across academic fields: faculty in fields that were in high demand in the general economy (for instance, some engineering and natural science fields, computer science, accounting, and finance) began to be recruited at "market" scale rather than the flatter "union" scale. This increased "marketization" of compensation has had two important effects. First, it has meant that institutions have had to reallocate salary funds from low-demand fields to high-demand fields, especially for new hires, a strategy that has tended to depress overall compensation in the low- and medium-demand fields. This effect has been especially notable in public systems, which typically have less flexibility in the reallocation of funds for salaries.

Second, market forces tend to be felt most keenly at the point of recruitment, so that new hires—usually made at the junior level—have been influenced disproportionately by those market forces. This development has contributed to a marked "salary compression" in the high-demand fields (as distinguished from across all disciplines), because in those fields new hires must be paid in relation to industry norms rather than to faculty salaries in the senior academic ranks in the particular field. One can see how clearly market scale—the centrifugal force—has intruded on and counteracted the centripetal, leveling pressures of "union" scale.

A snapshot of 2001–2 salaries broken out by disciplines reveals evidence of fields that have fared well and others that have fared poorly. Drawing on recent AAUP data (2003–4), full- and new assistant professor average salaries generally can be compared with their counterparts in English. (English is a useful reference because salaries of full professors of English fall at the midpoint among full professors' salaries in the twenty-seven fields listed by the AAUP, as shown in figure 8.12.) Taking the average salaries of English faculty, both full professors and new assistant professors, as separate baselines (100.0%), figure 8.12 depicts wide variations in salaries among fields. Thus, for example, full professors of business management and administrative services on the whole earn about one-third more than their colleagues in English do (134.3:100). However, new assistant professors in business management and administrative services do even better—earning more than double—compared with their counterparts in English (213.5:100). In computer and information science the premium for full professors is significant: 19.1% more than English salaries. And there are similar advantages in economics (17.4%) and engineering (16.5%). Comparing new assistant professors in computer and information science with their counterparts in English, the advantage is much more pronounced, a whopping 70%. The comparable edge for assistant professors in economics is 50.5% and in engineering 47.1%. Figure 8.12 makes clear both the "winners" and "losers" by field and the edge that new entrants enjoy in all illustrated fields compared to their senior colleagues.

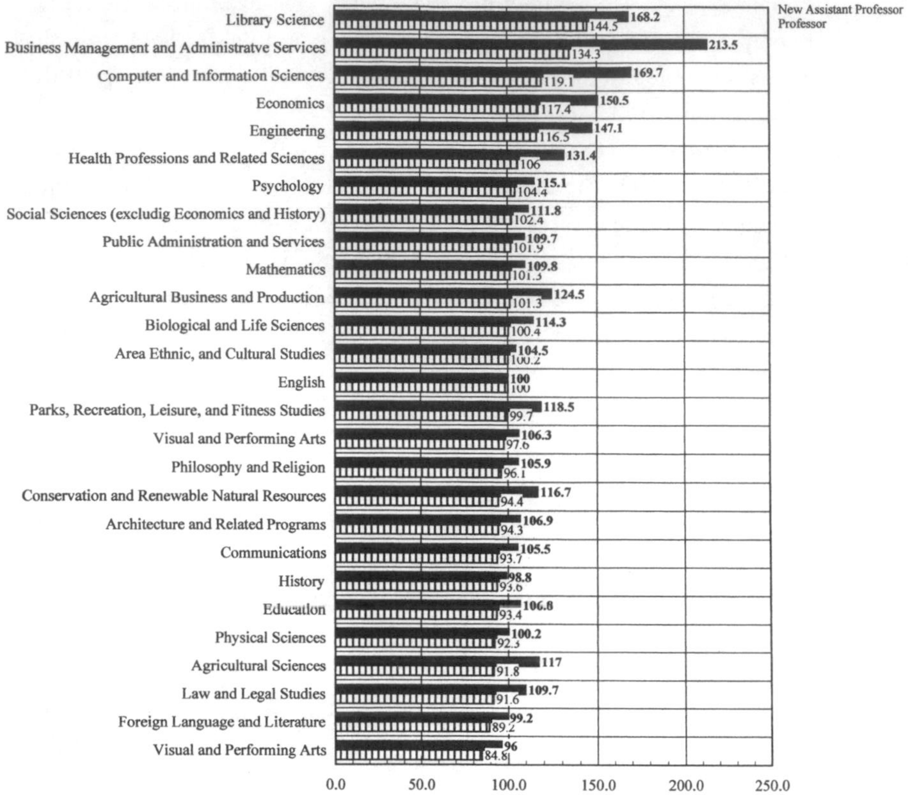

Fig. 8.12. Average salaries of professors, by discipline, as a percentage of the average salaries of professors of English, 2001–2002. From AAUP, 2004, tables C and D, using faculty and salary data from the Office of Institutional Research and Information Management, Oklahoma State University.

Collective Bargaining

The influence of collective bargaining on faculty salaries and overall compensation—the "CB effect"—is a much-analyzed phenomenon. It appears that roughly one-quarter of the approximately 1 million faculty members (including both full-time and part-time faculty) belong to faculty unions or associations that engage in collective bargaining. Information provided by the national organizations in 2005 indicates that the American Federation of Teachers has 140,000 higher education members (out of a total of about 1.3 million members, mostly schoolteachers), divided roughly half-and-half between four-year and two-year institutions, which are predominantly in the public sector. The National Education Association has about 100,000 higher education members in its total membership of 2.7 million. The American Association of University Professors has about 44,000 members, all in higher education, split between public and private mostly four-year institutions.

Because the unionization of faculty is more prominent in those states in which incomes (and living costs, as well) tend to be higher, it is a challenge to isolate the effects of collective bargaining on faculty salaries. Further complicating the effort is this fact: it is commonly the case that within a state that has enacted enabling legislation that authorizes collective bargaining among public-sector employees, most, if not all, public institutions of higher education in that state have unionized faculties. These factors mean that it is difficult to identify for comparison purposes colleges and universities that are similarly situated, even roughly, in which *some* faculty are represented by a bargaining agent but others are not.

Nevertheless, it is clear that faculty unionization generates some material advantage in most fields. Faculty salary data for 1998–99 can be generated from the NSOPF-99 by discipline and by union status, as shown in figure 8.13. These

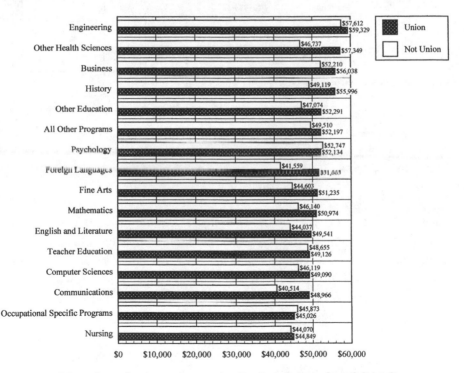

Fig. 8.13. Comparison of union and not-union faculty salaries, selected disciplines, 1998. Data from NSOPF-99. The data were generated using the NCES Data Analysis System.

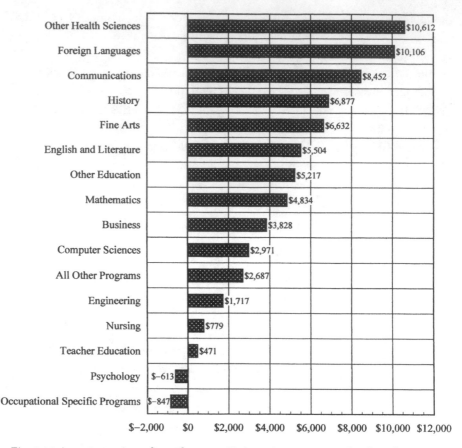

Fig. 8.14. Apparent union salary advantage: Union minus not-union faculty salaries, selected disciplines, 1998. Data from NSOPF-99. The data were generated using the NCES
Data Analysis System.

data indicate that in most fields, belonging to a union provides a salary advantage. The additional salary associated with union membership appears to
amount to more than $10,000 in health sciences and foreign languages. But in
a few fields, such as psychology and occupational programs, faculty who do *not*
belong to a union are reported to have slightly more income than those who do
belong, as illustrated also in figure 8.14.

Under closer scrutiny, however, such generalizations must yield to more
complex analyses. Thus, although the overall salary advantage of unionized versus nonunionized faculty does appear to vary considerably by discipline, the
absence of adequate control groups limits such comparisons. Even so, it does

appear, drawing on NSOPF data, that unionized faculty members receive the largest boost in relatively low-demand academic fields (perhaps especially the humanities). Correspondingly, faculty members appear to benefit less—or even, in some instances, experience a negative effect—in some high-demand fields.

TYPES OF ACADEMIC APPOINTMENTS

Beyond the increasingly strong effects of discipline-based markets, new directions in the types of academic appointments over the past quarter century have had important effects on patterns of faculty compensation. The effects among different types of full-time appointees are not yet fully discernible, as discussed below. More obvious, and of longer standing, are the differences between full- and part-time faculty.

Salaries of Part-Time Faculty

The substantial increase in the number of part-time faculty has significantly outpaced that for full-time faculty in recent years. In the 1990s, the growth in numbers of faculty employed part-time was spectacular; such appointments increased by almost 150,000, or by about half, in less than ten years. More than 70% of the increase in the total number of faculty employed during the 1990s was accounted for by part-timers. (Chapter 3 provides a picture of the huge expansion of part-time faculty.) In all, colleges and universities are paying considerably less per unit of teaching to the part-time faculty than they are to the full-time faculty. Hiring part-time employees is thus a significant element of cost-containing management strategies currently being implemented extensively in higher education.

It is interesting to note, however, that colleges and universities are containing costs by employing part-timers mostly for teaching functions. Hiring part-time employees is twice as prevalent among the faculty as among the nonprofessional staff (fig. 8.15). As of 2001, 44.5% of the total number of faculty (by head count) are employed part-time, compared with fewer than 4% of the executive/administrative/managerial staff and less than 15% of other (nonfaculty) professionals. There is another important aspect. Virtually all of the teaching and research assistants are employed on a part-time basis. By combining the part-time faculty with the teaching assistants, who, in fact, do much of the teaching in many institutions, one finds that over half of the instructional staff in American colleges and universities are now employed part-time. For purposes

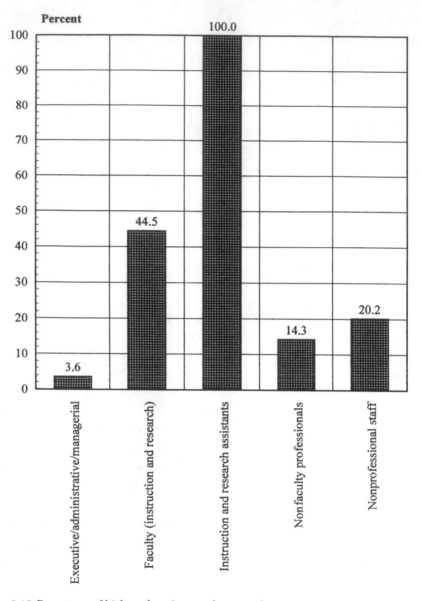

Fig. 8.15. Percentage of higher education employment that is part-time, by major occupation, 2001. Calculated using data obtained from the National Center for Education Statistics, *Digest of Education Statistics: 2003,* table 228, from the NCES Web site, http://nces.ed.gov.

of thinking about compensation, therefore, it is clear that a very substantial proportion of the faculty, at least according to the crude measure of head count, are
paid at a rate much less than that of traditional full-time faculty.

Full-Time Term versus Tenurable Appointments

The phenomenon of full-time term appointments off the tenure track, discussed at length in chapter 7, is rapidly adding a new dimension to the pattern
of faculty compensation. It is likely that over time the differences in compensation practices between full-time faculty who are on the tenure track (tenured
or tenure-eligible) and those full-timers who are off-track will become important. Unlike *part*-time faculty, who rarely receive fringe benefits as part of their
compensation, full-time faculty, whether on-track or off-track, appear to receive
benefits almost invariably. However, we cannot provide detailed analysis of the
compensation differences because data that distinguish between these types of
full-time appointments and adequately control for seniority and field are (to our
knowledge) not yet available.

THE CHANGING OCCUPATIONAL MIX IN HIGHER EDUCATION

More broadly, changing appointment practices, significant as they are, constitute but one manifestation of the changing occupational mix within higher
education's total employment. These trends have served to affect the proportion
of faculty—certainly of regular faculty—among all college and university employees. This development may be a factor affecting faculty leverage (formally
or informally) on college and university campuses and, consequently, on compensation patterns.

Consider the unevenness in the growth patterns of occupation groups within
higher education. Total employment in higher education was estimated in 2000
to be close to 3 million, up sharply from roughly 2 million in 1980. Thus, total
employment surged by about half over twenty years. Of the nearly 3 million total employment in higher education, only about 1 million, or just one-third, are
faculty members (fig. 8.16). In 1976 there were about 633,000 faculty, including
both full- and part-timers. The total number of faculty increased by about one-
quarter, or 160,000 from 1976 to 1987. Then from 1987 to 1999 the number of
faculty increased again by two-fifths, in this period by some 320,000, pushing
the total number of faculty, by 1999, to above 1 million.

A breakout of all the components of total employment in higher education
will be instructive. This total employment is conventionally divided among five

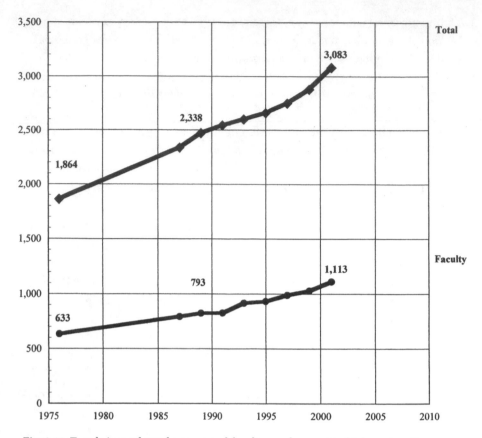

Fig. 8.16. Trends in total employment and faculty employment in higher education, 1976 and 1987–2001, biannually. From U.S. Department of Education, National Center for Education Statistics, *Digest of Education Statistics: 2003,* table 228, from the NCES Web site, http://nces.ed.gov and earlier editions. Note: Gaps in the data are spanned.

occupational groups: executive/administrative/managerial staff, faculty, teaching and research assistants (faculty plus TAs and RAs equal "instructional staff"), other (nonfaculty) professionals, and nonprofessional staff. The employment growth in each of these higher education occupation groups over two different time periods is shown in figure 8.17. The percentage growth differs greatly not only by occupation but also by time period. Growth over the thirteen-year period from 1976 to 1989 is quite different from the pattern extending over the twelve years from 1989 to 2001 (the latest year for which these occupational data are now available). From 1976 to 1989, the greatest percentage increase by far was among the nonfaculty professionals: 123.4% compared to a much more modest 30.2% for faculty. And over the period from 1989 to 2001, once again, the number of other (nonfaculty) professionals increased at a much faster rate than did the number of faculty (51.9% compared to 35.1% for faculty). The *percentage increases* by occupation group over the two periods are compared in figure 8.17, and the *percentage distribution of the increases* by category of employment are compared in figure 8.18.

Percent

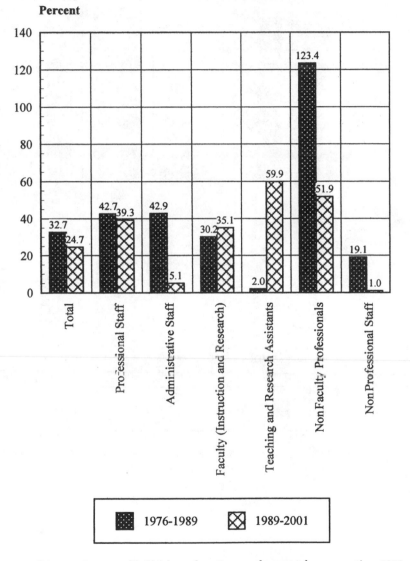

Fig. 8.17. Comparative growth of higher education employment, by occupation, 1976–1989 compared with 1989–2001. Calculated using data from the National Center for Education Statistics, *Digest of Education Statistics: 2003,* from the NCES Web site, http://nces.ed.gov and previous editions. Note: A = B + G; B = C + D + E + F.

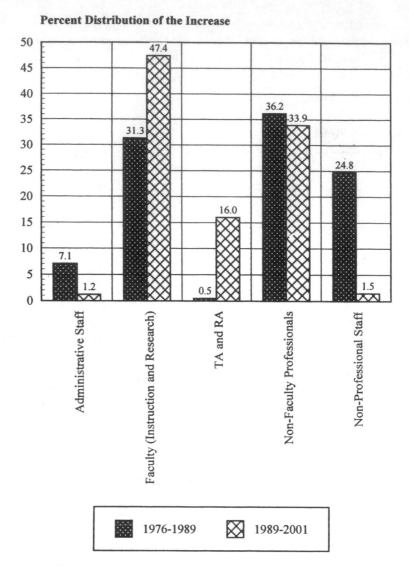

Percent Distribution of the Increase

Legend: 1976-1989, 1989-2001

Fig. 8.18. Distribution of Higher Education Employment Increases, by Occupation, 1976–1989 compared with 1989–2001. Calculated using data from the National Center for Education Statistics, *Digest of Education Statistics: 2003,* from the NCES Web site, http://nces.ed.gov and previous editions. Note: Because the total adds to 100%, including professional staff would result in double counting.

Staff compensation (all five employment components combined) is the largest single component of current fund expenditures of both public and private colleges and universities, generally accounting for 60% to 80% of these expenditures. Although dominant among expenditure categories, staff compensation is also the component of current fund expenditures that is considered to be relatively more controllable than many nonstaff costs, such as utilities. Thus, the growth of the pool of funds for staff compensation may be limited. The conclusion we reach, therefore, is that the changing distribution of staff by occupation group—specifically the increase among nonfaculty staff—within the institutions has weakened the relative position of the faculty in making claims on the limited pool of funds that could be allocated for faculty salaries. This development may have exerted additional downward pressure on faculty salaries during recent decades, slowing the adjustments that would have been necessary to make up for the earlier substantial losses to inflation.

Combining both time periods and calculating the percentage increases from 1976 to 2001, it can be seen that administrative staff employment in colleges and universities increased substantially, by about 50.1%. During the same period, the employment of nonfaculty professionals mushroomed by a whopping 239.3%—that is, at a *much* faster rate than that of the faculty (75.8%) and of teaching and research assistants (about 63.1%).

In the earlier period, from 1976 to 1989, not only were the *numbers* of administrative staff growing faster than the numbers of faculty, but their *salaries* were also higher and growing faster than the salaries of the faculty. In the later period, from 1989 to 2001, the growth in the numbers of administrative staff slowed dramatically, though their salaries exceeded those of the faculty.

Over this span, from 1976 to 2001, the huge increase in the number of nonfaculty professionals relative to the number of faculty entailed commensurate increases in demands for money to pay for them—all from a comparatively limited pool of funds available for all staff salaries. Over the period from 1976 to 2001, the number of nonfaculty professionals grew by about 427,000, almost as much as did the number of faculty, which grew by about 480,000. Thus, nonfaculty professionals accounted for one-third of the increase in total employment in higher education over this period. Accordingly, this explosion in the numbers of nonfaculty professionals is likely to have resulted in even greater crowding of the faculty in their claims for institutional resources for salaries than did even the sharp expansion in the numbers of administrative staff.

In the most recent period, from 1989 to 2001, the instructional staff (faculty plus teaching and research assistants) increased by 39.2%. Interestingly, within this component the number of teaching and research assistants grew much faster than the number of faculty, so that this 39% increase in instructional staff was made up of a 35.1% increase in the number of faculty but a 59.9% increase in the number of teaching and research assistants. (We recognize that the research assistants do not teach, but they are folded in with the TAs and reported by NCES as a single category.)

Percentages aside, over the past quarter-century (1976–2001), the total employment in higher education increased by more than 1.2 million. Of these employees, about 480,000 were faculty and almost as many—427,000—were nonfaculty professionals. Notably, the increase in the number of administrative staff during this period was only about 51,000. As can be seen, and contrary to widespread perception, the number of nonfaculty professionals mushroomed by more than eight times the growth of the administrative staff.

This much greater growth in the number of teaching and research assistants in the more recent period may be a consequence, in part, of increasing the numbers of class sections taught by teaching assistants and thereby substituting lower-cost graduate students for much more expensive professors. The increase in the number of teaching assistants could be interpreted as one more management attempt to hold down costs of higher education by using a strategy that relies heavily on low-cost instruction. Such a strategy may well also be in part a function of faculty preferences both to contain intradepartmental costs and to delegate more responsibility for instruction in introductory-level courses. In any event, shifting more of the teaching responsibilities to lower-cost teaching assistants, if used as a cost-saving strategy, *could* in effect free up resources that could be used to augment faculty salaries.

RESEARCH AND TEACHING AS DETERMINANTS OF SALARY

Yet a third major axis along which change in faculty salaries is being shaped—in addition to the pull of disciplinary market forces and the redistribution of types of academic appointments—is that of type of faculty activity. In *Faculty Work and Public Trust*, James Fairweather (1996) examined trends in the salary rewards that accrue to different types of faculty activities. He found that research generally trumps teaching and that quantity of research publications typically trumps quality, as the desiderata of prestige in the discipline. Although it is difficult to isolate the relative effects on faculty compensation attributable to research productivity and teaching effectiveness, the evidence suggests that at those institutions that expect more of their faculty than being instructors, the rewards of research are significant.

Any conclusions about the complex trends in faculty compensation depend significantly on at least three critical considerations:

1. *The time period covered.* Thus, for example, if the period selected to analyze trends in faculty salaries begins in 1980, the average salaries of full-time instructional faculty appear to have increased over the last two-plus decades in real terms. However, if the period of analysis starts earlier, in 1970, the conclusion is considerably different because real faculty income in the early 1970s has barely been exceeded in recent years. Thus, spanning the entire period from 1970 to the early 2000s, real faculty income has improved only marginally. See figure 8.2. So, employing different time frames produces different "stories."

2. *Faculty rank.* Examining trends in faculty salaries by rank shows that, on average, the salaries in the early 2000s of faculty at a particular rank—professor, associate professor, or assistant professor—only marginally exceed the real value of the salaries earned by that rank in the early 1970s. See figure 8.3. Once more, the importance of disaggregation is crucial; lumping together "all faculty" for analytical purposes almost always glosses over underlying realities.

3. *The compensation of other professionals.* It is clear that most other highly educated professionals earn substantially more than do faculty who teach in American colleges and universities. The gap is large and it is continuing to widen. See table 8.2.

Although faculty compensation continues to be fundamentally shaped along the lines of academic rank and institutional type and by race and gender, the 1990s and early 2000s have featured the increasing influence of several additional significant factors: diverging disciplinary markets, a dramatic new mix in types of academic appointments (in part a function of a continuing buyer's market for faculty services and the changing occupational mix in higher education), and differing values the market has been placing on different kinds of faculty work activities (particularly in honoring research and publications over teaching). These factors have molded academic compensation during the past several decades and have spurred the kinds of shifts increasingly evident in more recent years. We now turn to the outlook for academic compensation, being mindful that projecting economic conditions is at best hazardous if not foolhardy.

FUTURE PROSPECTS FOR FACULTY SALARIES

Faculty salaries in the future will be affected by many factors, both internal and external to higher education. A projection of salary levels might be more accurate if such factors as the probable demand for, and supply of, people qualified to teach at the postsecondary level could be taken into consideration. Demand for faculty is itself affected by a myriad of factors, often interrelated, including such variables as population growth, college-going rates, student-faculty ratios, the cost of college and the ability of students to pay for it, the attractiveness of U.S. higher education to foreign nationals (and obstacles to foreigners' gaining entry to the country), and domestic "competition" for students from proprietary and distance-learning entities, as well as trends in revenues (especially revenues from federal and state governments), operating costs, and nongovernment funding sources, both public and private, that are available to satisfy the insatiable appetite for "more and better."

In addition, a major driver of demand is faculty retirement rates and patterns and the perceived need to replace retired faculty. This variable is enormously important, but its impact is much less predictable than it was before 1994 when the amendment to the Age Discrimination in Employment Act took effect for colleges and universities, thereby ending the imposition of any mandatory retirement age for faculty members.

Factors that are external to the institutions that employ faculty but nevertheless heavily influence faculty salaries are elusive to project yet unquestionably will be far-reaching in their effects. In this category are the overall economic conditions and, relatedly, the educational and training needs of workers in a knowledge-based economy; inflation rates; competition *within* the academic labor market; and competition for talent from *outside* the academy, whether from industry and such professions as law and medicine or from the public (government agencies, including research laboratories) and the nonprofit sectors.

But pervading all these factors is a huge unknown variable: the future impact of information technology on the academic world. Surely the rate of technological change moves more swiftly than our capacity to measure the effects. Although we speculate about these effects in our concluding chapters, we are acutely aware that any projections are heavily freighted with uncertainties.

Taken together, these are all factors contributing, positively or negatively, to the overall financial health of colleges and universities. The pressures are incessant to control expenditures and expand revenues. For many institutions, philanthropy is a vitally important source of revenues, and the generosity of pa-

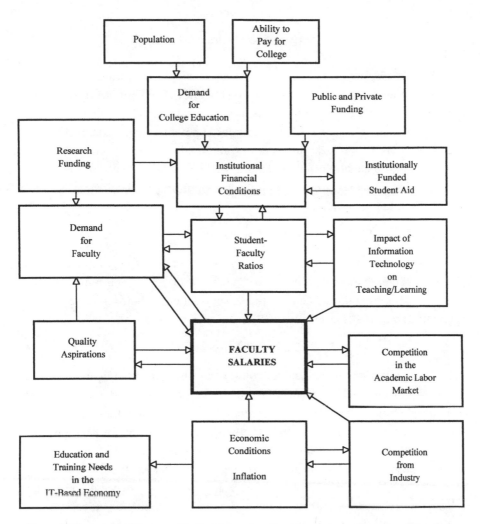

Fig. 8.19. Overview of factors affecting future faculty salary trends. Courtesy of Carol Frances and Associates.

trons, linked in turn to the economy and to governmental policies that promote charitable giving, mold institutional endowments. The ability to draw on such resources to directly compensate faculty or to pay for other activities and thereby free up moneys for salaries can make an enormous difference. These complex, interrelated internal and external factors that will affect the future prospects for faculty salaries are depicted by a rough diagram in figure 8.19. Some of the most important variables are highlighted there.

The Demand for Higher Education

Faculty salary increases will depend significantly on the future financial condition of the colleges and universities that employ the people who teach. That financial condition will turn, in large part, on the demand for higher education, which depends most basically on the pool of potential matriculants and their ability to pay for college: numbers of traditional college-age and older adult prospects. The usual place to begin projecting demand for college is to project the population by age group and apply current or projected college-going rates for each of the age groups.

Population Projections

Basic projections indicate that the traditional college-age group (ages 18 to 24) will increase dramatically in the coming decade, at an even faster rate than the adult population that contributed so substantially to enrollment growth in the 1980s and 1990s (see figure 8.20).

Student-Faculty Ratios

After projecting the demand for college education, the next logical step is to make at least a rough estimate of the number of faculty needed to teach the anticipated number of students. Conventionally, this has been done by projecting student-faculty ratios. From 1970 to 1990, as shown in figure 8.21, student-faculty ratios have edged slightly downward in both public and private institutions, meaning that faculty were teaching slightly fewer students on average than in previous years. Since 1990 the reduction in student-faculty ratios has been somewhat more marked, on average down from about 19 students per faculty member to 16 or so in the public colleges and universities and down from 13 students to 11 in the private institutions. These are admittedly crude, aggregated measures that fail to distinguish among the many subsectors that make up the undifferentiated whole. Nonetheless, this trend, should it continue, would lead to increasing demand for faculty and, accordingly, should exert some upward pressure on faculty salaries. But then there is the IT factor . . .

The IT Factor

As noted above, the great unknown in projections about higher education and its financing is the likely impact of instructional technology on the traditional relationships between students and teachers, in both on-campus classes and off-campus distance education. Will instructional technology permit mean-

Percent Increase

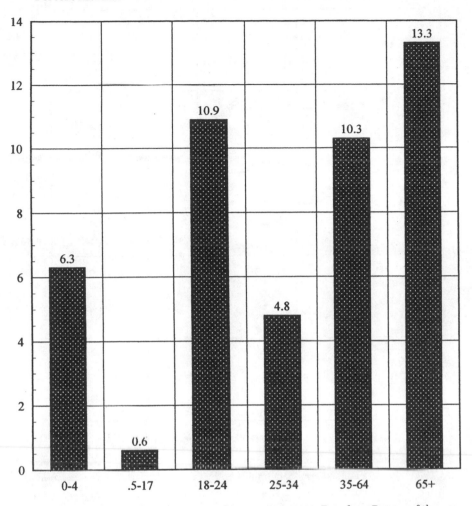

Fig. 8.20. Projected population increases, by age, 2001–2010. Data from Bureau of the Census, *Projections of the Resident Population by Age, Sex, Race, and Hispanic Origin: 1999–2100* (Washington, DC: Government Printing Office, 2000).

ingful cconomies of scale that will enable faculty to reach and teach significantly larger numbers of students—thereby *reducing* the need for faculty? Or will IT create the need (and opportunity) for frequent career shifts and continuous learning—and thereby potentially increase sharply the demand for postsecondary education and, consequently, the need for additional faculty? These developments surely will also exert even more upward pressure on the number of professionals needed to facilitate technology-mediated teaching and learning;

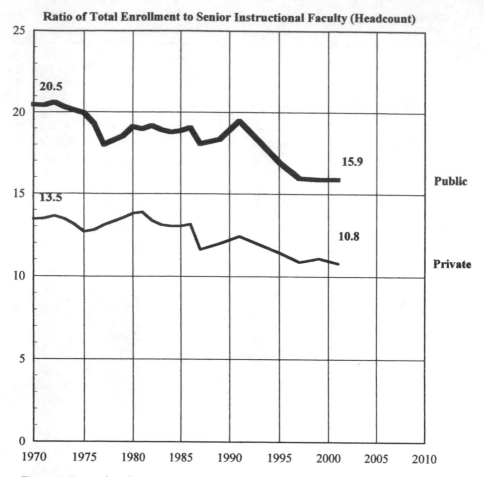

Ratio of Total Enrollment to Senior Instructional Faculty (Headcount)

Fig. 8.21. Ratio of total enrollment to senior instructional faculty (head count), by sector, 1970–2001. Calculated from data published by the U.S. Department of Education, National Center for Education Statistics, *Digest of Education Statistics: 2003*, from the NCES Web site, http://nces.ed.gov. Note: The student-faculty ratios are based on headcount data for both students and faculty. Student-faculty ratios based on full-time equivalents are about the same.

many such professionals do, and will, have faculty status and responsibilities. Strikingly different scenarios are plausible.

The Condition of College and University Finances

Additional factors that can be expected to affect faculty compensation include the following.

Cyclical Economic Activity

A strong national economy in the 1990s contributed to the financial strength of colleges and universities and helped boost real faculty compensation. Positive outcomes included students' increasing ability and willingness to pay higher tuition, which increased net revenues, even after greater allowances for compensatory increases in student aid. Also, state budget surpluses created a more favorable environment for public support of public institutions. A stock market boom created capital gains, which are the principal source of major private gifts to both private and public colleges and universities. These robust economic conditions began to contract in 2000 and then to fade rapidly. At this writing, state budgetary pressures and uncertainties are adversely affecting higher education, especially through constrained state appropriations for public institutions, in a variety of ways. Among these factors are the effects of declining equity markets on abilities or propensities to make gifts to institutions of higher education. Although markets rebounded somewhat in 2004 and into 2005, and expanding institutional endowments reflected that development, the outlook, as always, is laced with unknowns. The surging costs of defense and security-related activities that compete for the federal dollar and the unprecedented federal budget deficits serve to chill prospects for expanding existing federal support or launching new initiatives.

This recent downward swing in the economy, which may persist or may reverse itself soon, serves to underscore the reality that our ability to predict the future strength of the economy is circumscribed. The fluctuations of a cycle-prone market economy will always obscure the vision of even the wisest financial prognosticators (Schuster, 2002). The muscular national economy of the last half of the 1990s seemed to evaporate with remarkable swiftness; the hallmarks of an official recession were on hand even before the national tragedy of September 2001. The most exuberant forecasts that technology-fueled productivity has all but insulated the U.S. economy from serious setbacks appear, at this writing, to have been quite myopic. So recessions come—and go. In the period that our study covers, significant recessions in the early 1970s, early 1980s, and early 1990s and the weak economy in the early 2000s, as well as runaway inflation in the late 1970s, have all created hardships for higher education, its students, and its employees.[11] But the economy snaps back—or struggles back—and the higher education enterprise, over the longer term, grows and grows. This is likely to be the pattern for the foreseeable future, and despite the cyclical ups and downs, the economy, over time, is more likely than not to be a friend, not a foe, of academic compensation.

Dampening of Inflation

This positive outlook depends in no small measure on whether inflation—quite moderate in recent years—continues to be contained. The dampening of inflation has stemmed, for now, the erosion of the financial base of higher education institutions. This could, and should, create an economic environment for gains in the relative economic position of faculty on American campuses. It is certainly *not* a matter of higher education's costs somehow having been "tamed." Although inflation in the overall economy has receded for now, some components of the Higher Education Price Index continue to escalate sharply. Thus, whereas costs of utilities, supplies, and equipment have increased only moderately, the costs of some factors, particularly library acquisitions and fringe benefits, have much more than doubled in the two decades since 1983 (fig. 8.22).

There are also *negative trends* that could offset the positive influences.

Privatization

The trend with the greatest potential ramifications for the finance of colleges and universities is the pervasive move toward ever more privatization of higher education finance. There is a shift away from public sources of funds (that is, from federal, state, and local governments) and toward greater reliance on private funding (tuition, gifts, endowment income, and income from auxiliary enterprises like bookstores and residence halls). This trend takes many forms. Perhaps most conspicuous is the extent to which public institutions of higher education have succeeded in tapping into private philanthropic sources. Over the past several decades these institutions—most notably the great flagship state universities—have attracted billions of private dollars from individuals, corporations, and foundations. Such sources were never the exclusive preserve of private colleges and universities, but neither were the privates, until a few decades ago, accustomed to having to compete seriously with their public siblings for the philanthropic dollar. And so numerous public universities now derive only a minority of their total revenue from the states of which they are—at least nominally—an integral part. A few of them assert that less than one-fifth of their revenues are drawn directly from the state. (In these instances, much of the nonstate revenue is nonetheless public funds, primarily in the form of large infusions of federal dollars for research and for student financial aid.) This privatization has engendered and perhaps made inevitable the "entrepreneurial university." Whatever benefits accrue as a result of additional resources and

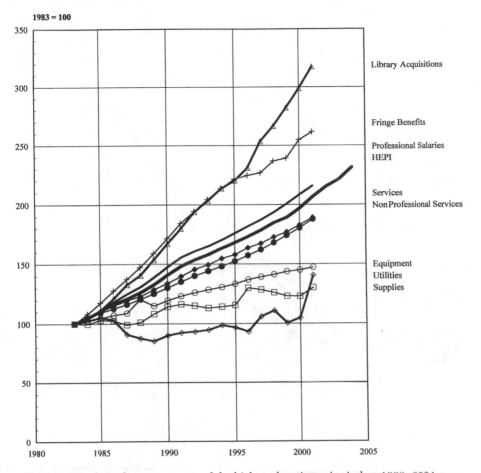

Fig. 8.22. Trends in the components of the higher education price index, 1983–2004. Data from Research Associates of Washington, D.C., Higher Education Price Index, 2004 Update.

new innovative activity, they seem almost always to come at a cost: the pre-occupation of university management with issues falling outside of the purely academic realm.

Tuition Discounting

The intensification of competition in education markets is leading institu-tions to engage in the virtually universal practice of tuition discounting. In its most extreme form, tuition discounting cuts deeply into revenues and, reveal-ingly, exposes the sensitive connection between student tuition revenues and faculty salaries.

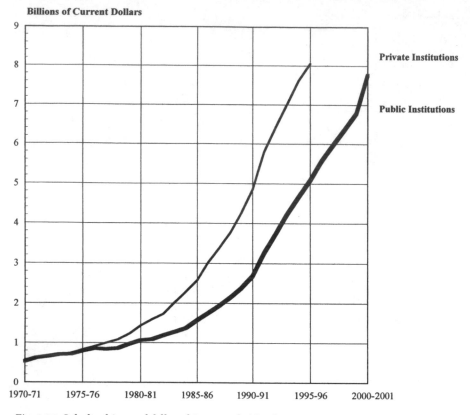

Billions of Current Dollars

Private Institutions

Public Institutions

1970-71   1975-76   1980-81   1985-86   1990-91   1995-96   2000-2001

Fig. 8.23. Scholarships and fellowships awarded by degree-granting institutions, 1970–1971 to 2000–2001. Data from National Center for Education Statistics, *Digest of Education Statistics: 2003,* from the NCES Web site at www.ed.gov.

Student Aid Shortfalls

Shortfalls in federal student financial aid could reduce demand for higher education. Although federal student aid is, in the aggregate, at record high levels, increases in the costs to students far outpace increases in student aid. Thus, significant shortfalls persist and have induced colleges and universities—whether out of genuine commitment to broadening educational opportunities or in an attempt to maximize revenues—to provide ever greater amounts of institutionally funded student aid. This institutional aid is usually drawn from general funds—the same funds from which faculty salaries are paid. So the need to tap general funds for student aid exerts some downward pressure on faculty salary increases. The growth of institutionally funded scholarships and fellowships in both public and private institutions is shown in figure 8.23.

Changes in Research Funding

Another possibly significant factor exerting downward pressure on faculty salaries at major research universities stems from changes in the way research is funded. Over several decades, the federal government has funded a smaller and smaller share of the research performed by faculty at the universities. As a consequence, universities have had to support more of the research with their own funds. (This is a major motivation for public institutions to seek and obtain funds from nonpublic sources, as noted above.) The erosion of the federal share of support for research at universities can be seen in figure 8.24. As research absorbs more of the universities' own resources, fewer funds are available for faculty salaries.

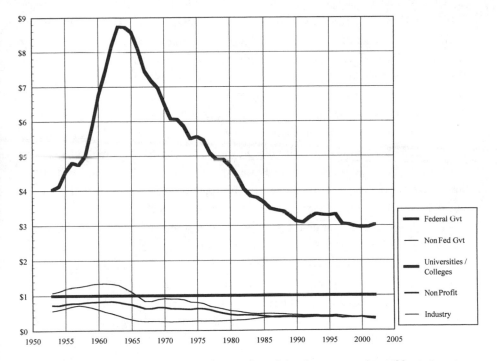

Fig. 8.24. Sources of funds to pay for research and development performed by universities and colleges, per dollar of institutional R&D expenditures, 1953–2002. Data from National Science Foundation, Science Resources Web site.

Further Reflections on Instructional Technology's Impact

The champions of technology—this great unknown obscuring the future of higher education—argue that technology will create economies of scale, drive down costs, and increase demand for higher education. However, increased demand for higher education does not necessarily translate into greater need for faculty and higher salaries. The drive to intensify the use of information technology in higher education is, in reality, a drive to substitute capital for labor—that is, to substitute technology for faculty.

Up to this point, the increased use of technology has not resulted in fewer faculty. The impact of technology on most faculty members has been, instead, a considerable increase in their workload, which results from the greater demands made on them in the transition to on-line learning: reconstructing their knowledge bases, creating Web sites, and responding to student e-mail (Finkelstein et al., 2000).

Information technology greatly affects the way faculty use their time. The most profound impact of technology on faculty is the deconstruction of their old knowledge bases and the resulting need to establish new forms of intellectual authority. Faculty may lose control over—that is, may lose their near-monopoly on—relevant information sources as students gain direct access to more current information, using better research tools and locating more Web-based sources.

In some fields IT can make textbooks obsolete. It takes an enormous amount of faculty time to evaluate the quality of the new sources of information and reconstruct a new knowledge reservoir, or, more profoundly, to generate entirely new roles and relationships to facilitate student learning. It also takes faculty members more time to implement technology-based teaching and learning strategies than it does to prepare a traditional class.

In the new IT era, ever-changing, cascading torrents of information demand constant updating, organizing, and continuous exploration. The additional faculty preparation time that these activities require is rarely recognized at the time faculty salaries are negotiated and becomes another "hidden cost" of IT. Another very important hidden cost is the time it takes for faculty to respond to the significantly greater demands, and still rising expectations, of students for more direct contact with faculty members.

Much faculty work now requires substantial additional commitments of time, in most cases without commensurate increases in compensation. Thus, the compensation per unit of faculty time, viewed in this way, is actually being eroded. IT's promise of greater productivity through freeing up resources that can be used to increase faculty salaries is far from being realized. On the contrary, faculty may have to compete more aggressively for funds, as many institutions experience huge costs—and, too often, major cost overruns—in implementing their new administrative information systems. (See chapter 4, on faculty work, and chapters 10 and 11.)

SOME CONCLUDING REMARKS ON FACULTY REWARDS

The above analysis suggests a few clear—and a few less clear—conclusions. First, it is evident that, overall, faculty salaries, in terms of real purchasing power, have only barely increased beyond the level that had been attained as far back as the early 1970s. Upon closer inspection, one finds that only in the rank of full professor has the real constant dollar value of salaries increased, albeit quite modestly. Thus, the apparent catching up is a function more of the upward redistribution of appointments—tilting toward full professorships (itself a function largely of aging)—that drives upward the average salary for all ranks.

Academic salaries continue to lag behind those in other "comparable" professions by roughly 30%. In the 1990s academic salaries began to trail the salaries of all workers with advanced degrees for the first time in the past quarter century. Faculty are increasingly turning to supplemental sources of income both from their primary employing institution and from outside. Moreover, faculty salaries have not kept up with administrative salaries paid by colleges and universities.

A second clear conclusion is that the *structure* of faculty salaries has in some basic respects remained fairly stable. That is, salaries continue to vary in predictable ways by institutional type, academic rank, employment status, and, unfortunately, gender. Full professors make appreciably more than associate professors, and associate professors earn more than assistant professors. Similarly, research university faculty at each rank earn more than faculty at other doctorate-granting universities; and the latter faculty, in turn, earn more than faculty at comprehensive colleges and at four-year liberal arts colleges. Women faculty continue to earn lower salaries than male faculty, though the gender gap varies when one controls for time in rank and field.

More significantly, however, the past quarter century has seen a fundamental restructuring of rewards *by academic discipline* or program area. Whereas there were formerly (with a few outlier exceptions) only small and stable differences among fields, beginning in the 1970s a large and accelerating divergence among disciplines has emerged that, in the main, places primarily academic-based fields (most notably in the humanities) at a disadvantage relative to some fields that are primarily anchored in the broader economy. Thus, market forces have come to increasingly displace institutional scales and even the union scales that served as a powerful centripetal force for convergence in salaries within ranks and across fields in the same institution.

These disciplinary differences have been particularly noticeable at the point of hiring, so that new assistant professors (and the smaller number of "new" senior faculty hires) in high-demand fields have been the chief beneficiaries of this market-propelled trend. The result has been a reallocation of faculty salary funds from low-demand to high-demand fields, depressing salaries for faculty in the majority of fields (which are in relatively low or moderate demand outside the university).

A second axis upon which faculty salaries are being restructured through management strategy is the *type of appointment*. Part-time teaching has become the preferred mode for reducing the marginal costs of faculty salaries. But even aside from the obvious part-time strategy, higher education management has developed a two-tier system of full-time salaries by type of appointment, distinguishing tenure-track from tenure-ineligible, as well as escalating difference by discipline. Moreover, faculty salaries as a proportion of total institutional salary funds have been declining.

Less clear is how these new management strategies will interact with broader economic factors, in particular the realignment of the competitive landscape as many for-profit providers emerge (paying lower faculty salaries), the increasing feminization of the profession (and the attendant risk of depressing average salaries), and, again, the least predictable wild card of all, the role of information technology. It does seem clear, however, that market forces will increasingly rule; the only question is precisely what form these influences will take. The prospect for faculty compensation is probably not as promising as it once was. The outlook for individuals in certain favored fields, however, as well as for those faculty members with entrepreneurial proclivities and skills, may be better than ever. For most new entrants to the academic profession, their respective fields and type of academic appointment will likely define their compensation prospects to a considerable degree.

As was once wisely observed, the greatest gift to American colleges in the 1800s was the willingness of professors to teach for very low wages (see again Horowitz, 1984). And so the same can be said, as well, albeit with less force, of the American faculty's contribution during the twentieth century. The first decades of the twenty-first century elude prediction in terms of faculty compensation. The variables are identifiable; their respective weights are not. Perhaps the one verity upon which most observers can agree is this: the faculty of America's colleges and universities have made a vital contribution to the nation's culture and competencies; the future will be linked significantly to the ability of higher education to educate the nation's populace—and the prospect for attracting and retaining a suitable corps of faculty members is linked to the capacity and willingness to compensate them fairly.

NOTES

1. These items are included, along with basic salary, by the employing institution in the income information (Form W-2) submitted each year for income tax purposes to federal and state agencies. However, few if any studies exist that report institutional records of distributions of *total* institutional income received by faculty (as distinguished from surveys in which faculty members themselves report their institutionally derived income—a method not likely to be nearly so reliable). Such data would help us to better understand faculty members' overall economic relationship to their principal employer.

2. This calculation is derived by subtracting the average salary for all faculty (all ranks) from the average salary for continuing faculty (all ranks), in AAUP data in Committee Z's annual reports (appearing as either table A or table 1). Thus, for the 29-year span from 1974–75 to 2003–4, the annual difference ranged between 0.5 and 1.5% in 26 instances and exceeded 1.5% (between 1.6 and 1.9%) in only 3 instances. The average year-to-year difference for these 29 years is 1.1%.

3. As Howard R. Bowen noted, "Compensation policy is . . . influenced by the weak market position of most academic personnel, especially faculty and administrators" (1980, p. 53).

4. According to Andrew Carnegie biographer Joseph Wall: "To discover that college professors might teach for several decades and not achieve a salary above $400 a year, with no provisions for retirement, was for Carnegie a shocking revelation. Office clerks at Carnegie Steel earned as much or more than this." (Wall, 1970, p. 870)

5. In their pioneering study of compensation from 1904 to 1953, Ruml and Tickton found that "salaries paid to the most eminent professors . . . show[ed] drastic deterioration" (1955, p. 18) and that "as the compensation at the higher levels of teaching in colleges and universities deteriorated, additional emphasis was placed on security. In many situations, permanent tenure was given instead of additional compensation" (p. 21).

Their data on salaries of professors and presidents are confined to large public universities, in part because reliable data were unavailable for private universities. Ruml and Tickton thought that salaries at private colleges and universities were even worse (p. 14).

The half century was an economic roller-coaster ride. Professors at large universities saw their real purchasing power increase some 33% from 1904 to 1933 but then plummet 32% from 1933 to 1947 and begin to rebound from 1947 to 1953 (by 8%). The net change was a 2% decrease. During this fifty-year period, other faculty at large universities fared somewhat better: associate professors gained 6% and assistant professors 3%. Relative to blue-collar workers, though, faculty salaries suffered miserably; for example, the salaries of automobile workers improved by 140% in real earnings, bituminous coal miners by 163%, and telephone operators by 111% (pp. 37–38).

6. Bowen delineates twelve periods or "episodes" in the history of faculty compensation from 1903–4 to 1977–78 (1980, pp. 54–59, esp. table 9, p. 55).

7. To illustrate: Assume that throughout a fifteen-year period, full professors earn (in constant dollars) $80,000 annually and assistant professors $50,000. Further assume that in year 1 there were four professors and six assistant professors, but by year 15 the distribution by rank had progressed to seven full professors and only three assistants. The *average* salary across those ranks will have increased over that time from $62,000 to $71,000 (an increase of 14.5%), but in fact only the distribution *by rank* has shifted; the compensation for the *individual* faculty members has *not* increased, because full professors and assistant professors are still paid at exactly the same rate as they were fifteen years earlier. (Of course, the *institution's* payroll will have increased as a function of the redistribution of rank.)

8. Thus, in 1970–71 the ratio of average salaries of all assistant professors ($11,176) to salaries of elementary and secondary teachers ($9,268) was 1.21:1. By 2000–2001, the ratio, having previously dropped as low as 1.04:1, had rebounded to 1.09:1 (calculated from NCES, 2003).

9. Although typically considered to be fringe benefits, and tabulated as such, payments by employer and employee for social security (Federal Insurance Compensation Act or "FICA" on most pay stubs), as suggested earlier, may be more properly characterized as a *tax* on current employment, since those payments do not actually create an individual account that the retiree (or her or his dependents) can draw on upon retirement.

10. The AAUP data are for full-time instructional faculty at AAUP Category I (i.e., doctoral) institutions. The same pattern exists for NCES data for full-time instructional faculty across types of institutions: associate professors salaries were 75.6% of full professors' salaries in 1970–71 but only 68.2% in 1998–99. For assistant professors the comparable figures are 62.2% for 1970–71 and 58.2% for 1998–99 (NCES, 2001a, table 23B).

11. Note well that following the unprecedented expansion of higher education that extended from the mid-1950s through the 1960s, growth in the national economy abruptly slowed. The effect was felt almost immediately by colleges and universities, and thus before the glow of the previous decades' boom had faded, Earl F. Cheit was prompted to publish one of the more influential studies in the Carnegie Commission on Higher Education series: *The New Depression in Higher Education* (1971).

CHAPTER NINE

Pathways to the Professoriate

We have analyzed through many different lenses the developments and trends that have affected the quality of academic life. Some of those developments, moderately improved compensation, for instance, presumably have made the prospect of an academic career marginally more attractive (chapter 8). Other developments, such as the shrinkage in the proportion of academic appointments that serve as the gateway to traditional, relatively secure academic careers, may discourage a person from choosing "the life academic" (chapter 7). In addition to such speculations about the attractiveness of academic careers, a stream of survey data helps to identify the areas of satisfaction and dissatisfaction that faculty members express about their work and their careers; sometimes an item asks specifically whether faculty members would choose an academic career if they had the opportunity to make that choice again (see especially chapter 5). And, more to the present point, an occasional survey item directly asks faculty members whether they would encourage their students to seek an academic career.

In this chapter we focus on what is known about the attractiveness of academic careers to talented young people contemplating their career options. More fundamentally, we try to determine whether probative evidence exists that bears on this complicated question. Can we determine whether adequate numbers of very talented young people are choosing academic careers? And for that matter, by what criteria would one judge whether new entrants to academic careers are better qualified than, or as well qualified as, their predecessors?

These are hardly new concerns; they may be as old as universities themselves. It is perhaps worth noting that a century ago this issue was raised in terms of needing to avoid hiring candidates who too often were "irredeemably mediocre" (Veysey, 1965, p. 178).

There are formidable obstacles to setting forth academic-career qualifications. To begin with, the qualities that are susceptible to measurement—those that are quantifiable—likely are not so important as intangibles such as dedication, a love of learning, a capacity and a commitment to reach culturally diverse learners, and so on; these attributes cannot be measured readily—if at all. Then there is the question, even more difficult to answer, of whether among the recruits to the academy there are some, at least, who have the intellectual gifts and creativity to make important intellectual breakthroughs: for instance, fresh insights in interpreting some aspect of society (perhaps a "new paradigm," as academics are fond of saying), or rearranging molecules in some unprecedented but consequential way. And more fundamental still are the "so what" questions: Does it really make a difference whether the academy attracts *very* strong new entrants? Do we actually *know* that students would learn more and that the prospects for "advancing the frontiers of knowledge" are served better—not to mention significantly better—by faculty members who appear by conventional indicators to be better qualified?

So a whole tangle of questions arise that challenge anyone who attempts to assess whether higher education is getting its "fair share" of highly talented young people. There are no clear answers. Ambiguities permeate the issues, and so it must be conceded at the outset that the kinds of evidence marshaled here will not settle the issue one way or another. Yet there are some ways in which relevant data can be brought to bear. It is our contention that the type of evidence we proffer sheds at least some light on the question, How is higher education doing in its efforts to attract to academic careers persons of high quality? Stating it more broadly (as was done two decades ago), "What do we know about the quality of persons now being attracted to academic careers?" (Bowen and Schuster, 1986, p. 201).

Underlying this inquiry is the concern that the changing realities of academic work and academic careers—or, more precisely, the *perceptions* of those realities among persons who contemplate academic careers—may be dissuading significant numbers of "prospects" from opting for such a commitment. Opinions about this issue abound. Anecdotal evidence flourishes. But efforts to systematically evaluate whether the situation is better or worse, from the perspective of the academy, are sparse. Perhaps this is so because such efforts are doomed to be suggestive at best and cannot answer definitively such complex and value-laden questions. Perhaps. But we assume otherwise: that a methodical analysis of available data, despite its inevitable limitations, is useful and likely will suggest, through discernible patterns, tentative, albeit inconclusive, answers to the questions posed herein.

It is also important at the outset to establish that excellence among faculty members is hardly unidimensional. For instance, to attract an intellectual elite into the corps of college and university teaching is desirable but, we submit, certainly not sufficient. We need to be wary of claiming too much for our admittedly "right-tail analysis," that is, assuming more than we should about an analysis that is more or less confined to just the very high end of a distribution of talent that is already restricted to high achievers. Such a preoccupation fails to accord adequate weight to the other qualities that are essential in fielding the huge million-plus instructional corps that is required to serve 15 or 16 million students. In more prosaic (if perhaps provocative) terms, the qualities needed in a faculty member to optimize learning among students enrolled at, say, Cal Tech or Wellesley are not necessarily the same qualities that may be crucial in most other academic venues. With that distinction made, we now turn to five further premises that need to be established.

First, having persons of "high quality" in faculty positions does make a positive difference in the extent to which colleges and universities are able to accomplish their mission. (By "high quality" we mean, though in oversimplified terms, persons of exceptional competence and dedication to their academic tasks.) Accordingly, this chapter focuses largely on the extraordinarily gifted. This does not mean, as just noted, that we are interested only in attracting the exceptionally talented to academic careers. With well over a half million full-time faculty members (and nearly that many part-timers) needed to staff the academy, it would be entirely unrealistic to set a standard for entry to the academic career so high as to exclude all but those possessing truly exceptional intellectual skills. We do strongly believe, however, that the academy must nonetheless succeed in drawing into academic careers adequate numbers of the truly gifted, lest higher education lose much of its capacity to provide intellectual leadership in research and social analysis and criticism. We note, too, that the many studies of the academic labor market have been concerned primarily with numbers—measures of demand and supply—and, accordingly, have infrequently engaged issues of *quality* rather than *quantity* (Schuster, 1995; National Research Council, 2000).

Second, particular groups of high academic-intellectual achievers do have excellent potential for academic careers, and their expressed career preferences and their ultimate choices among careers constitute indicators of the relative attractiveness to them of an academic career. A corollary of this observation is that persons who make up these select populations almost always have other attractive career options, at least up through their undergraduate years; thus, choosing an academic career, despite their presumed career mobility, constitutes a "vote" in favor of the appeal of such a career. Opting for some other career direction, at least to some degree, thereby casts a "negative vote."

Third, a more direct measure of perceived faculty quality can be found in the judgments of seasoned academics whose experience enables them to speak to issues of current (and would-be) faculty quality relative to the quality of faculty in the past. Such assessments are more expert and flow from direct observation, although their value is tempered by their inevitable subjectivity.

Fourth, expressions of interest in an academic career, even at an early age (say, while a person is still in high school), are relevant to the task at hand even though those interests may later be channeled into other pursuits—and most often are.

Fifth, even though there is no absolute measure by which to judge whether the academy is attracting its "fair share" of highly able persons into faculty careers, viewing how the career-related interests of key populations have shifted over time—gravitating toward or away from academic careers—yields indicators of whether academic careers are becoming more or less attractive relative to careers in other sectors (for example, law, medicine, and business) that compete for exceptional talent. Such indicators are suggestive of the academy's pull.

Further motivation for our current endeavor flows from the opportunity to extend earlier work that sought to answer the same questions. In chapter 11, "The Flow of Exceptional Talent into Academe," of their book *American Professors* (1986), Bowen and Schuster tried to determine whether higher education was losing its ability to attract highly talented individuals into academic careers. Toward that end those authors conducted secondary analyses of a number of data sets and undertook several original surveys and analyses. The present effort builds directly on that foundation and extends most of the original analyses over the intervening two decades. In the methods used here, we have sought to replicate insofar as possible the earlier efforts in order to optimize comparability of results. In addition, the current authors identified some populations not included earlier and thus the mid-1980s inquiry is now augmented by fresh analyses.

ORGANIZING THE NEW EVIDENCE

Our examination is divided into two main sections. First, we have identified a number of populations of highly talented persons whose career choices, we believe, reflect the relative attractiveness of academic careers, and we track how the career interests among those cohorts have shifted over time, that is, the interests of able persons who have not yet embarked on academic careers. This task entails tracking the career plans of high school students and college undergraduates. Second, we look at the quality of advanced graduate students contemplating academic careers via an expert assessment made by chairs of "leading" academic departments. These experts evaluate both their own advanced graduate students and the new entrants to academic careers. We compare the assessment of the quality of these advanced graduate students and the new faculty members with an earlier assessment made of their predecessors.

Taken together, these several explorations will suggest whether the pathways into the professoriate have become strewn with more or fewer obstacles, real or perceived, than was the case in the mid-1980s when reasons for concern were evident.

CAREER PREFERENCES OF UNDERGRADUATES

By the time undergraduates settle on their postbaccalaureate plans, their career trajectory is often set, at least initially. There are innumerable ways into the professoriate, as our earlier discussion of career trajectories shows (see especially chapter 6), and it is clear that the traditional, relatively narrow route to an academic career—while still modal—is not so dominant as it once was. That is to say, increasing numbers of faculty members are taking more circuitous routes into academic careers. Even so, an undergraduate's decision about immediate postbaccalaureate goals is closely associated with plans for and the likelihood of an academic career. Thus, for present purposes, the decision whether to (1) enter graduate school or (2) enter a professional school (law, medicine, business, education, and the like) or (3) enter the workforce directly is a reasonably good indicator of which persons are maintaining the option of pursuing an academic career and which are heading in other directions. To be sure, a degree in law, medicine, business, education, and so on, rather than advanced work in the arts and sciences, does not preclude an academic career, but the proportion of JDs, MDs, MBAs, and other professional degree earners that turn up in full-time academic work is extremely small.[1] Also, it must be recognized that most persons earning doctorates in some fields—such as chemistry and clinical psychology—do not seek academic careers.[2] But with the caveat in mind that either an expression of interest in becoming a faculty member or knowing one's ultimate degree aspirations—especially as early as the high school years or at the beginning stages of college—probably does not correlate very strongly with subsequent career decisions, we turn first to expressions of interest among entering college freshmen.

Career Leanings of Beginning College Students

One of the most remarkable and useful databases in higher education is the survey of entering college freshmen conducted for many years by the Cooperative Institutional Research Program (CIRP) at UCLA.[3] This Annual Freshmen Survey, begun at the American Council on Education in 1966, reaches large numbers of new freshmen each fall, most often during orientation activities or very soon after classes have begun. Accordingly, it only minimally reflects any influences that the college experience itself has imparted. Instead, the survey responses of these neophyte collegians are indicators of what "packages" of attributes—demographic, experiential, and attitudinal—the colleges are importing from the secondary schools. And so, tracking responses to the same questionnaire items spread over the decades can be quite revealing. The survey addresses many topics, but the ones relevant to our purposes are those dealing with degree aspirations and career plans.

Table 9.1 indicates that the proportion of entering freshmen who indicate that they want to become a "college teacher" has always been very small. When the responses were plotted in the mid-1980s, Bowen and Schuster noted a steady downturn in interest, dipping to historic lows of 0.3% or 0.2% (only several students per thousand respondents) for the stretch of years 1978–84 (1986, p. 203). Since then, however, there has been a modest uptick in interest both among men (from 0.3% in 1984 to 0.6% in 1996, and still at 0.6% in 2002 and 2003) and among women (0.2% in 1984, to 0.5% in 1996, to 0.4% in 2002 and 2003).

A related development, shown in table 9.2, is the preference among entering freshmen for becoming a "scientist researcher."[4] Interest in such careers appears to have bottomed out in the mid 1980s for both men and women freshmen but has rebounded somewhat for the women (from a range of 1.1 to 1.3% in 1980–90, rising to 1.7 to 1.8% in 1992–96, and to 1.7% in 2003). However, no comparable resurgence is evident among the men (1.8% in 1982, 1994, 1996, and 2003).

A related indicator that translates, however loosely, into prospective interest in an academic career is the response of entering freshmen to the question, "What is the highest academic degree you intend to obtain?" The proportion of those who over the years identify the PhD or the EdD as their goal greatly exceeds the subsequent realities. (If the 10% or so of freshmen who indicate doc-

TABLE 9.1
*College Freshmen Indicating a Probable Career
as a College Teacher, Selected Years, 1966–2004*
(percent)

	Men	Women	All
1966	2.1	1.5	1.8
1968	1.3	0.9	1.1
1970	1.2	0.9	1.0
1972	0.7	0.6	0.6
1974	0.7	0.8	0.7
1976	0.4	0.3	0.4
1978	0.3	0.3	0.3
1980	0.2	0.2	0.2
1982	0.2	0.2	0.2
1984	0.3	0.2	0.3
1986	0.4	0.3	0.3
1988	0.4	0.3	0.4
1990	0.4	0.3	0.4
1992	0.5	0.4	0.5
1994	0.5	0.5	0.5
1996	0.6	0.5	0.5
1998	0.5	0.4	0.5
2000	0.6	0.5	0.5
2001	0.5	0.5	0.5
2002	0.6	0.4	0.5
2003	0.6	0.4	0.5
2004	0.6	0.5	0.5

Sources: Annual reports since 1966. Most recent report: Sax et al., 2004.

toral aspirations actually went on to earn doctorates, given some 2 million freshmen who begin each year . . . well, you do the math.) Nevertheless, the responses to that same question, spanning more than three decades, are instructive. From 1970 to 1986, the percentage of entering freshmen who maintain that their educational goal is a doctorate held steady within a narrow range: 7.9% to 9.7% (table 9.3). But a gradual rise began after 1986 and has continued, almost doubling to 15.1% in 1996, peaking at 18.7% in 2000, and settling between 17.3% and 17.5% in 2001 through 2004. These aspiring doctorate-earners are about evenly divided—as has been the case throughout the 1990s—between men (17.2% in 2001–3) and women (17.7% in 2003). (Prior to the 1980s, the proportion of male freshmen aspiring to doctorates substantially exceeded the proportion of females.)

This upswing surely reflects the more recent collegians' responses to the omnipresent message that the world of work is becoming increasingly knowledge-based, rather than a more narrowly focused preference specifically for an academic career. Yet it is interesting to note that the *proportional* increase since the

TABLE 9.2
College Freshmen Indicating a Probable Career
as a Scientific Researcher, Selected Years,
1966–2004
(percent)

	Men	Women	All
1966	4.9	1.9	3.5
1968	3.8	1.7	2.9
1970	3.5	1.6	2.6
1972	3.1	1.5	2.3
1974	2.7	1.4	2.1
1976	3.0	1.7	2.4
1978	2.7	1.7	2.2
1980	2.2	1.3	1.7
1982	1.8	1.2	1.5
1984	1.9	1.2	1.5
1986	1.8	1.1	1.4
1988	2.0	1.3	1.6
1990	1.7	1.2	1.4
1992	2.0	1.5	1.7
1994	1.8	1.6	1.7
1996	1.8	1.8	1.8
1998	1.5	1.5	1.5
2000	1.8	1.8	1.8
2001	1.8	1.9	1.8
2002	1.9	1.6	1.8
2003	1.8	1.7	1.7
2004	2.0	1.8	1.9

Sources: Annual reports since 1966. Most recent report: Sax et
al., 2004.
   Note: From 1966 to 1976, the term *research scientist* was
used.

mid-1980s among freshmen leaning toward an academic career is roughly parallel to the increase among those who aspire to earning a doctorate. In all, the
new collegians' interest both in college teaching as a career and in earning the
credential that effectively functions as a prerequisite for a regular faculty appointment at a four-year institution has been building over the past decade or
so, thereby seeming to reverse a trend of dwindling interest that characterized
the 1970s and most of the 1980s.

A Further Note on the Methodology

An important caveat needs to be asserted at this juncture. The challenge to
ascertain whether "the best and the brightest" are being attracted to academe in
adequate numbers necessarily entails tracking the career choices over time of
cohorts of high achievers. This exercise, in turn, depends on identifying groups
whose patterns of career choices would indicate how well the academy is do-

TABLE 9.3
*College Freshmen Planning to Obtain a PhD
or EdD, Selected Years, 1966–2004*
(percent)

	Men	Women	All
1966	13.7	5.2	9.8
1968	14.0	6.1	10.6
1970	12.3	6.5	9.7
1972	10.6	6.8	8.9
1974	10.0	6.9	8.5
1976	9.8	7.6	8.7
1978	9.8	8.1	8.9
1980	8.5	7.3	7.9
1982	8.8	7.6	8.2
1984	9.6	8.7	9.2
1986	10.3	9.2	9.7
1988	12.1	11.4	11.7
1990	12.3	12.5	12.4
1992	10.5	10.4	10.5
1994	13.9	13.9	13.9
1996	15.1	15.0	15.1
1998	13.1	13.8	13.5
2000	18.4	19.0	18.7
2001	17.2	17.4	17.3
2002	17.2	17.5	17.4
2003	17.2	17.7	17.5
2004	17.3	17.5	17.4

Sources: Annual reports since 1966. Most recent report: Sax et
al., 2004.

ing vis-à-vis the "competition," that is, other occupations, particularly professions, that would be attractive and accessible to highly able young adults. The
populations that we have identified for these purposes—including, for example, Rhodes Scholars, Watson Fellows, and Phi Beta Kappa members—are
among the nation's highest-achieving undergraduates. They are exceptionally
able as measured in large part by their extraordinary academic records. To be
sure, each program we have tracked employs its own selection criteria with its
distinctive emphases, but very high academic performance is a shared characteristic. And so, how these academically talented persons distribute themselves
between academic careers and careers in, say, law, medicine, and business is
one important indicator of whether, over time, the academy is holding its own
in "the recruitment competitions." It is not exactly the case that academic "re-
cruiters" from the Wharton School and Harvard Divinity School and Stanford
Medical School and the Berkeley Anthropology Department are all prowling
Williamstown and Williamsburg in dogged pursuit of super-talented, "blue-
chip" academic undergraduates, but you get the idea: at some level, in some

sense, the professions *are* vying with one another. (But if you're wanting to keep score at home, don't try!)

Here is where our caveat enters in—in two ways. The first is quantitative. Taken together, these extraordinary undergraduate achievers constitute a tiny fraction among all very high achievers, the vast majority of whom do not rise to the widespread visibility associated with these various highly competitive programs that recognize superior achievement. Indeed, many talented students do not attend the prestigious colleges and universities that are home to so many of "the chosen."

Moreover, these elite undergraduates make up an insignificant proportion of the number of new academics who must be recruited each year to fill campus faculty vacancies, as noted earlier. So even if a disproportionately large percentage of those undergraduates who attain a measure of national recognition via selection by one of these nationally prominent programs do in fact commit themselves to academic careers, the *quantitative* challenge, as noted earlier, is not thereby addressed.

More nuanced still is the issue of "multiple intelligences" and aptitudes. Even if higher education were to attract its "fair share" of high academic achievers, we should have no illusion that that would suffice. The academy's instructional staff must encompass persons with many aptitudes and diverse cultural experiences to effectively advance scholarship and to connect engagingly with the millions of students, a spectacularly rich mosaic of talent.

Accordingly, the pathways to the professoriate that lead through the enclaves of the undergraduate superstars do not begin to solve the challenges of securing either adequate numbers *or* multifaceted diversity. Nevertheless—and this is the premise underlying this chapter—just how those highest mobility undergraduate elites are eventually apportioned among various career options *is* a meaningful barometer by which to gauge "how well are we doing."

Career Preferences among Selected College Seniors

The changes over time in career preferences of highly talented college seniors provide a useful vantage point from which to assess the magnetism of academic careers. Of course, highly talented undergraduates are dispersed throughout the complex world of higher education. Among more than 15 million undergraduates enrolled in nearly four thousand accredited colleges and universities, exceptionally able students can be found everywhere. But it may be more relevant, for present purposes, to probe the career preferences of graduating seniors at colleges and universities that are some of the most selective in admitting students from secondary schools. Although this indicator—like any other indicator—is an imperfect measure, it does speak to career destinations of individuals whose talents and personal qualities enabled them to attain access to particularly selective colleges and universities, and whose academic credentials presumably often translate into a broader range of career options.

Consortium on Financing Higher Education

Founded in 1974, the Consortium on Financing Higher Education (COFHE) is an association whose members are thirty-one independent colleges and universities that are highly selective in their admissions policies.[5] COFHE was initially concerned primarily with easing financial barriers to attending their relatively costly institutions. The association has for many years conducted studies that address, among other topics, the experience of their undergraduate students; and to better understand that experience, it periodically has sponsored surveys of graduating seniors and of alumni.

During the past two decades COFHE has coordinated six surveys of seniors who were about to graduate from their institutions. Conducted at somewhat irregular intervals (1982, 1989, 1994, 1996, 1998, and 2002), these questionnaires ordinarily have included items that ask for respondents' highest degree plans and their "anticipated long-term career."[6] The relevance of patterns that emerge over this period is reasonably clear: one can assume that the substantial majority of these graduating seniors had exhibited notable talent, academic or otherwise, in order to have attained admission to these very selective institutions some four years earlier. Their intended careers are suggestive, at least roughly speaking, of the pull among the professions and other career options. That is, because the COFHE institutions are so selective, their very talented undergraduates can be assumed to have considerable latitude in choosing among career paths. Accordingly, the choices this aristocracy of talent makes, over time, are one indicator of the ebb and flow of academic life as an attractive career option.

Here we are not hampered by the serious limitation that applies in attempting to discern shifts in career interests among a relative handful of award recipients (say, Rhodes or Watson selectees), because the number of seniors responding to each of these six most recent surveys has numbered between about nine thousand and nineteen thousand (varying with the number of COFHE institutions that participated in a given survey). Thus, relatively speaking, the numbers are robust.

Perhaps the most striking aspect of responses that emerges is the consistency in the pattern of anticipated long-term careers. Because these surveys are con-

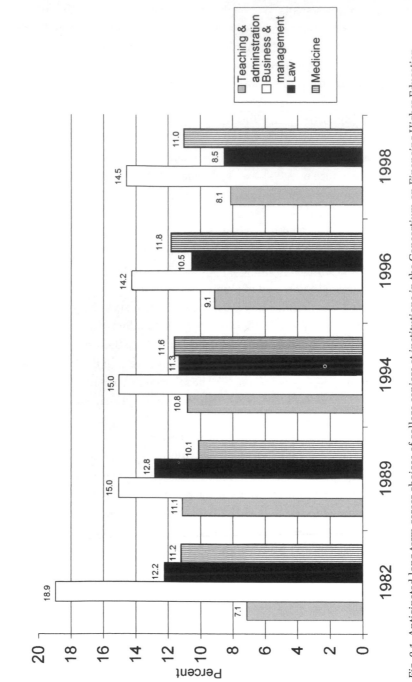

Fig. 9.1. Anticipated long-term career choices of college seniors at institutions in the Consortium on Financing Higher Education.

ducted near the very end of students' undergraduate experience, responses to applications to graduate and professional schools are likely to have been received and to have influenced these seniors' immediate postbaccalaureate career plans. The first thing to note here is that respondents consistently plan for careers in business, law, medicine, and college teaching or administration more than in any other field. Indeed, those four intended careers together account regularly for between 42% and 49% of all the responses.

The next observation is that while there has been some, but not much, ebb and flow among the combined four's attractiveness relative to all the others, there has not been much movement *among* the four (see fig. 9.1). That is, the rank order in attractiveness among them has been quite stable. Business has consistently led the way as a career objective, though its popularity may have peaked in the early 1980s, declining since then from about 19% to a steady 14% to 15%. The proportions of students anticipating careers in law and medicine have remained within quite narrow ranges. For aspirants to legal careers the percentage has fluctuated between 8.5% and 12.8%, with signs of possibly trending downward in popularity (about 12% over the first three senior surveys, but slipping to 10.5 and 8.5% for the two most recent ones). The interest in medical careers has been remarkably steady, staying within a 10.1% to 11.8% band throughout. With those variances as a backdrop, the interest in pursuing academic careers can be seen, like interest in these three "competing" careers, as not having shifted very much. However, at the risk of overinterpreting the results, one could say that the appeal of an academic career increased from a low of about 7% (during the early 1980s when various observers posited a diminishing interest in the academy) to more than 11% by 1989, then drifted modestly downward to about 8% by 1998. (The most recent measure of these graduating seniors, it should be noted, was for the class of 1998; perceptions of the attractiveness of an academic career since then may have shifted noticeably— up or down—for this population.)

To summarize, if the career inclinations of COFHE seniors are one useful gauge of how the academy's magnetism has fared during the past two decades, it can be argued that there has been neither significant recovery from the difficulties of the early 1980s nor further erosion. The academy appears to be holding its own, at least insofar as talented seniors at extraordinarily selective schools describe their plans.

The analysis of career choices of recipients of prestigious national awards is limited to a handful of programs. Several criteria have shaped our choices, including these: (1) The program should be sufficiently prestigious and visible to attract very high quality candidates. The Rhodes and Marshall Scholarships are obvious choices. (2) The program needs to have existed for enough years to allow tracking of results over a meaningful span of time. (3) The program's recipients should *not* be predestined for academic careers. Thus, for example, Mellon Fellowships are awarded to exceptionally able undergraduates or recent graduates, but they are restricted to persons who indicate that they plan to earn a doctorate in the humanities and then intend to teach in a postsecondary institution. The caliber of persons over time who apply for, and win, Mellons is directly relevant to the question of who is embarking on academic careers, but since all are committed to such careers, an analysis would not reveal differences over time in career choices. (4) The program should not be either so small in number of awardees or so focused on a particular field of study (e.g., Morris K. Udall Scholarships primarily are for environmental studies) or career (e.g., Harry S. Truman Scholarships are restricted to those with a commitment to careers in government or public service) as to limit its relevance for present purposes. (5) Finally, the office that administers the program must be willing to cooperate with the researchers (one prestigious program opted not to participate).

Phi Beta Kappa Members

Founded in 1776 at the College of William and Mary in Williamsburg, Virginia, Phi Beta Kappa is the oldest undergraduate honors organization in the United States. Roughly fifteen thousand students, almost all of them undergraduate seniors, have been inducted annually in recent years. With more than a half million living members, the Phi Beta Kappa Society represents a large pool of talent with potential to enter various demanding fields. By qualifying for Phi Beta Kappa membership at one of the 270 member institutions, they represent, in some respects, the top academic achievers at highly respected colleges and universities in the United States. Consequently, a survey of the occupations that Phi Beta Kappa members have chosen to pursue over time, along with data on the proportion of them who have opted for a faculty career, provides important insights for understanding the relative attractiveness of the academic profession. Indeed, the changing patterns of pursuit of academic careers by Phi Beta Kappa members over time is an important indicator of the degree to which high-performing undergraduates seek faculty positions. Furthermore, knowledge of the reasons why academic careers were *not* pursued, together with how those Phi Beta Kappa members currently employed in academe feel about their chosen profession, will also be helpful in illuminating the changing status of the American professoriate.

This survey, conducted in 2000, replicates a 1984 survey that queried Phi

Beta Kappa members who had been selected from 1945 to 1983 about their career choices. Their career choices, over time, were analyzed; the major finding
from the 1984 survey was that in the 1970s and early 1980s there was a significant dip in the proportion of Phi Beta Kappa members who chose an academic
career (Bowen and Schuster, 1985; 1986, pp. 224–28). Additionally, that study
found that about five times as many Phi Beta Kappa graduates had chosen careers in business, law, and medicine, taken together, as the number who had
opted for academic careers. A clear pattern of declining interest in the academy
was evident within this high-achieving, career-mobile population (Bowen and
Schuster, 1986, table 11-18, p. 227; figure 11-1, p. 228).

To conduct the 2000 survey of Phi Beta Kappa scholars, a random sample of
2,400 was requested from the Phi Beta Kappa national office, from among scholars selected from 1980 to 1997. In 1984 a 1% random sample was used. The 2000
survey in effect used a 1.14% random sample. Of 2,160 possible returned surveys, the number of returned usable surveys was 875, representing a 40.5% rate
of return.[7]

The results of this survey reveal that following a clear decline in interest
among Phi Beta Kappa members in pursuing careers in higher education during
the late 1970s and early 1980s, there appears to have been something of a turn-
around (table 9.4). However, the upswing in interest has not reached the level
demonstrated in the 1950s or 1960s. In speculating on the various reasons for
the results, one should recognize that the primary reasons for not pursuing academic careers were identified as a lack of financial return and the perceived un-
availability of appropriate positions. Consequently, it is likely that perceived (if
not actual) changes in the potential financial reward and the future labor market in higher education played significant roles in limiting this moderate recovery.

In assigning weight to the data collected in these two surveys, issues of data
maturity and the characteristics of the population responding to the survey
should be considered. The timing of the two surveys in relationship to when
Phi Beta Kappa members received their bachelor degrees surely played a role in
the apparent decline of interest in academic careers among those members most
recently receiving degrees. This could be a result of career indecision directly
following a four-year degree. But much more likely, the drop-off reflects the fact
that the lengthy process of pursuing a doctoral degree—and, accordingly, becoming eligible for many faculty positions—often would not have been completed. This pattern was dealt with for graduates in the 1980–84 period by using the 2000 survey results to identify respondents' career choices, rather than
using the much lower proportion from the 1984 survey figures of respondents

TABLE 9.4

Phi Beta Kappa Members, *Selected Career Choices, 1945–1997*
(percent)

	Year Bachelor's Degree Received										
	1945–49	1950–54	1955–59	1960–64	1965–69	1970–74	1975–79	1980–84	1985–89	1990–94	1995–97
Educator											
College	20.6	22.6	19.4	24.2	21.7	8.6	7.2	16.8	18.6	13.0	12.9
Elementary	1.3	4.3	2.0	1.7	1.2	3.9	2.9	2.1	2.6	3.6	5.8
Secondary	5.2	8.6	6.1	8.3	4.2	3.5	1.0	3.4	2.2	4.5	3.9
School principal or supervisor	1.3	1.1	1.0	0.8	0.0	0.4	0.7	0.0	0.0	0.0	0.0
Subtotal K–12[a]	7.8	14.0	9.1	10.8	6.4	7.4	4.3	5.5	4.8	8.1	9.7
Subtotal all educators[b]	28.4	36.6	28.5	35.0	28.1	16.0	11.5	22.3	23.4	21.1	22.6
Other Selected Careers											
Accountant/actuary	1.3	1.1	0.0	3.3	2.4	2.4	1.0	3.4	2.6	0.4	0.6
Business[c]	7.8	14.0	9.1	9.2	9.0	12.3	9.5	8.8	7.8	7.7	5.2
Clergy[d]	3.9	2.2	3.1	2.5	0.0	2.4	0.7	0.8	0.9	2.0	0.0
Computer programmer or analyst	0.0	1.1	3.1	3.3	3.0	3.5	4.2	3.8	3.5	5.3	3.9
Engineer	2.6	2.2	2.0	0.8	0.6	0.8	2.0	3.4	3.0	1.2	1.3
Homemaker	14.3	11.8	5.1	6.7	8.4	4.7	4.2	5.5	4.3	3.2	0.6
Journalist or writer	5.2	1.1	3.1	1.7	1.2	2.7	3.6	3.4	2.2	4.5	1.9
Lawyer or judge	5.2	6.5	5.1	5.8	9.6	15.3	20.2	13.0	10.4	9.3	12.9
Physician or dentist	3.9	10.0	15.3	10.0	7.8	16.1	18.9	13.9	15.6	13.8	14.2
Social or welfare worker	1.3	1.1	2.0	0.8	3.6	0.8	1.6	0.8	0.9	1.2	1.3
Other occupation	26.1	12.3	23.6	22.4	27.1	22.6	22.3	19.8	25.4	30.3	35.5
Total all careers	100	100	100	100	100	100	100	100	100	100	100

Sources: 1945–83 data based on Bowen and Schuster, 1986, chap. 11, table 11-18; 1984–97 data from Survey of Phi Beta Kappa Recipients, 2000, by the authors.

[a] Includes only the three K–12 entries (elementary, secondary, and school principal/supervisor).

[b] Includes all four "educators" entries.

[c] Includes business clerical, business executive, business proprietor, and business sales.

[d] Includes minister/priest and clergy miscellaneous.

who indicated current employment in an academic career so soon after receiving a baccalaureate degree. Furthermore, data on those members graduating after 1997 was not used. Nevertheless, one should be careful in evaluating the data from the years most closely preceding the survey dates (1984 and 2000). It should also be noted that those who work in higher education might well be more likely to respond to a survey about careers in academe, and thus tilt the survey results.

Finally, college educators, at 15.7%, made up the largest single group of specific career members in this more recent study, for the period 1980–97. (Physicians or dentists were second at 14.1%.) Clearly, those who perform best in higher education (judged by earning membership in the Phi Beta Kappa Society) are still pursuing careers in academe. However, this study shows that they are pursuing careers as college educators at roughly a 10% lower rate than in the 1950s and 1960s. Importantly, although the trend in choosing academic careers reveals a rebound in interest from the decline in the 1970s, it does not demonstrate a return to former interest levels.

Luce Scholars

Luce Scholars were first selected in 1974, and thus the program's existence roughly coincides with the era that this study examines. Fifteen persons under age 30 are selected each year, from among nominations submitted by sixty-five designated colleges and universities, to work in one-year professional internships in an East or Southeast Asian country. As the Luce Scholars Program Web site explains, the program's purpose is focused: "to increase awareness of Asia among future leaders in American society." In accordance with the program's design, individuals having "significant experience in Asia or Asian studies" are ineligible to participate. Through 2004, close to five hundred persons have been designated Luce Scholars. Thus, although an interest, but not expertise, in Asia is a common thread, the rigorous selection process emphasizes qualities that could lead in various career directions.

Aggregating the Scholars' career decisions, based on entries in the Luce Scholars directory, by half-decade intervals provides some indication suggestive of the popularity of various careers among this talented group of young people. The appeal of an eventual academic career appears to be diminishing. As seen in table 9.5, careers in higher education were a hallmark of the earliest Luce Scholars (27% among selectees who received their baccalaureates in 1969–74), although that high proportion might have been a fluke or a reflection of selection criteria of an earlier day. The proportion of Luce Scholars subsequently opt-

TABLE 9.5
Luce Scholars, Selected Career Choices, 1969–1999
(percent)

Career[b]	Year Bachelor's Degree Received[a]							
	1969–74	1975–79	1980–84	1985–89	1990–94	1995–99	Total %	Total No. of Cases
Education (college)[c]	26.9	20.5	12.2	15.9	6.3[d]	0.0[d]	14.8	53
Business[e]	15.4	21.9	27.0	33.3	25.0	19.2	24.6	88
Lawyer or judge	19.2	12.3	20.3	7.2	10.9	7.7	13.4	48
Physican or dentist	7.7	15.1	10.8	8.7	10.9	3.8[d]	10.3	37
Total[f]	69.2	69.8	70.3	65.1	53.1	30.7	63.1	226[g]

[a]If no bachelor's degree date was listed, the year of the Luce Scholarship Award was used.

[b]If more than one career choice was listed, the career classification was made according to the first one listed.

[c]Includes teachers and administrators.

[d]The time required to complete academic degrees and related training tends to reduce the numbers of Scholars engaged in these careers.

[e]Includes clerical, executives, managers, proprietors, salespeople, buyers, business partners, financial services, principals, and associates.

[f]Total is for these 4 occupations ($N = 226$ of total N of 418).

[g]The total 226 Luce Scholars in these four occupations represent 63.1% (226/358) of all Luce Scholars for whom an occupation could be determined (1969–99) and 54.1% (226/418) of all Luce Scholars, including those who were listed as graduate students ($N = 29$) and those whose occupation was unknown ($N = 31$).

ing for academic careers has consistently been lower. The most recent half-decade for which relevant data exist (1990–94) shows academic careers sharply down (to 6.3%), trailing all of the principal "competitor" career choices.

Watson Fellows

Each year some sixty-five to seventy-five college seniors are selected to be Watson Fellows. Established in 1968, The Thomas J. Watson Fellowship was created for college graduates to study abroad independently for twelve months following their graduation. The students, drawn from fifty eligible institutions (mostly smaller, private colleges), are chosen primarily on the basis of character, integrity, vision, excellence within a field, and potential for success, as well as academic record. Their choice of careers to be pursued following their fellowship shows general consistency over time. As can be seen in table 9.6, about one-seventh to one-fifth of the fellows appear to opt for academic careers during each half-decade. By comparison, roughly 10% choose legal careers, and 5% pursue medical careers. The popularity of business careers may have faded during this three-decade period; consistent at about 20% from 1969 to 1979, the percentage looks to be shrinking.

TABLE 9.6
Watson Fellows, Selected Career Choices, 1969–1999
(percent)

Career[b]	Year Designated as Watson Fellows[a]							
	1969–74	1975–79	1980–84	1985–89	1990–94	1995–99[c]	Total %	No. of Cases
Education (college)[d]	19.9	21.2	19.9	13.4	10.7	5.6	16.8	238
Business[e]	20.6	18.4	15.5	13.4	14.2	4.5	16.0	226
Lawyer or judge	9.8	9.9	5.9	9.7	5.1	2.2[c]	7.6	112
Physican or dentist	9.8	9.9	5.9	9.7	5.1	2.2	7.6	68
Total	60.1	59.4	47.2	46.2	35.1	12.3	48.0	644[f]

[a]Does not include the 60 Watson Fellows selected in 2000, all of whom were identified as "Current Fellows."

[b]If more than one career choice was listed, the career classification was made according to the first one listed.

[c]The time required to complete academic degrees and related training tends to reduce the numbers of Scholars who are engaged in these careers.

[d]Includes faculty, administrators, and researchers.

[e]Includes clerical, executives, managers, proprietors, salespeople, buyers, business partners, financial services, principals, and associates.

[f]The total 226 Watson Scholars in these four occupations represents 45.6% (644/1,413) of all Watson Scholars for whom an occupation could be determined (1969–1999) and 31.1% (644/2,073) of all Watson Scholars, including those who were listed as graduate students ($N = 216$) or whose occupation was unknown ($N = 444$).

Leading Graduate Departments

In the study two decades ago on how well the academy was doing at attracting exceptional talent, a key element of the authors' analysis was an original survey of chairs of "leading graduate departments." That survey queried the department chairs for their assessment of the quality of their advanced graduate students (many of whom aspired to a faculty career) and their junior faculty (mainly tenure-track assistant professors) (see Bowen and Schuster, 1986, pp. 212–16, 219–24, 292–93). The method was to identify the highest-ranking 15% of departments in each of thirty-two academic fields, drawn from the National Research Council's *Assessment of Quality-Related Characteristics of Research-Doctorate Programs in the U.S.* (1982). Questionnaires were addressed individually to each of the 404 chairs of the departments that we had identified. On average, this top 15% consisted of 12–13 departments per field, ranging from the low 20s for larger fields (e.g., 22 departments each in chemistry and psychology) to a mere handful in smaller fields (5 each in classics and linguistics). There was quite a high response rate; usable responses were received from 316 departments (316/404 = 78.2%).

On the basis of those survey results (including respondents' open-ended comments), Bowen and Schuster concluded regarding advanced graduate students in those departments: "Quality is being maintained at the very top. Moreover, even though higher education will make relatively few new hires in the proximate future . . . , these top departments exude confidence that they can avoid any erosion in quality. They seem to be saying that they will be able to remain highly selective, while lesser departments will have to scramble to recruit worthwhile graduate students" (1986, p. 216). Survey items also asked these chairs about the quality of recently hired junior faculty members. The authors observed that "many respondents in these academic centers of excellence indicated that they felt themselves to occupy 'privileged' positions within American higher education, given their departments' elite ranking within their respective disciplines" (p. 223). At the top, among these very highly regarded graduate programs, it seems clear, there was no cause for alarm. It seemed that "in this very strong buyer's market, many institutions are convinced that they have never done better in recruiting new faculty. Their enthusiasm is understandable" (pp. 223–24).

Fifteen years later, in 1999, the current authors essentially replicated the earlier survey. This time, the top 15% of departments were identified based on the 1995 report titled *Research-Doctorate Programs in the United States: Continuity and Change* (Goldberger, Maher, and Flattau). The National Research Council had gathered data on forty fields this time (eight more than for their earlier study). With more academic fields in the mix, the top 15% of programs resulted in a larger number of department chairs for the survey: 547 compared to 404. This time there were 369 usable responses, for a return rate of 67.5%, down somewhat from the earlier 78.2% but still quite a respectable rate, given who the respondents were.

On the whole, the results of our 1999 inquiry are remarkably similar to the 1984 findings, in regard to both advanced graduate students and junior faculty members as reported by the chairs of these exceptionally strong departments. It is important to note that the wording on the items in the 1999 questionnaire was identical to that used in 1984 (except, of course, for the years referenced in the items themselves).

Respondents judged the quality of advanced students in 1999 (see table 9.7), in comparison with students in the earlier period of 1983–87, to be 4.5 on a 7-point scale (4 is "almost the same," 7 is "much better"). Note that the item measures perceptions of *change* in quality, and that the comparison is to a time, roughly a decade and a half earlier, when these leading departments were in the main quite satisfied with the quality of doctoral students they were able to attract. (In 1984 the mean score was 4.7, but this indicator was an assessment in

TABLE 9.7

Change in Quality of Advanced Graduate Students, 1999, Compared with 1983–1987, as Reported by Leading Graduate Departments

(percent)

	Much Better 7	6	5	Almost the Same 4	3	2	Much Worse 1	No Response[a]	N^b	Mean 1999	Compare Mean 1983–87
Social/behavioral sciences	4	21	21	32	18	3	0	1	72	4.5	4.4
Humanities	5	33	30	16	16	0	0	0	57	5.0	4.6
Mathematics/ physical sciences	1	7	22	41	25	2	0	1	83	4.1	4.6
Biological sciences	2	22	33	26	17	0	0	0	94	4.7	4.7
Engineering	0	11	27	38	17	5	0	3	64	4.2	5.0
Unidentified field	0	31	15	38	8	8	0	0	13	4.5	—
All	2	21	25	32	17	3	0	1	383	4.5	4.7

Source: Survey of Chairpersons of Leading Graduate Departments, 1999, by authors (Q1).

Note: Rows may not add to 100% because of rounding.

[a]Includes "no opinion" or no usable response.

[b]Number of responding programs (including "no opinion" or no usable response).

comparison to the cohort of advanced graduate students in the 1968–72 era.) Put another way, these department chairs found modest improvements in quality in 1984 compared to 1968–72 and also in 1999 compared to 1983–87. In 1999 the highest mean (5.0) was for the fields comprising the humanities, while the lowest (4.1) was for mathematics and the physical sciences.

A breakout for all forty research-doctorate fields is shown in table 9.8. The fields in which the chairs seemed most enthusiastic, compared to the students they recalled from the 1983–87 era, were classics (6.0), art history (5.7), and anthropology (5.5). Most of the humanities fared very well, although, anomalously, linguistics was near the bottom (3.5) and German language and literature was dead last (3.3).

In terms of the *number* of advanced graduate students (1999 compared to 1983–87), most hovered around the middle to somewhat worse, that is, lower numbers of advanced graduate students. The overall mean of 3.9 was divided, in a sense, between "winners" (biological sciences [4.6] and engineering [4.0]) and "losers" (humanities was lowest at 3.2) (see table 9.9). Thus it seems apparent that the high marks that the humanists gave to the *quality* of their graduate students was to some degree a function of a self-imposed diet that limited the *quantity* of the graduate students they would accommodate.

An indicator of the outlook for attracting well-qualified advanced students (from whose ranks the faculty of the future would presumably be drawn) is seen

TABLE 9.8

Change in Quality of Advanced Graduate Students Enrolled, by Research-Doctorate Field, 1999, Compared with 1983–1987, as Reported by Leading Graduate Departments

(percent)

Rank	Research-Doctorate Field	General Area	N^a	Mean Scores^b		Difference
				1999	1983–87	
1	Classics	Humanities	3	6.0	5.2	0.8
2	Art history	Humanities	3	5.7	4.6	1.1
3	Anthropology	Social/behavioral science	4	5.5	5.1	0.4
4	Music	Humanities	8	5.4	3.7	1.7
5	English language & literature	Humanities	15	5.3	4.9	0.4
T6	Sociology	Social/behavioral science	9	5.2	4.4	0.8
	Spanish & Portugese language	Humanities	5	5.2	3.8	1.4
T8	History	Social/behavioral science	12	5.1	3.9	1.2
	French language & literature	Humanities	4	5.0	4.8	0.2
	Religion	Humanities	3	5.0	—^{c}	
11	Ecology, evolution & behavior	Biological science	14	4.9	4.4, 5.2^d	
T12	Pharmacology	Biological science	14	4.8	—^{c}	
12	Political science	Social/behavioral science	12	4.8	3.9	0.9
T14	Neurosciences	Biological science	8	4.7	—^{c}	
	Oceanography	Mathematics/physical science	4	4.7	—^{c}	
Mean for 32 Research-Doctorate Fields (1983–84) = 4.62						
T16	Molecular & general genetics	Biological science	11	4.6	4.4^e	0.2
	Philosophy	Humanities	7	4.6	4.9	−0.3
	Civil engineering	Engineering	12	4.6	5.3	−0.7
Mean for 40 Research-Doctorate Fields (1999) = 4.52						
T19	Physiology	Biological science	14	4.5	4.7	−0.2
	Biochemistry & molecular biology	Biological science	16	4.5	4.9, 5.1^f	

	Field	Broad field	N			
	Cell & developmental biology	Biological science	17	4.5	4.4[e]	0.1
	Computer sciences	Mathematics/physical science	11	4.5	5.2	−0.7
T23	Industrial engineering	Engineering	6	4.4	—[c]	
	Comparative literature	Humanities	4	4.4	—[c]	
T25	Statistics & biostatistics	Mathematics/physical science	9	4.3	4.3	0
	Chemical engineering	Engineering	12	4.3	5.6	−1.3
T27	Electrical engineering	Engineering	12	4.2	4.8	−0.6
	Mathematics	Mathematics/physical science	12	4.2	4.2	0
	Physics	Mathematics/physical science	15	4.2	4.6	−0.4
	Economics	Social/behavioral science	12	4.2	4.6	−0.4
	Mechanical engineering	Engineering	12	4.2	4.4	−0.2
T32	Aerospace engineering	Engineering	4	4.0	—[c]	
	Geosciences	Mathematics/physical science	10	4.0	4.9	−0.9
	Psychology	Social/behavioral science	19	4.0	4.2	−0.2
T35	Chemistry	Mathematics/physical science	19	3.8	4.7	−0.9
	Materials science	Engineering	6	3.8	—[c]	
	Geography	Social/behavioral science	4	3.8	5.2	−1.4
T38	Linguistics	Humanities	2	3.5	3.0	0.5
	Astrophysics & astronomy	Mathematics/physical science	3	3.5	—[c]	
40	German language & literature	Humanities	3	3.3	4.2	−0.9

Source: Survey of Chairpersons of Leading Graduate Departments, 1999, by the authors (Q1).

Notes: No response was received from the 6 programs in biomedical engineering that were sent surveys; thus 40 (of total of 41 fields in the NRC study) are listed here.

Standard deviation for 40 fields (1999) is 0.61.

[a] N = Number of usable responses received from Leading Graduate Departments.

[b] On the seven-point scale, 7 is "Much Better," 4 is "About the Same," and 1 is "Much Worse."

[c] A field having no corresponding counterpart in 1999.

[d] Compare botany (4.4), zoology (5.2).

[e] Compare cellular/molecular biology (4.4).

[f] Compare biochemistry (4.9), microbiology (5.1).

TABLE 9.9

Change in Number of Advanced Graduate Students, 1999, Compared with 1983–1987, as Reported by Leading Graduate Departments

(percent)

	Much Better 7	6	5	Almost the Same 4	3	2	Much Worse 1	No Response[a]	N[b]	Mean 1999	Compare Mean 1983–87
Social/behavioral sciences	0	4	8	32	35	18	0	3	72	3.4	3.1
Humanities	0	2	16	25	26	26	5	0	57	3.2	2.9
Mathematics/ physical sciences	0	4	21	29	36	10	0	1	83	3.7	4.2
Biological sciences	4	21	26	30	16	2	1	0	94	4.6	4.2
Engineering	3	3	25	3	62	28	0	3	64	4.0	4.7
Unidentified field	0	8	38	3	12	30	0	0	13	4.3	—
All	1	7	22	31	26	11	1	1	383	3.9	3.8

Source: Survey of Chairpersons of Leading Graduate Departments, 1999, by authors (Q2).

  Note: Rows may not add to 100% because of rounding.

  [a]Includes "no opinion" or no usable response.

  [b]Number of responding programs (including no opinion/no usable response).

in table 9.10. Here the chairs, looking ahead from 1999, anticipated the quality of their doctoral students in 2002–5. The mean of 4.4 suggests that most of these chairs forecast modest gains in quality (41% foresaw improvement; 11% anticipated slight decline). The five academic areas were closely clustered, ranging only from 4.3 (social/behavioral sciences and engineering) to 4.7 (for biological science).

Turning now from advanced graduate students to junior faculty, the chairs were generally quite enthusiastic about the current (1999) cohort. The mean score of 4.8 translated into 53% reporting improvements in the quality of their junior faculty (compared to those in 1983–87) as against only 7% of chairs indicating a decline in quality. The best "report card," a mean of 5.1, came from the chairs in the biological sciences (table 9.11).

By individual fields, the highest mean scores—indicating greatest satisfaction comparing the current cohort of junior faculty to their predecessors in the 1983–87 era—were found in quite a mix of fields: classics and anthropology (though both had low *N*'s) were at the high end, followed by electrical engineering, neurosciences, and music (see table 9.12). At the other end of the spectrum, indicating less enthusiasm, were linguistics, aerospace engineering, astrophysics and astronomy, art history, and chemical engineering. (The first four of these were based on few responses.)

In terms of *numbers* of junior faculty, the average was exactly 4.0, that is, no change, in the aggregate, from 1983–87 to 1999. Some numerical gains were re-

TABLE 9.10

Predicted Change in Quality of Doctoral Students to Be Enrolled 2002–2005, Compared with 1999, as Reported by Leading Graduate Departments

(percent)

	Much Better 7	6	5	Almost the Same 4	3	2	Much Worse 1	No Response[a]	N^b	Mean 1999	Compare Mean 1983–87
Social/behavioral sciences	0	4	28	51	11	0	0	6	72	4.3	4.7
Humanities	2	5	28	54	7	0	0	4	57	4.4	4.3
Mathematics/ physical sciences	0	8	31	49	10	0	0	1	83	4.4	4.7
Biological sciences	1	14	38	45	1	0	0	1	94	4.7	4.6
Engineering	0	6	23	60	5	2	0	3	64	4.3	4.7
Unidentified field	8	15	31	15	31	0	0	0	13	4.5	—
All	2	9	30	46	11	0	0	2	383	4.4	4.6

Source: Survey of Chairpersons of Leading Graduate Departments, 1999, by authors (Q3).

Note: Rows may not add to 100% because of rounding.

[a]Includes "no opinion" or no usable response.

[b]Number of responding programs (including no opinion/no usable response).

TABLE 9.11

Change in Quality of Junior Faculty (on Tenure Track), 1999, Compared with 1983–1987, as Reported by Leading Graduate Departments

(percent)

	Much Better 7	6	5	Almost the Same 4	3	2	Much Worse 1	No Response[a]	N^b	Mean 1999	Compare Mean 1983–87
Social/behavioral sciences	6	13	44	24	11	0	0	3	72	4.8	4.8
Humanities	2	23	35	28	7	0	0	5	57	4.8	4.7
Mathematics/ physical sciences	1	18	33	42	4	0	0	2	83	4.7	5.0
Biological sciences	9	28	27	35	0	1	0	1	94	5.1	4.9
Engineering	0	25	28	36	5	2	0	5	64	4.7	5.1
Unidentified field	0	15	15	46	8	0	0	15	13	4.5	—
All	3	20	30	35	6	1	0	5	383	4.8	4.9

Source: Survey of Chairpersons of Leading Graduate Departments, 1999, by authors (Q4).

Note: Rows may not add to 100% because of rounding.

[a]Includes "no opinion" or no usable response.

[b]Number of responding programs (including no opinion/no usable response).

TABLE 9.12

Change in Quality of Junior Faculty (on Tenure Track), by Research-Doctorate Field, 1999, Compared with 1983–1987, as Reported by Leading Graduate Departments

(percent)

Rank	Research-Doctorate Field	General Area	N^a	Mean Scores[b]		Difference
				1999	1983–87	
1	Classics	Humanities	3	5.7	5.4	0.3
2	Anthropology	Social/behavioral science	4	5.5	5.1	0.4
3	Electrical engineering	Engineering	12	5.5	5.2	0.3
T4	Neurosciences	Biological science	8	5.4	—[c]	
	Music	Humanities	8	5.4	4.8	0.6
6	English language & literature	Humanities	15	5.3	5.3	0
T7	Pharmacology	Biological science	14	5.3	—[c]	
	Computer sciences	Mathematics/physical science	11	5.2	4.7	0.5
T9	Mechanical engineering	Engineering	12	5.1	5.1	0
	Molecular & general genetics	Biological science	11	5.1	4.6	0.5
T11	German language & literature	Humanities	3	5.0	5.2	-0.2
	Political science	Social/behavioral science	12	5.0	4.2	0.8
	Ecology, evolution & behavior	Biological science	14	5.0	5.0, 5.0[d]	
	Biochemistry & molecular biology	Biological science	16	5.0	4.4, 5.7[e]	
	History	Social/behavioral science	12	5.0	4.8	0.2
	Physiology	Biological science	14	5.0	4.7	0.3
17	Industrial engineering	Engineering	6	4.9	—[c]	

Mean for 32 Research-Doctorate Fields (1983–87) = 4.85

Rank	Research-Doctorate Field	General Area	N^a	1999	1983–87	Difference
T18	Mathematics	Mathematics/physical science	12	4.8	5.0	-0.2
	Cell & developmental biology	Biological science	17	4.8	4.6[f]	0.2
	Physics	Mathematics/physical science	15	4.8	4.8	0
	Sociology	Social/behavioral science	9	4.8	4.7	0.1
	Spanish & Portugese Language	Humanities	5	4.8	4.3	0.5

T23	Psychology	Social/behavioral science	19	4.8	4.7	0.1
	Geography	Social/behavioral science	4	4.8	6.0	-1.2

Mean for 40 Research-Doctorate Fields (1999) = 4.75

T25	Geosciences	Mathematics/physical science	10	4.7	—[c]	
	Chemistry	Mathematics/physical science	19	4.7	5.1	-0.4
28	Materials science	Engineering	6	4.7	—[c]	
	Civil engineering	Engineering	12	4.6	4.1	0.5
T29	Comparative literature	Humanities	4	4.5	—[c]	
	French language & literature	Humanities	4	4.5	4.2	0.3
	Philosophy	Humanities	7	4.3	3.3	1.0
	Religion	Social/behavioral science	3	4.3	—[c]	
	Oceanography	Mathematics/physical science	4	4.3	—[c]	
	Statistics & biostatistics	Mathematics/physical science	9	4.3	4.8	-0.5
	Economics	Social/behavioral science	12	4.3	4.2	0.1
36	Chemical engineering	Engineering	12	4.2	4.9	-0.7
	Art history	Humanities	3	4.0	4.8	-0.8
T37	Astrophysics & astronomy	Mathematics/physical science	4	4.0	—[c]	
39	Aerospace engineering	Engineering	3	3.7	—[c]	
40	Linguistics	Humanities	2	3.5	4.0	-0.5

Source: Survey of Chairpersons of Leading Graduate Departments, 1999, by the authors (Q4).
Notes: No response was received from the 6 programs in biomedical engineering that were sent surveys; thus 40 (of total of 41 fields in the NRC study) are listed here.
Standard deviation for 40 fields (1999) is 0.49.
[a]N = Number of usable responses received from Leading Graduate Departments.
[b]On the seven-point scale, 7 was "Much Better," 4 was "About the Same," and 1 was "Much Worse."
[c]A field having no corresponding counterpart in 1999.
[d]Compare botany (5.0), zoology (5.0).
[e]Compare biochemistry (4.4), microbiology (5.7).
[f]Compare cellular/molecular biology (4.6).

TABLE 9.13

Change in Number of Junior Faculty (on Tenure Track), 1999, Compared with 1983–1987, as Reported by Leading Graduate Departments

(percent)

	Much Better 7	6	5	Almost the Same 4	3	2	Much Worse 1	No Response[a]	N^b	Mean 1999	Compare Mean 1983–87
Social/behavioral sciences	3	17	22	38	14	6	0	19	72	4.4	3.2
Humanities	0	4	16	35	19	21	2	4	57	3.5	3.0
Mathematics/ physical sciences	1	8	14	40	20	11	1	4	83	3.9	3.6
Biological sciences	6	14	18	36	18	6	0	19	4	4.3	3.7
Engineering	0	6	14	44	25	6	0	5	64	3.9	4.3
Unidentified field	0	8	31	31	15	0	15	0	13	3.8	—
All	2	10	19	37	19	8	3	2	383	4.0	3.6

Source: Survey of Chairpersons of Leading Graduate Departments, 1999, by authors (Q5).

Note: Rows may not add to 100% because of rounding.

[a]Includes "no opinion" or no usable response.

[b]Number of responding programs (including no opinion/no usable response).

ported by 31%; some decline in numbers by 30%. By fields, the social and behavioral sciences (4.4) and biological sciences (4.3) did best. The humanities fared poorest in numbers of junior faculty (3.5), but this perhaps explains, at least in part, the humanities chairs' overall enthusiasm for the quality of their new hires (table 9.13). This parallels exactly the lower numbers among humanities advanced graduate students—and the corresponding enthusiasm about *quality.*

How optimistic were these nearly four hundred chairs of leading graduate departments in 1999 about the quality of the tenure-track junior faculty they anticipated being able to employ in 2002–5? In fact, optimism was rampant as seen in a mean score of 4.9 (table 9.14). All areas did well, with mathematics and physical sciences and the biological sciences leading the way (both at 5.1), while the laggard among the areas, engineering, nonetheless rated, on average, 4.6 on the 7-point scale. In more vivid terms, fully 60% of the chairs anticipated improvements in quality among their junior faculty (improving, that is, from an already strong base), while a practically invisible 2% foresaw decline.

Finally, we sought to discover how tenure was holding up at these "elite" academic departments. Our question asked, as it had in the 1984 survey, "What is the percentage of faculty in your department who are tenured?" This wording does not define what precisely is meant by "faculty," but the other faculty items on the questionnaire referred specifically to "tenure-track junior faculty," and presumably it is the full-time faculty, but possibly only the full-time tenure-

TABLE 9.14

Anticipated Change in Quality of Junior Faculty (on Tenure Track) to Be Employed 2002–2005, Compared with 1999, as Reported by Leading Graduate Departments

(percent)

	Much Better 7	6	5	Almost the Same 4	3	2	Much Worse 1	No Response[a]	N^b	Mean 1999	Compare Mean 1983–87
Social/behavioral sciences	3	18	25	43	4	1	0	6	72	4.7	4.1
Humanities	0	18	33	39	4	0	0	7	57	4.7	3.9
Mathematics/ physical sciences	7	24	35	30	1	0	0	2	83	5.1	4.2
Biological sciences	3	30	39	27	0	0	0	1	94	5.1	4.0
Engineering	3	6	31	52	2	0	6	6	64	4.6	4.7
Unidentified field	0	15	62	15	0	0	0	8	13	5.0	—
All	3	19	38	33	2	0	0	5	383	4.9	4.2

Source: Survey of Chairpersons of Leading Graduate Departments, 1999, by authors (Q7).

Note: Rows may not add to 100% because of rounding.

[a]Includes "no opinion" or no usable response.

[b]Number of responding programs (including no opinion/no usable response).

TABLE 9.15

Tenure Rates at Leading Graduate Departments, 1968–1972, 1983–1984, and 1999

	Cumulative %		
% of Faculty Tenured	1968–72*	1983–87*	1999
At least 50	82.3	88.3	88.5
At least 60	67.1	82.6	85.4
At least 70	42.1	64.9	73.6
At least 80	17.4	42.4	50.4
At least 90	4.1	15.2	20.4
100	1.6	2.5	2.6

Source: Survey of Chairpersons of Leading Graduate Department, 1999, by the authors (Q6).

*From 1983–84 Survey of Leading Graduate Departments (figures from 1968–72 period derived from department chairs' recollections in 1983–84). See Bowen and Schuster, 1986, table 11-15, p. 223.

track faculty, on whom the chairs based their responses (table 9.15). That ambiguity aside, it is worth notice that the proportion of faculty who were tenured had advanced percentage-wise from 1968–72 to 1983–84 and again to 1999. Thus, at the "top," among these institutions there is no indication from *these* data of any erosion of tenure. The higher proportions of tenured faculty over this approximately thirty-year period is undoubtedly a function in part, probably in large part, of faculty members being granted tenure and then years later deferring retirement in an era of "uncapping" of mandatory retirement.

TABLE 9.16

American Rhodes Scholars, Selected Career Choices, 1978–1992, Five-Year Periods

	1978–82			1983–87			1988–92[a]		
	Number	% of All Cases	% of Leading Areas[b]	Number	% of All Cases	% of Leading Areas[b]	Number	% of All Cases	% of Leading Areas[b]
Higher education	34	7.6	42.0	20	4.5	25.3	10	2.2	16.7
Law	18	4.0	22.2	22	4.9	27.8	17	3.8	28.3
Business	18	4.0	22.2	22	4.9	27.8	19	4.3	31.7
Medicine	11	2.5	13.6	15	3.4	19.0	14	3.1	23.3
Total	81	18.1	100.0	79	17.7	100.0	60	13.4	100.0

[a]The time required to complete academic degrees and related training tends to reduce the numbers of Scholars who are engaged in certain areas, especially higher education and medicine.
[b]The leading areas are higher education, law, business, and medicine.

From the data describing the assessment by these 369 department chairs of "leading graduate departments," it is clear that for most of them there is satisfaction, ranging mostly upward to enthusiasm; and this applies to their perceptions for both their advanced doctoral students and their junior faculty. This picture bodes very well for stocking the top echelon of academic departments. The current concerns, judged by these responses, are few. But the issue of how wide and deep the optimism of these chairs either does obtain or should obtain is perhaps another matter—touched on at the conclusion of this chapter.

Rhodes Scholars

Among the highly selective, highly visible programs that recognize undergraduates with great promise, the American Rhodes Scholar program probably heads the list in prestige, and not without reason. Cecil Rhodes's magnificent gift to endow those scholarships enabled a number of countries, mainly in the British Commonwealth (from India to New Zealand but including also Germany, Nigeria, and the United States), to select a small number of exceptional college or university seniors (until 1976, men only). Since the first American Rhodes Scholars were chosen in 1904, thirty-two Americans have been selected each year, four from each of eight regions, in a fierce competition.

In *American Professors,* Bowen and Schuster (1986) analyzed trends in the occupations pursued by American Rhodes Scholars who had been selected from 1945 to 1983.[8] The authors, noting what appeared to be a trend away from the pursuit of an academic career over this 39-year stretch, expressed concern because these cohorts, though tiny in number, had enormous mobility in choosing a career path: "Over the period 1945–59, almost twice as many Rhodes Scholars chose academic careers as opted for a career in the competing fields of law, medicine, and business. But for the period 1965–79, the situation has been reversed: 2.3 times as many Scholars have taken up careers in one of the three competing fields as have chosen an academic career."

As table 9.16 indicates, the proportion of American Rhodes Scholars who have opted for academic careers appears to have diminished markedly over three recent five-year periods. Although there are various ways to view this phenomenon, one way that is revealing is through the lens of higher education careers versus the "competing" professions. By classifying the Scholars' careers on the basis of their biographical sketches in the Rhodes directory, it can be seen that during the first of these three half-decades, the number of scholars who chose careers in higher education was almost twice as large (34) as the number who chose the next most popular careers (law and business, each at 18). During the second period, though, both law and business (at 22 each) pulled slightly ahead of the academy (20). And by the third period, only one in six Scholars selected from 1988–92 opted for an academic career, trailing law, business, and medicine. To repeat, not much should be made of these choices over time, given the miniscule numbers, but the results are nonetheless suggestive.

"SO, HOW ARE WE DOING?"

This excursion to determine whether the academic profession is at risk of not being able to attract qualified successors to replenish itself—adequate both in number and "quality"—has led to two principal conclusions. And they are conclusions somewhat in tension with one another.

First, the record that we have developed shows no diminution in the quality of persons being drawn to academic careers. Yes, our instruments of measurement are imperfect; the evidence at best is suggestive rather than conclusive. But, compared to the findings of nearly two decades before, few indicators of slippage are evident. The occasional warning sign surfaces, as seen, for example, in the apprehension voiced by some of the chairs of very high-powered academic departments. But on the whole, there is no visible decay—not to mention collapse—in the aspirations of the most academically talented when it comes to opting for an academic career. The academy appears to be holding its own. Yes, but . . .

Viewing an earlier era—that is, comparing the decades *prior* to the 1970s and 1980s with the mid-1980s—it *appears* that colleges and universities in the mid-1980s were more competitive vis-à-vis "the competition" (other professions that draw the highly educated) (Bowen and Schuster, 1986), although the evidence was inconclusive. More recently, at the outset of the twenty-first century, higher education, in competitive terms, appears to be no worse off (or better off) than it was in the mid-1980s. That conclusion should *not* be construed, however, to mean that the academy now enjoys competitive parity, much less a competitive edge. This cautionary note is essential because of the substantial, pervasive influence of the conditions that obtain in the academic labor market. The past several decades have been host to a fierce buyer's market. That is, in almost all academic fields, the supply of PhD-qualified would-be faculty exceeds—sometimes hugely exceeds—the demand for them. Quite plainly, this *buyer*-friendly circumstance enables the hirers of academic talent to pick and choose. There are many casualties among the *un*chosen as career aspirations are sundered or compromised amid the harsh realities of the academic marketplace. But that, in a sense, is a different issue; from the *academy's* vantage point, the "pickin's" are (for the most part) good to very good.

Put another way, prevailing labor market conditions—that is, the fact that relatively few new faculty are being hired—not only shape, but in important ways distort, the results of the so-called competition among the professions. Application pools can be quite thin (a frequent observation of prevailing conditions in the mid-1980s [Bowen and Schuster, 1986]), but now, as then, at least in most fields, the top stratum of candidates is usually highly attractive. And so the new hires, for the most part, are warmly welcomed. Contrariwise, anecdotal evidence abounds regarding unsuccessful searches and, certainly in some fields (though relatively few), application pools range from uninspiring to barely existent. But those are the exceptional situations. On the whole, excess supply enables very positive hiring results. This is the point: As the demand curve reflecting replacement needs for faculty members rises to approach the supply curve (especially as increasing numbers of faculty retire), the results of faculty searches, presumably less frequently able to skim just the topmost layer of applicants, may come to generate decreasing enthusiasm. In other words, long-prevailing marketplace conditions favorable to the buyers of academic talent undoubtedly have artificially inflated the "results"; if or when the supply-to-demand ratio slips, the current level of candidates' attractiveness to academic buyers may come to be viewed in another, less favorable light. Under those circumstances the ability of academic employers to channel mostly top-quality candidates into academic appointments may well diminish, possibly even to a disturbing degree. For now, though, the word seems to be, "What, me worry?"

NOTES

1. Some advanced professional degrees are pursued very largely by existing or aspiring faculty and thus can be differentiated from the vast majority of professional degrees, which only infrequently lead to academic careers. An example would be the doctorate in jurisprudential science (JSD or SJD) which is associated almost exclusively with academics at law schools.

2. In fact, considerably smaller proportions of all PhD-earners now enter academic careers than was once the case. Several decades ago, obtaining a PhD essentially was tantamount to pursuing an academic career. But times have changed, in part because of a long-prevailing tight academic labor market, which cannot accommodate the surplus of PhDs in most fields, and in part because of the relatively recent receptivity of other employment sectors—government, finance, and corporate research and development, for instance—to

hiring PhDs. And so, as the National Research Council's Surveys of Earned Doctorates attest, smaller proportions of PhDs aspire to and enter academic ranks.

3. The authorship of the annual reports changes. Of particular interest, because it reports conveniently on the survey's first thirty years, is Astin, Parrott, et al., 1997, especially, for present purposes, pp. 48, 49, 78, 108, and 109. The most recent volume, reporting on freshmen entering in 2004, is Sax et al., 2004).

4. The comparable term (that is, questionnaire option) in earlier years (prior to 1977) was "research scientist." The extent to which neophyte collegians may have distinguished between a career as a "research scientist" or as a "scientific researcher" and a career as a college or university teacher-researcher in the natural sciences is unclear.

5. COFHE evolved from the Sloan Study Consortium, created in 1971 with support from the Alfred P. Sloan Foundation.

6. The 2002 COFHE senior survey, however, did not include an item asking for respondents' anticipated long-term career.

7. The sample of 2,400 Phi Beta Kappa members consisted of 800 each who had been selected in 1980–85, 1986–91, and 1992–97. Those with international addresses were excluded. The rate of return was calculated as follows:

2,400 surveys distributed − 194 undeliverable (incorrect addresses) = 2,206 − 46 respondents (ineligible because they reported receiving their baccalaureate degree outside the study's range of 1980 to 1997) = 2,160

921 returned surveys − the 46 ineligibles = 875 usable responses

875/2,160 = 40.5%

8. The method used was to classify each Scholar according to the biographical entry provided for each of them in the directory ("Register") published periodically by the American Rhodes Scholars organization. The first directory examined covered the years 1903 to 1981. The current assessment, based on comparable autobiographical entries in the subsequent directory (1996), covers the years 1903 to 1995. Because it often takes a number of years after completing the Rhodes Scholarship for a Scholar's career choice to become evident through such autobiographical entries, our calculations extend only through 1992 in order not to classify a Scholar's career prematurely.

PART FOUR

Assessing Contemporary Academic Life

CHAPTER TEN

American Academic Life Restructured

The foregoing analysis has painted a grounded portrait of a complex enterprise—the sprawling domain of American higher education—and of an academic profession in rapid transformation. The evidence suggests not only an arguably unprecedented rate of change but also dimensions of a restructured sector that are already in place—with much more change likely to unfold in the foreseeable future. The gist is this: Three fundamental, interrelated elements of restructuring have begun in earnest, and, largely in consequence of those developments, a fourth overarching shift is gathering momentum. These developments constitute the central elements of how academic life is being restructured in the United States; accordingly, they identify the principal axes of the ongoing transformation of the American faculty.

ACADEMIC APPOINTMENTS

Writ large, academic staffing is moving, seemingly inexorably, toward becoming a contingent workforce. A *majority* contingent workforce, no less. More specifically, as of 2004, perhaps two in five of all instructional staff hold contingent appointments. The exact number is not known; current counts are unavailable. Taking the IPEDS Fall Staff Survey for fall 2003 as likely the most accurate and most recent enumeration, among about 630,000 full-time faculty, approximately 219,000 (34.8%) are appointed off the tenure track. To these must be added roughly 543,000 part-time faculty (leaving aside the challenges of accurately counting part-timers and the inevitability of multiple counting of persons who teach at more than one postsecondary institution), yielding a total of

TABLE 10.1

Summary of Faculty Appointments, by Type of Appointment, Fall 2003

	Number of Faculty*	% of All Full-Time Faculty
Full-time faculty	630	100
On tenure track	411	65.2
Tenured	283	44.9
Probationary	128	20.3
Off tenure track	219	34.8
Part-time faculty	543	
All faculty	1,173	

Source: IPEDS Fall 2003 Survey.
*In thousands.

1,173,000 faculty of all stripes. Furthermore, although full-time *probationary* faculty may come to obtain a secure appointment (via tenure or the like), they are, for now, term appointees in the sense that their appointment contracts are subject to not being extended. They number approximately 128,000. So, as of 2003, the contingent off-track appointees accounted for roughly 34.8% of all full-time faculty—or 55.1% if on-track but as yet untenured faculty (20.3%)are added in (table 10.1). Every indication suggests that the number and proportion of contingent appointees has continued to expand. In fall 2003, more than 26,000 of 45,000 newly hired full-time faculty were appointed off the tenure track—a whopping 58.6%. Thus it is very likely that the contingent proportion of all full-time faculty, across all types of institutions and fields, may soon exceed one-half.

While part-time appointments have risen relentlessly over the past three decades to constitute nearly half the academic workforce (by head count), contingent or term appointments have become during the past decade the *modal form* of new full-time faculty appointments. Staffing arrangements for the system show clear lines of bifurcation. To be sure, there are marked differences by institutional type. Research and other doctoral universities and the elite liberal arts colleges, though increasingly resorting to contingent staffing, nonetheless retain a substantial majority core of traditional full-time, permanent or tenure-track appointments. Among other four-year institutions and in the two-year sector (together constituting the vast majority of American higher education), however, contingent full-time and part-time staffing are now the chief modes of institutional operation. In these venues the result is a shrinking core of permanent instructional staff augmented by a host of part-time and full-time term appointments.

The differences in the trend's penetration is manifest also by academic field. Several fields in the humanities—most notably English and foreign languages—and others, including mathematics and business, are on their way to becoming collections of potential transients, even at the research universities. Moreover, both of these lines of demarcation are affected by a third variable, that of gender, the proportion of women faculty in a given type of institution or academic field. The profusion of women into most precincts of postsecondary teaching that we have documented elsewhere is substantially accounted for by these temporary (possibly transient) positions. That is simply a descriptive fact and offers no judgment about the extent to which these developments depict either an exploitation of women, who may be less geographically mobile than men, or an accommodation "en masse" of many women's preferences for more flexible and "balanced" careers and lives.

And so, the distribution of academic appointments is in flux and is destined to skew further—and significantly—in the proximate future.

ACADEMIC WORK

Quite beyond the duration of academic employment contracts—the temporal-legal dimension—is the matter of the substance of the work itself. The data we have presented demonstrate conclusively that although research requirements have suffused throughout the four-year sector, the research function for the most part has been limited to the work of the regular, full-time, core faculty and has largely been squeezed out of the workload of those holding contingent appointments. (There are exceptions, of course: faculty who hold research-only appointments, often supported by "soft money," including research professorships and postdoctoral appointments, mainly in the natural and health sciences.) Thus contingent appointees in the four-year sector are predominately teaching faculty. And that role encapsulation is reinforced by a related trend: the decline in the proportion of time that most faculty, but especially the contingent faculty, dedicate to matters of administration and governance. Institutional administration and governance are shrinking spheres of faculty work or responsibility or involvement (notwithstanding, or, more to the point, precisely *because of,* the increase in the number of administrative staff hired to do administrative work). Accordingly, the familiar triumvirate of teaching, research, and service, for the contingent faculty, has largely morphed into a single-function role—teaching or research, for the less numerous research-only appointments and postdocs.

In all, the mix of tasks expected of academics is shifting, becoming more specialized. The implications for the future include the prospect that only a shrinking proportion of faculty will carry out the traditional variety of responsibilities.

ACADEMIC CAREERS

There are several striking highlights, among them that academic careers in several fields, including English and education, are becoming women's careers. Indeed, as established in chapter 3, the *majority* of recent full-time appointees throughout the humanities have been women. Entry-level compensation (as a percentage of median family income) is declining in comparison with that of other professions (see chapter 8). New entrants begin their academic careers later than ever and, in many cases, as a second career or a secondary branch of a primary career in fields such as nursing and accounting. Perhaps most consequential for academic career trajectories, though, is the ongoing transformation of the profession into a majority of contingent employees. It is too soon to foretell whether the careers of this ever-growing cadre of full-time off-track faculty will be more similar or more dissimilar to their traditionally appointed counterparts, in terms of persistence and satisfaction; the data simply do not yet exist. But the possibility—even the probability—that the relationship between the faculty member and his or her employing institution will have weakened surely has hugely important implications for what an academic career means.

HIGHER EDUCATION'S INSTITUTIONAL SYSTEM

In addition to the ongoing, interrelated restructuring of academic appointments, work, and careers, there exist economic forces with still further enormous potential for transforming the very essence of higher education. Already new providers of higher education have begun to make a difference; the consumer orientation and convenience that characterize much of the movement would appear to have considerable and growing influence. Beyond the pressures that will be exerted by these focused convenience providers on traditional institutions is the impact of the instructional technology revolution. IT has facilitated the entry of these new, nontraditional providers, which are organized not on the basis of traditional teaching-learning models but rather on business models. As they develop for-profit nontraditional academic programs, they are determining the market price of academic programs with which traditional institutions will need to find ways to compete (Ruch, 2001; Sperling, 2000). The higher education sector undoubtedly will evolve to respond to the threats and opportunities posed by newer entrants.

If the data, in fact, document to varying degrees the extant restructuring of academic staffing along the lines of appointments, work roles and activities, and career trajectories—as well as, ultimately, the institutional system itself—what does all this mean for the future of academic life and, perforce, for the American academy? What does such restructuring of academic life portend for the attractiveness of academic careers, their ability to both draw talented persons into careers and retain them? How temporary or durable will such careers be? How will such restructuring "play out" in the decades ahead—a time of inevitable turbulence in American and global higher education? Will this restructuring abate? Accelerate? Will it affect all segments of the system more or less equally, or will there be havens buffered from, but not unaffected by, these powerful, unrelenting forces? What quality assurance issues will be (are being) raised by these realities? How will they affect fundamental public policy and institutional policy questions? Academic quality? Access and equity? Costs? The vitality of the nation's university-based research enterprise?

Such questions call us to turn our focus from our detailed retrospective analysis of the documented, empirical trends, past and current, to the *prospective* analysis of how these trends are likely to play out, be affected by, and in turn affect the current and future environment for American higher education. How can that environment be described? What are the critical forces shaping it? To answer these questions, let us first look at broad-brush projections of the demand for and supply of higher education as the basic economic forces that will drive its development in the proximate to intermediate future.

DEMAND FOR HIGHER EDUCATION

Nearly all analysts agree that over the next decade, the demand for higher education *worldwide* will rise spectacularly. In industrialized western countries, such as Britain, other western European nations, and Australia, the rates of participation in higher education are fast approaching, or even surpassing, those in the United States. In China, among developing nations, the sharp increase in participation rates has been astonishing.[1] Because the United States has experienced by far the highest rate of participation in the last half of the twentieth century, the projected rate of expansion here is likely to be slower than that in much of the rest of the world. Nevertheless, even though the level of participation in U.S. postsecondary education is extraordinary by worldwide standards,

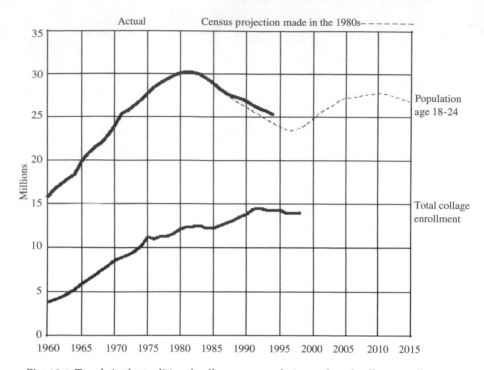

Fig. 10.1. Trends in the traditional college-age population and total college enrollment, 1960–2015 (projected). Data from Bureau of the Census, "U.S. Population Estimates, by Age, Sex, Race, and Hispanic Origin," *Current Population Reports,* ser. P25, PPL-21; National Center for Education Statistics, *Digest of Education Statistics, 1996* (NCES 96-133), 176, table 169; and unpublished updates. Graph from Frances, 1998. Courtesy of Carol Frances.

and although the potential for further upward movement is therefore limited, participation rates in the United States continue to increase, moving inexorably, it appears, from mass to universal access (Trow, 1973).

What kind of demand can be expected within the United States? Whereas the past twenty years have seen relatively higher growth in nontraditional, working adult–oriented higher education, over the next decade we expect to see an important variation materialize in that pattern. As figure 10.1 illustrates, the children of the baby-boom generation have been arriving at traditional college age (i.e., turning 18) in record numbers since about 1996, and that wave is expected to continue through at least 2010. The result is a sudden and steep increase in demand for traditional higher education (i.e., a residential, full-time learning experience) that is likely to persist for several more years (Frances, 1998). The talk of "Tidal Wave II" is widespread in many sunbelt states, beginning with California.

This is not to suggest that demand for higher education oriented toward working adults will fall off. We expect significant increase in demand in that area, too, as the workplace evolves and "serial" careers become more the norm. We are merely suggesting that the relative rates of growth of these two segments of American higher education will reverse themselves. And that reversal has important implications for those who are undertaking strategic planning on our nation's campuses.

One further word about demand and faculty careers, has to do with how information technology, in particular the rise of the Internet, will affect demand for higher education. Most analysts believe that the growth of the World Wide Web (and the communication capabilities that it offers) will open up a whole new channel of demand for higher education, essentially unlimited by time and space constraints (Daniel, 1996; Finkelstein et al., 2000). There is no reason to assume any geographic boundedness to this demand. That is, it seems fair to assume that the United States will experience in the decade ahead increased demand for higher education coming not only from indigenous sources, but from sources outside the country as well. For instance, the dampened demand for American graduate degrees earned *in residence* (an enormously expensive proposition for foreign governments) following the Asian economic downturn of the late 1990s may be more than offset by the much less costly possibility of earning the increasingly available "distance" or on-site graduate degrees from American universities offered on-site in foreign countries.

SUPPLY OF HIGHER EDUCATION

On the face of it, at least in the United States, there appears to be no shortage of "suppliers" or "providers" on the horizon. Traditional suppliers (traditional colleges and universities) remain numerous, even by some reckoning too (inefficiently) numerous. And the supply of traditional and part-time faculty, as a function of the steady growth in PhDs in the last quarter of the twentieth century, remains robust, arguably excessive in many fields. However, perhaps the single most defining change in higher education over the past ten years or so has been the surge of nontraditional suppliers who have built on the capabilities of the World Wide Web as well as other distance technologies. Included are the for-profit entities (like the ubiquitous University of Phoenix [the Apollo Group]), whose purpose is to provide content to learners in the most cost-effective and convenient fashion possible (Ruch, 2001; Sperling, 2000; Berg, 2002). This has amounted to a reconfiguration of the competitive landscape in American higher education (some would describe the development as a realignment of the market for higher education). It is less and less possible for a single institution to claim near-hegemonic ownership of a geographical niche. It now has potential competitors (even though electronic) from around the world, let alone from the adjacent state. Thus, instructional technology undermines the geographic niches of colleges and universities, greatly expanding the arena of interinstitutional competition. There is no such thing anymore as a purely local institution. As a result "adaptive" pressures (the need for greater flexibility) on colleges and universities have increased, especially so for less prestigious, purely teaching institutions.

If supply is not limited by the availability of willing providers, it *is* limited by cost. Certainly cost is the single greatest barrier to expanding access in the developing world. National "open" universities on the British model have been spawned in response, across most of the industrialized *and* developing world, at an accelerating rate (Daniels, 1996). For that matter, cost is emerging as the single greatest barrier to higher education access in the United States, as well. Most states in recent years have resisted as too costly the strategy of adding substantially to the physical capacity of their higher education system and rather have sought to enhance their capacity either electronically or by means of a consortium offering distance education, in anticipation of the baby boomlet. Relevant examples include Florida Gulf Coast University, Thomas Edison State College in New Jersey, the University of Massachusetts On-Line, Maine Open University, and Michigan Virtual University.

U.S. data reveal that the actual per student costs of higher education, adjusted for inflation, have continued to increase annually since 1976–77; the issue of college costs (and, on the other side of the coin, college affordability) has risen to prominence in the national debate about higher education (see, for example, the report of the National Commission on the Cost of Higher Education, 1998; Ehrenberg, 2000; and recurrent congressional hearings). The arrival en masse of alternative providers will realign the competitive market for academic programs and perhaps become the major force (in place of the "real" costs incurred by traditional colleges and universities) in shaping (reshaping) the "prices" for academic programs. We can expect some academic program realignment at most traditional institutions over the coming decade as they seek to adjust to the new competitive marketplace, especially for career-oriented programs, which are the primary emphasis of most nontraditional providers.

What do these developments mean for academic work and careers? Some implications can be suggested. We can anticipate a remarkable increase and diversification of nontraditional instructional staff and academic support staff.

Many are part-timers in an academic discipline in which traditional full-time faculty appointments are hard to come by. So we expect that jobs such as course facilitators, mentor-coaches, and course designers will increase. This diversification and specialization of roles will proceed not only demographically (spurred by the growing presence of women and the increasing availability of foreign-born scholars), but also in terms of the qualifications and skills required. It will lead to the greater acceptability of nontraditional credentials (with more emphasis on competencies other than the usual academic credentials), prompted in part by the growing emphasis on outcomes rather than input- or throughput-based measures. This attention to outcomes is in turn being reinforced by the accrediting agencies' intensifying focus on demonstrated educational effectiveness. One highly consequential, if unintentional, byproduct: Although traditional academic careers will continue to be modal at the "elite" institutions, at the "mass" and "convenience" institutions (see Finn, 1999), the proportion of instructional staff entering upon and able to pursue traditional academic careers will shrink to minority status.

COST PRESSURES AND THE INFLUENCE OF INFORMATION TECHNOLOGY

The three basic elements we have identified as driving developments in higher education in the early twenty-first century are: (1) a rising demand for higher education, spanning traditional and nontraditional modalities, amid proportionately declining government funding (Brenemen and Finney, 1997); (2) a ready availability of supply, fueled by the rise of nontraditional providers and substantially boosted by the need to contain costs (indeed the imperative to reduce per student costs); and (3) the impact of information technology, principally through the rise of the World Wide Web as an instrument of communication and education.

It is basic, we believe, to identify these elements as forming the crucible within which academic life and work will be reshaped over the coming decade or so. What we propose to do here is develop descriptively the parameters of that crucible. Once we have done so, we will return to the three axes of restructuring—academic appointments, work, and careers—and ask, How will restructuring along these three basic dimensions be affected by rising demand, cost pressures associated with supply, and information technology? To what extent are these vectors of change likely to be neutralized, undone, or reinforced?

Cost Pressures

The extraordinary cost pressures on American higher education come from several concurrent sources, all part of the general trend toward privatization in the Western democracies:

1. A proportionate decline in state government funding for higher education as other public funding priorities (Medicare benefits, criminal justice and corrections, etc.) ascend in precedence;
2. A proportionate decline in federal funding for research that requires universities to allocate more of their own discretionary funds to research;
3. The costs of information technology; and
4. Persistent staffing inflexibility associated with a substantial corps of tenured faculty no longer subject to mandatory retirement.

Several analysts have already documented quite vividly the decline in public funding (see, for example, Breneman and Finney, 1997; Slaughter and Leslie, 1997; Meyer, 1998; Frances, 1998; Zumeta, 2004), but less analysis is available of the fixation on information technology within the costs of higher education (Finkelstein et al., 2000). Those costs entail a number of major components:

1. The costs of hardware and network construction and maintenance (traditionally capital items with very short half-lives);
2. The costs of software for both the administrative and the academic side of the organization and the staff to maintain same;
3. Training for all campus constituencies;
4. Round-the-clock (24/7) technical support; and
5. The recruitment and retention of highly paid professional staff to oversee and operate the system.

Although precise figures are hard to come by, available data suggest that the proportionate share of campus instructional budgets devoted to information technology has swelled from 2–3% in the early 1990s to 10% and more by 2000 (Finkelstein et al., 2000). It is important to underscore that historically these funds have come from capital budgets (for equipment) and from discretionary operating budgets (not basic operating items). Only now are many campuses beginning to understand that the financing of IT will require a large built-in annual operating expenditure. The net effect of all of these cost pressures has been to place severe constraints on faculty salaries and full-time faculty lines—as the largest part of instructional operating budgets.

Ironically, of course, IT has often been touted as a vehicle for saving money, on the administrative side through achieving efficiencies and on the academic side by permitting the substitution of capital for labor in the instructional process (e.g., via centralizing the development of course content and paying only for actual delivery, including interaction with students and assessment). There surely have been some savings on the administrative side, but there have also been significant associated costs (the hiring of new staff and the tremendous challenges of making new operations software, e.g., PeopleSoft, work efficiently). On the academic side, as we are learning, the result has been nearly all additional costs (Finkelstein et al., 2000). IT has actually *driven up* instructional costs. And the conditions under which capital may be substituted effectively for labor are quite peculiar and limited (see the discussion of "economies of scale" in Jewett, 2000).

The upshot is that IT has emerged as a serious *competitor* for resources with and within academic affairs. Together with the other trends we discussed above, an environment of constrained resources on campus is hard upon us and will almost surely continue over the coming decade.

The Non-Fiscal Concomitants of IT

Aside from increasing dollar costs on the academic side, IT contributes to at least three further new developments with profound, if less clear, implications for academic staffing. In the first place, IT reduces traditional institutional boundaries on the deployment of faculty. Institutions can "share" faculty resources in many low-demand fields, increasing the potential "efficiency" of staffing arrangements. (Foreign languages, for example, do not need to be staffed with full-time faculty in all languages an institution might wish to offer but cannot afford. Nor does an English department that largely offers "service" courses need to have, say, its own medievalist/Chaucerian or Tolstoy or Joyce scholar.) Moreover, since IT weakens the role of the individual faculty member as "gatekeeper" of knowledge (the "best" content authorized by disciplinary associations and/or authored by renowned scholars is increasingly available directly on the Web unmediated by local faculty), institutions anywhere in the world can offer courses taught by highly regarded faculty members with whom they have contracted. This possibility reinforces faculty "entrepreneurialism," providing more opportunities for the "best" faculty outside their own employing institutions and limiting opportunities for the more journeyman variety of content experts on individual campuses.

Second, IT permits—indeed, greatly accelerates—the "unbundling" of traditional faculty instructional functions, especially the separation of content generation from presentation/interaction with learners, allowing for "division of labor" and specialization in the instructional function. This structurally facilitates hiring more part-time and teaching-only full-time faculty; it thus accelerates the trend toward unbundling that the movement to part-time and full-time term staffing represents and, correspondingly, furthers the progressive shrinking of the traditional tripartite faculty role (teaching, research, and service) that crystallized in the post–World War II period.

Third, IT extends issues about intellectual property from the research and development realm deeply into the instructional arena (who owns a professor's course content as it resides in her or his Web site, the professor and/or the institution?) and thereby raises new questions about the nature of the employment relationship between faculty members and their institution. To be sure, IT may be viewed as a boon to faculty research and scholarship; after all, it greatly democratizes access to others' scholarship and facilitates dissemination of individual faculty scholarship, potentially cutting costs associated with travel to professional meetings and providing new avenues for nonresearch university faculty to connect with, and contribute to, scholarship in their field. However, as IT extends issues of intellectual property to teaching material and encourages faculty entrepreneurialism, it has at least the potential to realign the faculty-institution employment relationship as well as to redefine the parameters of academic citizenship, including interaction with students. More generally, IT allows faculty to do ever more work at home and makes it all the more tempting and easier to stay "a safe distance" from campus. Although IT may increase the *frequency* of faculty-student interaction, it may also change the nature—the *quality*—of such interaction (toward more superficial, less face-to-face).

HOW ARE THESE DEVELOPMENTS LIKELY TO IMPACT THE DIMENSIONS OF RESTRUCTURING?

Table 10.2 charts the effects of the supply-demand forces that we have identified on academic staffing, work roles, and careers. These forces are conceptualized as either reinforcing (+), mitigating (−), or having no effect (N) on restructuring in the pivotal areas of academic appointments, academic work, and academic careers.

A glance at table 10.2 suggests first that the trio of external forces (increasing cost pressures, increasing competition among traditional and nontraditional suppliers, and the unbundling of faculty roles that IT facilitates) are all operating in the same direction, that is, reinforcing the trend toward more specialized

TABLE 10.2

Anticipated Effects of Supply and Demand Forces on the Dimensions of Academic Restructuring

	Supply and Demand Forces						
Dimensions of Restructuring	Government Funding (Proportionate Decline)	Traditional Enrollment Demand[a]	Nontraditional Enrollment Demand[b]	Entry of New Institutional Providers	Growth in Number and Type of Content Providers	Intellectual Property Rights & Faculty Entrepreneurship	IT as % of Campus Education & General Expenditures
Appointments							
Temporary, full-time	+	−	+	+	N	N	+
Part-time	+	−	+	+	N	N	+
New cadres of nonfaculty professional staff with teaching responsibilities	N	N	+	+	+	N	+
Academic work							
Unbundling of teaching from research & service	+	−	+	+	+	+	+
Differentiation and more specialized job descriptions	+	−	+	+	N	N	N
Resituating faculty-institutional relationship	N	−	+	+	+	+	N
Academic careers							
Increasing feminization	N	N	N	N	N	N	N
Later career entry	?	?	?	+	?	?	?
2nd or nonexclusive career	N	N	N	+	N	N	N

Notes: "+" indicates reinforcing restructuring; "−" indicates mitigating restructuring; "*N*" indicates no effect.
[a]Mainly middle-class 18–22-year-olds.
[b]Including students age 25 and over.

teaching-only faculty appointments as well as the further diversification of instructional staffs to include new cadres of nonfaculty instructional designers, course facilitators, and the like.

Similarly, as far as the scope and substance of faculty work is concerned, the external forces, especially the advent of on-line and distance education, clearly all reinforce the unbundling of faculty work roles (teaching split off from research and service) and the differentiation of professional tasks. Moreover, the restructuring of work roles and the resort to new types of appointments reinforce each other. That is, restructured (more specialized) work roles encourage the new kinds of part-time and temporary full-time appointments, while these new types of restructured appointments, in turn, foster significantly different, more specialized work roles. Restructured appointments and reconfigured work roles, are, to use the jargon, "tightly coupled."

The relationship of restructured appointments and work roles (job descriptions) to the restructuring of academic careers is perhaps less clear, more loosely coupled. The increasing modality of nontraditional appointments (including full-time, teaching-only appointments without the associated pressures of competing for tenure) promises to appeal to more married women with families, as well as to seasoned workers in other fields, ranging from the military to law enforcement to business and accounting, who may be seeking opportunities heretofore unavailable for second or later careers in higher education. The key point here is that the restructuring of academic careers is subject to the broader socioeconomic restructuring of work in our society at the dawn of the twenty-first century (Handy, 1994).

In sum, table 10.2 clearly reveals a preponderance of pluses, suggesting that the restructuring of academic staffing, and the concomitant shift in the nature of the faculty-institutional contract (relationship) that we have documented in this volume, is likely to accelerate rather than slow down over the coming decade. However, what the chart does not show is how the effects of these supply-demand forces are likely to be mediated according to institutional type, academic field, and even gender (although we have broadly hinted at the contours of such mediation). In the sections that follow we offer two sets of staffing scenarios, based as fully as possible on available data: in the first set we look at research and other doctoral universities and elite liberal arts colleges versus other four-year and two-year institutions; in the second set we consider low-demand fields (perhaps especially the humanities) versus higher-demand fields in the professions.

Differentiated Patterns by Institutional Type

There are two broad dimensions along which institutions may be classified. We begin with a variation on the traditional, "mission-based" classification. These differentiations are rough, of course, because many institutions do some of nearly everything, sometimes with objectives clearly in tension with one another. Most institutions, nevertheless, would seem to have a center of gravity, a central thrust, that best characterizes what they do. Institutions may seek to educate a highly selective clientele (elite students), to provide traditional career education to a mass clientele, or to make "convenience education" available to all in the workforce, so we can distinguish among elite, mass-provider, and convenience (universal) institutions. This trichotomy has been advanced by Massey and Zemsky (Finn, 1999). The *elite* institutions are roughly equivalent to the research universities and selective liberal arts colleges identified in the older Carnegie classification (CFAT, 1984). The *mass providers* approximate the regional universities and include many nonresearch doctoral universities, the public master's-granting institutions, and some independent liberal arts colleges (the former Liberal Arts II category). And the *convenience* institutions comprise the two-year community colleges and other proprietary institutions that offer career education to high school graduates.

Independent of mission, campuses have also developed strategic responses to instructional challenges of information technology. The strategies might be loosely defined as a commitment to remain a primarily residential ("brick") institution, a commitment to remain or become a primarily distance-education ("click") institution, or a dual commitment to development as a "brick and click" institution. Theoretically, at least, any of the three mission orientations might adopt any of the IT strategies, yielding nine types—a nine-cell matrix—defined by mission and IT strategy. We do not attempt here to project staffing developments at all nine types of institutions; we simply want to recognize that elite and mass providers, especially, may adapt very different IT strategies; and indeed some institutions, even elite institutions, may find themselves operating concurrently as nearly separate components—compartmentalized brick and click enterprises—with staffing strategies to fit each. (The breadth of distance learning is apparent in a 2003 National Center for Education Statistics publication authored by Waits and Lewis [USDE, 2003a].)

Within these basic parameters, what can we say about staffing patterns and institutional type? In the first place, it appears that the elite providers, including the Ivy League and other major research institutions, are most likely of all types to maintain the most traditional staffing patterns. The data suggest that though nontraditional full-time appointments continue to increase at even the elite providers, this set of institutions continues by and large to maintain predominantly traditional, tenured, full-time faculties. The research universities, in particular, have always made room for a modicum of specialized (research-only) appointments, to which some teaching-only appointments are now being added, especially in a few predominantly "service" fields such as foreign languages, composition, and mathematics. And further, we note that a considerable portion of undergraduate instruction at these research universities is borne not by actual faculty but by graduate student teaching assistants.

To the extent that such institutions develop substantial "click" presences, it seems likely that they will attempt to involve their traditional faculty in such nontraditional instruction modes (although the possibility remains of separate, semi-autonomous click operations).

The cases of the mass-provider and convenience institutions are clearer. The latter, principally the community colleges, years ago had already transitioned to a contingent workforce: a small cadre of permanent faculty buttressed by a growing corps of part-time faculty (see Gappa and Leslie, 1993; Palmer, 1999). The mass-provider institutions, principally four-year campuses, have typically moved to a contingent workforce in a different way: while they have expanded their part-time workforce marginally, they have moved increasingly to a system of full-time *term* appointments; the majority of their new hires in the 1990s fit into this category. We can anticipate, however, that before the end of the first decade of the twenty-first century, some of these institutions will gradually move to a predominantly full-time contingent faculty and that others will maintain a bare majority of core full-time faculty. It is in the category of the *mass-provider* institutions that we are likely to see the most frenetic staff restructuring on campus as well as the development of autonomous click components that operate entirely with a contingent and part-time staff.

Differentiated Patterns by Academic Field

We have already suggested in our discussion of the elite providers that *academic field* may provide, independent of institutional mission or institutional type, a second axis around which academic work, careers, and appointments are restructured. The data in previous chapters, especially chapter 7, suggest that a differential is emerging between, on the one hand, career and professional fields, which have substantial numbers of student majors, and, on the other hand, what have become increasingly service fields, such as English, history, foreign languages, philosophy, and physics (predominantly in the humanities), which have relatively few student majors. In the latter, we find a markedly higher incidence of restructuring of academic appointments and academic work. The majority of new full-time appointments in these fields are now non-tenure-eligible; in addition, part-time appointments are increasingly common. This development suggests, perhaps shockingly, that outside of the elite providers, traditional academic careers in the humanities and other largely service fields may be becoming anachronisms at most institutions.

SO WHAT? ASSESSING THE SCOPE AND MEANING OF ACADEMIC RESTRUCTURING

In table 10.3 we sketch a preliminary framework for thinking through *both* the costs and the benefits of academic restructuring in *both* the short term and the longer term. A basic assumption of this framework is, first, that complex change is rarely all good or all bad. Change, rather, necessitates identifying what some of the major consequences are likely to be, in the long run as well as the proximate future, especially for those aspects of academic life that we hold to be most valuable. We must be clear about what is important to us and what we hope can be preserved in the current state of transition (even, by some measures, upheaval). We have to be at once be as analytical as possible in projecting consequences, that is, be as realistic as we can be in assessing both the long-term outcomes and the immediate consequences, and in identifying what our needs and priorities really are. We must undertake to understand what stakes pertain to each of the various constituencies on campus (as well as to the broader society) in the ways these changes are managed and the resulting realignment of the higher education enterprise. This analysis is unavoidably fraught with risks; accelerating changes in the environment, especially in technological advances, make projections into the future all the more tenuous. Nevertheless, the future of the academy demands that we begin the task.

Six basic academic constituencies, both internal to campuses and across the sprawling academic enterprise, are identified in table 10.3: (1) individual institutions of higher education as organizational entities; (2) the faculty of individual campuses; (3) students and their learning needs (undergraduate as well as graduate and professional students); (4) more generally, the national academic profession; (5) the national research and development enterprise and the academic disciplines upon which it depends; and (6) the general impact on a knowledge-based society that can optimize opportunities for training and technology transfer from the laboratory to the economy and can maintain the his-

TABLE 10.3
Summary of the Consequences (Benefits and Costs) of Academic Restructuring

Constituency	Short-Term Benefits and Costs	Long-Term Benefits and Costs
Institutions of higher education	■ Financial flexibility (better assures responsiveness to student & other interests) ■ Increased ability to redeploy instructional staff ■ Increased competitiveness (esp. vis-à-vis nontraditional providers)	■ Replacement of academic disciplines by "client services" as "organizing" principle for instructional delivery ■ Corporatization (includes faculty as managed professionals and less emphasis on academic values for high-level administrators)
Campus faculties	■ Greater social/status stratification of staff (core vs. periphery) ■ Increased workload for smaller core faculty ■ Declining influence of faculty as internal constituent ■ More efficient staffing (i.e., functionally more specialized) ■ Fewer "all positions" faculty (teaching, research, campus service)	■ Renegotiation of faculty-institutional "social contract" (e.g., declining mutual loyalty; increased administrative oversight of academic affairs); ■ Diminished faculty ownership and control of intellectual property ■ Increasingly flexible accreditation standards, which serve to accommodate flexible portions of academic staffing (e.g., less emphasis on full-time faculty)
Students & undergraduate education	■ Increasingly student-centered vs. faculty-centered focus (focus on clients, not providers) ■ More cost-efficient instruction (cost/credit hour), which moderates cost increases to students	■ Market-set standards for academic programs (standards no longer set by the academic professions) ■ Replacement of provider expertise by "client" needs as desideratum for organizing instruction ■ Greater responsiveness to needs of demographically diverse student body
Academic profession	■ Limited opportunity for traditional academic careers ■ Stratification of fields by level of market demand (e.g., business over physics) ■ Further undermining of "one faculty" ideal	■ Chronic depressed job market in the traditional arts and sciences ■ Increased difficulty recruiting and retaining the "best and brightest" ■ "Withering" of select low-demand fields (physics, philosophy, literature) ■ Diminished protection of academic freedom as fewer positions are protected by tenure ■ Promotion of academic star system undergirded by a vast new "academic proletariat"

(continued)

TABLE 10.3 (*continued*)

Constituency	Short-Term Benefits and Costs	Long-Term Benefits and Costs
National research and development enterprise	■ More efficient "research" expenditures; less encouragement/support for "esoteric" research ■ Greater market responsiveness of research activities	■ Increasing separation of research function from teaching function (drift toward national academy model) ■ Research corporatization (a result of corporate support and subject to increased reliance on corporate needs)
The larger society	■ Increased efficiency in achieving definable outcomes ■ Increased responsiveness to societal needs as defined by market	■ Increased capacity to manage costs of higher education ■ Increased access to higher education (via increased efficiency and greater diversity of institutions and greater use of distance learning modes) ■ Increased polarization of higher education into elite, traditional, and residential venues and "streamlined," accessible market-responsive venues ■ Diminished number of higher education institutions primed to carry out cutting-edge research and social critique ■ Unknown costs to society of higher education's diminished ability to attract/retain top talent as faculty

torical capacity of the academy to critique all aspects of society. Our examination of these constituencies posits that for each of them, the anticipated changes result in a mix of costs and benefits. Each of the six arenas in effect serves as a vital lens through which the changes, ongoing and impending, must be viewed in order to obtain an overview of the complex trade-offs that are taking shape. Moreover, we maintain that the cost-benefit mix needs to be assessed temporally—that is, that the mix may tilt in either direction in both the short and the long term. We turn now to the presumed impact.

Institutions of Higher Education

Our assessment suggests that the restructuring of appointments and the search for new "cost-conscious" teaching and learning strategies promises for individual *institutions* increased financial flexibility in responding to student needs and greater competitiveness vis-à-vis emergent nontraditional providers—in the short term, at least. Institutions must reckon with the impact of "business" models of their operation on what might be described (by impatient critics) as a heretofore "labor-intensive" boutique academic enterprise. The new realities, replete with pressures, appear to require the institution to adopt a different mind-set, a different conception of itself.

Campus Faculties

For the *faculties* of our colleges and universities and for the academic profession generally, the prospects are decidedly less "balanced." In the short term, we can predict that the workload of full-time tenure-eligible faculty will continue to increase (as a shrinking core assumes the burden for nonteaching functions historically assumed by a larger portion of the faculty), academic staffing will continue to become more functionally specialized, the corporate faculty as a force on campus will decline, and the teaching staff will be fragmented between the relatively few core regulars and the expanded academic proletariat.

Students and Undergraduate Education

For *students* a different mix of trade-offs pertains. Perhaps most portentous, the kinds of restructuring described thus far are likely to mean, in the short term, an intensified, student-learning focus rather than *faculty*-oriented, academic discipline–focused learning experiences. These realignments may also yield a more cost-effective (or at least cost-conscious) approach to instruction that over time may potentially moderate spiraling costs for students' higher education. On the longer-term side of the ledger, however, students will increasingly find their own perceived needs, rather than provider expertise, serving as the desideratum for identifying course offerings and organizing instruction. (That is to say, students will be more likely to receive what they *seek* than what they are thought to need). Put another way, the standards for academic programs will more and more likely be set not by the content experts but rather by the marketplace or, more precisely, by students' perceptions of it.

The Academic Profession

With respect to the academic profession more generally, the prospects for traditional academic careers will shrink, and, in particular, differences among academic fields (those in high versus low demand) will continue to be magnified. This will at once raise concerns about the health of scholarship in the lower-demand fields and the long-term attractiveness of academic careers to the nation's most gifted youth—thus posing a serious challenge to America's intellectual and scientific leadership in the world. On a more positive note, it is likely that the academic profession will continue to diversify demographically and that the availability of more flexible roles will bring heretofore underrepresented groups and cultural vantage points increasingly into the academic fold.

The National Research and Development Enterprise

With respect to the *national research and development enterprise,* there is the promise (especially in the short term) of achieving greater "efficiencies" in research expenditures and greater market responsiveness, including the likely discouragement of more esoteric types of research that are not clearly related to defined national interests. The downside of this development is, of course, the increasing separation of research from teaching and the broader education function and the increasing "corporatization" of research. This is occurring when most national systems that have historically separated teaching from research functions are now moving to more nearly American models of integrating the two functions as the most effective and synergistic. It also comes at a time when concerns are being expressed about the effects of shifting support for research from government to predominantly corporate sponsorship. Prominent among these concerns is that such a shift in sponsorship and priorities may threaten the viability as well as the quality of more basic research.

The Larger Society

Finally, there is the matter of *broader social impact.* And here the balance appears at first blush to favor the benefits above the costs. There is the promise of targeting public dollars more efficiently to the achievement of desired social outcomes—in terms both of training and research and development—and thus fitting the wildly diverse (messy) enterprise more closely to public needs. There is the further promise of increasing the capacity to manage the costs of higher education and of boosting access. On the other side, however, are a number of imponderables. At what point does the shrinking number of educational institutions primed to carry out cutting-edge research reach the point of diminishing returns—wherein the benefits of efficiency are outweighed by effectiveness costs? At what point does an increasingly stratified institutional system begin "disserving" the goals of human resource development and social mobility? And at what point does the declining opportunity for academic careers diminish our broader social capability to mobilize the best available scientific and intellectual talent in the nation? Still further out lies perhaps the most consequential of the outcomes of restructuring for the general society. It is also probably the most elusive to gauge. This is the extent to which this reengineering of American higher education, as we have described it, will curtail the capacity of the academy to engage in the invaluable (though often highly controversial) activity of critiquing aspects of society, from arts to politics, from commerce to the academy itself. The premise underlying this concern is that fewer universities will be able to maintain a cadre of faculty employed to do more than teach.

In all, what these axes of analyses suggest is that American higher education, poised as it is on the cusp of a significant, even sweeping, restructuring, faces a very complex assessment and sorting-out task. Depending on where one is located in the institutional and disciplinary system, the calculus of the costs and benefits of restructuring vary substantially. How does each individual institution (or college faculty or student body) optimize the benefit-to-cost yield? And how does the broader society go about that complicated task? What seems clear from our analysis of variation by institutional type, academic field, and campus constituency, is that each campus, each group of faculty, each student body, and each academic field will need to undertake thoroughgoing assessments of the cost-benefit mix in relation to the values it holds most dear. There is no substitute for such sober and tough-minded assessment.

CONCLUDING THOUGHTS

In chapter 11 we identify some of the major policy issues that the restructuring of academic staffs, work, and careers raise for colleges and universities. We do so with no preconception of impending disaster, but rather with the conviction that our institutions need to thoughtfully address the trends we have identified and to develop policies that minimize costs to quality and access while maximizing functionality and excellence. Disaster *is* likely to ensue if higher education is swept downstream on the swirling currents of societal change without having sorted out, prioritized, and protected its own core values.

Our analysis suggests that the restructuring of academic appointments, work roles, and careers depicted in incipient evidence from national survey data is likely over the coming decade or so to accelerate. Outside the elite institutions, we are likely to see in the near term the marginalization of traditional academic careers, especially in the humanities and other predominantly service fields. What do these trends mean for the health of our colleges and universities, for the health and vitality of the academic disciplines, and for the prospects for continued growth of the nation's knowledge-based economy? These questions are immensely important and terribly complex, and the answers to them are unknowable in large measure—but the broad outlines can be sketched.

NOTE

1. From 1985 to 2003 (the latest year for which data are available from the Education Ministry of China), the growth of participation in higher education has been explosive. Undergraduate enrollments have swelled from 1.7 million to 11.1 million and PhD enrollments from 3,600 to 136,700.

CHAPTER ELEVEN

What's Ahead?

Agendas for Policy Analysis, Research, and Action on Academic Staffing

We began with the observation that American higher education—and higher education throughout most of the rest of the world—is undergoing a swift and sweeping transformation. The pace and scope of change, across so many basic features of higher education, is, we contend, unprecedented. And we believe that these changes are taking place at such a rapid rate that it is difficult to "keep score," to measure just how much change is occurring—much less to divine the innumerable implications. Nonetheless, the dimensions of change that we discern and the impacts that we foresee arising therefrom have led to our apprehension concerning the future of the academic profession and, perforce, the academy itself. This constitutes the enormous stakes. Nothing less.

Within this volatile environment, we have discerned that the direction in which American higher education appears to be heading is being driven, most generally, by twin challenges: (1) to continue to expand access while (2) containing or reducing operating costs, in order to achieve economic efficiencies. Three salient developments reflect efforts to realize these overarching goals: first, the rise of a significant and increasingly competitive for-profit sector, of both the "brick" and "click" variety (Adelman, 2000); second, the further bifurcation of public higher education systems (as well as the independent sector) into elite, more traditional institutions and mass or convenience producers; and, third, the increasing privatization of the public sector. In addition to trends of escalating interinstitutional competition and a focus on cost containment, the most problematic change—with potentially enormous long-term consequences—is the differentiation and restructuring of academic staffing (work roles, types of appointments, and careers) designed to support the "new" educational production function.

Although the precise complexion of the "new equilibrium" remains unclear, as does its exact timing and trajectory, what is clear is that we can expect over the coming decade and beyond a period of tension and realignment as the new higher education order takes root and familiar staffing policies lurch toward adjustment. Movement toward this new equilibrium will require throughout higher education—at individual academic units and campuses, in entire systems, and among external stakeholders—responding to two congeries of challenges: to create appropriate policy and to design relevant research to probe what is transpiring and assess the results.

POLICY CHALLENGES

The broad contours of the period of adjustment will present a number of tricky policy challenges to the nation and to our colleges and universities. We have identified at least five sorts of policy challenges that we anticipate will, in the aggregate, redefine the character of the academic profession—encompassing the faculty's expectations, obligations, opportunities, and constraints.

First are nationwide challenges pertaining to *recruitment* to academic careers, especially in the sciences and the humanities, and subsuming the crucial goal of expanding faculty diversity throughout the academy.

Second are challenges to *graduate education* to better prepare prospective candidates for the new academic workforce.

A third set of challenges centers on *staffing arrangements:* how to manage adroitly the transition to a more sharply polarized system (elite versus open-access institutions; this will require recalibration of the access-excellence calculus) and how to define and institute optimum policies for the new staffing arrangements.

Fourth are campus and system challenges to renegotiate the *basic social contract* between faculty and their institutional employers. These tasks will entail, in part, managing the inexorable movement toward a more stratified distribution among faculty ranks into what may become a de facto "star and chorus" system.

A fifth major challenge will revolve around getting *quality assurance* right in the new era, namely, tailoring processes to preserve effective voluntary regional accreditation—and an influential role for faculty—in the face of accelerating governmental and market-driven pressures.

Recruitment to Academic Careers

The challenges posed to recruitment are several. First, how is the nation to recruit the "best and brightest" to what will become for the most part, from the systems perspective, much more of a teaching, rather than a research or hybrid teaching-research, career? If only a small number of spaces for traditional "all-around" faculty positions will remain, mainly at the research universities and elite liberal arts colleges, how can we assure the steady flow of the best talent to those positions? Moreover, how will we manage to do so especially in those fields where demand by students (and for faculty) is soft? We can anticipate a pipeline with no dearth of, for example, computer scientists, some types of engineers, and accountants (though they may be pricey). But what of the physicists, astronomers, and mathematicians and those in the more "academic" fields of the natural sciences? An even more urgent matter: how can we ensure the infusion of talented humanists into the academy when compensation weakens and when many English, history, and philosophy departments—except at the research universities and the elite liberal arts colleges—have devolved into basically service departments dominated by teaching-focused term appointees?

If we witness the clearer bifurcation of the academic profession itself into a small cadre of academic stars who are reasonably well paid and a much larger corps of teaching-oriented "journeypeople," what incentive will prospective faculty have to pursue, against considerable odds, a traditional academic career? In particular, as we seek to diversify the faculty with new hires who are women and underrepresented minorities, how will we attend to inequalities in their distribution among the stars and the academic proletariat? (We know that underrepresented faculty, especially women, are already *over*represented among the part-time faculty and the non-tenure-eligible full-timers.) How will we maintain momentum toward diversification of the national corps of faculty? Although considerable progress toward diversifying the faculty is evident, it is clear that much more remains to be done before the faculty's characteristics begin to approximate the diversity of students.

The Challenges to Graduate Education

Two things became abundantly clear about the academic labor market during the 1990s. The number of candidates for academic jobs (represented most succinctly by the torrent of PhDs awarded annually) continued to grow faster than the number of newly created (or replacement) positions. And the substantial majority of institutions of higher education (but generally not the research universities) moved both teaching experience and teaching skill (including facility with instructional technology) to the top of their criteria for hiring.

Both of these developments—the oversupply of PhDs in almost all fields and deepening doubts about the suitability of their traditional "teaching-free" preparation for the newish faculty role—pose formidable challenges to graduate education. Significant policy questions about the scope and focus of graduate training abound and must be addressed. Should doctoral programs, especially in low-demand fields, curtail their enrollments, be forced to diet? Should marginal programs in those low-demand fields simply close? And how shall graduate programs, typically dependent on supplies of cheap graduate student labor, manage the further reduction in academic opportunities to which any such "academic birth control" measures lead?

Whatever the numbers of doctoral graduates that should be produced to satisfy anticipated demand, major issues attend the nature of graduate preparation in the disciplines. Among them are the following: What sort of preparation is most useful for the kinds of academic jobs that will be available in colleges and universities, including those in nontraditional postsecondary programs and institutions? How can graduate students be better prepared to become effective teachers? How can graduate schools better ensure the development of critical skills in the use of instructional technology? Or for teaching students with low English proficiency or substandard academic skills? Projects such as the Association of American Colleges and Universities' Preparing Future Faculty have been developing fresh approaches for faculty preparation that are more clinically focused. Yet serious challenges remain. In all, just how difficult it will be to transform graduate education more broadly to satisfy current and future needs still remains to be seen.

Reconceptualizing Staffing at the System and Institutional Levels

Policies will need to be developed to reflect how institutions reconceive their staffing needs and reallocate faculty roles, and then how they will redevelop and presumably differentiate faculty compensation and other personnel policies, particularly the terms and duration of employment agreements, as well as design appropriate performance reviews.

In addition to the imponderables of how best to calibrate supply and demand to produce the right numbers of appropriately trained college faculty for the nation at large, there remains a barrage of questions that public and independent institutions will need to address. As globalization proceeds, to what extent will academic labor markets truly become global at the very time when the job markets for part-time and term faculty are becoming more local? What combination of types of appointments and work roles will best serve evolving institutional missions? To what extent must institutions plan for new mixes of tenured, temporary full-time, and part-time faculty? And to what extent must institutions plan to staff new instruction-related but non-discipline-based roles associated with the new instructional technologies? By what process will such strategic staffing plans be arrived at? And once developed, how will the strategies be implemented? Will institutions develop separate sets of faculty recruitment strategies and personnel policies? Separate sets of policies are already evolving, of course, for both part-timers (see Gappa and Leslie, 1993) and term appointees (see Baldwin and Chronister, 2001). Yet the hard work remains to be done.

How will the internal dynamics of systems and individual campuses change as the ranks of instructional staff continue to diversify and ultimately stratify? Will the boundaries between strata within and across institutions be relatively permeable or rigid? And how will competitive cost pressures of the market for academic programs affect these stratification dynamics? Even more importantly, how will institutions develop the capacity to monitor the effects of changing staffing arrangements (Chait, 2002)? These types of questions lead directly to new questions related to the basic social contract between faculty and their respective campuses.

The Changing Faculty-Institution Social Contract

Perhaps the most fundamental impact of the realignment of faculty appointments and roles that we are witnessing is the associated "renegotiation" of the historical social/employment contract between American academics and their institutions. Three basic tenets or principles of the academic social contract as it developed in the twentieth century have shaped that relationship:

1. *Mutual* loyalty. The tenure system is one of mutual commitment. In response to the commitment of tenure that faculty receive from their institution, they are expected to display increasing loyalty to the institution and act in accordance with its overall best interests (when those collide with their own personal best interests as reflected in conflict-of-interest policies).

2. *Academic* oversight. As professionals in their fields, faculty—and *only*

faculty—have the special expertise required to formulate and implement educationally sound academic and curricular policy: faculty are essential custodians of all aspects of academic policy.

3. *Intellectual* property. As scholars and researchers whose basic function is intellectual production, individual scholars own the intellectual property they produce (in terms of course materials and publications in scholarly venues).

All three of these basic premises are now in the process of renegotiation and have been for at least a generation. The faculty role in academic governance generally and, more specifically, in the formulation of academic policy, admissions, and curricular decision making has shrunk, with more and more areas now increasingly subject to administrative determination.

The development of the Internet and on-line education has raised new questions about intellectual property ownership and has led to business partnerships between faculty and institutions, pertaining most visibly to technology transfer. Faculty at the research universities have been increasingly spinning off their own for-profit ventures in partnership with their campuses. For larger numbers of faculty, the social contract, it appears, is turning into a business contract—with the faculty member becoming the solo entrepreneur.

We must ask, What will all this mean over time for institutions and for faculty members themselves?

Challenges to Academic Quality Control

The challenges posed to traditional measures of and mechanisms for quality control are more nuanced. The regional accrediting associations have been under increasing pressure over the past decade to connect their standards for accreditation explicitly to student learning and educational effectiveness. In so doing, the regional associations, including perhaps most notably the North Central Association, the Western Association, and the Middle States Association, have revised their standards for accreditation, moving away from a traditional focus on institutional "capacity" as reflected in visible educational resource inputs (for example, faculty credentials, student selectivity measures, library volumes, and endowments) toward demonstrable evidence of actual educational effectiveness. Thus, at precisely the moment when academic appointment policies and practices are experiencing their greatest flux in perhaps a century (and maybe ever), the "voluntary" upholders of quality in higher education have been diluting their insistence on venerable measures of educational capacity.

The appeal of shifting attention from mere measures of capacity to actual "results" as meaningful indicators of "effectiveness" is perhaps irresistible in the prevailing political and economic climate, but proponents of this change should not lose sight of some of the attendant (if difficult to measure) likely costs. Three interrelated developments spring readily to mind.

First, as standards have shifted to de-emphasize the necessity of a core full-time faculty, the sharp rise both of part-time and off-track full-time faculty has resulted in a smaller proportion of all faculty members who are available for a wide range of responsibilities.

Second, among these responsibilities, faculty participation in governance likely will diminish further as the burden of devoting time to governance now must be borne by a smaller cadre of faculty.

Third, as fewer faculty members become tenured or tenure-eligible in this extraordinary ongoing redistribution of faculty appointments, the traditional value of academic freedom—whether used to espouse controversial or unpopular ideas or to challenge campus management—is also susceptible to being compromised.

Are these actual consequences, even if unintended, of the more "flexible" views of accrediting associations? The hard data to answer this question are scant to nonexistent, at least thus far. But the possibility—even the likelihood—of accreditation's long reach, is surely real. And prudence, correspondingly, surely requires close monitoring of these developments.

CHALLENGES TO RESEARCHING THE FACULTY

We turn now to issues that urgently need more research.[1] Our aim is to help prioritize a useful research agenda for the proximate to intermediate future. Throughout our study, we have been obliged to acknowledge that the data are too thin to establish in important instances just what is going on, much less to ascertain the long-term effects. But in developing an agenda for meaningful research relating to the academic profession, a threshold challenge is evident.

A limitless number of "worthy" discrete research topics that focus on research-amenable issues can be identified and, according to one's preferences, can be prioritized and pursued. This approach, however, runs a risk of scrutinizing the proverbial trees without contemplating the changes that are sweeping through the forest and altering its character. The challenge evokes a familiar image: the blind men each feeling parts of a great beast—a tusk, the tail, an ear, a leg—and then reporting their disparate findings to one another. Being tactilely proficient, each examiner's report is accurate, and in research terms, each particular finding would be valid and reliable, as far as it goes. But of course their respective reports fail abysmally to capture the physical nature of the whole elephant. The parts may be adequately described while the Big Picture goes entirely wanting.

Issues of Substance

It is not much of a stretch to find a direct parallel to the challenges of the exercise at hand. In the quest to understand better the changing nature of the faculty and their work, many important topics can be and will be identified, and appropriate research methodologies can readily be suggested that, taken together, will yield useful insights about faculty members and their work life. But the crucial overview may suffer from inattention, and the deeper meanings that inhere in the Big Picture likely will be obfuscated in the process.

Perhaps such an outcome is unavoidable, given the kinds of topics that are readily researchable—and most easily fundable—in contrast to the kinds of nuanced issues that cannot be researched in any conventional sense. And perhaps the overarching issues can be—indeed, need to be—addressed by the likes of historians and philosophers who are more adept than most at placing the contemporary phenomena in a larger, more meaningful context. Consider for now several aspects of this contention.

A commonplace theme in efforts to describe the contemporary academic workplace is the unbundling of faculty work into discrete tasks and the appointment of specialized personnel to implement them. Unbundling is everywhere. The reasons for it are multiple and reasonably well understood. It's not that this is a new phenomenon. Various aspects have been described for years. Examples include the mushrooming of postdoctoral appointments and the regular faculty's shucking off less desirable tasks (e.g., academic advising and the teaching of developmental or remedial and introductory, lower-division courses). But the pace of unbundling has quickened, and the downstream consequences of such large-scale changes surely are largely unknown. This development requires very serious attention. The point here is that unbundling should not simply be accepted either as inevitable *or* as desirable (even though it may be tempting for some to suggest that it represents progress beyond "the tired old ways") without a broader, deeper contemplation of what this apparent sea change means.

In some ways, arguably centrally important ways, the unbundling movement represents a regression, a retrograde action. This is not the place to develop the historical-philosophical argument at length, so a brief suggestion must suffice.

Two historical lenses may be relevant. First, by shrinking the proportion of faculty who hold regular academic appointments, the academy regresses toward a discredited old European model featuring an imminent central figure in an academic program, surrounded by concentric circles of lesser beings whose professional status is marginalized. Second, by splitting off research from teaching (this is what is happening in many contemporary academic appointments), we flirt with the prospect of divorcing functions that were fruitfully joined in the twentieth-century American academy. This melding no doubt has accounted for remarkable academic strengths in the United States in contrast to the French–Soviet–eastern European–Chinese model of separate academies or institutes to house "serious" research apart from teaching. Paradoxically, a blending of these functions appears to be the direction in which these other national systems are now moving.

The argument here is not that we are in imminent danger of so drastic a reversion as divorcing teaching from research. However, these American trends do need to be understood and evaluated in a much broader context, extending well beyond finite, readily researchable, "tree-by-tree" investigations. Accordingly, researchers on academic life should conceive of their tasks more broadly than is often done: to include essays, likely anchored in historical and philosophical perspectives, that contemplate the bigger picture and its implications for the academic profession, the academy, and the society that the academy serves.

Other large-scale multidimensional topics include these:

Diversity in the Faculty

There are a host of questions about the scope and dynamics of truly diverse academic communities that need to be addressed. One issue is the matter of unit of analysis. To what extent is diversity a characteristic of academic programs, academic departments, schools within universities, and entire colleges and universities? Can an academic unit support diversity within a larger organization that does not? What about diversity as a characteristic of academic fields? At each level of analysis, how is diversity reflected in the student body, the instructional staff, the administrative staff? What does it mean to support diversity? At what point does the presence of diversity—whether in race, gender, ethnicity, religion, sexual orientation, language, or political persuasion—translate into what one might consider to be a truly open and tolerant community, for minority as well as majority members?

More concretely, there are issues to be addressed regarding faculty, students, and their interactions. In all, what does it mean to truly support diversity in the academic workplace?

Academic Labor Market Effects

The pervasive effects of the academic labor market constitute another sprawling topic. Just how much is faculty work shaped by marketplace conditions? The short answer is, Plenty! How much of this phenomenon is susceptible to research? The answer, Not much. Models of the academic marketplace can be tried and tested, for what they are worth. (And, for what it is worth, such models appear to have been of quite limited value in the past [Committee on Methods, 2000].) Yes, supply can be more or less readily measured (that is, the availability of qualified would-be faculty), and enrollment- and replacement-driven demand can be approximated. But we have scant understanding about how much *academic work* is shaped by the conditions of a lopsided buyer's market (long prevalent in most academic fields) and, accordingly, affected by the leverage that this condition of oversupply affords the employers of academic talent ("management") to dictate work content and performance expectations. Were academic talent to become scarce (as is the case in some fields), then, it is clear, the balance would shift and, likely, so would the content of work—in addition, of course, to improvements in compensation. In sum, it is apparent that labor market conditions profoundly shape the *fundamentals* of academic work, beginning with who gets responsibility for which academic tasks, as well as the level of expectations for faculty performance and productivity. Surely this complex phenomenon needs to be examined in greater depth to understand how demand-supply imbalances shape the content of, and standards for, academic work.

On the complicated but very important—and neglected—topic of who chooses to pursue an academic career and why (or why not), it would be very useful to try to understand, through studies based on interviews, what anticipated aspects of academic careers were attractive and what factors were regarded as obstacles. There are many aspects of this vital "pipeline" phenomenon that could be valuable if more evidence were gathered. There is a need to develop three-dimensional narratives about career choices involving whether to pursue or forgo an academic career and why. Such findings would provide helpful insights into "how we (the academic profession) are doing."

Academic Appointments

Conceivably the most consequential but most underinvestigated faculty-related phenomenon of the past several decades is the dramatic—even radical—redistribution in the types of academic appointments, as we have asserted repeatedly. This phenomenon is closely related to labor market conditions, but it is a more discrete, research-amenable topic. That the number and proportion of part-time appointments has continued to climb (from about 22% by head count in the early 1970s to perhaps some 45% or more in 2000) is old news. Less visible but hugely significant is the change in the nature of *full-time* appointments. As noted elsewhere, they have undergone a rapid and huge shift: we have emphasized that the *majority* of *new* full-time appointments in the 1990s and into the 2000s have been term appointments, that is, off the tenure track: "temporary" appointments (at least technically). Such appointments were essentially unknown in the not-distant past and were so rare, in fact, as to be practically invisible (fewer than 2%) only three decades ago. Put in other terms, only a *minority* of full-time faculty appointments currently being made in the academy are traditional, that is, either tenured or tenurable. And that minority share of traditional appointments is steadily shrinking. (This development is examined in detail in chapter 7.)

In this context the obvious research question is catapulted to the forefront: So what? Does this redeployment compromise student learning, as some have argued (Benjamin, 2003)? Does it retard student academic progress, as suggested by the small negative beta coefficient of the proportion of faculty who are part-time with six-year college graduation rates, reported by Ehrenberg and Zhang (2004) and based on the IPEDS annual graduation rate survey? Or does this seismic shift in appointments have no measurable effect on the *quality* of the instructional experience in a college course, as suggested by the findings of many studies comparing the student course evaluations of part-time and full-time faculty (Cross and Goldenberg, 2003, pp. 49–69). Or does it perhaps provide a net long-term *gain* owing to student exposure to faculty who may have more diverse experiences and points of view and whose continuation is likely more explicitly linked to favorable student ratings?

More generally, does this redeployment make a meaningful difference in the nature of faculty work or in faculty career trajectories? Behind that question lie more detailed inquiries: Are there significant differences in faculty demographics among appointment categories? In the values they hold? In their job satisfaction? In how the two contingents compare in the way they spend their time at work? What, if anything, does the reconfiguration of appointments portend for the *attractiveness* of academic careers among career choosers vis-à-vis the professions (such as law and medicine) that compete for top intellectual talent? And to what extent is the widely observed unbundling of faculty work linked directly to a proliferation of term appointments in which these appointees are hired for teaching-only or research-exclusive duties? (Most term appointments, as noted, are for specialized purposes, jobs that entail teaching *or* research responsibilities but usually not both.)

All of these are important questions that have only begun to be addressed, in this volume and in the work of Baldwin and Chronister (2000). It may turn out, pursuant to adequate investigations, that the redeployment of faculty into different types of appointments makes little difference per se in the content of academic work and its consequences. But it may very well develop that this restructuring of appointments is highly consequential, rich with both intended and unintended effects, and from these insights might flow a reconsideration of institutional appointment policies.

Accreditation, or Quality Assurance

Regional accrediting associations, as noted, are in the midst of rewriting standards. There have been sweeping revisions in order, among other objectives, to better enable colleges and universities to accommodate to the new technologies and to respond to pressures to give higher priority to teaching—in short, to adapt to the new ways of "doing academic business." Are there links between revised measures of quality (whether traditional input measures or outcomes) and the work of faculty? Probably. In at least several instances, regional accrediting associations' revisions in standards have potentially reshaped the distribution or content of faculty work. Consider these two: the revised standards' de-emphasis on the importance of a core, full-time faculty, as well as a similar de-emphasis on the faculty's decision-making role in academic matters (i.e., governance). In such instances, the result may significantly alter what category of faculty members do what kind of academic work. And so the larger question arises: what are the effects of quality assurance policies on the allocation of faculty work among faculty and on the effectiveness of the work?

Redefining Scholarship

One of the most important efforts designed to affect faculty work in recent years derives from Ernest Boyer's *Scholarship Reconsidered* (2000), in which he (among others) argued for a much more expansive notion of what should "count" as scholarship for purposes of the faculty reward system. This proposed break with narrow, more traditional conceptions of scholarship—centered on "discovery" research and published results—had the potential to significantly shift faculty work efforts from conventional research toward more teaching-oriented "scholarly" activities. But has anything much happened since *Scholarship Reconsidered* was first published in 1990 that in fact tilted campus policies and practices in the direction of the "other scholarships"? Anecdotal information pops up in the literature, but nothing systematic. Investigations at a sample of selected campuses that attempted to sell the idea internally—probably in the form of small-scale case studies—would have the potential to go beyond the episodic reports and beyond the usual survey data about how faculty spend their time. Such studies could yield useful three-dimensional pictures of how it is that some campuses may have succeeded while others may have failed in their efforts to reprioritize what counts in faculty academic work.

Faculty-Administration Cultural Clashes

Another Big Picture topic that affects academic life in profound ways is the perceived growing tension between two putative cultures on campus: managerial and academic. The former is said to be attuned more to achieving efficiencies and being responsive to pressures emanating from the political environment (e.g., accountability in demonstrating results); the latter clings more to traditional academic values and implicitly embraces certain inefficiencies as necessary for spawning good academic work. Managerial imperatives also give rise to engaging nontraditional academics or "proto-academics" to design and implement programs, including distance-education programs—a movement that is in tension with traditional faculty prerogatives. In any event, the perceived clash of cultures affects academic work in many ways. Once again, more nuanced explorations of what has happened on particular campuses attempting to balance these countervailing pressures would provide important insights about the changing priorities of academic work.

Governance

Almost no one is pleased with the way campuses are governed: not faculty, not administrators, not governing boards, not external observers (Schuster et al., 1994). The differences in satisfaction among the various institutional types are differences in the degree of unhappiness. Given the kinds of changes evident in faculty work in "the new era," including the functional respecialization and the influence on the curriculum (content and delivery) of instructional technology specialists, it is important to ascertain what the effects are on how campuses are governed. Who is making the decisions? Are faculty curriculum committees continuing to do what they have (or haven't) done in the past? What is becoming of the traditional tripartite division of faculty work among teaching, research, and service? To what extent, if any, is the "managerial culture" driving faculty to the periphery of campus governance? Is "shared governance," whatever its historical flaws, receding further from reality? Too little is known about either the extent of meaningful faculty participation in governance or faculty attitudes about their own involvement. These are significant matters that shape the distribution of academic work—and they are ripe for further explication.

Issues of Organization and Process

Having identified a number of "substantive" areas that deserve much closer attention by investigators into the well-being of the academy, we turn now to several important topics, sometimes rather technical, that can help or hinder effective research.

Models of Good Practice

Research should be encouraged that identifies "models of good practice" and that yields policy recommendations. Some research on faculty work stops short of translating findings into direct implications for campus policymaking, yet such efforts would be particularly valuable for practitioners. Research about faculty work that fails to connect to policy and its implementation is of dubious value. Among the innumerable topics that could illustrate this point is that of whether adequate support is made available to faculty for using instructional technology. Faculty members complain almost universally that they fail to get adequate assistance. Yet there surely are models of good practice that, if identified and more widely shared, could make a very positive difference. A good example of this approach is provided by the Institute for Effective Educational Practices of the National Study of Student Engagement (NSSE). Under programmatic banners including Project DEEP (Documenting Effective Educational Practices) and, more recently, Project BEAMS (Building Engagement and Attainment of Minority Students), NSSE, in collaboration with the American Association for Higher Education and the Lumina Foundation, has sought to document educational practices associated with higher student retention and graduation rates and to disseminate them throughout the higher education community. Another example of disseminating models of good practice would be to identify institutional structures and processes for monitoring the relationship among academic staffing patterns, student course evaluations, and academic achievement, and then to build an institutional capacity to translate these findings into academic staffing policies (see Honan and Trower, 2002).

Stimulating Coordination

There are several areas in which heightened attention and coordination within the research community are urgently needed. The importance of such collaborative efforts transcends the topic of faculty work and is crucially important in at least three related quests: to seek agreement on the definition of basic terms; to strive for coordination—little appears now to exist—among the major surveyors of the faculty; and to develop a classification scheme for institutions that will enable continuities in particular lines of research.

Definitions of Terms. The semantic swampland of definitions of terms basic to research on faculty and their work creates obvious obstacles to effective research. This is not the place to lay out the argument in detail; however, the absence of some basic standardized terminology limits the comparability of research findings. (This problem especially plagues efforts to compare faculty characteristics [demographics, for instance] and faculty activity across national boundaries.) There are innumerable examples, starting with the most basic: just who is a faculty member? To what extent should having faculty *status* determine who is "counted"—and therefore who is to be surveyed and tabulated—as faculty members? (Faculty status is often conferred, for instance, pursuant to collective bargaining agreements for persons who neither teach nor engage in academic research.) There are many variations on this theme, but some understanding among major research entities, particularly among faculty survey providers, would enable more meaningful trend-line analyses. Another example—one that is so specific as to be easily (but wrongly) dismissed—is illustrative of the "little things" that hinder research: could not the research community agree that age intervals for faculty be delineated in a consistent way (e.g., 35–39, 40–44, 45–49 instead of sometimes 36–40, 41–45, 46–50)? With major surveyors using different age intervals, trend analyses (involving not just age itself but many cross-tabulations of age with other variables) are hampered, at least at the edges.

Collaboration among Surveyors. Little collaboration exists among the principal entities that conduct periodic national faculty surveys, for example among the U.S. Department of Education's National Center for Education Statistics, the National Science Foundation, the Carnegie Foundation for the Advancement of Teaching, the UCLA Higher Education Research Institute, the American Association of University Professors, the National Education Association, and the Teachers Insurance and Annuity Association–College Retirement Equity Fund. Coordination issues related to faculty work (indeed, much more far-reaching than just faculty work) commonly arise. For instance, seeking greater consistency in the wording of questionnaire items would be a significant plus. Still further, some coordination among major survey providers regarding just *when* they conduct their surveys—in order to make possible more evenly spaced intervals among the surveys—would be very useful, too. There is a need and opportunity to establish meaningful coordination at no significant impairment to the goals of the major surveying organizations.

Two additional points should be noted here. First, the proposed coordination among major surveyors would not limit in any significant way their latitude in pursuing their respective research agendas and, in fact, would enhance their respective investigations because findings in the aggregate would be more meaningful. Second, it is important that a convener step forward to initiate a process that presumably would span both the task of moving toward common definitions and facilitating coordination among the principal surveyors. Any of several foundations or, perhaps, the TIAA-CREF Institute and/or the Carnegie Foundation for the Advancement of Teaching, could well serve as such a convener. The kind of coordination herein envisioned would serve well researchers and policymakers everywhere.

Classifying Institutions for Research Purposes and Differentiation by Institutional Type. The kinds of changes that are reshaping faculty work, as outlined above, appear to be affecting types of institutions differently, as would be expected. Nevertheless, it is worth emphasizing here that any analyses of faculty work must be broken out by institutional type. The point is that the Carnegie Foundation for the Advancement of Teaching's departure, in 2000, from their typology for classifying institutions that had existed since 1976 (with some adjustments) could seriously complicate trend analyses. This challenge is destined to intensify significantly as CFAT proceeds with its plan to radically redo the classifications for 2005, unless certain precautions are taken (McCormack, 2004). Specifically, it is important that Carnegie preserve the opportunity for researchers to use, among other options, the classifications that have been employed over the past several decades. Accordingly, it would seem very desirable for the research community to advise CFAT about what classification-related issues have been, and will be, important for research purposes. This is an issue that extends well beyond just faculty work. But at the same time, understanding changes over time in the nature of academic life—and how faculty work varies from one type of institution to another—can be undermined if the classification scheme that has prevailed generally for nearly three decades cannot readily be recaptured by the research community.

In each of the areas just discussed, the efforts required to achieve important enhancements in research results are modest. The potential payoff for more effective research, though, is considerable.

In sum, research is increasingly needed that, as suggested earlier, will seek to address the larger, more complex aspects of how faculty work is changing, why it is changing, and with what consequences. Such explorations are not going to be tidy and likely will raise as many questions as they answer. But it will be better to grapple with such complexities even in an inevitably inconclusive way than to seek to definitively answer relatively less important questions. The American academy is undergoing rapid and far-reaching changes, and the shifting nature of faculty work and careers is centrally important to what is emerging. Our hope is that the research community will strive harder to understand and interpret this larger picture. We hope, too, that the policy and practice community will raise such questions and will use research results to develop staffing and other strategies that appropriately balance faculty and other institutional interests.

In 1968 two respected sociologists and commenters on higher education, Christopher Jencks and David Riesman, wrote a book with the provocative title *The Academic Revolution.* In it they described the ways by which the faculty had captured control of the reins of the academy, asserting their authority over the academic core of the enterprise. Their choice of "Revolution" in the title was timely, although it did not refer to the turbulence on campuses that was widespread in the late sixties. Nor did their chronicle of the faculty's rise to power constitute a "revolution" at all; rather, it depicted a more gradual *evolution,* spread over nearly one hundred years beginning with the emergence of a research university model on American soil.

Thus, in our view, there had been no revolution. And for that matter, Riesman himself recanted some years later what he conceded to have been a premature declaration of victory of the faculty in their age-old struggle to achieve primacy over academic matters: what should be taught and how, who should be hired, and so forth (Riesman, 1981, p. xx).

By way of contrast, we have argued throughout this volume that the current, volatile condition of higher education reflects a profound transformation of higher education and its faculty—and that these changes are occurring with unprecedented velocity. The changes now under way, we submit, amount to a pervasive restructuring of academic appointments, academic work, and academic careers. Taken together, these reconfigurations are indeed revolutionary; they amount to nothing less than a new order for the academic profession. The vectors reshaping higher education and the faculty press relentlessly: a globalized, knowledge-based economy (with millions of "conventional" manufacturing jobs in the United States being exported to the developing world); ascendant privatization and marketization forces that now permeate higher education as never before; and stunning new modalities for information technology that constantly reinvent the means of teaching and learning.

Historically, the faculty has functioned in large measure as a single indivisible corporate entity with membership roles traditionally defined by a predominantly unitary structure. At institutions such as the University of Pennsylvania, those roles and prerogatives were established by charter and bylaws (Cowley, 1980). Thus, it was not so long ago that one could speak of *the* faculty, not just as a romanticized image, but as a reflection of how the faculty as an organizational entity was regarded. This is not to suggest that there were not always some differences in status. But the centrifugal pressures on academic life, often market-driven, that increasingly differentiate among faculty, render the concept of *the faculty* more and more hollow. Will the corporate faculty simply wither away, to be displaced by a more variegated, more specialized, less cohesive academic body? Will faculty roles and functions be ever more unevenly distributed over different subgroups? The direction and effectiveness of the academic profession will be determined in the coming years in considerable measure by how much remains of *the faculty.*

NOTE

1. This portion of the chapter, on challenges for research, is a revised version of a paper for which Schuster was commissioned by the National Center for Postsecondary Improvement, Stanford University. He presented the paper at a meeting on December 10, 2001. We appreciate NCPI's permission to reuse the paper in modified form.

List of Appendixes

The National Faculty Surveys

OVERVIEW, BY JESUS FRANCISCO GALAZ-FONTES

With the expansion of U.S. higher education in the twentieth century, there was a concomitant growth and development of the faculty, an element critical to higher education quality (Bowen and Schuster, 1986). The need to better understand the faculty was explicitly recognized by 1942 when Logan Wilson published *The Academic Man* in an effort to systematize what was known of these professionals responsible for teaching, research, and service in higher education. By the end of the next decade, Lazarsfeld and Thielens had reported their study (1958) on social scientists in four-year accredited institutions, and Caplow and McGee (1958) had inaugurated the analysis of "the academic marketplace" by describing the way in which academic positions were made available and filled in liberal arts divisions of nine major universities. Berelson (1960), as part of a Carnegie study on graduate education carried out in 1959, explored several aspects of faculty working in graduate departments. Then in 1965 the American academic profession was more closely scrutinized by Parsons and Platt (1968); however, only high-prestige institutions were considered by these authors.*

Although highly relevant in establishing a research agenda in relation to faculty, these studies had three serious limitations when considered as sole resources in delineating a profile of U.S. faculty. In the first place, all of them dealt with faculty working in four-year institutions, usually of good reputation and commonly known as *research universities* (CFAT, 1994). Research universities are a vital component of the U.S. higher education system, of course, but they no longer can be regarded as the typical higher education institution, especially after the 1960s (Clark, 1987). Second, disciplines and program levels were carefully selected, and so none of the studies mentioned can claim to be truly representative in relation to discipline or program level. Finally, these studies focus on full-time faculty, who, though central to higher education, are not the only ones who must be taken into account, especially now that the proportion of part-time faculty has increased significantly (Schuster, 1998).

It was in 1969, through the joint effort of the Carnegie Commission on Higher Ed-

---

*Appendix A is adapted from a qualifying examination paper prepared by Jesus Francisco Galaz-Fontes and presented to Dr. David E. Drew, Claremont Graduate University, 1997.

ucation and the American Council on Education, that the first national faculty survey was carried out. In what became a standard procedure in later surveys, a two-step sampling technique was used to assure the representativeness of the sample. In the first step of this particular survey, 310 higher education institutions were selected from a universe of 2,615 that were stratified into seven strata for sampling purposes. In the second step, a sample of 100,290 faculty was drawn from the institutions selected. Out of this faculty sample, 60,028 survey instruments were returned (Trow and associates, 1975). This massive study set the standard for subsequent national faculty surveys in two respects: it contemplated all types of higher education institutions, and, because faculty were drawn at random from each institution selected, all disciplines had the potential to be included in the final sample. So two limitations of earlier surveys were thus overcome. The inclusion of the part-time faculty is much more recent; not until the 1988 National Survey of Postsecondary Faculty was an explicit effort made to ensure that this faculty sector was adequately represented (Selfa et. al., 1997).

Because this book relies on the data generated by an important set of faculty surveys, we supply in this appendix basic information regarding the most visible of them implemented since 1955. In addition to the reports generated by the Carnegie Foundation for the Advancement of Teaching and by the National Center for Education Statistics, the works of Drew and Tronvig (1988) and of Blackburn and Mackie (1992) served as a departure point for our search of material. With their help we were able to locate twenty-eight potentially useful faculty studies, which are listed below.*

Following the list, more detailed information on each survey is presented. We have tried to provide the reader with a general sense of the main characteristics of each survey, including identification information, content, and details regarding the sampling and response rates attained (see Creswell, Chronister, and Brown, 1991, for a similar structure in summarizing faculty surveys). The variation in the categories of information provided for different surveys reflects the extent to which our sources made the relevant facts available. Also, in several surveys the reported numbers for some aspects (e.g., number of returned questionnaires and response rates) vary even within the same source. In such cases the figures reported are those that the principal investigators presented in a more consistent manner as the appropriate index. In addition, for every survey we have listed the references used in building its summary, as well as other works based on the data generated by it. Although considerable effort has gone into the identification of these references, our search cannot be said to be exhaustive; it must be considered as a starting point for further bibliographic searches.

---

*There are other sources of information on faculty in higher education institutions. However, these efforts are usually limited to a basic quantitative description of the faculty universe or subpopulations of it, and to faculty employment characterization. For example, each year the Department of Education publishes the latest data regarding the number of faculty working in higher education (e.g., NCES, 1996). Another kind of information source is represented by the National Science Foundation's surveys dealing specifically with scientists and engineers that include those working in higher education (e.g., Wilkinson, 1994).

We hope that the information compiled here on faculty surveys carried out during the last four decades will serve other scholars by saving time and effort and sparking some new insights for further research.

NATIONAL SURVEYS OF FACULTY IN
U.S. HIGHER EDUCATION INSTITUTIONS

— LT-55: 1955 Lazarsfeld and Thielens Study of Social Scientists
— SGEUS-59: 1959 Study of Graduate Education in the United States
— SCOCF-63: Status and Career Orientations of College Faculty, Spring 1963
— PP-65: 1965 Parsons and Platt Study of the American Academic Profession
— Carn-69: 1969 Carnegie Commission National Survey of Faculty and Student Opinion
— SPAG-71: 1971 Stanford Project on Academic Governance
— ACE-72: Teaching Faculty in Academe, 1972–73
— LL-72: 1972 Ladd-Lipset Survey on Academics, Politics, and the 1972 Election
— CFAT-75: 1975 Carnegie Council National Surveys of Higher Education
— LL-75: 1975 Ladd-Lipset Survey of the American Professoriate
— LL-77: 1977 Ladd-Lipset Survey of the American Professoriate
— HERI-80: 1980 HERI Faculty Survey
— NSSA-82: 1982 Sources of Stress in Academe: A National Perspective
— CFAT-84: 1984 National Survey of Faculty
— CIC-86: The Future of the Academic Workplace in Liberal Arts Colleges: Survey of the Academic Workplace (1986)
— NCRIPTAL-88: 1988–1989 Study of Faculty at Work: A Survey of Motivations, Expectations, Satisfactions
— NSOPF-88: 1988 National Survey of Postsecondary Faculty
— CFAT-89: 1989 National Survey of Faculty
— HERI-90: 1989–90 HERI Faculty Survey
— CFAT-93: The International Survey of the Academic Profession, 1991–93
— HERI-93: 1992–93 HERI Faculty Survey
— NSOPF-93: 1993 National Study of Postsecondary Faculty
— HERI-96: 1995–96 HERI Faculty Survey
— CFAT-97: The National Survey of Faculty 1996–1997
— HERI-99: 1998–99 HERI Faculty Survey
— NSOPF-99: 1999 National Study of Postsecondary Faculty
— TIAA-CREF-99: The American Faculty Poll (1999)
— HERI-02: 2001–02 HERI Faculty Survey
— NSOPF-04: 2004 National Study of Postsecondary Faculty

DETAILED DESCRIPTIONS OF THE SURVEYS

LT-55: 1955 Lazarsfeld and Thielens Study of Social Scientists

Sponsor	Fund for the Republic
Principal investigators	Paul F. Lazarsfeld, and Wagner Thielens Jr.
Contents of survey	Faculty productivity, pressures on the college administration, worry, caution, apprehension, concern for civil liberties, faculty intimidation, permissiveness, and occupational self-esteem
Institutional population	904 (all accredited four-year institutions)
Institutional sample size	182
Institutions represented	165
Faculty population	14,000 (faculty of undergraduate social sciences courses in four-year accredited institutions; faculty teaching exclusively at professional schools were not considered)
Faculty sample size	2,451
Interviews completed	2,059
Response rate reported	90%
Reference	Lazarsfeld and Thielens, 1958

SGEUS-59: 1959 Study of Graduate Education in the United States

Sponsor	Carnegie Corporation of New York
Principal investigator	Bernard Berelson
Contents of survey	Background data, conception and evaluation of graduate work, and criticism and reforms
Institutional population	92 (all institutions in the Association of Graduate Schools and all other institutions awarding at least 10 doctorates a year)
Institutional sample size	92
Institutions represented	92
Faculty sample size	4,440
Returned questionnaires	2,176
Usable questionnaires	1,821
Response rate reported	41%
Reference	Berelson, 1960

SCOCF-63: Status and Career Orientation of College Faculty, Spring 1963

Sponsors	U.S. Office of Education and National Science Foundation
Principal investigators	Ralph E. Dunham, Patricia S. Wright, and Marjorie O. Chandler
Contents of survey	Earnings, personal background, position, assignment, workload, education, previous employment experience, summer activities, and occupational plans
Institutional population	1,174 (universities, liberal arts colleges, independently organized teachers colleges, and technological institutions)
Institutional sample size	360
Institutions represented	360
Faculty population	138,203 (only full-time faculty)
Faculty sample size	15,494
Returned questionnaires	14,711
Usable questionnaires	13,017

(continued)

SCOCF-63: Status and Career Orientation of College Faculty, Spring 1963
(continued)

Response rate reported	95%
Reference	Dunham, Wright, and Chandler, 1963

PP-65: 1965 Parsons and Platt Study of the American Academic Profession

Sponsor	National Science Foundation
Principal investigators	Talcott Parsons and Gerald M. Platt
Contents of survey	Background and other characteristics, academic role, and decision making
Institutions represented	8 (institutions were chosen from the top of the prestige spectrum)
Faculty sample size	639 (only arts and sciences full-time faculty from physics, biology, economics, sociology, history, and English departments)
Returned questionnaires	420
Response rate reported	66%
Reference	Parsons and Platt, 1968

Carn-69: 1969 Carnegie Commission National Survey of Faculty and Student Opinion

Sponsors	Carnegie Commission on Higher Education and American Council on Education
Principal investigators	Martin Trow and Seymour M. Lipset
Contents of survey	Background information, political and social issues, political and academic issues, campus political issues, unionization, campus governance, campus educational issues, and satisfaction with institution
Institutional population	2,615
Institutional sample size	310
Institutions represented	303
Faculty population	446,296
Faculty sample size	100,290
Returned questionnaires	60,028 (full-time faculty: 80%)
Response rate reported	60%
References	Bayer, 1970; Fulton, 1975; Fulton and Trow, 1975a, 1975b; Ladd and Lipset, 1975a; Roizen, Fulton, and Trow, 1978; Steinberg, 1975; Trow and associates, 1975

SPAG-71: 1971 Stanford Project on Academic Governance

Sponsor	National Institute of Education
Principal investigator	J. Victor Baldridge
Contents of survey	Organizational characteristics of colleges and universities, diversity in the academic system, patterns of management and governance, bureaucracy and autonomy in academic work, institutional climates and faculty morale, impact of bargaining on campus management, and women faculty in higher education
Institutional sample size	249

(continued)

SPAG-71: 1971 Stanford Project on Academic Governance (continued)

Institutions represented	249
Faculty sample size	17,296
Usable questionnaires	9,237
Response rate reported	53 %
References	Baldridge, 1971; Baldridge et al., 1978

ACE-72: Teaching Faculty in Academe, 1972–73

Sponsor	American Council on Education
Principal investigator	Alan E. Bayer
Contents of survey	Demographic background, educational background, work history, current position, and faculty opinions and attitudes
Institutional population	2,433
Institutional sample size	301
Institutions represented	301
Faculty population	518,849
Faculty sample size	108,722
Returned questionnaires	53,034
Usable questionnaires	42,345 (full-time faculty: 95%)
Response rate reported	49%
Reference	Bayer, 1973

LL-72: 1972 Ladd-Lipset Survey on Academics, Politics, and the 1972 Election

Sponsor	American Enterprise Institute for Public Policy Research
Principal investigators	Everett Carl Ladd Jr. and Seymour Martin Lipset
Contents of survey	Personal characteristics (age, religious background, academic discipline, publications, etc.), voting intention and behavior, and political self-description and opinions
Institutional population	All four-year colleges and universities included in Carn-69
Faculty population	All full-time faculty at the four-year colleges and universities considered in Carn-69
Faculty sample size	523
Interviews completed	472
Usable questionnaires	472
Response rate reported	90%
References	Ladd and Lipset, 1973, 1975a

CFAT-75: 1975 Carnegie Council National Surveys of Higher Education

Sponsor	Carnegie Foundation for the Advancement of Teaching (Carnegie Council for Policy Studies in Higher Education)
Principal investigators	Martin Trow, Oliver Fulton, and Judy Roizen
Contents of survey	Background; status; behavior; attitudes; collective bargaining; affirmative action; academic governance; academic reform; student financial support; career plans; relationships between students, faculty, and institutions; and funding of university-based research
Institutional population	2,883
Institutional sample size	514
Institutions represented	340
Faculty population	475,723

(continued)

CFAT-75: 1975 Carnegie Council National Surveys of Higher Education
(continued)

Faculty sample size	47,753
Returned questionnaires	25,445
Usable questionnaires	25,262 (full-time faculty: 93%)
Response rate reported	53%
References	CFAT, 1989; Roizen, Fulton, and Trow, 1978; Stadtman, 1980

LL-75: 1975 Ladd-Lipset Survey of the American Professoriate

Sponsors	National Institute of Education, the Spencer Foundation, and the Earhart Foundation
Principal investigators	Everett Carl Ladd Jr. and Seymour Martin Lipset
Contents of survey	Personal description (background, career experiences, attainments, and aspirations), professional norms, and ideology and opinion on issues confronting higher education and on major social and political issues that the United States faces
Institutional sample size	111
Faculty population	366,326
Faculty sample size	7,800
Returned questionnaires	3,500
Response rate reported	51%
References	Ladd and Lipset, 1975a, 1975b; Lipset and Ladd, 1979.

1975 articles by E. C. Ladd and S. M. Lipset, all in *Chronicle of Higher Education,* vol. 11:

"What Professors Think." No. 1: 2, 9.
"Professors' Religious and Ethnic Backgrounds." No. 2: 2.
"Faculty Women: Little Gain in Status." No. 3: 2.
"Faculty Income Favorably Compared." No. 4: 2.
"How Professors Spend Their Time." No. 5: 2.
"Academics: America's Most Politically Liberal Stratum." No. 6: 1–2.
"The Academy: Politically Split." No. 7: 2.
"Professors, Politics, and Academe's 'Internal Logic.'" No. 8: 2.
"Faculty Opinion on Watergate." No. 9: 2.
"War's Dramatic Impact on Faculty Behavior." No. 10: 14.
"World Role Losing Faculty Support." No. 11. 10.
"War-Shy Professors Divided over Middle East." No. 12: 10.
"Republicans Are Few and Far Between on U.S. College Faculties." No. 13: 15.
"Faculty Democrats Disagree with Party's Rank and File." No. 14: 11.
"How Do Faculty Members Take Their Responsibilities as Citizens?" No. 15: 13.

1976 articles by E. C. Ladd and S. M. Lipset, all in Chronicle of Higher Education:

"Which Groups Are Most Influential in Public Affairs?" 11, no. 16: 14.
"The General Periodicals Professors Read." 11, no. 17: 14.
"The Growth of Faculty Unions." 11, no. 18: 11.
"Faculty Unions Find Greatest Support on Most Conservative Campuses." 11, no. 19: 14.
"How Faculty Unions Rate with Professors." 11, no. 20: 12.

(continued)

LL-75: 1975 Ladd-Lipset Survey of the American Professoriate (continued)

"Militancy of Unionized Faculty Members Is Related to the Unions They Belong To." 11, no. 21: 13.

"Faculty Members Note Both Positive and Negative Aspects of Campus Unions." 11, no. 22: 11.

"How Faculty Members Feel about Equality." 12, no. 1: 12.

"Egalitarianism on the Campus." 12, no. 2: 13.

"Should Any Research Topics Be Off-Limits?" 12, no. 3: 11.

"Students in Campus Decision-Making." 12, no. 4: 12.

"What Do Professors Like Best about Their Jobs? Surprise: It Isn't Research." 12, no. 5: 10.

"98 to 2, That Professor in a Saab Is a Liberal." 12, no. 6: 18.

"When Colleges Retrench, Where Should Cutbacks Come?" 12, no. 7: 7.

"Only 12 per cent of U.S. Faculty Members Think 'Intellectual' Describes Them Best." 12, no. 8: 14.

"Professors Found Far More Receptive to Change in Academe." 12, no. 9: 12.

"Nearly All Professors Are Satisfied with Their Choice of an Academic Career:." 12, no. 10: 11.

"Sex Differences in Academe." 12, no. 11: 18.

"Professors and Society Strata." 12, no. 12: 11.

"The Aging Professoriate." 12, no. 13: 16.

"U.S. Professors." 12, no. 14: 1, 12.

LL-77: 1977 Ladd-Lipset Survey of the American Professoriate

Principal investigators	Everett Carl Ladd Jr. and Seymour Martin Lipset
Contents of survey	Background, opinions, and attitudes on a diversity of higher education (income, student activism, research support, retirement, etc.) and political issues (faculty unionism, voting behavior, etc.)
Institutional population	2,406
Institutions represented	161
Faculty sample size	8,697
Returned questionnaires	4,607
Usable questionnaires	4,607 (full-time faculty: 100%)
Response rate reported	53%
References:	Ladd and Lipset, 1977, 1981.

1977 articles by E. C. Ladd and S. M. Lipset, all in *Chronicle of Higher Education,* vol. 15:

"The Faculty Mood: Pessimism Is Predominant: Professors Are Troubled about Their Students, Their Colleges, Their Paychecks." No. 5: 1, 14.

"How Professors Rate Their Departments' Facilities and Resources." No. 6: 2.

"How Professors View Today's Students." No. 7: 2.

"Professors' Attitudes toward State Aid to Private Colleges. "No. 8: 2.

"Professors' Views on Federal Support for Research." No. 9: 2.

(continued)

LL-77: 1977 Ladd-Lipset Survey of the American Professoriate (continued)

"Many Professors Would Postpone Retirement If Law Were Changed." No. 10: 7–8.

"Does U.S. Provide Enough Support for Basic Research?" No. 11: 2.

"Professors' Output of Books and Monographs." No. 12: 12.

"The Scholarly Articles Published by Professors." No. 13: 2.

"Professors Give 'Fairly High Marks' to U.S. Agencies." No. 15: 11.

1978 articles by Ladd and Lipset, all in *Chronicle of Higher Education:*

"Professors Found to Be Liberal but Not Radical." 15, no. 18: 9.

"Faculty Support for Unionization: Leveling Off at about 75 per cent." 15, no. 22: 8.

"The Big Differences among Faculty Unions." 16, no. 3: 14.

"Professors' Interests in Research, Teaching." 16, no. 5: 2.

"Faculty Members Who Travel Abroad." 16, no. 9: 8.

HERI-80: 1980 HERI Faculty Survey

Sponsor	Higher Education Research Institute, UCLA
Principal investigator	Alexander W. Astin
Institutional population	The sampling frame used was that of the Carn-69 (2,615) and ACE-72 (2,433) surveys
Institutional sample size	96
Institutions represented	96
Faculty sample size	31,302
Usable questionnaires	9,948
Response rate reported	32%
References	Astin, 1980; Bentley, Blackburn, and Bieber, 1990; Drew and Tronvig, 1988

NSSA-82: 1982 Sources of Stress in Academe: A National Perspective

Principal investigators	Walter H. Gmelch, Nicholas P. Lovrich, and Phyllis Kay Wilke
Contents of survey	Background information and sources of faculty stress (teaching, research, service, etc.)
Institutional population	184 doctorate-granting institutions
Institutional sample size	80 (40 public and 40 private)
Institutions represented	80 (40 public and 40 private)
Faculty population	Full-time faculty at all doctorate-granting institutions
Faculty sample size	1,920
Returned questionnaires	1,221 (full-time faculty: 100%)
Usable questionnaires	1,221
Response rate reported	67%
Reference	Gmelch, Lovrich, and Wilke, 1984

(*continued*)

CFAT-84: 1984 National Survey of Faculty

Sponsor	Carnegie Foundation for the Advancement of Teaching
Principal investigator	Opinion Research Corporation
Contents of survey	Background information and a diversity of opinions and attitudes, including job satisfaction
Institutional population	2,559
Institutional sample size	310
Institutions represented	190
Faculty sample size	9,968
Returned questionnaires	5,248
Usable questionnaires	5,057 (full-time faculty: 92%)
Response rate reported	51%
References	Clark, 1987; Opinion Research Corporation, 1984

CIC-86: The Future of the Academic Workplace in Liberal Arts Colleges: Survey of the Academic Workplace (1986)

Sponsor	Council of Independent Colleges
Principal investigators	R. Eugene Rice and Ann E. Austin
Contents of survey	Career patterns and issues, participation in institutional decision-making, evaluating the performance of faculty, satisfaction, importance of work experience, the culture of the respondent's college, and demographic data
Institutional population	Small liberal arts colleges that were members of CIC
Institutional sample size	Small liberal arts colleges that were members of CIC
Institutions represented	142
Faculty population	Faculty mostly at small liberal arts colleges
Faculty sample size	9,204
Returned questionnaires	4,271 (full-time faculty: 98%)
Response rate reported	46%
References	Austin, Rice, and Splete, 1987, 1991; Austin, Rice, Splete, and associates, 1991a, 1991b; Rice and Austin, 1988

NCRIPTAL-88: 1988–1989 Faculty at Work: A Survey of Motivations, Expectations, Satisfactions

Sponsor	National Center for Research to Improve Postsecondary Teaching and Learning, U.S. Department of Education
Principal investigator	Robert T. Blackburn
Contents of survey	Background information, work environment, teaching, scholarly activities, university service, student learning, feedback, and use of time
Institutional sample size	250
Institutions represented	236
Faculty population	Full-time faculty from eight disciplines (English, history, psychology, sociology, political science, biology, chemistry, and mathematics)
Faculty sample size	8,000
Usable questionnaires	3,972
Response rate reported	50%
References	Blackburn and Lawrence, 1989, 1995

NSOPF-88: 1988 National Survey of Postsecondary Faculty

Sponsor	National Center for Education Statistics
Principal investigator	SRI International
Contents of survey	Employment, job satisfaction, academic-professional background, responsibilities and workload, benefits and professional development, compensation, sociodemographic characteristics, and academic interests and values
Institutional population	3,159
Institutional sample size	480
Institutions represented	424
Faculty population	664,753
Faculty sample size	11,071
Returned questionnaires	8,382
Usable questionnaires	7,408 (full-time faculty: 67%)
Response rate reported	76%
References	Cox, R. S., S. H. Russell, and C. Williamson. 1989. *1988 National Survey of Postsecondary Faculty. Descriptive Report: Survey of Institutions.* A report prepared for the National Center for Education Statistics. Menlo Park, CA: SRI International.
	Russell, S. H., R. S. Cox, J. M. Boismier, and J. T. Porter. 1990. "A Descriptive Report of Academic Departments in Higher Education Institutions." Contractor report to the National Center for Education Statistics, Washington, DC.
	Russell, S. H., R. S. Cox, J. Fairweather, C. Williamson, and J. Boismier. 1989. *1988 National Survey of Postsecondary Faculty: Descriptive Report: Survey of Faculty.* A report prepared for the National Center for Education Statistics, second draft. Menlo Park, CA: SRI International.
	Russell, S. H., R. S. Cox, C. Williamson, J. Boismier, H. Javitz, J. Fairweather, and L. J. Zimbler. 1990. "Faculty in Higher Education Institutions, 1988." Contractor report to the National Center for Education Statistics, Washington, DC.
	Russell, S. H., R. S. Cox, C. L. Williamson, and J. T. Porter. 1990. "Institutional Policies and Practices Regarding Faculty in Higher Education." Contractor report to the National Center for Education Statistics, Washington, DC.
	Russell, S. H., J. S. Fairweather, and R. M. Hendrickson. 1990. *Special Issue Reports from the 1988 National Survey of Postsecondary Faculty.* A report prepared for the National Center for Education Statistics. Menlo Park, CA: SRI International.
	Russell, S. H., J. S. Fairweather, R. M. Hendrickson, and L. J. Zimbler. 1991. "Profiles of Faculty in Higher Education Institutions." Contractor report to the National Center for Education Statistics, Washington, DC.

CFAT-89: 1989 National Survey of Faculty

Sponsor	Carnegie Foundation for the Advancement of Teaching
Principal investigator	Wirthlin Group
Contents of survey	Attitudes on goals of collegiate education; academic standards; student life, teaching, research, and service; status of the profession; views of the institution; participation in decision-making; and general observations

(*continued*)

CFAT-89: 1989 National Survey of Faculty (continued)

Institutional population	2,747
Institutional sample size	306
Institutions represented	306
Faculty sample size	9,996
Usable questionnaires	5,450 (full-time faculty: 92%)
Response rate reported	55%
References	CFAT, 1989; Wirthlin Group, 1989

HERI-90: 1989–90 HERI Faculty Survey

Sponsor	American Council on Education through the Cooperative Institutional Research Program, Higher Education Research Institute, UCLA
Principal investigator	Alexander W. Astin
Contents of survey	Background characteristics, professional goals, teaching, research, job satisfaction, stress, and perceptions of the institution
Institutional population	2,528
Institutional sample size	432
Institutions represented	392
Faculty population	401,431
Faculty sample size	93,479
Returned questionnaires	51,574
Usable questionnaires	35,478 (full-time faculty: 100%)
Response rate reported	55%
Reference	Astin, Korn, and Dey, 1991

CFAT-93: The International Survey of the Academic Profession, 1991–93

Sponsor	Carnegie Foundation for the Advancement of Teaching
Principal investigator	Philip G. Altbach
Contents of survey	Demographics; work activities; satisfaction with careers; students, classes, and teaching styles (instructional activity within and outside the classroom; teaching styles); the research cadre (activities and publications [articles, books authored, books edited, research reports and monographs]); perceived quality of training for professional roles; mobility; and internationalism (attitudes and activities)
Institutional population	2,022
Institutional sample size	40
Institutions represented	40
Faculty population	584,000
Faculty sample size	7,588
Returned questionnaires	3,528 (full-time faculty: 89%)
Response rate reported	47%
References	Altbach and Lewis, 1995, 1996; Boyer, Altbach, and Whitelaw, 1994; Haas, 1996; Lewis and Altbach, 1996

(continued)

HERI-93: 1992–93 HERI Faculty Survey

Sponsor	American Council on Education through the Cooperative Institutional Research Program, Higher Education Research Institute, UCLA
Principal investigator	Alexander W. Astin
Contents of survey	Background characteristics, professional and personal goals, teaching and research environment, teaching goals and practices, job satisfaction and stress, and perception of the institution
Institutional population	2,582
Institutional sample size	344
Institutions represented	289
Faculty population	416,911
Faculty sample size	72,417
Returned questionnaires	43,940
Usable questionnaires	29,771 (full-time faculty: 100%)
Response rate reported	61%
Reference	Dey et al., 1993

NSOPF-93: 1993 National Study of Postsecondary Faculty

Sponsor	National Center for Education Statistics
Principal investigator	National Opinion Research Center, University of Chicago
Contents of survey	Nature of employment, academic/professional background, institutional responsibilities and workload, job satisfaction issues, compensation, sociodemographic characteristics
Institutional population	3,256
Institutional sample size	974
Institutions represented	817
Faculty population	885,796 (fall 1992)
Faculty sample size	31,354 (1,590 were ineligible)
Returned questionnaires	25,780 (full-time faculty: 67%)
Response rate reported	87%
References	Abraham, S. Y., N. A. Suter, B. D. Spencer, R. A. Johnson, D. A. Zahs, S. L. Myers, and L. J. Zimbler. 1994. *1993 National Study of Postsecondary Faculty (NSOPF-93): 1992–93 National Study of Postsecondary Faculty Field Test Report.* Washington, DC: National Center for Education Statistics. Conley, V. M., and L. J. Zimbler. 1997. *1993 National Study of Postsecondary Faculty (NSOPF-93): Characteristics and Attitudes of Instructional Faculty and Staff in the Humanities.* Washington, DC: National Center for Education Statistics. Kirshstein, R. J., N. Matheson, Z. Jing, and L. J. Zimbler. 1996. *1993 National Study of Postsecondary Faculty (NSOPF-93): Institutional Policies and Practices Regarding Faculty in Higher Education.* Washington, DC: National Center for Education Statistics. ———. 1997. *1993 National Study of Postsecondary Faculty (NSOPF-93): Instructional Faculty and Staff in Higher Education Institutions: Fall 1987 and Fall 1992.* Washington, DC: National Center for Education Statistics.

(continued)

NSOPF-93: 1993 National Study of Postsecondary Faculty (continued)

Selfa, L. A., N. Suter, S. Myers, S. Koch, R. A. Johnson, D. A. Zahs, B. D. Kuhr, S. Y. Abraham, and L. J. Zimbler. 1997a. *1993 National Study of Postsecondary Faculty (NSOPF-93): Data File User's Manual Public-Use Institution File and Restricted-Use Faculty File.* Washington, DC: National Center for Education Statistics.
———. 1997b. *1993 National Study of Postsecondary Faculty (NSOPF-93): Methodology Report.* Washington, DC: National Center for Education Statistics.
Zimbler, L. J. 1994. *1993 National Study of Postsecondary Faculty (NSOPF-93): Faculty and Instructional Staff: Who Are They and What Do They Do?* Washington, DC: National Center for Education Statistics.

HERI-96: 1995–96 HERI Faculty Survey

Sponsor	American Council on Education through the Cooperative Institutional Research Program, Higher Education Research Institute, UCLA
Principal investigator	Alexander W. Astin
Contents of survey	Background characteristics and salary, professional goals, teaching goals and practices, personal goals, stress, and diversity issues
Institutional population	2,551
Institutional sample size	403
Institutions represented	384
Faculty population	418, 213
Faculty sample size	143,816
Returned questionnaires	59,933
Usable questionnaires	33,986 (full-time faculty: 100%)
Response rate reported	42%
References	Astin et al., 1997; Sax et al., 1996

CFAT-97: The National Survey of Faculty, 1996–1997

Sponsor	Carnegie Foundation for the Advancement of Teaching
Principal investigator	Wirthlin Worldwide
Contents of survey	Personal information, working conditions, professional activities, governance, higher education goals, campus community, and higher education and society
Institutional population	2,873
Institutional sample size	306
Faculty population	794,960
Faculty sample size	9,991
Returned questionnaires	5,194
Usable questionnaires	5,151 (full-time faculty: 87%)
Response rate reported	52%
References	Huber, 1997; Wirthlin Worldwide, 1997

HERI-99: 1998–99 HERI Faculty Survey

Sponsor	American Council on Education through the Cooperative Institutional Research Program, Higher Education Research Institute, UCLA
Principal investigator	Linda J. Sax
Contents of survey	Background characteristics; information technology; tenure attitudes; academic climate; community service, social activism, and gender equity; use of time; interaction with students; teaching and evaluation methods; and job satisfaction
Institutional population	2,618
Institutional sample size	429
Institutions represented	378
Faculty population	440,850
Faculty sample size	128,423
Returned questionnaires	55,081
Usable questionnaires	33,785 (full-time faculty: 100%)
Response rate reported	43%
Reference	Sax, Astin, Korn, and Gilmartin, 1999

NSOPF-99: 1999 National Study of Postsecondary Faculty

Sponsor	National Center for Education Statistics
Principal investigator	Gallup Organization
Contents of survey	Nature of employment, academic/professional background, institutional responsibilities and workload, job satisfaction issues, compensation, sociodemographic characteristics, and opinions
Institutional population	3,396
Institutional sample size	959
Institutions represented	819
Faculty population	1,073,667
Faculty sample size	19,213
Usable questionnaires	17,600 (full-time faculty: 57%)
Response rate reported	92%
References	Abraham et al., 2002; Glover, Parsad, and Zimbler, 2002; Parsad, Glover, and Zimbler, 2002; Warburton et al., 2002

TIAA-CREF-99: The American Faculty Poll (1999)

Sponsor	TIAA-CREF
Principal investigator	National Opinion Research Center, University of Chicago
Contents of survey	Satisfaction with work and career, interfering factors, opinions about institutional policies and priorities, and sociodemographic information
Institutional population	All accredited, nonproprietary U.S. postsecondary institutions that grant a two-year or higher degree, included in the latest IPEDS
Institutional sample size	294
Institutions represented	285
Faculty population	Full-time faculty teaching at the undergraduate level
Faculty sample size	4,116 individuals called to request an interview (2,290 turned out to be eligible)

(*continued*)

TIAA-CREF-99: The American Faculty Poll (1999) (continued)

Interviews completed	1,511
Usable interviews	1,511
Response rate reported	66%
References	Pena and Mitchell, 2000; Sanderson, Phua, and Herda, 2000

HERI-02: 2001–2002 HERI Faculty Survey

Sponsor	American Council on Education through the Cooperative Institutional Research Program, Higher Education Research Institute, UCLA
Principal investigator	Jennifer A. Lindholm
Contents of survey	Background characteristics, tenure attitudes, institutional climate, views about undergraduate education, use of time, interaction with students, teaching and evaluation methods, diversity issues, personal goals, and sources of stress and satisfaction
Institutional population	2,617
Institutional sample size	416
Institutions represented	358
Faculty population	442,449
Faculty sample size	134,905
Returned questionnaires	55,521
Usable questionnaires	32,840 (full-time faculty: 100%)
Response rate reported	41%
Reference	Lindholm et al., 2002

NSOPF-04: 2004 National Study of Postsecondary Faculty

Sponsor	National Center for Education Statistics
Principal investigators	RTI International and MPR Associates
Contents of survey	Nature of employment, academic/professional background, institutional responsibilities and workload, scholarly activities, job satisfaction, compensation, sociodemographic characteristics, and opinions
Institutional population	3,380
Institutional sample size	1,080
Institutions represented	980
Faculty population	1,211,800
Faculty sample size	35,629
Usable questionnaires	26,110 (full-time faculty: 56%)
Response rate reported	76%
Reference	Forrest Cataldi et al., 2005

Selected National Faculty Surveys

A Concordance of Contents

This concordance (table B.1) is offered to provide investigators with a roadmap for collecting information efficiently from the national faculty surveys. The rows are labeled with the key variables on which the various surveys have collected data over the years; the columns identify the ten major national surveys that have served as the bases for our analyses in this volume. For each variable we give the item number of the actual survey question(s) that produced the data in each particular survey. Each column, furthermore, amounts to a content map of the variables on which that survey offers data. We have taken the liberty of including a column for NSOPF-04, since the instrument, though not the results, was available prior to publication of this volume.

When used in tandem with Appendix H ("Note on Accessing the Survey Instruments"), the concordance guides the reader in identifying trends in the data across surveys. It does not, of course, purport to provide guidance in the interpretation of that data; that is the principal task of chapters 3–8 of this volume. The data presented in our many tables and figures are best understood—put into proper context, that is—when viewed alongside Appendixes A and C. The former ("The National Faculty Surveys") is intended to apprise the reader of the essential details about each survey upon which we draw (sampling, response rate, characterization of contents, and so on), as well as additional surveys. The latter ("Interpreting Faculty Surveys: Challenges and Strategies") is, in effect, an extended technical note on the opportunities and limitations for divining trends from often disparate surveys.

The rows of table B.1 are organized to correspond roughly with our chapter outline, albeit not in sequence. Thus, the concordance begins with basic demographic data (treated in chapter 3) and proceeds to current appointment status and conditions of employment (chapter 7), compensation (chapter 8), educational and career background (chapter 6), work role and effort (chapter 4), and attitudes and values (chapter 5).

The first survey selected for inclusion in the concordance was conducted in 1969—a somewhat arbitrary beginning point, to be sure, but the one that has undergirded the conception of this entire volume. We recognize, of course, that several important national surveys of faculty were conducted before 1969, most notably Lazarsfeld and Thielen's survey of social scientists (Lazarsfeld and Thielens, 1955) and Parsons and Platt's survey of academics at fifteen major universities (Parsons and Platt, 1968). These we view as "special purpose" inquiries: Lazarsfeld and Thielens were attempting to document the reactions of academic social scientists to Mc-Carthyism, and Parsons and Platt were testing their theory of institutional differentiation in American higher education. (See Appendix A for further descriptions of those two surveys.) For our purposes (as we explain in chapter 1 and elsewhere), the systematic initiative to portray the American faculty via survey research effectively began in 1969. Moreover, and even more relevant, the 1969 survey is the most robust faculty survey that could be found to serve as one bookend of the era we scrutinize—the end of the explosive growth of the 1950s and 1960s and the onset of more moderate growth, further institutional differentiation, and expanded faculty professionalization and specialization.

A further comment may be in order. This concordance does not purport to include all items or all surveys during the post-1969 era. And it is important to note that our organization of the variables and, indeed, our decisions on which items "belong" to which variable are to some degree arbitrary. Nevertheless, within these limitations, we hope the concordance will prove to be a useful tool for researchers in examining many key dimensions of the evolution of the American faculty during a period of remarkable development and change.

TABLE B.1
Concordance of Faculty Surveys

	1969 Carn-69	1972 ACE-72	1975 CFAT-75	1984 CFAT-84	1987 NSOPF-88	1988 NCRIPTAL-88	1992 NSOPF-93	1997 CFAT-97	1998 NSOPF-99	2004 NSOPF-04
Demographics & background										
Gender	88	28	71	73	41	8i	51	65	81	71
Race/ethnicity	89	27	70	72	43, 44	8s	53, 54	67	83, 84	73, 74
Country of birth	—	—	—	—	—	—	56	—	89	80
Citizenship	65	14	—	—	46	—	57	—	90	81
Age	87	13	69	69	42	8j	52	66	82	72
Disability status	—	—	—	—	—	—	—	—	85, 86	75
Parents' education and occupation	79, 80	26	59	58, 59	47	—	58	—	91	—
Spouse's education and occupation	79	26	59	58, 59	47	—	—	—	88, 91	—
Marital status	85	14	66	66	45	—	55	—	87	77
Number of dependents	—	—	—	—	—	—	50	—	80	—
Dependent children	86	14	67	67	—	—	—	—	—	79
Persons in household (number)	—	—	—	—	—	—	48	—	78	—
Religion										
Background	78	—	54	54	—	—	—	—	—	—
Identification, current	78	—	55	55	—	—	—	—	—	—
Involvement	74, 76, 77	25	56	22, 56	—	—	—	—	—	—
Appointment status & conditions of employment										
Employment status (full- or part-time)	—	2	61	61	4	—	4	9	5	5
Rank	1	3	1	1	12	8k	9	7	8	10
Visiting/adjunct	2	—	4	2	14	8m	11	—	12	—
Contract duration	—	—	—	—	11	8m	8	9	11	12
Tenure status	2	13	4	2	9	8m	7	9	10	12
Tenure, year of	—	13	69	71	10	—	7	—	10	13
Tenure-track status	—	14	5	3	9	8n	7	9	10	12
Tenure, at another institution	—	—	—	—	15	—	—	—	24	—
Sabbatical	—	—	—	—	3, 8	—	2	—	3	4

(continued)

TABLE B.1 (continued)

	1969 Carn-69	1972 ACE-72	1975 CFAT-75	1984 CFAT-84	1987 NSOPF-88	1988 NCRIPTAL-88	1992 NSOPF-93	1997 CFAT-97	1998 NSOPF-99	2004 NSOPF-04
Compensation										
Gross compensation	81, 82, 84	29	62, 64	62, 64	40	—	47	10, 11	76	66b
Benefits	—	—	—	—	38	—	—	—	61	62c
Household income, total	—	29	62, 64, 65	62, 64, 65	—	—	49	—	79	70a, 70b
Concurrent employment										
Yes/no	—	—	—	7	5	—	17	41, 42	21	—
Number of outside jobs	—	—	—	—	6	—	17	—	22	—
Sector of main other job	—	—	—	—	6	—	18	—	28	—
Year other main job begun	—	—	—	—	—	—	18	—	28	—
Primary responsibility at other job	—	—	—	7	6	—	18	—	28	—
Full- or part-time status of other job	—	—	—	7	6	—	18	—	28	19a
Consulting activities	55	14, 15	21	7, 17	6	—	18	43	20	—
Preparation & careers										
Degrees										
Highest degree earned	32	9	25	21	26	8a	16	4	16	17a1
Institution of highest degree	34	10	72	74	26	8a	16	—	16	17a4
Age (or year) at award of highest degree	30	13	69	70	26	8a	16	—	16	17a2
Other degrees held	32	9	25	21	26	—	16	—	16	17a1b
Years of receipt	—	13	69	—	26	—	16	—	16	17a2
Fields	33	12	30	23	26	—	16	5	16	17a3
Institutions	32, 34	9	72	74	26	—	16	—	16	—
Years between bachelor's and highest degree	31	13	—	—	26	—	16	—	16	17d
Undergraduate honors	—	—	—	—	27	—	14	—	—	—
Graduate school support	68	14	—	—	28	—	15	—	—	—
Employment history, previous										
Previous employment										
Year (age) at first full-time teaching position	—	—	—	—	29	—	19	—	24	23

Total no. previous full-time faculty positions	36	—	—	—	29	—	8h	—	24	—
Years employed in higher education	35	—	57	57	29	57	—	19	25	28
Sector	—	—	57	57	29	57	—	19	24, 28	28
Primary responsibility	41	24	57	57	29	57	—	19	24, 28	24
Full- or part-time	—	—	57	57	29	57	—	19	24, 28	24
Retired from other job? yes/no	—	—	—	—	—	—	—	—	72	64
Employment history, current										
Age (year) at appointment to current position	—	13	—	—	13	—	8l	10	9	—
Beginning year of faculty job	35	13	—	57	29	—	8e	6	7	9
Years job held	35	—	57	57	29	57	—	19	7	9
Work role & effort										
Workload distribution										
% hours (actual) in teaching, research, admin.	45	—	15	—	37	—	13a	37	31	32
% hours (preferred) in teaching, research, admin.	—	—	—	—	—	—	13b	37	31	—
Total no. hours spent in all work activities	3	4	8	6	36	8	13c	36	30	31
Hours in paid and unpaid activities	45	—	15	—	36	15	—	36	30	31
Teaching										
Principal field	33	12	30	23	16	30	8b	12	14	16
Classes/sections taught (no.)	—	6	—	—	—	—	—	22	33	35
Classes taught for credit (no.)	—	6	—	23	—	—	—	22	40	35
Academic disciplines of classes taught	3	12	30	23	32	30	—	23	41	—
Hours per week of classes taught	3, 6, 7	4	8	—	32	8	—	23	41	37
Hours/TAs/no. of students in classes taught	3	—	—	—	32	—	—	23	41	37
Primary level of students in classes taught	4	7	7	5	32	7	—	23	41	37
Undergraduate courses for credit? (yes/no)	—	7	—	—	32	—	—	23	41	37

(continued)

TABLE B.1 *(continued)*

	1969 Carn-69	1972 ACE-72	1975 CFAT-75	1984 CFAT-84	1987 NSOPF-88	1988 NCRIPTAL-88	1992 NSOPF-93	1997 CFAT-97	1998 NSOPF-99	2004 NSOPF-04
Primary instructional methods	—	—	—	—	32	—	23	—	41	38
Other instructional methods	6	—	16	—	—	3	24	—	42–45	38
Individualized instruction (no. of students, contact hours)	—	4	—	6	33	—	25	12	49	46, 47
Office hours	—	—	8	6	—	—	26	—	51	—
Theses/comprehensives/certifications/committees (chaired)	—	—	33	—	31	—	21	—	32, 62	—
Informal contact hours with students	—	—	—	—	—	—	27	—	—	—
Research										
Principal field	33	12	30	23	—	8c	13	—	15	54
Publications/presentations (total in last 2 yrs.)	47, 48, 49	17, 18, 19	12, 13, 14	10, 11, 12	30	8cc, 8dd, 8ee	20	36	29	52
Professional research/writing? (yes/no)	51	20	17	13	—	—	28	35	52	52
Description of professional research	—	22	—	—	—	—	29	—	53	56
Engaged in funded research? (yes/no)	—	—	—	—	—	—	30	37	54	55
P.I. or co-P.I. for grants/contracts? (yes/no)	—	—	—	—	34	—	31	—	55	—
Personnel supported by grants/contracts (no.)	53	—	20	16	—	—	32	—	56	—
Funding sources of grants and contracts	54	21	19	15	35	8x	33	39	57	—
Funding sources (no.)	54	21	—	15	35	—	33	—	58	—
Funding sources (P.I./co-P.I./staff)	—	—	—	—	—	—	33	—	55	—
Funding sources (total $)	—	—	—	—	35	—	33	38	59	—
Funding sources (how used in Research/Prog. Dev./other)	—	—	—	—	—	—	33	—	59	—
Attitudes & values										
Campus environment										
Undergraduate education	9, 26	8, 14, 25	31	32–35	19, 48, 49	1, 10	39, 60	26–27, 58	65, 93	—
Equity issues	9, 27	25	9	52	48	—	59	23, 59	92	—

Work pressures	42	25	22, 31	29	—	1	39, 40, 60	22, 32, 40	65, 92, 93	—
Facilities and resources	—	—	45	48	19	1d, 1e, 13f	34	13, 15	60	—
Faculty roles & rewards										
Interests in teaching *vs.* research	50	—	11	9	—	8w	—	28	—	—
Teaching as primary criterion for promotion	42	25	9	28	48	—	59	32	92	—
Research & publication as primary criterion for promotion	42	25	—	—	48	—	59	—	92	—
Difficulty of receiving tenure without publishing	42	25	31	31	48	—	—	40	—	—
Research more rewarded than teaching	—	—	—	—	48	—	59	—	92	—
Governance										
Consistency between expectations and rewards	—	—	—	—	—	—	—	54	—	—
Influence on departmental policies	17	—	38	39	—	—	—	50	—	—
Influence on institutional policies	17	—	38	39	—	—	—	50	—	—
Participation in meetings	16	—	37	43	—	6b, 6c	—	51	—	—
Leadership by top-level administrators	11	27	39	40	19	1m	—	52	—	—
Student participation	26	27	9, 42	28	—	—	—	52	—	—
Junior faculty participation	27, 70	—	9	42	—	—	—	52	—	—
Nontenured faculty participation	—	—	41	31	—	—	—	52	—	—
Effectiveness of faculty governance	—	—	45	—	19, 48	1n	—	53	66	—
Institution managed effectively	27	—	45	—	—	—	—	52	—	—
Communication between faculty and administration	—	—	—	—	19	—	—	52	—	—
Administration supports academic freedom	27	—	9	28	—	—	—	53	—	—
Clarity of mission, goals, and activities	—	—	9	—	—	—	—	53, 54	—	—
Collective bargaining and unions	27	25	9	28	19, 48	—	—	—	64	—
Job satisfaction										
Global	38	—	28	27	19	8u	39, 40	21	66	62d
Instructional duties	8, 42	14, 25	22, 45, 9, 31, 38, 39, 40, 41, 45	29, 32, 48	19	—	39	21, 33, 53	65	61a
Quality of students	9	25	28	30, 32	19	8u	39	26, 27	65	—
Feeling about institution	38	—	28	27	—	8u	—	24	—	—

(continued)

TABLE B.1 (*continued*)

	1969 Carn-69	1972 ACE-72	1975 CFAT-75	1984 CFAT-84	1987 NSOPF-88	1988 NCRIPTAL-88	1992 NSOPF-93	1997 CFAT-97	1998 NSOPF-99	2004 NSOPF-04
Job security	—	—	—	—	19	—	40	21	66	—
Job as source of strain	42	—	—	29	—	—	—	22, 23	—	—
Career satisfaction	40	25	22	25, 30	—	8v	59	22	92	83
Opinion/Academic Interests (list)	9, 42	8, 25	9, 22, 31	28, 29	48, 49	1	59, 50	32, 40	92, 93	82
Job departure & retirement										
Leaving Job										
Likelihood in 3 yrs.	—	—	29	26	20	—	41	—	67	—
Important factor if leaving	—	23	—	—	22	—	43	—	69	—
Amount of work desired if leaving	—	—	—	—	21	—	41	—	67	—
Where would you go if leaving?	—	—	—	—	23	—	41	—	67	—
Retirement										
What age most likely to stop working	—	—	—	—	24	—	42	—	74	65
Retirement or part-time teaching? (yes/no)	—	—	—	—	—	—	44	25	67	—
Early retirement? (yes/no)	—	—	—	—	—	—	45	25	73	—
What age retirement?	—	—	—	—	25	—	46	—	68	—

Interpreting Faculty Surveys

Challenges and Strategies

National surveys undertaken during the past three decades have generated information about the American faculty that is unprecedented in breadth and richness. These surveys recognized the growing importance of this occupational group in an increasingly knowledge-based economy and, accordingly, the importance of understanding changes and continuities within the academic profession. To be sure, faculty surveys of national scope were conducted prior to 1969,* but the "modern era" of examining the faculty via surveys can fairly be said to have begun in 1969 with the landmark collaboration between the Carnegie Commission on Higher Education and the American Council on Education.

Among the considerable number of national faculty surveys conducted since 1969, three series, or strands, have emerged: the Carnegie strand, begun in 1969, repeated in 1975, and then continued by the Carnegie Foundation for the Advancement of Teaching (CFAT) in 1984, 1989, and 1997; the U.S. Department of Education's National Study of Postsecondary Faculty (NSOPF), first undertaken by the National Center for Education Statistics (NCES) in 1988, then repeated in 1993, 1999, and 2004; and the faculty surveys of the Higher Education Research Institute (HERI) at UCLA, initiated in 1980, resumed in 1990, and continued at three-year intervals in 1992–93, 1995–96, 1998–99, and 2001–2. To these three major strands can be added other less systematic strands and several significant individual surveys. They include studies of academic scientists undertaken periodically by the National Science Foundation and the National Research Council; occasional studies of particular issues (for example, faculty politics and political activism, by Ladd and Lipset in the 1970s), and several broad-gauged assessments of the faculty (see Bowen and Schuster, 1986; Clark, 1987). Another important source of insight into the profession has been provided by federally sponsored, university-based collaborative research centers, such as the National Center for Research to Improve Postsecondary Teaching and Learning (NCRIPTAL, University of Michigan, 1987–92); the National Center for Teaching, Learning, and Assessment (NCTLA, Pennsylvania State University,

---

*These include the 1955 Lazarsfeld and Thielens survey of social scientists (Lazarsfeld and Thielens, 1958), the 1960 Association of Graduate Education survey of graduate education in the United States (Berelson, 1960), the 1963 U.S. Office of Education survey of faculty in universities and four-year colleges (Dunham, Wright, and Chandler, 1963), and the 1965 Parsons and Platt study of the American academic profession (Parsons and Platt, 1968).

1992–97); and, most recently, the National Center for the Improvement of Postsecondary Education, headquartered at Stanford University.

There have been four major reputational studies of graduate education, including faculty quality and program effectiveness. The American Council on Education sponsored studies in 1966 and 1970, and the National Research Council sponsored studies in 1982 and 1995.* Both studies used quantitative analysis suggesting strong positive correlation between reputational ratings and indicators of quality, such as federal research funding.

Although the scope and volume of reliable national data is unprecedented in the United States (according to Altbach [1996], it exceeds national databases on faculty anyplace else in the world), the dissemination and use of these resources have been far more circumscribed. There are notable exceptions: the 1969 Carnegie survey served as the empirical foundation for several major publications, including Trow's *Teachers and Students* (though that work did not appear until 1975), Ladd and Lipset's *The Divided Academy* (1975a), and Steinberg's *The Academic Melting Pot* (1974), all of them "official" publications of the Carnegie Commission on Higher Education. The 1984 Carnegie survey served as a partial foundation for Clark's *The Academic Life* (1987) and, along with the 1975 survey, underpinned Boyer's *College: The Undergraduate Experience in America* (1987); and the 1997 Carnegie survey was utilized by Glassick, Huber, and Maeroff to support *Scholarship Assessed* (1997). The NSOPF surveys are the basis of Fairweather's *Faculty Work and Public Trust* (1996), Gappa and Leslie's *The Invisible Faculty* (1993), and our own *The New Academic Generation* (1998), as well as a host of National Center for Education Statistics monographs. The HERI survey data, largely proprietary, have been reported primarily in HERI's own triennial monographs. HERI data are also the source of several works by Helen Astin, including "Women and Achievement: Occupational Entry and Persistence" (1978), "Career Development of Young Women during the Post-High School Years" (Astin and Myint, 1971), "Gender Roles in Transition: Research and Policy Implications for Higher Education" (Astin and Kent, 1983), and "Sex Discrimination in Academe" (Astin and Bayer, 1972).

The point here is that despite the existence of these databases, this extraordinary lode has been generally underutilized. The surveys for the most part have not served as a visible foundation for the major research and policy analyses undertaken in the 1980s and 1990s on the American faculty, nor have they, viewed as a collective, been employed to comprehensively record the enormous changes that have permeated American higher education and its faculty members during this era. Perhaps the most significant exception is Blackburn and Lawrence's *Faculty at Work* (1995), which draws on several surveys to examine key motivational and performance variables for faculty in eight disciplines (chemistry, mathematics, biology, psychology, sociology, political science, English, and history).

This relative "invisibility" may be a function in some instances of the proprietary character of the data and, accordingly, its restricted accessibility to the research com-

---

*See Cartter, 1966; Roose and Anderson, 1970; Jones, Lindzey, and Coggeshall, 1982; Goldberger, Maher, and Flattau, 1995.

munity. That may be true in particular for the HERI databases, but it does not account for the limited use of the widely accessible NSOPF survey data.* Nor does it account for the underutilization of the more recent Carnegie surveys. (See Appendix H for information on accessing the Carnegie surveys.) The limited use of these data in public discourse, we believe, is due more to their complexity—even "inscrutability"—than to inaccessibility. This challenge is described variously by Drew and Tronvig (1988); Creswell, Chronister, and Brown (1991); and Leslie and Fygetakis (1992), all of whom have examined the characteristics of these surveys and identified serious methodological obstacles that must be hurdled before the data can be reliably mined for insights about trends.

The challenges center on issues of comparability both within and across the surveys. The three survey strands (as well as individual examples within each strand) differ from one another (1) in their topical content (that is, the topics that are addressed); (2) in the construction of the items/questions and in the response alternatives to them; (3) in their sampling strategies (both of institutions and of faculty members); (4) in the response rates they generate; (5) in sample size; and (6) in the weighting of cases. Having significant variations among the surveys is important because to administer the same survey time and again would be foolishly limiting. No single survey can or should attempt to cover all useful topics (after all, who will take the time to respond to a thirty-page questionnaire?). Moreover, most topics can and should be probed from different angles. Survey variety is indisputably desirable—up to a point. But greater efforts to achieve much-needed coordination among major surveys—in order to circumvent the most serious pitfalls—could facilitate substantially the efforts of researchers who seek to understand faculty-related developments. With those considerations as a backdrop, the following comments provide an overview of similarities and contrasts among the surveys and delineate the challenges that confront researchers.

CONTENT COMPARABILITY

The salient content-related issues have to do with the topics that each survey addresses and, more specifically, how the individual survey items are constructed.

Topical Content

The three national survey strands differ systematically in the types of questions they pose. Table C.1 displays the major differences in content emphasis across the three major survey strands.

In addition, the Concordance (Appendix B), perhaps the first of its kind, provides a detailed cross-listing of content items from a number of surveys. A review of that detailed matrix suggests that although all surveys share a staple of basic demographic

---

*Although NSOPF data are directly available on the NCES Web site for users for download, the USDE's Data Analysis System (DAS) permits running only rudimentary bivariate crosstabs. More sophisticated analyses require application to USDE for a restricted file license, requirements for which are described on the Web site.

TABLE C.1
The Depth of Focus of Three National Faculty Survey Strands, 1969–1999

	NSOPF[a]	CFAT[b]	HERI[c]
Demographics (age, gender, nativity, etc.)	average	strong	average
Career educational background (highest degree; previous employment)	strong	weak	weak
Appointment status/conditions (part- or full-time; tenure eligibility)	strong	weak	weak
Workload activities (teaching, research, service, % time allocation)	strong	weak	weak
Governance	weak	strong	weak
Job satisfaction	strong	average	strong
Departure plans or retirement	strong	weak	weak
Status of U.S. higher education	weak	strong	strong
Campus environment	weak	strong	strong
Faculty roles	weak	strong	weak

[a]NSOPF-88, -93, -99, -04.
[b]Carn-69, CFAT-75, -84, -89, -93, -97.
[c]HERI-90, -93, -96, -99, -02.

items (age, gender, rank, citizenship, etc.), each strand has its particular foci. The CFAT surveys tend to emphasize attitudinal items, including faculty members' perceptions of their institution, their discipline, and, more generally, American higher education; levels of satisfaction with various aspects of their current job and career; attitudes about politics and religion; and, more recently, views concerning issues directly related to the Carnegie Foundation's teaching-centric agenda in higher education (e.g., faculty roles and rewards and the evaluation of faculty). The Carnegie surveys are less attentive to career histories and information about faculty workload.

The NSOPF surveys are spare on attitudinal items (and absolutely proscribe questions about politics and religion). However, they do inquire into aspects of job satisfaction, instructional responsibilities (including detailed questions on each course taught and numbers of independent studies supervised), research funding and publication, compensation (from within and from outside the institution), and career history.

The HERI surveys resemble the CFAT surveys in that they concentrate on attitudinal items; however, the nature of these items tends to differ from Carnegie's thrust, focusing more on relations with students and on job stressors, with less attention directed to overall perceptions of higher education and views about one's academic field. There are few items on workload and career history.

Item Format

The format or wording of questions and the structure of response alternatives are related matters. The CFAT strand has the longest history, and the CFAT items tend to be the most consistent. A considerable number of identically worded questions have appeared since 1975 (a few going back to 1969) and have become standards within the Carnegie surveys. Some of the Carnegie item wording has been picked up by other surveys. For example, the question about faculty orientation to teaching versus research is posed as "Do your interests lie primarily in teaching or in research?" (Choices: very heavily in research; in both but leaning toward research; in both but leaning toward teaching; very heavily in teaching.) This question has appeared in nearly every faculty survey, no matter what sponsorship, since 1969. The thrust of many other questions has been maintained, but they sometimes undergo changes in wording and/or in response options. Thus, for example, the response alternatives to the question about type of academic appointment have changed, undoubtedly as a reflection of changing appointment practices in the academic world. In the case of some other items, such as age, the numerical clusters or intervals have changed. On attitudinal items, a "neutral" or "not applicable" response has sometimes been added to—or deleted from—options of agreement or disagreement, thereby providing five or six response possibilities instead of four (or vice versa).

The NSOPF surveys have been relatively consistent in how questions about workload and attitudinal items are presented, but they have changed the scaling on job satisfaction questions. The career history item has been modified, shifting from questions about the respondents' two or three immediately preceding jobs to questions about their previous job, their first full-time job, and the job that immediately preceded their current appointment. The HERI surveys have been relatively consistent since at least 1990 on attitudinal items.

The crucial point here is that item format may affect the data in unpredictable ways. Leslie and Fygetakis (1992) found, for example, that on a particular item, such as faculty attitudes toward maintaining or abolishing tenure, responses during the same year but from two different surveys varied markedly depending on how the item had been framed, that is, whether the wording was positive (for maintaining the tenure system) or negative (in terms of abolishing tenure). Whether such wording choices are "innocent" or reflect the item framer's agenda is a matter left for speculation, but surely such spinning of questions has a long if ethically questionable history in political surveys. Consider another complexity. Many surveys include items about faculty workload. Whereas some questionnaires ask faculty to allocate percentages of their time across various work responsibilities, others inquire about the number of hours per week spent in each of those activities. This variation complicates finding a common denominator that will enable comparisons of workload-related items.

Even the format of basic demographic items across survey strands poses analytical challenges. For example, age data may be reported as date of birth or as the respondent's age. Also, age intervals change from one survey to another (for example, 45 to 49 versus 46 to 50), thereby limiting precise comparisons. Furthermore, race and ethnicity items maintain no constancy across surveys; but then, too, government data collection on race and ethnicity is in constant flux as public consciousness and political sensibilities evolve. Nationality items, also, vary considerably (citizenship status versus nativity). In a word, analysts are all too frequently saddled with the challenge of comparing "apples and oranges" in striving to interpret similar but non-identical content across surveys.

SAMPLING AND WEIGHTING OF CASES

In the matter of sampling populations and in assigning weightings to subgroups, the surveys differ in at least four ways: sampling strategy, response rates, sample sizes, and weighting schemes. Table C.2 summarizes differences among the surveys in three of those areas.

Sampling Strategy

The CFAT and NSOPF surveys share a similar two-stage sampling design. They select a sample of institutions, stratified by type. Then, from the selected institutions, they draw a sampling of faculty, stratified by rank and/or field. But even as these two strands share the same basic strategy, they differ in their institutional sampling frames. CFAT stratifies its institutional sample—naturally enough—using the Carnegie classification scheme (CFAT, 1984), whereas NCES bases its institutional sample on the U.S. Department of Education's Integrated Postsecondary Education Data System (IPEDS). The HERI survey, in contrast, draws its sample exclusively from the group of institutions that participate in the Cooperative Inter-Institutional Research Program (CIRP), a program whose principal activity over the years has been conducting and reporting the annual national freshman surveys. (Astin et al., 1992; survey data was also published for 1986, 1985, 1984, 1983, and 1981.) The HERI surveys bypass the community colleges until 1989.

Response Rates

The three survey strands differ substantially in average response rates. At the high end, NSOPF surveys have varied from 76% to 92%; this is extraordinary—unprecedented in the authors' experience—and reflects the exceptional follow-up efforts directed at initial nonrespondents, on the part of the contractors who conduct the actual survey for NCES.* At the lower end, the CFAT surveys have hovered around 50%, as have the HERI surveys, whose response rates have fluctuated from 42% to 61%. Response rates, of course, are critical because they vitally affect one's confidence that the sample utilized can credibly serve as a source of population estimates.

Sample Size

Another basic variable is sample size. The 1969 and 1975 Carnegie surveys set the gold standard for large-sample faculty surveys, generating 60,028 (Trow, 1975)

---

*Among the faculty surveys, the NSOPF-99 response rate was the highest, at 92%. NSOPF surveys were designed and conducted by external consultants SRI International in Palo Alto, California (1988), the National Opinion Research Center in Chicago (1993), the Gallup Organization (1999), and the Research Triangle Institute in North Carolina (2004).

TABLE C.2
The Sampling Frames of Three Strands of National Faculty Surveys

Survey	Institutions			Faculty (in thousands)			Response Rate %	Representativeness
	Pop.	Sample	Represented	Pop.	Sample	Responded		
Carn-69	2,615	310	303	446.3	100.3	60.0	60	Low part-time; low 2-yr.
CFAT-75	2,883	514	340	475.7	47.8	25.4	53	Low part-time; low 2-yr.
CFAT-84	2,559	310	190	—	10.0	5.2	51	Low part-time; low 2-yr.
CFAT-89	2,747	306	306	—	10.0	5.4	55	Low part-time
CFAT-97	2,873	306	—	795.0	10.0	5.2	52	Low part-time
HERI-90	2,528	432	392	401.4	93.5	51.6	55	FT undergraduate faculty only
HERI-93	2,582	344	289	416.9	72.4	43.9	61	FT undergraduate faculty only
HERI-96	2,551	403	384	418.2	143.8	59.9	42	FT undergraduate faculty only
HERI-99	2,618	429	378	440.8	128.4	55.1	43	FT undergraduate faculty only
HERI-02	2,617	416	358	442.4	134.9	55.5	41	FT undergraduate faculty only
NSOPF-88	3,159	480	424	664.8	11.1	7.4	76	Low minority
NSOPF-93	3,256	974	817	885.8	31.4	25.8	87	Minorities oversampled
NSOPF-99	3,396	959	819	1073.7	19.2	17.6	92	Minorities oversampled
NSOPF-04	3,380	1080	980	1211.8	35.6	26.1	76	Methodology report not yet available

and 25,262 (Roizen, Fulton, and Trow, 1970) usable responses, respectively. Such robust numbers support a wide array of "fine-tuned" analyses of faculty subgroups. That is, it became possible with such response numbers to compare, for example, minority women in the social sciences with minority men or nonminority women. But beginning in 1984, the Carnegie surveys, for practical reasons of cost, allowed sample sizes (and ipso facto usable response numbers) to plunge to as little as one-tenth the size of the 1975 survey. This has hampered efforts to probe faculty subgroups after 1975 and to compare subgroups in the present with similar subgroups in the past: cells that had numbered in the hundreds now often number in the tens, or less).

The NSOPF surveys utilized large sample sizes and had large usable responses in 1988 and 1993 (7,408 [Russell, Hancock, and Williamson, 1990] for the former and 25,780 [Zimbler et al., 1994] for the latter). Owing to cost factors, the Department of Education was obliged to reduce the 1999 sample by one-half to 19,213, partly because of the National Science Foundation's decision not to contribute to funding the survey. Nonetheless, as a strand, the NSOPF surveys provide an excellent opportunity to examine subgroup trends over time. The HERI surveys have consistently maintained relatively large usable response numbers (ranging from 51,000 in 1990 to 32,000 in 2002), but the fact that they are convenience samples clouds their generalizability.

Weighting Schemes

Each of the strands (and even sometimes individual surveys within a given strand) may weight the sample cases differently in estimating population parameters. That means, first, that the population estimates across surveys may vary as a function of how much weight is attached to a particular variable (based on institutional type, academic field, gender, race or ethnicity, full- or part-time appointment, etc.). As a result, population estimates differ, sometimes significantly, even for a given year, and even on such basic faculty demographics as age and gender. For example, Leslie and Fygetakis (1992), in comparing the nearly simultaneous 1988 NSOPF and 1989 CFAT surveys, found substantial differences in faculty age distribution and even in gender estimates. Moreover, the same survey may yield different findings when different weighting schemes are applied. Thus, in the interesting case of the 1969 Carnegie survey, two data files survive: one with ACE weightings, the other with Carnegie/Berkeley weightings. The difference in population estimates between the two files are displayed in table C.3. Although generally not large, the differences nevertheless suggest the need for caution in interpreting the findings when different files exist based on the *same* survey.

THE METHODOLOGICAL RISKS RESEARCHERS FACE:
AN OVERVIEW AND RESPONSE

What does all of this mean for the researcher seeking to describe the faculty at a particular time, and especially for the task of discerning trends over time? Typically, we ask three kinds of questions of these large national data bases:

1. What is the status of the American faculty (or one subset thereof) on any one variable at any one point in time? For example, what was the age distribution of full-time academics in 1969? Or, what was the proportion of women or members of minority groups in a particular academic field in 1998?

    Or, in a variation on the basic question, we might ask about the relationship between two or more faculty variables at any one point in time. This is in some sense merely a "multivariate" variation. Thus, we might ask how gender is associated with type of faculty appointment or with involvement in research and publication in 1988.

2. The second basic question, also in univariate and multivariate versions, is, Does the faculty differ between *t1* and *t2* on a single variable or on a multivariate relationship? Thus: How does the faculty's age distribution in 1969 compare with that of 1999? Or, how does the relationship between gender and publication rate in 1975 compare with the same relationship in 1993?

TABLE C.3

Demographic Characteristics of All Faculty, Full-Time and Part-Time: Carn-69 Results from Two Weighting Systems, ACE-Bayer's and Carnegie/Berkeley's

(percent)

| | All Institutions | | | | | |
| | Men | | Women | | Total | |
Variable	ACE-Bayer	Carnegie/Berkeley	ACE-Bayer	Carnegie/Berkeley	ACE-Bayer	Carnegie/Berkeley
Race						
White	96.6	95.6	94.7	92.4	96.3	94.9
Black	1.8	2.6	3.9	6.0	2.2	3.3
Oriental	1.3	1.4	1.1	1.2	1.3	1.4
Other	0.3	0.4	0.3	0.3	0.3	0.4
Father's education						
8th grade or less	30.0	30.3	25.5	27.0	29.1	29.6
Some high school	14.4	14.4	13.7	13.9	14.3	14.3
Completed high school	17.5	17.3	17.4	17.0	17.5	17.2
Some college	12.4	12.2	13.7	13.5	12.6	12.5
Graduated from college	9.6	9.4	10.0	9.6	9.7	9.4
Attended graduate or professional school	5.0	5.2	7.1	6.6	5.4	5.5
Attained advanced degree	11.1	11.2	12.6	12.5	11.4	11.4
Religious background						
Protestant	63.9	66.2	65.4	65.5	64.1	66.0
Catholic	15.9	17.2	21.3	23.4	16.9	18.5
Jewish	10.4	9.4	6.7	5.6	9.7	8.7
Other	3.4	3.7	2.7	2.9	3.3	3.6
None	3.3	3.4	2.6	2.6	3.2	3.2
Current religion						
Protestant	47.1	48.4	51.4	51.7	47.9	49.1
Catholic	12.2	13.3	19.2	21.2	13.5	14.9
Jewish	7.3	6.4	5.4	4.7	7.0	6.0
Other	6.1	6.3	5.2	5.2	5.9	6.1
None	21.9	22.7	15.6	14.8	20.7	21.1
Marital status						
Currently married	87.0	86.9	47.4	46.3	79.3	78.8
Divorced, separated, widowed	3.0	2.9	12.4	12.1	4.8	4.8
Never married	10.0	10.2	40.1	41.5	15.9	16.5

Source: Bayer, 1970.

3. A third basic question asks, What is the magnitude of any such difference over time? And what is the significance (statistical or otherwise) of that difference?

The methodological risks—challenges—posed by the complexities outlined above need to be understood precisely in terms of how they affect our ability to answer these three questions (and their variations) with reasonable confidence.

The methodological risks are multiple. In the first place, different surveys in the same or proximate years may yield significantly different population estimates of the American faculty depending on differences in instrumentation (measurement error) and sampling/weighting schemes (sampling error). As Leslie and Fygetakis (1992) have shown, even basic demographic estimates such as gender and age can vary by 4% to 10%—largely, it would appear, as a function of sampling differences. Attitudinal indices can vary even more wildly. For example, the same authors show how faculty attitudes toward the tenure system appear to vary depending on whether the question is framed negatively (that is, expressing support for the *abolition* of tenure) or positively (expressing support for the *maintenance* of tenure). The same appears to be true for questions about faculty members' plans for retirement. Here measurement error may exacerbate any sampling or weighting effects. Indeed, as the 1969 Carnegie-ACE survey demonstrates, even different weighting schemes applied to the very same data set can lead to different results. The corollary, of course, is that apparent *similarities* in estimates across surveys or data files may actually *obscure* real *differences* when measurement and/or sampling errors happen to offset one another.

This basic risk is compounded when we seek to compare trends on the same or similar items over time, thus effectively compounding any error (or potential error) at point *t1* with an error (or potential error) at point *t2*. If the risk is obvious in efforts to compare items at two temporal points from quite different surveys, it is less obvious, but no less real, when comparing items at two temporal points *within the same survey strand*. How is one to interpret a comparison, say, of faculty racial or ethnic distribution in 1969 to that in, say, 1989—when the study sample has plummeted from 60,000 to less than 6,000, yielding very small cells? And when the 1969 survey does not break out Hispanics as a separate category? Or, how should a decline in faculty satisfaction over a decade be understood when one of the surveys has added a fifth "neutral" category to an earlier four-point response alternative (thereby letting respondents off the hook of having to report either satisfaction or dissatisfaction)? Finally, there is the matter of interpreting the magnitude of any differences that may emerge. How "significant," statistically or practically, is, say, a 3% versus a 6% versus a 10% difference over time in the estimate of a single population parameter? Or in the estimate of a multivariate relationship (e.g., the publication activity of women at research universities versus such activity at another institutional type)? How do we compare the difference between an estimate yielded by a large-sample study (such as NSOPF-93, where a 3% difference between subgroups nearly always attains statistical significance) and an estimate derived from a smaller-sample study (where subgroup differences as great as 10% ordinarily do *not* attain statistical significance)?

Taken together, the methodological pitfalls are substantial enough to have deterred most researchers from combing the collective evidentiary record embedded in the national faculty surveys. As experienced researchers, we have chosen a riskier, and arguably even foolhardy, path. But the road we have chosen does have a methodological foundation, one that we believe has proved over the past several decades to be sound, albeit rarely neat and routine. In particular, we build upon and adapt the evolving methodology of what has been called meta-analysis (Glass, 1976) or integrative research (Boyer, 1990; Glassick, Huber, and Maeroff, 1997). This general approach has yielded some impressive exemplars in the higher education literature, among them the pioneering work of Feldman and Newcomb's *The Impact of College on Students* (1976), Finkelstein's *The American Academic Profession* (1984), Blackburn and Lawrence's *Faculty at Work* (1995), and Pascarella and Terenzini's *How College Affects Students* (1991). What these projects share is a commitment to *optimizing the comparability* among the different studies and data files, seeking, as Feldman and Newcomb (1976) put it, to find "a common metric" for reporting findings, or, at the least, attempting through a variety of strategies to "reduce" the differences across studies that weaken the comparability of findings.

METHODOLOGICAL STRATEGIES FOR OPTIMIZING COMPARABILITY AND REDUCING INCOMPARABILITY

With those challenges as backdrop, we turn now to describing strategies that we have used to optimize *comparability* with respect to item content (including response alternatives) and with respect to sampling.

Item Content and Response Alternatives

In our effort to discern changes across the panoply of surveys, we have sought whenever possible to develop a common metric to enable comparisons of different studies' findings. Several basic examples should suffice to clarify our approach and the scope of "data transformation" that we have attempted. In the area of faculty publication, for instance, we found that different studies employ different response categories. They differ even in the basic taxonomy of publication categories (some ask generally about publications, others about books or journal articles, etc.) and, too, in the details of the distinctions drawn (e.g., between refereed and nonrefereed journals). We tested the possibility of reducing this variation (and the attendant measurement error) by developing a least common metric: the percentage of faculty reporting *no* publications of any kind over a two-year period. As it turned out, there were sufficient variations in this group when analyzed by institutional type, academic field, career stage, and gender to yield a serviceable—albeit crude—common metric that spanned the surveys. This example represents a typical simple transformation that we undertook to reduce differences among the response categories of basic survey items. That is, we sometimes selected a common extreme of the distributions from the various surveys—in the example, no publications during the past two years—to enable *some* useful comparisons that would surmount the barriers that otherwise cordon off the surveys from each other. The test of utility that we applied was to determine whether sufficient variation emerged when reporting these common (albeit extreme) measurements to make the findings meaningful.

In the area of workload distribution, we undertook a more "extended" transformation. The Carnegie strand typically asks respondents to estimate the *percentage of time* they allocate to particular basic tasks (such as teaching, research, administration, and consulting). The NSOPF strand asks respondents to estimate the total *number of hours* they work weekly and then allocate those hours across activity categories—categories, as it happens, that are not identical from one survey to the next. To maximize comparability, we chose to use NSOPF's total hours and hours spent in each activity category to create a new, common metric that melded the percentage-of-time and the actual-hours categories. This yielded a new category: "percentage distribution of time in teaching, research, and administration" (reducing, in that process, the response categories to just those three common ones). Following an empirical examination of the distribution of responses for each category, we then selected subcategories for which to make actual comparisons across the surveys. These subcategories ultimately included ""percentage with less than 10% in administration," "percentage with 10% or more in research," and so on—subcategories that, although simplified, nevertheless proved useful in terms of offering sufficient variation. The measurement is imperfect and arbitrary (there are lots of ways the measurements could have been sliced and diced), but this represents our best judgment of how best to report trends over time for this particular aspect of academic life.

Sampling and Weighting Cases

Comparability may be achieved not only with respect to content items or response alternatives, but also with respect to sampling, thus minimizing the effects of sampling error. There are several strategies for optimizing comparability among samples. Most obvious—and most time consuming—is the selection from different surveys of identical faculty subgroups for analysis. This most often means delineating faculty in one common set of disciplines or in one type of institution. This was the basic strategy adopted by Blackburn and Lawrence in *Faculty at Work* (1995). They analyzed trends across surveys among faculty in eight disciplines. In our own analysis, we have sought to describe faculty trends, *controlling for* different institutional types and different academic fields (for example, community college faculty or humanities faculty). This strategy by no means *eliminates* sampling error, but it does *reduce* it. Another basic strategy for maximizing comparability among samples is to examine trends in population parameters or multivariate relationships *within survey strands*—thus, for instance, examining changes across Carnegie surveys or HERI surveys as discrete strands. Although sampling is not identical within a given survey strand, sampling strategies *within strands* are more consistent than not. Once again, this tactic is a way to reduce sampling error, not eliminate it.

Search for Triangulation

In addition to reducing measurement and sampling error, we have observed as a basic analytic strategy the imperative to triangulate data sources, especially estimates of population parameters, by actively juxtaposing the estimates of population parameters in any one year with, when available, population censuses (for example, employing the IPEDS data). How large are the differences between estimates derived from survey sampling and census-based data sets? What likely accounts for them? And how are we to interpret them? The triangulation strategy forces us to consider the variability in estimates and provides an appropriately cautious context within which to interpret differences. Having said all this, we should note that most of the differences in estimates of population parameters across surveys identified by Leslie and Fygetakis were "under 5%." This finding suggests that very large differences, say on the order of 20–30% over time, are unlikely to be primarily attributable to "error"—however many times compounded, by resort to however many different sources.

PROMOTING A FOCUS ON TRENDS IN MULTIVARIATE RELATIONSHIPS

While exercising caution against "overinterpreting" differences between population estimates of individual variables (or subgroup means on such variables) in a given year, we have used a related strategy to offset error: focusing on trends in multivariate relationships, rather than on discrete population parameters across surveys. Thus, for example, we have avoided emphasizing trends in single demographic or work activity variables *that cannot be corroborated or triangulated with other reliable census sources* (e.g., IPEDS). Instead, we have concentrated on trends in bivariate or multivariate relationships.

This strategy is anchored in two related foundations. First, Leslie and Fygetakis (1992) suggest that multivariate analysis is more stable and less subject to measurement and sampling error than estimates of individual population parameters.

Second, this strategy builds also on Paul Lazarsfeld's classic work on the "interchangeability" of social indicators (see Lazarsfeld and Thielens, 1958). The basic premise here is that although differences between items, or combinations of items, in a survey may result in classifying individual subjects differently on any one index, the relationship between such a "classification" variable and a second variable would remain largely unaffected.

INTERPRETING MAGNITUDES OF DIFFERENCE

When empirical differences do emerge between subgroups of faculty on any one survey or between such faculty subgroups over time (for example, the publication activity of women faculty), the question remains, On what basis do we determine when such a difference is meaningful? Traditionally, the desideratum of "meaningfulness" has been empirical/statistical, which is to say that the probability is small (variously defined, usually, as less than 5% or 1%) that such a difference could occur by chance in a similarly drawn sample of the same size. This statistical "standard" appears to allow for clear and definitive judgments for intergroup comparisons in any individual survey, but our current work is complicated by sampling differences among the various surveys. Thus, for example, a 3% or 4% difference between groups nearly always attains statistical significance in the large-sample surveys (such as the Carn-69 and -75; NSOPF-88 and -93; and all HERI surveys), whereas a 10% difference may not attain statistical significance in one of the smaller-sample surveys (CFAT-84, -89, -97; NSOPF-99). The larger the number of cells, that is, the number of categories of the particular variable being compared, and the smaller the sample, the more difficult the application of a conventional statistical standard becomes. For instance, how does one compare a 4% intergroup difference in 1969 with a 15% intergroup difference in 1989?

Although we have chosen not to devote our attention to copious significance testing, we have developed several "rules of thumb" that we have applied in reaching judgments about significance, broadly defined:

- In large-sample surveys, we have attributed significance to differences of 5% or greater.
- In smaller-sample studies, we have required differences of 10% or more (depending on sample size).
- When comparing faculty subgroups over time, we have, whenever possible, used the most reasonable "conservative" standard to judge significance.

Accordingly, we have opted for caution in attributing significance (or, in less formal statistical terms, meaningful differences). But we recognize that our interpretations of trends would be greatly curtailed if, given the difference among survey methodologies, we restricted ourselves to applying strict statistical tests of significance.

SUMMARY

We have attempted to unearth (and document) the changes and continuities in the American academic profession over the past three decades. We present our results in this volume with a view not only of highlighting heretofore largely inaccessible or, at least, underutilized, national data sources, but also of chronicling trends in academic work, academic careers, and values that have shaped the platform—the foundation—from which the next academic generation will emerge. Although megatrends such as globalization and the rise of the Internet are assuredly scrambling the academic order, we have sought to provide a detailed map of that order, which, as we see it, often masks important, long-term changes that lie just below the surface.

In this effort to bring all the available evidence together, we are aware of the challenges, both technical and more broadly methodological, that we face. They include a lack of comparability in the content, response alternatives, sampling, and weighting across the potpourri of national faculty surveys. Specifically, we face the possibility that significant amounts of measurement or sampling error are entering the equation as we seek to compare faculty subgroups or to identify trends. We have been sobered but undeterred by these challenges. Instead of backing off, we have sought to explicate the challenges and to develop strategies for minimizing the threats they pose. Building on the methodology of meta-analysis and integrative research, we have employed strategies to enhance comparability among the surveys in content, response alternatives, and sampling. The strategies include assorted data transformations, the realignment of sampling frames, and so on, described in some detail above. Moreover, at the same time that we have sought to increase comparability, we have also sought to reduce the effects of measurement and sampling error by triangulating data sources (especially when census data for the population are available, as they are in the IPEDS database) and by focusing on trends in multivariate relationships rather than on individual population estimates of discrete parameters (e.g., age and gender). When possible, we have sought to test empirically the effect of various data transformations on the findings, including assuring that sufficient variation exists in the outcome variables of interest. We have been guided by such empirical tests on a routine basis.

We recognize, however, that all of our strategies have combined not to eliminate the intrusion of error into the findings, but merely to reduce error. We are heartened by the pioneering methodological work of David Drew and David Leslie and their associates that demonstrates just how much consistency actually exists in the findings among the surveys. To be sure, they focus on the items that show the greatest disparities; but, when one realizes how many hundreds of variables are included in each of these data files, and yet how relatively few show striking disparities, we are encouraged to view a "glass half full." That is, despite the tremendous potential for error, most of the incongruities from survey to survey seem to make little difference in the overall findings. And this fact reinforces in our minds the experience of methodologists such as Gene Glass, whose work demonstrates quite conclusively, we think, that the findings of "bad" studies, that is, methodologically flawed, typically differ little from the findings of the "best" studies. Methodological risks are just that—risks. They are not always fully realized; in fact, it appears, they rarely are.

In sum, we have opted for a strategy to facilitate interpretation of data that spills across nearly a score of surveys and that entails many scores of variables, exhibiting vexing inconsistencies from database to database. In so doing we have attempted to strike an acceptable balance between objectives ever in tension: (1) to enable reasonably defensible interpretations of highly complex (not to say erratic and inconsistent) data while (2) respecting principles of statistical analysis that are designed to safeguard against overreaching interpretation. Our strategy of balance incurs risk, employs a degree of arbitrary—though we believe grounded—judgments or decision "rules," and, perhaps inevitably, invites controversy. The alternatives are less appealing for researchers such as ourselves struggling to grasp just what are the nuanced but tangible changes and continuities that characterize the dynamic era that spans these past three decades: to surrender to strict statistical guidelines that would inhibit all but the most obvious interpretations or, more tempting, to forgo the effort to wring meaning out of the unruly tangle of numbers—in a word, to succumb to analytical paralysis.

Variables for Classifying Faculty Subgroups

If there is one generalization that can be unequivocally applied to the faculty—and increasingly so—it is their diversity. Burton Clark was among the first to emphasize the "small worlds, different worlds" of American academics; his theme highlighted differences among faculty *primarily on the basis of institutional type and academic field* (Clark, 1987). Since Clark's evocation, entirely new bases have emerged upon which to "dissect" and analyze the faculty. And as these grounds for differentiating faculty subgroups multiply, it becomes more necessary than ever to resist generalizations based on aggregate data and, rather, to be very thoughtful in selecting those variables upon which to disaggregate faculty subgroups.

Our analyses of three decades of national faculty survey data suggest that two critical, increasingly important bases for distinguishing among faculty subgroups are employment status (full-time versus part-time) and type of appointment (eligibility for tenure versus fixed-term appointment). Describing full-time and part-time faculty in the same breath is sometimes like mixing the proverbial apples and oranges. Let us then take a first cut at differentiating the full- and part-timers, a distinction long made in the literature but for which more revealing analyses are now possible.

Full-Timers. Among the full-time faculty, there are several critical lines of cleavage that need to be recognized in any data analysis. The first concerns *type of appointment.* Are we talking about tenured or tenure-track faculty *or* about full-timers on term, that is, off-track appointments? If the latter, are these individuals on functionally specialized appointments (teaching-only, research-only or administrative types of appointments), *or* do their responsibilities entail the traditional threefold mandate of teaching, research, and service? To mix these different types of appointees indiscriminately in a single analysis is likely to provide more murkiness than light. Among these types of full-time appointees, it is almost always necessary to distinguish among academic fields or clusters of academic fields, for the differences among the subcultures, as well as the variegated nature of their work, are manifest. So, too, are the differences from one type of institution to another. Thus, a social science generalist at a two-year institution and, say, a research university microbiologist probing the frontiers of knowledge likely share some important characteristics but probably sharply differ in most aspects of how they spend their work time.

Career stage and *gender* are also critical classificatory variables. Gender has always had important explanatory power as a differentiator of academic work preferences, performance, rewards, and so on. Career stage now comes more to the fore as the very structure of academic careers undergoes profound changes; and it can be badly misleading, for example, to mix, for analytical purposes, term appointees at the beginning of an academic career with faculty members who are nearing the final stages of historically more traditional careers.

Full-time faculty need to be classified by *race and ethnicity as well. Whatever progress the academic profession may have made in becoming more inclusive—at least at the entry level—the available data suggest that the work roles or activities, the values and orientations, and the experiences of institutional climate differ substantively for faculty who are white or Asian, on the one hand, and black or Hispanic, on the other.*

Part-Timers. Building upon the work of Tuckman (1978) and Gappa and Leslie (1993), our analyses suggest that there is about as much diversity among part-time as among full-time faculty, if not more. That diversity stems not so much from institutional type, field, gender, and career cohort as it does from the differing levels of commitment to and engagement with part-time faculty work. The range extends from involvement that is no more than incidental to the faculty member's work and career to being as all-consuming as that experienced by many full-time faculty. Accordingly, we have delineated four principal types of part-time faculty members, using a typology similar to Gappa and Leslie's.

To date, the major published supplement to Tuckman's classification scheme has been Gappa and Leslie's (1993). Based on a limited sample of some one hundred interviews at twenty campuses, Gappa and Leslie "loosely" (p. 45) collapsed Tuckman's seven categories into four: (1) career enders (retirees or semiretirees), (2) professionals/experts/specialists (faculty employed full-time outside the academy who choose to teach mainly for their own edification), (3) aspiring academics (Tuckman's "hopeful full-timers," plus graduate students), and (4) freelancers (those who concurrently work more than one part-time job). They were not, of course, in a position to estimate the relative proportion of each type of part-timer, nor to adjust those distributions to particular institutional types, fields, career stages, and so on. More recently, Berger and Kirshstein (2001) have developed a simpler classification scheme of part-time faculty based on whether their part-time position constituted their primary employment (careerists) or not (moonlighters). The strength of their work is its empirical grounding in the NSOPF-99 survey data, which they use to generate numbers for each of the two categories. The major limitation is their reliance on a single criterion for classification, which yields two subgroups that are still quite heterogeneous, plus a large residual (nonclassifiable) group, among whom there are relatively minor demographic and work-related differences.

We developed empirically a more differentiated taxonomy of part-time faculty, based on the addition of several variables we considered critical, including (1) whether respondents had retired from another job; (2) whether they had other concurrent employment and, if so, whether that concurrent employment was full-time or part-time, in or outside higher education; (3) whether they were pursuing a graduate degree; (4) what their marital status was; and (5) whether or not they had children. The flowchart in figure D.1 details how we identified our subgroups of part-

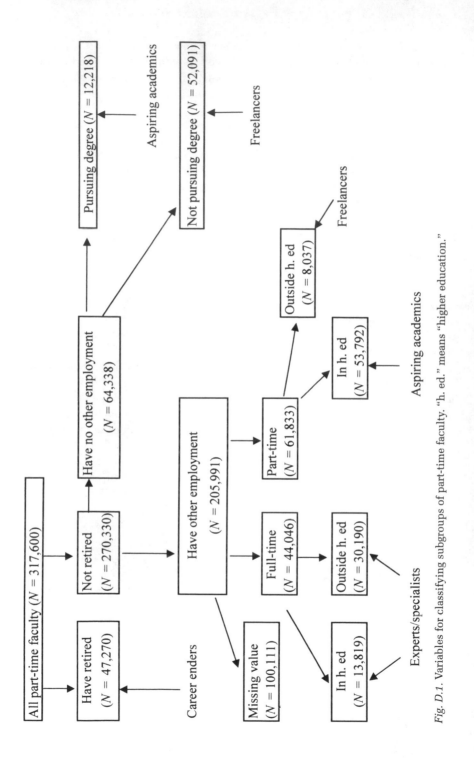

Fig. D.1. Variables for classifying subgroups of part-time faculty. "h. ed." means "higher education."

time faculty based on the 1999 NSOPF variables. Our categories are largely congruent with those originally developed by Gappa and Leslie (1993). The first is *Career
enders,* individuals who have retired from one career and have moved into part-time
college teaching as a second career. The other three consist of part-timers who have
not retired from another position: *experts/specialists* who are employed full-time in
other settings, either outside higher education (e.g. in industry or government) or inside (e.g. faculty at another institution), and whose part-time teaching represents an
extension of their professional practice; *aspiring academics,* including graduate students as well as those with multiple part-time teaching assignments; and *freelancers,*
the most internally diverse subgroup, including persons who report other part-time
employment that is outside higher education, homemakers, and individuals pursuing nontraditional freelance careers. Our taxonomy yields a reasonably small residual group that we have classified as *unknown*-about 10–15% of the total part-time
population.

Table D.1 explicitly compares the distribution of part-timers in 1998 with their
distribution a quarter century earlier in Tuckman's study (as well as in general comparison with Gappa and Leslie's categories, recalling that they did not provide an estimate of subgroup size). As can be seen there, the diversification within the part-
timers continues.

- *Career enders.* We found that 14.8% of part-timers in 1998 could be classified
  as semiretirees in Tuckman's terminology and as career enders in Gappa and
  Leslie's; this constitutes a substantial increase from the mere 1.8% that Tuckman found in 1976.
- *Experts/specialists.* Another 15%, we concluded, were experts, specialists,
  and professionals. These correspond to the "full-mooners" in Tuckman's taxonomy.
- *Aspiring academics.* We divided the aspiring academics category into two
  main subcategories: graduate students with or without other concurrent part-
  time employment, and "seekers," whose multiple part-time roles and either
  current graduate degree pursuit or recent graduate degree receipt suggested as-
  piration to full-time academic careers.
- *Graduate students.* The proportion of part-time faculty who were primarily
  graduate students, as derived by us, is much smaller than the proportion so
  identified by Tuckman (5.7% versus 21.2%). (For our purposes, persons who
  functioned as teaching assistants at the institution where they were enrolled
  as graduate students did not count as part-time *faculty.* Also, if graduate students were employed, in addition to their part-time teaching, at another institution in another nonteaching job, we did not classify them as graduate students.) Thus, we applied a strict definition to identifying as part-time faculty
  persons who were also graduate students. Concomitantly, we also observed an
  increase in the number of "seekers" or "freeway flyers," the "hopeful full-
  timers" (Tuckman, 1978) or "aspiring academics" (Gappa and Leslie, 1993).
- *Freelancers.* Our subgroup of freelancers was heavily representative of homemakers (Tuckman, 1978). The percentage of homemakers seems to have stayed
  relatively steady: 6.4% in 1976, 10.7% in 1998. Meanwhile, only 2.0% of fac-

TABLE D.1
The Distribution of Part-Time Faculty by Type, 1976 and 1998

	1976		Gappa & Leslie's Categories		1998		% Change 1976–98
	N	%			N	%	
All part-time faculty	3,763	100.0			317,210	100.0	—
Semiretired	107	1.8	Career enders	Career enders	47,233	14.8	13.0
Graduate students	796	21.2	Aspiring academics	Graduate students	18,090	5.7	−15.5
Hopeful full-timers	624	16.6	Aspiring academics	Seekers (active & presumed)	72,590	22.8	6.2
Full-mooners	1,039	27.6	Experts/specialists/professionals	Specialists (academic & other)	47,580	15.0	−12.6
Homemakers	240	6.4	Freelancers	Homemakers	33,846	10.7	4.3
Part-mooners	512	13.6	Freelancers	Other instructors	6,260	2.0	−11.6
Unknown*	445	11.8	Freelancers	Other	91,611	28.9	17.1

Categories	1976	1998
Career enders	1.8	14.8
Aspiring academics	37.6	28.5
Freelancers	31.8	41.6
Specialists	27.6	15.0

*Insufficient information was available either to assign these individuals to one of the known groups or to develop a "meaningful" new group.

ulty members in 1998 were considered to be "part-mooners," compared to 13.6% in 1976. Again, the definition applied to derive this group could be the reason for the huge discrepancy.

Tables D.2 and D.3, taken together, compare some key demographic, career, and work-related characteristics among the subgroups of part-time faculty in 1976 (table D.2) and 1998 (table D.3). These data again demonstrate the diversification among the various groups of part-time faculty members, regardless of the time frame applied. The semiretirees (career enders) and hopeful full-timers (aspiring academics) were more likely in 1976 to hold the PhD and to have published; by 1998 the active seekers (hopeful full-timers) were still most likely to hold the PhD and to have published; however, it is now the academic specialists (full-mooners) rather than the career enders (semiretirees) who are significantly more likely to hold the PhD and to have published. Homemakers, who in 1976 were the least likely (except for graduate students) to hold the PhD and to have published, are by 1998 among the most likely groups to do so—reflecting the widespread entry of women into graduate education in the 1980s and 1990s. Women were disproportionately represented among the homemakers both in 1976 and in 1998 (although in 1998 by significantly smaller margins) but increased from one-seventh of the academic specialists (full-mooners) in 1976 to 52% in 1998. A high, albeit declining, proportion of part-time faculty were teaching in two-year colleges in both 1976 and 1998. Most of the part-time faculty members taught one or two courses, and the average hours they spent at the institutions ranged from twelve to twenty hours in 1976. Although the majority of part-timers in 1976 were teaching in evening and continuing education divisions, by 1998 the vast majority were teaching within the regular academic program in the liberal arts and sciences and in the professions.

What is demonstrably clear is the enormous and rapid diversification of the academic workforce in our colleges and universities. Not only have the faculty split into relatively independent full-time and part-time career tracks (see chapter 7); but among the full-time faculty, we have seen tremendous diversification by demography (gender, race, nativity) and type of appointment. The part time professoriate has at once grown explosively and continued to represent a wide diversity of motivations, commitments, and qualifications.

TABLE D.2

Characteristics of Part-Time Faculty, by Type, 1976

Characteristics	All Part-Timers	Semiretired	Student	Hopeful Full-Timers	Full-Mooners	Homemakers	Part-Mooners	Unknown*
					Type of Part-Timer			
% with PhD	19.7	31.4	3.9	30.3	21.1	15.8	23.8	24.9
% female	38.7	25.2	48.5	52.6	14.1	96.7	31.6	39.3
% married	76.5	77.6	66.8	66.8	84.1	96.7	74.3	81.6
% with dependent	58.8	23.4	51.5	49.4	68.3	98.3	55.9	53.7
% who have published an article	19.5	26.2	15.5	23.6	20.4	12.9	20.3	20.0
% in evening or continuing education division	59.7	45.7	55.6	51.4	74.9	34.0	64.0	56.0
% at universities	13.4	16.8	13.9	9.0	12.1	22.5	12.7	16.6
% at other 4-yr. institutions	34.0	38.3	35.2	39.7	29.3	35.0	36.5	30.6
% at 2-yr. colleges	52.6	44.9	50.9	51.3	58.7	42.5	50.8	52.8
Average courses taught	1.5	1.6	1.6	1.9	1.2	1.6	1.5	1.3
Average total hours	13.5	15.1	15.4	18.0	9.5	17.5	11.6	13.8

Source: Tuckman, 1978, tables 2, 3.
*Insufficient information was available either to assign these individuals to one of the known groups or to develop a "meaningful" new group.

TABLE D.3

Characteristics of Part-Time Faculty, by Type, 1998

Characteristics	All Part-Timers	Career Enders	Specialists		Seekers				Graduate Students		Homemakers	
			Academic Specialists	Other Specialists	Active Seekers		Presumed Seekers		With Other Part-Time Concurrent Job	With No Other Concurrent Job	With Dependents	Without Dependents
					Pursuing Doctorate or 1st Prof. Degree	Have Doctorate or 1st Prof. Degree	Pursuing Non-Doctorate	Have Non-Doctorate				
Total N	317,210	47,233	22,710	24,870	6,450	16,580	5,440	44,120	5,910	12,180	21,602	12,244
% with Ph.D.	47.3	23.8	35.7	12.4	3.6	73.1	1.4	0.0	6.7	1.1	24.0	20.5
% female	19.3	32.2	51.7	36.8	46.6	30.1	45.9	54.9	45.3	57.6	67.3	76.7
% married*	73.3	82.8	62.7	78.6	67.9	65.4	68.7	71.3	74.8	52.8	87.8	100.0
% with dependents	57.2	54.9	53.6	66.9	45.6	61.4	63.2	56.4	64.2	32.5	100.0	0.0
% who have published an article in career	31.6	37.2	47.7	12.4	34.0	60.3	7.6	17.5	27.2	22.9	36.4	33.8
% who have taught continuing education	11.0	11.5	9.3	13.3	6.6	4.6	19.5	15.7	16.4	13.6	10.7	5.2
% at universities	20.7	18.5	27.5	16.9	15.4	26.2	11.5	12.8	11.0	18.9	24.2	21.4
% at other 4-yr. institutions	30.2	34.5	29.3	31.4	36.5	29.3	12.7	23.8	25.5	34.5	38.6	37.3
% at 2-yr. colleges	40.6	39.9	34.6	42.8	34.8	26.8	68.0	54.0	59.7	39.6	34.0	39.1
% at other types of institutions	8.6	7.1	8.6	9.0	13.3	17.7	7.8	9.4	3.8	6.9	3.2	2.3
% in liberal arts and sciences	57.1	50.5	62.1	46.2	70.1	67.3	58.4	62.2	59.5	60.7	50.0	61.2
% in professions	26.2	33.3	22.4	35.7	21.6	13.6	25.6	20.7	21.7	16.2	30.3	26.7
% in other program areas	16.6	16.2	15.4	18.1	8.3	19.1	15.9	17.1	18.8	23.2	19.7	12.1
Average total courses taught	1.6	1.6	1.5	1.5	1.6	1.6	2.0	1.6	1.8	1.8	1.5	1.5
Average total hours worked per week	37.1	30.6	42.0	39.8	35.6	43.0	39.0	36.8	40.9	32.1	29.2	26.6

Source: NSOPF-99.

*"Married" includes living with someone in a marriage-like relationship.

Definitions of Terms Used in Tables and Figures

Defining Faculty. Who are the faculty for purposes of our analyses? This definitional issue is complicated by the fact that different surveys define *faculty* in different ways, and the U.S. Department of Education's HEGIS/IPEDS biennial census of colleges and universities adds still another definition of faculty.

For the Integrated Postsecondary Education Data System (IPEDS), which until 1989 was known as the Higher Education General Information System (HEGIS), *faculty* is defined inclusively: individuals with the title of professor, associate professor, assistant professor, instructor, lecturer, assisting professor, adjunct professor, or interim professor. IPEDS excludes graduate assistants (including teaching assistants and research assistants) from the category of faculty.

Turning now to the three major faculty survey strands (NSOPF, Carnegie, and HERI), for the U.S. Department of Education's National Study of Postsecondary Faculty (NSOPF) surveys, faculty are defined as persons (other than graduate assistants) teaching one or more courses *for academic credit* during the term in which the survey was conducted. NSOPF clearly distinguishes between full-time, part-time, and visiting faculty as self-reported by the respondent. (By 1999 the two latter categories constituted nearly half the sample.) For our own analytical purposes, we have established two additional criteria in order to more strictly define faculty: we have restricted the faculty category to those individuals whose responsibilities entail typical faculty work. Thus, persons teaching one or more for-credit courses must *also* report that they have *faculty status* and that their *principal activity* is *teaching, research,* or *academic administration* (including deans, chairs, directors/heads/coordinators), or that they are *currently on sabbatical.* (See "Principal Activity: Research" and "Principal Activity: Administration" below.) Our filtering thereby excludes, for our calculations, some full-time administrators who may teach a for-credit course but who are not in a specified *academic* administrative role, as defined in "Principal Activity: Administration." This screening also excludes certain professional staff—for example, librarians, counselors, and student affairs administrators—who may have faculty status (often by virtue of a collective bargaining agreement) but who do not also teach a for-credit course.

For the various Carnegie surveys, faculty are defined inclusively: individuals offering courses in any academic department. "Visiting" faculty are clearly self-identified, but the landmark 1969 Carnegie–American Council on Education survey did not provide the opportunity for explicit self-reported distinction between full-time and part-time status.

The Higher Education Research Institute (HERI) surveys rely on the participating institutions to define faculty according to their own criteria, making it impossible to identify with confidence a common definitional standard across institutions. However, since its inception in 1989, although providing no clear definition, HERI has permitted faculty respondents to self-identify as full-time or part-time.

We have systematically excluded *medical school faculty* members from our calculations by not including persons who identified their principal field of teaching as medicine (or one of its branches). Accordingly, we systematically *excluded* from our analyses of the NSOPF and Carnegie surveys those faculty who identified themselves as being primarily affiliated with a medical school. For NSOPF surveys, this was accomplished by filtering out those who indicated medicine (including psychiatry) to be their principal field of teaching. For Carnegie surveys, this exclusion was accomplished by excluding those who reported that their appointment for teaching purposes was medicine. No such exclusion was possible for the HERI surveys, since the actual data files were not available to us. However, since the HERI faculty survey samples are restricted to faculty who teach undergraduate courses, it seems safe to assume that few, if any, medical school faculty would be included.

Academic term. This refers to the fall academic term in the focal year. All years listed are for the fall term of the year indicated, unless otherwise noted.

Employment status. Historically, the HEGIS/IPEDS biennial censuses have provided the most reliable national head counts of *part-time faculty* (i.e., those employed less than full-time) broken out by institutional type and gender. The national faculty surveys did not begin to elicit data on the employment status of faculty until CFAT-75—with the singular exception of the ACE-72 survey, which included a specific item that allowed respondents to classify their employment status in one of four ways: less than half-time, half-time, more than half-time, or full-time. (Most surveys since then have simply treated employment status as a dichotomous variable, either full-time for nine months or *not*). Moreover, the sampling strategies of all national surveys prior to NSOPF-88 did not explicitly address the issue of sampling part-timers as a subpopulation (see "Defining Faculty" above). As a result, it is fair to say that part-timers almost certainly have been undercounted and undersampled at least until NSOPF-88. Accordingly, although HEGIS/IPEDS, ACE-72, and CFAT-75 do provide limited data on employment status, we have usually employed 1988 as a baseline year for analyzing a variety of variables by employment status.

For the Carnegie surveys prior to 1989—that is, 1969, 1972, 1975, and 1984—the survey sponsors estimate that about 8% of "faculty" were part-time faculty.

See "Defining Faculty" for the HERI surveys' treatment of full- and part-time faculty.

Institutional type. The categories for classifying by type of institution have changed over the years, driven in part by the changing topography of higher education. Whereas most of the national surveys report data in terms of a modified Carnegie classification (CFAT, 1974), the Carn-69 survey used a tripartite division according to the highest academic degree that the institution offered: (1) universities offering graduate degrees, (2) baccalaureate-granting institutions, and (3) two-year, associate-degree-granting institutions. Each of the first two degree-level types was further distinguished by a purported level of quality (high, medium, or low), which was based roughly on student selectivity. This division roughly corresponds to the HERI surveys' three-way division into universities, other four-year colleges, and two-year colleges.

In reporting data by institutional type across this mix of surveys, we have chosen to collapse institutional types for most purposes into three aggregated categories of *universities, other four-year institutions,* and *two-year colleges* when that has been necessary to achieve commonality across surveys. In some instances, however, we report by a five-fold division that reflects the modified Carnegie classification: universities subdivided into (1) *research universities* and (2) *other doctorate-granting universities;* other four-year institutions, subdivided into the two subcategories of (3) *comprehensive institutions* and (4) *liberal arts colleges;* and (5) *two-year colleges.*

Sample Size. National faculty surveys differ in absolute sample sizes, ranging (among the surveys we most rely on) from about 4,000 (CFAT-97) to approximately 60,000 (Carn-69). The surveys differ also in regard to whether they report the data in terms of sample statistics or as weighted population parameters. Whereas the NSOPF surveys of 1988, 1993, and 1999 and Carn-69 report data as estimates projected for the *total* population, the Carnegie surveys after 1969 report only the weighted numbers of respondents in the sample. These reported N's, accordingly, are much smaller than the population estimates provided by the other surveys. In order to avoid confusion that would result from the incongruity between the smaller *sample* numbers and the *population* estimates if they were to be reported in the same row in our tables, we have shown *only* the population estimates; and, accordingly, we have excluded from those tables the number of respondents in the actual sample. Thus, in those instances in which the survey sponsor has reported the data only in terms of *sample N's* (CFAT-1975, -1984, and -1997), we report row or column *percentages,* but not the raw sample numbers from which those percentages were derived.

For the sample sizes of the various surveys, see Appendix A.

Program Area. The breakout (taxonomy) of individual program areas varies, sometimes considerably, across the surveys (and even within survey strands). In our effort to find a common metric for reporting data by program area, we have collapsed academic fields into two broad categories: (1) liberal arts and sciences and (2) the professions. Modifying slightly the practice we used in *The New Academic Generation* (Finkelstein and Schuster, 1998a), we have further subdivided the liberal arts and sciences and the professions into the following eight categories, plus a "catchall" for other areas:

Liberal arts and sciences:
    Fine arts
    Humanities

Social sciences
Natural sciences
Professions:
   Business
   Engineering
   Education
   Health sciences (excluding medical school faculty)
All other program areas

As with almost all variables that we use, this simplified taxonomy for academic fields is, of course, arbitrary—an attempt to balance complex realities with more streamlined aggregations. In particular, we are aware of the substantial differences (in academic cultures, as well as essentially all other respects) that are obscured when, as practicality sometimes dictates, we lump together various professional fields into a single aggregated "Professions" category.

Career Cohort. This variable is one of our own devising (see, e.g., *The New Academic Generation*). We find career cohort to be a useful lens through which to view differences and similarities among faculty members. It adds the dimension of how much *full-time* faculty experience they have had—that is, for how long they have been full-time faculty members. In other words, *career cohort* refers to the temporal *stage* of an individual faculty member's career. In much of the higher education literature, this concept is defined by either the number of years elapsed since the respondent's receipt of a terminal degree (usually the PhD) or the number of years since appointment to the person's first academic job beyond graduate (teaching or research) assistant positions. It is important to underscore that we measure faculty career experience for these purposes based *only* on *full-time* teaching.

While recognizing that it is necessarily somewhat arbitrary, we have conceptualized a tripartite division for faculty cohorts: (1) *new entrants* (faculty in the first 7 years of full-time teaching), (2) *midcareer faculty* (8 to 14 years of full-time teaching experience), and (3) *senior* faculty (15 or more years of full-time teaching experience).

The seven-year standard approximates the typical probationary period for a full-time faculty appointee at a four-year college or university. Our career-cohort construct varies slightly depending on the data available in a particular national survey as well as the constraints of the data file. Thus, for NSOPF surveys we are able to use the seven-year standard (0 to 7 years). Because some questionnaires (e.g., Carn-69) use predetermined ranges or bands for reporting years of experience, it is not always possible to maintain the criterion of the first 7 years; thus, we have been obliged to use a 6-year standard (the closest reasonable standard allowed by the questionnaire's response categories) when the respondent had to choose, say, between 0–6 years and 7–14 years. Empirically, this occasional use of a 6-year criterion for the new-entrant cohort has resulted in perhaps 5% of the new entrants (those with 7 years experience) being reclassified into another, more experienced cohort. However, in our view this occasional "reassignment" from new-entrant cohort to midcareer cohort does not significantly affect bivariate relationships between the career-cohort variable and other variables. And so, in our view, the *inter*cohort comparisons we use do hold up reasonably well.

Race/Ethnicity. The issue of how best to report breakouts of faculty by race and ethnicity is complicated both by the constantly changing categories employed in the national faculty surveys and by the need—by designers of survey instruments and by the authors—to simplify the potentially infinite array of categories. Accordingly, these matters are addressed in greater detail in Appendix I.

Nativity/Citizenship. Both *nativity* (that is, country of origin) and *citizenship status* provide important lenses through which to view changing faculty demographics. Our own analyses of faculty demographics take into account both nativity and U.S. citizenship status (the latter ordinarily broken out by the subcategories U.S. citizen, naturalized citizen, holder of a permanent visa, and holder of a temporary visa).

NSOPF-88 was the first national survey to ask respondents about their citizenship status (and that questionnaire item has been continued in NSOPF-93 and -99). Country of birth was not asked until NSOPF-93, and that item remains a part of subsequent NSOPF questionnaires.

Neither the Carnegie nor the HERI surveys ask about citizenship or nativity per se—although the 1975 Carnegie asks respondents to report the country in which their secondary school was located, as well as that of their baccalaureate-granting and highest-degree-granting institutions. From that information, it is possible to crudely estimate nativity patterns.

These demographic patterns are undoubtedly in flux. Immigration barriers were substantially eased for faculty (teachers and researchers) by the U.S. Immigration Act of 1990. But current concerns with "homeland security" in the United States may serve to inhibit the international flow of faculty and students.

Age. Age is not consistently recorded across national faculty surveys. Most surveys ask for date of birth, leaving the calculation of age to the analyst. Sometimes, however, surveyors collect age-related data by bands, but these age ranges are not always consistent. One questionnaire may ask respondents to choose from, say, 35–39, 40–44, and so forth, while another may provide somewhat different options (e.g., 36–40, 41–45, etc.). Thus, Carn-69 elicits age data in bands that differ from those employed by other surveys (e.g., CFAT-84). This constraint has required on occasion that we use broader age categories that cut across the differing categories available from the individual surveys.

Type of Appointment. The principal challenge here is to distinguish, based on survey data, between faculty appointments that are eligible for tenure consideration and those that are not. Although a minuscule proportion of part-time faculty, especially in professional fields, may be eligible for tenure (as much as 8–9% of all part-timers nationally in NSOPF-99), eligibility for tenure is overwhelmingly an issue with respect to full-time appointments; and we have chosen to restrict our analyses of appointment type to full-time faculty.

Surveys prior to CFAT-84, perhaps surprisingly, did not explicitly ask about the tenure status of respondents. To indicate a nonregular appointment, surveys routinely included *only* the category of "adjunct, visiting" faculty. Once survey designers recognized that nonregular *full-time* appointments were becoming more numerous, distinctions were frequently drawn between two types of full-time but nontenurable faculty: (1) those who are ineligible for tenure because there is no tenure option available at a campus, that is, because institutional policy precludes tenure as an option on a given campus and (2) those whose *particular* appointment is nontenurable although a tenure system does exist at a campus, that is, the respondent's *particular* appointment is tenure-ineligible. When appropriate, we maintain this distinction in our analyses; for the most part, however, we limit our analyses to the second type above, that is, off-track positions at those campuses that maintain tenure systems.

Principal Activity: Research. Surveys often ask respondents to identify their principal activity, as between research, teaching, and administration. The first of these, *research* (as well as *scholarship* and *publishing*) is among the terms very widely used by and about faculty (with reference to their attitudes, preferences, and actual work behavior). It is important to underscore, however, that such terms connote quite different types of activity as well as different "standards" of activity to different faculty. That is, faculty understandings of just what qualifies to be described as, say, research-related activity, and what constitutes a publication, may, and frequently does, differ substantially across institutional types and academic fields. Some faculty may choose to report as a legitimate publication a short piece in a newsletter or a letter to the local newspaper. Others may restrict "publication" to refereed journal articles. Thus, the "standard," given the generality of many questionnaire items, is vague and needs to be interpreted with the institutional and disciplinary context within which it is embedded.

Principal Activity: Administration. Although *administration* refers in NSOPF to administrative activities defined broadly (both nonacademic administration and academic administration), we count as faculty, for our analytical purposes, only those whose administrative work is explicitly academic in nature. In *academic* administration we include the titles *program director, department chair, academic dean* (as distinguished from, say, dean of students), and *chief academic officer* (whether vice president or provost), provided that the individual bearing any of these identified titles taught at least one for-credit course during the academic term of the survey.

Data Sources. The analysis that has been carried out on the basis of the faculty surveys demanded, in general, direct access to the corresponding data files. So, although we referred to information contained in reports and publications, the original data, as supplied to us by the appropriate agency, was employed to generate our tables. More specifically, the survey sources included the following (in chronological order by survey).

— Martin Trow et al., "Carnegie Commission National Survey of Higher Education: Faculty Study, 1969," computer file produced by Survey Research Center, University of California, Berkeley, CA, 1971; "Study 7501," distributed by Inter-University Consortium for Political and Social Research, Ann Arbor, MI, 1978. The original file provided was recoded into an SPSS format by an external contractor, October 25, 1997. This survey is referred to as Carn-69.

— American Council on Education, "Teaching Faculty in Academe, 1972–1973," computer file, ICPSR version, produced by American Council on Education, Office of Research, Washington, DC, 1973; "Study 7914," distributed by Inter-University Consortium for Political and Social Research, Ann Arbor, MI, 2002. This survey is referred to as ACE-72.

— Carnegie Commission on Higher Education, "1975 Carnegie Council National Surveys of Higher Education, Faculty Sample," computer file produced by Survey Research Center, University of California, Berkeley, CA, 1975; "Study USMISCHED1975-CARN-FAC," distributed by the Roper Center for Opinion Research, University of Connecticut, Storrs, CT, n.d. This survey is referred to as CFAT-75.

— Carnegie Foundation for the Advancement of Teaching, "1984 Carnegie Foundation National Surveys of Higher Education, Faculty Sample," computer file produced by Survey Research Center, University of California, Berkeley, CA, 1984; "Study USMISCHED1984-CARN-FAC," distributed by the Roper Center for Opinion Research, University of Connecticut, Storrs, CT, 1990. This survey is referred to as CFAT-84.

— Robert T. Blackburn and Janet H. Lawrence, "Faculty at Work, 1988–1989," computer file produced by National Center for Research to Improve Postsecondary Teaching and Learning, Ann Arbor, MI, 1989; "Study 9713," distributed by Inter-University Consortium for Political and Social Research, Ann Arbor, MI, 1992. This survey is referred to as NCRIPTAL-88.

— National Center for Education Statistics, "1988 National Survey of Postsecondary Faculty," computer file produced by SRI International, Menlo Park, CA, 1989 (Public Access Data Analysis System developed by JHC & Associates, 2001); "Study NSOPF:88," distributed by National Center for Education Statistics, Washington, DC, 2001. This survey is referred to as NSOPF-88.

— National Center for Education Statistics, "1993 National Study of Postsecondary Faculty," computer file produced by National Opinion Research Center, University of Chicago, Chicago, IL, 1994 (Public Access Data Analysis System developed by JHC & Associates, 2001); "Study NSOPF:93," distributed by National Center for Education Statistics, Washington, DC, 2001. This survey is referred to as NSOPF-93.

— National Center for Education Statistics, "1993 National Study of Postsecondary Faculty," restricted computer file obtained under license agreement 9807290399 between U.S. Department of Education and Claremont Graduate University, Jack H Schuster, principal investigator; "Study NSOPF:93," distributed by National Center for Education Statistics, Washington, DC, 2001. This survey is referred to as NSOPF-93.

— Carnegie Foundation for the Advancement of Teaching. "1997 National Survey of Faculty," computer file produced by the Wirthlin Group, McLean, VA, 1997; "Study USMISCHED1997-CARN-FAC," distributed by the Roper Center for Opinion Research, University of Connecticut, Storrs, CT, 2002. This survey is referred to as CFAT-97.
— National Center for Education Statistics. "1999 National Study of Postsecondary Faculty," computer file produced by the Gallup Organization, 2002 (Public Access Data Analysis System developed by JHC & Associates, 2001); "Study NSOPF:99," distributed by National Center for Education Statistics, Washington, DC, 2001. This survey is referred to as NSOPF-99.
— National Center for Education Statistics. "1999 National Study of Postsecondary Faculty," restricted computer file obtained under license agreement 951300177E between U.S. Department of Education and Seton Hall University, Martin J. Finkelstein, principal investigator; "Study NSOPF:99," distributed by National Center for Education Statistics, Washington, DC, 2001. This survey is referred to as NSOPF-99.

Academic Appointments

Historical Milestones

In order to provide the reader with a sense of the evolution of opinions and practices related to faculty appointments in the United States over the past three and a half centuries, we have constructed a timeline that points out some of the milestones. Any selection of "critical events" from those that make up this history must necessarily be viewed as somewhat arbitrary, since it is almost always possible to identify "counter" or "contrary" events. We have tried, nonetheless, to be judicious in reflecting the climate of opinion and practice prevailing in any historical period and to select as illustrative those events that in our judgment are—or soon became—prototypical or modal for the era in question. With these caveats in mind, it seems possible to identify several discernible stages in the evolution of faculty appointments in the United States.

The Harvard Charter of 1650 took as its point of departure the English college model of the faculty as comprising the corporate university. That characterization did not long endure, however: no sooner had the 1650 charter been issued than challenges to the model of "faculty as corporation" arose from several quarters (see, for example, Herbst, 1982). Thus, within a brief half century, charter modifications were being proposed that at once limited the terms of Fellows (i.e., the faculty) and specified a nonresident corporate body—that is, the *lay governing board*—as authoritative for purposes of making faculty renewal decisions (including specification of the grounds for denying renewal). By the second decade of the eighteenth century, the Harvard Corporation had instituted the first formal three-year term appointments for all tutors (after having restricted Fellowships to just a few senior tutors a decade earlier), thereby, in effect, eclipsing the traditional English system and leaving it behind. During the first quarter of the nineteenth century, the preference spread for term appointments, subject to renewal by the nonresident board of trustees. Thus, New York State's 1810 charter for Columbia College provided that "teachers are to hold their office at the pleasure of the Trustees," jettisoning the earlier requirement in cases of dismissal for stating a cause and holding a hearing (Metzger, 1973, p. 127); this development echoed a landmark case, *Bracken v. Visitors of William and Mary*, decided twenty years earlier.

The first quarter of the nineteenth century was pivotal in another respect: widespread establishment of the first "professorships." In contradistinction to the previously modal tutorship, the terms for these endowed faculty positions were intended to be indefinite, but nonetheless they were clearly subject to the pleasure of the board and thus far from being permanent. These professional positions were established in specific fields of study, and the incumbent was expected to have prior, or at least concurrent, academic preparation in his particular subject matter (the professors were invariably men). The point here is simply that the endowed professorship emerged as a new kind of appointment, one that frequently did not specify a length of term, in contrast to the then dominant model of term appointments for those not holding full professorial rank (even some full professors still had term appointments, e.g., at state universities such as Wisconsin and Michigan). Certainly by the last quarter of the nineteenth century, the basic principle of "at the pleasure of the board" pertained to most faculty appointments at most institutions, even in the increasingly frequent cases of those "indefinite" appointments not explicitly limited by prespecified terms.

It was in this context of opinion and practice that the American Association of University Professors (AAUP) in the first quarter of the twentieth century recognized—conceded, really—the prerogative of governing boards to undertake summary dismissals in cases of gross misconduct. To be sure, the AAUP also argued for the desirability of predismissal hearings and stressed, as well, the distinction between privileges that should pertain to long-term, indefinite appointments as distinguished from short-term, non-professorial-ranked appointments. In effect, the AAUP was recognizing a two-tier system of faculty appointments.

The AAUP's landmark 1940 "Statement on Academic Freedom and Tenure," which had been revised from earlier versions (1915 and 1925), represents a radical departure from the then prevailing climate of opinion and practice in stipulating an expected career progression and timetable for decision on reappointment for all faculty. The key notion of the faculty as a body on permanent appointment following a monitored probationary period and a reasoned tenure decision process is a creation of the second half of the twentieth century, as it relates to practice. This is a concept with only minimal legal standing and one whose long-term viability arguably depends at least in part on a "seller's" market for academic services, that is, faculty (more or less) in demand. The explosive growth of part-time appointments and the sharp increase in full-time but contingent appointments in the last decades of the twentieth century represent in some sense a return, a reversion, to much earlier American academic practice.

Nonetheless, this transformation in the deployment of academic appointments, now featuring a contingently appointed *majority* by head count, thereby constitutes a dramatic departure from practice in the pre-1975 period. The trade-offs therein entailed are multifaceted, and the consequences—for the future of the academic profession and for the quality of higher education—remain to be seen. This metamorphosis of the academic profession, perhaps best documented by the changing deployments of faculty appointments, is indeed ongoing.

TIMELINE

1650   A Harvard charter incorporates tutors as "Fellows" of the corporation.
1696–1700   New charters are proposed for Harvard College, limiting the terms of

Fellows (and, ipso facto, tutors) to seven years, with the option of renewal.

1701   At Yale, trustees agree that the rector and masters shall continue in office "quamdium bene se gesseriut" (during good behavior) (Metzger, 1973, p. 126).

1707   At Harvard, the corporation begins restricting its Fellowships to senior tutors (and appointing the rest without Corporate Fellow status).

1716   The Harvard Corporation passes a rule that "all Tutors, now or hereafter chosen" shall hold their position for no longer than three years, "except continued by a new election" (the first term appointment) (ibid., p. 117).

1720s   The donor of the Hollis Professorship (at Harvard) specifies grounds for termination as "want of ability to execute the trust or misbehavior in the office or immoral and scandalous behavior out of it" (ibid., pp. 120–21).

1722   Edward Wigglesworth is appointed to the first professorship in America (Hollis Professor of Divinity at Harvard) with no time limit (an indefinite appointment).

1727   William and Mary College completes the hiring of its first faculty and instruction begins.

1734   At Harvard, the corporation and the Board of Overseers agree to a three-year term of appointment for tutors.

1745   Yale's second charter specifies that dismissal is now allowable for cause, that is, "any misdemeanor, . . . default or incapacity" (ibid., p. 126).

1754   At Kings College, the first charter leaves open whether faculty will hold office "during good behavior" or "at will of the Governors" (ibid.).

1756   Naphtali Daggett is appointed Yale's first professor (of divinity).

1767   At Princeton, professors achieve numerical parity with tutors (three of each).

1790   In *Bracken v. Visitors of William and Mary,* a Virginia court refuses to accept the argument that professors have a "freehold" in their office as members of the corporation; rather, "the will of the Visitors is decisive" and they may dismiss a professor without a trial.

1791   William and Mary appoints its first professor.

1802   At Harvard, the number of professors for the first time reaches parity with the number of tutors (five of each); there are two separate career tracks.

     At Yale, two tutors, Benjamin Silliman and Jeremiah Day, are "promoted" from tutors to professors (the first such promotions), giving professors nearly numerical parity with tutors (although only one-tenth of Yale tutors were subsequently appointed to professorships in the eighteenth century, all six Yale professors served first as tutors).

     At Brown, three professors have joined the five tutors (about one-fifth of the tutors in the eighteenth century went on later to professorships; but less than half of the Brown professors were former tutors).

Who were professors? Typically they went into college teaching from a career in the ministry, medicine, or law; typically they pursued an institutional career at their alma mater; the average tenure by the turn of the nineteenth century was in generations (thirty to forty years); half "died in office"; only one-fourth left to pursue another career.

1810   Harvard appoints its first instructor (as distinguished from tutors and professors); over the next generation almost no instructors come from tutorships or move into professorships.

The New York legislature's new charter for Columbia College provides that teachers are to "hold their offices at the pleasure of the Trustees" (dropping the requirement for cause and a hearing in event of dismissal) (Metzger, 1973, p. 126).

1820   Professors outnumber tutors at Harvard and Yale by ten to six; at Brown, by three to one. Professors outnumber instructors at Harvard by ten to five.

1824   Yale appoints its first instructor; only four others are appointed over the next generation.

Francis Gilmer returns to the United States from Europe with five professors recruited for the first University of Virginia faculty.

Harvard faculty are "temporarily" reorganized into academic departments (the Ticknor Plan).

1828   In *Murdoch v. Visitors of Theological Institute of Phillips Academy at Andover,* the Massachusetts Supreme Court, though deferring to the Board on one charge, holds that three other charges against a professor do *not* justify dismissal (seemingly suggesting that substantive bases of dismissal were open to challenge).

1835   Henry Rodgers is appointed first professor of geology and mineralogy at the University of Pennsylvania (nonsalaried).

The first assistant professor is appointed at Brown; few additional faculty are appointed with that rank until the 1890s.

At Yale, tutors are first assigned to departments of instruction.

1842   The first assistant professor is appointed at Yale; only four more such appointments occur in the next three decades.

The first instructor is appointed at the University of Michigan; few other such appointments are made until the 1870s.

1844   Brown appoints its first instructor; few additional instructors are appointed until the 1860s; tutors disappear.

1846   Harvard establishes two new professorships (agricultural chemistry and chemistry).

1856   Professor Benjamin Hedrick is dismissed from the University of North Carolina for supporting the U.S. presidential candidacy of John Fremont.

1857   The first assistant professor is appointed at the University of Michigan; few additional such appointments are made until the 1880s.

1858	The Board of Regents of the University of Wisconsin, acting according to bylaws that require professors to be elected at each annual meeting, terminates all faculty contracts.
1860	At Harvard, the corporation limits the total time one can serve as a tutor to eight years.
1859–1914	Only six of sixty-eight dismissals at 122 institutions are preceded by a hearing.
1860s	One-quarter of Harvard instructors/assistant professors are "promoted" to full professorships.

One-third of Yale instructors/assistant professors are "promoted" to full professorships.

Junior faculty begin leaving their first employers for better jobs or promotions elsewhere.

1867	The University of Wisconsin Board of Regents declares that the "terms of office of every officer of the University" are to be continued "at pleasure, unless otherwise expressly provided" (Metzger, 1973, p. 133).
1868	At Cornell, the Board of Trustees adopts the policy of offering annual contracts, renewable unless it is "displeased" (ibid., p. 123).
1869	Courses at Harvard are listed for the first time by department rather than by class.
1870s	The majority of junior faculty (instructors and assistant professors) are "promoted" to professorships at Harvard, Yale, Brown, and Michigan (ibid., pp. 128–31).

At Harvard, the rule is adopted that all professors appointed without express limitation of time can be dismissed for "inadequate performance of duty and misconduct."

1878	In *Mudge v. Board of Regents of Kansas State Agricultural College,* the Kansas Supreme Court rules that regents must abide by bylaws requiring a three-month notice prior to dismissal despite the legislative statute granting absolute discretion to the board.
1880	Harvard offers its first sabbatical leave; junior faculty outnumber full professors by eight to five.

Junior faculty attain numerical parity with full professors at Michigan and Brown; at Michigan, the majority are working on, or have completed, their doctoral degree.

1881	Fifteen of Dartmouth's resident faculty petition the Board of Trustees for removal of President Bartlett (over faculty academic appointment prerogatives).
1892	In *McAuliffe vs. Mayor of New Bedford,* 29 NE 517, Justice Holmes establishes the "privilege doctrine" that certain governmentally bestowed advantages, for example, employment, are not rights, but rather privileges that may be granted or withdrawn for any reason (effectively blocking state university faculty from judicial review in cases of dismissal).
1894	In *Gillan v. Board of Regents of Normal Schools,* 88 Wisconsin 7, a state

court rules that the plenary powers granted to the Board of Regents absolve it of any obligation to offer teachers a predismissal hearing.

1898   In *Kelsey v. New York Medical School*, a state appellate court rules that conflicting bylaw requirements in cases of dismissal are to be resolved in favor of the "pleasure of the Board" as an ultimate principle.

1899   In *DeVol v. Board of Regents of the University of Arizona*, a state court rules that the statute giving the Board of Regents the power to dismiss "when in their judgement the interests of the University required it" lays a positive obligation on the board not to delay for even three months, or any period "Which would be in direct violation of the interests of the institution as the legislature has created it." (This ruling contradicted Mudge, of 1878, and came to set the law.)

1901   In *Hartigan vs. Board of Regents of West Virginia University*, a court rules that it does *not* have the right to exercise judicial review over judgments of a board of regents.

1910   The Van Hise survey of twenty-two American Association of Universities members reports that *none* made all faculty subject to annual appointments, although most did so for the rank of instructor.

1914   Cornell reports that although faculty appointments are technically for one year, "it is the established policy of the University that a man once installed continues indefinitely" (Metzger, 1973, p. 123).

    The Sanderson survey of forty-three land grant colleges reports only two with strict one-year appointment policies.

1915   The AAUP issues its General Report on Academic Freedom and Academic Tenure, setting down rules for "fair procedures" in dismissal cases (ibid., p. 148).

1925   The AAUP issues its 1925 Conference Statement on Academic Freedom and Tenure, establishing the "desirability" of predismissal hearings and consultation with department faculty; the organization recognizes summary dismissals by the board in cases of "gross immorality or treason, when the facts are admitted," and distinguishes between the privileges of long-term, indefinite versus short-term appointments (no rank criterion is mentioned) (ibid., p. 151).

1932   The first "dry promotions" (without salary increase) are made by campuses in response to the Great Depression.

    Several colleges assign full-load faculty to "part-time" salaried positions.

1940   The AAUP issues its 1940 Statement on Academic Freedom and Tenure, positing a seven-year probationary period (i.e., setting a timeline to regulate institutional decision making on term versus tenured appointments), which could count service at other institutions.

1950   *Bailey vs. Richardson*, 182 F 2nd 46, upholds the "privilege doctrine" for public employees.

1956   The U.S. Supreme Court in *Slochower vs. Board of Higher education*, 350 US 551, strikes down a statute permitting dismissal of a teacher for exercising his Fifth Amendment right against self-incrimination as a "violation of due process," effectively challenging/superseding the "privilege doctrine."

1958   The AAUP issues its 1958 Conference Statement on Academic Freedom and Tenure, including specification of procedural standards in faculty dismissal hearings.

In *Worzella vs. Board of Regents,* 93 NW 2nd 411, a court upholds the dismissal of a tenured professor for "insubordination" by South Dakota State College without statement of charges, notice, or hearing.

1969   Part-time faculty reach 25% of all appointments at the rank of instructor or above.

1972   In *Roth vs. Board of Regents,* 92 S.CT. 2694, the Supreme Court rejects the "privilege doctrine," that public employment is a "privilege" that can be retracted without infringing on Fourteenth Amendment protections.

Sources of the information in the timeline include Davis, 1976; Finkelstein, 1983; and Metzger, 1973.

Faculty Compensation

Data Sources

There are several sources of national data on faculty compensation. A prominent one is the National Center for Education Statistics (NCES) of the U.S. Department of Education, which collects faculty salary data as part of the Integrated Postsecondary Education Data System (IPEDS) annual data collection for institutions of higher education. NCES has also conducted detailed periodic surveys of individual faculty members, including salary data, in 1987–88, 1992–93, 1998–99, and 2003–4; these are known respectively as the 1988 National Survey of Postsecondary Faculty and the 1993, 1999, and 2004 National Studies of Postsecondary Faculty (NSOPF). The 2003–4 survey is available as of 2005.

Several of the educational associations also collect salary data. These associations include most notably the American Association of University Professors (AAUP), the American Federation of Teachers (AFT), the National Educational Association (NEA), and the College and University Professional Association for Human Resources (CUPA-HR), which has added a series on faculty members to the surveys of administrative salaries that CUPA-HR has conducted for decades.

Each of these sources of faculty salary data is described here.

NATIONAL CENTER FOR EDUCATION STATISTICS, U.S. DEPARTMENT OF EDUCATION (NCES)

NCES currently conducts eleven surveys to obtain data relating to postsecondary education, including data on institutions and students. The two surveys that pertain primarily to postsecondary faculty are the Integrated Postsecondary Education Data System (IPEDS) and the periodic NSOPF (National Study of Postsecondary Faculty). The IPEDS survey is completed by institutions of higher education on an annual cycle entailing several collection periods per year. IPEDS is the successor, since 1986, to a previous annual survey, the Higher Education General Information System (or HEGIS).

IPEDS Faculty Data

IPEDS is the core postsecondary education data collection program of NCES. It obtains data from institutions in the fifty states, the District of Columbia, and outlying areas that participate in Title IV (of the federal Higher Education Act) student financial aid programs. IPEDS currently collects data from approximately 9,900 post-secondary institutions. Postsecondary institutions are defined for IPEDS purposes as those institutions whose primary purpose is to provide instruction to students beyond the high school level. Included are academic, vocational, and continuing education programs, but not avocational or adult basic education programs.

The postsecondary institutions are grouped into nine categories structured as a three-by-three matrix: three variables for control (public, private nonprofit, and private for-profit) and three for institutional type (institutions offering baccalaureate or higher degrees, two-year colleges, and institutions offering a less-than-two-year program [often for an occupation certificate]).

IPEDS ordinarily collects data annually (but did not do so in 2000) for full-time instructional faculty at degree-granting institutions that award AA, BA, MA, doctoral, or first professional degrees. Data are collected on salaries and fringe benefits and are broken out by rank, gender, tenure status, and length of contract. In 1998–99 the survey response rate from institutions was about 95%, and data for the missing institutions were imputed based on the returns from responding institutions. Additional information about IPEDS can be obtained from the National Center for Education Statistics Web site at www.nces.ed.gov/ipeds/.

National Surveys of Postsecondary Faculty (NSOPF)

The NSOPF series was inaugurated to respond to the need for richer data on college and university faculty. Four "cycles" of NSOPF have been conducted thus far. The institutional and faculty sample sizes of the four cycles compare as follows:

	1987–88	1992–93	1998–99	2003–4
Sample Size				
Institutions	480	974	960	
Chairpersons	3,000+	—	—	
Faculty	11,000	31,354	18,000	35,000
Response Rates (in %)				
Institutions	88	94	93	
Chairpersons	80	—	—	
Faculty Subsample	76	84	83(?)	76

Some data from the fourth survey cycle (NSOPF-04), conducted in 2003–4, are available in 2005.

NSOPF Survey Design.

As described by NCES, the NSOPF uses a two-stage stratified, clustered probability design, stratifying the 3,396 institutions in the universe on the basis of the highest degree offered and the amount of federal research dollars they received.

Institutional sample and survey instrument. The institutions included in the survey are drawn from the universe of public and private not-for-profit institutions located in the United States that confer formal associate, bachelor's, or advanced degrees and which participate in the Title IV student aid programs. The survey excludes for-profit institutions.

The institutional survey seeks, for the given year, numbers of faculty, faculty hires and departures, tenure policies and tenure status of faculty, and retirement and other benefits of faculty.

Faculty member sample and survey instrument. The universe of faculty, for purposes of the NSOPF-93, NSOPF-99, and NSOPF-04 sampling, includes all those persons who were designated as faculty, whether or not their responsibilities included instruction, plus nonfaculty personnel with instructional responsibilities. Administrators and researchers who held faculty positions, even if they did not teach, were included in the samples. Teaching assistants, however, were not included in the samples.

In addition to asking sampled individuals to report on their own salary and benefits, the faculty member survey asked for demographic and social characteristics of the faculty and their academic and professional background; employment history and current employment status, including rank and tenure; workload; field of instruction; publications; job satisfaction and attitudes; and career and retirement plans.

The survey forms can be downloaded from the NCES/NSOPF Web site, www.nces.ed.gov/surveys/nsopf/.

The NCES has developed for public use a particularly useful Data Analysis System (DAS) that provides not only public access to NCES survey data but also analytic capabilities. DAS can generate and print tables drawn from the NSOPF survey items, including straight counts, percentages, means, and correlation coefficients.

DAS is a Windows software application and is also available from NCES as a CD-ROM. More information about the DAS, and downloads, can be obtained from the DAS Web site, www.nces.ed.gov/das/.

A note on reconciling data from IPEDS and NSOPF is in order. A challenge to interpreting faculty compensation data arises from the differences between IPEDS and NSOPF data. Different results are to be expected because the data sources are so different: for IPEDS purposes, the data are institution-wide salary data, derived from "official" institutional payrolls, but for NSOPF purposes, data are provided by the individual faculty member, who may not have at hand his or her precise salary information at the time of responding to the questionnaire. More problematic is that the sampling frame for faculty members can be an issue; in any event, the NSOPF response rates, although impressively high compared to those of other surveys, are consistently lower than IPEDS *institutional* response rates.

In addition to the public-use data file, researchers deemed qualified by the Department of Education may obtain a restricted-access CD-ROM that details analytical options.

AMERICAN ASSOCIATION OF UNIVERSITY PROFESSORS (AAUP)

The AAUP, founded in 1915, is a nonprofit professional organization with a membership in 2005 of approximately 44,000. AAUP represents faculty, librarians, and academic professionals at four-year and two-year accredited public and private colleges and universities.

The AAUP conducts each fall a widely used survey of institutions of higher education regarding faculty salaries and benefits. The results are published in an issue of the AAUP journal, *Academe,* usually in the March–April issue, as "The Annual Report on the Economic Status of the Profession." (The 2004–5 report is based on responses from 1,416 institutions representing 1,715 campuses.)

The AAUP uses the following definitions for its survey.

Instructional Faculty: those members of the staff who are employed on a full-time basis and whose major regular assignment is instruction, including those with released time for research. Faculty who teach only part of the year, or part-time, are excluded. Faculty in preclinical or clinical medicine, administrative officers, and teaching assistants are also excluded.

Salary: AAUP salary data represent the contracted salary for the standard nine-month academic year. Salaries for eleven- or twelve-month contracts are prorated.

Major Fringe Benefits: These include benefits for which payments are made by the institution (or via a public agency for some public institutions) on behalf of an individual faculty member. They include social security, retirement contributions, medical and dental insurance, group life insurance, disability income protection, unemployment compensation, and worker's compensation. Also included are tuition waivers or remissions for faculty or dependents, and benefits, either in kind or with cash alternatives, such as moving expenses, housing, or cafeteria plans with cash options.

The faculty salary data is grouped into five institutional categories:

Category I   Doctoral-Level Institutions
Category IIA   Comprehensive Institutions
Category IIB   General Baccalaureate Institutions
Category III   Two-Year Institutions with Academic Ranks
Category IV   Two-Year Institutions without Academic Ranks

AAUP provides data on average salary and average compensation broken out for all ranks combined as well as by each rank and by rank and gender. AAUP also calculates faculty salaries in two ways: for all faculty and for "continuing" faculty, that is, those faculty members who were employed by the institution both in the current and the preceding year. Year-to-year percentage changes, calculated in these two ways, provide different lenses: the former method, by substituting ordinarily lower-paid new faculty for ordinarily higher-paid exiting faculty, shows how *the* faculty as a whole did from one year to the next, whereas the calculation that is limited to continuing faculty members indicates how the ongoing instructional staff has fared from one year to the next.

The 2004–5 Economic Report on the Status of the Profession is shown on the AAUP Web site and can be reached by accessing *Academe,* then "Past Issues," and then the March–April 2005 issue.

AMERICAN FEDERATION OF TEACHERS (AFT)

The American Federation of Teachers is a labor union with about 1.3 million members, most of whom are elementary and secondary public schoolteachers, nurses, and other health care workers. AFT membership includes approximately 140,000 higher education faculty and staff as well. Most of the AFT's higher education members are faculty at two-year colleges. First organized in 1916, the AFT is affiliated with the AFL-CIO, with headquarters in Washington, D.C.

The AFT Research Department annually publishes trend data primarily on teachers' salaries. For comparison purposes, the AFT also publishes data derived from the U.S. Department of Labor's Bureau of Labor Statistics in each year's March issue of *Employment and Earnings,* and from the most recent National Survey of Professional, Administrative, Technical, and Clerical Pay (PATC), on salaries in selected white-collar occupations.

Data on salaries of white-collar occupations can be found in the section of the AFT Web site dedicated to its Research Department, www.aft.org, and at www.aft.org/higher_ed/.

NATIONAL EDUCATION ASSOCIATION (NEA)

The NEA membership is approximately 2.7 million, the vast majority of whom are employees of public school districts. About 100,000 of the members are from higher education institutions.

Although the NEA does not collect original compensation data from individuals or institutions, it publishes secondary analyses; for years these analyses have been conducted by JBL Associates in Bethesda, Maryland (www.jblassoc.com). The NEA publishes an annual almanac with data relevant to faculty compensation issues, the most recent being *The NEA 2005 Almanac of Higher Education* (Washington, DC: National Education Association, 2004). See especially Suzanne B. Clery and Amelea M. Topper, "Faculty Salaries: 2003–04," pp. 7–26, and the CD-ROM included with the almanac.

The NEA Higher Education Web site is located at www2.nea.org/he/.

COLLEGE AND UNIVERSITY PROFESSIONAL ASSOCIATION FOR HUMAN RESOURCES (CUPA-HR)

CUPA-HR is a professional association based in Washington, D.C. CUPA-HR surveys institutions to obtain data on administrative salaries and benefits and, more recently, data on faculty salaries by rank and discipline. CUPA-HR publishes separate reports, one for faculty at private institutions and the other for faculty at public institutions, with data shown separately for five ranks and eighty disciplines or fields. Data for 2004–5 became available in 2005.

Although questionnaires can be downloaded from the CUPA-HR Web site, the reports themselves must be purchased. For the CUPA-HR Web site, go to www.cupahr.org. For survey data: www.cupahr.org/surveys/salarysurveysinfo.html.

OKLAHOMA STATE UNIVERSITY / NATIONAL ASSOCIATION OF STATE UNIVERSITIES AND LAND-GRANT COLLEGES (NASULGC)

A Faculty Salary Survey by Discipline has been conducted by the Office of Planning, Budget, and Institutional Research at Oklahoma State University (OSU) since 1974. Institutions participating in the survey are members of the National Association of State Universities and Land-Grant Colleges that award doctoral degrees in at least five different disciplines; they tend to be the flagship public institutions in each state. OSU attempts to include institutions from every state so that a national sample of average public faculty salaries by discipline can be generated.

In 2003−4 OSU's invitation to participate in the survey was extended to 105 institutions, of which 92 responded in time to be included in the analysis. Institutions are asked to provide data on average, high, and low salaries of faculty. (Institutions that are surveyed are limited to members of the National Association of State Universities and Land Grant Colleges.)

To help in identifying the impact on average faculty salaries of the salaries of health professionals, the data are provided in three sections: Section A, major fields grouped into discipline categories; Section B, major fields but excluding health professions; and Section C, health professions only. The data are also provided for institutions grouped by three Carnegie classifications: Research I, Research II, and Other (which combines Doctoral I and II institutions). The OSU Faculty Salary Survey Web site is located at http://it.okstate.edu/irim/FacultySalary.html.

OTHER NATIONAL FACULTY SURVEYS

The Higher Education Research Institute (HERI) at UCLA and the Carnegie Foundation for the Advancement of Teaching (CFAT) publish, as a small part of their much broader periodic surveys, survey data on faculty compensation as well as items on faculty members' level of satisfaction or dissatisfaction with their salaries and fringe benefits. These series are not as extensive in coverage as the AAUP and the U.S. Department of Education data. However, the attitudinal items in these surveys provide a basis for assessing how compensation issues fit into faculty members' overall work experience.

COMMON DATA SET (CDS)

The Common Data Set (CDS) is a collaborative effort to develop reporting standards and definitions to be used by those in the higher education community who provide information requested by private publishers, such as the College Board, U.S. News and World Report, Peterson's, or Wintergreen/Orchard House. The purpose of the CDS is to improve the quality and to assure the accuracy and comparability of information provided to various publishers, as well as to reduce the reporting burden on participating institutions.

Two of the thirty-one pages of CDS instructions are devoted to defining instructional faculty and class size. The definition of *instructional faculty* used is the one specified by the AAUP: *Instructional faculty* as defined by AAUP refers to those members of the instructional and/or research staff whose major regular assignment is instruction, including those with released time for research. Participants are asked to report on the number of faculty by full-time and part-time employment, minority status, gender, and highest degree attained.

Some faculty salary data are generated by institutions analyzing trends in their own salaries over time, or for the purposes of assessing salary equity or progress toward affirmative action goals. Faculty salary data are also generated for studies comparing an institution's own salary levels with those of a peer group. These data are commonly used by public institutions or systems in efforts to influence annual appropriations deliberations.

SUMMARY

There is a wide variety of sources for ascertaining levels and trends in faculty compensation, spanning both "hard" figures and softer attitudinal measures. Of these sources, arguably the most consistent and most useful standard for measuring faculty compensation—certainly over the three-decade period upon which this study focuses—is the AAUP's Annual Report on the Economic Status of the Profession.

Note on Accessing
the Survey Instruments

In recent years, organizations that conduct surveys of faculty have been choosing more and more to make survey data (and the survey instruments themselves) available electronically in lieu of relying exclusively, or even principally, on printed material for dissemination.

The information we provide here is intended to offer step-by-step guidance in gaining access to key data sets, both those maintained by the federal government and those of nongovernmental entities. Of course, Web sites change, along with the specifics of how to reach them, and entire technologies emerge to supplant existing modalities; accordingly, all we can promise is that the steps that follow are current at the time this is written. In order to keep this information from becoming obsolete too quickly, we give short rather than long Uniform Resource Locator (URL) addresses for each step.

U.S. DEPARTMENT OF EDUCATION

The U.S. Department of Education has been increasingly attentive to making databases accessible electronically—via Web sites—at no charge to users. Among the data sets of particular interest to those whose research and policy interests pertain to the American faculty are these:

- The National Center for Education Statistics' National Survey of Postsecondary Faculty (1988) and National Studies of Postsecondary Faculty (1993, 1999, and 2004), including both the survey instruments and the data files derived from them.
- The series of Integrated Postsecondary Education Data Systems (IPEDS) data reports, for years going back to 1986.

For the U.S. Department of Education's Web-based data, most relevant to faculty research,

- Go to www.ed.gov
- Select *Research & Statistics*
- Select *National Center for Education Statistics*

Then, for access to the National Study of Postsecondary Faculty (NSOPF),

- Select *Survey & Program Areas*

- Select *Postsecondary*
- Select *National Study of Postsecondary Faculty (NSOPF)*
- Select information on a particular survey form or select Data Analysis System (DAS) for survey data. DAS was developed by the U.S. Department of Education to allow for basic access to its survey data files. It permits the user to go to subgroups of faculty for analysis and to perform basic bivariate operations. The data available through DAS will suffice for many, perhaps most, analytical purposes.

For more complex data analyses, it may be necessary to apply for an *NCES Restricted Data License.* Simply select that icon for application information and to learn about relevant restrictions.

For Integrated Postsecondary Education Data Systems (IPEDS),

- Select *Survey & Program Areas*
- Select *Postsecondary*
- Select *Integrated Postsecondary Education Data Systems (IPEDS)*
- Select *Survey Forms* or *Data*

For IPEDS data before 1986, in the IPEDS data archives at the University of Michigan,

- Select *Postsecondary Education Data IPEDS*
- Select *Data*
- Select *Data Archive at International Archive of Education Data housed at the University of Michigan*

For the Digest of Education Statistics,

- Select *NCES Electronic Catalogue*
- Enter "Digest of Education Statistics"
- Select *Digest* year

For Condition of Education,

- Select *Electronic Catalogue*
- Enter "Condition of Education"
- Select Condition of Education report year

OTHER GOVERNMENT-SPONSORED DATA

For the National Science Foundation,

- Go to www.nsf.gov
- Under *Program Areas,* select *Education*
- Select *Graduate Education (DGE),* or
- Select *Undergraduate Education (DUE)*

For the National Academies,

- Go to www.nas.edu

- Select *Education*
- Select a particular National Academies office. These include *Board on Higher Education and Workforce* and *Committee on Research in Education.*

PRIVATELY SPONSORED SURVEYS

In addition to the surveys sponsored by the federal government, the Carnegie Foundation for the Advancement of Teaching (CFAT) and the Higher Education Research Institute (HERI) of UCLA conduct important surveys periodically. However, accessing their survey forms and the data files is not so convenient.

For the Carnegie Foundation,

- Go to www.carnegiefoundation.org
- Select *Publications*
- Select *Survey Research*
- Select *Community College Faculty: Attitudes and Trends 1997* for this report based on Carnegie's 1997 Survey of Faculty. (Note that this 1997 survey, and the report, cover faculty at many types of institutions, not just community college faculty.)
  Or,
- Select *The Roper Center* (University of Connecticut)
- Select *Online Access to Data*

The Higher Education Research Institute (HERI) Web site includes the Cooperative Institutional Research Program (CIRP).

- Go to www.ucla.edu
- Select *Academics*
- Select *Graduate School of Education and Information Studies (GSEIS)*
- Select *Research*
- Select *Higher Education Research Institute (HERI)*
- Select *HERI Surveys*
- Select *HERI Faculty Survey*

You will be provided with a program overview of the Faculty Survey, normative results of the 2001–2 Survey, and a copy of the 2004–5 survey form.

OTHER SURVEYS

Beyond the four major survey strands (NSOPF, IPEDS, Carnegie, and HERI), there are a number of important individual surveys. Here is information about how to access some of the most prominent of these surveys.

For the 1972 American Council on Education Faculty Survey,

- Go to the Education Resources Information Center (ERIC) database at www .eric.ed.gov
- Select *ERIC Search*

- Enter Eric no. "ED288484"
- Follow the instructions

For the 1975 Ladd and Lipset survey,

- Go to the Education Resources Information Center (ERIC) database at www .eric.ed.gov
- Select *ERIC Search* Enter Eric no. "ED109957"
- Follow the instructions

For the 1986 National Center for Research to Improve Postsecondary Teaching and Learning (NCRIPTAL) Survey,

- Go to the Education Resources Information Center (ERIC) database at www .eric.ed.gov
- Select *ERIC Search*
- Enter Eric no. "ED287438"
- Follow the instructions

For the 2000 TIAA Faculty Poll,

- Go directly to the report at the National Opinion Research Center: www .norc.uchicago.edu/online/tiaa-fin.pdf.

OTHER METHODS FOR ACCESSING SURVEYS

These other means can be cumbersome, but they may prove to be fruitful.

Review of Major Publications Based on the Carnegie Surveys

The *1969 and 1975 Carnegie Faculty Surveys* served as a basic data source for several major publications sponsored by one of the Carnegie entities (see Appendix A). Examples include

— Everett Carl Ladd and Seymour M. Lipset, *The Divided Academy* (New York: McGraw-Hill, 1975)
— Stephen Steinberg, *The Academic Melting Pot* (New York: McGraw Hill, 1974)
— Martin Trow, ed., *Teachers and Students* (New York: McGraw-Hill, 1975)

The actual questionnaires are available as appendixes in each of these volumes, and some data analysis results are reported as well.

The *1984 Carnegie Faculty Survey* served as a basis for

— Burton R. Clark, *The Academic Life: Small Worlds, Different Worlds* (Princeton, NJ: Carnegie Foundation for the Advancement of Teaching, 1987) (The survey form together with some basic data analyses appear in that volume.)
— Ernest Boyer, *College: The Undergraduate Experience in America* (New York: Harper and Row, 1987)

The *1989 Carnegie Survey* served as the basis for

— *The Condition of the Professoriate, 1989* (Princeton, NJ: Carnegie Foundation for the Advancement of Teaching, 1989)

The *1992 International Faculty Survey* forms the basis for

— Ernest Boyer, Philip G. Altbach, and Mary Jane Whitelaw, *The Academic Profession: An International Perspective* (Princeton, NJ: Carnegie Foundation for the Advancement of Teaching,,1994)
— Philip Altbach, ed., *The International Academic Profession: Portraits of Fourteen Countries* (Princeton, NJ: Carnegie Foundation for the Advancement of Teaching, 1996)

The *1997 Faculty Survey* served, in part, as the basis for

— Charles Glassick, Mary Taylor Huber, and Gene I. Maeroff, *Scholarship Assessed* (San Francisco: Jossey-Bass, 1997)

Consortium of Social Science Associations

• Go to www.cossa.org
• Select *COSSA Members* or *Research Support*

Faculty Diversity

Race and Ethnicity Categories

The attempt to report changes over time in the characteristics, activities, and values of faculty members by racial and ethnic categories presents researchers with some formidable challenges. (The issue, and the consequent challenge, affects many different kinds of research, of course. Any perusal of the changing categories used by the U.S. Census Bureau will attest to the constantly evolving historical realities and sensibilities in matters of race and ethnicity.) Over the past three decades, there have been considerable, even dramatic, changes in the conventions for labeling racial and ethnic groups, as well as in the relative inclusiveness or exclusiveness of categories for grouping individuals. Sometimes the pace of change has exceeded the capacity of social science research to adapt and interpret, given the half-life of categories from inception to publication. Moreover, in the current study, with its focus on mining historical data files, we have been limited by the naming and categorizing conventions built into, and thereby constraining, the data collection at different historical moments.

In 1969 the Carnegie Council/American Council on Education simply identified three racial categories: *white/Caucasian, black/Negro/Afro-American,* and *Oriental.* By 1975 that taxonomy had expanded to include the new categories *other Asians* and *Native Americans/American Indians,* as well as two new categories for Hispanics/Latinos: *Mexican-American/Chicano* and *Puerto Rican.* By 1984 *Hispanic* had been added as a new, separate category in contradistinction to *Mexican-American* and *Puerto Rican.* And in 1988–89 each of three roughly concurrent national faculty surveys "resolved" the classification confusion in three slightly different directions. The first HERI survey (1989–90) mirrored the 1975 Carnegie survey categories (i.e., no separate or inclusive *Hispanic* category), whereas the Carnegie Foundation for the Advancement of Teaching (1989) eliminated the separate *Mexican* and *Puerto Rican* categories and subsumed them under the more inclusive *Hispanic* category. Finally, the U.S. Department of Education, in its first national faculty survey (NSOPF-88, based on 1987 data) distinguished, by way of illustration, among three subgroups of Native Americans (*Indians, Aleuts,* and *Eskimos*) and among ten subgroups of Asians or Pacific Islanders—although respondents were provided with only a single inclusive response category to indicate *Native American* or *Asian/Pacific Islander.* Most importantly, the USDE created a "derived" variable, *Hispanic,* which included both blacks and whites of Hispanic descent. This convention has continued in subsequent NSOPF surveys.

By 1992 the U.S. Department of Education, for purposes of administering NSOPF-93, had replaced *black* with the descriptor *African-American/Black* (to distinguish native-born blacks from foreign-born blacks), and the *Asian/Pacific Islander* category offered more elaborated response categories for self-identification as *Chinese, Filipino, Japanese, Korean, Southeast Asian* (Vietnamese, Cambodian, Thai, etc.), or *Pacific Islander.* By 1998 (with NSOPF-99), although the distinction was maintained between Hispanic ethnicity and the racial categories of *black* and *white,* the racial categories were simplified to five groups: *Native American, Asian, Pacific Islander* (now distinguished from *Asian*), *black,* and *white.*

When we attempt to discern trends using these kinds of historical data, the basic challenge is to identify a common metric for reporting results across surveys that at once permits "faithful" reporting of the data and respects the evolving conventions for naming and categorizing racial groups. Given the competing desiderata—accuracy specific to a given survey and sense-making across varied data sets—our decision, to allow for the best "fit" across time, was to adopt the following five categories: (1) *American Indian/Native American;* (2) *Asian,* including Pacific Islander; (3) *black/African American;* (4) *Hispanic* (as a single broad category including Mexicans, Puerto Ricans, Cubans, and others of Hispanic descent; and (5) *white.* We believe that this taxonomy is most responsive to the ever-changing lineup, survey-to-survey, of racial names and categories. We have not distinguished for Hispanics between race and ethnicity (although we ourselves recognize that distinction), nor have we distinguished between *black* as a racial category and blacks' nativity (i.e., American versus foreign-born). These are limitations of the data; and we have accepted them—although we have run cross-tabulations on race and nativity to allow us at least to crudely estimate their interaction (and to estimate the proportion of those who are classified as black who likely are African American).

Once having established these five basic racial and ethnic categories, we addressed the question of how best to aggregate among them for analytical purposes when either the N's for individual racial groups were too low to permit meaningful analysis, or the presentation of multivariate relationships demanded some collapsing of table rows or columns to enhance readability or emphasize a particular point. Often these considerations led us to contrast the experience and characteristics of Asians with those of historically underrepresented racial and ethnic groups. In doing so, we tried to adopt the principle of "losing" as little salient information as possible; that is, we sought to ensure that the presentation of data reflected, as far as possible, the actual variation in the full data set. On these bases, we collapsed several categories for particular tables and figures in order to highlight the experience of underrepresented groups. This resulted in *Asian, other nonwhite* (that is non-Asian, nonwhite, by which we tried to aggregate historically underrepresented groups), and *white.* We recognize the inherent limitations in anchoring any classification scheme in the majority racial group terminology (thereby defining nonmajority as a kind of "residual" group). In the end, we were persuaded that this trichotomy best reflected, for certain limited purposes, the realities of the underlying data. When we discerned significant differences *among* the subgroups that we thus aggregated for a particular table or figure, we attempted to duly note those differences.

Appendix Tables

TABLE A-3.1
Full-Time Faculty, by Institutional Type, 1969–1998

	1969	1975*	1984*	1987	1992	1998
All full-time faculty	302,584	—	—	493,690	470,320	449,190
Institutional type						
Universities	146,067	—	—	225,073	198,710	202,405
	48.3%	38.2%	37.0%	45.6%	42.3%	45.1%
Research	—	—	—	(143,713)	(130,589)	(142,124)
		(26.6%)	(24.6%)	(29.1%)	(27.8%)	(31.6%)
Other doctorate-granting	—	—	—	(81,360)	(68,121)	(60,281)
		(11.7%)	(12.4%)	(16.5%)	(14.5%)	(13.4%)
Other 4-yr. institutions	117,412	—	—	172,446	168,144	152,545
	38.8%	40.9%	39.2%	34.9%	35.8%	34.0%
Comprehensive	—	—	—	(134,037)	(130,718)	(109,647)
		(29.1%)	(31.3%)	(27.2%)	(27.8%)	(24.4%)
Liberal arts colleges	—	—	—	(38,409)	(37,426)	(42,943)
		(11.8%)	(7.9%)	(7.8%)	(8.0%)	(9.6%)
2-yr. colleges	39,105	—	—	96,170	103,467	94,195
	12.9%	17.4%	23.7%	19.5%	22.0%	21.0%

Sources: Carn-69, CFAT-75, CFAT-84, NSOPF-88, NSOPF-93, NSOPF-99 (see Appendix A for key).
Notes: Parentheses denote subsets of larger total.
For definitions of row label terms, see Appendix E.
*Data for 1975 and 1984 are based on sample N's, not weighted N's.

TABLE A-3.2A
Part-Time Faculty, by Institutional Type, 1969–1998

	1969	1975*	1984*	1987	1992	1998
All part-time faculty	68,507	—	—	233,190	255,720	290,090
Institutional type						
Universities	25,217	—	—	54,892	53,982	65,531
	36.8%	26.9%	22.8%	23.5%	21.1%	22.6%
Research	—	—	—	(28,776)	(30,328)	(37,364)
	—	(17.0%)	(15.5%)	(12.3%)	(11.9%)	(12.9%)
Other doctorate-granting	—	—	—	(26,117)	(23,680)	(28,168)
	—	(9.9%)	(7.3%)	(11.2%)	(9.3%)	(9.7%)
Other 4-yr. institutions	28,749	—	—	73,758	75,182	95,904
	42.0%	45.7%	49.6%	31.6%	29.4%	33.1%
Comprehensive	—	—	—	(56,828)	(59,532)	(68,519)
	—	(27.1%)	(40.5%)	(24.4%)	(23.3%)	(23.6%)
Liberal arts colleges	—	—	—	(16,930)	(15,650)	(27,385)
	—	(18.6%)	(9.1%)	(7.3%)	(6.1%)	(9.4%)
2-yr. colleges	14,541	—	—	104,539	126,555	128,655
	21.2%	19.0%	27.6%	44.8%	49.5%	44.4%

Sources: Carn-69, CFAT-75, CFAT-84, NSOPF-88, NSOPF-93, NSOPF-99 (see Appendix A for key).
Note: Parentheses denote subsets of larger total.
*Data for 1975 and 1984 are based on sample N's, not weighted N's.

TABLE A-3.2B
Part-Time Faculty within Institutional Types, 1969–1998
(percent)

	1969	1987	1992	1998	Change in % 1969 (1987)– 1998
Institutional type					
Universities	14.7	19.6	22.1	24.5	9.8
Research	—	16.7	19.6	20.8	4.1
Other doctorate-granting	—	24.3	26.1	31.8	7.5
Other 4-yr. institutions	19.7	30.0	30.9	38.6	18.9
Comprehensive	—	29.8	31.5	38.5	8.7
Liberal arts colleges	—	30.6	28.8	38.9	8.3
2-yr. colleges	27.1	52.1	55.3	57.7	30.6
All other institutions	—	50.0	43.4	47.1	−2.9

Sources: Carn-69, NSOPF-88, NSOPF-93, NSOPF-99 (see Appendix A for key).

TABLE A-3.3A
Full-Time Faculty, by Program Area, 1969–1998

	1969	1975[a]	1984[a]	1988	1992	1998
All faculty	302,585	–	—	515,230	483,226	480,090
	100.0%	100%	100%	100.0%	100.0%	100.0%
Program area						
Liberal arts and sciences	205,127	—	—	257,100	266,944	270,452
	67.8%	59.9%	60.6%	49.9%	55.2%	56.4%
Fine arts	(23,763)	—	—	(32,975)	(31,045)	(31,654)
	7.9%	7.9%	9.5%	6.4%	6.4%	6.6%
Humanities	(66,423)	—	—	(75,224)	(74,779)	(77,265)
	22.0%	18.5%	18.7%	14.6%	15.5%	16.1%
Natural sciences	(72,457)	—	—	(93,772)	(103,382)	(106,761)
	23.9%	21.3%	16.9%	18.2%	21.4%	22.3%
Social sciences	(42,484)	—		(55,645)	(57,738)	(54,723)
	14.0%	12.3%	11.9%	10.8%	11.9%	11.4%
Professions	94,643	–	—	200,940	145,648	139,615
	31.3%	38.0%	34.1%	39.0%	30.1%	29.1%
Business	(17,061)	—	—	(39,673)	(39,442)	(37,314)
	5.6%	5.6%	—	7.7%	8.2%	7.8%
Education	(28,039)	—	—	(40,703)	(35,152)	(34,340)
	9.3%	11.7%	7.9%	7.9%	7.3%	7.2%
Engineering	(20,563)	—	—	(26,277)	(25,116)	(23,645)
	6.8%	5.4%	6.3%	5.1%	5.2%	4.9%
Health sciences	(8,030)	—	—	(94,287)	(45,758)	(44,316)
	2.7%	6.1%	11.2%	18.3%	9.5%	9.2%
Other professions	(20,950)	—	—	—	—	—
	6.9%	9.2%	6.7%	—	—	—
All other program areas[b]	(2,812)	—	—	(57,191)	(70,815)	(69,495)
	0.9%	2.1%	5.3%	11.1%	14.7%	14.5%

Sources: Carn-69, CFAT-75, CFAT-84, NSOPF-88, NSOPF-93, NSOPF-99 (see Appendix A for key).
Note: Parentheses denote subsets of larger total.
[a]Data for 1975 and 1984 are based on sample N's, not weighted N's.
[b]"All other program areas" includes agriculture & home economics, communications, law, occupationally specific programs, and all other program areas.

New-Entrant Full-Time Faculty, by Program Area, 1969–1998
(percent)

	1969	1975	1992	1998
All new-entrant faculty	45.4	28.3	28.9	18.4
Program area				
Liberal arts and sciences	45.7	24.6	27.4	17.1
Fine arts	41.9	22.3	24.1	14.7
Humanities	45.8	20.0	25.2	15.3
Natural sciences	45.2	24.3	29.2	18.8
Social sciences	48.7	33.3	28.7	17.5
Professions	44.5	33.7	31.2	20.6
Business	50.1	36.8	29.9	15.9
Education	44.9	30.6	28.8	22.7
Engineering	42.2	25.7	33.1	22.4
Health sciences	51.8	44.3	33.1	21.9
Other professions	38.9	34.1	—	—
All other programs	55.9	45.0	30.0	19.0

Sources: Carn-69, CFAT-75, NSOPF-93, NSOPF-99 (see Appendix A for key).

TABLE A-3.3C
Part-Time Faculty, by Program Area, 1969–1998

	1969	1975[a]	1984[a]	1988	1992	1998
All part-time faculty	68,507	—	—	254,700	273,480	317,579
	100.0%	100.0%	100.0%	100.0%	100.0%	100.0%
Program area						
Liberal arts and sciences	37,577	—	—	124,294	147,406	181,222
	54.9%	57.3%	60.6%	48.8%	53.9%	57.1%
Fine arts	(6,207)	—	—	(26,744)	(27,621)	(33,466)
	9.1%	14.2%	19.3%	10.5%	10.1%	10.6%
Humanities	(12,840)	–	—	(38,205)	(48,132)	(60,238)
	18.7%	19.2%	18.6%	15.0%	17.6%	19.0%
Natural sciences	(12,167)	—	—	(43,808)	(46,218)	(52,276)
	17.8%	11.6%	13.0%	17.2%	16.9%	16.5%
Social sciences	(6,362)	—	—	(15,537)	(25,434)	(35,242)
	9.3%	12.4%	9.7%	6.1%	9.3%	11.1%
Professions	29,713	—	—	93,730	80,950	83,172
	43.4%	38.9%	31.0%	36.8%	29.6%	26.2%
Business	(4,896)	—	—	(32,092)	(25,981)	(25,884)
	7.1%	6.3%	—	12.6%	9.5%	8.2%
Education	(8,765)	—	—	(15,791)	(22,152)	(23,822)
	12.8%	10.6%	12.3%	6.2%	8.1%	7.5%
Engineering	(4,592)	—	—	(10,442)	(9,572)	(6,979)
	6.7%	3.9%	5.4%	4.1%	3.5%	2.2%
Health sciences	(3,894)	—	—	(35,403)	(23,245)	(26,519)
	5.7%	7.7%	10.8%	13.9%	8.5%	8.4%
Other professions	(7,566)	—	—	—	—	—
	11.0%	10.5%	2.5%	—	—	—
All other program areas[b]	1,218	—	—	36,677	45,397	52,815
	1.8%	3.8%	8.5%	14.4%	16.6%	16.7%

Sources: Carn-69, CFAT-75, CFAT-84, NSOPF-88, NSOPF-93, NSOPF-99 (see Appendix A for key).
Note: Parentheses denote subsets of larger total.
[a]Data for 1975 and 1984 are based on sample N's, not weighted N's.
[b]All other program areas include agriculture & home economics, communications, law, occupationally specific programs, and all other program areas.

TABLE A-3.4A

Female Full-Time Faculty by Institutional Type and Career Cohort, 1969–1998
(percent)

	1969	1975	1984	1987	1992	1998
All female faculty	17.3	21.2	24.8	27.3	33.2	35.9
New entrants	20.0	27.4	35.9	—	42.0	44.2
Midcareer & senior faculty	15.1	18.7	22.4	—	29.6	33.9
Midcareer faculty	15.3	—	—		37.7	42.9
Senior faculty	14.8	—	—		26.8	29.1
Institutional type						
Universities						
New entrants	14.3	21.4	29.9	—	34.0	39.7
Midcareer & senior faculty	10.3	11.4	15.5	—	23.1	26.9
Midcareer faculty	10.8	—	—	—	30.9	34.5
Senior faculty	9.9	—	—	—	20.5	23.2
Research	—	12.3	16.8	20.8	25.2	27.7
New entrants	18.8	31.8	—	—	32.8	40.0
Midcareer & senior faculty	10.1	12.5	—	—	21.6	24.9
Midcareer faculty	—	—			29.6	31.2
Senior faculty	—	—			18.9	21.9
Other doctorate-granting	—	18.2	22.2	23.6	28.9	33.3
New entrants	26.7	25.7	—	—	36.4	39.3
Midcareer & senior faculty	14.7	21.3	—	—	25.8	31.8
Midcareer faculty	—	—			33.2	42.3
Senior faculty	—	—			23.4	26.3
Other 4-yr institutions	21.4	24.5	25.7	28.6	35.0	36.8
New entrants	23.7	30.4	39.1	—	46.1	48.3
Midcareer & senior faculty	19.4	22.2	23.2	—	30.8	34.3
Midcareer faculty	18.9	—	—		38.0	46.1
Senior faculty	20.0	—	—		28.7	28.4
Comprehensive	—	21.3	24.4	28.5	33.9	36.6
New entrants	26.4	37.9	—	—	44.9	47.3
Midcareer & senior faculty	19.4	21.8	—	—	29.8	34.4
Midcareer faculty	—	—			38.8	48.2
Senior faculty	—	—			27.3	28.1
Liberal arts colleges	—	32.7	31.3	28.9	39.0	37.3
New entrants	38.8	43.6	—	—	49.9	50.4
Midcareer & senior faculty	29.8	28.7	—	—	34.5	34.0
Midcareer faculty	—	—			35.7	41.5
Senior faculty	—	—			34.1	29.4
2-yr. colleges	25.1	31.1	33.4	38.0	44.2	48.8
New entrants	26.5	36.5	44.2	—	53.7	53.6
Midcareer & senior faculty	23.4	28.7	31.4	—	40.3	47.8
Midcareer faculty	22.4	—	—		49.6	53.6
Senior faculty	25.1	—	—		36.6	44.0

Sources: Carn-69, CFAT-75, CFAT-84, NSOPF-88, NSOPF-93, NSOPF-99 (see Appendix A for key).

TABLE A-3.4B

Female Full-Time Faculty, by Program Area and Career Cohort, 1969–1998
(percent)

	1969	1975	1984	1987	1992	1998
All female faculty	17.3	21.2	24.8	27.3	33.2	35.9
New entrants	20.0	27.4	35.9	—	42.0	44.2
Midcareer & senior faculty	15.1	18.7	22.4	—	29.6	34.1
Midcareer faculty	15.3	—	—		37.7	43.3
Senior faculty	14.8	—	—		26.8	29.2
Program area						
Liberal arts and sciences	15.7	17.0	21.2	23.3	29.2	32.3
New entrants	18.8	21.1	32.0	—	39.5	41.3
Midcareer & senior faculty	13.1	15.7	19.5	—	25.3	30.4
Midcareer faculty	12.8	—	—		35.2	40.2
Senior faculty	13.3	—	—		22.5	25.9
Fine arts	21.0	21.8	33.3	30.5	33.0	31.9
New entrants	26.3	26.2	48.9	—	49.4	39.5
Midcareer & senior faculty	17.2	20.6	30.6	—	27.8	30.6
Midcareer faculty		16.2	—		31.0	40.0
Senior faculty	18.2	—	—		26.8	26.4
Humanities	23.0	23.8	26.8	29.1	41.2	43.9
New entrants	28.3	30.0	40.7	—	53.8	55.3
Midcareer & senior faculty	18.5	22.2	25.3	—	37.0	41.9
Midcareer faculty	19.1	—	—		57.8	50.4
Senior faculty	17.9	—	—		32.4	38.1
Natural sciences	9.5	11.0	10.2	17.8	20.5	24.2
New entrants	11.4	14.8	18.7	—	28.3	30.5
Midcareer & senior faculty	7.9	9.7	8.9	—	17.3	22.7
Midcareer faculty	7.2	—	—		26.8	30.7
Senior faculty	8.7	—	—		14.0	18.7
Social sciences	12.1	15.0	18.4	20.7	27.1	31.9
New entrants	13.2	19.4	28.1	—	38.9	47.7
Midcareer & senior faculty	11.0	12.8	16.4	—	22.3	28.5
Midcareer faculty	11.1	—	—		29.7	45.2
Senior faculty	10.8	—	—		20.3	21.3
Professions	21.0	28.0	30.6	33.3	43.1	43.8
New entrants	23.2	35.2	37.1	—	48.6	49.5
Midcareer & senior faculty	19.3	24.3	28.2	—	40.6	42.4
Midcareer faculty	20.8	—	—		45.6	50.9
Senior faculty	17.9	—	—		38.6	36.8

(*continued*)

TABLE A-3.4B (*continued*)

	1969	1975	1984	1987	1992	1998
Business	13.8	19.9	—	28.1	30.3	34.4
New entrants	15.6	23.5	—	—	31.7	35.5
Midcareer & senior faculty	12.0	17.8	—	—	29.7	34.2
Midcareer faculty	12.2	—	—		41.6	42.6
Senior faculty	11.8	—	—		24.8	28.8
Education	28.6	32.4	34.7	46.2	51.8	56.7
New entrants	29.1	37.0	56.6	—	65.1	67.6
Midcareer & senior faculty	28.1	30.4	28.6	—	46.4	53.5
Midcareer faculty	28.0	—	—		56.8	65.6
Senior faculty	28.2	—	—		43.0	43.5
Engineering	1.0	0.8	1.9	2.9	6.0	8.2
New entrants	1.2	1.5	3.4	—	12.6	14.2
Midcareer & senior faculty	0.8	0.5	1.4	—	2.7	6.5
Midcareer faculty	0.8	—	—		2.7	14.2
Senior faculty	0.9	—	—		2.8	1.9
Health sciences	58.8	63.7	56.2	38.5	67.7	66.3
New entrants	67.6	72.7	50.4	—	70.3	68.9
Midcareer & senior faculty	49.1	56.4	59.2	—	66.5	65.6
Midcareer faculty	56.8	—	—		64.8	67.3
Senior faculty	38.5	—	—		67.2	64.4
All other program areas	9.6	18.1	22.4	23.7	28.2	31.6
New entrants	8.0	21.5	22.9	—	38.3	41.5
Midcareer & senior faculty	11.6	15.4	22.2	—	23.9	29.2
Midcareer faculty	10.5	—	—		30.0	32.5
Senior faculty	13.0	—	—		21.4	27.5

Sources: Carn-69, CFAT-75, CFAT-84, NSOPF-88, NSOPF-93, NSOPF-99 (see Appendix A for key).

TABLE A-3.5A

Minority (Nonwhite) Full-Time Faculty, by Institutional Type, Program Area, and Career Cohort, 1969–1998

(percent)

	1969		1987*		1992		1998
	All Faculty	New Entrants	All Faculty	All Faculty	New Entrants	All Faculty	New Entrants
All minority faculty	3.8	3.7	10.7	13.3	17.0	14.5	19.8
Universities	2.8	3.3	11.2	12.9	18.7	14.7	22.6
Liberal arts and sciences	2.6	3.0	9.9	12.0	15.7	15.1	23.2
Fine arts	1.5	1.6	8.2	14.3	18.4	11.2	13.7
Humanities	2.3	3.0	9.2	11.5	22.1	18.7	32.6
Natural sciences	3.4	3.5	10.9	13.1	14.9	14.8	21.6
Social sciences	2.0	2.5	9.8	9.5	12.5	13.6	19.4
Professions	3.2	3.9	13.0	14.5	20.8	16.0	24.0
Business	1.0	1.9	8.5	11.7	14.7	16.5	30.0
Education	2.5	2.7	10.5	9.1	19.7	10.6	17.1
Engineering	6.1	8.1	16.6	25.4	30.9	25.1	33.3
Health sciences	3.6	4.0	13.6	11.3	16.4	11.6	14.4
All other program areas	0.9	1.2	8.2	9.3	15.9	10.2	16.5
Other 4-yr. institutions	5.9	4.9	11.4	13.8	17.0	14.2	18.5
Liberal arts and sciences	5.6	4.6	10.2	13.9	17.3	14.0	18.0
Fine arts	4.1	4.7	7.5	10.8	11.6	8.9	20.6
Humanities	5.0	4.5	9.5	12.1	13.9	14.2	18.7
Natural sciences	5.4	4.0	11.6	16.9	24.3	13.5	15.7
Social sciences	7.8	5.7	11.0	13.7	15.2	18.0	18.6
Professions	7.0	5.7	13.8	13.4	16.5	14.4	21.1
Business	9.0	11.0	21.3	11.7	17.2	14.6	20.2
Education	6.8	5.2	12.4	14.0	17.3	16.1	28.8
Engineering	2.0	2.7	17.7	27.0	32.1	18.8	low N
Health sciences	7.8	1.8	6.1	9.5	10.1	9.1	8.9
All other program areas	6.3	10.4	10.6	14.1	16.8	14.5	14.6
2-yr. colleges	1.4	1.8	9.6	14.1	14.8	14.3	17.4
Liberal arts and sciences	1.2	1.4	9.9	13.1	15.5	16.0	20.0
Fine arts	0.4	0.8	5.6	8.1	6.4	9.5	low N
Humanities	0.8	1.1	16.5	13.0	12.0	17.1	32.1
Natural sciences	1.6	2.3	4.5	12.2	19.1	14.8	15.1
Social sciences	2.0	0.7	14.0	18.0	17.9	22.0	low N
Professions	1.9	2.5	9.9	15.5	16.0	12.4	12.6
Business	2.4	3.9	9.2	11.0	18.6	9.4	low N
Education	0.9	2.1	9.7	25.0	16.1	21.1	low N
Engineering	—	—	1.2	17.4	13.4	22.7	low N
Health sciences	4.0	3.7	5.6	13.9	15.4	9.8	10.5
All other program areas	—	—	8.1	12.9	8.5	12.6	18.4

Sources: Carn-69, NSOPF-88, NSOPF-93, NSOPF-99 (see Appendix A for key).
  Note: Asian Americans and Pacific Islanders are included.
  *The NSOPF-88 survey (1987 data) did not provide the data required to create the career cohort variable.

TABLE A-3.5B

Selected Characteristics of Full-Time Faculty, by Race or Ethnicity, 1969–1998

	1969	1975	1984	Change in % 1969–84	1987	1992	1998	Change in % 1987–98
Native American								
% of all faculty	—	0.2	0.2	—	0.7	0.5	0.7	0.0
% of new-entrant faculty	—	0.2	0.5	—	—	0.6	1.2	—
% of nonwhite faculty	—	3.4	4.5	—	6.8	3.6	5.1	-1.7
Native Amer. new entrants as % of Native Amer. faculty	—	24.2	33.1	—	—	35.1	29.2	—
% of doctorates awarded	—	0.2	0.1	—	0.6	0.4	0.6	0.0
Asian								
% of all faculty	1.3	2.0	2.4	1.1	4.4	5.3	5.5	1.1
% of new-entrant faculty	1.5	2.0	3.4	1.9	—	7.6	8.0	—
% of nonwhite faculty	34.1	35.2	37.4	3.3	41.0	40.0	38.1	-2.9
Asian new entrants as % of Asian faculty	53.4	27.7	24.8	-28.6	—	42.3	26.6	—
% of doctorates awarded	1.7	1.1	3.1	1.4	5.2	6.6	7.2	2.0
Black/African American								
% of all faculty	2.2	2.4	2.1	-0.1	3.2	5.0	5.0	1.8
% of new-entrant faculty	1.8	3.8	2.5	0.7	—	5.7	6.6	—
% of nonwhite faculty	57.9	45.1	34.3	-23.6	29.7	37.3	34.9	5.2
Black/African Amer. new entrants as % of Black/African Amer. faculty	36.8	45.4	24.1	-12.7	—	33.7	23.9	—
% of doctorates awarded	1.6	1.6	1.1	-0.5	2.5	4.0	4.2	1.7

(continued)

TABLE A-3.5B (*continued*)

	1969	1975	1984	Change in % 1969–84	1987	1992	1998	Change in % 1987–98
Hispanic/Latino								
% of all faculty	—	0.3	1.1	—	2.4	2.5	3.2	0.8
% of new-entrant faculty	—	0.4	2.2	—	—	3.1	4.1	—
% of nonwhite faculty	—	6.0	18.2	—	22.4	19.0	21.9	−0.5
Hispanic/Latino new entrants as % of Hispanic/Latino faculty	—	41.5	33.3	—	—	35.8	23.8	—
% of doctorates awarded	—	0.3	0.8	—	2.4	2.3	3.3	0.9
Other nonwhite								
% of all faculty	0.3	0.5	0.4	0.1	—	—	—	—
% of new-entrant faculty	0.4	0.8	0.5	0.1	—	—	—	—
% of nonwhite faculty	8.0	10.3	5.6	−2.4	—	—	—	—
Other nonwhite new entrants as % of other nonwhite faculty	56.2	44.8	26.7	−29.5	—	—	—	—
% of doctorates awarded	0.3	0.6	0.3	0.0	—	—	—	—
White								
% of all faculty	96.2	94.6	93.7	−2.5	89.3	86.7	85.5	−3.8
% of new-entrant faculty	96.3	92.8	90.8	−5.5	—	83.0	80.2	—
White new entrants as % of white faculty	45.4	27.8	17.7	−27.7	—	28.2	17.2	—
% of doctorates awarded	96.3	94.6	94.6	−1.7	89.3	86.8	84.7	−4.6

Source: Hoffer et al. 2003.
Note: The "Other nonwhite" category includes, in every case, the overall "Other" category.

TABLE A-3.5C

Percentage of Females among All and New-Entrant Faculty and of Female New Entrants among All Female Faculty, by Race or Ethnicity, Full-Time Faculty, 1969–1998

	1969			1975			1984			1987*	1992			1998		
	% of All Faculty	% of All New Entrants	% New Entrants of All Females	% of All Faculty	% of All New Entrants	% New Entrants of All Females	% New All Faculty	% of All New Entrants	% New Entrants of All Females	% of All Faculty	% of All Faculty	% of All New Entrants	% New Entrants of All Females	% of All Faculty	% of All New Entrants	% New Entrants of All Females
All female faculty	17.4	20.1	52.5	22.1	27.5	36.7	25.7	35.8	26.1	27.3	33.2	42.0	37.2	35.8	44.2	22.7
Race/ethnicity																
All nonwhite faculty	25.9	28.6	48.0	27.9	32.7	43.8	29.0	32.8	29.7	29.0	34.8	39.5	42.6	37.2	44.6	30.1
American Indian	—	—	—	14.7	11.1	16.7	27.3	—	—	51.6	31.0	39.0	44.2	29.4	20.7	20.6
Asian	16.9	24.1	75.0	14.5	26.3	45.6	16.0	14.8	26.7	19.9	25.1	28.3	47.6	29.4	37.9	34.3
Black	32.7	33.3	37.0	41.9	39.3	43.1	44.3	72.2	33.3	37.1	47.7	54.2	38.3	46.5	60.1	30.9
Hispanic	—	—	—	18.1	26.1	60.0	26.9	23.5	28.6	27.9	30.8	40.3	46.9	37.9	39.4	24.8
Other	15.1	24.4	92.6	21.9	24.1	41.2	31.3	50.0	40.0	—	—	—	—	—	—	—
All non-Asian, nonwhite faculty	30.6	31.8	38.5	35.4	35.4	43.2	36.6	46.3	31.7	35.5	41.2	48.7	30.1	42.1	49.1	28.4
White	17.0	19.8	52.8	21.8	27.1	36.2	25.5	36.0	25.8	27.1	33.0	42.6	36.4	35.5	44.1	21.4

Sources: Carn-69, CFAT-75, CFAT-84, NSOPF-88, NSOPF-93, NSOPF-99 (see Appendix A for key).
*The NSOPF-88 survey did not provide the data required to create the career cohort variable.

TABLE A-3.6

Selected Characteristics of Foreign-Born Full-Time Faculty, 1969, 1992, and 1998

		1969	1992	1998	Change in % 1969−98
All faculty	N =	282,588	495,061	479,610	
% in universities		48.3	40.1	42.5	−5.8
% in natural sciences and engineering		31.3	26.6	27.2	−4.1
% in all other fields		68.7	73.4	72.8	4.1
% female		17.3	33.2	35.8	18.5
% Asian		1.3	5.3	5.5	4.2
All foreign-born faculty	N =	28,276	68,587	74,220	
% in universities		64.1	56.9	58.8	−5.3
% in natural sciences and engineering		39.9	42.9	43.5	3.6
% in all other fields		60.1	57.1	56.5	−3.6
% female		13.5	24.0	29.7	16.2
% Asian		11.2	32.1	29.6	18.4
New-entrant foreign-born faculty	N =	12,310	25,671	16,410	
% in universities		59.2	61.9	67.9	8.7
% in natural sciences and engineering		37.2	46.7	46.5	9.3
% in all other fields		62.8	53.3	53.5	−9.3
% female		16.7	27.9	36.4	19.7
% Asian		14.3	37.4	36.4	22.1

Sources: Carn-69, NSOPF-93, NSOPF-99 (see Appendix A for key).

TABLE A-3.7
Age of Full-Time Faculty, 1969–1998
(percent)

	1969*	1975	1984	1987	1992	1998
All faculty						
35 or under	33.1	24.8	12.8	13.0	9.7	8.5
60 or over	6.9	8.1	12.7	12.4	13.2	16.1
Career cohort						
New entrants						
35 or under	64.4	60.5	50.9	—	26.8	33.8
60 or over	1.0	1.1	1.7	—	4.8	2.1
Midcareer & senior						
35 or under	7.2	10.6	4.3	—	2.6	2.8
60 or over	11.8	10.9	15.1	—	16.7	19.2
Gender						
Female						
35 or under	32.6	30.3	19.6	17.5	12.2	10.9
60 or over	8.6	8.4	10.9	8.6	8.5	10.1
Male						
35 or under	33.1	28.0	12.9	11.4	8.4	7.2
60 or over	6.5	6.9	12.3	13.9	15.5	19.4
Race/ethnicity						
White						
35 or under	33.1	28.3	14.0	12.8	8.9	8.1
60 or over	6.8	7.4	12.6	13.0	13.5	16.8
All nonwhite						
35 or under	28.2	32.5	23.0	14.9	14.7	11.2
60 or over	10.1	4.8	4.9	7.6	11.1	12.0

Sources: Carn-69, CFAT-75, CFAT-84, NSOPF-88, NSOPF-93, NSOPF-99 (see Appendix A for key).
  *Because of the limitation of the categories, 1969 data report faculty who are 61 or over instead of 60 or over.

TABLE A-3.8

Formal Education of Full-Time Faculty Members' Parents and Spouses, 1969, 1992, and 1998
(percent)

| | Less than College Degree[a] | | | | | | | | College Degree[b] | | | | | | | | Graduate or Professional Degree[c] | | | | | | | |
| | Father | | | Mother | | | Spouse[d] | | Father | | | Mother | | | Spouse[d] | | Father | | | Mother | | | Spouse[d] | |
	1969	1992	1998	1969	1992	1998	1969	1998	1969	1992	1998	1969	1992	1998	1969	1998	1969	1992	1998	1969	1992	1998	1969	1998
All faculty	72.4	63.6	57.4	81.7	71.7	67.3	30.9	12.9	15.5	17.0	19.4	14.9	19.4	21.5	41.9	31.3	12.1	19.4	23.2	3.4	8.9	11.2	27.2	55.8
Institutional type																								
Universities	68.4	57.9	52.2	79.9	67.8	62.5	28.3	9.9	17.4	18.9	21.1	16.3	21.8	23.8	42.9	27.9	14.2	23.2	26.7	3.8	10.5	13.6	28.8	62.2
Other 4-yr. institutions	74.4	64.2	58.8	82.2	71.8	68.7	30.2	11.4	14.8	16.6	19.6	14.5	19.0	20.8	42.4	31.9	10.8	19.2	21.6	3.3	9.2	10.5	27.4	56.7
2-yr. colleges	81.4	72.9	64.3	87.3	78.6	73.7	43.3	20.6	10.4	14.0	16.5	10.6	15.9	18.6	36.8	36.5	8.2	13.0	19.2	2.1	5.5	7.7	19.9	42.9
Program area																								
Liberal arts and sciences	69.6	60.4	54.1	80.3	69.2	63.5	27.6	10.3	16.6	17.7	19.8	15.9	20.5	23.2	42.5	30.6	13.7	21.9	26.1	3.9	10.3	13.3	29.9	59.1
Professions	78.1	69.0	61.6	84.9	75.4	72.3	37.7	15.5	13.2	17.5	19.3	12.7	18.2	19.7	40.6	32.2	8.7	15.5	19.1	3.6	6.5	8.1	21.7	52.3
All other program areas	80.8	65.4	61.5	82.2	74.5	72.2	37.2	18.0	11.0	15.6	18.3	14.3	17.8	18.4	42.5	32.0	8.2	17.0	20.2	2.4	7.7	9.4	19.3	50.0
Gender																								
Female	69.2	61.1	55.8	76.8	68.5	64.2	16.5	11.7	17.0	18.9	20.0	18.0	21.3	23.2	23.0	28.0	13.8	20.0	24.2	5.2	10.3	12.6	60.5	60.3
Male	73.0	64.8	58.2	82.7	73.3	69.0	32.7	13.5	15.2	16.1	19.1	14.2	18.5	20.6	44.2	33.0	11.8	19.1	22.7	3.0	8.2	10.4	23.1	53.4

Race/ethnicity																									
Asian	57.8	52.9	46.4	86.0	76.3	63.8	20.0	7.2	28.4	25.6	25.1	12.0	16.3	22.7	38.8	29.8	13.8	21.5	28.5	2.0	7.4	13.4	41.2	63.0
Other nonwhite	76.0	75.9	62.9	81.2	76.9	69.3	17.4	13.9	13.5	10.0	19.0	14.3	14.7	20.3	38.8	26.7	10.5	14.1	18.1	4.4	8.4	10.4	43.8	59.4
White	72.5	63.1	57.5	81.7	71.0	67.3	31.4	13.2	15.4	17.1	19.1	14.9	20.0	21.6	42.1	31.9	12.1	19.8	23.4	3.4	9.0	11.1	26.6	55.0
Career cohort																									
New-entrant	70.5	58.0	47.7	78.7	67.0	60.5	30.4	13.9	16.9	18.6	22.3	16.9	21.6	23.7	42.3	33.2	12.6	23.4	30.0	4.4	11.5	15.8	27.3	52.9
Midcareer & senior																									
senior	73.9	65.9	59.5	84.2	73.7	68.8	31.4	12.7	14.4	18.9	18.8	13.2	18.5	21.0	41.6	30.9	11.7	17.8	21.7	2.6	7.8	10.2	27.0	56.5
Midcareer	74.0	63.3	54.4	82.8	72.0	65.4	31.6	12.8	14.5	18.9	19.6	14.0	19.4	21.9	41.8	32.5	11.5	17.8	26.0	3.2	8.6	12.7	26.6	54.7
Senior	73.7	66.7	62.2	85.7	74.3	70.6	31.1	12.6	14.3	15.5	18.4	12.3	18.2	20.6	41.4	30.0	12.0	17.7	19.4	2.0	7.6	8.8	27.4	57.4

Sources: Carn-69, NSOPF-93, NSOPF-99 (see Appendix A for key).

[a] The "Less than College Degree" category includes less than high school diploma, high school diploma, and some college.

[b] The "College Degree" category includes associate degree and bachelor's degree.

[c] The "Graduate or Professional Degree" category includes master's degree, doctorate, and 1st professional degree.

[d] Data not available in NSOPF-93 (for 1992).

TABLE A-3.9

Religious Background and Current Religious Identification of Full-Time Faculty, 1969, 1975, and 1984

(percent)

Religion	1969		1975		1984	
	Religious Background	Current Religious Identity	Religious Background	Current Religious Identity	Religious Background	Current Religious Identity
All faculty						
Protestant	67.7	49.6	63.4	44.6	62.5	41.2
Catholic	16.6	13.4	20.6	15.4	20.8	14.1
Jewish	8.6	5.9	7.7	5.7	7.3	5.5
Other	3.5	6.5	4.0	7.1	5.2	8.7
None	3.6	19.0	4.2	27.2	4.2	30.5
University faculty						
Protestant	65.9	45.5	65.0	41.7	63.1	38.9
Catholic	13.7	10.2	15.6	10.6	16.5	11.1
Jewish	12.1	8.2	9.8	6.9	8.5	6.3
Other	3.7	6.7	3.8	6.0	6.5	9.6
None	4.6	29.4	5.8	34.8	5.4	34.2
Faculty in liberal arts and sciences						
Protestant	65.5	43.7	62.0	38.8	61.6	36.4
Catholic	17.3	13.4	20.9	14.8	21.5	12.4
Jewish	9.5	6.3	8.8	6.1	7.9	5.6
Other	3.4	6.8	3.6	7.1	4.6	8.9
None	4.3	29.8	4.8	33.2	4.4	36.8
Faculty in professional fields						
Protestant	72.2	62.1	65.6	53.6	63.6	46.0
Catholic	15.2	13.5	20.4	16.3	21.2	17.3
Jewish	6.8	5.3	6.2	4.9	6.7	5.1
Other	3.7	5.6	4.8	7.1	5.8	7.9
None	2.1	13.5	3.1	18.2	2.7	26.8
New-entrant faculty						
Protestant	64.5	44.3	62.1	41.4	59.0	35.8
Catholic	19.1	14.9	22.6	15.9	23.8	16.1
Jewish	9.0	6.2	7.4	5.7	7.5	5.8
Other	3.7	7.0	4.4	7.8	6.0	9.6
None	3.8	27.6	3.5	29.2	3.6	32.7

Sources: Carn-69, CFAT-75, CFAT-84 (see Appendix A for key).

TABLE A-3.10

Marital Status of Full-Time Faculty, 1969, 1992, and 1998
(percent)

	Single, Never Married			Married			Living with Someone in a Marriage-like Relationship*		Widowed, Divorced, and Separated		
	1969	1992	1998	1969	1992	1998	1992	1998	1969	1992	1998
All faculty	15.5	11.0	11.9	79.7	74.8	73.9	2.4	3.0	4.9	11.8	11.2
New-entrant	17.5	15.0	20.7	78.1	70.9	66.4	3.2	3.1	4.4	10.8	9.8
Midcareer	13.3	10.6	12.8	81.7	75.9	73.5	2.0	3.4	5.1	11.5	10.3
Senior	14.4	8.9	8.4	80.2	76.7	76.7	2.0	2.8	5.4	12.4	12.2
All female faculty	41.9	17.7	16.9	44.7	61.5	63.2	3.4	4.3	13.5	17.4	15.6
New-entrant	34.9	19.2	21.8	53.4	61.2	60.7	4.2	4.4	11.7	15.4	13.1
Midcareer	42.8	15.0	16.0	42.2	63.2	64.7	3.5	4.6	15.0	18.3	14.7
Senior	56.7	17.8	15.0	27.3	61.0	63.3	2.6	4.1	15.9	18.6	17.6
All male faculty	10.0	7.6	9.1	87.0	81.5	79.9	1.8	2.3	3.0	9.0	8.8
New-entrant	13.2	12.0	19.9	84.3	78.0	70.8	2.4	2.0	2.5	7.5	7.3
Midcareer	8.0	8.0	10.4	88.7	83.6	80.2	1.1	2.5	3.3	7.3	7.0
Senior	6.9	5.6	5.7	89.5	82.4	82.2	1.8	2.2	3.6	10.2	9.9

Sources: Carn-69, NSOPF-93, NSOPF-99 (see Appendix A for key).
*This response category not available in Carn-69.

TABLE A-3.11

Dependents of Full-Time Faculty, 1969, 1992, and 1998
(percent)

	Number of Dependents								
	None			1 or 2			3 or more		
Career Cohort	1969	1992	1998	1969	1992	1998	1969	1992	1998
All faculty	35.1	32.5	37.7	40.3	46.4	43.6	24.5	21.2	18.6
New-entrant	38.2	37.7	44.5	42.1	42.5	37.8	19.8	19.8	17.7
Midcareer	25.0	29.2	33.1	41.2	47.4	44.0	33.8	23.4	22.8
Senior	40.4	30.6	37.8	36.5	48.2	45.4	23.1	21.1	16.8
All female faculty	66.2	48.3	49.6	25.5	42.5	40.0	8.3	9.2	10.4
New-entrant	61.3	47.3	52.7	28.9	42.9	38.9	9.8	9.7	8.5
Midcareer	61.5	44.3	44.1	29.4	46.9	44.1	9.1	8.8	11.8
Senior	83.2	51.0	52.3	13.0	39.9	37.5	3.8	9.0	10.2
All male faculty	28.7	24.6	31.1	43.4	48.3	45.6	27.9	27.1	23.3
New-entrant	32.4	30.7	37.9	45.3	42.2	37.0	22.3	27.2	25.0
Midcareer	18.6	20.0	24.9	43.3	47.6	44.0	38.2	32.3	31.1
Senior	33.4	23.2	31.9	40.4	51.2	48.7	26.2	25.6	19.5

Sources: Carn-69, NSOPF-93, NSOPF-99 (see Appendix A for key).
Note: For 1969 the item (86) asks "How many dependent children do you have?" For 1992 the item (50) asks "For the calendar year 1992, how many dependents did you have?" For 1998 the item (80) asks "For the calendar year 1998, how many dependents did you have?"

TABLE A-3.12
Selected Characteristics of Full-Time Faculty, 1969–1998
(percent)

	1969	1975	1984	1987	1992	1998
All faculty						
Female	17.3	21.2	24.8	27.3	33.2	35.8
Nonwhite	3.8	5.4	6.2	10.7	13.3	14.5
Non-Asian, nonwhite	2.5	3.3	3.7	6.3	8.0	9.0
Foreign-born	10.0	—	—	—	13.9	15.5
Age 35 or under	33.1	28.5	14.6	13.0	9.7	8.5
Age 60 or over	6.9	7.2	12.1	12.4	13.2	16.1
White male	79.8	73.7	69.7	65.1	58.1	55.2
"Nontraditional"*	54.1	—	—	—	70.1	71.2
New entrants						
Female	20.0	27.4	35.9	—	42.0	44.2
Nonwhite	3.7	7.2	9.2	—	17.0	19.8
Non-Asian, nonwhite	2.2	5.2	5.8	—	9.3	11.8
Foreign-born	9.6	—	—	—	17.6	18.6
Age 35 or under	64.4	60.5	50.9	—	26.8	33.8
Age 60 or over	1.0	1.1	1.7	—	4.8	2.1
White male	77.3	67.8	58.3	—	47.8	44.8
"Nontraditional"*	54.8	—	—	—	78.4	79.5
Midcareer & senior faculty						
Female	15.1	18.7	22.4	—	29.6	33.9
Nonwhite	3.9	4.7	5.6	—	11.8	13.3
Non-Asian, nonwhite	2.8	2.6	3.3	—	7.4	8.3
Foreign-born	10.3	—	—	—	12.3	14.8
Age 35 or under	7.2	10.6	4.3	—	2.6	2.8
Age 60 or over	11.8	10.9	15.1	—	16.7	19.2
White male	82.0	77.8	73.4	—	62.4	57.5
"Nontraditional"*	53.6	—	—	—	66.6	69.3
Midcareer faculty						
Female	15.3	—	—		37.7	42.9
Nonwhite	3.6	—	—		12.2	16.7
Non-Asian, nonwhite	2.2	—	—		8.0	9.7
Foreign-born	11.3	—	—		12.2	19.1
Age 35 or under	14.2	—	—		3.8	8.1
Age 60 or over	2.4	—	—		8.1	3.7
White male	81.9	—	—		54.6	46.4
"Nontraditional"*	53.5	—	—		74.7	78.5
Senior faculty						
Female	14.8	—	—		26.8	29.2
Nonwhite	4.2	—	—		11.6	11.5
Non-Asian, nonwhite	3.5	—	—		7.2	7.6
Foreign-born	9.3	—	—		12.3	12.5
Age 35 or under	0.0	—	—		2.1	0.0
Age 60 or over	21.4	—	—		19.6	27.4
White male	82.1	—	—		65.0	63.2
"Nontraditional"*	53.6	—	—		63.9	64.5

Sources: Carn-69, CFAT-75, CFAT-84, NSOPF-88, NSOPF-93, NSOPF-99 (see Appendix A for key).
*Nontraditional faculty are those who are not "native-born white males in the liberal arts and sciences."

TABLE A-4.1A
Weekly Hours Worked inside Home Institution by Full-Time Faculty, 1972–1998

	1972	1984	1987	1992	1997	1998
Mean total hours worked in institution (all faculty)	42.9	40.2	46.4	47.0	41.8	48.6
Institutional type						
Universities	43.7	40.3	50.2	50.6	43.9	50.6
Research	44.1	40.4	51.2	51.4	44.2	50.9
Other doctorate-granting	42.6	40.3	48.4	49.2	42.9	49.9
Other 4-yr. institutions	41.2	40.0	45.5	46.9	41.2	48.3
Comprehensive	41.2	40.0	45.1	46.7	41.4	47.6
Liberal arts colleges	41.2	40.1	46.9	47.4	40.6	50.0
2-yr. colleges	40.4	40.3	40.0	41.8	39.9	45.1
Program area						
Liberal arts and sciences	43.6	40.3	47.8	47.7	43.1	49.0
Fine arts	40.6	37.1	43.5	43.0	39.2	47.1
Humanities	43.8	41.9	48.4	47.1	44.1	48.1
Social sciences	44.2	40.2	47.8	48.1	43.0	48.4
Natural sciences	43.9	40.3	49.2	49.6	43.4	50.5
Professions	41.8	40.2	48.7	46.5	40.7	48.0
Business	42.1	—	45.8	44.4	42.0	45.8
Education	39.5	42.0	44.3	45.7	38.8	49.0
Health sciences	41.8	35.5	50.9	45.6	37.7	47.3
Engineering	43.5	43.8	48.8	49.8	44.8	50.2
Gender						
Female	40.7	38.5	44.4	45.8	40.9	47.9
Male	43.3	40.8	47.2	47.7	42.3	48.9
Race/ethnicity						
Asian	44.2	40.8	45.0	48.3	42.5	48.9
Black/African American	38.0	40.0	40.8	42.5	42.6	46.5
Hispanic	41.9	38.4	42.3	44.6	43.8	47.7
Native American	low N	low N	44.4	44.6	low N	46.1
White	43.0	40.2	46.9	47.4	41.7	48.7
Career cohort						
New-entrant (0–6 yrs.)	—	40.1	—	48.2	41.4	49.0
Midcareer & senior (7 or more yrs.)	—	40.3	—	46.7	41.8	48.5
Midcareer (7–14 yrs.)		—		46.5	43.2	48.5
Senior (15 or more yrs.)		—		46.7	41.3	48.5

Sources: ACE-72, CFAT-84, NSOPF-88, NSOPF-93, CFAT-97, NSOPF-99 (see Appendix A for key).
   Note: For definitions of row and column label terms, see Appendix E.

TABLE A-4.1B
Weekly Hours Worked outside Home Institution by Full-Time Faculty, 1984–1998

	1984	1987	1992	1997	1998
Mean total hours worked					
outside institution (all faculty)	3.4	6.3	4.8	3.8	4.4
Institutional type					
Universities	3.6	5.61	4.6	3.2	4.4
Research	3.8	5.5	4.5	3.1	4.2
Other doctorate-granting	3.4	5.8	4.7	3.6	4.9
4-yr. institutions	3.3	6.5	4.9	3.8	4.2
Comprehensive	3.5	6.8	5.1	3.8	4.4
Liberal arts colleges	2.5	5.4	4.4	3.8	3.6
2-yr. colleges	3.0	7.0	5.0	4.5	4.2
Program area					
Liberal arts and sciences	2.7	5.6	4.2	2.8	3.8
Fine Arts	5.8	8.4	7.1	6.2	7.4
Humanities	1.9	4.5	3.3	1.9	3.1
Social sciences	2.8	6.1	5.0	3.1	4.4
Natural sciences	1.7	5.1	3.3	2.3	2.9
Professions	4.5	6.3	5.3	4.9	4.9
Business	—	7.5	6.2	3.3	5.1
Education	4.5	7.6	5.1	5.5	5.4
Health sciences	4.8	5.8	5.4	8.3	5.0
Engineering	3.7	6.2	4.7	2.3	4.4
Gender					
Female	3.1	5.8	4.2	4.4	3.9
Male	3.4	6.4	5.1	3.5	4.6
Race/ethnicity					
Asian	3.6	6.4	3.5	2.0	3.0
Black/African American	3.6	8.2	6.1	3.7	5.7
Hispanic	4.4	8.3	5.6	2.8	4.2
Native American	low N	4.7	7.9	low N	6.2
White	3.3	6.1	4.7	3.9	4.4
Career cohort					
New-entrant (0–6 yrs.)	3.3	—	4.3	4.0	3.7
Midcareer & senior					
(7 or more yrs.)	3.4	—	5.0	3.7	4.5
Midcareer (7–14 yrs.)	—		5.6	3.4	4.5
Senior (15 or more yrs.)	—		4.8	3.8	4.5

Sources: CFAT-84, NSOPF-88, NSOPF-93, CFAT-97, NSOPF-99 (see Appendix A for key).

TABLE A-4.2
Full-Time Faculty Allocating More than 10 Percent of Total Work Time to Consulting, 1969–1998
(percent)

	1969	1975	1984	1987	1992	1997	1998
Faculty with >10% in consulting	17.5	17.4	12.2	6.6	6.2	7.9	5.9
Institutional type							
Universities	16.7	15.5	16.0	5.9	6.1	9.3	5.0
Research	—	15.1	17.2	5.9	6.3	9.3	4.6
Other doctorate-granting	—	16.6	13.7	5.9	5.8	9.6	6.0
4-yr. institutions	18.6	17.5	11.7	7.1	6.2	8.6	5.7
Comprehensive	—	17.6	12.3	7.5	6.6	9.8	6.5
Liberal arts colleges	—	17.1	9.0	5.9	4.9	5.7	3.7
2-yr. colleges	16.9	20.3	7.1	6.7	6.6	5.6	6.5
Program area							
Liberal arts and sciences	14.3	14.4	7.8	6.3	4.5	4.9	5.0
Fine arts	21.2	20.9	10.2	11.4	8.5	6.6	8.4
Humanities	14.4	15.2	4.0	3.3	3.1	2.1	4.0
Social sciences	17.8	17.2	13.6	5.3	5.2	8.2	7.3
Natural sciences	10.0	9.8	6.7	7.3	3.9	4.3	3.4
Professions	21.3	21.8	18.1	6.2	8.0	10.3	6.5
Business	22.2	20.9	—	11.5	13.6	13.5	10.2
Education	26.7	25.6	18.4	7.0	5.6	10.4	5.0
Health sciences	16.5	20.0	20.3	3.5	4.4	7.3	4.9
Engineering	18.7	22.0	16.5	10.6	8.1	11.3	5.0
Gender							
Female	22.3	18.3	11.1	4.4	3.6	6.9	4.4
Male	16.5	17.1	12.6	7.5	7.5	8.5	6.7
Race/ethnicity							
Asian	19.8	20.4	10.3	4.6	3.1	5.9	4.3
Black/African American	29.0	23.4	9.1	5.6	5.8	13.9	8.5
Hispanic	—	24.6	13.5	7.7	5.2	8.2	4.9
Native American	—	18.8	low N	6.0	9.2	low N	14.1
White	17.1	17.1	12.2	6.8	6.4	7.7	5.8
Career cohort							
New-entrant (0–6 yrs.)	17.3	17.9	12.2	—	5.3	5.9	5.6
Midcareer & senior (7 or more yrs.)	17.6	16.8	12.3	—	6.6	8.1	6.0
Midcareer (7–14 yrs.)	17.4	—	—		6.8	8.8	5.0
Senior (15 or more yrs.)	17.8	—	—		6.5	7.8	6.5

Sources: Carn-69, CFAT-75, CFAT-84, NSOPF88, NSOPF93, CFAT-97, NSOPF-99 (see Appendix A for key).

TABLE A-4.3

Full-Time Faculty Leaning or Heavily Oriented to Teaching and Research, 1969–1997

(percent)

	1969	1975	1984	1988	1997
All faculty					
Teaching	74.7	74.3	69.5	65.5	72.0
Research	25.3	25.7	30.6	34.5	27.7
Institutional type					
universities					
Teaching	59.4	52.8	46.2	34.9	45.0
Research	40.6	47.2	53.8	65.1	54.4
Research univs.					
Teaching	—	47.9	38.3	24.2	40.4
Research	—	52.1	61.7	75.8	59.1
Other doctorate- granting universities					
Teaching	—	64.1	61.8	49.5	60.4
Research	—	35.9	38.2	50.5	39.3
Other 4-yr. institutions					
Teaching	86.0	85.1	77.0	77.5	78.0
Research	14.0	14.9	23.0	22.5	21.4
Comprehensive					
Teaching	—	83.6	75.0	76.2	76.0
Research	—	16.4	25.0	23.8	23.4
Liberal arts colleges					
Teaching	—	88.6	84.8	80.8	83.2
Research	—	11.4	15.2	19.2	16.1
2-yr. colleges					
Teaching	95.7	95.1	93.6	93.4	96.3
Research	4.3	4.9	6.4	6.6	3.7
Program area					
Liberal arts and sciences					
Teaching	71.1	70.9	66.7	—	66.7
Research	28.9	29.1	33.3	—	32.7
Fine arts					
Teaching	82.4	82.9	83.9	—	71.6
Research	17.6	17.1	16.1	—	27.9
Humanities					
Teaching	81.8	78.6	70.2	69.3	74.2
Research	18.2	21.4	29.8	30.7	25.4
Social sciences					
Teaching	64.7	66.0	63.7	56.6	61.8
Research	35.3	34.0	36.3	43.4	37.1
Natural sciences					
Teaching	61.4	62.7	55.2	68.7	63.2
Research	38.6	37.3	44.8	31.3	36.6
Professions					
Teaching	81.0	79.5	72.1	—	77.2
Research	19.0	20.5	27.9	—	22.4
Business					
Teaching	87.5	85.3	57.8	—	78.3
Research	12.5	14.7	16.0	—	21.1

(continued)

TABLE A-4.3 (*continued*)

	1969	1975	1984	1988	1997
Program area					
Education					
Teaching	89.3	87.3	80.6	—	79.5
Research	10.7	12.7	19.4	—	20.5
Health sciences					
Teaching	82.6	85.3	69.6	—	85.8
Research	17.4	14.7	30.4	—	14.2
Engineering					
Teaching	68.0	62.0	72.0	—	55.6
Research	32.0	38.0	28.0	—	44.0
Gender					
Female					
Teaching	87.6	87.0	78.1	70.0	79.3
Research	12.4	13.0	21.9	30.0	20.1
Male					
Teaching	71.9	70.7	66.2	64.0	67.5
Research	28.1	29.3	33.8	36.0	32.3
Race/ethnicity					
Asian					
Teaching	43.1	50.1	48.5	43.7	51.6
Research	56.9	49.9	51.5	56.3	48.4
Black/African American					
Teaching	86.8	81.6	52.6	66.5	72.6
Research	13.2	18.4	47.4	33.5	26.4
Hispanic					
Teaching	—	66.7	56.7	53.3	74.1
Research	—	33.3	43.3	46.7	23.5
Native American					
Teaching	—	76.9	90.0	77.8	82.6
Research	—	23.1	10.0	22.2	17.4
White					
Teaching	74.9	74.7	70.9	66.4	73.1
Research	25.1	25.3	29.1	33.6	26.6
Career cohort					
New-entrant (0–6 yrs.)					
Teaching	73.6	71.0	61.3	50.9	66.9
Research	26.4	29.0	38.7	49.1	32.3
Midcareer & senior					
(7 or more yrs.)					
Teaching	75.6	74.8	71.1	68.0	72.8
Research	24.4	25.2	28.9	32.0	26.8
Midcareer (7–14 yrs.)					
Teaching	73.5	—	—	60.2	68.4
Research	26.5	—	—	39.8	31.0
Senior (15 or more yrs.)					
Teaching	77.6	—	—	70.7	74.6
Research	22.4	—	—	29.3	25.2

Sources: Carn-69, CFAT-75, CFAT-84, NCRIPTAL-88, CFAT-97 (see Appendix A for key).

TABLE A-4.4

Ratio of Full-Time Faculty Leaning or Heavily Oriented to Teaching, to Those Leaning or Heavily Oriented to Research, 1969–1997

	1969	1975	1984	1988	1997	Difference in Ratios 1969–97*
All faculty	3.0	2.9	2.3	1.9	2.6	−0.3
Institutional type						
Universities	1.5	1.1	0.9	0.5	0.8	−0.6
Research	—	0.9	0.6	0.3	0.7	−0.2
Other doctorate-granting	—	1.8	1.6	1.0	1.5	−0.2
Other 4-yr. institutions	6.1	5.7	3.3	3.4	3.6	−2.5
Comprehensive	—	5.1	3.0	3.2	3.2	−1.8
Liberal arts colleges	—	7.8	5.6	4.2	5.2	−2.6
2-yr. colleges	22.3	19.4	14.6	14.2	26.0	3.8
Program area						
Liberal arts and sciences	2.5	2.4	2.0	—	2.0	−0.4
Fine arts	4.7	4.8	5.2	—	2.6	−2.1
Humanities	4.5	3.7	2.4	2.3	2.9	−1.6
Social sciences	1.8	1.9	1.8	1.3	1.7	−0.2
Natural sciences	1.6	1.7	1.2	2.2	1.7	0.1
Professions	4.3	3.9	2.6	—	3.4	−0.8
Business	7.0	5.8	—		3.7	−3.3
Education	8.3	6.9	4.2		3.9	−4.5
Health sciences	4.7	5.8	2.3		6.0	1.3
Engineering	2.1	1.6	2.6		1.3	−0.9
Gender						
Female	7.1	6.7	3.6	2.3	3.9	−3.1
Male	2.6	2.4	2.0	1.8	2.1	−0.5
Race/ethnicity						
Asian	0.8	1.0	0.9	0.8	1.1	0.3
Other nonwhite	5.1	3.4	1.1	1.9	2.6	−0.8
Native American	—	3.3	—	—	—	—
Black/African American	6.6	4.4	1.1	2.0	2.8	−3.8
Hispanic	—	2.0	1.3	1.1	3.2	1.2
White	3.0	3.0	2.4	2.0	2.7	−0.2
Career cohort						
New-entrant (0–6 yrs)	2.8	2.4	1.6	1.0	2.1	−0.7
Midcareer & senior (7 or more yrs.)	3.1	3.0	2.5	2.1	2.7	−0.4
Midcareer (7–14 yrs.)	2.8	—	—	1.5	2.2	−0.6
Senior (15 or more yrs.)	3.5	—	—	2.4	3.0	−0.5

Sources: Carn-69, CFAT-75, CFAT-84, NCRIPTAL-88, CFAT-97 (see Appendix A for key).

*The difference 1969–97 for research, other doctorate-granting, comprehensive, and liberal arts institutions, as well as for Hispanic faculty, is really a 1975–97 difference.

TABLE A-4.5
Mean Percentage of Full-Time Faculty Effort Allocated to Teaching and Research, 1972–1998

	1972	1984	1987	1988	1992	1997	1998
All faculty							
Teaching	65.5	65.8	55.7	57.8	55.9	64.1	60.8
Research	24.8	15.0	16.0	15.4	18.9	19.2	15.1
Institutional type							
Universities							
Teaching	59.5	53.8	43.0	42.8	42.5	50.0	50.2
Research	30.8	25.8	27.1	27.1	32.4	33.1	25.6
Research							
Teaching	57.2	50.3	42.0	38.2	39.3	48.2	49.2
Research	32.9	28.9	29.3	30.9	35.6	35.2	27.4
Other doctorate-granting							
Teaching	65.9	60.5	44.8	49.0	48.2	56.0	52.6
Research	24.8	19.7	23.2	22.0	26.5	26.3	21.3
Other 4-yr. institutions							
Teaching	77.8	68.5	62.5	62.3	60.7	65.8	65.6
Research	12.5	11.2	10.0	10.6	13.6	16.9	10.0
Comprehensive							
Teaching	77.4	67.4	62.0	60.8	60.1	64.5	64.6
Research	13.1	12.0	10.4	11.4	14.2	17.9	10.6
Liberal arts colleges							
Teaching	78.4	73.2	64.3	66.2	63.0	69.2	68.1
Research	11.7	8.2	8.5	8.4	11.7	14.2	8.6
2-yr. colleges							
Teaching	88.5	79.9	71.5	72.3	71.3	78.7	4.4
Research	4.9	4.7	3.3	4.4	4.8	5.3	3.7
Program area							
Liberal arts and sciences							
Teaching	64.5	65.7	56.6	57.7	56.0	64.7	61.4
Research	26.3	17.3	18.7	15.5	21.1	21.9	16.9
Fine arts							
Teaching	73.8	66.6	54.0	—	56.9	65.0	63.6
Research	10.3	0.3	9.8	—	15.1	16.9	11.6
Humanities							
Teaching	72.0	70.2	60.9	59.4	61.7	69.8	66.2
Research	19.7	14.7	16.0	12.7	16.7	16.9	12.7
Social sciences							
Teaching	62.0	62.6	54.2	52.0	52.4	60.8	57.9
Research	28.1	20.3	20.8	19.0	22.6	24.8	18.2
Natural sciences							
Teaching	57.8	62.4	55.7	60.5	53.1	63.5	59.0
Research	33.0	22.7	23.3	15.1	27.2	24.9	20.8
Professions							
Teaching	68.6	62.2	45.2	—	56.2	62.3	60.0
Research	21.1	14.2	20.8	—	16.1	16.5	13.3
Business							
Teaching	71.9	—	57.8	—	57.1	65.4	63.5
Research	18.6	—	16.0	—	15.2	16.6	11.7

(*continued*)

TABLE A-4.5 (continued)

	1972	1984	1987	1988	1992	1997	1998
Program area							
Education							
Teaching	74.8	66.3	58.1	—	55.9	64.0	60.2
Research	13.6	9.7	11.4	—	11.9	15.0	10.7
Health sciences							
Teaching	67.9	59.4	34.1	—	59.8	58.8	61.1
Research	20.8	13.4	24.4	—	12.4	10.6	11.0
Engineering							
Teaching	63.7	64.8	56.2	—	53.0	58.15	6.0
Research	26.1	15.4	21.0	—	22.3	28.3	20.4
Gender							
Female							
Teaching	78.8	70.0	60.7	61.0	61.5	66.2	64.0
Research	12.8	10.4	11.6	13.2	13.9	14.6	11.8
Male							
Teaching	63.2	64.3	53.9	56.7	53.1	62.8	59.0
Research	27.0	16.7	17.6	16.1	21.4	21.8	16.9
Race/ethnicity							
Asian							
Teaching	57.5	57.3	49.2	59.4	55.4	57.1	56.1
Research	35.9	24.9	24.9	18.1	26.5	31.5	24.2
Black/African American							
Teaching	76.1	71.8	58.8	59.0	58.4	65.16	2.0
Research	13.9	7.3	11.3	12.9	13.2	17.4	10.9
Hispanic							
Teaching	66.6	66.3	57.0	57.7	57.2	72.5	61.4
Research	23.3	12.0	13.9	18.0	19.3	13.9	16.9
Native American							
Teaching	64.6	68.3	60.5	58.3	61.3	69.36	5.4
Research	21.3	8.0	9.1	14.4	12.5	15.6	10.5
White							
Teaching	65.5	65.9	55.9	57.7	55.8	64.3	61.0
Research	24.8	14.9	15.8	15.4	18.8	18.7	14.7
Career cohort							
New-entrants (0–6 years)							
Teaching	—	63.2	—	56.6	54.6	64.9	61.3
Research	—	18.8	—	19.6	20.6	20.4	18.1
Midcareer & senior (7 or more yrs.)							
Teaching	—	66.1	—	57.9	56.5	64.0	60.1
Research	—	14.4	—	14.7	18.2	19.0	14.8
Midcareer (7–14 yrs.)							
Teaching	—	—	—	55.0	53.4	64.4	60.8
Research	—	—	—	17.3	20.0	19.8	15.6
Senior (15 or more yrs.)							
Teaching	—	—	—	59.5	57.5	63.9	59.7
Research	—	—	—	13.7	17.6	18.6	14.3

Sources: ACE-72, CFAT-84, NCRIPTAL-88, NSOPF-88, NSOPF-93, CFAT-97, NSOPF99 (see Appendix A for key).

TABLE A-4.6

Ratio of Full-Time Faculty Teaching Effort to Research Effort, 1969–1998

	1972	1984	1988*	1992	1997	1998
All faculty	3.6	8.1	6.0	5.0	5.2	7.0
Institutional type						
Universities	2.2	2.4	1.7	1.3	1.6	2.2
Other 4-yr. institutions	11.0	10.7	8.0	7.0	5.5	8.5
2-yr. colleges	84.9	58.1	60.0	46.5	46.9	60.0
Program area						
Liberal arts and sciences	3.0	5.8	—	4.0	4.0	6.0
Fine arts	6.7	11.6	—	5.0	5.1	7.0
Humanities	4.8	6.7	7.0	6.0	5.6	8.0
Social sciences	2.4	3.8	4.0	3.0	2.8	4.3
Natural sciences	1.9	3.5	7.0	3.0	3.6	5.7
Professions	4.8	9.5	—	6.8	6.6	7.5
Business	4.8	—		6.7	6.3	11.4
Education	9.4	15.7		7.0	6.5	7.5
Health sciences	8.7	10.6		14.0	13.5	10.0
Engineering	2.6	7.4		3.2	2.2	3.8
Gender						
Female	12.6	17.0	7.9	8.9	8.2	9.0
Male	3.0	6.3	6.0	3.8	4.0	5.5
Race/ethnicity						
Asian	1.9	2.7	4.7	3.0	2.2	3.1
Other nonwhite	6.2	15.8	7.0	7.0	6.4	7.4
White	3.6	8.3	6.0	5.0	5.5	7.0
Career cohort						
New-entrant (0–6 yrs.)	—	5.3	4.0	5.0	5.2	7.0
Midcareer & senior (7 or more yrs.)	—	9.0	6.0	5.0	5.3	7.0

Sources: ACE-72, CFAT-84, NCRIPTAL-00, NSOPF-93, CFAT-97, NSOPF-99 (see Appendix A for key).

Note: For each case, the figure given here is the ratio of percentage of time involved in teaching to percentage of time involved in research. When either percentage was 0, 1 was used for calculating the ratio. The median was then obtained for the ratios thus calculated. For 1972, 1984, and 1997 the percent time measures were derived from weekly worked hours reported, whereas for 1988, 1992, and 1998, those measures were based on the reported percentages of time spent in each type of actitivity.

*In 1988 only faculty from humanities and social and natural sciences were sampled. Usually humanities and social sciences are characterized as having fewer gender differences in a number of aspects (including the one reported in this table) as compared to faculty in other program areas.

TABLE A-4.7

Full-Time Faculty Spending 10 Percent or Less Time in Administration, 1969–1998

(percent)

	1969	1972	1984	1987	1988	1992	1997	1998
All faculty	52.8	66.7	55.5	66.6	60.0	71.4	71.2	68.9
Institutional type								
Universities	51.5	65.7	52.6	63.4	58.1	70.1	67.4	67.6
Research	—	64.8	51.9	63.4	57.1	69.7	68.1	68.1
Other doctorate-granting	—	68.0	53.8	63.3	59.4	70.8	65.0	66.6
Other 4-yr. institutions	53.0	67.6	53.0	66.2	56.2	71.4	69.2	68.8
Comprehensive	—	70.0	53.6	67.4	56.5	72.4	70.0	70.1
Liberal arts colleges	—	64.5	50.9	61.7	55.5	67.8	67.2	65.6
2-yr. colleges	57.0	80.4	63.9	75.6	69.2	74.9	77.7	73.8
Program area								
Liberal arts and sciences	56.0	67.9	59.7	66.1	—	72.9	75.4	70.0
Fine arts	53.0	65.6	59.2	72.1	—	71.1	80.1	68.7
Humanities	59.1	71.8	62.5	62.8	56.8	73.4	71.0	69.9
Social sciences	54.4	64.4	57.3	63.0	58.9	70.8	76.0	66.5
Natural sciences	55.0	67.6	58.6	68.5	63.2	74.4	77.1	72.2
Professions	47.5	64.6	45.8	61.3	—	70.7	65.6	68.3
Business	55.4	67.4	—	70.9	—	73.9	63.0	72.2
Education	41.9	61.0	46.0	56.1	—	65.5	56.4	63.7
Health sciences	42.3	59.2	36.3	57.1	—	70.0	69.1	66.5
Engineering	50.7	63.9	54.5	70.7	—	72.5	77.0	71.0
Gender								
Female	61.3	72.4	51.8	67.3	58.5	73.5	66.8	68.3
Male	51.1	65.8	56.6	66.4	60.5	70.4	73.8	69.2
Race/ethnicity								
Asian	69.5	78.6	61.8	74.0	64.1	80.8	79.7	76.4
Other nonwhite	46.6	68.2	50.3	66.8	64.7	72.9	70.8	74.7
Native American	—	low *N*	low *N*	58.8	low *N*	67.2	low *N*	70.9
Black/African American	44.3	67.2	44.6	69.7	63.7	70.6	67.4	72.9
Hispanic	—	64.5	53.1	65.2	low *N*	78.8	78.3	78.5
White	52.8	66.4	55.2	66.3	59.5	70.7	70.7	67.8
Career cohort								
New-entrant (0–6 yrs.)	64.1	—	59.5	—	67.0	72.0	78.1	78.2
Midcareer & senior								
(7 or more yrs.)	43.6	—	54.3	—	58.7	71.2	70.2	66.8
Midcareer (7–14 yrs.)	46.3		—		56.0	69.5	72.7	68.9
Senior (15 or more yrs.)	40.9		—		59.7	71.8	69.2	65.7

Sources: Carn-69, ACE-72, CFAT-84, NSOPF-88, NCRIPTAL-88, NSOPF-93, CFAT-97, NSOPF-99 (see Appendix A for key).

TABLE A-4.8
Ratio of High to Low Teaching Loads among Full-Time Faculty, 1969–1998

	1969	1975	1984	1987	1992	1997	1998	Difference in Ratios 1969–98*
All faculty	1.5	2.2	2.0	1.7	1.3	2.0	2.0	0.6
Institutional type								
Universities	0.6	0.8	0.7	0.6	0.4	0.6	0.7	0.1
Research	—	0.6	0.4	0.4	0.2	0.4	0.5	−0.1
Other doctorate-granting	—	1.5	1.5	1.2	0.7	1.2	1.2	−0.3
Other 4-yr. institutions	3.2	4.0	3.0	3.6	2.7	3.2	3.9	0.7
Comprehensive	—	4.1	2.9	3.7	2.6	3.1	3.9	−0.2
Liberal arts colleges	—	3.8	3.8	3.3	2.8	3.3	3.9	0.1
2-yr. colleges	6.9	6.0	6.9	8.1	4.7	7.3	11.9	5.0
Program area								
Liberal arts and sciences	1.6	2.8	2.4	1.4	1.3	2.1	2.1	0.4
Fine arts	4.7	7.1	5.7	2.7	2.3	4.4	4.1	−0.6
Humanities	2.7	3.9	3.8	2.0	1.9	2.6	2.7	0.1
Social sciences	1.0	2.4	1.8	1.0	1.2	1.6	1.6	0.6
Natural sciences	1.1	1.9	1.3	1.1	0.9	1.8	1.6	0.5
Professions	1.2	1.6	1.0	1.0	1.3	1.7	1.9	0.7
Business	2.0	4.0	—	1.5	2.2	2.6	3.6	1.6
Education	1.4	1.9	1.5	1.5	1.4	2.1	1.9	0.6
Health sciences	0.8	0.8	0.7	0.8	1.3	1.1	1.6	0.8
Engineering	0.9	1.7	1.6	1.0	0.9	1.0	1.0	0.2
Gender								
Female	2.5	2.4	2.2	2.2	1.6	2.1	2.5	0.0
Male	1.3	2.2	2.0	1.5	1.2	1.9	1.8	0.5
Race/ethnicity								
Asian	0.9	1.7	1.3	1.2	1.0	1.2	1.3	0.4
Other nonwhite	2.5	2.1	1.3	1.8	2.2	3.2	2.7	0.2
Black/African American	2.7	1.8	0.8	2.0	1.6	2.7	2.6	−0.1
Native American	—	9.7	—	1.7	2.4	—	2.7	−6.9
Hispanic	—	1.8	2.3	1.7	1.5	6.1	2.9	1.0
White	1.4	2.3	2.1	1.7	1.3	2.0	2.0	0.6
Career cohort								
New-entrant (0–6 yrs.)	1.9	2.1	1.3	—	1.1	2.1	1.9	0.0
Midcareer & senior								
(7 or more yrs.)	1.2	2.2	2.3	—	1.4	2.0	2.0	0.8
Midcareer (7–14 yrs.)	1.3	—	—		1.2	2.1	2.3	1.0
Senior (15 or more yrs.)	1.1	—	—		1.5	1.9	1.9	0.8

Sources: Carn-69, CFAT-75, CFAT-84, NSOPF-88, NSOPF-93, CFAT-97, NSOPF-99 (see Appendix A for key).
Notes: High teaching load ≥ 9 hrs/week; low teaching load ≤ 6 hrs/week.
*The difference 1969–98 for research, other doctorate-granting, comprehensive, and liberal arts institutions, as well for Native American and Hispanic faculty, is really a 1975–98 difference.

TABLE A-4.9

Research and Publication Activity as Reported by Full-Time Faculty, 1969–1998
(percent)

	1969	1972	1975	1984	1987	1988	1992	1997	1998	Difference in % 1969–98
All faculty										
No publications over past 2 yrs.	49.5	35.6	47.7	44.6	54.7	38.2	40.4	30.5	33.4	−16.1
No publications over entire career	32.6	19.4	30.4	38.2	38.0	18.0	26.5	—	21.4	−11.2
5 or more publications over past 2 yrs.	11.1	18.0	11.3	14.8	14.2	19.5	12.7	18.1	22.5	11.4
Engaged in funded research over past 2 yrs.	37.1	48.9	38.9	40.6	21.9	63.7	27.4	47.6	33.9	−3.2
Institutional type										
No publications over past 2 yrs.										
Universities	28.8	23.1	23	20.0	9.1	12.0	21.0	9.1	14.0	−14.8
Other 4-yr. institutions	62.5	59.2	55.7	45.6	64.4	42.9	40.1	26.3	35.1	−27.4
No publications over entire career										
Universities	17.2	11.4	12.1	24.3	16.2	3.0	12.0	—	6.9	−10.3
Other 4-yr. institutions	40.7	32.8	34.2	37.6	42.1	15.4	23.1	—	18.2	−22.5
5 or more publications over past 2 yrs.										
Universities	19.4	24.2	23.1	29.6	28.6	40.6	26.4	38.0	40.9	21.5
Other 4-yr. institutions	4.3	4.7	4.8	8.8	4.5	10.7	5.5	11.3	13.5	9.2
Engaged in funded research over past 2 yrs.										
Universities	57.7	59.0	63.4	65.5	37.9	80.3	49.3	68.4	52.4	−5.3
Other 4-yr. institutions	23.0	29.1	29.4	36.5	12.4	61.9	18.2	48.4	26.3	3.3
Program area										
No publications over past 2 yrs.										
Natural and social sciences	39.7	25.1	38.7	36.7	39.6	39.5	33.2	26.2	27.7	−12.0
All other program areas	54.0	42.0	52.3	44.9	61.2	35.0	43.6	32.6	35.9	−18.1
No publications over entire career										
Natural and social sciences	23.3	10.6	21.1	29.3	20.1	17.0	18.2	—	14.4	−8.9
All other program areas	37.7	24.6	35.2	39.3	45.2	19.7	30.2	—	24.6	−13.1
5 or more publications over past 2 yrs.										
Natural and social sciences	16.1	25.2	15.5	20.8	20.2	20.5	19.6	26.4	30.1	14.0
All other program areas	8.4	13.3	9.2	14.2	16.3	17.5	9.6	14.1	19.5	11.1
Engaged in funded research over past 2 yrs.										
Natural and social sciences	53.3	62.7	53.8	57.2	34.4	65.7	38.1	54.3	44.1	−9.2
All other program areas	28.9	40.5	31.3	38.1	22.5	59.4	22.6	44.3	29.5	0.6

	Carn-69	ACE-72	CFAT-75	CFAT-84	NCRIPTAL-88	NSOPF-88	NSOPF-93	CFAT-97	NSOPF-99	Change
Gender										
No publications over past 2 yrs.										
Female	70.3	59.66	7.15	5.6	68.6	44.1	50.2	37.3	39.6	−30.7
Male	45.1	31.3	42.4	40.5	49.5	36.3	35.5	26.6	29.5	−15.6
No publications over entire career										
Female	52.3	39.4	50.5	49.1	53.7	26.6	35.8	—	28.2	−24.1
Male	28.3	16.0	24.7	34.3	32.2	15.2	21.8	—	17.3	−11.0
5 or more publications over past 2 yrs.										
Female	3.5	5.9	3.0	7.6	7.2	13.6	6.6	12.8	15.5	12.0
Male	12.7	20.2	13.7	17.4	16.8	21.4	15.7	21.4	27.4	14.7
Engaged in funded research over past 2 yrs.										
Female	16.3	26.0	21.4	31.4	14.2	58.9	20.6	45.1	30.4	14.1
Male	41.6	53.3	43.9	44.1	24.8	65.3	30.8	48.8	37.0	−4.6
Career cohort										
No publications over past 2 yrs.										
New entrants[a]	56.0	—	51.6	42.2	—	28.3	40.4	32.2	38.1	−17.9
Midcareer & senior faculty[b]	44.3	—	45.2	45.0	—	40.0	40.4	30.2	32.0	−12.3
No publications over entire career										
New entrants[a]	46.5	—	41.6	48.1	—	20.9	30.4	—	30.8	−15.7
Midcareer & senior faculty[b]	21.2	—	23.6	35.0	—	17.5	24.9	—	19.1	−2.1
5 or more publications over past 2 yrs.										
New entrants[a]	7.8	—	9.1	17.1	—	24.2	14.3	18.2	20.0	12.2
Midcareer & senior faculty[b]	13.7	—	12.9	14.6	—	18.7	12.0	18.1	23.9	10.2
Engaged in funded research over past 2 yrs.										
New entrants[a]	34.8	—	38.7	46.4	—	70.9	31.3	54.2	34.0	−0.8
Midcareer & senior faculty[b]	39.1	—	39.9	39.6	—	62.4	25.8	46.5	34.8	−4.3

Sources: Carn-69, ACE-72, CFAT-75, CFAT-84 NCRIPTAL-88, NSOPF-88, NSOPF-93, CFAT-97, NSOPF-99 (see Appendix A for key).

Notes: For 1987 the DAS system provides data only for "articles in refereed journals" in last 2 years.

For 1997 the item asking for publications uses a 3-year period.

For 1972 the % reporting being engaged in funded research was derived from all sources of research funds considered, as opposed to the response to the alternative of no support received.

Surveys for the following years asked for the past 12 months: 1969 (item 54), 1972 (item 21), 1975 (item 19), 1984 (item 15), and 1988 (item 8.x). For 1987 item 34 asked for the 1987 fall term as principal investigator or project director. For 1992 item 30 asked for the 1992 fall term. For 1997 item 37 asked for the past 3 years (as principal or coprincipal investigator). For 1998 item 54 asked for the 1998 fall term.

[a] 0–6 years in faculty appointment.

[b] 7 or more years in faculty appointment

TABLE A-4.10

Publication Prolificity as Reported by Full-Time Faculty, 1969–1998
(percent)

	1969	1972	1975	1984	1987	1988	1992	1997*	1998
All faculty									
≥ 5 publications	11.1	18.0	11.3	14.8	14.2	19.5	12.7	9.2	22.5
No publications in past 2 yrs.	49.5	35.6	47.7	44.6	54.7	38.2	40.4	41.5	33.4
No publications over entire career	32.6	19.4	30.4	38.2	38.0	18.0	26.5	—	21.4
Gender									
≥ 5 publications									
Females	3.5	5.9	3.0	7.6	7.2	13.6	6.6	5.8	15.1
Males	12.7	20.2	13.7	17.4	16.8	21.4	15.7	11.3	26.6
No publications in past 2 yrs.									
Females	70.3	59.6	67.1	55.6	68.6	44.1	50.2	49.7	39.7
Males	45.1	31.3	42.4	40.5	49.5	36.3	5.5	36.9	29.9
No publications over entire career									
Females	52.3	39.4	50.5	49.1	53.7	26.6	35.8	—	28.2
Males	28.3	16.0	24.7	34.3	32.2	15.2	21.8	—	17.6
Institutional type									
Universities									
≥ 5 publications									
Females	5.9	8.8	6.4	20.2	16.4	33.8	16.5	17.7	29.3
Males	21.2	26.3	26.0	32.0	32.0	42.2	29.9	23.3	44.6
No publications in past 2 yrs.									
Females	54.5	48.1	47.2	30.8	44.6	14.7	29.6	15.6	19.1
Males	25.2	19.8	18.7	17.4	24.8	11.4	18.0	13.3	12.4
No publications over entire career									
Females	37.9	30.0	34.3	31.3	30.8	6.1	18.7	—	11.4
Males	14.4	8.9	8.3	22.5	12.1	2.3	9.6	—	5.2
Research univs.									
≥ 5 publications									
Females	—	10.7	7.6	25.5	18.3	40.6	21.3	20.7	32.7
Males	—	29.2	30.0	37.6	34.3	51.8	34.4	26.2	47.8
No publications in past 2 yrs.									
Females	—	44.0	41.3	24.5	37.6	9.4	26.4	12.2	16.2
Males	—	16.7	15.7	13.6	21.8	7.6	15.8	11.5	9.8
No publications over entire career									
Females	—	25.2	28.2	27.8	22.1	6.1	17.5	—	9.8
Males	—	7.1	6.5	22.0	10.6	1.2	9.2	—	4.0
Other doctorate-granting universities									
≥ 5 publications									
Females	—	4.8	4.4	12.5	13.6	24.1	9.0	9.0	22.7
Males	—	17.5	16.1	20.1	27.6	28.9	21.3	13.8	36.3
No publications in past 2 yrs.									
Females	—	56.3	56.8	39.8	54.7	22.3	34.5	25.5	24.9
Males	—	28.8	26.1	25.5	30.5	16.7	22.2	19.6	19.0
No publications over entire career									
Females	—	39.7	44.2	36.2	43.5	6.0	20.5	—	14.5
Males	—	14.2	12.7	23.7	15.0	3.7	10.3	—	8.4
Other 4-yr. institutions									
≥ 5 publications									
Females	2.9	2.8	2.0	4.5	3.7	7.8	3.2	3.1	11.8
Males	4.6	5.4	5.8	10.3	4.9	11.7	6.7	4.4	14.5
No publications in past 2 yrs.									
Females	73.4	69.5	67.7	52.2	72.5	45.7	45.0	40.5	35.8
Males	59.4	56.1	51.9	42.8	61.2	42.2	37.3	34.9	34.4

(continued)

TABLE A-4.10 (*continued*)

	1969	1972	1975	1984	1987	1988	1992	1997*	1998
No publications over entire career									
Females	55.0	46.5	48.0	46.5	53.8	21.1	28.6	—	21.0
Males	36.6	29.1	29.5	34.3	37.4	13.5	20.0	—	16.2
Comprehensive insts.									
≥ 5 publications									
Females	—	3.2	2.2	4.0	4.6	9.6	3.7	3.5	13.6
Males	—	5.8	6.4	11.0	5.8	12.0	7.1	4.8	15.2
No publications in past 2 yrs.									
Females	—	67.0	64.6	50.9	69.7	41.1	43.1	36.5	34.0
Males	—	55.5	49.6	40.9	58.7	39.3	36.7	30.8	32.8
No publications over entire career									
Females	—	46.6	44.0	45.6	49.8	14.6	27.5	—	19.1
Males	—	28.4	27.8	31.7	34.1	12.0	19.4	—	15.1
Liberal arts colleges									
≥ 5 publications									
Females	—	2.3	1.8	7.0	0.9	5.4	1.9	1.9	7.3
Males	—	4.7	4.0	7.2	1.5	10.7	5.4	3.3	12.7
No publications in past 2 yrs.									
Females	—	72.0	72.9	55.7	82.3	52.0	50.7	50.9	40.3
Males	—	56.9	58.6	51.1	69.4	50.8	39.5	46.3	38.4
No publications over entire career									
Females	—	46.4	54.5	49.1	67.7	30.4	32.0	—	25.8
Males	—	30.1	34.5	45.6	48.8	17.9	22.2	—	19.3
2-yr. colleges									
≥ 5 publications									
Females	0.8	0.2	0.8	0.3	0.9	2.3	0.7	0.0	3.0
Males	1.6	0.9	1.5	2.6	0.9	3.8	1.6	0.0	3.6
No publications in past 2 yrs.									
Females	90.7	91.7	87.5	83.0	92.9	72.6	76.3	83.0	69.8
Males	84.6	86.1	79.3	80.4	91.2	72.9	71.1	78.3	67.9
No publications over entire career									
Females	70.6	70.0	71.7	68.1	80.2	57.3	60.6	—	58.4
Males	61.1	60.2	55.1	56.9	73.8	44.4	52.3	—	51.5
Program area									
Professions									
≥ 5 publications									
Females	3.3	4.0	2.3	10.9	12.2	—	5.8	5.2	14.7
Males	11.5	19.6	13.7	23.3	28.1	—	15.8	12.0	28.6
No publications in past 2 yrs.									
Females	72.3	64.8	73.2	50.8	57.7	—	54.4	56.2	42.2
Males	44.0	32.4	42.6	33.8	31.7	—	37.1	35.9	27.7
No publications over entire career									
Females	53.5	41.6	56.9	48.0	44.7	—	40.9	—	31.7
Males	26.1	15.8	24.6	30.5	18.2	—	25.0	—	17.4
Business									
≥ 5 publications									
Females	1.4	0.6	2.7	—	3.9	—	5.5	5.5	9.3
Males	7.4	14.7	9.2	—	6.9	—	10.5	3.5	17.2
No publications in past 2 yrs.									
Females	84.6	77.6	76.9	—	70.1	—	66.7	60.8	46.0
Males	55.0	38.1	53.5	—	43.5	—	38.4	45.1	37.1
No publications over entire career									
Females	68.8	50.0	67.3	—	62.3	—	55.9	—	38.7
Males	36.8	21.5	38.0	—	30.5	—	26.3	—	25.5

(*continued*)

TABLE A-4.10 (*continued*)

	1969	1972	1975	1984	1987	1988	1992	1997*	1998
Education									
≥ 5 publications									
Females	4.0	5.1	2.6	19.8	6.1	—	6.1	6.3	14.3
Males	10.5	14.6	9.2	14.5	10.5	—	7.8	9.4	17.6
No publications in past 2 yrs.									
Females	68.3	62.0	66.8	39.5	64.1	—	46.8	42.0	34.4
Males	48.6	40.4	45.0	41.6	46.6	—	36.0	33.6	25.7
No publications over entire career									
Females	49.3	37.5	46.0	38.8	51.8	—	32.0	—	23.8
Males	29.5	19.3	24.4	29.6	25.9	—	21.3	—	13.0
Health sciences									
≥ 5 publications									
Females	1.8	3.1	1.0	7.5	15.8	—	4.9	4.4	14.7
Males	21.8	37.3	25.2	41.8	43.3	—	26.0	11.3	40.6
No publications in past 2 yrs.									
Females	74.0	67.7	80.0	55.1	54.4	—	57.7	63.4	48.1
Males	29.7	15.5	27.1	21.5	20.6	—	34.0	38.2	24.2
No publications over entire career									
Females	57.4	47.9	66.3	51.7	41.6	—	43.0	—	35.7
Males	13.3	5.3	14.0	35.9	10.5	—	21.6	—	15.2
Engineering									
≥ 5 publications									
Females	5.1	low *N*	low *N*	low *N*	low *N*	—	9.5	11.4	42.0
Males	13.3	22.1	18.5	19.5	18.0	—	23.1	26.8	41.3
No publications in past 2 yrs.									
Females	61.4	low *N*	low *N*	low *N*	low *N*	—	59.2	65.8	22.8
Males	35.9	26.9	36.5	44.1	40.6	—	33.7	22.1	23.4
No publications over entire career									
Females	61.1	26.9	low *N*	low *N*	low *N*	—	50.3	—	17.6
Males	20.5	11.3	17.6	28.5	21.2	—	20.8	—	13.7
Liberal arts and sciences									
≥ 5 publications									
Females	3.9	7.5	3.6	7.5	7.5	—	7.3	7.4	15.5
Males	13.6	20.5	13.8	17.4	16.3	—	16.5	11.8	28.5
No publications in past 2 yrs.									
Females	68.3	54.4	60.7	53.5	59.3	—	46.1	42.4	37.9
Males	43.9	30.3	41.9	40.8	44.9	—	34.6	34.0	28.6
No publications over entire career									
Females	52.0	36.9	43.5	46.9	40.4	—	30.9	—	24.9
Males	28.6	15.5	24.5	31.6	25.4	—	19.6	—	14.6
Fine arts									
≥ 5 publications									
Females	1.8	2.4	1.8	0.0	9.1	—	3.3	3.6	13.9
Males	6.7	6.0	7.5	8.0	3.8	—	5.2	3.1	17.2
No publications in past 2 yrs.									
Females	74.6	71.8	73.9	73.1	71.3	—	62.8	66.8	46.7
Males	63.3	61.3	62.3	59.9	71.1	—	56.0	59.8	53.4
No publications over entire career									
Females	60.7	53.7	54.8	67.0	50.3	—	48.5	—	39.2
Males	47.7	41.1	43.3	50.7	58.3	—	43.0	—	37.9
Humanities									
≥ 5 publications									
Females	3.3	5.2	2.9	6.3	5.2	15.0	3.8	6.3	9.0
Males	8.7	11.6	9.5	13.2	8.5	18.7	7.8	3.9	20.3

(*continued*)

TABLE A-4.10 (*continued*)

	1969	1972	1975	1984	1987	1988	1992	1997*	1998
No publications in past 2 yrs.									
Females	72.3	58.7	64.5	50.9	55.2	43.1	47.0	32.1	35.0
Males	49.9	36.0	43.7	41.5	52.4	31.4	33.5	29.6	29.1
No publications over entire career									
Females	59.1	44.4	48.5	43.7	36.5	28.8	30.0	—	21.0
Males	36.0	20.8	27.6	29.9	29.5	15.7	18.6	—	14.0
Social sciences									
≥ 5 publications									
Females	5.7	10.8	4.1	11.5	8.7	18.2	9.1	9.9	22.4
Males	15.3	20.8	11.7	15.5	14.6	24.3	11.4	11.0	26.3
No publications in past 2 yrs.									
Females	55.3	39.4	49.5	41.8	49.2	31.4	34.1	33.7	27.3
Males	37.1	24.6	36.6	39.0	34.0	28.9	29.2	28.7	22.0
No publications over entire career									
Females	37.4	22.5	35.2	36.4	36.4	18.2	21.2	—	15.8
Males	24.0	12.0	23.0	24.7	18.9	12.9	15.0	—	11.4
Natural sciences									
≥ 5 publications									
Females	5.5	13.4	5.7	18.6	8.8	8.5	13.8	8.2	20.0
Males	18.5	29.6	20.1	26.4	27.5	21.5	28.1	18.2	36.8
No publications in past 2 yrs.									
Females	64.7	46.0	53.7	42.4	67.3	55.2	45.5	57.7	45.5
Males	37.4	22.8	37.0	33.1	36.3	44.8	32.3	34.1	24.7
No publications over entire career									
Females	41.1	21.5	33.4	33.9	44.0	30.4	30.8	—	30.8
Males	19.9	8.2	17.3	29.6	13.8	16.1	16.1	—	10.2
Race/ethnicity									
Asian									
≥ 5 publications									
Females	4.8	7.1	4.9	low N	32.8	11.1	8.2	2.8	23.4
Males	24.8	32.9	25.6	26.7	32.2	24.4	27.5	24.1	42.1
No publications in past 2 yrs.									
Females	64.7	57.1	58.3	62.5	43.9	40.7	50.9	low N	30.2
Males	25.2	16.1	28.7	23.3	27.9	28.0	27.3	18.0	18.3
No publications over entire career									
Females	50.1	39.1	41.1	low N	32.3	29.6	36.4	—	19.9
Males	13.6	9.0	15.6	25.8	17.0	3.4	18.1	—	8.5
Black/African American									
≥ 5 publications									
Females	2.6	2.6	1.3	0.0	0.6	8.5	3.1	4.5	9.2
Males	2.6	6.7	7.4	3.8	6.7	10.3	9.4	3.0	20.8
No publications in past 2 yrs.									
Females	80.7	77.4	74.1	69.8	81.8	63.4	60.8	51.9	41.4
Males	67.0	57.7	60.8	69.8	59.3	39.3	48.0	28.9	38.3
No publications over entire career									
Females	60.7	57.1	57.6	65.9	65.9	33.7	48.4	—	31.4
Males	41.3	37.3	43.8	62.7	39.6	14.3	35.6	—	23.8
Hispanic									
≥ 5 publications									
Females	—	low N	low N	low N	3.1	28.6	9.8	9.4	17.0
Males	—	15.4	5.1	23.7	19.6	31.8	13.2	6.7	28.9
No publications in past 2 yrs.									
Females	—	low N	low N	low N	70.7	low N	46.6	low N	41.1
Males	—	33.8	51.7	52.6	44.4	low N	37.7	56.8	28.6

(*continued*)

TABLE A-4.10 (*continued*)

	1969	1972	1975	1984	1987	1988	1992	1997*	1998
No publications over entire career									
Females	—	low N	low N	low N	45.5	low N	36.2	—	28.7
Males	—	21.2	30.9	45.9	30.1	low N	24.5	—	18.8
Native American									
≥ 5 publications									
Females	—	low N	low N	low N	low N	low N	3.4	low N	low N
Males	—	low N	6.7	low N	low N	low N	13.4	low N	23.7
No publications in past 2 yrs.									
Females	—	low N	low N	low N	low N	low N	43.3	low N	low N
Males	—	low N	53.3	low N	low N	low N	55.4	low N	48.8
No publications over entire career									
Females	—	low N	low N	low N	low N	low N	24.7	—	low N
Males	—	low N	low N	low N	low N	low N	32.1	—	41.2
White									
≥ 5 publications									
Females	3.6	5.9	3.0	7.8	6.7	14.0	6.7	5.7	15.0
Males	12.7	19.9	13.5	17.0	16.3	21.5	15.3	10.9	25.8
No publications in past 2 yrs.									
Females	69.9	58.9	66.9	55.1	68.6	42.8	49.4	50.3	40.2
Males	44.9	31.4	42.3	40.5	50.4	36.7	35.3	37.5	30.2
No publications over entire career									
Females	51.9	38.6	50.2	48.3	53.8	26.0	34.7	—	28.4
Males	28.3	15.8	24.5	34.0	32.8	15.7	21.3	—	17.6
Career cohort									
New entrants (0–6 yrs.)									
≥ 5 publications									
Females	2.8	—	2.0	9.9	—	16.8	6.5	5.6	13.7
Males	9.1	—	11.8	21.6	—	28.6	20.1	8.7	25.0
No publications in past 2 yrs.									
Females	75.5	—	68.4	50.0	—	33.6	50.7	49.1	43.0
Males	51.0	—	44.9	37.5	—	25.8	32.8	35.0	34.2
No publications over entire career									
Females	66.3	—	60.1	56.0	—	28.8	39.5	—	36.2
Males	41.5	—	34.3	43.7	—	16.2	23.7	—	26.5
Midcareer & senior (7 or more yrs.)									
≥ 5 publications									
Females	4.3	—	3.8	6.6	—	12.5	6.6	5.8	16.0
Males	15.5	—	15.0	17.0	—	20.4	14.3	11.7	27.9
No publications in past 2 yrs.									
Females	65.0	—	65.7	58.5	—	47.2	49.9	49.7	38.6
Males	40.4	—	40.7	40.8	—	38.0	36.4	37.0	28.6
No publications over entire career									
Females	37.8	—	42.5	46.8	—	25.8	33.6	—	25.9
Males	18.1	—	19.4	31.5	—	15.1	21.2	—	15.5
Midcareer (7–14 yrs.)									
≥ 5 publications									
Females	4.0	—	—	—	—	15.0	7.7	5.6	14.9
Males	15.7	—	—	—	—	28.1	18.3	15.7	28.6
No publications in past 2 yrs.									
Females	65.2	—	—	—	—	39.9	52.0	47.7	39.3
Males	39.9	—	—	—	—	28.8	33.3	33.1	26.5
No publications over entire career									
Females	46.3	—	—	—	—	26.1	39.0	—	29.0
Males	22.3	—	—	—	—	12.4	24.2	—	19.0

(*continued*)

TABLE A-4.10 (*continued*)

	1969	1972	1975	1984	1987	1988	1992	1997*	1998
Senior (15 or more yrs.)									
≥ 5 publications									
Females	4.7	—	—	—	—	11.0	6.0	5.9	16.9
Males	15.3	—	—	—	—	18.2	13.2	10.4	27.6
No publications in past 2 yrs.									
Females	64.7	—	—	—	—	51.8	48.8	51.0	38.0
Males	41.0	—	—	—	—	40.7	37.3	38.3	29.5
No publications over entire career									
Females	28.9	—	—	—	—	25.6	31.1	—	23.5
Males	14.0	—	—	—	—	15.9	20.3	—	14.1

Sources: Carn-69, ACE-72, CFAT-75, CFAT-84, NSOPF-88, NCRIPTAL-88, NSOPF-93, CFAT-97, NSOPF-99 (see Appendix A for key).

*For CFAT-97 the corresponding items asked for a three-year period. In the case of no publications the "0" figure was simply maintained. In the case of 5 or more publications, the answer provided by each respondent was multiplied by (2/3) in order to obtain a figure comparable with those of the other surveys. The reported answer was kept for the item relative to funded research.

TABLE A-4.11

Full-Time Faculty Engaged in Funded Research, 1969–1998

(percent)

	1969	1972[a]	1975	1984	1987[b]	1988	1992	1997[c]	1998
All faculty	37.1	48.9	38.9	40.6	21.9	63.7	27.4	47.6	33.9
Female	16.3	26.0	21.4	31.4	14.2	58.9	20.6	45.1	29.7
Male	41.6	53.3	43.9	44.1	24.8	65.3	30.8	48.8	36.3
Institutional type									
Universities	57.7	59.0	63.4	65.5	37.9	80.3	49.3	68.4	51.3
Female	29.7	32.9	38.8	54.6	27.5	78.8	40.6	68.9	45.9
Male	61.5	62.9	67.7	68.2	40.9	80.8	52.4	67.9	53.6
Research	—	62.5	68.1	71.1	42.9	83.6	55.7	72.1	54.7
Female		36.1	43.6	59.1	34.2	83.6	47.2	73.6	48.0
Male		65.9	71.9	73.7	45.1	83.8	58.6	71.3	57.4
Other doctorate-granting univs.	—	49.3	52.6	54.4	29.1	75.8	37.4	56.1	43.4
Female		26.5	31.3	48.0	17.6	72.2	30.0	55.0	41.6
Male		53.8	57.6	56.2	32.9	76.7	40.4	56.3	44.2
Other 4-yr. institutions	23.0	29.0	29.4	36.5	12.4	61.9	18.2	48.4	26.1
Female	12.2	19.2	20.2	33.3	8.4	60.1	16.3	50.1	27.6
Male	26.1	32.5	32.5	38.1	13.9	62.4	19.3	47.2	25.2
Comprehensive	—	27.1	30.4	38.5	12.8	62.1	18.9	50.0	26.7
Female		16.8	20.2	35.7	9.1	59.3	17.1	52.6	20.4
Male		30.0	33.3	39.7	14.2	62.7	19.9	47.9	25.7
Liberal arts colleges	—	31.9	27.0	28.8	11.0	61.4	15.9	44.4	24.7
Female		21.4	20.3	25.2	6.3	61.4	14.0	43.5	25.7
Male		36.0	30.3	30.9	12.8	61.4	17.1	44.8	24.2
2-yr. colleges	4.9	10.3	9.5	8.7	6.1	39.2	5.7	22.5	13.7
Female	2.7	9.6	5.9	8.1	6.0	34.1	6.4	24.0	14.3
Male	5.6	10.7	11.0	8.9	6.1	41.3	5.1	21.1	13.1
Program area									
Liberal arts and sciences	39.7	49.9	41.6	43.2	24.0	—	28.1	51.0	35.4
Female	18.3	30.9	26.6	35.7	18.2		22.3	52.6	30.1
Male	43.7	52.7	44.9	45.6	25.6		30.5	50.1	37.9
Fine Arts	16.9	27.6	20.8	21.4	9.7	—	17.3	51.8	28.0
Female	11.9	19.5	14.9	19.8	14.2		15.8	42.5	27.7
Male	18.2	30.2	22.6	22.2	8.2		17.9	56.5	28.1
Humanities	24.1	30.7	28.0	32.6	10.3	59.4	12.7	43.2	20.2
Female	10.7	20.8	19.9	35.3	9.5	55.5	12.7	47.0	22.3
Male	28.2	32.9	30.8	32.0	10.6	61.1	12.8	40.2	18.6
Social sciences	48.6	55.5	48.9	44.7	23.0	69.2	28.5	50.3	37.5
Female	30.6	43.2	41.1	46.8	27.4	68.8	27.7	61.4	38.1
Male	51.1	57.1	50.5	44.4	21.9	69.4	28.8	44.8	37.2
Natural sciences	56.0	67.1	56.6	66.0	42.1	63.2	44.3	57.1	47.5
Female	30.9	49.7	35.8	50.8	25.4	54.7	37.5	58.0	35.9
Male	58.5	68.6	59.1	68.4	45.1	65.4	46.0	56.9	51.2
Professions	35.2	48.3	34.9	45.8	30.5	—	26.7	43.8	34.6
Female	12.7	20.0	16.4	32.4	18.8		18.5	37.3	29.9
Male	41.3	55.7	42.2	52.1	35.1		31.7	49.1	38.5
Business	26.3	35.9	25.4	—	5.9		14.3	35.6	17.4
Female	3.3	13.4	11.3		6.1		8.3	39.0	14.5
Male	30.3	39.5	28.3		5.8		16.9	33.5	18.9
Education	22.7	31.9	27.4	32.6	18.3		22.3	44.3	33.9
Female	13.0	17.2	18.7	33.3	13.5		22.7	43.6	36.1
Male	26.6	38.5	31.6	32.7	21.3		21.9	44.4	30.9

(*continued*)

TABLE A-4.11 (*continued*)

	1969	1972[a]	1975	1984	1987[b]	1988	1992	1997[c]	1998
Health sciences	31.9	47.4	28.7	46.5	36.5		24.4	37.3	34.0
Female	12.4	19.8	12.8	31.0	21.8		17.9	33.3	28.9
Male	59.4	72.8	58.2	67.1	43.3		44.2	52.4	49.4
Engineering	58.6	68.7	59.8	50.5	41.6		43.8	69.6	54.2
Female	45.3	50.0	low *N*	low *N*	low *N*		22.4	48.7	58.6
Male	58.7	69.2	59.3	50.2	41.3		46.5	74.0	53.9
Race/ethnicity									
Asian	52.0	59.2	56.0	59.8	37.4	65.5	38.6	57.5	49.6
Female	14.9	32.2	33.3	low *N*	19.3	low *N*	33.0	60.5	40.4
Male	58.6	62.7	60.4	61.8	42.0	62.2	40.5	56.6	53.3
Black/African American	20.2	31.6	26.7	22.7	13.8	58.9	20.3	44.1	29.8
Female	12.4	21.7	21.4	25.6	12.3	54.4	17.5	45.9	28.6
Male	23.8	36.5	30.6	20.8	14.6	61.8	22.9	41.9	30.8
Hispanic	—	42.3	33.8	34.0	17.7	low *N*	30.5	36.5	36.3
Female		low *N*	low *N*	low *N*	8.9	low *N*	27.5	46.9	29.1
Male		43.9	35.1	35.1	21.3	low *N*	31.9	28.8	40.7
Native American	—	low *N*	29.4	low *N*	7.7	low *N*	18.2	low *N*	34.4
Female		low *N*	low *N*	low *N*	low *N*	low *N*	19.6	low *N*	low *N*
Male		low *N*	low *N*	low *N*	low *N*	low *N*	17.7	low *N*	31.7
White	37.4	49.3	38.9	40.5	21.7	63.8	27.1	47.2	33.1
Female	16.5	26.0	21.2	31.0	14.5	58.8	20.2	44.5	29.2
Male	41.7	53.3	43.8	44.1	24.4	65.4	30.5	48.8	35.2
Career cohort									
New-entrant (0–6 yrs.)	34.8	—	38.7	46.4	—	70.5	31.3	54.2	34.0
Female	14.4		22.8	36.4		68.8	23.6	55.6	29.9
Male	40.0		44.8	52.5		71.4	37.0	52.3	37.2
Midcareer & senior (7 or more yrs.)	39.1	—	39.9	39.6	—	62.5	25.8	46.5	34.8
Female	18.3		19.9	28.9		55.6	18.9	43.2	30.5
Male	42.9		44.0	42.9		64.4	28.7	48.2	37.0
Midcareer (7–14 yrs.)	41.4		—	—		68.5	30.3	52.1	36.3
Female	17.9					61.6	20.5	46.1	31.5
Male	45.8					71.8	36.3	57.8	40.0
Senior (15 or more yrs.)	36.7		—	—		60.3	24.3	44.1	34.0
Female	18.7					51.9	10.2	41.5	29.8
Male	40.0					61.2	26.5	45.3	35.7

Sources: Carn-69, ACE-72, CFAT-75, CFAT-84, NSOPF-88, NCRIPTAL-88, NSOPF-93, CFAT-97, NSOPF-99 (see Appendix A for key).

[a]The variable was derived from all sources of research funds considered, as opposed to the response to the alternative of no support received.

[b]The corresponding item in this survey asked for the last 3 years. Therefore, the answer provided by each respondent was multiplied by 2/3 in order to obtain a figure comparable with those of the other surveys.

[c]The corresponding item asked for funds received as principal or coprincipal investigator.

TABLE A-4.12A

Full-Time Faculty Reporting "More than Average" Involvement in Department Governance, 1969, 1975, and 1997

(percent)

	1969	1975	1997
All faculty	58.8	65.1	91.7
Institutional type			
Universities	55.5	59.7	90.0
Research	—	58.0	89.6
Other doctorate-granting	—	63.5	91.2
Other 4-yr. institutions	61.4	68.9	93.9
Comprehensive	—	68.1	93.7
Liberal arts colleges	—	70.7	94.0
2-yr. colleges	62.8	68.5	91.5
Program area			
Liberal arts and sciences	57.7	63.5	90.7
Fine arts	68.4	71.3	93.0
Humanities	54.3	65.0	90.9
Social sciences	68.7	63.0	89.7
Natural sciences	56.6	59.5	91.0
Professions	62.7	67.5	93.0
Business	59.3	58.5	93.3
Education	66.6	52.1	92.9
Health sciences	65.8	61.5	93.8
Engineering	58.3	36.0	93.2
Gender			
Female	54.2	67.6	92.6
Male	59.8	64.4	91.2
Race/ethnicity			
Asian	37.8	47.7	89.4
Black/African American	60.0	64.9	89.0
Hispanic	—	55.7	82.7
Native American	—	78.0	100.0
White	59.1	65.6	92.4
Career cohort			
New-entrant (0–6 years)	51.5	59.7	87.7
Midcareer & senior			
(7 or more years)	64.7	67.8	92.3
Midcareer (7–14 years)	65.0	—	93.7
Senior (15 or more years)	64.4	—	91.8

Sources: Carn-69, CFAT-75, CFAT-97 (see Appendix A for key).

TABLE A-4.12B

Full-Time Faculty Reporting "More than Average" Involvement in Campus Governance, 1969, 1975, and 1997

(percent)

	1969	1975	1997
All faculty	31.4	37.2	39.8
Institutional type			
Universities	25.4	29.3	26.3
Research	—	28.4	23.9
Other doctorate-granting	—	31.2	34.4
Other 4-yr. institutions	34.7	41.2	50.2
Comprehensive	—	38.8	43.1
Liberal arts colleges	—	47.2	68.8
2-yr. colleges	43.6	43.7	44.4
Program area			
Liberal arts and sciences	32.5	39.1	38.8
Fine arts	28.8	32.2	35.7
Humanities	35.2	44.0	46.3
Social sciences	34.6	40.8	36.3
Natural sciences	31.1	36.5	35.8
Professions	39.8	36.5	41.7
Business	36.0	38.4	41.7
Education	31.5	39.4	47.2
Health sciences	20.8	26.1	42.1
Engineering	37.0	31.4	32.1
Gender			
Female	23.9	35.1	47.5
Male	33.0	37.7	35.2
Race/ethnicity			
Asian	11.9	20.5	14.4
Black/African American	34.5	39.8	45.0
Hispanic	—	38.0	49.4
Native American	—	50.0*	34.8
White	31.6	37.4	41.0
Career cohort			
New-entrant (0–6 years)	21.4	27.5	34.1
Midcareer & senior			
(7 or more years)	39.6	42.0	40.7
Midcareer (7–14 years)	37.0	—	40.7
Senior (15 or more years)	42.2	—	40.8

Sources: Carn-69, CFAT-75, CFAT-97 (see Appendix A for key).

Notes: The Carn-69 (item 16b) and the CFAT-75 (item 37b) asked, "How active are you in the faculty government of your institution (committee membership, etc.)? and asked respondents to choose among the following responses: (1) Much more than average, (2) Somewhat more than average, (3) About average, (4) Somewhat less than average, and (5) Much less than average. The "more than average involvement" category was created by combining options (1) and (2).

The CFAT-97 asked for the "Extent to which you participate in meetings of each of the following type of organization at your institution: a. Faculty senate; b. Campus-wide committee"; and respondents were to choose among "(1) Often/usually, (2) Sometimes, (3) Rarely, and (4) Never."
The "more than average involvement" category was created by the following steps:

1. If a case reported (1) for either (a) or (b), then the case was included in the "more than average" category.

2. If a case did not report (1) in (a) or (b), but reported (2 or more) for either (a) or (b), then it was a "average or less than average" case.

3. If a case presented missing values in (a) and (b), then it was a missing value in this variable also.

*N = 40

TABLE A-4.13A

Full-Time Faculty Reporting High Influence on Department Governance, 1969–1997

(percent)

	1969	1975	1984	1997
All faculty	63.4	68.2	62.9	64.0
Institutional type				
Universities	59.3	62.0	56.2	57.7
Research	—	61.1	55.0	56.6
Other doctorate-granting	—	64.1	58.5	61.4
Other 4-yr. institutions	65.7	72.1	67.2	70.0
Comprehensive	—	68.9	64.4	68.2
Liberal arts colleges	—	80.0	78.4	74.6
2-yr. colleges	71.7	71.6	66.3	64.8
Program area				
Liberal arts and sciences	64.2	67.5	63.5	63.7
Fine arts	67.3	69.6	59.4	55.7
Humanities	61.7	65.6	60.9	62.7
Social sciences	67.2	68.6	66.4	63.6
Natural sciences	63.8	67.8	66.3	66.6
Professions	64.2	69.0	60.5	63.0
Business	65.5	69.6	—	62.9
Education	64.5	69.7	59.3	66.7
Health sciences	68.0	73.0	61.0	59.7
Engineering	62.8	66.1	62.0	62.2
Gender				
Female	55.6	64.0	62.3	64.4
Male	65.2	69.4	63.1	63.8
Race/ethnicity				
Asian	37.1	44.9	44.9	36.0
Black/African American	56.6	60.0	45.7	62.8
Hispanic	—	57.7	44.0	45.9
Native American	—	85.0	53.8	43.5
White	64.1	69.1	64.3	66.3
Career cohort				
New-entrant (0–6 years)	56.2	62.1	47.9	51.4
Midcareer & senior				
(7 or more years)	69.4	71.8	66.6	65.6
Midcareer (7–14 years)	67.7	—	—	62.3
Senior (15 or more years)	71.1	—	—	67.0

Sources: Carn-69, CFAT-75, CFAT-84, CFAT-97 (see Appendix A for key).

TABLE A-4.13B

Full-Time Faculty Reporting High Influence on Campus Governance (Affairs), 1969–1997

(percent)

	1969	1975	1984	1997
All faculty	17.6	18.9	14.3	14.7
Institutional type				
Universities	12.7	14.0	9.9	11.7
Research	—	13.9	9.7	11.8
Other doctorate-granting	—	14.2	10.3	11.5
Other 4-yr. institutions	21.3	16.0	15.9	16.0
Comprehensive	—	16.0	13.2	12.8
Liberal arts colleges	—	32.3	26.9	24.3
2-yr. colleges	23.9	22.1	18.4	16.7
Program area				
Liberal arts and sciences	18.6	19.4	14.3	14.9
Fine arts	15.0	17.3	11.7	10.9
Humanities	20.6	20.9	14.1	15.5
Social sciences	19.8	20.2	16.0	16.3
Natural sciences	17.1	18.3	14.6	14.5
Professions	16.0	18.1	14.3	15.5
Business	20.2	21.7	—	18.1
Education	17.5	19.9	21.2	15.0
Health sciences	13.6	16.1	14.0	15.4
Engineering	12.7	15.2	9.5	12.2
Gender				
Female	12.5	16.7	15.1	15.8
Male	18.7	19.3	14.0	14.0
Race/ethnicity				
Asian	6.8	9.8	2.9	6.8
Black/African American	20.2	20.9	30.5	17.7
Hispanic	—	20.8	5.8	12.9
Native American	—	35.0	38.5	20.8
White	17.7	18.9	14.3	15.1
Career cohort				
New-entrant (0–6 years)	11.1	12.7	6.2	9.5
Midcareer & senior				
(7 or more years)	22.8	22.2	15.8	15.4
Midcareer (7–14 years)	19.9	—	—	11.1
Senior (15 or more years)	25.8	—	—	17.1

Sources: Carn-69, CFAT-75, CFAT-84, CFAT-97 (see Appendix A for key).

TABLE A-5.1

Full-Time Faculty Interested in Education of Undergraduates, 1969 and 1997

(percent)

	1969	1997	Change in % 1969–97
All faculty	61.6	82.0	20.4
Somewhat agree	(42.7)	(41.6)	−1.1
Strongly agree	(18.9)	(40.4)	21.5
Institutional type			
Universities	52.3	73.5	21.2
Other 4-yr. institutions	68.3	86.2	17.9
2-yr. colleges	75.8	86.9	11.1
Program area			
Liberal arts and sciences	60.9	81.5	20.6
Professions	63.2	81.9	18.7
Gender			
Female	69.7	87.2	17.5
Male	59.9	79.1	19.2
Race/ethnicity			
Asian	58.9	72.3	13.4
Other nonwhite	60.3	76.5	16.2
White	61.7	83.0	21.3
Career cohort			
New-entrant	59.5	80.8	21.3
Midcareer & senior	63.3	82.2	18.9

Sources: Carn-69, CFAT-97 (see Appendix A for key).

Notes: Item wording: The Carn-69 (item 9o) reads, "Please indicate your agreement or disagreement with the following statement: Most faculty here are strongly interested in the academic problems of undergraduates." Reported result combines responses of "strongly agree" and "agree with reservations" on a 4-point scale (strongly agree, agree with reservations, disagree with reservations, strongly disagree). The CFAT-97 (item 27f) reads, "Regarding undergraduates at your institution, please indicate your agreement or disagreement with the following statement: Faculty here are concerned with the academic progress of their undergraduate students." Reported result combines responses of "strongly agree" and "somewhat agree" on a 5-point scale (strongly agree, somewhat agree, neutral, somewhat disagree, strongly disagree).

For definitions of row and column label terms, see Appendix E.

1969: N = 302,585; 1997: N = 4,430.

Parentheses denote subsets of larger percentages.

Full-Time Faculty Reporting New Methods for Evaluating Faculty Work, 1997
(percent)

	Teaching	Research and/or Other Creative Work	Applied Scholarship	Services to the College or University
All faculty	38.0	13.0	10.5	14.6
Institutional type				
Universities	36.3	16.4	10.7	11.5
Other 4-yr. institutions	37.4	15.9	12.5	14.9
2-yr. colleges	40.4	5.0	7.8	17.9
Program area				
Liberal arts and sciences	37.0	13.0	9.1	13.7
Professions	39.4	14.3	12.6	16.7
Gender				
Female	40.1	12.7	11.2	15.8
Male	36.4	13.3	9.9	13.7
Race/ethnicity				
Asian	29.8	16.9	1.8	9.7
Other nonwhite	38.7	15.2	11.1	19.4
White	38.1	12.8	10.8	14.2
Career cohort				
New-entrant	38.8	13.4	10.6	13.7
Midcareer & senior	38.0	13.0	10.4	14.7

Source: CFAT-97 (see Appendix A for key).

Notes: Item wording: CFAT-97 (item 47) reads, "In the past several years, have new methods of evaluating faculty in your department been developed in the following areas?" Reported results are responses of "yes" from 3 categories (yes, no, don't know).

1997: $N = 4,430$.

TABLE A-5.3

Full-time Faculty Agreeing That Tenure Is Difficult to Attain without Research/Publications, 1969–1997

(percent)

	1969	1975	1984	1989	1997	Change in % 1969–97
All faculty	39.9	44.9	54.5	54.0	65.0	23.1
Agree with reservations	(19.6)	(16.2)	(14.7)	—	(14.4)	−5.2
Strongly agree	(20.3)	(28.6)	(39.9)	—	(50.5)	28.2
Institutional type						
Universities	69.1	80.0	89.1	—	94.4	25.3
Other 4-yr. institutions	19.8	29.0	49.2	—	63.8	44.0
2-yr. colleges	5.6	6.9	7.1	6.0	3.1	−2.5
Program Area						
Liberal arts and sciences	43.3	45.4	55.1	—	68.6	25.3
Professions	39.1	43.9	62.7	—	63.6	24.5
Gender						
Female	32.3	35.8	47.5	45.0	57.1	24.8
Male	44.0	47.4	57.3	57.0	69.3	25.3
Race/ethnicity						
Asian	55.8	51.7	67.0	—	73.0	17.2
Other nonwhite	25.7	38.9	46.9	—	52.3	26.6
White	42.2	45.0	54.7	—	65.8	23.6
Career cohort						
New-entrant	40.6	46.0	62.7	—	59.7	19.1
Midcareer & senior	43.1	45.7	52.9	—	65.7	22.6

Sources: Carn-69, CFAT-75, CFAT-84, CFAT-89, CFAT-97 (see Appendix A for key).

Notes: Item wording: Carn-69 (item 42n), CFAT-75 (item 31m), CFAT-84 (item 32-11), CFAT-89 (item 23d), and CFAT-97 (item 40b) read, "Opinion about the following statement: 'In my department it is difficult for a person to achieve tenure if he or she does not publish.'" For Carn-69, CFAT-75, and CFAT-84, reported results combine responses of "strongly agree" and "agree with reservations" on a 4-point scale (strongly agree, agree with reservations, disagree with reservations, strongly disagree). For CFAT-89 and CFAT-97, reported results combine responses of "strongly agree" and "agree with reservations" on a 5-point scale (strongly agree, agree with reservations, neutral, disagree with reservations, strongly disagree).

1969: $N = 302,585$; 1975: $N = 20,788$; 1984: $N = 4,479$; 1989: $N = 9,996$; 1997: $N = 4,430$.

Parentheses denote subsets of larger percentages.

TABLE A-5.4

Full-Time Faculty Rating "Broad Liberal Arts Education" as an Important Goal of Undergraduate Education, 1975–1997

(percent)

	1975	1984	1989	1997	Change in % 1975–97
All faculty	86.7	89.8	91.0	90.9	4.2
Fairly important	49.7	42.7	41.0	42.2	−7.5
Very important	37.0	47.1	50.0	48.7	11.7
Institutional type					
Universities	86.2	88.6	91.0	91.1	4.9
Research	86.0	87.3		91.3	5.3
Other doctorate-granting	86.5	91.0	90.2		3.7
Other 4-yr. institutions	90.8	92.4	94.0	93.6	2.8
Comprehensive	89.5	91.2		92.7	3.2
Liberal arts colleges	94.3	96.9		95.5	1.2
2-yr. colleges	78.2	87.4	88.0	88.0	9.8
Program area					
Liberal arts and sciences	92.2	94.5	—	94.7	2.5
Fine arts	98.0	98.1		97.4	−0.6
Humanities	97.4	97.6		97.9	0.5
Natural sciences	87.2	90.7		92.0	4.8
Social sciences	89.4	92.2		94.2	4.8
Professions	78.3	83.8	—	87.4	9.1
Business	73.2	—		89.2	16.0
Education	86.8	96.2		90.8	4.0
Engineering	63.8	67.8		77.5	13.7
Health sciences	83.0	84.4		85.2	2.2
All other program areas	79.6	88.6	—	85.4	5.8
Gender					
Female	1.1	92.8	94.0	93.0	1.9
Male	85.4	88.9	89.0	89.6	4.2
Race/ethnicity					
Asian	83.3	87.8	—	81.5	−1.8
Other nonwhite	86.7	90.3	—	93.9	7.2
Black/African American	87.6	94.7		95.5	7.9
Hispanic	88.6	94.2		89.6	1.0
Native American	82.5	69.2		83.3	0.8
White	86.8	89.8	—	91.1	4.3
Career cohort					
New-entrant	84.0	84.8	—	89.0	5.0
Midcareer & senior	88.0	90.7	—	91.2	3.2

Sources: CFAT-75, CFAT-84, CFAT-89, CFAT-97 (see Appendix A for key).

Notes: Item wording: CFAT-75 (item 48a), CFAT-84 (item 34-1), CFAT-89 (item 32a), and CFAT-97 (item 55a) read, "Many goals have been proposed for undergraduate education. On the following list, please indicate how important you consider each of the following possible outcomes for the undergraduate: Appreciation of literature and the arts." For CFAT-75, CFAT-84, CFAT-89, and CFAT-97, results combine responses of "very important" and "fairly important" on a 4-point scale (very important, fairly important, fairly unimportant, very unimportant).

1975: $N = 20,788$; 1984: $N = 4,479$; 1989: $N = 9,666$; 1997: $N = 4,430$.

TABLE A-5.5
Full-Time Faculty Rating "Increasing Tolerance for Diversity" as an Important Goal of Undergraduate Education, 1975–1997
(percent)

	1975	1984	1997	Change in % 1975–97
All faculty	95.7	93.7	91.3	−4.4
Fairly important	(31.4)	(31.7)	(31.1)	−0.3
Very important	(64.3)	(61.9)	(60.2)	−4.1
Institutional type				
Universities	95.2	93.4	89.5	−5.7
Research	95.3	92.9	89.7	−5.6
Other doctorate-granting	95.2	94.2	88.7	−6.5
Other 4-yr. institutions	96.6	95.0	92.7	−3.9
Comprehensive	96.4	94.9	92.3	−4.1
Liberal arts colleges	97.1	95.7	94.0	−3.1
2-yr. colleges	94.5	91.9	91.8	−2.7
Program area				
Liberal arts and sciences	96.1	95.1	91.5	−4.6
Fine arts	97.0	97.8	96.0	−1.0
Humanities	96.6	95.0	94.4	−2.2
Natural sciences	94.7	93.7	88.6	−6.1
Social sciences	97.1	95.2	90.6	−6.5
Professions	95.1	92.5	90.9	−4.2
Business	94.2	—	84.1	−10.1
Education	96.7	97.0	95.9	−0.8
Engineering	92.5	81.2	84.1	−8.4
Health sciences	96.7	94.8	95.9	−0.8
All other program areas	96.1	91.6	91.5	−4.6
Gender				
Female	97.9	95.9	95.8	−2.1
Male	95.1	92.8	88.5	−6.6
Race/ethnicity				
Asian	93.0	93.1	92.1	−0.9
Other nonwhite	95.5	94.4	92.4	−3.1
Black/African American	96.1	95.9	96.5	0.4
Hispanic	93.0	92.3	88.0	−5.0
Native American	100.0	100.0	73.9	−26.1
White	95.8	93.6	91.2	−4.6
Career cohort				
New-entrant	96.8	92.6	92.6	−4.2
Midcareer & senior	95.2	93.7	91.1	−4.1

Sources: CFAT-75, CFAT-84, CFAT-97 (see Appendix A for key).

Notes: Item wording: CFAT-75 (item 48f), CFAT-84 (item 34-6), and CFAT-97 (item 55e) read, "Many goals have been proposed for undergraduate education. On the following list, please indicate how important you consider each of the following possible outcomes for the undergraduate: "Tolerance of diversity." Reported results combine responses of "very important" and "fairly important" on a 4-point scale (very important, fairly important, fairly unimportant, very unimportant).

1975: $N = 20,788$; 1984: $N = 4,479$; 1997: $N = 4,430$.

Parentheses denote subsets of larger percentages.

TABLE A-5.6
Full-Time Faculty Rating "Career Preparation" as an Important Goal of Undergraduate Education, 1975–1997
(percent)

	1975	1984	1989	1997	Change in % 1975–97
All faculty	84.5	77.9	75.0	88.1	3.6
Fairly important	(46.7)	(43.4)	(44.0)	(43.1)	−3.6
Very important	(37.8)	(34.5)	(31.0)	(45.0)	7.2
Institutional type					
Universities	82.4	75.7	—	84.3	1.9
Research	81.3	73.8		84.4	3.1
Other doctorate-granting	85.1	79.2		83.8	−1.3
Other 4-yr. institutions	82.8	75.7	—	85.4	2.6
Comprehensive	83.4	76.4		85.9	2.5
Liberal arts colleges	81.1	73.1		84.3	3.2
2-yr. colleges	92.5	84.9	—	95.4	2.9
Program area					
Liberal arts and sciences	79.4	70.8	—	83.6	4.2
Fine arts	82.0	77.7		83.1	1.1
Humanities	72.7	63.1		82.6	9.9
Natural sciences	86.8	78.5		87.3	0.5
Social sciences	75.2	66.1		79.5	4.3
Professions	92.4	84.3	—	94.2	1.8
Business	93.0	—		93.3	0.3
Education	92.0	83.4		90.6	−1.4
Engineering	94.2	87.1		96.0	1.8
Health sciences	93.8	84.7		98.4	4.6
All other program areas	86.5	79.5	—	90.5	4.0
Gender					
Female	89.8	86.2	79.0	92.3	−4.3
Male	82.9	75.0	73.0	85.5	9.4
Race/ethnicity					
Asian	88.4	83.0	—	89.8	1.4
Other nonwhite	91.9	85.4	—	89.6	−2.3
Black/African American	95.1	85.6		90.4	−4.7
Hispanic	91.5	81.1		85.5	−6.0
Native American	94.9	92.9		100.0	5.1
White	84.1	77.5	—	87.7	3.6
Career cohort					
New-entrant	86.1	78.6	—	92.4	6.3
Midcareer & senior	83.9	77.4	—	87.5	3.6

Sources: CFAT-75, CFAT-84, CFAT-89, CFAT-97 (see Appendix A for key).

Notes: Item wording: CFAT-75 (item 48e), CFAT-84 (item 34-5), CFAT-89 (item 32e), and CFAT-97 (item 55d) read, "Many goals have been proposed for undergraduate education. On the following list, please indicate how important you consider each of the following possible outcomes for the undergraduate: "Preparation for a career." Reported results combine responses of "very important' and "fairly important" on a 4-point scale (very important, fairly important, fairly unimportant, very unimportant).
1975: N = 20,788; 1984: N = 4,479; 1989: N = 9,666; 1997: N = 4,430.

TABLE A-5.7

Full-Time Faculty Rating "In-Depth Knowledge of One Subject" as an Important Goal of Undergraduate Education, 1975–1997

(percent)

	1975	1984	1989	1997	Change in % 1975–97
All faculty	85.9	81.3	77.9	80.6	−5.3
Fairly important	(50.8)	(47.9)	(46.0)	(48.0)	−2.8
Very important	(35.1)	(33.4)	(32.0)	(32.5)	−2.6
Institutional type					
Universities	85.8	81.9	—	81.6	−4.2
Research	85.3	81.8		81.4	−3.9
Other doctorate-granting	87.0	82.3		82.2	−4.8
Other 4-yr. institutions	87.4	83.6	—	83.7	−3.7
Comprehensive	86.5	83.6		82.5	−4.0
Liberal arts colleges	89.6	83.6		86.8	−2.8
2-yr. colleges	83.9	76.5		76.1	−7.8
Program area					
Liberal arts and sciences	85.5	82.6	—	82.0	−3.5
Fine arts	86.5	85.5		79.4	−7.1
Humanities	84.6	78.0		82.6	−2.0
Natural sciences	87.7	89.5		83.8	−3.9
Social sciences	82.6	77.8		79.6	−3.0
Professions	86.9	78.8	—	80.3	−6.6
Business	85.2			79.9	−5.3
Education	87.9	82.3		83.8	−4.1
Engineering	86.2	76.6		82.2	−4.0
Health sciences	86.4	79.6		82.8	−3.6
All other program areas	79.9	88.6		76.2	−3.7
Gender					
Female	86.7	84.3	—	80.8	−5.9
Male	85.7	80.3	—	80.5	−5.2
Race/ethnicity					
Asian	86.0	77.6	—	83.5	−2.5
Other nonwhite	87.1	75.3	—	87.6	0.5
Black/African American	90.0	68.0		88.1	−1.9
Hispanic	85.9	88.5		90.4	4.5
Native American	80.0	76.9		78.3	−1.7
White	85.9	81.5	—	79.8	−6.1
Career cohort					
New-entrant	83.6	77.0	—	79.2	−4.4
Midcareer & senior	87.0	82.6	—	80.7	−6.3

Sources: CFAT-75, CFAT-84, CFAT-89, CFAT-97 (see Appendix A for key).

Notes: Item wording: CFAT-75 (item 48h), CFAT-84 (item 34-8), CFAT-89 (item 32g), and CFAT-97 (item 55g) read, "Many goals have been proposed for undergraduate education. On the following list, please indicate how important you consider each of the following possible outcomes for the undergraduate: "Knowledge of a subject in depth." For CFAT75 and CFAT84, reported results combine responses of "very important" and "fairly important" on a 4-point scale (very important, fairly important, fairly unimportant, very unimportant). For CFAT-89 and CFAT-97, respondents were offered a fifth point in the response scale (no opinion).

1975: N = 20,788; 1984: N = 4,479; 1989: N = 9,666; 1997: N = 4,430.

Parentheses denote subsets of larger numbers.

TABLE A-5.8

Full-Time Faculty Rating "Developing Moral Values" as an Important Goal of Undergraduate Education, 1975–1997

(percent)

	1975	1984	1989	1997	Change in % 1975–97
All faculty	82.3	79.3	85.0	83.8	1.5
Fairly important	(36.3)	(38.3)	(44.0)	(36.3)	0.0
Very important	(46.0)	(41.0)	(41.0)	(47.5)	1.5
Institutional type					
Universities	77.0	74.4	—	78.1	1.1
Research	75.8	73.0		77.7	1.9
Other doctorate-granting	79.7	77.4		79.1	−0.6
Other 4-yr. institutions	84.4	83.9	—	86.0	1.6
Comprehensive	82.7	82.6		84.4	1.7
Liberal arts colleges	88.6	89.0		90.1	1.5
2-yr. colleges	87.2	79.4	—	87.8	0.6
Program area					
Liberal arts and sciences	80.5	76.4	—	79.9	−0.6
Fine arts	85.0	83.9		90.0	5.0
Humanities	84.1	78.9		81.5	−2.6
Natural sciences	81.2	74.5		81.8	0.6
Social sciences	71.0	69.3		71.1	0.1
Professions	85.4	84.2	—	87.5	2.1
Business	86.1			88.4	2.3
Education	82.9	80.7		86.3	3.4
Engineering	86.7	83.7		81.4	−5.3
Health sciences	87.3	86.5		95.3	8.0
All other program areas	78.9	74.3		88.7	9.8
Gender					
Female	85.3	82.7	88.0	84.8	−0.5
Male	81.5	78.1	84.0	83.0	1.5
Race/ethnicity					
Asian	88.1	88.7	—	89.5	1.4
Other nonwhite	84.1	89.2	—	85.2	1.1
Black/African American	85.0	92.6		86.6	1.6
Hispanic	79.7	82.7		88.6	8.9
Native American	89.5	85.7		91.3	1.8
White	82.2	79.0	—	83.2	1.0
Career cohort					
New-entrant	79.8	76.7	—	82.3	2.5
Midcareer & senior	83.9	79.8	—	83.9	0.0

Sources: CFAT-75, CFAT-84, CFAT-89, CFAT-97 (see Appendix A for key).

Notes: Item wording: CFAT-75 (item 48b), CFAT-84 (item 34–2), CFAT-89 (item 32b), and CFAT-97 (item 55b) read, "Many goals have been proposed for undergraduate education. On the following list, please indicate how important you consider each of the following possible outcomes for the undergraduate: "Firm moral values." Reported results combine responses of "very important" and "fairly important" on a 4-point scale (very important, fairly important, fairly unimportant, very unimportant).

1975: N = 20,788; 1984: N = 4,479; 1989: N = 9,666; 1997: N = 4,430.

Parentheses denote subsets of larger numbers.

TABLE A-5.9
Agreement that "Respect for Academic Profession Has Declined," Full-Time Faculty, 1969, 1988, and 1997
(percent)

	1969	1987	1997	Change in % 1969–97
All faculty	57.8	36.8	71.7	13.9
Somewhat agree	37.0	—	48.9	11.9
Strongly agree	20.8	—	22.8	2.0
Institutional type				
Universities	54.4	34.9	71.6	17.2
Other 4-yr. institutions	60.7	38.2	72.4	11.7
2-yr. colleges	62.0	39.2	71.2	9.2
Program area				
Liberal arts and sciences	56.5	39.8	72.9	16.4
Professions	60.5	33.2	70.9	10.4
Gender				
Female	62.8	37.7	74.2	11.4
Male	56.7	36.4	70.2	13.5
Race/ethnicity				
Asian	68.0	29.4	74.1	6.1
Other nonwhite	76.4	32.0	68.4	−8.0
White	57.2	37.5	71.8	14.6
Career cohort				
New-entrant	54.4	—	70.6	16.2
Midcareer & senior	60.6	—	71.9	11.3

Sources: Carn-69, NSOPF-88, CFAT-97 (see Appendix A for key).

Notes: Item wording: Carn-69 (item 27w) reads, "Please indicate your agreement or disagreement with the following statement: Respect for the academic profession has declined over the past 20 years." Reported results combine responses of "strongly agree" and "agree with reservations" on a 4-point scale (strongly agree, agree with reservations, disagree with reservations, strongly disagree). NSOPF-88 (item 49f) reads, "Please indicate your opinion regarding whether the following has worsened, improved, or stayed the same in the recent years: Respect for the academic profession, generally." Reported result is the response of "worsened" on a 3-point scale (worsened, stayed the same, improved, and the category "have no idea"). CFAT-97 (item 61c) reads, "Now we would like to know how you feel about the status and role of higher education in this country: Respect for the academic profession is declining." Reported result combines responses of "strongly agree" and "somewhat agree" on a 5-point scale (strongly agree, somewhat agree, neutral, somewhat disagree, strongly disagree).

1969: N = 302,585; 1987: N = 491,500; 1997: N = 4,430.

TABLE A-5.10
Agreement that "Faculty Are Free to Express Relevant Ideas in Class," Full-Time Faculty, 1969–1998
(percent)

	1969	1975	1984	1987	1992	1997	1998	Change in % 1969–98
All faculty	83.9	87.5	84.1	80.1	81.7	77.1	62.9	−21.0
Somewhat agree	35.4	35.4	35.5	38.1	59.7	36.5	52.7	17.3
Strongly agree	48.5	52.1	48.6	42.0	22.0	40.6	10.2	−38.3
Institutional type								
Universities	84.7	88.7	82.5	81.8	80.3	78.7	62.8	−21.9
Other 4-yr. institutions	84.6	87.5	85.4	81.0	82.8	79.9	63.4	−21.2
2-yr. colleges	78.5	84.6	84.4	76.1	82.7	72.1	61.8	−16.7
Program area								
Liberal arts and sciences	87.0	89.8	88.1	84.7	81.4	81.8	63.6	−23.4
Professions	77.3	83.8	80.3	74.5	81.5	70.1	61.6	−15.7
Gender								
Female	86.3	90.1	85.5	78.8	81.6	76.4	63.6	−22.7
Male	83.5	86.8	83.7	80.5	81.8	77.6	62.5	−21.0
Race/ethnicity								
Asian	88.0	90.3	81.1	84.4	84.1	77.7	60.9	−27.1
Other nonwhite	90.4	84.7	81.1	79.2	81.6	81.4	62.7	−27.7
White	83.7	87.5	84.2	79.9	81.6	76.9	63.0	−20.7
Career cohort								
New-entrant	87.2	90.0	82.7	—	81.5	76.2	66.3	−20.9
Midcareer & senior	81.1	86.4	84.1	—	81.8	77.3	62.1	−19.0

Sources: Carn-69, CFAT-75, CFAT-84, NSOPF-88, CFAT-97, NSOPF-99 (see Appendix A for key).

Notes: Item wording: Carn-69 (item 27z), CFAT-75 (item 9o), CFAT-84 (item 28-5), NSOPF-88 (item 48f), and CFAT-97 (item 53d) read, "Please indicate your agreement or disagreement with each of the following statements: Faculty members should be free to present in class any idea that they consider relevant." For Carn-69, CFAT-75, and CFAT-84, reported results combine responses of "strongly agree" and "agree with reservations" on a 4-point scale (strongly agree, agree with reservations, disagree with reservations, strongly disagree). For NSOPF-88, reported result combines responses of "somewhat agree" and "agree strongly" on a 4-point scale (strongly disagree, somewhat disagree, somewhat agree, strongly agree). NSOPF-93 (item F60h) reads, "Please indicate your opinion regarding whether each of the following has worsened, stayed the same, or improved in recent years at this institution: The atmosphere for free expression of ideas" Reported result combines responses of "stayed the same" and "improved" on a 4-point scale (worsened, stayed the same, improved, don't know). For CFAT-97, reported result combines responses of "strongly agree" and "somewhat agree" on a 5-point scale (strongly agree, somewhat agree, neutral, somewhat disagree, strongly disagree). NSOPF-99 (item 93d) reads, "Please indicate the extent to which you agree or disagree with each of the following statements. Over recent years at this institution the atmosphere is less conducive to free expression of ideas." Reported result combines responses of "strongly disagree" and "disagree" on a 4-point scale (strongly disagree, disagree, agree, strongly agree).

1969: N = 302,585; 1975: N = 20,788; 1984: N = 4,479; 1987: N = 491,500; 1992: N = 495,061; 1997: N = 4,430; 1998: N = 483,690.

TABLE A-5.11

Agreement that the Administration at Their Institution Supports Academic Freedom, Full-Time Faculty, 1969–1997

(percent)

	1969	1975	1984	1989	1997	Change in % 1969–97
All faculty	76.1	74.4	76.8	67.0	55.3	−20.8
Somewhat agree	38.3	46.6	47.2	—	33.6	−4.7
Strongly agree	37.8	27.8	29.6	—	21.7	−16.1
Institutional type						
Universities	78.0	75.5	78.8	—	53.3	−24.7
Other 4-yr. institutions	76.5	73.6	76.1	—	54.5	−22.0
2-yr. colleges	68.1	73.6	75.1	—	58.5	−9.6
Program area						
Liberal arts and sciences	74.5	73.0	76.5	—	55.5	−19.0
Professions	79.4	76.5	77.6	—	54.9	−24.5
Gender						
Female	73.4	75.6	75.7	65.0	56.7	−16.7
Male	76.6	74.0	77.1	68.0	44.5	−32.1
Race/ethnicity						
Asian	70.9	70.5	69.5	—	40.7	−30.2
Other nonwhite	74.0	69.8	74.6	—	56.5	−17.5
White	76.2	74.7	77.2	—	56.0	−20.2
Career cohort						
New-entrant	69.4	71.9	76.0	—	48.7	−20.7
Midcareer & senior	81.6	76.8	77.0	—	56.1	−25.5

Sources: Carn-69, CFAT-75, CFAT-84, CFAT-89, CFAT-97 (see Appendix A for key).

Note: Item wording: Carn-69 (item 27j) and CFAT-97 (item 53a) read, "Please indicate your agreement or disagreement with each of the following statements: The administration here has taken a clear stand in support of academic freedom." For Carn-69, reported results combine responses of "strongly agree" and "agree with reservations" on a 4-point scale (strongly agree, agree with reservations, disagree with reservations, strongly disagree). For CFAT-97, reported result combines responses of "strongly agree" and "somewhat agree" on a 5-point scale (strongly agree, somewhat agree, neutral, somewhat disagree, strongly). CFAT-75 (item 9v) and CFAT-84 (item 28-8) read, "Please indicate the extent of your agreement or disagreement with each of the following statements: The administration here strongly supports academic freedom." Reported results combine responses of "strongly agree" and "agree with reservations" on a 4-point scale (strongly agree, agree with reservations, disagree with reservations, strongly disagree). CFAT-89 (item 30b) reads, "Please indicate the extent of your agreement or disagreement with each of the following statements: The administration here supports academic freedom." Reported result combines responses of "strongly agree" and "agree with reservations" on a 5-point scale (strongly agree, agree with reservations, neutral, disagree with reservations, strongly disagree).

1969: N = 302,585; 1975: N = 20,788; 1984: N = 4,479; 1989: N = 9,666; 1997: N = 4,430.

TABLE A-5.12

Agreement that Female and Minority Faculty Are Treated Fairly at Their Institutions, Full-Time Faculty, 1975–1998

(percent)

	1975	1987	1992	1997	1998
All faculty					
Women faculty	20.3	76.7	75.8	78.6	80.2
Somewhat agree	15.2	41.0	37.3	35.6	53.4
Strongly agree	5.1	35.7	38.5	43.0	26.8
Minority faculty	—	84.0	81.4	78.1	83.5
Somewhat agree	—	42.4	39.3	32.0	58.4
Strongly agree	—	41.6	42.1	46.1	25.1
Institutional type					
Universities					
Women faculty	17.9	75.3	73.0	74.1	77.8
Minority faculty	—	81.3	78.6	74.8	81.4
Research univs.					
Women faculty	17.1	74.4	72.8	74.3	78.0
Minority faculty	—	81.2	78.4	74.1	81.4
Other doctorate-granting					
Women faculty	19.7	76.8	73.4	73.5	77.5
Minority faculty	—	81.6	78.9	77.1	81.4
Other 4-yr. institutions					
Women faculty	19.1	74.6	74.5	75.3	80.8
Minority faculty	—	83.8	81.0	75.1	84.4
Comprehensive institutions					
Women faculty	19.8	73.8	72.8	74.5	80.7
Minority faculty	—	82.7	80.0	74.1	84.7
Liberal arts colleges					
Women faculty	17.5	77.6	80.2	77.7	81.3
Minority faculty	—	87.8	84.5	77.6	83.7
2-yr. colleges					
Women faculty	27.6	83.1	82.4	87.0	84.3
Minority faculty	—	89.8	86.7	85.1	86.5
Program area					
Liberal arts & sciences					
Women faculty	18.9	76.5	76.5	79.6	81.2
Minority faculty	—	83.0	82.0	78.0	83.6
Professions					
Women faculty	22.8	77.4	74.8	78.3	78.6
Minority faculty	—	85.3	81.0	79.9	83.2
Gender					
Female					
Women faculty	12.7	60.0	59.7	68.9	65.3
Minority faculty	—	75.1	72.7	73.2	75.3
Male					
Women faculty	22.5	83.0	83.8	84.4	88.6
Minority faculty	—	87.2	85.7	81.1	88.1

(*continued*)

TABLE A-5.12 (*continued*)

	1975	1987	1992	1997	1998
Race/ethnicity					
Asian					
Women faculty	34.8	84.2	80.9	67.6	84.8
Minority faculty	—	72.0	70.1	60.8	69.8
Other nonwhite					
Women faculty	19.2	73.5	68.9	66.0	74.0
Minority faculty	—	70.3	65.9	62.6	67.4
White					
Women faculty	20.1	76.6	76.1	80.4	80.6
Minority faculty	—	85.5	83.5	80.5	86.1
Career cohort					
New-entrant					
Women faculty	18.0	—	73.7	73.2	79.0
Minority faculty	—	—	78.7	67.6	80.8
Midcareer & senior					
Women faculty	21.6	—	76.6	79.3	80.5
Minority faculty	—	—	82.5	79.6	84.1

Sources: CFAT-75, NSOPF-88, NSOPF-93, CFAT-97, NSOPF-99 (see Appendix A for key).

Notes: Item wording: CFAT-75 (item 9ii) reads, "Please indicate your agreement or disagreement with the following statement: On the whole, women have not been discriminated against in academic life." Reported results combine responses of "strongly agree" and "agree with reservations" on a 4-point scale (strongly agree, agree with reservations, disagree with reservations, strongly disagree). NSOPF-88 (item 48l), NSOPF-93 (item F59e), CFAT-97 (item 59b), and NSOPF-99 (item 92f) read, "Please indicate your agreement or disagreement with the following statement: Female faculty are treated fairly at this institution." For NSOPF-88, reported result combines responses of "strongly agree" and "somewhat agree" on a 4-point scale (strongly agree, somewhat agree, somewhat disagree, strongly disagree.) For NSOPF-93, reported result combines responses of "agree somewhat" and "agree strongly" on a 4-point scale (disagree strongly, disagree somewhat, agree somewhat, agree strongly). For CFAT-97, reported result combines responses of "strongly agree" and "somewhat agree" on a 5-point scale (strongly agree, somewhat agree, neutral, somewhat disagree, strongly disagree). For NSOPF-99, reported result combines responses of "agree" and "strongly agree" on a 4-point scale (strongly disagree, disagree, agree, strongly agree). NSOPF-88 (48m), NSOPF-93 (F59f), CFAT-97 (item 59a), and NSOPF-99 (item 92g) read, "Please indicate your agreement or disagreement with the following statement: Faculty who are members of racial or ethnic minorities are treated fairly at this institution." Reported result combines responses of "agree somewhat" and "agree strongly" on a 4-point scale (disagree strongly, disagree somewhat, agree somewhat, agree strongly." For CFAT-97, reported result combines responses of "strongly agree" and "somewhat agree" on a 5-point scale (strongly agree, somewhat agree, neutral, somewhat disagree, strongly disagree). For NSOPF-99, reported result combines responses of "agree" and "strongly agree" on a 4-point scale (strongly disagree, disagree, agree, strongly agree).

1975: $N = 20,788$; 1987: $N = 491,500$; 1992: $N = 495,061$; 1997: $N = 4,430$; 1998: $N = 483,690$.

TABLE A-5.13

Agreement that the Personal Relations among Faculty
in Their Departments Are Good, Full-Time Faculty, 1969–1997

(percent)

	1969	1975	1984	1997	Change in % 1969–97
All faculty	73.9	69.8	65.5	81.1	7.2
Good	43.8	42.1	43.1	41.4	−2.4
Excellent	30.1	27.7	22.4	39.7	9.6
Institutional type					
Universities	72.8	66.6	62.6	74.5	1.7
Research	—	67.1	64.5	73.9	—
Other doctorate-granting	—	65.4	58.8	76.5	—
Other 4-yr. institutions	74.0	69.6	64.7	82.2	8.2
Comprehensive	—	66.2	62.4	81.4	—
Liberal arts colleges	—	77.8	73.7	84.5	—
2-yr. colleges	77.7	73.8	71.5	87.3	9.6
Program area					
Liberal arts and sciences	73.5	69.4	64.2	79.4	5.9
Professions	74.6	70.3	66.0	82.4	7.8
Gender					
Female	69.4	65.9	63.6	83.8	14.4
Male	74.9	70.9	66.5	79.5	4.6
Race/ethnicity					
Asian	60.8	55.2	58.1	76.3	15.5
Other nonwhite	67.3	62.6	56.5	78.9	11.6
White	74.3	70.4	66.2	81.7	7.4
Career cohort					
New-entrant	71.8	69.1	66.6	76.1	4.3
Midcareer & senior	75.6	70.5	65.3	81.8	6.2

Sources: Carn-69, CFAT-75, CFAT-84, CFAT-97 (see Appendix A for key).

Notes: Item wording: Carn-69 (item 75n), CFAT-75 (item 45m), and CFAT-84 (item 47-10) read, "How would you rate the following: Personal relations among faculty in your department." Reported results combine responses of "excellent" and "good" on a 4-point scale (excellent, good, fair, poor). CFAT-97 (item 21d) reads, "To what extent are you satisfied with the following aspect of your job: Relationships with colleagues." Reported result combines responses of "very satisfied" and "somewhat satisfied" on a 5-point scale (very satisfied, somewhat satisfied, neutral, somewhat dissatisfied, very dissatisfied).

1969: $N = 302,585$; 1975: $N = 20,788$; 1984: $N = 4,479$; 1997: $N = 4,430$.

TABLE A-5.14

Full-Time Faculty Rating the Sense of Community at Their Institution as Good/Excellent or Important/Very Important, 1989–1999

(percent)

	1989	1989–90	1992–93	1995–96	1997	1998–99	% Change 1989–97
All faculty	37.0	41.0	47.7	44.3	26.9	47.4	−10.1
Good or important (somewhat agree)	—	—	—	—	22.0	—	—
Excellent or very important (strongly agree	—	—	—	—	4.9	—	
Institutional type							
Universities	—	—	—	—	25.1	—	
Research	—	—	—	—	27.7	—	
Other doctorate-granting	—	—	—	—	17.7	—	
Other 4-yr. institutions	—	38.8	46.5	44.1	28.3	46.5	—
Comprehensive	—	—	—	—	21.2	—	—
Liberal arts colleges	—	—	—	—	46.8	—	—
2-yr. colleges	45.0	48.5	51.7	44.7	27.6	50.1	−17.4
Program area							
Liberal arts and sciences	—	—	—	—	25.2	—	—
Professions	—	—	—	—	29.3	—	—
Gender							
Female	38.0	46.5	52.5	47.7	27.3	51.6	−10.7
Male	35.0	38.7	45.5	42.5	26.7	44.9	−8.3
Race/ethnicity							
Asian	—	—	—	—	27.1	—	—
Other nonwhite	—	—	—	—	26.7	—	—
White	—	—	—	—	27.0	—	—
Career cohort							
New-entrant	—	—	—	—	31.2	—	—
Midcareer & senior	—	—	—	—	26.4	—	—

Sources: CFAT-89, HERI-90, HERI-93, HERI-96, CFAT-97, HERI-99 (see Appendix A for key).

Notes: Item wording: CFAT-89 (item 40i) and CFAT-97 (item 58e) read, "How would you rate each of the following at your institution: The sense of campus community." Reported result combines responses of "excellent" and "good" on a 4-point scale (excellent, good, fair, poor). HERI-90 (item 27d), HERI-93 (item 27d), HERI-96 (item 26d), and HERI-99 (item 28d) read, "Indicate how important you believe each priority listed below is at your college or university: To develop a sense of community among students and faculty."

1989: $N = 9,666$; 1989–90: $N = 29,771$; 1992–93: $N = 35,748$; 1995–96: $N = 33,968$; 1997: $N = 4,430$; 1998–99: $N = 33,785$.

TABLE A-5.15

Agreement that the Faculty-Student Relations in Their Departments Are Good, Full-Time Faculty, 1969, 1975, and 1997

(percent)

	1969	1975	1997	Change in % 1969–97
All faculty	80.7	82.2	78.1	−2.6
Good	56.0	55.4	59.9	3.9
Excellent	24.7	26.8	18.2	−6.5
Institutional type				
Universities	78.2	78.1	71.8	−6.4
Research	—	77.5	71.7	—
Other doctorate-granting	—	79.7	72.5	—
Other 4-yr. institutions	81.7	83.1	80.1	−1.6
Comprehensive	—	80.7	76.0	—
Liberal arts colleges	—	89.2	90.8	—
2-yr. colleges	87.5	86.9	83.2	−4.3
Program area				
Liberal arts and sciences	79.5	81.2	76.3	−3.2
Professions	83.2	83.6	79.7	−3.5
Gender				
Female	80.6	82.1	81.6	1.0
Male	80.8	82.2	76.2	−4.6
Race/ethnicity				
Asian	69.0	67.3	61.7	−7.3
Other nonwhite	70.2	75.3	72.4	2.2
White	81.2	82.8	79.7	−1.5
Career cohort				
New-entrant	77.8	81.1	78.2	0.4
Midcareer & senior	83.2	83.1	78.2	−5.0

Sources: Carn-69, CFAT-75, CFAT-97 (see Appendix A for key).

Notes: Item wording: Carn-69 (item 75o), CFAT-75 (item 45n), and CFAT-97 (item 58i) read, "How would you rate the following: Faculty/student relations in your department." Reported results combine responses of "excellent" and "good" on a 4-point scale (excellent, good, fair, poor).

1969: $N = 302,585$; 1975: $N = 20,788$; 1997: $N = 4,430$.

TABLE A-5.16

Satisfaction with Administration, Full-Time Faculty, 1969–1997

(percent)

	1969	1975	1984	1987	1989	1997	Change in % 1969–97
All faculty	52.2	36.5	33.7	57.0	36.0	46.5	−5.7
Good	42.0	31.5	29.3	39.8	—	34.5	−7.5
Excellent	10.2	5.0	4.4	17.2	—	12.0	1.8
Institutional type							
Universities	52.0	35.8	35.8	56.7	—	42.6	−9.4
Research	—	37.3	37.4	54.9		43.3	
Other doctorate-granting	—	32.4	32.6	59.9	—	40.4	
Other 4-yr. institutions	53.2	35.2	30.6	56.2	—	47.7	−5.5
Comprehensive	—	31.3	27.1	53.5		45.1	
Liberal arts colleges	—	44.9	44.5	65.7		54.4	
2-yr. colleges	49.9	37.9	35.6	58.3	45.0	49.6	−0.3
Program area							
Liberal arts and sciences	49.0	32.9	31.1	53.9	—	43.4	−5.6
Professions	58.9	42.1	37.6	60.5	—	51.1	−7.8
Gender							
Female	54.7	40.7	35.6	56.8	—	49.1	−5.6
Male	51.7	35.3	32.8	57.5	—	44.9	−6.8
Race/ethnicity							
Asian	40.5	24.8	26.7	57.7	—	34.6	−5.9
Other nonwhite	44.3	41.0	37.2	58.4	—	48.9	4.6
White	52.6	36.6	33.8	56.8	—	46.9	−5.7
Career cohort							
New-entrant	47.9	35.0	32.3	—	—	49.2	1.3
Midcareer & senior	55.8	37.6	33.5	—	—	46.0	−9.8

Sources: Carn-69, CFAT-75, CFAT-84, NSOPF-88, CFAT-89, CFAT-98 (see Appendix A for key).

Notes: Carn-69 (item 75h), CFAT-75 (item 45h), CFAT-84 (item 47-8), and CFAT-89 (item 40g) read, "How would you rate the following: The administration at your institution." For Carn-69, CFAT-75, and CFAT-84, reported results combine responses of "excellent" and "good" on a 4-point scale. For CFAT-89, reported result combines responses of "excellent" and "good" on a 5-point scale (excellent, good, fair, poor, not applicable). NSOPF-88 (item 19p) reads, "How satisfied or dissatisfied do you personally feel about each of the following aspects of your job at this institution? Quality of chief administrative officers at this campus." Reported result combines responses of "somewhat satisfied" and "very satisfied" on a 4-point scale (very dissatisfied, somewhat dissatisfied, somewhat satisfied, very satisfied, and a category for "does not apply"). CFAT-97 (item 52a) reads, "Please indicate how you feel about the following statements which relate to management and the decision-making process: Top-level administrators are providing competent leadership." Reported result combines responses of "strongly agree" and "somewhat agree" on a 5-point scale (strongly agree, somewhat agree, neutral, somewhat disagree, strongly disagree).

1969: N = 302,585; 1975: N = 20,788; 1984: N = 4,479; 1987: N = 491,500; 1989: N = 9,666; 1997: N = 4,430.

TABLE A-5.17
Reported Left/Liberal Views, Full-Time Faculty, 1969–1997
(percent)

	1969	1975	1984	1997	Change in % 1969–97
All faculty	48.4	41.1	39.7	56.6	8.2
Female	43.3	41.4	41.9	64.8	21.5
Male	49.4	40.2	39.0	51.5	2.1
Program area					
Liberal arts and sciences	55.4	48.9	48.9	63.9	8.5
Female	51.9	50.8	54.8	74.6	22.7
Male	56.0	48.5	47.3	59.0	3.0
Fine arts	51.5	45.1	46.7	71.6	20.1
Female	43.6	38.2	50.0	81.0	37.4
Male	53.6	47.0	45.1	66.7	13.1
Humanities	61.3	56.6	56.3	74.7	13.4
Female	54.7	55.4	55.9	79.0	24.3
Male	63.3	56.9	57.1	71.0	7.7
Natural sciences	43.6	37.0	37.6	49.8	6.2
Female	39.7	35.4	41.4	55.8	16.1
Male	44.1	37.2	37.2	48.1	4.0
Social sciences	68.4	60.4	55.1	69.8	1.4
Female	68.0	69.4	65.4	85.0	17.0
Male	68.5	58.7	52.6	63.9	−4.6
Professions	33.5	29.2	30.5	45.8	12.3
Female	29.4	29.4	33.7	53.0	23.6
Male	34.6	29.1	29.1	39.2	4.6
Business	29.8	23.1	—	31.1	1.3
Female	17.3	12.9	—	45.2	27.9
Male	31.8	25.6	—	24.0	−7.8
Education	36.1	33.1	38.8	59.4	23.3
Female	30.4	32.4	44.2	60.7	30.3
Male	38.4	33.4	36.2	58.1	19.7
Engineering	28.7	24.8	25.0	32.6	3.9
Female	51.2	50.0	50.0	45.7	−5.5
Male	28.5	24.6	24.3	30.4	1.9
Health sciences	31.8	28.5	28.6	46.0	14.2
Female	30.0	27.9	25.7	48.1	18.1
Male	34.4	29.6	32.7	35.9	1.5
All other program areas	33.2	37.6	39.5	55.1	21.9
Female	49.8	59.5	41.5	69.1	19.3
Male	31.3	32.8	38.8	45.6	14.3

Sources: Carn-69, CFAT-75, CFAT-84, CFAT-97 (see Appendix A for key).

Notes: Item wording: Carn-69 (item 61a), CFAT-75 (item 52), CFAT-84 (item 53), and CFAT-97 (item 68) read, "How would you characterize yourself politically at the present time?" Carn-69, CFAT-75, and CFAT-84 categories are "left," "liberal," "middle of the road," "moderately conservative," and "strongly conservative." CFAT-97 categories are "liberal," "moderately liberal," "middle of the road," "moderately conservative," and "conservative."

1969: $N = 302,585$; 1975: $N = 20,788$; 1984: $N = 4,479$; 1997: $N = 4,430$.

TABLE A-5.18
Reported Various Political Views, Full-Time Faculty, 1969–1997
(percent)

	1969	1975	1984	1989	1997	Change in % 1969–97
All faculty						
Left/liberal	48.3	41.1	39.5	57	56.5	8.3
Left	5.5	5.4	5.5	25	23.1	17.6
Liberal	42.8	35.7	34.0	32	33.4	−9.4
Middle of the road	26.3	28.1	26.7	16	19.7	−6.6
Moderately/strongly conservative	25.3	30.8	33.9	27	23.8	−1.5
Moderately conservative	23.0	27.7	29.5	21	17.4	−5.6
Strongly conservative	2.3	3.1	4.4	6	6.4	4.1
Institutional type						
Universities						
Left/liberal	53.3	45.3	41.4	—	64.6	11.3
Middle of the road	24.5	27.3	26.7	—	18.5	−6.0
Moderately/strongly conservative	22.3	27.3	31.9	—	16.9	−5.4
Research univs.						
Left/liberal	—	47.4	43.0	—	67.6	—
Middle of the road	—	27.5	26.1	—	17.3	—
Moderately/strongly conservative	—	25.1	30.8	—	15.1	—
Other doctorate-granting univs.						
Left/liberal	—	40.7	38.1	—	54.6	—
Middle of the road	—	26.8	27.7	—	22.5	—
Moderately/strongly conservative	—	32.5	34.2	—	22.8	—
Other 4-yr. institutions						
Left/liberal	46.7	42.4	42.2	—	60.1	13.4
Middle of the road	27.7	28.7	26.6	—	19.4	−8.3
Moderately/strongly conservative	25.6	28.9	31.2	—	20.5	−5.1
Comprehensive insts.						
Left/liberal	—	41.8	42.2	—	59.8	—
Middle of the road	—	29.1	25.8	—	19.3	—
Moderately/strongly conservative	—	29.1	32.0	—	20.9	—
Liberal arts colleges						
Left/liberal	—	43.8	42.1	—	60.4	—
Middle of the road	—	27.8	29.8	—	19.9	—
Moderately/strongly conservative	—	28.4	28.1	—	19.7	—
2-yr. colleges						
Left/liberal	34.9	31.1	32.1	48	43.7	8.8
Middle of the road	29.0	28.8	26.8	26	21.2	−7.8
Moderately/strongly conservative	36.1	40.1	41.1	35	35.1	−1.0

(*continued*)

TABLE A-5.18 (*continued*)

	1969	1975	1984	1989	1997	Change in % 1969−97
Program area						
Liberal arts and sciences						
Left/liberal	55.4	48.8	48.7	—	63.9	8.5
Middle of the road	24.3	26.6	24.8	—	18.1	−6.2
Moderately/strongly conservative	20.3	24.6	26.6	—	17.9	−2.4
Fine arts						
Left/liberal	51.5	44.9	46.7	—	71.9	20.4
Middle of the road	24.9	28.7	27.3	—	10.8	−14.1
Moderately/strongly conservative	23.6	26.4	26.0	—	17.3	−6.3
Humanities						
Left/liberal	61.3	56.4	56.1	—	74.8	13.5
Middle of the road	21.6	23.6	24.6	—	14.5	−7.1
Moderately/strongly conservative	17.1	20.1	19.3	—	10.7	−6.4
Natural sciences						
Left/liberal	43.7	37.0	37.1	—	49.8	6.1
Middle of the road	29.1	31.5	27.1	—	23.8	−5.3
Moderately/strongly conservative	27.2	31.4	35.7	—	26.4	−0.8
Social sciences						
Left/liberal	68.4	60.4	55.0	—	69.7	1.3
Middle of the road	19.9	21.1	19.5	—	16.9	−3.0
Moderately/strongly conservative	11.7	18.5	25.5	—	13.4	1.7
Professions						
Left/liberal	33.5	29.3	30.7	—	45.7	12.2
Middle of the road	30.7	30.6	28.6	—	22.2	−8.5
Moderately/strongly conservative	35.8	40.1	40.7	—	32.1	−3.7
Business						
Left/liberal	29.7	22.8	—	—	31.2	1.5
Middle of the road	31.0	31.0	—	—	20.6	−10.4
Moderately/strongly conservative	39.3	46.1	—	—	48.2	8.9
Education						
Left/liberal	36.2	33.2	24.6	—	59.4	23.2
Middle of the road	32.6	31.3	22.3	—	18.5	−14.1
Moderately/strongly conservative	31.2	35.5	53.1	—	22.1	−9.1
Engineering						
Left/liberal	28.8	25.4	24.6	—	32.6	3.8
Middle of the road	29.2	30.2	22.3	—	31.8	2.6
Moderately/strongly conservative	42.0	44.4	53.1	—	35.6	−6.4
Health sciences						
Left/liberal	31.6	28.9	28.7	—	45.7	14.1
Middle of the road	30.5	32.2	28.7	—	23.1	−7.4
Moderately/strongly conservative	37.9	38.8	42.6	—	31.1	−6.8

(*continued*)

TABLE A-5.18 (*continued*)

	1969	1975	1984	1989	1997	Change in % 1969–97
All other program areas						
Left/liberal	33.4	37.8	38.8	—	55.0	21.6
Middle of the road	27.4	26.0	21.8	—	19.5	−7.9
Moderately/strongly conservative	39.2	36.2	39.4	—	25.5	−13.7
Gender						
Female						
Left/liberal	43.3	40.2	41.9	62.0	64.8	21.5
Middle of the road	29.1	30.2	27.8	14.0	16.8	−12.3
Moderately/strongly conservative	27.6	29.6	30.2	24.0	18.4	−9.2
Male						
Left/liberal	49.4	41.4	39.0	54.0	51.5	2.1
Middle of the road	25.7	27.4	26.2	17.0	21.4	−4.3
Moderately/strongly conservative	24.9	31.2	34.8	28.0	27.2	2.3
Race/ethnicity						
Asian						
Left/liberal	51.5	42.2	38.9	—	43.6	−7.9
Middle of the road	33.5	34.4	40.7	—	37.8	4.3
Moderately/strongly conservative	14.9	23.4	20.4	—	18.6	3.7
Other nonwhite						
Left/liberal	67.0	54.4	56.7	—	61.5	−5.5
Middle of the road	22.3	27.6	21.9	—	24.4	2.1
Moderately/strongly conservative	10.7	18.1	21.3	—	14.0	3.3
Black/African American						
Left/liberal	—	59.0	65.6	—	64.6	—
Middle of the road	—	26.2	21.9	—	24.0	—
Moderately/strongly conservative	—	14.8	12.5	—	11.5	—
Hispanic						
Left/liberal	—	43.5	36.5	—	67.5	—
Middle of the road	—	37.7	28.8	—	19.3	—
Moderately/strongly conservative	—	18.8	34.6	—	13.3	—
Native American						
Left/liberal	—	31.7	30.8	—	23.8	—
Middle of the road	—	31.7	23.1	—	33.3	—
Moderately/strongly conservative	—	36.6	46.2	—	42.9	—
White						
Left/liberal	47.8	40.6	38.6	—	56.8	9.0
Middle of the road	26.3	27.9	26.6	—	18.3	−8.0
Moderately/strongly conservative	25.9	31.5	34.8	—	24.9	−1.0

(*continued*)

TABLE A-5.18 (*continued*)

	1969	1975	1984	1989	1997	Change in % 1969–97
Career cohort						
New-entrant						
Left/liberal	51.7	43.8	44.0	—	47.3	−4.4
Middle of the road	24.8	26.5	27.3	—	19.1	−5.7
Moderately/strongly						
conservative	23.5	29.6	28.7	—	33.6	10.1
Midcareer & senior						
Left/liberal	45.5	38.9	38.0	—	57.8	12.3
Middle of the road	27.6	29.1	26.6	—	19.8	−7.8
Moderately/strongly						
conservative	26.9	31.9	35.4	—	22.4	−4.5

Sources: Carn-69, CFAT-75, CFAT-84, CFAT-89, CFAT-97 (see Appendix A for key).

Notes: Item wording: Carn-69 (item 61a), CFAT-75 (item 52), CFAT-84 (item 53), CFAT-89 (item 51), and CFAT-97 (item 68) read, "How would you characterize yourself politically at the present time?" Carn-69, CFAT-75, and CFAT-84 categories are "left," "liberal," "middle of the road," "moderately conservative," and "strongly conservative." CFAT-89 categories are "left," "liberal," "middle of the road," "moderately conservative," and "conservative." CFAT-97 categories are "liberal," "moderately liberal," "middle of the road," "moderately conservative," and "conservative."

1969: $N = 302{,}585$; 1975: $N = 20{,}788$; 1984: $N = 4{,}479$; 1989: $N = 9{,}666$; 1997: $N = 4{,}430$.

TABLE A-5.19A

Tenured and Nontenured Faculty Very Satisfied with Their Job, 1969–1998
(percent)

	1969	1975	1984	1987	1992	1997	1998
All faculty	47.7	49.8	41.6	35.4	36.6	48.2	37.6
Tenured	—	54.8	43.6	38.5	40.8	50.0	39.0
Nontenured	—	41.9	36.0	30.8	30.9	44.0	35.6
Institutional type							
Universities							
Research	—	50.6	45.4	39.6	38.1	41.5	38.3
Tenured	—	56.4	47.6	41.6	42.9	42.7	40.1
Nontenured	—	40.0	39.6	35.9	28.4	38.0	35.0
Other doctorate-granting	—	44.8	34.2	27.4	33.0	35.4	30.9
Tenured	—	50.5	35.2	31.8	36.5	37.5	34.5
Nontenured	—	36.0	31.7	21.8	28.2	30.4	26.5
Other 4-yr. institutions							
Comprehensive	—	45.5	35.0	28.0	32.0	40.3	33.3
Tenured	—	49.9	36.2	31.1	34.6	39.8	33.7
Nontenured	—	36.9	31.2	22.6	27.9	41.5	32.8
Liberal arts colleges	—	51.9	46.8	37.3	36.2	49.8	38.2
Tenured	—	59.7	52.1	45.5	44.8	52.2	42.6
Nontenured	—	43.6	37.3	28.9	28.2	46.7	35.1
2-yr. colleges	55.6	57.6	48.6	44.2	42.9	63.1	45.0
Tenured	—	60.3	50.8	45.9	47.5	66.5	45.6
Nontenured	—	53.1	40.6	41.6	37.2	53.9	44.4
Program area							
Liberal arts and sciences	45.3	46.7	38.2	30.9	35.6	46.1	36.3
Tenured	—	51.9	39.7	34.3	39.8	47.5	38.4
Nontenured	—	37.2	33.4	23.8	28.7	42.6	33.1
Professions	52.0	54.9	44.2	35.3	37.6	49.6	37.3
Tenured	—	59.9	46.3	40.2	41.8	52.3	38.2
Nontenured	—	48.0	39.9	29.9	32.7	44.1	36.2
Gender							
Female	49.6	51.2	42.7	32.9	33.3	51.6	35.7
Tenured	—	56.0	45.9	35.4	36.8	55.9	36.1
Nontenured	—	46.9	37.4	30.8	30.6	44.5	35.5
Male	47.5	49.4	40.8	36.4	38.3	46.3	38.6
Tenured	—	54.7	42.5	39.3	42.1	47.0	40.2
Nontenured	—	39.5	34.8	30.8	31.1	44.3	35.7
Race/ethnicity							
Nonwhite	36.3	39.6	36.3	26.8	31.7	42.3	32.5
Tenured	—	46.7	32.7	35.1	35.6	42.8	37.0
Nontenured	—	33.3	43.6	17.9	27.9	41.3	27.7
White	48.4	50.5	42.1	36.4	37.4	49.3	38.4
Tenured	—	55.3	44.2	38.9	41.4	51.1	39.3
Nontenured	—	42.6	35.8	32.7	31.4	45.0	37.2
Career cohort							
New-entrant	39.4	43.2	37.4	—	32.4	47.6	36.2
Tenured	—	48.8	43.0		40.3	63.3	40.2
Nontenured	—	41.4	35.2		30.1	45.1	35.9
Midcareer & senior	54.6	54.2	43.0	—	38.4	48.3	37.9
Tenured	—	56.0	43.8		40.8	49.7	39.0
Nontenured	—	44.6	37.4		31.8	43.5	35.4

Sources: Carn-69, CFAT-75, CFAT-84, NSOPF-88, NSOPF-93, CFAT-97, NSOPF-99 (see Appendix A for key).

Notes: The CFAT questionnaire asked respondents, "In general, how do you feel about this institution?" Valid response alternatives were "It is a very good place for me," "It is a fairly good place for me," and "It is not the place for me." The NSOPF questionnaire asked, "How satisfied or dissatisfied do you personally feel about each of the following aspects of your job at this institution? My job here, overall." Valid response alternatives were "very dissatisfied," "somewhat dissatisfied," "somewhat satisfied," and "very satisfied."

1969: N = 337,250; 1975: N = 20,789; 1984: N = 4,313; 1987: N = 489,260; 1992: N = 476,328; 1997: N = 4,444; 1998: N = 483,690.

TABLE A-5.19B
Tenured and Nontenured Faculty Dissatisfied with Their Job, 1969–1998
(percent)

	1969	1975	1984	1987	1992	1997	1998
All faculty	9.0	7.3	10.0	14.8	15.7	8.1	15.3
Tenured	—	4.6	8.7	12.7	13.6	6.5	14.0
Nontenured	—	11.6	13.4	17.9	18.6	11.6	17.0
Institutional type							
Universities							
Research	—	6.6	7.8	14.0	16.2	10.8	16.0
Tenured	—	3.9	6.3	12.3	14.4	8.6	14.3
Nontenured	—	11.6	12.0	17.3	19.7	17.3	19.1
Other doctorate-granting	—	7.6	10.0	17.0	18.4	11.2	17.0
Tenured	—	5.0	8.1	16.7	16.2	10.0	15.5
Nontenured	—	11.5	14.6	17.3	21.3	14.0	18.8
Other 4-yr. institutions							
Comprehensive	—	8.9	13.1	17.6	17.2	8.1	17.5
Tenured	—	6.0	12.0	14.7	15.5	6.5	16.8
Nontenured	—	14.5	16.5	22.6	19.9	11.2	18.5
Liberal arts colleges	—	7.4	8.2	14.4	16.9	9.1	16.2
Tenured	—	3.9	6.5	11.0	10.1	5.5	14.3
Nontenured	—	10.8	11.1	17.8	23.4	13.8	17.5
2-yr. colleges	8.5	5.7	8.3	9.7	10.6	4.3	10.7
Tenured	—	3.8	7.5	7.7	9.4	3.7	9.6
Nontenured	—	8.6	11.2	12.7	12.0	5.9	12.0
Program area							
Liberal arts and sciences	10.1	8.6	10.9	18.5	17.4	8.6	16.4
Tenured	—	5.6	9.7	16.1	15.2	7.3	15.0
Nontenured	—	14.3	15.1	23.5	21.1	12.3	18.4
Professions	6.9	5.2	8.6	12.9	13.4	7.0	14.4
Tenured	—	3.0	7.6	10.4	11.2	5.2	13.2
Nontenured	—	8.3	10.6	15.7	16.0	10.8	15.8
Gender							
Female	8.6	7.5	9.4	16.4	17.2	7.1	16.1
Tenured	—	4.8	8.0	13.9	15.1	5.1	14.6
Nontenured	—	10.1	11.8	18.4	18.7	10.6	17.3
Male	9.1	7.3	10.2	14.2	15.0	8.4	14.0
Tenured	—	4.7	8.9	12.4	13.0	7.0	13.7
Nontenured	—	12.2	14.6	17.6	18.6	12.6	16.7
Race/ethnicity							
Nonwhite	7.9	10.1	9.3	16.1	17.4	10.4	17.3
Tenured	—	5.5	8.2	12.6	13.7	9.0	16.7
Nontenured	—	14.2	11.6	19.9	21.0	13.3	18.0
White	9.0	7.2	9.6	14.6	15.4	7.4	15.0
Tenured	—	4.6	8.6	12.7	13.5	5.9	13.6
Nontenured	—	11.4	12.5	17.6	18.3	11.1	16.8
Career cohort							
New-entrant	13.7	10.8	12.8	—	17.8	11.6	36.2
Tenured	—	7.0	11.7		14.8	2.4	40.2
Nontenured	—	11.9	13.2		18.7	13.1	35.9
Midcareer & senior	5.2	5.3	9.1	—	14.9	7.6	37.9
Tenured	—	4.2	8.5		13.4	6.6	39.0
Nontenured	—	10.9	14.1		18.6	10.9	35.4

Sources: Carn-69, CFAT-75, CFAT-84, NSOPF-88, NSOPF-93, CFAT-97, NSOPF-99 (see Appendix A for key).

Notes: The CFAT questionnaire asked respondents, "In general, how do you feel about this institution?" Valid response alternatives were "It is a very good place for me," "It is a fairly good place for me," and "It is not the place for me." The NSOPF questionnaire asked, "How satisfied or dissatisfied do you personally feel about each of the following aspects of your job at this institution? My job here, overall." Valid response alternatives were "very dissatisfied," "somewhat dissatisfied," "somewhat satisfied," and "very satisfied."

1969: $N = 337,250$; 1975: $N = 20,789$; 1984: $N = 4,313$; 1987: $N = 489,260$; 1992: $N = 476,328$; 1997: $N = 4,444$; 1998: $N = 483,690$.

Tenured and Nontenured Faculty Somewhat Satisfied with Their Job, 1969–1998
(percent)

	1969	1975	1984	1987	1992	1997	1998
All faculty	43.1	42.7	48.5	49.8	47.7	43.8	47.1
Tenured	—	40.6	47.7	48.8	45.6	43.6	47.0
Nontenured	—	46.5	50.6	51.3	50.4	44.3	47.4
Institutional type							
Universities	43.5						
Research	—	42.8	46.7	46.4	45.7	47.7	45.8
Tenured		39.7	46.1	46.2	42.6	48.7	45.6
Nontenured		48.4	48.4	46.9	51.9	44.7	46.0
Other doctorate-granting	—	47.7	55.8	55.6	48.7	53.4	52.1
Tenured		44.5	56.7	51.5	47.3	52.5	49.9
Nontenured		52.5	53.7	60.8	50.5	55.6	54.7
Other 4-yr. institutions	45.1						
Comprehensive	—	45.6	51.9	54.4	50.8	51.5	49.2
Tenured		44.1	51.7	54.2	49.9	53.7	49.5
Nontenured		48.6	52.3	54.8	52.2	47.3	48.7
Liberal arts colleges	—	41.1	45.0	48.4	46.9	41.1	45.6
Tenured		36.4	41.4	43.5	45.2	42.3	43.1
Nontenured		45.6	51.6	53.3	48.4	39.5	47.3
2-yr. colleges	35.9	36.8	43.1	46.1	46.5	32.6	44.2
Tenured		35.9	41.6	46.4	43.1	29.7	44.9
Nontenured		38.3	48.1	45.7	50.8	40.2	43.5
Program area							
Liberal arts and sciences	44.6	44.6	50.9	50.6	47.0	45.2	47.4
Tenured	—	42.5	50.7	49.6	45.0	45.3	46.6
Nontenured	—	48.5	51.6	52.8	50.2	45.1	48.5
Professions	41.2	39.9	47.2	51.8	49.0	43.4	48.3
Tenured	—	37.1	46.1	49.5	47.0	42.6	48.6
Nontenured	—	43.7	49.4	54.4	51.3	45.1	48.0
Gender							
Female	41.7	41.2	47.8	50.8	49.5	41.2	48.1
Tenured	—	39.2	46.0	50.7	48.1	39.0	49.3
Nontenured	—	43.0	50.8	50.8	50.6	44.9	47.2
Male	43.4	43.3	49.1	49.4	46.7	45.3	46.6
Tenured	—	40.6	48.6	48.3	44.9	46.0	46.0
Nontenured	—	48.3	50.6	51.6	50.3	43.1	47.5
Race/ethnicity							
Nonwhite	55.8	50.3	54.5	57.1	50.9	47.3	50.2
Tenured	—	47.8	59.2	52.3	50.7	48.2	46.3
Nontenured	—	52.5	44.8	62.3	51.1	45.5	54.3
White	42.5	42.3	48.4	48.9	47.2	43.3	46.6
Tenured	—	40.1	47.3	48.4	45.0	43.0	47.1
Nontenured	—	46.0	51.6	49.7	50.3	43.8	46.0
Career cohort							
New-entrant	46.9	46.0	49.9	—	49.8	40.8	46.4
Tenured	—	44.1	45.3		44.8	34.3	44.1
Nontenured	—	46.6	51.6		51.2	41.8	46.6
Midcareer & senior	40.2	40.5	47.8	—	46.8	44.1	47.3
Tenured	—	39.7	47.7		45.8	43.7	47.0
Nontenured	—	44.5	48.5		49.5	45.6	47.9

Sources: Carn-69, CFAT-75, CFAT-84, NSOPF-88, NSOPF-93, CFAT-97, NSOPF-99 (see Appendix A for key).

Notes: The CFAT questionnaire asked respondents, "In general, how do you feel about this institution?" Valid response alternatives were "It is a very good place for me," "It is a fairly good place for me," and "It is not the place for me." The NSOPF questionnaire asked, "How satisfied or dissatisfied do you personally feel about each of the following aspects of your job at this institution? My job here, overall." Valid response alternatives were "very dissatisfied," "somewhat dissatisfied," "somewhat satisfied," and "very satisfied."

1969: N = 337,250; 1975: N = 20,789; 1984: N = 4,313; 1987: N = 489,260; 1992: N = 476,328; 1997: N = 4,444; 1998: N = 483,690.

TABLE A-6.1
Full-Time Faculty Holding Doctorate, 1969–1998
(percent)

	1969	1975	1984	1987	1992	1997	1998	Change in % 1969–98
All faculty	57.3	59.0	62.9	54.3	58.8	62.8	62.8	5.5
Institutional type								
Universities	73.7	76.6	78.8	65.2	76.3	86.8	79.8	6.1
Research	—	78.4	79.7	70.3	78.4	87.6	81.7	
Other doctorate-granting	—	72.4	76.7	56.0	72.5	84.0	75.5	
Other 4-yr. institutions	52.2	62.2	70.5	62.2	66.1	74.7	69.2	17.0
Comprehensive	—	64.4	71.9	62.6	67.7	76.1	71.3	
Liberal arts colleges	—	56.9	64.9	61.0	60.3	71.2	64.0	
2-yr. colleges	10.2	15.2	25.9	17.9	16.8	22.4	18.8	8.6
Program area								
Liberal arts and sciences	62.3	67.7	71.9	67.9	66.9	70.7	69.8	7.5
Fine arts	35.1	39.2	44.9	40.3	35.2	30.2	34.1	−1.0
Humanities	58.1	67.0	72.4	66.0	65.7	73.7	67.5	9.4
Natural sciences	70.9	75.4	83.4	71.5	71.4	74.4	75.3	4.4
Social sciences	69.0	73.6	75.8	80.6	77.1	78.3	82.8	13.8
Professions	47.1	46.0	51.4	40.0	52.2	56.8	57.0	9.9
Business	43.4	39.2	—	47.9	53.6	52.5	49.8	6.4
Education	55.1	60.4	77.1	58.1	65.5	71.6	75.0	19.9
Engineering	61.9	62.9	63.5	65.2	73.2	80.6	75.8	13.9
Health sciences	23.6	20.7	23.1	21.9	29.2	32.5	39.0	15.4
All other program areas	33.4	46.7	52.7	42.5	43.1	48.7	47.4	14.0

(continued)

TABLE A-6.1 (continued)

	1969	1975	1984	1987	1992	1997	1998	Change in % 1969–98
Gender								
Female	34.0	36.4	46.5	43.0	44.9	50.5	52.2	18.2
Male	62.3	65.4	68.7	58.5	65.7	70.2	68.8	6.5
Race/ethnicity								
Asian	76.0	78.3	79.8	63.7	72.7	79.1	80.4	4.4
Other nonwhite	45.0	41.9	37.8	47.4	48.8	59.5	57.4	12.4
White	57.4	59.3	63.4	54.3	58.8	62.3	62.2	4.8
Career cohort								
New-entrant	45.6	53.9	55.0	—	53.3	58.4	56.7	11.1
Midcareer & senior	67.0	62.8	65.5	—	61.0	63.4	64.2	-2.8
Midcareer	64.7	—	—		53.1	—	58.2	-6.5
Senior	69.5	—	—		63.7	—	67.4	-2.1

Sources: Carn-1969, CFAT-75, CFAT-84, NSOPF-88, NSOPF-93, CFAT-97, NSOPF-99 (see Appendix A for key).
Notes: Doctorate refers to PhD, EdD, etc.; it does not include first professional degree.
For definitions of row label terms, see Appendix E.

1969: N = 302,585; 1975: N = 20,788; 1984: N = 4,479; 1987: N = 491,500; 1992: N = 495,061; 1997: N = 4,430; 1998: N = 483,690.

TABLE A-6.2

Full-Time Faculty Receiving Fellowships or Scholarships, Teaching Assistantships, or Research Assistantships during Graduate Study, 1969–1992

(percent)

	1969	1987	1992	Change in % 1969–92
Fellowship	52.5	33.2	31.1	−21.4
Scholarship	—	22.4	18.5	—
Fellowship or scholarship*	—	55.6	49.6	−2.9
Teaching assistantship	58.2	48.4	51.5	−6.7
Research assistantship	37.9	30.3	31.5	−6.4
Fellowship and/or scholarship				
Institutional type				
Universities	60.7	67.9	54.5	−6.2
Other 4-yr. institutions	49.6	53.1	44.1	−5.5
2-yr. colleges	29.5	29.8	22.6	−6.9
Program area				
Liberal arts and sciences	56.5	62.8	49.7	−6.8
Fine arts	43.9	54.6	43.9	0.0
Humanities	53.0	63.3	49.8	−3.2
Natural sciences	60.4	60.9	47.6	−12.8
Social sciences	62.2	70.2	56.3	−5.9
Professions	43.9	48.4	37.5	−6.4
Business	40.4	42.9	31.3	−9.1
Education	38.5	39.5	31.5	−7.0
Engineering	52.6	53.4	39.5	−13.1
Health sciences	56.7	53.2	46.7	−10.0
All other program areas	40.8	46.8	36.5	−4.3
Gender				
Female	45.9	56.5	41.5	−4.4
Male	53.9	55.4	45.1	−8.8
Race/ethnicity				
Asian	65.4	61.4	43.1	−22.3
Other nonwhite	60.0	57.7	46.5	−13.5
White	52.1	55.2	43.7	−8.4
Career cohort				
New-entrant	55.8	—	43.9	−11.9
Midcareer & senior	49.7	—	43.9	−5.8
Teaching assistantship				
Institutional type				
Universities	66.1	48.1	56.6	−9.5
Other 4-yr. institutions	56.0	58.0	58.1	2.1
2-yr. colleges	35.1	31.6	32.1	−3.0
Program area				
Liberal arts and sciences	63.1	62.3	62.3	−0.8
Fine arts	57.6	59.8	56.7	−0.9
Humanities	55.9	61.1	62.8	6.9
Natural sciences	72.2	63.4	62.9	−9.3
Social sciences	61.7	63.5	63.6	1.9

(*continued*)

TABLE A-6.2 (*continued*)

	1969	1987	1992	Change in % 1969–92
Professions	47.9	32.1	38.7	−9.2
Business	47.3	43.8	44.3	−3.0
Education	52.9	46.8	48.2	−4.7
Engineering	56.5	49.3	50.5	−6.0
Health sciences	33.5	16.0	19.7	−13.8
All other program areas	36.4	40.3	37.9	1.5
Gender				
Female	44.0	42.5	43.4	−0.6
Male	61.2	50.5	55.5	−5.7
Race/ethnicity				
Asian	61.0	47.9	56.5	−4.5
Other nonwhite	40.1	41.5	38.9	−1.2
White	58.6	48.9	52.4	−6.2
Career cohort				
New-entrant	57.3	—	51.4	−5.9
Midcareer & senior	59.0	—	51.6	−7.4
Research assistantship				
Institutional type	49.6	38.4	44.3	−5.3
Universities	30.6	29.1	29.4	−1.2
Other 4-yr. institutions	15.4	12.6	11.3	−4.1
2-yr. colleges				
Program area				
Liberal arts and sciences	38.8	33.0	33.6	−5.2
Fine arts	13.3	10.4	11.1	−2.2
Humanities	18.1	14.2	17.0	−1.1
Natural sciences	54.7	47.8	45.6	−9.1
Social sciences	55.5	47.2	45.8	−9.7
Professions	36.1	26.1	28.0	−8.1
Business	31.6	32.8	30.7	−0.9
Education	26.7	21.8	25.3	−1.4
Engineering	55.4	56.6	54.2	−1.2
Health sciences	21.6	16.8	13.1	−8.5
All other program areas	27.3	32.9	29.4	2.1
Gender				
Female	21.4	22.2	22.1	0.7
Male	41.3	33.3	36.2	−5.1
Race/ethnicity				
Asian	65.4	51.3	54.9	−10.5
Other nonwhite	29.6	23.8	23.0	−6.6
White	37.7	29.7	30.9	−6.8
Career cohort				
New-entrant	38.4	—	36.3	−2.1
Midcareer & senior	37.5	—	29.6	−7.9

Sources: Carn-69, NSOPF-88, NSOPF-93 (see Appendix A for key).

Note: No similar items are available for 1998.

*Data for 1969 consider fellowships alone, since no survey item on scholarships is available; data for 1987 computes responses on fellowships plus responses on scholarships, because the Data Analysis System does not allow recoding two variables into one variable; data for 1992 calculates responses on either fellowships or scholarships.

TABLE A-6.3
Full-Time Faculty Reporting Various Types of Previous Employment, 1969–1998
(percent)

	1969	1975	1992	1998	Change in % 1969–98
All faculty					
C/U teaching	76.2	98.6	53.5	62.1	−14.1
C/U administration	6.1	18.2	26.2	7.3	1.2
Postdoc. or other research	16.8	11.6	—	—	
K–12	25.8	15.5	13.9	13.9	−11.9
Outside of education	49.9	41.7	49.7	43.0	−6.9
Institutional type					
Universities					
C/U teaching	78.7	98.2	49.9	64.0	−14.7
C/U administration	6.2	22.1	38.1	6.8	0.6
Postdoc. or other research	24.8	17.9	—	—	—
K–12	14.7	6.3	6.8	9.7	−5.0
Outside of education	52.7	42.4	47.0	39.1	−13.6
Research					
C/U teaching	—	97.8	47.9	62.8	—
C/U administration	—	23.3	41.1	6.7	—
Postdoc. or other research	—	19.7	—	—	—
K–12	—	5.3	5.6	8.9	—
Outside of education	—	42.8	46.5	38.0	—
Other doctorate-granting					
C/U teaching	—	98.9	53.4	61.2	—
C/U administration	—	19.5	32.9	5.0	—
Postdoc. or other research	—	14.0	—	—	—
K–12	—	8.8	9.0	11.5	—
Outside of education	—	41.7	48.0	41.6	—
Other 4-yr. institutions					
C/U teaching	75.3	99.2	61.9	64.7	−10.6
C/U administration	6.4	16.7	21.7	8.2	1.8
Postdoc. or other research	11.2	9.3	—	—	—
K–12	32.2	17.6	15.9	17.1	−15.1
Outside of education	47.1	37.1	45.7	42.2	−4.9
Comprehensive insts.					
C/U teaching	—	99.0	61.6	63.4	—
C/U administration	—	16.5	21.8	8.4	—
Postdoc. or other research	—	8.9	—	—	—
K–12	—	18.2	15.6	17.2	—
Outside of education	—	37.6	45.9	42.5	—
Liberal arts colleges					
C/U teaching	—	99.5	63.1	67.1	—
C/U administration	—	17.0	21.4	6.4	—
Postdoc. or other research	—	10.2	—	—	—
K–12	—	16.1	16.7	17.0	—
Outside of education	—	35.8	45.2	41.6	—
2-yr. colleges					
C/U teaching	69.4	98.6	46.8	53.2	−16.2
C/U administration	4.5	13.2	13.1	6.2	1.7
Postdoc. or other research	4.0	3.8	—	—	—
K–12	47.8	32.1	24.8	17.0	−30.8
Outside of education	47.9	49.1	59.0	49.8	1.9

(*continued*)

TABLE A-6.3 (*continued*)

	1969	1975	1992	1998	Change in % 1969–98
Program area					
Liberal arts and sciences					
C/U teaching	77.5	99.2	59.5	66.0	−11.5
C/U administration	5.0	16.4	28.5	5.5	0.5
Postdoc. or other research	18.6	14.8	—	—	—
K–12	22.9	13.4	13.2	12.1	−10.8
Outside of education	44.9	35.6	38.6	33.5	−11.4
Fine arts					
C/U teaching	75.3	99.6	69.9	65.5	−9.8
C/U administration	4.2	11.3	11.4	2.8	−1.4
Postdoc. or other research	5.0	4.2	—	—	—
K–12	36.4	22.3	19.1	15.1	−21.3
Outside of education	49.3	45.3	46.2	37.2	−12.1
Humanities					
C/U teaching	79.1	99.5	73.8	66.8	−12.3
C/U administration	5.6	11.3	15.9	6.7	1.1
Postdoc. or other research	8.5	7.5	—	—	—
K–12	27.6	15.8	18.5	14.4	−13.2
Outside of education	40.4	29.7	29.9	31.9	−8.5
Natural sciences					
C/U teaching	75.8	99.1	48.5	63.3	−12.5
C/U administration	3.0	21.9	41.0	3.0	0.0
Postdoc. or other research	31.6	28.1	—	—	—
K–12	18.6	11.6	11.4	11.2	−7.4
Outside of education	43.0	34.7	38.6	31.4	−11.6
Social sciences					
C/U teaching	79.2	98.9	56.8	66.3	−12.9
C/U administration	7.6	18.1	30.0	5.2	−2.4
Postdoc. or other research	19.8	9.6	—	—	—
K–12	15.2	7.4	6.9	8.7	−6.5
Outside of education	52.8	39.7	45.3	37.5	−15.3
Professions					
C/U teaching	73.8	97.8	48.9	56.7	−17.1
C/U administration	8.5	20.6	22.6	9.9	1.4
Postdoc. or other research	13.2	6.8	—	—	—
K–12	32.2	19.0	16.1	17.1	−15.1
Outside of education	60.1	51.1	59.4	56.0	−4.1
Business					
C/U teaching	77.2	99.1	50.4	61.1	−16.1
C/U administration	9.3	18.6	20.1	11.6	2.3
Postdoc. or other research	8.3	3.7	—	—	—
K–12	21.8	16.0	9.5	8.0	−13.8
Outside of education	63.4	51.7	61.2	62.0	−1.4
Education					
C/U teaching	75.9	98.2	49.9	56.0	−19.9
C/U administration	12.1	23.6	28.7	12.8	0.7
Postdoc. or other research	10.4	6.2	—	—	—
K–12	71.4	36.6	48.8	50.3	−21.1
Outside of education	41.1	37.8	34.6	32.8	−8.3

(*continued*)

TABLE A-6.3 (*continued*)

	1969	1975	1992	1998	Change in % 1969–98
Engineering					
C/U teaching	76.3	98.8	47.7	49.3	−27.0
C/U administration	5.4	20.2	26.7	7.1	1.7
Postdoc. or other research	19.9	9.7	—	—	—
K–12	4.2	5.2	2.1	1.5	−2.7
Outside of education	73.5	66.2	64.8	53.1	−20.4
Health sciences					
C/U teaching	67.7	98.3	47.3	55.8	−11.9
C/U administration	5.5	17.3	18.1	5.4	−0.1
Postdoc. or other research	16.0	10.1	—	—	—
K–12	8.9	5.9	4.7	5.9	−3.0
Outside of education	73.7	56.3	73.3	69.1	−4.6
All other program area					
C/U teaching	61.9	96.8	47.1	56.6	−5.3
C/U administration	5.3	25.1	21.8	8.2	2.9
Postdoc. or other research	11.8	5.2	—	—	—
K–12	21.0	10.5	12.8	14.5	−6.5
Outside of education	71.7	46.8	66.1	53.8	−17.9
Gender					
Female					
C/U teaching	71.6	98.1	53.6	60.3	−11.3
C/U administration	4.3	15.3	21.9	6.7	2.4
Postdoc. or other research	10.1	6.4	—	—	—
K–12	43.1	23.6	20.9	18.4	−24.7
Outside of education	49.0	37.3	51.9	47.0	−2.0
Male					
C/U teaching	77.3	98.8	53.4	63.0	−14.3
C/U administration	6.5	19.0	28.7	7.6	1.1
Postdoc. or other research	18.3	13.1	—	—	—
K–12	22.1	13.1	10.0	11.3	−10.8
Outside of education	50.1	42.9	48.5	40.7	−9.4

Sources: Carn-69, CFAT-75, NSOPF-93, NSOPF-99 (see Appendix A for key).
Note: "C/U" means "College or university."

TABLE A-6.4

Distribution of Academic Ranks, Full-Time Faculty, 1969–1998

	1969	1975	1984	1987	1992	1997	1998	Change in % 1969–98
All faculty								
Full professor	27.1	28.8	38.0	34.9	33.1	39.0	33.4	6.3
Associate professor	23.4	26.8	27.5	25.1	24.8	25.5	25.1	1.7
Assistant professor	29.6	30.4	22.1	24.6	23.5	18.8	22.5	−7.1
Instructor	16.5	11.8	10.6	12.5	13.8	12.8	13.8	−2.7
Lecturer	2.3	1.3	1.2	1.9	2.0	1.5	2.4	0.1
Other ranks	1.2	0.9	0.6	1.1	2.7	2.5	2.8	1.6
Gender								
Female								
Full professor	12.5	13.7	18.1	15.4	16.8	27.4	19.9	7.4
Associate professor	18.1	21.2	26.8	22.5	23.1	25.4	24.6	6.5
Assistant professor	31.6	37.8	34.3	35.4	31.8	25.4	28.7	−2.9
Instructor	32.1	23.9	17.8	20.7	20.7	16.1	19.8	−12.3
Lecturer	3.8	1.9	1.7	4.0	3.9	2.6	3.9	0.1
Other ranks	1.8	1.5	1.3	2.1	3.6	3.1	3.2	1.4
Male								
Full professor	30.1	33.1	44.8	41.9	41.1	46.1	40.9	10.8
Associate professor	24.4	28.4	27.7	26.0	25.7	25.6	25.5	1.1
Assistant professor	29.2	28.3	18.0	20.7	19.4	14.7	19.1	−10.1
Instructor	13.2	8.3	8.2	9.5	10.5	10.7	10.5	−2.7
Lecturer	2.0	1.1	1.0	1.2	1.1	0.8	1.5	−0.5
Other ranks	1.1	0.7	0.4	0.7	2.2	2.1	2.6	1.5
Career Cohort								
New-entrant								
Full professor	3.1	4.2	4.0	—	11.8	3.5	2.7	−0.4
Associate professor	14.0	15.9	12.8	—	13.8	9.8	7.9	−6.1
Assistant professor	47.6	51.8	55.9	—	44.8	59.0	55.6	8.0
Instructor	30.9	24.0	23.2	—	21.4	21.6	24.4	−6.5
Lecturer	3.1	2.3	3.4	—	3.0	2.7	4.0	0.9
Other ranks	1.3	1.8	0.7	—	5.1	3.5	5.3	4.0
Midcareer & senior								
Full professor	46.7	44.2	48.1	—	42.0	44.0	40.3	−6.4
Associate professor	31.0	32.6	31.8	—	29.5	27.7	29.0	−2.0
Assistant professor	15.0	17.3	12.3	—	14.5	13.1	15.1	0.1
Instructor	4.6	4.7	6.7	—	10.7	11.6	11.4	6.8
Lecturer	1.6	0.7	0.6	—	1.6	1.3	2.0	0.4
Other ranks	1.1	0.5	0.6	—	1.7	2.3	2.3	1.2
Midcareer								
Full professor	25.7	—	—	—	23.4	—	11.5	−14.2
Associate professor	41.2	—	—	—	40.9	—	36.2	−5.0
Assistant professor	23.5	—	—	—	14.8	—	29.2	5.7
Instructor	6.3	—	—	—	15.6	—	18.2	11.9
Lecturer	2.0	—	—	—	2.1	—	2.2	0.2
Other ranks	1.2	—	—	—	3.2	—	2.7	1.5
Senior								
Full professor	68.0	—	—	—	48.3	—	55.5	−12.5
Associate professor	20.6	—	—	—	25.6	—	25.2	4.6
Assistant professor	6.3	—	—	—	14.4	—	7.6	1.3
Instructor	2.8	—	—	—	9.0	—	7.8	5.0
Lecturer	1.2	—	—	—	1.5	—	1.8	0.6
Other ranks	1.0	—	—	—	1.2	—	2.1	1.1

Sources: Carn-69, CFAT-75, CFAT-84, NSOPF-88, NSOPF-93, CFAT-97, NSOPF-99 (see Appendix A for key).

TABLE A-7.1

Principal Activities of Full-Time Faculty, by Appointment Status, Institutional Type, Program Area, and Career Cohort, 1992 and 1998

(percent)

	1992					1998				
	All	Teaching	Research	Admin.	Sabbatical	All	Teaching	Research	Admin.	Sabbatical
All faculty	100.0	76.9	11.7	8.5	2.9	100.0	78.5	11.4	9.1	1.0
Tenured/tenure track	88.7	77.4	11.2	8.4	3.1	85.5	78.6	11.5	8.7	1.2
Non-tenure-track	11.3	73.0	16.3	9.8	0.9	14.5	78.0	10.6	11.4	0.0
Institutional type										
Universities	100.0	61.0	25.5	10.1	3.4	100.0	64.5	23.6	10.4	1.5
Tenured/tenure track	(88.5)	61.5	24.6	10.1	3.8	(83.6)	63.3	24.5	10.5	1.8
Non-tenure-track	(11.5)	56.6	32.8	10.3	0.3	(16.4)	70.9	18.9	10.2	0.0
Research	100.0	55.9	30.8	9.7	3.7	100.0	60.9	27.4	10.1	1.6
Tenured/tenure track	(88.9)	56.9	29.5	9.6	4.1	(84.5)	60.1	27.9	10.1	1.9
Non-tenure-track	(11.1)	47.8	41.1	10.7	0.4	(15.5)	65.1	24.5	10.5	0.0
Other doctorate-granting univs.	100.0	70.8	15.5	10.9	2.9	100.0	73.3	14.4	11.0	1.3
Tenured/tenure track	(87.8)	70.6	15.1	11.1	3.3	(81.5)	71.2	15.9	11.4	1.6
Non-tenure-track	(12.2)	71.9	18.3	9.5	0.2	(18.5)	82.6	7.8	9.6	0.0
Other 4-yr. institutions	100.0	87.2	1.5	8.2	3.1	100.0	89.4	1.0	8.9	0.7
Tenured/tenure track	(89.2)	87.1	1.6	8.1	3.2	(84.5)	89.9	1.0	8.3	0.9
Non-tenure-track	(10.8)	88.2	0.8	8.9	2.1	(15.5)	86.6	1.2	12.2	0.0
Comprehensive	100.0	87.2	1.7	8.6	2.5	100.0	89.0	1.2	9.0	0.9
Tenured/tenure track	(89.7)	86.8	1.8	8.8	2.6	(86.0)	89.5	1.1	8.4	1.0
Non-tenure-track	(10.3)	90.7	0.8	6.8	1.6	(14.0)	85.7	1.4	12.9	0.0
Liberal arts colleges	100.0	87.4	0.7	6.5	5.4	100.0	90.8	0.5	8.3	0.3
Tenured/tenure track	(87.3)	88.5	0.7	5.2	5.7	(80.1)	91.4	0.5	7.7	0.4
Non-tenure-track	(12.7)	80.3	0.7	15.6	3.4	(19.9)	88.4	0.8	10.8	0.0

(continued)

TABLE A-7.1 (continued)

	1992					1998				
	All	Teaching	Research	Admin.	Sabbatical	All	Teaching	Research	Admin.	Sabbatical
2-yr. colleges	100.0	92.9	0.4	5.7	1.0	100.0	94.3	0.4	5.0	0.3
Tenured/tenure track	(94.2)	93.0	0.4	5.5	1.1	(92.4)	95.1	0.2	4.4	0.3
Non-tenure-track	(5.8)	91.0	0.6	8.4	—	(7.6)	85.2	2.6 1	2.2	0.0
Program area										
Liberal arts and sciences	100.0	77.7	12.3	6.6	3.4	100.0	78.2	12.9	7.8	1.1
Tenured/tenure track	(91.3)	77.6	12.1	6.7	3.6	(87.1)	78.5	12.7	7.5	1.3
Non-tenure-track	(8.7)	78.1	14.7	5.7	1.5	(12.9)	76.4	14.2	9.4	0.0
Fine arts	100.0	88.9	1.4	5.6	4.2	100.0	91.7	0.5	7.1	0.7
Tenured/tenure track	(91.2)	88.4	1.6	5.8	4.2	(89.3)	91.8	0.5	7.0	0.8
Non-tenure-track	(8.8)	93.4	—	3.1	3.6	(10.7)	90.7	0.8	8.6	0.0
Humanities	100.0	84.6	3.5	7.9	4.0	100.0	86.6	3.1	9.2	1.1
Tenured/tenure track	(90.1)	83.9	3.9	8.0	4.2	(84.1)	86.3	3.4	8.9	1.4
Non-tenure-track	(9.9)	90.5	—	7.4	2.0	(15.9)	87.7	1.5	10.8	0.0
Natural sciences	100.0	69.3	22.6	5.4	2.7	100.0	68.7	23.9	6.3	1.1
Tenured/tenure track	(91.5)	69.8	21.7	5.6	2.9	(87.3)	69.6	22.9	6.2	1.2
Non-tenure-track	(8.5)	64.5	31.5	2.8	1.2	(12.7)	62.3	30.5	7.2	0.0
Social sciences	100.0	78.5	10.2	7.7	3.5	100.0	77.5	12.1	9.0	1.5
Tenured/tenure track	(92.3)	78.6	10.0	7.5	3.8	(89.4)	77.5	12.2	8.6	1.6
Non-tenure-track	(7.7)	76.5	13.2	10.3	—	(10.6)	77.2	10.7	12.1	0.0
Professions	100.0	78.3	9.2	10.5	2.0	100.0	78.6	9.8	10.7	0.9
Tenured/tenure track	(88.4)	78.4	9.2	10.2	2.3	(83.6)	78.3	10.5	10.1	1.1
Non-tenure-track	(11.6)	77.0	9.3	13.4	0.3	(16.4)	79.9	6.3	13.9	0.0
Business	100.0	81.8	7.8	9.0	1.4	100.0	85.7	5.4	7.8	1.2
Tenured/tenure track	(91.0)	81.4	8.5	8.6	1.5	(83.4)	86.1	6.2	6.2	1.4
Non-tenure-track	(9.0)	86.0	0.9	12.6	0.5	(6.6)	83.4	1.1	15.6	0.0

Education	100.0	82.0	3.7	12.5	1.7	100.0	81.2	4.3	14.0	0.6
Tenured/tenure track	(88.2)	83.4	3.7	11.2	1.8	(84.0)	81.7	4.3	13.3	0.7
Non-tenure-track	(11.8)	72.3	4.1	22.7	0.9	(16.0)	78.4	4.2	17.4	0.0
Engineering	100.0	71.2	16.7	8.0	4.0	100.0	0.3	21.0	7.6	1.0
Tenured/tenure track	(94.9)	71.5	16.5	7.7	4.2	(93.6)	69.9	21.3	7.8	1.1
Non-tenure-track	(5.1)	65.4	21.1	13.5	—	(6.4)	69.9	21.3	7.8	1.1
Health sciences	100.0	76.1	10.3	11.8	1.7	100.0	75.5	11.2	12.4	0.8
Tenured/tenure track	(82.2)	75.8	9.6	12.5	2.1	(77.6)	74.5	12.0	12.5	1.1
Non-tenure-track	(17.8)	77.5	13.8	8.6	—	(22.4)	79.0	8.7	12.3	0.0
All other fields	100.0	7.5	10.2	9.8	2.5	100.0	79.7	8.3	11.4	0.7
Tenured/tenure track	(90.6)	77.1	10.4	9.8	2.7	(82.6)	79.7	8.4	11.1	0.8
Non-tenure-track	(9.4)	81.6	7.5	9.9	1.1	(17.4)	79.5	7.8	12.7	0.0
Career cohort										
New-entrant	100.0	70.4	19.4	8.9	1.3	100.0	78.9	16.1	4.9	0.1
Tenured/tenure track	(80.2)	70.4	19.1	8.9	1.5	(69.2)	79.4	17.5	2.9	0.2
Non-tenure-track	(19.8)	70.2	20.4	8.8	0.6	(30.8)	77.7	13.1	9.2	0.0
Midcareer & senior	100.0	79.5	8.7	8.4	3.4	100.0	78.5	10.3	10.1	1.2
Tenured/tenure track	(93.5)	79.7	8.5	8.2	3.6	(89.0)	78.5	10.5	9.7	1.3
Non-tenure-track	(6.5)	76.2	11.5	11.0	1.4	(11.0)	78.2	9.1	12.7	0.0
Midcareer	100.0	71.8	14.2	8.9	5.1	100.0	78.5	14.4	6.1	1.0
Tenured/tenure track	(89.7)	72.7	14.1	7.9	5.4	(82.3)	78.5	15.3	5.0	1.2
Non-tenure-track	(10.3)	64.3	15.2	17.9	2.6	(17.7)	78.7	10.3	11.1	0.0
Senior	100.0	81.9	6.9	8.3	2.9	100.0	78.4	8.3	12.0	1.3
Tenured/tenure track	(94.7)	81.8	6.8	8.4	3.1	(92.3)	78.5	8.3	11.8	1.4
Non-tenure-track	(5.3)	83.5	9.2	6.7	0.6	(7.7)	77.7	7.7	14.6	0.0

Sources: NSOPF-93, NSOPF-99 (see Appendix A for key).
Notes: For definitions of row and column label terms, see Appendix E.
"Non-tenure-track" does not include faculty in institutions with no tenure system.
Parentheses denote subset of larger percentages.

TABLE A-7.2

Selected Characteristics of Full-Time Faculty, by Appointment Status, Institutional Type, and Program Area, 1992 and 1998

(percent)

Characteristics	1992								1998							
	All		Principal Activity						All		Principal Activity					
			Teaching		Research		Admin.				Teaching		Research		Admin.	
	TT	NTT	TT	NTT	TT	NTT	TT	NTT	TT	NTT	TT	NTT	TT	NTT	TT	NTT
All faculty																
Highest degree																
PhD	66.2	37.3	61.4	31.2	89.2	70.2	75.6	29.5	71.5	38.5	67.3	32.8	94.4	83.1	76.9	35.7
Gender																
Women	29.0	50.8	30.5	54.6	18.3	31.7	28.1	53.4	31.9	50.5	33.5	52.3	22.0	32.8	30.2	54.8
Marital status																
Married*	78.4	70.4	76.9	70.0	84.3	72.8	83.5	68.2	77.3	72.9	76.5	72.0	79.8	77.3	79.8	75.5
Race/ethnicity																
Asian	5.2	7.3	5.2	5.5	7.5	18.5	2.4	2.4	6.2	4.0	5.7	3.6	12.6	10.6	3.1	0.5
Other nonwhite	8.1	9.8	8.6	10.8	4.2	5.1	9.3	8.7	8.4	9.9	8.9	10.5	9.4	5.8	6.0	9.8
White	86.7	82.9	86.2	83.6	88.3	76.5	88.3	88.8	84.9	86.1	84.9	85.9	81.4	83.6	89.0	89.7
Age																
<45 years	34.9	58.9	32.3	57.8	52.0	75.6	14.7	40.7	28.4	44.4	28.0	44.2	44.7	57.5	11.0	33.8
Rank																
Full professor	38.3	4.5	35.4	4.4	40.4	3.5	58.2	7.9	39.5	6.4	37.1	5.3	41.3	14.9	57.0	5.6
Associate professor	27.6	8.1	27.3	6.8	29.6	12.3	24.5	10.1	29.1	5.9	28.7	5.0	31.4	7.4	27.4	10.9
Assistant professor	23.0	30.9	24.3	31.9	28.1	31.1	8.4	23.1	22.0	24.9	23.4	24.4	25.7	38.0	6.6	16.2
Institutional type																
Universities																
Degree																
PhD	81.8	49.2	77.9	41.3	89.8	69.6	85.0	26.5	85.8	50.4	82.8	42.4	94.7	84.7	82.1	42.8
Gender																
Women	21.9	49.8	22.9	58.5	18.2	32.7	21.6	54.8	25.4	48.9	27.3	51.4	21.5	30.3	24.4	65.7
Marital status																
Married*	82.3	71.8	80.9	75.8	84.2	73.1	85.5	60.7	79.5	73.2	79.0	72.0	79.8	81.1	80.8	67.4

Race/ethnicity																
Asian	6.5	10.0	6.7	6.6	7.7	18.1	2.9	3.2	8.0	5.1	7.2	4.3	12.6	11.0	2.4	0.0
Other nonwhite	5.7	5.7	6.4	5.6	3.7	5.0	6.4	6.5	6.9	9.0	7.6	10.3	5.7	2.7	5.4	11.9
White	87.8	84.3	86.9	87.9	88.6	76.9	90.7	90.3	85.2	85.8	85.2	85.4	81.7	86.3	92.3	88.1
Age																
<45 years	36.8	62.0	34.2	59.4	52.8	76.2	14.3	32.5	31.2	44.0	29.5	42.6	44.8	57.4	9.4	29.0
Rank																
Full professor	45.0	4.84	2.9	4.6	40.4	2.9	65.6	11.8	44.0	7.5	41.7	5.8	41.3	13.8	62.6	7.4
Associate professor	29.4	8.8	30.1	7.4	29.5	11.7	23.0	8.4	32.4	6.6	33.3	5.9	31.3	7.7	28.5	9.8
Assistant professor	23.5	30.7	24.9	32.2	28.4	31.6	8.0	21.1	21.6	25.3	23.3	22.4	26.0	39.1	3.6	19.8
Other 4-yr. institutions																
Highest degree																
PhD	73.3	30.2	72.1	29.8	86.6	100.0	81.3	31.9	78.6	26.8	77.6	25.0	97.4	low N	85.3	34.4
Gender																
Women	31.7	53.5	31.9	53.4	18.2	2.2	31.7	59.0	33.9	53.7	33.0	55.0	36.6	low N	35.4	43.4
Marital status																
Married*	75.4	70.9	74.7	70.1	85.3	42.3	81.2	80.7	74.8	73.6	74.2	73.3	82.2	low N	78.5	80.8
Race/ethnicity																
Asian	4.3	4.8	4.7	5.1	2.8	29.4	0.8	1.3	5.0	3.1	5.0	3.4	12.8	low N	2.9	0.0
Other nonwhite	9.1	14.9	8.8	15.2	12.4	13.2	13.7	13.5	9.6	11.3	9.2	11.3	18.3	low N	13.4	9.7
White	86.6	80.3	86.5	79.7	84.8	57.4	85.6	85.7	85.3	85.6	85.8	85.3	69.0	low N	83.7	90.3
Age																
<45 years	30.9	56.8	32.5	57.5	40.1	86.8	12.1	48.7	27.1	47.0	28.6	48.2	36.6	low N	11.5	38.4
Rank																
Full professor	37.8	3.8	35.8	3.6	40.2	13.2	56.9	5.7	38.0	6.2	36.8	6.1	47.0	low N	50.6	4.5
Associate professor	31.2	5.5	31.0	4.5	36.6	55.1	29.3	9.6	31.9	6.3	32.0	5.2	37.4	low N	27.9	15.3
Assistant professor	27.3	36.2	29.6	36.9	23.3	2.2	9.1	30.3	27.3	28.0	28.9	30.0	15.6	low N	13.4	12.6
2-yr. colleges																
Highest degree																
PhD	18.9	10.5	18.7	9.3	29.2	—	21.6	23.4	21.6	12.5	21.7	12.5	low N	low N	18.9	low N
Gender																
Women	41.3	51.7	41.2	53.9	42.5	—	45.3	31.3	46.7	56.2	46.1	52.9	low N	low N	59.8	low N
Marital Status																
Married*	74.8	58.0	74.2	57.3	81.1	100.0	83.8	59.3	74.2	70.4	74.4	69.2	low N	low N	71.2	low N

(continued)

TABLE A-7.2 (continued)

Characteristics	1992 All TT	1992 All NTT	1992 Teaching TT	1992 Teaching NTT	1992 Research TT	1992 Research NTT	1992 Admin. TT	1992 Admin. NTT	1998 All TT	1998 All NTT	1998 Teaching TT	1998 Teaching NTT	1998 Research TT	1998 Research NTT	1998 Admin. TT	1998 Admin. NTT
Race/ethnicity																
Asian	4.1	2.3	4.1	2.5	—	—	5.3	—	4.3	2.4	4.0	2.8	low N	low N	11.1	low N
Other nonwhite	11.8	11.6	12.0	12.3	1.1	—	9.9	4.7	11.9	11.0	12.1	9.0	low N	low N	8.3	low N
White	84.1	86.1	84.0	85.1	98.9	100.0	84.7	95.3	83.8	86.6	84.0	88.1	low N	low N	80.6	low N
Age																
<45 years	28.9	57.3	29.5	56.4	21.1	—	23.0	71.1	25.4	43.0	25.4	40.8	low N	low N	23.3	low N
Rank																
Full professor	24.5	4.3	23.4	4.7	62.3	—	36.7	—	29.3	2.8	29.5	2.5	low N	low N	25.1	low N
Associate professor	16.2	10.5	16.4	11.0	—	—	13.7	5.8	16.1	0.9	15.5	0.7	low N	low N	29.9	low N
Assistant professor	13.5	13.2	14.0	13.8	1.1	—	6.3	7.6	13.1	12.1	13.5	14.2	low N	low N	5.7	low N
Program area																
Liberal arts and sciences																
Highest degree																
PhD	73.6	41.2	69.5	36.9	91.8	71.5	80.8	24.7	76.0	49.9	71.4	43.0	95.4	91.7	88.3	42.4
Gender																
Women	25.7	48.8	26.8	50.7	17.6	32.9	23.8	34.1	28.5	49.9	30.7	52.0	19.8	33.8	20.3	57.6
Marital status																
Married*	78.1	68.7	76.9	69.4	82.6	72.7	83.2	47.5	76.0	71.7	74.8	69.1	78.6	80.2	82.5	80.1
Race/ethnicity																
Asian	5.1	7.8	5.3	7.3	5.7	12.2	1.6	5.9	6.5	5.6	6.0	5.1	11.9	11.4	3.1	1.1
Other nonwhite	7.6	10.7	8.2	11.7	3.6	4.9	9.0	6.5	9.0	10.0	9.8	11.5	4.8	3.3	8.6	8.0
White	87.4	81.5	86.5	81.0	90.7	82.9	89.4	87.7	84.5	84.4	84.3	83.4	83.4	85.3	88.3	90.9
Age																
<45 years	31.8	65.4	30.5	65.2	50.7	79.4	12.6	39.3	29.6	47.8	28.8	47.5	46.6	55.9	9.8	37.8
Rank																
Full professor	42.2	2.9	39.8	2.7	43.7	4.4	63.4	3.1	42.6	6.0	40.2	4.0	44.3	17.6	64.2	4.7
Associate professor	27.1	7.2	26.8	5.2	28.8	11.8	23.6	17.9	27.4	4.8	27.0	3.6	29.1	6.6	25.9	12.2
Assistant professor	21.3	29.9	22.2	30.5	26.9	32.0	5.6	15.5	21.9	24.6	23.2	22.8	26.1	41.7	4.6	13.7

Professions																
Highest degree																
PhD	60.6	33.9	55.5	26.8	86.3	82.9	74.6	41.2	68.1	29.2	64.4	23.6	92.6	low N	68.7	37.1
Gender																
Women	25.5	47.2	39.9	62.9	20.1	39.6	34.2	62.6	41.3	56.2	43.0	58.5	27.2	low N	42.6	55.0
Marital status																
Married*	78.9	74.1	77.5	75.2	86.3	65.0	83.2	73.0	81.2	76.2	81.3	75.5	83.2	low N	78.2	81.5
Race/ethnicity																
Asian	6.4	5.1	5.7	4.1	14.9	9.2	3.6	—	7.0	3.3	6.4	3.3	15.5	low N	2.3	0.0
Other nonwhite	8.7	7.6	9.0	8.1	5.8	14.0	9.5	8.0	8.4	10.6	8.3	10.9	9.2	low N	8.3	12.3
White	84.9	87.4	85.3	87.8	79.3	76.9	86.9	92.0	84.6	86.1	85.3	85.7	75.3	low N	89.4	87.7
Age																
<45 years	35.1	50.6	34.4	48.4	62.8	70.3	13.2	48.4	27.9	37.7	27.4	38.6	46.4	low N	14.1	27.7
Rank																
Full professor	31.4	4.8	28.1	4.7	31.4	2.1	54.9	7.2	31.5	4.2	29.3	3.5	32.3	low N	46.6	6.2
Associate professor	30.7	10.1	31.0	9.2	30.3	21.7	27.0	7.3	34.8	7.8	35.1	6.7	35.5	low N	29.7	10.8
Assistant professor	26.7	33.8	28.3	33.8	34.9	39.8	9.7	28.3	23.8	29.1	25.3	29.5	27.2	low N	10.5	23.2
All other program areas																
Highest degree																
PhD	49.0	25.6	41.9	22.4	85.2	68.7	66.9	21.7	57.6	21.7	53.5	20.8	92.3	low N	59.0	low N
Gender																
Women	25.7	48.8	26.2	48.8	15.7	44.7	25.3	50.3	27.2	41.6	26.5	41.4	22.9	low N	35.8	low N
MaritalsStatus																
Married*	78.5	66.0	76.2	60.6	87.6	89.8	85.7	88.6	74.9	70.5	74.3	73.5	79.1	low N	74.7	low N
Race/ethnicity																
Asian	3.4	3.2	3.8	2.7	2.6	4.6	0.4	6.3	3.8	0.6	3.0	0.0	9.4	low N	4.9	low N
Other nonwhite	8.7	13.1	9.6	14.	5.1	—	8.0	10.0	9.2	8.2	10.2	6.6	6.1	low N	5.1	low N
White	87.9	83.7	86.6	82.4	92.3	95.4	91.6	83.7	87.0	91.2	86.8	93.4	84.5	low N	90.0	low N
Age																
<45 years	33.3	52.7	34.6	55.3	38.9	61.2	22.0	18.4	24.2	46.9	25.9	45.1	28.0	low N	8.7	low N
Rank																
Full professor	37.7	8.8	33.9	9.4	44.3	—	59.1	11.6	42.1	11.6	39.5	12.5	44.5	low N	55.7	low N
Associate professor	23.2	8.7	22.4	6.9	30.7	22.1	19.9	14.2	24.6	5.7	23.1	5.9	36.0	low N	27.5	low N
Assistant professor	22.6	32.3	24.2	31.0	22.8	37.8	11.5	42.0	18.9	18.1	20.9	19.7	19.5	low N	5.2	low N

Sources: NSOPF-93, NSOPF-99 (see Appendix A for key).
Notes: "TT" means "Tenurable or tenured"; "NTT" means "Non-tenure-track."
"Non-tenure-track" does not include faculty in institutions with no tenure system.
*Married includes living with someone in a marriage-like relationship.

Mean Weekly Hours Worked by Full-Time Faculty, by Appointment Status, Gender, and Institutional Type, 1992 and 1998

| | 1992 | | | | 1998 | | | |
| | Principal Activity | | | | Principal Activity | | | |
	All	Teaching	Research	Admin.	All	Teaching	Research	Admin.
All faculty								
Female								
Tenured/tenure-track	41.3	40.6	49.5	46.2	45.6	45.0	50.2	48.6
Tenured	40.5	39.9	48.6	45.6	44.9	44.2	49.9	48.7
Tenure-track	42.6	41.8	50.5	48.4	46.9	46.4	50.6	48.3
Non-tenure-track	39.1	37.5	48.6	43.2	42.4	41.3	47.2	47.0
Male								
Tenured/tenure-track	43.5	42.3	50.9	48.0	46.7	45.5	52.0	50.6
Tenured	43.0	41.9	49.7	48.2	46.4	45.2	51.3	50.3
Tenure-track	45.1	43.5	53.7	46.7	47.8	46.4	53.9	54.3
Non-tenure-track	41.1	38.7	48.0	42.7	42.9	41.1	48.1	48.7
Institutional type								
Universities								
Female								
Tenured/tenure-track	45.9	45.2	50.2	49.4	49.1	48.7	50.5	51.2
Tenured	45.1	44.6	49.4	49.1	48.5	47.8	50.5	51.2
Tenure-track	47.0	45.9	50.9	50.1	50.2	50.1	50.6	low *N*
Non-tenure-track	42.0	39.4	48.7	44.8	43.5	41.9	47.7	48.5
Male								
Tenured/tenure-track	47.5	46.3	51.0	50.6	49.3	48.3	52.2	51.0
Tenured	46.9	46.1	49.8	50.8	49.1	48.2	51.5	50.9
Tenure-track	49.5	47.1	54.1	45.2	50.5	48.5	54.1	low *N*
Non-tenure-track	44.3	40.8	48.4	43.4	43.5	41.2	48.2	low *N*
Other 4-yr. institutions								
Female								
Tenured/tenure-track	41.6	41.6	44.1	46.5	46.2	46.2	low *N*	48.2
Tenured	41.0	41.1	43.3	46.2	46.0	46.1	low *N*	47.5
Tenure-track	42.3	42.2	45.5	47.6	46.5	46.2	low *N*	low *N*
Non-tenure-track	36.2	36.1	40.0	40.7	41.1	40.6	low *N*	low *N*
Male								
Tenured/tenure-track	41.8	41.8	50.7	46.3	45.2	44.7	low *N*	50.5
Tenured	41.5	41.5	51.8	46.0	44.6	44.1	low *N*	49.6
Tenure-track	42.8	42.8	47.6	47.7	47.1	46.6	low *N*	low *N*
Non-tenure-track	37.9	37.6	36.6	42.1	43.2	42.2	low *N*	low *N*
2-yr. colleges								
Female								
Tenured/tenure-track	35.7	35.6	29.2	40.0	39.8	39.5	low *N*	43.6
Tenured	35.6	35.5	29.4	39.5	39.6	39.2	low *N*	low *N*
Tenure-track	35.8	35.7	28.5	45.2	40.4	40.6	low *N*	low *N*
Non-tenure-track	35.6	35.1	—	44.8	41.7	40.9	low *N*	low *N*
Male								
Tenured/tenure-track	35.6	35.6	32.4	40.4	41.0	41.0	low *N*	low *N*
Tenured	35.2	35.2	24.7	40.3	40.4	40.5	low *N*	low *N*
Tenure-track	37.6	37.4	49.4	41.8	43.0	42.8	low *N*	low *N*
Non-tenure-track	34.2	33.2	45.0	40.4	39.5	38.5	low *N*	low *N*

Sources: NSOPF-93, NSOPF-99 (see Appendix A for key).
Notes: The hours worked include all paid activities at this institution in teaching, research, and administration.
"Non-tenure-track" does not include faculty in institutions with no tenure system.

TABLE A-7.4

Allocation of Effort by Full-Time Faculty, by Appointment Status, Gender, and Institutional Type, 1992 and 1998
(percent)

Characteristics	1992								1998							
	All		Principal Activity						All		Principal Activity					
			Teaching		Research		Admin.				Teaching		Research		Admin.	
	TT	NTT	TT	NTT	TT	NTT	TT	NTT	TT	NTT	TT	NTT	TT	NTT	TT	NTT
All faculty																
Female																
Teaching	59.1	58.7	67.5	71.6	27.0	8.8	23.3	13.7	62.1	65.9	68.5	74.3	34.9	24.8	31.2	33.7
Research	22.7	26.5	11.6	8.6	55.1	71.4	9.1	10.2	13.6	10.1	10.2	5.9	47.0	64.5	9.7	6.8
Administration	11.6	12.0	7.7	6.3	7.6	3.3	55.7	65.8	13.2	10.8	10.3	6.4	8.8	5.4	47.2	42.0
Professional growth	5.3	6.0	5.4	5.4	2.6	11.0	3.3	3.7	4.7	5.4	4.8	5.2	2.9	2.7	3.9	7.8
Consulting	1.7	2.0	1.8	2.3	1.2	0.6	1.3	0.7	2.4	3.5	2.3	3.7	2.2	0.7	3.1	3.9
Service	5.9	5.6	5.9	5.7	4.9	5.0	7.3	5.9	4.1	4.4	4.0	4.4	4.2	1.9	5.0	5.8
Male																
Teaching	51.8	47.6	61.5	65.1	24.1	7.4	20.5	20.0	57.5	59.2	65.6	71.0	32.8	20.4	28.8	26.8
Research	22.7	26.5	17.0	11.3	56.6	81.1	11.4	4.4	18.6	15.1	14.1	7.4	47.1	60.9	11.6	7.0
Administration	12.9	12.7	8.5	8.6	9.5	3.1	58.6	66.5	12.5	14.0	8.9	9.1	9.6	8.4	48.5	56.4
Professional growth	4.4	5.3	4.6	6.0	2.7	3.2	2.7	3.0	4.0	4.2	4.2	4.3	2.6	3.4	3.2	4.0
Consulting	3.0	3.1	3.2	3.9	2.5	1.6	2.4	1.5	3.0	4.1	3.0	4.7	3.0	2.2	3.1	2.7
Service	5.0	4.8	5.1	5.2	4.3	3.6	4.5	4.6	4.3	3.5	4.2	3.4	5.0	4.7	4.8	3.2
Institutional type																
Universities																
Female																
Teaching	44.9	50.5	57.0	71.3	27.3	8.9	21.3	9.5	50.9	61.7	60.1	73.6	34.2	20.8	27.2	31.5
Research	29.2	25.3	21.0	11.7	54.9	71.3	13.2	14.1	23.9	14.5	17.5	7.5	48.1	69.0	14.0	6.1
Administration	12.6	12.0	8.4	5.5	7.8	3.3	52.7	67.5	14.0	11.4	11.0	6.1	8.5	5.2	46.8	45.1
Professional growth	3.9	5.9	4.3	4.7	2.3	11.0	2.3	3.2	3.4	4.7	3.6	4.6	2.7	2.7	2.6	6.4
Consulting	1.7	1.1	2.0	1.4	1.2	0.6	0.8	0.2	2.4	3.2	2.4	3.4	2.1	0.6	3.8	4.1
Service	6.8	5.3	7.3	5.3	4.8	5.0	9.7	5.5	5.4	4.7	5.5	4.7	4.4	1.7	5.8	6.8

(continued)

TABLE A-7.4 (continued)

Characteristics	1992								1998							
	All		Principal Activity						All		Principal Activity					
			Teaching		Research		Admin.				Teaching		Research		Admin.	
	TT	NTT	TT	NTT	TT	NTT	TT	NTT	TT	NTT	TT	NTT	TT	NTT	TT	NTT
Male																
Teaching	40.3	34.3	52.3	63.1	24.0	6.9	18.5	19.0	47.6	55.0	57.8	71.2	32.6	20.0	28.4	low N
Research	34.0	43.5	26.5	15.0	56.6	82.0	14.9	5.7	28.0	23.7	21.6	10.3	47.2	61.6	13.8	low N
Administration	13.7	11.3	8.5	7.9	9.5	3.1	57.4	67.0	13.5	10.7	9.7	7.4	9.7	8.5	46.7	low N
Professional growth	3.5	4.8	3.8	6.5	2.6	3.3	2.4	1.7	3.1	4.0	3.2	4.2	2.6	3.4	2.7	low N
Consulting	3.1	2.2	3.3	3.2	2.5	1.1	2.5	1.6	2.9	3.5	2.7	4.3	3.0	2.0	3.1	low N
Service	5.1	4.0	5.4	4.3	4.3	3.5	4.3	5.1	5.0	3.2	5.0	2.6	5.0	4.6	5.3	low N
Other 4-yr. institutions																
Female																
Teaching	61.7	66.5	67.7	72.8	18.3	0.0	25.9	18.4	64.9	72.0	69.1	75.9	low N	low N	34.3	low N
Research	12.8	7.3	11.3	6.5	61.6	100.0	7.2	6.1	10.6	5.9	9.6	5.0	low N	low N	7.9	low N
Administration	11.9	11.8	8.1	6.2	4.2	0.0	56.4	64.0	13.2	9.1	10.1	6.0	low N	low N	46.6	low N
Professional growth	5.5	5.8	5.3	5.6	7.7	0.0	3.6	3.6	4.7	5.2	4.7	5.1	low N	low N	4.3	low N
Consulting	1.8	2.8	1.9	3.0	0.9	0.0	1.2	0.8	2.7	3.5	2.5	3.4	low N	low N	2.7	low N
Service	5.6	5.9	5.6	5.9	7.3	0.0	5.7	7.2	4.0	4.5	4.0	4.6	low N	low N	4.2	low N
Male																
Teaching	59.0	59.6	64.7	64.2	25.7	19.2	22.4	23.4	65.2	64.3	68.5	70.7	low N	low N	30.7	low N
Research	15.7	10.8	14.2	10.4	55.9	58.6	8.2	3.0	11.5	5.8	11.5	5.4	low N	low N	8.4	low N
Administration	12.6	12.8	8.6	8.5	7.8	1.5	59.2	64.3	12.1	18.2	8.7	11.5	low N	low N	51.0	low N
Professional growth	4.8	6.4	4.8	6.3	4.4	0.0	3.1	4.1	4.1	4.3	4.1	4.4	low N	low N	4.1	low N

Consulting	2.8	4.4	2.9	4.5	1.9	18.2	2.3	1.6	2.9	3.8	3.0	3.8	low *N*	low *N*	low *N*	1.7	low *N*
Service	4.8	6.0	4.8	6.2	4.2	2.5	4.6	3.7	4.2	3.7	4.2	4.0	low *N*	low *N*	low *N*	4.2	low *N*
2-yr. colleges																	
Female																	
Teaching	71.9	65.5	75.9	68.0	37.1		20.1	18.2	73.7	64.7	76.0	72.4	low *N*	low *N*	low *N*	35.6	low *N*
Research	4.6	6.1	4.4	6.3	41.8		5.2	0.8	4.0	4.6	4.0	2.7	low *N*	low *N*	low *N*	3.6	low *N*
Administration	9.8	11.7	6.5	8.5	11.4		61.5	72.3	11.4	13.8	9.3	9.2	low *N*	low *N*	low *N*	46.9	low *N*
Professional growth	6.5	7.1	6.4	7.4	4.3		4.7	2.0	6.2	8.9	6.2	7.0	low *N*	low *N*	low *N*	6.0	low *N*
Consulting	1.7	2.7	1.6	2.7	0.0		2.9	3.6	2.1	5.3	2.1	6.1	low *N*	low *N*	low *N*	2.2	low *N*
Service	5.3	6.9	5.1	7.1	5.4		5.7	3.1	2.6	2.8	2.5	2.6	low *N*	low *N*	low *N*	5.5	low *N*
Male																	
Teaching	68.9	65.5	72.2	72.5	19.5	40.0	24.3	17.0	75.2	65.7	76.8	70.3	low *N*	low *N*	low *N*	low *N*	low *N*
Research	5.6	6.4	5.1	6.1	59.4	60.0	2.7	3.4	4.1	1.9	4.0	1.9	low *N*	low *N*	low *N*	low *N*	low *N*
Administration	10.8	16.5	8.0	9.2	1.3	—	63.1	70.8	8.4	12.7	7.3	7.5	low *N*	low *N*	low *N*	low *N*	low *N*
Professional growth	5.9	3.2	5.7	3.1	10.9	—	2.8	4.1	6.5	4.6	6.4	5.0	low *N*	low *N*	low *N*	low *N*	low *N*
Consulting	3.5	4.3	3.6	4.6	2.4	—	1.7	1.9	3.7	10.1	3.4	10.8	low *N*	low *N*	low *N*	low *N*	low *N*
Service	5.4	4.2	5.3	4.4	6.6	—	5.4	2.8	2.2	5.0	2.1	4.5	low *N*	low *N*	low *N*	low *N*	low *N*

Sources: NSOPF-93, NSOPF-99 (see Appendix A for key).

Notes: "TT" means "Tenurable or tenured"; "NTT" means "Non-tenure-track."

"Non-tenure-track" does not include faculty in institutions with no tenure system.

Effort refers to all paid activities at this institution (teaching, research, administration, etc.).

TABLE A-7.5

Selected Work Activities of Full-Time Faculty, by Appointment Status, Gender, and Institutional Type, 1992 and 1998
(percent)

Work Activities	1992 All		Principal Activity Teaching		Research		Admin.		1998 All		Principal Activity Teaching		Research		Admin.	
	TT	NTT	TT	NTT	TT	NTT	TT	NTT	TT	NTT	TT	NTT	TT	NTT	TT	NTT
All faculty																
Female																
Teaching undergraduates only	39.8	39.9	44.6	45.8	10.6	8.8	30.4	29.5	52.9	57.9	59.8	62.4	7.3	22.0	38.6	54.9
No publications during career	28.5	41.6	31.5	45.1	8.5	28.5	20.5	29.8	20.9	37.5	23.4	40.4	1.2	8.0	17.2	35.0
No publications during past 2 years	42.6	56.2	46.9	59.3	13.1	34.0	35.1	56.8	32.1	50.2	35.8	53.3	2.3	15.4	26.4	49.6
Have funded research	64.2	65.1	29.0	23.8	78.6	87.4	39.0	27.5	24.1	34.3	18.3	29.1	84.2	74.6	28.5	42.7
No informal contact hours with students	13.4	19.2	10.9	13.5	20.2	44.6	14.3	30.1	29.9	46.4	29.4	47.5	31.7	49.0	28.1	37.8
Male																
Teaching undergraduates only	31.0	33.5	36.5	41.5	10.3	9.2	21.8	32.3	39.5	55.3	49.5	64.1	4.2	15.4	25.8	58.5
No publications during career	18.4	30.0	21.7	37.5	3.9	3.0	12.0	39.0	12.3	31.6	15.2	37.3	0.2	3.5	5.6	29.5
No publications during past 2 years	32.1	41.8	37.0	52.6	5.6	7.2	29.8	46.3	24.9	42.1	29.8	48.5	1.4	3.5	17.9	49.1
Have funded research	56.3	56.3	34.4	22.0	82.1	86.4	44.8	30.4	40.1	26.7	31.6	15.6	86.3	88.1	43.3	21.8
No informal contact hours with students	13.7	26.3	11.6	18.1	14.6	53.5	14.5	18.4	30.0	42.2	29.3	41.8	33.0	47.1	27.3	38.7

Institutional type

Universities																
Female																
Teaching undergraduates only	20.7	27.5	25.9	35.0	9.6	8.8	16.1	19.7	16.9	40.7	21.7	48.5	7.1	13.4	7.2	31.9
No publications during career	10.8	34.7	12.2	38.2	8.1	28.5	7.1	27.4	3.9	30.2	5.2	34.7	0.0	2.7	3.1	29.3
No publications during past 2 years	19.5	47.8	22.8	52.8	12.3	34.0	16.5	47.2	9.3	43.7	12.2	49.8	0.8	11.2	7.6	37.9
Have funded research	50.7	47.4	40.8	31.6	78.5	87.4	48.7	25.7	51.8	31.5	44.1	22.1	76.3	88.4	52.5	34.6
No informal contact hours with students	15.3	24.1	10.5	13.3	19.1	44.6	17.2	45.2	32.1	50.4	31.9	51.6	31.8	52.8	30.3	41.7
Male																
Teaching undergraduates only	15.5	18.8	19.4	24.4	9.0	9.1	12.9	36.5	15.4	39.9	21.4	50.3	3.7	15.8	14.8	low N
No publications during career	8.7	16.8	10.4	26.6	4.1	3.2	6.7	32.7	2.9	20.2	4.4	27.4	0.1	3.2	1.6	low N
No publications during past 2 years	16.9	27.7	20.8	43.8	5.7	7.0	18.9	42.6	9.8	28.3	13.4	38.9	1.4	3.2	10.1	low N
Have funded research	57.8	58.5	47.4	26.8	82.0	86.4	52.4	40.2	56.4	39.2	45.3	21.6	86.9	89.3	45.5	low N
No informal contact hours with students	14.9	35.7	12.3	19.6	14.7	55.4	15.8	22.9	33.0	45.1	32.6	43.4	33.3	48.7	27.8	low N
Other 4-yr. institutions																
Female																
Teaching undergraduates only	43.7	47.7	45.9	49.5	20.1	—	38.8	39.9	67.6	71.3	69.1	70.5	low N	low N	55.6	low N
No publications during career	23.5	42.2	24.4	42.7	8.4	—	17.6	38.4	14.1	40.1	14.3	40.9	low N	low N	14.6	low N
No publications during past 2 years	40.2	58.6	41.4	57.4	20.3	—	36.3	74.1	29.5	52.4	30.0	51.9	low N	low N	30.9	low N
Have funded research	26.2	15.8	23.8	15.4	86.5	100.0	32.2	22.5	30.9	18.0	28.7	15.9	low N	low N	39.6	low N
No informal contact hours with students	10.3	13.5	8.5	12.2	31.7	—	6.4	11.7	23.0	44.7	22.6	45.8	low N	low N	18.1	low N

(continued)

TABLE A-7.5 (continued)

| | 1992 | | | | | | | | 1998 | | | | | | | |
| | All | | Teaching | | Research | | Admin. | | All | | Teaching | | Research | | Admin. | |
Work Activities	TT	NTT	TT	NTT	TT	NTT	TT	NTT	TT	NTT	TT	NTT	TT	NTT	TT	NTT
Male																
Teaching under-graduates only	41.5	45.4	43.9	47.2	27.0	—	31.3	29.2	66.3	76.2	68.0	76.0	low N	low N	52.8	low N
No publications during career	17.8	38.6	18.7	38.3	1.1	—	13.3	44.3	11.8	40.0	12.5	40.9	low N	low N	5.8	low N
No publications during past 2 years	35.5	51.7	36.3	52.4	2.1	—	36.0	52.3	31.2	55.0	31.8	53.6	low N	low N	26.4	low N
Have funded research	27.2	21.7	24.5	19.9	82.0	100.0	29.7	27.9	26.7	13.9	25.3	11.8	low N	low N	38.1	low N
No informal contact hours with students	10.6	15.5	8.7	16.0	11.0	—	11.1	7.6	21.3	42.1	20.9	42.6	low N	low N	5.2	low N
2-yr. colleges																
Female																
Teaching under-graduates only	56.5	67.3	57.7	68.4	49.6		45.3	47.1	100.0	100.0	100.0	100.0	low N	low N	low N	low N
No publications during career	55.7	68.8	56.4	72.5	35.8		50.2	—	54.1	66.0	54.1	65.1	low N	low N	52.0	low N
No publications during past 2 years	73.1	83.4	74.0	86.3	41.3		64.9	28.8	66.2	76.4	66.4	76.8	low N	low N	60.8	low N

	1	2	3	4	5	6	7	8	9	10	11	12	13	14	15	16
Have funded research	20.1	19.8	19.3	20.4	64.7	—	27.5	—	15.4	13.4	15.1	14.7	low N	low N	22.2	low N
No informal contact hours with students	16.0	18.2	15.0	18.7	36.4	10.1	21.9	37.7	35.8	37.3	37.9	low N	low N	low N	44.5	low N
Male																
Teaching under-graduates only	53.0	60.0	54.1	62.0	47.2	100.0	43.2	41.5	99.7	low N	99.7	low N	low N	low N	low N	low N
No publications during career	48.7	61.1	50.0	62.4	—	—	34.2	57.5	45.1	65.1	45.1	66.6	low N	low N	low N	low N
No publications during past 2 years	68.7	72.8	69.1	74.5	—	100.0	67.8	57.5	63.2	77.7	63.0	78.0	low N	low N	low N	low N
Have funded research	15.9	9.9	14.7	11.0	68.7	—	28.1	6.7	14.9	4.2	15.4	4.6	low N	low N	low N	low N
No informal contact hours with students	17.7	28.8	16.8	27.5	21.5	100.0	21.9	31.4	45.1	30.1	45.2	32.9	low N	low N	low N	low N

Sources: NSOPF-93, NSOPF-99 (see Appendix A for key).
Notes: "TT" means "Tenurable or tenured"; "NTT" means "Non-tenure-track."
"Non-tenure-track" does not include faculty in institutions with no tenure system.

TABLE A-7.6
Institutional Support and Benefits of Full-Time Faculty, by Appointment Status and Principal Activity, 1992 and 1998
(percent)

Support/Benefits	1992								1998							
	Tenurable/Tenured				Non-Tenure-Track				Tenurable/Tenured				Non-Tenure-Track			
	All	T	R	A	All	T	R	A	All	T	R	A	All	T	R	A
Tuition remission																
Available	54.6	55.2	48.7	57.7	57.1	55.6	58.9	63.8	70.1	70.6	68.9	68.2	71.0	69.2	72.8	80.9
Used	24.0	23.2	30.3	22.9	27.2	25.0	31.8	35.2	18.9	18.5	25.4	14.8	21.4	21.7	24.9	17.6
Professional association membership																
Available	39.6	39.6	31.5	52.5	39.8	36.9	32.7	68.8	57.6	57.5	51.2	65.3	58.0	54.0	65.6	76.1
Used	79.5	77.2	84.5	89.9	74.3	71.4	75.0	87.1	47.3	46.8	41.1	57.8	44.6	40.9	45.4	67.0
Professional travel																
Available	80.5	81.1	72.7	88.6	72.1	71.5	63.7	89.8	90.3	91.0	82.5	94.1	85.1	83.5	85.4	95.6
Used	76.0	73.6	83.8	87.4	70.7	67.4	74.7	84.8	74.4	73.8	70.0	84.6	67.3	63.9	75.8	82.6
Training to improve research or teaching skills																
Available	51.2	52.1	40.0	58.5	49.4	47.2	48.4	65.3	74.4	75.1	64.1	79.7	68.5	66.6	67.3	80.0
Used	38.8	40.3	24.8	41.4	43.4	47.6	30.9	36.3	34.5	35.8	23.4	36.0	36.8	35.3	38.6	44.2

Retraining for field in higher demand								
Available	17.4	17.7	13.2	21.6	14.2	13.2	18.7	13.7
Used	14.3	14.0	16.1	14.9	18.2	16.6	21.9	18.5
Sabbatical								
Available	60.4	59.4	57.6	64.6	34.2	34.2	33.0	32.7
Used	18.4	15.5	15.4	13.2	4.3	3.0	—	1.8
Available	55.7	54.5	52.1	65.1	31.0	31.3	24.0	33.0
Used	9.0	8.0	8.9	8.1	2.3	2.3	3.5	0.9
Released time from teaching								
Available	53.8	53.6	46.9	63.7	36.7	36.4	24.4	46.4
Used	21.7	21.6	17.6	26.4	12.5	13.3	4.4	12.8

Sources: NSOPF-93, NSOPF-99 (see Appendix A for key).
Notes: "T" = "Teaching"; "R" = "Research"; "A" = "Administration."
"Non-tenure-track" does not include faculty in institutions with no tenure system.

Bibliography

Abraham, Sameer Y., Darby Miller Steiger, Margretha Montgomery, Brian D. Kur, Roger Tourangeau, Bob Montgomery, and Manas Chattopadhyay. 2002. *1999 National Study of Postsecondary Faculty (NSOPF:99): Methodology Report.* Washington, DC: National Center for Education Statistics.

Acuff, Gene, and Donald Allen. 1970. "Hiatus in Meaning: Disengagement for Retired Professors." *Journal of Gerontology* 25 (April): 126–28.

Adelman, Clifford. 2000. "A Parallel Universe: Certification in the Information Technology Guild." *Change* 32, no. 3 (May–June): 20–29.

Altbach, Philip G., ed., 1996. *The International Academic Profession: Portraits of Fourteen Countries.* Princeton, NJ: Carnegie Foundation for the Advancement of Teaching.

———. 2004. "The Past and Future of Asian Universities: Twenty-first Century Challenges." In *Asian Universities: Historical Perspectives and Contemporary Challenges,* ed. Philip G. Altbach and Toru Umakoshi. Baltimore: Johns Hopkins University Press.

Altbach, Philip G., and L. S. Lewis. 1995. "Professorial Attitudes: An International Survey." *Change* 27, no. 6 (November–December): 51–57.

———. 1996. "The Academic Profession in International Perspective." In Altbach, 1996, pp. 3–48.

American Association of University Professors (AAUP). 2004. "Don't Blame Faculty for High Tuition: The Annual Report on the Economic Status of the Profession, 2003–2004." *Academe,* special issue, March–April, pp. 20–46.

Ashenfelter, Orley, and David Card. 1998. "Faculty Retirement Behavior in the Post–Mandatory Retirement Era: New Evidence from the Princeton Retirement Survey." Paper presented at the TIAA-CREF and North Carolina State University Conference "Examining Life after the End of Mandatory Retirement," Washington, DC, May.

———. 2001. "Did the Elimination of Mandatory Retirement Affect Faculty Retirement Flows?" Working Paper 8378, July, National Bureau of Economic Research, Cambridge, MA.

Association of American Universities. 1998. *Committee on Graduate Education: Report and Recommendations.* New York: Association of American Universities.

Astin, Alexander, Eric Dey, William Korn, and Ellyne Riggs. 1992. *The American Freshman: National Norms for Fall 1991.* Los Angeles: UCLA Higher Education Research Institute.

Astin, Alexander W., William S. Korn, and E. L. Dey. 1991. *The American College Teacher: National Norms for the 1989–90 HERI Faculty Survey.* Los Angeles: Higher Education Research Institute, UCLA.

Astin, Alexander W., Leticia Oseguera, Linda J. Sax, and William S. Korn. 2002. *The American Freshman: Thirty-Five-Year Trends, 1966–2001*. Los Angeles: Higher Education Research Institute, UCLA.

Astin, Alexander W., Sarah A. Parrott, William S. Korn, and Linda J. Sax. 1997. *The American Freshman: Thirty Year Trends, 1966–1996*. Los Angeles: Higher Education Research Institute, UCLA.

Astin, Helen. 1978. "Women and Achievement: Occupational Entry and Persistence." *New Directions for Education and Work*, no. 4: 61–71.

———. *Factors Affecting Research Productivity of Academic Scientists*. Los Angeles: Higher Education Research Institute, UCLA.

Astin, Helen S., Antonio L. Antonio, Christine M. Cress, and Alexander W. Astin. 1997. *Race and Ethnicity in the American Professoriate, 1995–96*. Los Angeles: Higher Education Research Institute, UCLA.

Astin, Helen, and Alan Bayer. 1972. "Sex Discrimination in Academe," *Educational Record*, no. 53 (Spring): 101–18.

Astin, Helen, and Laura Kent. 1983. "Gender Roles in Transition: Research and Policy Implications for Higher Education." *Journal of Higher Education* 54, no. 3 (May–June): 309–24.

Astin, Helen, and Jeffrey Milem. 1997. "The Changing Composition of the Faculty." In *Academic Couples: Problems and Promises*, ed. Marianne A. Ferber and Jane W. Loeb. Urbana: University of Illinois Press.

Astin, Helen, and Thelma Myint. 1971. "Career Development of Young Women during the Post-High School Years." *Journal of Counseling Psychology*, no. 18 (July): 369–94.

Atkinson, Richard C. 1990. "Supply and Demand for Scientists and Engineers: A National Crisis in the Making," *Science* 248, no. 27.

Austin, Ann E., R. Eugene Rice, and Allen P. Splete. 1987. *Community, Commitment, and Congruence: A Different Kind of Excellence: A Preliminary Report on the Future of the Academic Workplace in Liberal Arts Colleges*. Washington, DC: Council of Independent Colleges.

———. 1991. *The Academic Workplace Audit*. Washington, DC: Council of Independent Colleges.

Austin, Ann E., R. Eugene Rice, Allen P. Splete, and associates. 1991a. "The Future of the Academic Workplace in Liberal Colleges: Survey of Faculty Views of the Academic Workplace." In Austin et al., 1991b, pp. 155–66.

Austin, Ann E., R. Eugene Rice, Allen P. Splete, and associates, eds. 1991b. *A Good Place to Work: Sourcebook for the Academic Workplace*. Washington, DC: Council of Independent Colleges.

Baldridge, J. Victor. 1971. *Power and Conflict in the University*. New York: John Wiley.

Baldridge, J. Victor, David Curtis, George Ecker, and Gary Riley. 1978. *Policy Making and Effective Leadership: A National Study of Academic Management*. San Francisco: Jossey-Bass.

Baldwin, Reginald Lawrence, and Rowena Tracy Blackburn. 1981. "The Academic Career as a Developmental Process: Implications for Higher Education." *Journal of Higher Education* 53, no. 6: 598–614.

Baldwin, Roger G., and Jay L. Chronister. 2001. *Teaching Without Tenure: Policies and Practices for a New Era.* Baltimore: Johns Hopkins University Press.

Bayer, A. E. 1970. *College and University Faculty: A Statistical Description.* ACE Research Reports, vol. 5, no. 5. Washington, DC: American Council on Education.

———. 1973. *Teaching Faculty in Academe: 1972–73.* ACE Research Reports, vol. 8, no. 2. Washington, DC: American Council on Education.

Benjamin, Ernst, ed. 2003. *Exploring the Role of Contingent Instructional Staff in Undergraduate Learning: New Directions for Higher Education, No. 123.* San Francisco: Jossey-Bass.

Bentley, Richard J., Robert T. Blackburn, and Jeffrey P. Bieber. 1990. "Some Corrections and Suggestions for Working with the National Faculty Survey Databases." *Research in Higher Education* 31, no. 6: 587–604.

Berelson, Bernard. 1960. *Graduate Education in the United States.* New York: McGraw-Hill.

Berg, Gary A. 2002. *Why Distance Learning? Higher Education Administrative Practices.* Westport, CT: Praeger.

Berger, Andrea R., and Rita J. Kirshstein. 2001. "Careerists and Moonlighters: Recognizing the Diversity of Part Time Faculty." Paper presented at the Association for the Study of Higher Education Conference, Richmond, VA, November 14–18.

Blackburn, Robert T., and Janet H. Lawrence. 1989. *Faculty at Work: Final Report of the National Survey.* Ann Arbor: National Center for Research to Improve Teaching and Learning, University of Michigan.

———. 1995. *Faculty at Work: Motivation, Expectation, Satisfaction.* Baltimore: Johns Hopkins University Press.

Blackburn, Robert T., and C. J. Mackie. 1992. Test-Retest Coefficients and the National Faculty Surveys. *Review of Higher Education* 16, no. 1: 19–39.

Bowen, Howard R. 1968. "Faculty Salaries: Past and Future." *Educational Record* (Winter): 9–21.

———. 1978. *Investment in Learning: The Individual and Social Value of American Higher Education.* San Francisco: Jossey-Bass.

———. 1980. *The Costs of Education: How Much Do Colleges and Universities Spend per Student and How Much Should They Spend?* Indianapolis: Jossey-Bass.

Bowen, Howard R., and Jack H. Schuster. 1985. "Whither the Gifted? Shifting Career Interests of the Nation's Intellectual Elite." *Key Reporter* 51, no. 1 (Autumn): 1–4.

———. 1986. *American Professors: A National Resource Imperiled.* New York: Oxford University Press.

Bowen, William G., and Julie Ann Sosa. 1989. *Prospects for Faculty in the Arts and Sciences: A Study of Factors Affecting Demand and Supply, 1987 to 2012.* Princeton, NJ: Princeton University Press.

Boyer, Carol M., and Darrell R. Lewis. 1985a. *And on the Seventh Day: Faculty Consulting and Supplemental Income.* ASHE-ERIC Higher Education Research Report no. 3. Washington, DC: Association for the Study of Higher Education.

———. 1985b. "Maintaining Faculty Vitality through Outside Professional Consulting." In *Faculty Vitality and Institutional Productivity,* ed. Shirley M. Clark and Darrell Lewis, pp. 177–97. New York: Teachers College Press.

Boyer, Ernest L. 1987. *College: The Undergraduate Experience in America*. New York: Harper and Row.

———. 1990. *Scholarship Reconsidered: Priorities of the Professoriate*. Princeton, NJ: Carnegie Foundation for the Advancement of Teaching.

Boyer, Ernest L., Philip G. Altbach, and Mary Jane Whitelaw. 1994. *The Academic Profession: An International Perspective*. Princeton, NJ: Carnegie Foundation for the Advancement of Teaching.

Breneman, David, and Joni Finney. 1997. "The Changing Landscape: Higher Education Finance in the 1990s." In *Public and Private Financing of Higher Education: Shaping Public Policy for the Future*, ed. Patrick M. Callan and Joni E. Finney. Phoenix: Oryx Press.

Brubacher, John, and Willis Rudy. 1968. *Higher Education in Transition*. Rev. ed. New York: Harper and Row.

Burke, Colin. 1982. *American Collegiate Populations*. New York: New York University Press.

Calhoun, Daniel. 1965. *Professional Lives in America*. Cambridge, MA.: Harvard University Press.

Caplow, Theodore, and Reece J. McGee. 1958. *The Academic Marketplace*. New York: Basic Books.

Carnegie Foundation for the Advancement of Teaching (CFAT). 1984. *A Classification of Institutions of Higher Education*. Princeton, NJ: Carnegie Foundation for the Advancement of Teaching.

———. 1989. *The Condition of the Professoriate: Attitudes and Trends, 1989*. Princeton, NJ: Carnegie Foundation for the Advancement of Teaching.

———. 1994. *A Classification of Institutions of Higher Education*. Princeton, NJ: Carnegie Foundation for the Advancement of Teaching.

Carrell, William. 1968. "American College Professors: 1750–1800." *History of Education Quarterly* 8:289–305.

Cartter, Allan M. 1965. "A New Look at the Supply and Demand for College Teachers." *Educational Record* 46, no. 3.

———. 1966. *An Assessment of Quality in Graduate Education*. Washington, DC: American Council on Education.

———. 1976. *Ph.D.s and the Academic Labor Market*. New York: McGraw-Hill.

Chait, Richard, ed. 2002. *The Questions of Tenure*. Cambridge, MA: Harvard University Press.

Cheit, Earl F. 1971. *The New Depression in Higher Education*. Carnegie Commission on Higher Education series. New York: McGraw-Hill.

Chevalier, Thierry. 2001. "Professional Diversity in a Centralized System: Academic Staff in France." In Enders, 2001.

Chronister, Jay L. 1997. *Faculty Retirement and Benefits: The NEA 1997 Almanac of Higher Education*. Washington, DC: National Education Association.

———. 2000. *Benefits and Retirement—Challenges for the New Century: The NEA 2000 Almanac of Higher Education*. Washington, DC: National Education Association.

Chronister, Jay L., Roger Baldwin, and Valerie Conley. 1997. *Retirement and Other Departure Plans of Instructional Faculty and Staff in Higher Education Institutions*.

Washington, DC: U.S. Department of Education, National Center for Education Statistics.

Chronister, Jay L., and Thomas R. Kepple Jr. 1987. *Incentive Early Retirement Programs for Faculty.* ASHE-ERIC Higher Education Report no. 1. Washington DC: Association for the Study of Higher Education.

Clark, Burton R. 1987. *The Academic Life: Small Worlds, Different Worlds.* Princeton, NJ: Carnegie Foundation for the Advancement of Teaching.

———. 1990. "The Entrepreneurial University," *Academe* 76, no. 5.

———. 1997. "Small Worlds, Different Worlds: The Uniqueness and Troubles of American Academic Professions." *Daedalus* 4, no. 126 (Fall): 21–42.

Clark, Robert L., Linda Ghent, and Juanita Kreps. 2001. "Faculty Retirement at Three North Carolina Universities." In Clark and Hammond, 2001.

Clark, Robert L., and P. Brett Hammond, eds. 2001. *To Retire or Not? Retirement Policy and Practice in Higher Education.* Philadelphia: University of Pennsylvania Press.

Clery, Suzanne. 2002. "Faculty Satisfaction." *Update: NEA Higher Education Research Center, Volume 8, Number 2, May.* Washington, D.C.: National Education Association.

CNN. 2003. "Distance Learning's Popularity Takes a Jump," July 22, 2003. CNN.com Education page at www.cnn.com/2003/EDUCATION/07/18/distance.learning.ap/, June 7, 2004.

Committee on Methods of Forecasting Demand and Supply of Doctoral Scientists and Engineers. 2000. *Forecasting Demand and Supply of Doctoral Scientists and Engineers: Report of a Workshop on Methodology.* Washington, DC: National Academy Press.

Conference Board. 2003. *Special Consumer Survey Report: Job Satisfaction Executive Action Report Number 68, September, 2003.* New York: Conference Board, Inc.

Conley, Valerie, and David Leslie. 2002. *Part-Time Instructional Faculty and Staff: Who They Are, What They Do, and What They Think.* Statistical Analysis Report NCES 2002-163. Washington, DC: U.S. Department of Education.

Council of Graduate Schools. 2004. *Ph.D. Completion and Attrition: Policy, Numbers, Leadership, and Next Steps.* Washington, DC: Council of Graduate Schools.

Cowley, William H. 1980. *Professors, Presidents, and Trustees.* Ed. Donald Williams. San Francisco: Jossey-Bass.

Creswell, John, Jay L. Chronister, and Dennis Brown. 1991. "The Characteristics and Utility of National Faculty Surveys." In *Using National Data Bases: New Directions for Institutional Research, No. 69,* ed. Charles S. Lenth, pp. 41–59. San Francisco: Jossey-Bass.

Cross, John G., and Edie N. Goldenberg. 2003. "How Does University Decision Making Shape the Faculty?" In Benjamin, 2003, pp. 20–29.

Cross, K. Patricia. 1994. "Academic Citizenship." *American Association for Higher Education Bulletin 1994–1995* 47, nos. 1–10: 3–5.

Curti, Merle E., and Vernon Carstensen, 1949. *The University of Wisconsin: A History.* Vol. 2, *1848–1925.* Madison: University of Wisconsin Press.

Daniel, John S. 1996. *Mega-Universities and Knowledge Media: Technology Strategies for Higher Education.* London: Kogan Page.

Davis, James A. 1964. *Great Aspirations: The Graduate School Plans of America's College Seniors.* Aldine, TX: Aldine.

Davis, William J. 1976. "A Timeline for the Development of Higher Education in America." Oklahoma State University, Stillwater. Unpublished manuscript.

De Weert, Egbert. 2001. "The End of Public Employment in Dutch Higher Education?" In Enders, 2001.

Dey, Eric L., Alexander W. Astin, and William S Korn. 1991. *The American Freshman: Twenty-Five-Year Trends, 1966–1990.* Los Angeles: Higher Education Research Institute, UCLA.

Dey, Eric L., C. E. Ramirez, W. S. Korn, and Alexander W. Astin. 1993. *The American College Teacher: National Norms for the 1992–93 HERI Faculty Survey.* Los Angeles: Higher Education Research Institute, UCLA.

Dorfman, Lorraine. 1978. "Professors in Retirement: A Study of the Activities and Reactions to Retirement of University of Iowa Emeritus Faculty." PhD diss., University of Iowa.

Drew, David E., and Jill A. Tronvig. 1988. "Assessing the Quality of National Data about Academic Scientists." Claremont Graduate School, Claremont, California. Unpublished manuscript.

Dunham, Ralph E., Patricia S. Wright, and Marjorie O. Chandler. 1963. *Teaching Faculty in Universities and Four-Year Colleges, Spring 1963.* Washington, DC: U.S. Department of Health, Education, and Welfare.

Dwight, Timothy. 1903. *Memories of Yale Life and Men, 1845–1899.* New York: Dodd, Mead.

Ehrenberg, Ronald G. 1991. "Academic Labor Supply." In *Economic Challenges in Higher Education,* ed. Charles T. Clotfelter, Ronald G. Ehrenberg, Malcolm Getz, and John J. Siegfried. Chicago: University of Chicago Press.

———. 2000. *Tuition Rising.* Cambridge, MA: Harvard University Press.

Ehrenberg, Ronald G., and Liang Zhang. 2004. "The Changing Nature of Faculty Employment." TIAA-CREF Institute paper. TIAA-CREF Institute, New York.

Eliot, Samuel. 1848. *A Sketch of the History of Harvard College.* Boston: Little and Brown.

Enders, Jürgen, ed. 2001. *Academic Staff in Europe: Changing Contexts and Conditions.* Westport, CT: Greenwood Press.

Fairweather, James S. 1996. *Faculty Work and Public Trust: Restoring the Value of Teaching and Public Service in American Academic Life.* Boston: Allyn and Bacon.

Feldman, Kenneth A., and Theodore M. Newcomb. 1976. *The Impact of College on Students: An Analysis of Four Decades of Research.* San Francisco: Jossey-Bass.

Finkelstein, Martin J. 1983. "From Tutor to Professor: The Development of the Modern Academic Role at Six Institutions during the Nineteenth Century." *History of Higher Education Annual* 3:99–121.

———. 1984. *The American Academic Profession: A Synthesis of Social Scientific Inquiry since World War II.* Columbus: Ohio State University Press.

Finkelstein, Martin J., Carol Frances, Frank Jewett, and Bernhard Scholz, eds. 2000. *Dollars, Distance, and On-Line Education: The New Economics of College Teaching and Learning.* Phoenix: American Council on Education/Oryx Press.

Finkelstein, Martin J., Robert K. Seal, and Jack H. Schuster. 1998a. *The New Academic Generation: A Profession in Transformation.* Baltimore: Johns Hopkins University Press.

———. 1998b. *New Entrants to the Full-Time Faculty of Institutions of Higher Education.* Statistical Analysis Report NCES no. 92-252. Washington, DC: National Center for Education Statistics.

Finn, Chester. 1999. "Today's Academic Market Requires a New Taxonomy of Colleges." *Chronicle of Higher Education* 44, no. 18: B-4.

Forrest Cataldi, Emely, Mansour Fahimi, Ellen M.Bradburn, and Linda Zimbler. 2005. *2004 National Study of Postsecondary Faculty (NSOPF:04) Report on Faculty and Instructional Staff in Fall 2003.* NCES 2005-172. U.S. Department of Education. Washington, DC: National Center for Education Statistics. http://nces.ed.gov//pubsearch, July 28, 2005.

Frances, Carol. 1998. "Higher Education: Enrollment Trends and Staffing Needs." *TIAA-CREF Research Dialogues* 55 (March).

Fulton, Oliver. 1975. "Rewards and Fairness: Academic Women in the United States." In Trow, 1975, pp. 199–248.

———. 2001. "Profession or Proletariat: Academic Staff in the United Kingdom after Two Decades of Change." In Enders, 2001.

Fulton, Oliver, and M. Trow. 1975a. "Research Activity in American Higher Education. In Trow, 1975, pp. 39–83.

———. 1975b. "Students and Teachers: Some General Findings of the 1969 Carnegie Commission Survey." In Trow, 1975, pp. 1–38.

Gappa, Judith M. 1984. *Part-Time Faculty: Higher Education at a Crossroad.* ASHE-ERIC Higher Education Research Report no. 3. Washington, DC: Association for the Study of Higher Education.

Gappa, Judith M., and David W. Leslie. 1993. *The Invisible Faculty: Improving the Status of Part-Timers in Higher Education.* San Francisco: Jossey-Bass.

Geiger, Roger. 1986. *To Advance Knowledge: The Growth of American Research Universities, 1900–1940.* New York: Oxford University Press.

Glass, Gene V. 1976. "Primary, Secondary, and Meta-Analysis of Research." *Educational Researcher* 6 (November): 3–8.

———. 1978. "Standards and Criteria." *Journal of Educational Measurement* 15:237–61.

———. 1982. "Meta-Analysis: An Approach to the Synthesis of Research Results." *Journal of Research in Science Teaching* 19, no. 2: 93–112.

Glassick, Charles, Mary Taylor Huber, and Gene I. Maeroff. 1997. *Scholarship Assessed: Evaluation of the Professoriate.* San Francisco: Jossey-Bass.

Glover, Denise, Basmart Parsad, and Linda J. Zimbler. 2002. *The Gender and Racial/Ethnic Composition of Postsecondary Instructional Faculty and Staff, 1992–98.* Washington, DC: National Center for Education Statistics.

Gmelch, Walter H., Nicholas P. Lovrich, and Phyllis Kay Wilke. 1984. "Sources of Stress in Academe: A National Perspective." *Research in Higher Education* 20, no. 4: 477–90.

Goldberger, Marvin L., Brendan A. Maher, and Pamela Ebert Flattau, eds. 1995. *Research-Doctorate Programs in the United States: Continuity and Change.* Washington, DC: National Academy Press.

Gordon, Margaret S., ed. 1974. *Higher Education and the Labor Market.* New York: McGraw-Hill.

Granger, David. 1990. "Open Universities." *Change* 22, no. 4: 44–51.

Green, Kenneth C. 1995. *The 1995 Campus Computing Survey.* Encino, CA: Campus Computing Project, www.campuscomputing.net.

———. 2002. *The 2002 Campus Computing Survey.* Encino, CA: Campus Computing Project, www.campuscomputing.net.

———. 2003. *The 2003 Campus Computing Survey.* Encino, CA: Campus Computing Project, www.campuscomputing.net.

———. 2004a. *The 2004 Campus Computing Survey.* Encino, CA: Campus Computing Project, www.campuscomputing.net.

———. 2004b. "The 2004 National Survey of Information Technology in U.S. Higher Education." www.campuscomputing.net/summaries.

Gruber, Marilyn. 1976. *Mars and Minerva.* Baton Rouge: Louisiana State University Press.

Gumport, Patricia. 1997. "Academic Restructuring: Organizational Change and Institutional Imperatives." *Higher Education* 39:67–91.

Haas, J. Eugene. 1996. "The American Academic Profession." In Altbach, 1996, pp. 343–88.

Haggerty, William, and George Works. 1939. *Faculties of Colleges and Universities Accredited by the North Central Association of Colleges and Secondary Schools, 1930–1937.* Publication no. 12. Chicago: Commission on Institutions of Higher Education, North Central Association.

Hammond, P. Brett, and Harriet P. Morgan, eds. 1991. *Ending Mandatory Retirement for Tenured Faculty: The Consequences for Higher Education.* Washington, DC: National Academy Press.

Handy, Charles. 1994. *The Age of Paradox.* Boston: Harvard Business School Press.

———. 1998. *The Age of Unreason.* Boston: Harvard Business School Press.

Hansen, W. Lee, and Karen C. Holden. 1981. "Effect of the Tenured Faculty Exemption in the 1978 ADEA Legislation." In *Abolishing Mandatory Retirement: Implications for America and Social Security of Eliminating Age Discrimination in Employment.* Washington, DC: Government Printing Office.

Harris, Seymour E. 1972. *A Statistical Portrait of Higher Education.* New York: McGraw-Hill.

Haskins, Charles Homer. 1976. *The Rise of Universities.* New York: Gordon Press.

Herbst, Jurgen. 1982. *From Crisis to Crisis: American College Government, 1636–1819.* Cambridge, MA: Harvard University Press.

Historical Catalogue of Brown University, 1764–1904. 1905. Providence, RI: Brown University.

Hoffer, Thomas B., Scott Sederstrom, Lance Selfa, Vince Welch, Mary Hess, Shana Brown, Sergio Reyes, Kristy Webber, and Isabel Guzman-Barron. 2003. *Doctorate Recipients from United States Universities: Summary Report, 2002.* Chicago: National Opinion Research Center, University of Chicago.

Hofstadter, Richard, and Walter Metzger. 1955. *The Development of Academic Freedom in the United States.* New York: Columbia University Press.

Holden, Karen C., and W. Lee Hansen, eds. 1989 *The End of Mandatory Retirement: Effects on Higher Education: New Directions for Higher Education, No. 65.* San Francisco: Jossey-Bass.

———. 2001. "What We Can Still Learn from an Earlier Study of Mandatory Retirement." In Clark and Hammond, 2001.

Honan, James P., and Cathy A. Trower. 2002. "How Might Data Be Used?" In Chait, 2002.

Horowitz, Helen Lefkowitz. 1984. *Alma Mater: Design and Experience in the Women's Colleges from Their Nineteenth-Century Beginnings to the 1930s.* New York: Knopf.

Huber, Mary Taylor. 1997. *Community College Faculty: Attitudes and Trends, 1997.* Menlo Park, CA: Carnegie Foundation for the Advancement of Teaching.

Jacobs, Jerry A. 2004. "The Faculty Time Divide." *Sociological Forum* 19, no. 1.

Jacobs, Jerry A., and Kathleen Gerson. 2004. *The Time Divide: Work, Family, and Gender Inequality.* Cambridge, MA: Harvard University Press.

Japan Ministry of Education, Culture, Sports, Science, and Technology. 2002. *Fact Book on Education in Japan.* Tokyo: MOESHI.

Jencks, Christopher, and David Riesman. 1968. *The Academic Revolution.* Garden City, NY: Doubleday.

Jewett, Frank. 2000. "A Framework for the Comparative Analysis of the Costs of Classroom Instruction vis-à-vis Distributed Instruction." In Finkelstein et al., 2000.

Jones, Lyle V., Gardner Lindzey, and Porter E. Coggeshall, eds. 1982. *An Assessment of Research-Doctorate Programs in the United States.* 5 vols. Washington, DC: National Academy Press.

Keefe, John. 2001."Survey of Early Retirement Practices in Higher Education." In Clark and Hammond, 2001.

Keller, George. 2001. "The New Demographics of Higher Education." *Review of Higher Education* 24:219–35.

Kerr, Clark. 1991. *The Great Transformation in Higher Education, 1960–1980.* Albany: State University of New York Press.

Kunkel, B. W. 1938. "A Survey of College Faculties." *American Association of University Professors Bulletin* 24 (March): 249–62.

Ladd, Everett C., Jr., and Seymour M. Lipset. 1973. *Academics, Politics, and the 1972 Election.* Washington, DC: American Enterprise Institute for Public Policy Research.

———. 1975a. *The Divided Academy: Professors and Politics.* New York: McGraw-Hill.

———. 1975b. *Technical Report: 1975 Survey of the American Professoriate.* Storrs: University of Connecticut.

———. 1977. *Technical Report: 1977 Survey of the American Professoriate.* Storrs: University of Connecticut.

———. 1981. A Reply to Lang. In *The File: Case Study in Correction (1977–1979),* ed. S. Lang, pp. 18–30. New York: Springer-Verlag.

Lazarsfeld, Paul F., and Wagner Thielens Jr. 1958. *The Academic Mind: Social Scientists in a Time of Crisis.* Glencoe, IL: Free Press.

Leslie, David W., and Elaine Fygetakis. 1992. "A Comparison of Carnegie and NCES Data on Postsecondary Faculty: Ambiguities and Disjunctures." *Research in Higher Education* 33, no. 4.

Leslie, David W., and Natasha Janson. 2005. "Phasing Away: How Phased Retirement Works for College Faculty and Their Institutions." A report to the Alfred Sloan Foundation. College of William and Mary, Williamsburg, VA.

Leslie, David W., Samuel E. Kellams, and Manuel G. Gunne. 1982. *Part-Time Faculty in American Higher Education.* New York: Praeger.

Leslie, David W., and James T. Walke. 2001. *Out of the Ordinary: The Anomalous Academic.* New York: Sloan Foundation.

Leslie, Larry L., and Gary Rhoades. 1995. "Rising Administrative Costs: On Seeking Explanations." *Journal of Higher Education* 66, no. 2: 187–212.

Leslie, Larry R., and Ronald L. Oaxaca. 1993. "Scientists and Engineering Supply and Demand." In *Higher Education: Handbook of Theory and Research,* vol. 9. New York: Agathon Press.

Lewis, L. S., and Philip G. Altbach. 1996. "The Professoriate in International Perspective: Who They Are and What They Do. *Academe* 82, no. 3 (May-June): 29–33.

Light, Barbara K. 1984. "Careers of American Rhodes Scholars and Phi Beta Kappa Members: A Methodological Note." Project on the Future of the Faculty, School of Educational Studies, Claremont Graduate University. Unpublished manuscript.

Light, Donald W., Jr., Lawrence R. Mardsen, and Thomas C. Corl. 1972. *The Impact of the Academic Revolution on Faculty Careers.* ERIC-AAHE Report no. 10. Washington, DC: American Association for Higher Education.

Lindholm, Jennifer A., Alexander W. Astin, Linda J. Sax, and William S. Korn. 2002. *The American College Teacher: National Norms for the 2001–02 HERI Faculty Survey.* Los Angeles: Higher Education Research Institute, UCLA.

Lipset, Seymour, and Everett C. Ladd Jr. 1979. "The Changing Social Origins of American Academics." In *Qualitative and Quantitative Social Research,* ed. Robert Merton, James S. Coleman, and Peter H. Rossi. Glencoe, IL: Free Press.

List, Murray D. 1956. "An Intensive Life History Study of Pre- and Post-Retirement Personality Factors of Retired College Professors." PhD diss., New York University.

Luskin, Bernard. 2002. *Casting the Net over Global Learning.* Irvine, CA: Griffin.

Lynton, Earnest A. 1995. *Making the Case for Professional Service.* Washington, DC: American Association for Higher Education.

Lynton, Earnest, and Sandra E. Elman. 1987. *New Priorities for the University.* San Francisco: Jossey-Bass.

Marver, James D., and Carl V. Patton. 1976. "The Correlates of Consultation: Academics in the Real World." *Higher Education* 5:319–35.

Mason, Mary Ann, and Marc Goulden. 2002. "Do Babies Matter? The Effect of Family Formation on the Lifelong Careers of Academic Men and Women." *Academe* 88, no. 6.

Mauch, James E., Jack W. Birch, and Jack Matthews. 1990. *The Emeritus Professor: Old Rank—New Meaning.* ASHE-ERIC Higher Education Report no. 2. Washington, DC: Association for the Study of Higher Education.

McCaughey, Robert M. 1974. "The Transformation of American Academic Life: Harvard University, 1821–1892." *Perspectives in American History* 8:239–334.

McCormack, Alexander. 2004. "Revision of the Carnegie Classification System." Paper presented to the Washington Higher Education Secretariat, Washington, DC, June 8.

McInnis, Craig. 2000. "Towards New Balance or New Divides? The Changing Work Roles of Academics in Australia." In *Academic Work and Life: What It Is to Be an Academic and How This Is Changing,* ed. Malcolm Tight. Amsterdam: JAI/Elsevier.

Metzger, Walter P. 1969. "Academic Freedom in Delocalized Institutions." In *Dimensions of Academic Freedom,* ed. Walter P. Metzger, pp. 1–33. Urbana: University of Illinois Press.

———. 1973. "Academic Tenure in America: An Historical Essay." In *Faculty Tenure,* by Commission on Academic Tenure in Higher Education. San Francisco: Jossey-Bass.

———. 1987. "The Academic Profession in the United States." In *The Academic Profession: National, Disciplinary, and Institutional Settings,* ed. Burton R. Clark. Berkeley: University of California Press.

Meyer, Katrina A. 1998. *Faculty Workload Studies: Perspectives, Needs, and Future Directions.* ASHE-ERIC Higher Education Research Reports, vol. 26, no. 1. Eric Clearinghouse on Higher Education. Washington, DC: George Washington University.

Morison, Samuel E. 1936. *Harvard College in the Seventeenth Century.* Cambridge: Harvard University Press.

National Center for Education Statistics (NCES). 1980. *The Condition of Education 1980, Statistical Report.* Washington, DC: U.S. Government Printing Office.

———. 1996. *Digest of Education Statistics, 1995.* Washington, DC: U.S. Department of Education, Office of Educational Research and Improvement.

———. 2001a. *Digest of Education Statistics, 2000.* NCES 2001-034. Washington, DC: U.S. Department of Education, Office of Education Research and Improvement.

———. 2001b. *Institutional Policies and Practices: Results from the 1999 National Study of Postsecondary Faculty, Institution Survey.* NCES 2001-201. Washington, DC: U.S. Department of Education.

———. 2002. *Digest of Education Statistics, 2001.* NCES 2001-083. Washington, DC: U.S. Department of Education, Office of Education Research and Improvement.

———. 2003. *Digest of Education Statistics, 2002.* NCES 2003-060. Washington, DC: U.S. Department of Education, Office of Education Research and Improvement.

———. 2004. *Digest of Education Statistics, 2003.* NCES 2005-025. Washington, DC: U.S. Department of Education, Office of Education Research and Improvement.

National Commission on the Cost of Higher Education. 1998. *Straight Talk about College Costs and Prices: The Report of the National Commission on the Cost of Higher Education.* Phoenix: Oryx Press.

National Research Council. 1982. *Assessment of Quality-Related Characteristics of Research Doctorate Programs in the U.S.* Washington, DC: National Academy of Sciences.

———. 2000. *Forecasting Demand and Supply of Doctoral Scientists and Engineers: Report of a Workshop on Methodology.* Washington, DC: National Academy of Sciences.

National Science Foundation. 1987. *U.S. Scientists and Engineers: 1986: Detailed Statistical Tables.* Washington, DC: National Science Foundation.

Nerad, Maresi, and Joseph Cerny. 2002. "Postdoctoral Appointments and Employment Patterns of Science and Engineering Doctoral Recipients Ten-Plus Years after Ph.D. Completion: Selected Results from the 'Ph.D.s Ten Years Later' Study." *Communicator* 35, no. 7, Council of Graduate Schools, Washington, DC.

Newman, Cardinal John Henry. 1907. *The Idea of a University: Defined and Illustrated.* New York: Longman's, Green, and Co.

Oleson, Alexandra, and Sanborn Brown, eds. 1976. *The Pursuit of Knowledge in the Early American Republic.* Baltimore: John Hopkins University Press.

Oleson, Alexandra, and John Voss, eds. 1979. *The Organization of Knowledge in Modern America, 1860–1880.* Baltimore: Johns Hopkins University Press.

Opinion Research Corporation. 1984. *Technical Report: 1984 Carnegie Foundation National Surveys of Higher Education.* Princeton, NJ: Opinion Research Corporation.

Organization of Economic Cooperation and Development (OECD). 2002. *Education at a Glance: OECD Indicators, 2002.* Paris: Organization of Economic Cooperation and Development.

Orr, Kenneth B. 1978. "The Impact of the Depression Years, 1929–39, on Faculty in American Colleges and Universities." PhD diss., University of Michigan, Ann Arbor.

Packard, Alpheus, ed. 1882. *History of Bowdoin College.* Boston: James Ripley Osgood and Co.

Palmer, James. 1999. "Part-time Faculty in Two Year Community Colleges." In *NEA Almanac on Higher Education, 1999,* ed. Harold Weschler. Washington, DC: NEA.

Parsad, Basmat, Denise Glover, and Linda J. Zimbler. 2002. *Tenure Status of Postsecondary Instructional Faculty and Staff: 1992–98.* Washington, DC: National Center for Education Statistics.

Parsons, Talcott, and Gerald M. Platt. 1968. *The American Academic Profession: A Pilot Study.* Cambridge, MA: Harvard University.

Pascarella, Ernest, and Patrick Terenzini. 1991. *How College Affects Students: Findings and Insights from Twenty Years of Research.* San Francisco: Jossey-Bass.

Patton, Carl V. 1977. "Early Retirement in Academia: Making the Decision." *Gerontologist* 17:347–54.

———. 1984. *Academia in Transition: Mid-Career Change or Early Retirement.* Lanham, MD: Rowman and Littlefield.

Pena, D., and D. Mitchell. 2000. "The American Faculty Poll." *NEA Higher Education Research Center Update* 6, no. 3: 1–6.

Radner, Roy, and Leonard S. Miller. 1975. *Demand and Supply in U.S. Higher Education.* New York: McGraw Hill.

Rees, Albert, and Sharon Smith. 1991. *Faculty Retirement in the Arts and Sciences.* Princeton, NJ: Princeton University Press.

Rhoades, Gary. 1998. *Managed Professionals: Unionized Faculty and Restructuring Academic Labor.* Albany: State University of New York Press.

Rhoades, Gary, and Christine Maitland. 2000. "Negotiating Technology: Support Personnel in Higher Education." *Journal of Collective Negotiations in the Private Sector* 29, no. 3: 207–19.

———. 2004. "Bargaining Workload and Workforce on the High Tech Campus." In *2004 Almanac of Higher Education.* Washington, DC: National Education Association.

Rice, R. Eugene, and Ann E. Austin. 1988. "High Faculty Morale: What Exemplary Colleges Do Right." *Change* 20, no. 2: 51–58.

Rice, R. Eugene, and Mary Deane Sorcinelli. 2002. "Improving the Tenure Process." In Chait, 2002.

Richardson, Leon D. 1932. *History of Dartmouth College.* Vol. 2. Hanover, NH: Dartmouth College Publications.

Riesman, David. 1981. *On Higher Education: The Academic Enterprise in an Era of Rising Student Consumerism.* San Francisco: Jossey-Bass.

Roizen, J., O. Fulton, and M. A. Trow. 1978. *Technical Report: 1975 Carnegie Council National Surveys of Higher Education*. Berkeley: Center for Studies in Higher Education, University of California, Berkeley.

Roman, P. B., and P. Taietz. 1967. "Organizational Structure and Disengagement: The Emeritus Professor." *Gerontologist* 7:147–52.

Roose, Kenneth D., and Charles Anderson. 1970. *A Rating of Graduate Programs*. Washington, DC: American Council on Education.

Rowe, Alan R. 1976. "Retired Academics and Research Activity." *Journal of Gerontology* 31:456–61.

Ruch, Richard S. 2001. *Higher Education, Inc.: The Rise of the For-Profit University*. Baltimore: Johns Hopkins University Press.

Rudolph, Frederick. 1956. *Mark Hopkins and the Log*. New Haven, CT: Yale University Press.

———. 1962. *The American College and University: A History.* New York: Random House.

———. 1991. *The American College and University: A History.* Athens: University of Georgia Press.

Ruml, Beardsley, and Sidney G. Tickton. 1955. *Teaching Salaries Then and Now: A 50-Year Comparison with Other Occupations*. New York: Fund for the Advancement of Education, Ford Foundation.

Russell, S. H., M. P. Hancock, and C. Williamson. 1990. *1988 National Survey of Postsecondary Faculty Methodology Report*. Menlo Park, CA: SRI International.

Salvucci, Sameena, Rita Bureika, George Carter, Dhiren Ghosh, Mindy Reiser, and Stephen Wenck. 1996. "Strategies for Improving Accuracy of Postsecondary Faculty Lists" (draft, December 3), National Center for Education Statistics, Washington, DC.

Sanderson, A., V. C. Phua, and D. Herda. 2000. *The American Faculty Poll*. Chicago: National Opinion Research Center.

Sax, Linda J., Alexander W. Astin, M. Arredondo, and William S. Korn. 1996. *The American College Teacher: National Norms for the 1995–96 HERI Faculty Survey*. Los Angeles: Higher Education Research Institute, UCLA.

Sax, Linda J., Alexander W. Astin, William S. Korn, and S. K. Gilmartin. 1999. *The American College Teacher: National Norms for the 1998–1999 HERI Faculty Survey*. Los Angeles: Higher Education Research Institute, UCLA.

Sax, Linda, Alexander W. Astin, William S. Korn, and Kathryn M. Mahoney. 1999. *The American Freshman: National Norms for Fall 1999*. Los Angeles: Cooperative Inter-Institutional Research Program, Higher Education Research Institute, UCLA.

Sax, Linda J., Alexander W. Astin, Jennifer A. Lindholm, William S. Korn, Victor B. Saenz, and Kathryn M. Mahoney. 1998. *The American Freshman: National Norms for Fall 2000*. Los Angeles: Higher Education Research Institute, UCLA.

———. 2000. *The American Freshman: National Norms for Fall 2000*. Los Angeles: Higher Education Research Institute, UCLA.

———. 2001. *The American Freshman: National Norms for Fall 2001*. Los Angeles: Higher Education Research Institute, UCLA.

———. 2002. *The American Freshman: National Norms for Fall 2002*. Los Angeles: Higher Education Research Institute, UCLA.

————. 2003. *The American Freshman: National Norms for Fall 2003.* Los Angeles: Higher Education Research Institute, UCLA.

Sax, Linda J., Sylvia Hurtado, Jennifer A. Lindholm, Alexander W. Astin, William S. Korn, and Kathryn M. Mahoney. 2004. *The American Freshman: National Norms for Fall 2003.* Los Angeles: Higher Education Research Institute, UCLA.

Schor, Juliet. 1991. *The Overworked American: The Unexpected Decline of Leisure.* New York: Basic Books.

Schuster, Jack H. 1995. "Whither the Faculty? The Changing Academic Labor Market." *Educational Record* 76, no. 4: 28–33.

————. 1998. "Reconfiguring the Professoriate: An Overview." *Academe* 84, no. 1 (January–February): 48–53.

————. 2001. "Higher Education in the United States: Historical Excursions." *Revista Electrónica de Investigación Educativa* 3, no. 2. Available at http://redie.ens.uabc.mx/search.

————. 2002. "Lurching Right Along." In "TIAA-CREF Benefit Plan Counselor," Special Report, p. 5. TIAA-CREF, New York.

————. 2003. "The Faculty Makeover: What Does It Mean for Students?" In Benjamin, 2003.

Schuster, Jack H., Daryl G. Smith, Kathleen Corak Sund, and Myrtle M. Yamada. 1994. *Strategic Governance: How to Make Big Decisions Better.* Phoenix: American Council on Education/Oryx Press.

Schuster, Jack H., and Daniel W. Wheeler. 1990. *Enhancing Faculty Careers: Strategies for Development and Renewal.* San Francisco: Jossey-Bass.

Scott, W. Richard. 1966. "Professionals in Bureaucracies—Areas of Conflict." In *Professionalization,* ed. Howard M. Vollmer and D. L. Mills. Englewood Cliffs, NJ: Prentice Hall.

Selfa, Lance A., Natalie Suter, Sharon Myers, Shaun Koch, Robert A. Johnson, Daniel A. Zahs, Brian D. Kuhr, and Sameer Y. Abraham. 1997. *1993 National Study of Postsecondary Faculty (NSOPF-93: Methodology Report.* Washington, DC: U.S. Department of Education, Office of Educational Research and Improvement, National Center for Education Statistics.

Shulman, Lee S. 2004. *Teaching as Community Property: Essays on Higher Education.* San Francisco: Jossey-Bass.

Skrabench, R. L. 1969. "Adjustment of Former University Faculty Members to Retirement." *Proceedings of the Southwestern Sociological Association,* pp. 65–69.

Slaughter, Sheila, and Larry Leslie. 1997. *Academic Capitalism: Politics, Policies, and the Entrepreneurial University.* Baltimore: Johns Hopkins University Press.

Slaughter, Sheila, and Gary Rhoades. 2004. *Academic Capitalism and the New Economy: Markets, State, and Higher Education.* Baltimore: Johns Hopkins University Press.

Sloan Foundation. 1998. *Part-time, Adjunct, and Temporary Faculty: The New Majority?* Report of the Sloan Conference on Part-time and Adjunct Faculty. New York: Alfred Sloan Foundation.

Smallen, David, and Karen Leach. 2000. "Understanding the Costs of Information Technology Support Services in Higher Education." In Finkelstein et al., 2000.

Smallwood, Scott. 2003. "American Women Surpass Men in Earning Doctorates." *Chronicle of Higher Education* 50, no. 16: 1.

Smelser, Neil J., and Robin Content. 1980. *The Changing Academic Market.* Berkeley: University of California Press.

Sperling, John. 2000. *Rebel with a Cause.* New York: John Wiley.

Stadtman, Verne. 1980. *Academic Adaptations Higher Education Prepares for the 1980s and 1990s.* San Francisco: Jossey-Bass.

Steinberg, Stephen. 1974. *The Academic Melting Pot: Catholics and Jews in American Higher Education.* New York: McGraw-Hill.

———. 1975. "Religious Involvement and Scholarly Productivity among American Academics." In Trow, 1975, pp. 85–112.

Syverson, Peter. 2003. "Bad News, Good News: Number of New Doctorates Decreases in 2001 While Job Market Indicators Improve." *Communicator,* January–February 2003, Council of Graduate Schools, Washington, DC.

Tickton, Sidney G. 1961. *Teaching Salaries Then and Now—A Second Look.* New York: Fund for the Advancement of Education, Ford Foundation.

Tobias, Marilyn. 1982. *Old Dartmouth on Trial.* New York: New York University Press.

Townsend, Robert B. 2003."Changing Relationships: Changing Values in the American Classroom." In Benjamin, 2003.

Trow, Martin. 1973. "Problems in the Transition from Elite to Mass Higher Education." In *Policies for Higher Education, from the General Report on the Conference on Future Structures of Post-Secondary Education.* Paris: Organization for Economic Cooperation and Development.

———, ed. 1975. *Teachers and Students: Aspects of American Higher Education.* New York: McGraw-Hill.

Trow, Martin, and associates. 1975. "A Technical Report on the 1969 Carnegie Commission Survey of Faculty and Student Opinion." In Trow, 1975, pp. 297–414.

Trower, Cathy. 2001. "Alleviating Tenure Torture." *Science Next Wave* (August 10). http://nextwave.sciencemag.org/search.dtl, accessed June 25, 2005.

Tuckman, Howard. 1978. "Who Is Part-Time in Academe." *AAUP Bulletin,* pp. 305–15.

Twigg, Carol. 2002a. "The Impact of the Changing Economy on Four-Year Institutions of Higher Education: The Importance of the Internet." In *The Knowledge Economy and Postsecondary Education: Report of a Workshop,* ed. PatriciaAlbjerg Graham and Nevzer G. Stacey. Washington, DC: National Academy Press.

Twigg, Carol. 2002b. "Report: Improving Quality and Reducing Costs, Designs for Effective Learning Using Information Technology." Observatory on Borderless Higher Education, London.

U.S. Department of Education (USDE). 1990. *Faculty in High Education Institutions, 1988.* NCES90-365. Washington, DC: National Center for Education Statistics.

———. 1995. *E.D. Tabs: Fall Staff in Postsecondary Institutions, 1991.* NCES 95-317. By Rose Fernandez. Washington, DC: National Center for Education Statistics.

———. 1996a. *Fall Staff in Postsecondary Institutions, 1993.* Statistical Analysis Report NCES 96-323. By Margaret Cahallan and Stephen Roey. Washington, DC: National Center for Education Statistics.

———. 1996b. *Integrating Research on Faculty: Seeking New Ways to Communicate about the Academic Life of Faculty,* NCES 96-849. Washington, DC: National Center for Education Statistics.

———. 1997. *Distance Education in Higher Education Institutions.* Statistical Analysis Report NCES 98-062. By Laurie Lewis, Debbie Alexander, Elizabeth Farris (Westat, Inc.). Project officer Bernie Greene. Washington, DC: National Center for Education Statistics.

———. 1998a. *E.D. Tabs: Fall Staff in Postsecondary Institutions, 1995.* NCES 98-228. By Stephen Roey and Rebecca Rak. Washington, DC: National Center for Education Statistics.

———. 1998b. *The National Study of Postsecondary Faculty, 1993.* Washington, DC: National Center for Education Statistics.

———. 2000. *E.D. Tabs: Fall Staff in Postsecondary Institutions, 1997.* NCES 2000-164. By Stephen Roey and Rebecca Rak Skinner. Washington, DC: National Center for Education Statistics.

———. 2001a. *The National Study of Postsecondary Faculty, 1999.* Washington, DC: National Center for Education Statistics.

———. 2001b. *Study of College Costs and Prices, 1988–89 to 1997–98.* Vol. 1. Statistical Analysis Report NCES 2002-157. By Alisa F. Cunningham, Jane V. Wellman, Melissa E Clinedinst, and Jamie P. Merisotis. Project officer C. Dennis Carroll. Washington, DC: National Center for Education Statistics.

———. 2001c. *Study of College Costs and Prices, 1988–89 to 1997–98.* Vol. 2. Statistical Analysis Report NCES 2002-158. By Alisa F. Cunningham, Jane V. Wellman, Melissa E. Clinedinst, and Jamie P. Merisotis. Project officer C. Dennis Carroll. Washington, DC: National Center for Education Statistics.

———. 2002a. *Part-Time Faculty in Institutions of Higher Education, 2002.* Washington, DC: National Center for Education Statistics.

———. 2002b. *Tenure Status of Postsecondary Instructional Faculty and Staff, 1992–1998.* Statistical Analysis Report NCES 2002-210. By Basmat Parsad and Denise Glover. Washington, DC: National Center for Education Statistics.

———. 2003a. *E.D. Tabs: Distance Education at Degree-Granting Postsecondary Institutions, 2000–01.* NCES 2003-17. By Tiffany Waits and Laurie Lewis. Washington, DC: National Center for Education Statistics.

———. 2003b. *E.D. Tabs: Fall Staff, 2001, and Salaries of Full-Time Instructional Faculty, 2001–02.* NCES 2004-159. By Laura G Knapp, Janice E. Kelly, Roy W. Whitmore, Shiying Wu, Seungho Huh, Burton Levine, and Susan G. Broyles. Washington, DC: National Center for Education Statistics.

———. 2005. *E.D. Tabs: Fall Staff, 2003, and Salaries of Full-Time Instructional Faculty, 2003–04.* NCES 2005-155. By Janice Kelly-Reid et al. Washington, DC: National Center for Education Statistics.

Vaill, Peter. 1996. *Learning as a Way of Being: Strategies for Survival in a World of Permanent White Water.* San Francisco: Jossey-Bass.

Veysey, Laurence R. 1965. *The Emergence of the American University.* Chicago: University of Chicago Press.

Wall, Joseph F. 1970. *Andrew Carnegie.* New York: Oxford University Press.

Warburton, E., X. Chen, E. M. Bradburn, and L. J. Zimbler. 2002. *Teaching with Technol-*

ogy: Use of Telecommunications Technology by Postsecondary Instructional Faculty and Staff in Fall 1998. Washington, DC: National Center for Education Statistics.

Wertenbaker, Thomas J. 1946. *Princeton, 1746–1896*. Princeton, NJ: Princeton University Press.

Wilkinson, R. K. 1994. *Characteristics of doctoral scientists and engineers in the United States: 1991*. Arlington, VA: National Science Foundation.

Wilson, Logan. 1942. *The Academic Man*. London: Oxford University Press.

Wirthlin Group. 1989. *Survey among College and University Faculty: The Technical Appendix*. Princeton, NJ: Wirthlin Group.

Wirthlin Worldwide. 1997. *The National Survey of Faculty, 1996–1997: The Technical Appendix*. McLean, VA: Wirthlin Worldwide.

Wolfle, Dale. 1972. *The Home of Science*. New York: McGraw-Hill.

Wolf-Wendel, Lisa, Susan B. Twombly, and Susan Rice. 2003. *The Two-Body Problem: Dual-Career Couple Hiring Policies in Higher Education*. Baltimore: Johns Hopkins University Press.

Wolf-Wendel, Lisa Ellen, and Kelly Ward. 2003. "Negotiating Work and Family: Parenting and Dual-Career Dilemmas." In *Gendered Futures in Higher Education: Critical Perspectives for Change,* ed. Becky Ropers-Huilman. Albany: State University of New York Press.

Yamanoi, Atsunori. 2003. *A Study of the Non-Tenure System for Faculty Members in Japan*. Hiroshima, Japan: Research Institute for Higher Education, Hiroshima University.

Zimbler, Linda, Rita J. Kirshstein, Nancy Matheson, and Zhongren Jing. 1994. *1993 National Study of Postsecondary Faculty: Institutional Policies and Practices Regarding Faculty in Higher Education*. Menlo Park, CA: Carnegie Foundation.

Zumeta, William. 2004. "Higher Education Funding: Stagnation Continues, Financial Restructuring Underway." In *NEA 2004 Almanac of Higher Education*. Washington, DC: National Education Association.

Index

Page numbers followed by *f* refer to figures, by *n* refer to notes, and by *t* refer to tables.

ABOUT THE AUTHORS

Jack H. Schuster is Professor of Education and Public Policy at Claremont Graduate University, Claremont, California. He previously served as Assistant Director of Admissions at Tulane University, Legislative and Administrative Assistant to U.S. Congressman John Brademas (D-IN), and Assistant to the Chancellor at the University of California, Berkeley, where he also was Lecturer in Political Science. He has held visiting appointments at the University of Michigan, the Brookings Institute, Oxford University, Harvard University, and the University of Melbourne. He is coauthor of *Enhancing Faculty Careers, American Professors, Governing Tomorrow's Campus, Strategic Governance,* and *The New Academic Generation.* Dr. Schuster received the Research Achievement Award of the Association for the Study of Higher Education and serves on the board of trustees of Mount St. Mary's College (California). He holds degrees from Tulane University (BA), Harvard Law School (JD), Columbia University (MA in Political Science), and the University of California, Berkeley (PhD in Education).

Martin J. Finkelstein is Professor of Higher Education, Seton Hall University, South Orange, New Jersey. He previously served as Executive Director of the New Jersey Institute for Collegiate Teaching and Learning (New Jersey Board of Higher Education) and as Associate Director of the University Council for Educational Administration. He has held faculty appointments at the University of Denver and at Teachers College, Columbia University, and visiting appointments at the Research Institute for Higher Education at Hiroshima University and at Claremont Graduate University. In addition to numerous articles and chapters, he wrote *The American Academic Profession* and coauthored *The Senior Faculty, The New Academic Generation,* and *Dollars, Distance, and On-Line Education.* Dr. Finkelstein received his BA (summa cum laude) at Columbia University. Following advanced study in French at Stanford and Columbia, he earned his PhD in higher education at the State University of New York at Buffalo.

Jesus Francisco Galaz-Fontes is Professor in the Faculty of Human Sciences at the Autonomous University of Baja California in Mexicali, Mexico, where he has served as dean and is currently head of the Department of Planning and Strategic Studies. His scholarly interests have spanned the areas of computer usage by children, moral development, and the condition and future of Mexican faculty. A member of Mexico's National System of Researchers, during 2005–6 he serves as Chair of International Higher Education (coconvened by the Consortium for North American Higher Education Collaboration and the National Association of Universities and Institutions of Higher Education of Mexico); in this capacity he is Visiting Professor at the University of Arizona's Center for the Study of Higher Education. Dr. Galaz-Fontes studied psychology at the National Autonomous University of Mexico in Mexico City, where he received his BA, and at the University of Guelph, Ontario, for his MA. He earned his PhD in higher education at Claremont Graduate University.

Mandy Liu is Deputy Director, International Affairs Division, Institute of Engineering Education Taiwan, a nonprofit, nongovernment organization that develops and promotes accreditation of engineering and technology programs in Taiwan. Prior to joining IEET, she was Research Associate at the Association of American Medical Colleges in Washington, D.C. Dr. Liu served as a teaching assistant for courses on international education and quantitative research methods at Claremont Graduate University and for English language laboratory classes at the Chinese Culture University, Taipei, where she earlier received her BA. She subsequently completed an MS in educational administration from California State University, Fullerton, and earned her MA and PhD in education at Claremont Graduate University.

Carol Frances is Professor of Education at Seton Hall University, New Jersey. She has also taught since 1998 at Claremont Graduate University. Her teaching and writing have focused on economics and finance of higher education and, in more recent years, on information technology's impact on higher education. She is coeditor of *Dollars, Distance, and On-Line Education*. Dr. Frances has been Chief Economist at the American Council on Education and director of ACE's Division of Policy Analysis. She holds degrees in international relations from UCLA (BA) and Stanford University (MA) and in economics from Yale University (MA) and Duke University (PhD).